ACCOUNTING
A Management Approach

WITHDRAWN

The Willard J. Graham Series in Accounting

Consulting Editor   ROBERT N. ANTHONY   *Harvard University*

Sixth Edition

Accounting
A Management Approach

GORDON SHILLINGLAW
Professor of Accounting
Graduate School of Business
Columbia University

MYRON J. GORDON
Professor of Finance
Faculty of Management Studies
University of Toronto

JOSHUA RONEN
Professor of Accounting
and Assistant Director
Vincent C. Ross Institute of Accounting Research
New York University

1979 **RICHARD D. IRWIN, INC.** Homewood, Illinois 60430
IRWIN-DORSEY LIMITED Georgetown, Ontario L7G 4B3

ISBN 0-256-02175-9
Library of Congress Catalog Card No. 78–70942

Printed in the United States of America

2 3 4 5 6 7 8 9 0 MP 6 5 4 3 2 1 0

LEARNING SYSTEMS COMPANY—
a division of Richard D. Irwin, Inc.—has developed a
PROGRAMMED LEARNING AID
to accompany texts in this subject area.
Copies can be purchased through your bookstore
or by writing PLAIDS,
1818 Ridge Road, Homewood, Illinois 60430.

*This edition is dedicated
to the memory of the late
Thomas M. Hill
coauthor, colleague, and friend*

Preface

The main objective of this textbook is to help the newcomer to accounting learn how to understand the principal financial information provided to managers and investors in publicly traded business corporations. To achieve this objective, we have tried to identify the major choices the accountants must make, the factors influencing them, and the effects of these choices on the information the accountants provide. We describe the methods and rules accountants use to develop this information and the standards set by authoritative bodies to guide this process, but we do this within a broader conceptual framework of accounting so that the role of methods and rules is placed in proper perspective.

We are convinced this is the best way to teach accounting to today's students. For those going no farther in accounting, further emphasis on detailed procedures would just get in the way. In fact, our conceptual approach leads many previously uncommitted students to think more favorably of future careers in accounting. Even students who enter the first course strongly committed to accounting careers are better off if they learn from the outset that accounting requires the use of judgment and analysis, not merely an ability to track the effects of transactions through a set of journals and ledgers.

This Sixth Edition, like its predecessors, has three parts. Part I establishes the basic concepts and structure of accounting. Chapter 1, for example, provides an overview of the field of accounting, including a description of those who call themselves accountants and a summary of the mechanisms by which accounting principles are established. The next four chapters explain how accountants analyze business transactions to derive data on which statements of income, financial position, and changes in financial position are based. Chapter 6 broadens this discussion to include manufacturing operations. Chapter 7 then sets the introductory discussion within a perspective of reporting on economic values of the company's net assets, while Chapter 8 addresses the crucial problem of deciding when changes in economic value should be recognized.

Part II delves in greater depth into the accounting treatment of specific aspects of the company's position and performance. We haven't taken the easy route, avoiding controversial issues by limiting ourselves to a statement of a set of rules that are or should be observed in practice. Instead, we have tried to present alternative solutions to measurement problems, together with their supporting arguments and some indications of their probable effects on the meaning of the information provided by the firm's financial statements. Whenever appropriate, we cite accepted practice and authoritative rulings, along with a brief summary of our evaluation of these positions. Part II concludes with a chapter on the elements of financial statement analysis.

Part III deals with the use of accounting information by the firm's own management. The first five chapters in this part examine the use of accounting data in various kinds of planning activities, while the final three chapters explore the bases on which accountants measure and report the results of operations to management.

How does this edition differ from the Fifth Edition? First, we have checked the entire text for consistency with standards issued by the Financial Accounting Standards Board since the Fifth Edition went to press, and have made changes as necessary. Second, we have rewritten the entire text, aiming at a more conversational style and greater clarity, with the aid of additional exhibits and text inserts. As part of this, we have made a special effort to make sure the problem material accompanying each chapter relates to and complements the material in the chapter itself.

Third, we have reorganized the chapter sequence, particularly in Part I. Our first discussion of manufacturing costs has been moved to Chapter 6 so we could go through the entire cycle of transactions analyses and statement preparation for a nonmanufacturing corporation first. Coverage of present value has been moved into Part I to provide a better background for the discussion of revenue recognition. We have eliminated the elementary chapter on manual recordkeeping systems and have moved the chapter on financial statement analysis to the end of Part II, where we could reflect the effects of differences in measurement bases.

Finally, we have moved the discussion of current costing from the inventory and depreciation chapters into an entirely new chapter on methods of adjusting for changes in individual resource prices and for the effects of inflation.

Although we have made every effort to make this book clear and readable, it's still no novel. In our own teaching, we try to persuade our students to study the illustrations carefully, verifying each figure and perhaps even duplicating the calculations on scratch paper. The next step is to work some of the independent study problems to be found at the end of each chapter. Once this has been done, the student should be in an excellent position to prepare a short summary of the main concepts or principles embodied in each chapter.

We are grateful to our public for the success previous editions have had. Many of our colleagues have been with us since the first edition appeared almost a generation ago. Much of whatever merit the present edition may have can be attributed to those who have taught us, criticized our work, and worked with us over the years. The links that go back farthest in time are those with Frank P. Smith, with William Cooper, and with our former colleague and coauthor, the late Thomas M. Hill, to whose memory this edition is dedicated.

Carl L. Nelson has been the most active of those now contributing actively to our work. In reading earlier drafts of the manuscript for Parts I and II, Professor Nelson asked the questions we should have asked ourselves. Sometimes a simple query on a single sentence led us to rewrite and reconsider whole pages of text. George Benston's comments on the Fifth Edition were highly useful as we tackled the revision of Part III, and Clyde Stickney made an equally helpful analysis of much of the problem material in Part I.

We are also indebted to Robert N. Anthony for his support and encouragement and for his insightful reviews of the manuscript for Part I, and to Lawrence Revsine, William A. Collins, and Alan R. Cerf for helping us see the faults in the Fifth Edition and the path to greater heights in the Sixth. Yoram Haft, Michael Karash, Stuart Karlinsky, and Etzman Rozen also helped us by reviewing early drafts of some of the text and problem material.

Material from the Uniform CPA Examinations (American Institute of Certified Public Accountants) and Certificate in Management Accounting Examination (Institute of Management Accounting) has been adapted or reproduced with permission, for which we are most grateful.

Finally, we should like to express our gratitude to John Burton, Charles Bastable, and Carl Nelson for their permission to use or adapt a number of their problems, and to the IMEDE management development institute in Lausanne, Switzerland, for its permission to reproduce a number of cases from its collection.

March 1979   GORDON SHILLINGLAW
                                                          MYRON J. GORDON
                                                          JOSHUA RONEN

Contents

17. Financial-Statement Analysis, 510

part III
ACCOUNTING DATA FOR MANAGEMENT PLANNING AND CONTROL

18. Budgetary Planning, 547

19. Analyzing Short-Term Planning Problems, 568

20. Cost Measurement: Full Costing, 595

xx   Contents

part 1

BASIC ACCOUNTING CONCEPTS

1

Purposes and Structure of Accounting Information

EVERY ORGANIZATION has an accounting system of some sort, designed to provide information to people directly interested in the organization and its operations. For example, in a business firm:

The treasurer needs to know whether the company's bank balance is big enough to cover the weekly payroll.

The marketing manager needs to know which products are profitable and which ones aren't covering their costs.

The owners need to know how well the managers have been doing their jobs.

Similar needs arise in not-for-profit organizations. The trustees of a museum, for example, need to know how much each museum program costs, who benefits from it, and how much money is available to pay for it.

Because these needs are so varied, the accounting system in any organization has to have several dimensions. In this introductory chapter, we'll take our first look at two of these dimensions—providing information to investors on the operations of a simple business firm and providing information on financial performance to the managers of a small service business. The chapter is divided into four sections:

1. A description of the *operating and financing cycles* of individual business firms—where they get their money and how they use it.

3

2. A description of the *financial statements* accountants prepare for individual business firms.
3. A short introduction to *management's use of accounting* data in planning and controlling business operations.
4. A view of the *environment* in which accounting measurements are made—who decides what measurements are necessary, how they are to be made, and who is to make them.

FINANCING AND OPERATING CYCLES

Accounting tries to mirror the conditions that actually exist in an organization. To understand accounting, therefore, we need to know something about what various kinds of organizations do. To keep this introductory description as simple as possible, we shall limit it to a discussion of the financing and operating functions of a small business firm, the XYZ Company. Larger companies and nonbusiness organizations have cycles that have most of the same elements in one form or another.

The Operating Cycle

The XYZ Company operates a store. It owns a building, equipped with shelves, counters, display racks, cash registers, and office equipment. The owners, Joe and Ann Dobson, invested some of their savings in the business to get it started; the rest of the money they needed they borrowed from banks.

Joe and Ann manage the store themselves. He orders merchandise from suppliers and places it on the shelves when it arrives. She sells the merchandise to customers. Some customers pay on the spot; others pay a short time later. The company pays its suppliers after it has received payment from its customers.

This simple set of activities constitutes the XYZ Company's operating cycle, defined as the "time intervening between the acquisition of materials or services . . . and the final cash realization."[1] It is diagrammed in Exhibit 1–1. The cycle begins when Joe buys merchandise from the company's suppliers. This has two consequences: (1) the store has something to offer its customers and (2) the company has an obligation to pay its suppliers. These are represented by the two rectangular blocks at the left of the diagram.

The cycle continues when Ann sells merchandise to a customer. This reduces the amount of merchandise available for sale to other customers but gives the company the right to receive money from

---

[1] American Institute of Certified Public Accountants, *Accounting Research Bulletin 43*, chap. 3, sec. A, para. 5; codified in *Professional Standards—Accounting, Current Text* (New York: Commerce Clearing House, Inc., 1978), sec. 2031.05.

EXHIBIT 1–1. XYZ Company: Operating Cycle

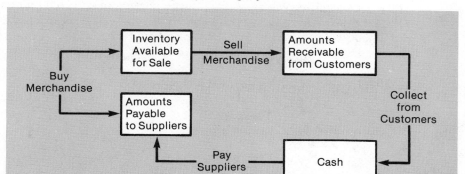

the customer who bought the merchandise. This change is indicated by the arrow at the top of the diagram. The next stage is reached when the customer pays and the company receives cash. This cash can then be used to pay suppliers, and the cycle is complete. In simpler terms, the cycle may be divided into three phases: cash to merchandise, merchandise to receivable, receivable to cash. When a customer pays cash immediately, the last two phases merge into one.

Different organizations, and even different parts of a single organization, have operating cycles of different lengths. The cycle for a cheese store may average only a few weeks because inventories are perishable and all sales are for cash, while a bicycle dealer may have a six-month cycle due to the large inventories necessary in this kind of business. A whiskey distiller may have an operating cycle several years long.

The Financing Cycle

Superimposed on the operating cycle is a second cycle, which we may call the *financing cycle*. It begins when an owner or owners invest money or other property in the business. They then appoint or elect managers, who may decide to borrow additional money from lenders of various sorts. In some cases, the owners may serve as their own managers, but this is rare in businesses of any substantial size.

Some of the money from the owners and from lenders is used to buy physical items, such as buildings, machinery, and merchandise to be offered to customers. Some is used to pay employees while the company is waiting for its customers to begin paying their bills. If the company is successful, the operating cycle will generate enough cash to pay the investors for the use of their money and, eventually, to repay the money they have invested. The owners of successful enterprises are likely to reinvest a large portion of the cash generated on their behalf, thereby starting the financing cycle over again.

These relationships are illustrated in Exhibit 1-2. The operating cycle is represented as both a user and as a supplier of cash, as

EXHIBIT 1-2.   XYZ Company: Financing Cycle

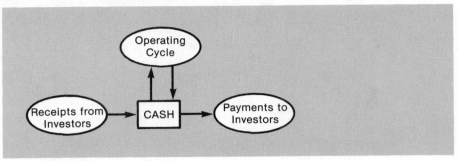

indicated by the arrows going in both directions between the cash box and the operating cycle.

THE FINANCIAL STATEMENTS

This simple illustration leaves out a number of elements, such as the purchase and use of equipment, but it should help us understand how accountants think of business firms. Accountants think of a business as a set of resources gathered together under a common control and used to generate profits for the owners of the business.[2] The relationship between the amount of resources the owners have invested in the business and the profits they produce is known as the *rate of return* on the owners' investment. Other things being equal, investors try to invest their money in businesses in which the rate of return on investment is high.

Accounting information about a business as a whole is conveyed to investors in a set of tables and explanatory notes, referred to as its *financial statements*. The part of accounting that is devoted to the preparation of financial statements for use by investors is known as

---

[2] Others see the firm differently. Employees see it as the source of their earnings and a consumer of their time. Customers see it as a source of goods and services and a consumer of part of their income. Economists see it as an element in a complex mechanism by which a nation's resources are allocated and the public welfare is benefited. Because these viewpoints don't help us understand the financial statements, we shall ignore them for the moment.

financial accounting. Companies prepare three main financial statements for this purpose:

1. The *balance sheet* or *statement of financial position,* summarizing two or more aspects of the resources invested in the firm *at a particular time.*
2. The *income statement,* sometimes called the *profit and loss statement* (*P&L,* for short), measuring how successfully management was able to use these resources *during a particular time period.*
3. The *funds statement,* or *statement of changes in financial position,* indicating where the company obtained resources *during a particular period of time* and how it invested those resources during that time period.

Statement of Financial Position

The statement of financial position consists of a list of *assets* owned or controlled by the company on a specific date, together with a list of the *liabilities* and *owners' equities* in the company at that time. Before going farther, we need to define each of these terms and see what they represent.

Assets and asset measurement. The assets of an organization are objects, claims, and other rights owned by and having value to that organization. They have value either because they can be exchanged for cash or other goods or services in the future or because the company can use them to increase the amount of cash or other assets at its disposal in the future.

Four kinds of assets are listed in the left-hand column of the balance sheet in Exhibit 1–3. The first two items are examples of *monetary assets,* representing enforceable claims on others for specified amounts of money. *Cash* is the amount of money the company has in its cash registers ("cash on hand") and in its bank accounts ("cash in

EXHIBIT 1–3

XYZ COMPANY
Statement of Financial Position
December 31, 19x1

Assets		*Liabilities and Owners' Equity*	
Cash	$ 30,000	Accounts payable	$ 50,000
Accounts receivable	50,000	Notes payable	20,000
Inventories	100,000	Bonds payable	80,000
Plant and equipment	160,000	Owners' equity	190,000
Total Assets	$340,000	Total Equities	$340,000

bank"). This amount measures the value of the company's claims against money-issuing authorities and banks. The second item, *accounts receivable*, represents the claims the company has against its customers. The amount shown is the estimated value of these claims, measured by the amount of cash the company expects to receive from these customers to satisfy these claims.

The third and fourth items are *nonmonetary assets*. *Inventories* are physical items the company intends to sell to its customers ("merchandise") or consume in operating the business (office supplies, raw materials, and so forth). *Plant and equipment* (often referred to as *fixed assets*) consists of any land, buildings, and machinery the company owns and intends to use rather than sell. (A real estate company would regard parcels of land held for resale as inventories.) For reasons we'll examine in the next few chapters, assets in these last two groups are measured on the basis of their *historical cost*—that is, the amounts the company has expended to acquire them.

COST AND VALUE

Cost and value may be very different quantities. For example, the Lucky Land Development Company bought 200 acres of farm land in 19x1 for $100,000. The company still owned the land four years later, and by that time its market value had risen to $250,000 due to its potential use for suburban housing. The company's accounting records, however, still listed the land at its $100,000 historical cost.

What we see, then, is a mixed bag: some of the assets (in this case, cash and accounts receivable) are measured by what they are worth to the company (their *values*); others are listed at their *cost* (in this case, inventories and plant and equipment). When the items in these two groups are added together, as they are on every statement of financial position, the total represents neither the cost nor the value of the company's assets, but a mixture of the two, as Exhibit 1–4 shows. The accountant usually uses the term *basis of valuation* to refer to the quantity an accounting figure represents; we prefer the term *basis of measurement* because many items are not measured at their values. We'll provide a more complete definition of the term *value* in Chapter 7.

Liabilities and owners' equity.   Individuals may be endowed by nature or other benefactors with various assets—good looks, talent, money, and so forth. Business firms aren't this lucky. A company's assets are provided by its owners and its creditors, who thereby acquire owners' or creditors' equities in the company. The statement of

EXHIBIT 1–4. Bases of Asset Measurement

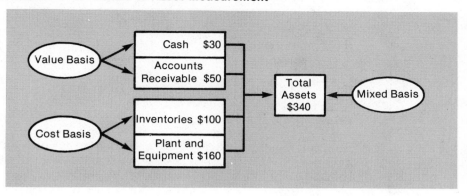

financial position includes a list of these equities, as in the right side of Exhibit 1–3.

A creditor is someone from whom the company has acquired assets or services for which the company is legally required to make payment or provide services in the future. A creditor's equity in a business is a *liability* of that business. Exhibit 1–3 listed three liabilities:

Accounts payable, measuring the amounts due to people or organizations who have not yet been paid for the goods or services they have supplied to the XYZ Company prior to the date of the statement and for which the company has an obligation to pay.

Notes payable, measuring the amounts lent to the company by banks or others for relatively short periods of time.

Bonds payable, a form of *long-term debt,* the amounts lent to the company by outsiders for relatively long periods of time in return for the company's agreement to pay specified amounts at specified future dates.

The final item on the right-hand side of Exhibit 1–3 is the *owners' equity,* the amount the owners have invested in the company. In choosing to be owners rather than creditors, investors put themselves in a different legal relationship to the company. The main differences in legal status are summarized in Exhibit 1–5.

In economic terms, the general idea is that creditors accept limits on the rewards they will receive and, in return, assume smaller risks than the owners. In practice, both the legal and risk/reward relationships are less clear-cut than this discussion suggests, but the variations are unimportant for our purposes.

EXHIBIT 1–5. Simplified Comparison of Owners and Creditors

Creditors	*Owners*
1. Make no decisions on how the company's resources are used.	1. Decide, either directly or through representatives they elect or appoint, how the company's resources are used.
2. Have a right to specified payments on specified dates and can bring legal action if a payment is not made when it is due.	2. Are entitled to receive payments from the company only after the company has provided adequately for the amounts due its creditors.
3. Will receive no more than the specified amounts, no matter how prosperous the company becomes.	3. Can receive very large amounts if the company prospers.
4. Have the right to receive specified amounts, and no more, if the company is liquidated.	4. Have the right to receive whatever is left over after all creditors' claims have been met; will receive nothing if the creditors' claims are not met in full.

Notice that the amounts shown as liabilities and owners' equity do not measure the *values* of these investors' equities in the company. Both the liabilities and the owners' equity in Exhibit 1–3 were measured on the same basis:

Liabilities:	Amounts Invested by Creditors
Owners' Equity:	Amount Invested by Owners

In other words, the money amount reported for each class of investors is the amount that class has invested in the firm, not the amount the creditor or owner will or may get out of the firm.

The accounting equation. The liabilities and owners' equity reported by the XYZ Company for December 31, 19x1, added up to $340,000:

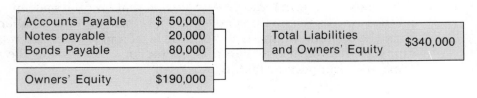

Accounts Payable	$ 50,000		
Notes payable	20,000	Total Liabilities and Owners' Equity	$340,000
Bonds Payable	80,000		
Owners' Equity	$190,000		

This is just equal to the total of the assets listed on the same balance sheet. This equality is not just a coincidence. In the accounting systems in use today, *the asset total must be identical to the total of the equities.* This identity is referred to as the accounting equation:

$$\boxed{\begin{array}{c}\text{Total}\\\text{Assets}\end{array}} = \boxed{\begin{array}{c}\text{Total}\\\text{Liabilities}\end{array}} + \boxed{\begin{array}{c}\text{Owners'}\\\text{Equity}\end{array}}$$

The accounting equation holds true for all balance sheets at all points in time. It holds because the list of assets and the list of liabilities and owners' equity merely represent two ways of looking at the same set of resources. The list of equities classifies the resources according to their source—that is, it answers the question, where did the resources come from? The list of assets, on the other hand, classifies the same set of resources according to their use—that is, it answers the question, what shape did the resources take on the balance sheet date?

Current assets and current liabilities. Some assets will be converted into cash much sooner than others and with less risk that something will prevent this conversion. To emphasize these differences in risk and convertibility, accountants usually divide a company's assets into two main groups: current assets and noncurrent assets.

Current assets are "cash and other assets or resources commonly identified as those which are reasonably expected to be realized in cash or sold or consumed during the normal operating cycle of the business." Assets that don't enter into the operating cycle, such as short-term investments in marketable securities, are also classified as current assets if they are expected to be exchanged for cash within a year; if the conversion date is to be later, they are classified as noncurrent assets.[3]

The XYZ Company's assets, for example, would be presented in the following groups:

Current Assets:
Cash	$ 30,000
Accounts receivable	50,000
Inventories	100,000
Total Current Assets	$180,000

Noncurrent Assets:
Plant and equipment	160,000
Total Assets	$340,000

---

[3] AICPA, *Accounting Research Bulletin 43,* chap. 3, sec. A, para. 4, and Accounting Principles Board, Statement 4, chap. 7, para. 25, in *Professional Standards— Accounting,* secs. 2031.04 and 1027.25.

Of the three current assets, cash is listed first, then accounts receivable, and then inventories. The receivables are listed before the inventories because they are one stage closer to cash in the operating cycle.

The only noncurrent asset in this case is plant and equipment. Whereas particular accounts receivable and particular items of merchandise are expected to flow through the operating cycle fairly quickly, the plant and equipment will be around for a long time. It will produce benefits not only in the next year but for many years to come. As a result, it is classified as a noncurrent asset.

Liabilities are also classified as either current or noncurrent. Current liabilities are those that are expected to be eliminated by the use of assets that are classified as current in the same balance sheet. In any case, current liabilities include all liabilities that will become payable during the next 12 months, no matter how short the operating cycle may be. For example, if a company has a liability that will be paid off in installments spread over several years, the portion that will have to be paid during the next 12 months will be classified as a current liability.

The XYZ Company had two current liabilities and one noncurrent liability on December 31, 19x1:

Current Liabilities:	
Accounts payable	$ 50,000
Notes payable	20,000
Total Current Liabilities	$ 70,000
Noncurrent Liabilities:	
Bonds payable	80,000
Total Liabilities	$150,000

This classification indicates that all the accounts payable and all the notes payable come due for payment within the next year, while none of the bonds will mature (come due for payment) within the year. In practice, of course, a company can have both current and noncurrent notes payable and bonds maturing within the next year as well as bonds with longer maturities.

Working capital.   Every business has to have at least some current assets. It needs cash to be able to pay its bills when they are due even if customers don't pay their bills on time. It usually has to have receivables because many customers won't buy if they have to pay cash immediately, and sales to these customers are important to the company. And it must have inventories so that customer orders can be filled promptly.

The company's creditors and owners provide it with the current assets it needs. Some of these are provided by short-term creditors, and this amount is measured by the company's current liabilities. The rest must be provided by the owners and long-term creditors. This latter amount is known as the company's working capital, the spread between the total of its current assets and the total of its current liabilities. For example, the XYZ Company had a working capital of $110,000 on December 31, 19x1:

Current assets	$180,000
Current liabilities	70,000
Working Capital	$110,000

Working capital is calculated partly in the belief that the current assets will be converted into cash soon enough to make them available to pay the current liabilities when they come due. It also measures the amounts of the current assets that must be financed from long-term sources. A large amount of working capital, in other words, is regarded as a useful safety device, and that may be good, but it also increases the need for long-term capital, and that is likely to be less good.

The Income Statement

The social purpose of the resources invested in a business is to produce goods and services that are demanded by other organizations or by individual consumers. The private purpose is to produce *income*—that is, to increase the owners' equity in the business. The income statement attempts to measure the amount of income the company has been able to generate during a specific period.

Economic income. In economic theory, the income of a firm during some period of time is the amount the owners could take out of the business and leave it as well off at the end of the period as at the beginning.[4]

To illustrate, suppose Mamie Arcaro transferred her entire fortune, $200,000, to an investment manager. The manager used this money to buy stocks and bonds and paid the dividends and interest on these investments to Ms. Arcaro as they came in during the year. By the end of the year, she had received $20,000, and the market value of the investments had risen to $210,000.

Ms. Arcaro's income for the year was $30,000, as illustrated in Exhibit 1–6. Although she received only $20,000 from the invest-

---

[4] The underlying definition can be found in J. R. Hicks, *Value and Capital* (London: Oxford University Press, 1939), p. 172. Further examination of this concept can be found in our Chapter 7 and also in Robert K. Jaedicke and Robert T. Sprouse, *Accounting Flows, Income, Funds, and Cash* (Englewood Cliffs, N.J.: Prentice-Hall, Inc., 1965), chap. ii.

EXHIBIT 1–6. Mamie Arcaro: Total Income for the Year

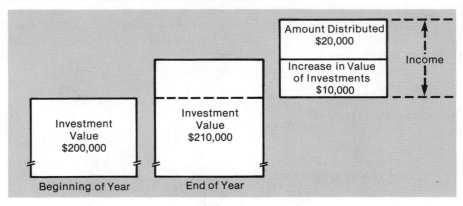

ment fund, she could have withdrawn another $10,000 without reducing the value of her holdings. Her income, therefore, was $20,000 + $10,000 = $30,000.

Accounting income. The accountant measures income in a slightly different way, by measuring various resources flowing into and out of the company. The accounting measure of income is labeled *net income*, defined as the difference between total revenue and total expense:

1. The *revenues* of a period are the resources received by the business as a result of providing products or services to outsiders during that period.
2. The *expenses* of a period are the resources consumed by the company in the creation of the revenues of that period.

The income statement in Exhibit 1–7 lists only one kind of revenue, the revenues arising from the delivery of merchandise to customers. The resources received are monetary assets—cash and cus-

EXHIBIT 1–7

XYZ COMPANY
Income Statement
For the Year Ended
December 31, 19x1

Revenue (from sales)		$900,000
Less expenses:		
Cost of goods sold	$600,000	
Salaries and wages expense	200,000	
Other operating expenses	45,000	
Interest expense	10,000	855,000
Net Income		$ 45,000

tomers' promises to pay cash or provide services in the future. The values of these resources can be determined fairly easily. As a result, revenues are measured by the *value* of the resources received.

The expenses are a different story. We don't know what the merchandise was worth when the XYZ Company sold it. Management obviously thought it was worth less than the $900,000 the company received in revenues—otherwise, management wouldn't have sold it for this amount. We don't know, however, how much less than $900,000 this merchandise was worth to the XYZ Company. Because value figures of this sort are so difficult to measure, the accountant usually falls back on historical cost. Expenses are measured by the *cost* of the resources consumed in the process of creating the revenues of the period. In the XYZ Company we have only four kinds of expenses:

Cost of goods sold: the amounts paid or to be paid in the future to buy the merchandise sold during the year.

Wages and salaries expense: the amounts paid or to be paid for the services of the employees who worked in the store, in the office, in the storeroom, and in the shipping room during the year.

Other operating expenses: the amounts paid or to be paid for other goods and services used up in the operation of the business during the year.

Interest expense: the amounts paid or to be paid for use of borrowed money during the year.

The difference between total revenue and total expense is income. Notice what the company has done to create income. It has received assets (mostly cash and receivables) in exchange for other assets (merchandise inventories) and services (employees' time) for which it has had to give up assets or incur liabilities. If the value of the assets it receives is greater than the cost of the assets and services used up, we say the company has a *net income* for the year; if the company gives up more than it gets, we say it has a *net loss*.

Accounting income and taxable income.   We should emphasize at this point that the income statement is not an income tax return. Company income statements are prepared to help investors decide whether to retain or increase the size of their investments in the company. Tax returns have an entirely different purpose—they are prepared to permit the government to determine the amounts of taxes the company must pay. "Income" for this purpose must be measured by the rules laid down by government.

Taxable income often differs substantially from accounting income before taxes. The reason: the legislature often uses income taxation as a way of influencing the actions of business managers and investors. For example, if the government wishes to encourage investments in oil exploration, it can rule that part of the spread between the revenues and the expenses of this kind of activity isn't "income" for tax purposes. Or, if the legislature wants to discourage political lobbying by business firms, it can rule that the costs of lobbying activities aren't deductible from revenues for tax purposes.

In both of these situations, adoption of the tax definition of income for financial reporting would mislead investors. This has been recognized quite clearly in the United States, not so clearly in some other countries. Differences between the income statement and the tax return are not necessarily fraudulent, either in purpose or in result. Beginning accounting students usually need to be reminded from time to time that the financial accounting principles they are studying are chosen with the investor in mind, not the tax agent. We start with the idea that the net income figure ought to be the best possible estimate of the difference between the amount of resources earned during the period and the amount of resources sacrificed to obtain them.

The Statement of Changes in Financial Position

The third major financial statement is the statement of changes in financial position, or funds statement. This shows where the company has obtained resources during the period and what it has done with them. A simple funds statement for the XYZ Company for 19x1 is shown in Exhibit 1–8. In this case, most of the new resources brought into the company during the year came from the operation of the company's store. This amount was more than enough to cover the dividend payments to the owners and buy some land. As a result, the company was able to increase its working capital slightly and

EXHIBIT 1–8

XYZ COMPANY
Statement of Changes in Financial Position
For the Year Ended December 31, 19x1

Resources Obtained:

By operating the business	$60,000
By borrowing	25,000
Total Resources Obtained	$85,000

Resources Committed:

To pay dividends to owners	$20,000
To repay old long-term bank loans	50,000
To purchase land	10,000
To increase working capital	5,000
Total Resources Committed	$85,000

reduce its long-term debt. This would be regarded as a fairly conservative set of financial actions, and investors would have to decide whether this conservatism seemed appropriate in the circumstances.

The funds statement is highly interrelated to the balance sheet and the income statement. It shows, for example, what the company has done to get from its financial position at the beginning of the year to its financial position at the end of the year. Like the income statement, it links the two balance sheets together. In fact, the item labeled "resources obtained by operating the business" can be calculated from items in a detailed income statement. We're not quite ready to deal with these interrelationships yet, but we'll begin to tackle them in Chapter 2, using a more complete illustration than we have room for here.

The Economic Role of Financial Accounting

Financial accounting plays a vital role in a private enterprise economy. It helps to direct money that is available for investment into activities that society values most highly. It does this because the financial statements of individual businesses are essential to the operations of markets in which individuals and others with money to invest get together with individuals and organizations who have ideas for using this money. A prudent investor will try to estimate the rates of return investments in different companies and in different industries are likely to produce. Financial statements don't foretell the future, but they do show the results of management's investment activities in the recent past. Companies with favorable financial statements are usually far more successful in raising funds than companies whose financial statements show low rates of return on their past investments. In other words, the financial statements have an effect on the allocation of available investment capital.

A number of prominent accountants and authorities on financial markets contend that the information contained in financial statements is already known to investors in various ways by the time the statements are issued. This doesn't mean, however, that the statements are unnecessary. Published financial statements confirm, quantify, or correct much of the other publicly available information. By doing this, they provide investors with a more reliable set of data than would otherwise be available.

Furthermore, statements containing "surprises"—that is, information the market is not already aware of—do affect prices investors are willing to pay for owners' shares in business firms. For these reasons, financial statements seem likely to be here to stay for the foreseeable future. Our main task in most of Parts I and II will be to try to make these statements more understandable.

MANAGERIAL ACCOUNTING

The second major branch of accounting is *managerial accounting*. Managerial accounting consists of the means by which an organization's accounting staff helps management plan and control the organization's activities. Our introductory description of managerial accounting will be brief because we won't take up the main threads of the discussion again until Part III. Some explanation is necessary here, however, not only to put financial accounting in perspective but also because many aspects of financial accounting have managerial implications.

Planning and Control Processes

Planning can be defined as the process of deciding how to use available resources. The key word in this definition is "deciding," because planning is essentially a matter of choosing the set of alternatives which seem most likely to enable the organization to meet its objectives. Several different kinds of planning processes can be identified, but the most important for our purposes is comprehensive, periodic planning for the activities of the organization as a whole.

Control is the complement of planning. It consists of management's efforts to prevent undesirable departures from planned results, to keep track of what is happening, to interpret this information, and to take action in response to it.

The main relationship between planning and control is diagrammed in Exhibit 1–9. Planning produces a plan. This becomes a

EXHIBIT 1–9. Planning and Control Loops

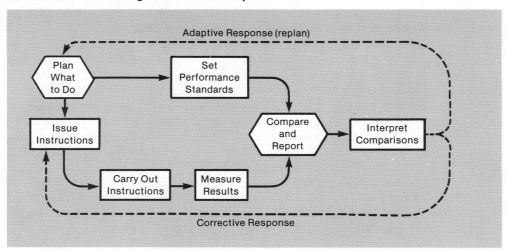

set of instructions to be executed. The results of the actions taken on the basis of the plan are then compared with the planned results. The differences from the plan are interpreted to determine what kind of response is appropriate. A corrective response requires a change in the way the plan is carried out, while an adaptive response requires replanning. Each of these leads back to an earlier phase of the process, and the loop is completed.

Accounting's Role

Accounting's most visible contribution to planning and control processes is in the accumulation of data and preparation of reports on the results of operations. For example, many companies have their accountants prepare income statements for individual groups of products or market segments. Exhibit 1–10 summarizes the reve-

EXHIBIT 1–10

ABC, SERVICE DIVISION
Income Statement
For the Month Ended April 30, 19x1

	Plan	Actual	Difference
Revenues	$17,000	$18,000	+$1,000
Expenses:			
Salaries	$10,000	$11,500	+$1,500
Supplies	1,000	800	– 200
Other expenses	2,000	2,300	+ 300
Total Expenses	$13,000	$14,600	+$1,600
Net Income	$ 4,000	$ 3,400	–$ 600

nues and expenses of the service division of an automobile dealership. This is generally similar in structure to the income statement for the company as a whole; the main difference is that it stresses differences from planned results rather than the absolute amounts. Management's job is to determine the causes of the departures from plan and to decide what action, if any, to take.

Control reporting of this sort seldom stops with the divisional income statement. Other, more detailed, statements are prepared for each responsible executive within the division. Some of them may have responsibility for revenues as well as for costs; others have cost responsibility only. In each case, the content of the report should correspond to the scope of the executive's responsibility.

Managerial accounting also has an important role to play in the planning process. For one thing, accounting data on the results of activities carried out in the past often prove very helpful to anyone trying to estimate the future effects of management's present decisions. Exhibit 1–11, for example, lists the costs incurred by a recordkeeping service company in processing a client's payrolls last month. A file of records of this sort, properly analyzed and inter-

EXHIBIT 1–11.   Papershufflers, Inc.: Cost Summary, Customer Job. No. 1776

	Hours	Amount
Senior accountant	4	$ 40
Keypunch operators	18	90
Processors	6	42
Computer charges		24
Other costs		78
Total Cost		$274

preted, can help management estimate costs of future jobs with characteristics similar to those of jobs performed in the past.

Managerial accounting makes another major contribution to the planning process. The accounting staff is ordinarily responsible for assembling, consolidating, and testing the tentative plans drawn up at the beginning of each period by the managers of the various segments of the organization. Inconsistencies must be identified and corrected, and the consolidated plan must be tested for feasibility and consistency with top management's objectives.

THE ACCOUNTING ENVIRONMENT

Making accounting measurements in any organization is the direct responsibility of the accountants who are employed and paid by the organization. Others, however, have a great deal to say about what measurements are necessary and how they are to be made. Before moving on, we need to describe these influences very briefly.

Influences on Financial Reporting to Investors

Responsibility for deciding what accounting measurements are necessary is shared in the United States by governmental and private bodies. The Securities and Exchange Commission is the governmental agency with the widest influence on financial reporting to investors. It establishes what information the major industrial and commercial corporations in the United States must report to the commission. This information is then made available to anyone who is interested in it.

The SEC has generally interpreted its role as one of deciding what must be disclosed and reported but has let organizations in the private sector determine how the variables are to be measured. For example, the commission requires companies to file income statements but provides only sketchy guidance on how revenues and expenses are to be measured.

One reason for this is that accounting was well established in the private sector before the legislation creating the SEC was enacted. The guidelines used by accountants emerged gradually, first without any formal rule-making body, then through the activities of committees and boards of the American Institute of Certified Public Accountants, the major professional association interested in financial reporting to investors. These guidelines are known individually as *financial accounting standards* and collectively as "generally accepted accounting principles." Responsibility for further development of accounting standards is now vested in the Financial Accounting Standards Board, created in 1973 with the support of the AICPA and other major professional associations of accountants and financial executives in the United States.

Another influence on financial accounting is exerted by the rules and regulations governing taxes on business income. As we have already said, published financial statements in the United States need not be identical to the statements that are submitted to the U.S. Internal Revenue Service and other taxing authorities. Differences are both frequent and substantial because the purposes of taxation and financial reporting are so different. Taxation does influence accounting measurements, however, at least partly because differences between accounting measurements and tax measurements increase the costs of operating accounting systems and partly because the ways accountants measure some elements may determine the company's taxes as well.

Influence on Managerial Accounting

The story in managerial accounting is very different. Management is free to design the measurement and reporting system for internal use in any way it pleases. Nobody has ever been constituted with authority to establish and enforce measurement and reporting standards in this area. (The National Association of Accountants has a Management Accounting Practices Committee which issues formal statements on these matters from time to time, but it has no enforcement power.)

The main constraint on management's freedom in system design is cost. Most accounting systems have to serve several purposes simultaneously, and clerical costs will skyrocket if every variable (for example, the cost of goods sold) has to be measured in several different ways, one for each purpose. Since externally oriented measurements have to be made anyway, the obvious solution is to use these for internal use as well, unless they are very badly suited to managerial needs.

Government has had a relatively minor influence on accounting for internal use. Statistical reporting requirements on such matters as employees' wages have undoubtedly affected the information base that is available to management, and income taxation also has affected the measurements of some variables, but the government's influence in a broad sense has been limited mainly to companies in regulated industries and to companies with substantial government contracts. Many of these contracts base the contract price on cost, and contractors have designed their systems to meet the government's demands for cost data. Such systems are often very different from those that otherwise might have been adopted. The government body with the widest responsibility for prescribing accounting standards for this purpose is the Cost Accounting Standards Board, established in 1972.

ACCOUNTING PRACTITIONERS

Most of the people who work in accounting are employed directly by business firms and other organizations. They prepare payrolls, record purchases and sales, and keep track of their employers' property. They prepare financial statements that summarize the effects on the organization of activities and events that have already taken place and help management develop budgetary plans for the future. They participate in the design of systems to do all this and help management understand the meaning of the figures that emerge from these systems.

The skills required by these activities vary widely. By far the largest number of people perform routine clerical functions for which high school or technical school education is adequate preparation. At the top of the pyramid, in contrast, is the chief accounting officer or *controller*, performing duties that in the large organization require extensive formal education and many years of practical experience.

Many of the people now moving up toward higher positions of this sort are *certified management accountants* (CMAs). The CMA certificate is granted to those who meet the experience, educational, and examination requirements of the Institute of Management Accounting, an offshoot of the National Association of Accountants. Possession of the certificate is not an official requirement for advancement in controllership, however. Anyone can serve who can perform the functions to management's satisfaction.

The second group of accounting practitioners are the public accountants who provide services to their clients for a fee. Some of this is helping the client develop information for use in resolving income tax questions. Some is "management services," helping the client design record-keeping systems and planning and control systems or analyzing the client's business problems and opportunities.

None of these activities is unique to public accounting. The unique role of public accountants is to *audit* the financial statements of business corporations and other organizations. No matter how competent and honest the company's own accountants are, the investor and other outsiders need an independent representative who will state that:

1. The figures representing the organization's financial status and performance are measured on the basis of agreed-upon measurement principles.
2. Enough information is available to insure that the figures are reasonably accurate.

The people who provide these assurances are known as *auditors* or *independent public accountants*. Auditing for this purpose has been defined as "an exploratory, critical review by a public accountant of the underlying internal controls and accounting records of a business enterprise or other economic unit, precedent to the expression . . . of an opinion of the propriety ('fairness') of its financial statements."[5]

Most audits of the financial statements of publicly owned businesses in the United States are performed by large and medium-sized organizations known as *public accounting firms*. As Exhibit 1–12 shows, each of the big firms has three main divisions—audit,

EXHIBIT 1–12. Divisions of Public Accounting Firms

_____

[5] Eric L. Kohler, *A Dictionary for Accountants*, 4th ed. (Englewood Cliffs, N.J.: Prentice-Hall, Inc., 1970), p. 40.

tax, and management services. The audit division is the largest division by far. Each firm is organized as a partnership, and the largest among them have more than a thousand partners, operating in offices throughout the United States and in many other countries.

All of the partners in the audit divisions of these firms and most of the professional staff are *certified public accountants* (CPAs). CPAs are individuals who have satisfied the educational, experience, and examination requirements that have been established by the states in which they wish to practice.

Casual readers of financial statements often assume that the auditing firm prepares the statements. This is not true. The company's own accountants prepare the statements on the basis of the company's records. The auditors then examine the records and the judgments the company's accountants have made. If they are satisfied with the statements as a result of this examination, they will write a letter (known as an *opinion*) similar to the one in Exhibit 1–13, to be attached to the financial statements and published with

EXHIBIT 1–13.

Opinion of Independent Certified Public Accountants

To the Board of Directors and Stockholders of Uniroyal, Inc.:

We have examined the consolidated balance sheets of Uniroyal, Inc. and subsidiary companies as of January 1, 1978 and January 2, 1977 and the related statements of consolidated income, reinvested earnings, capital surplus and changes in financial position for the fiscal years then ended. Our examinations were made in accordance with generally accepted auditing standards and, accordingly, included such tests of the accounting records and such other auditing procedures as we considered necessary in the circumstances.

In our opinion, such financial statements present fairly the financial position of the companies at January 1, 1978 and January 2, 1977 and the results of their operations and changes in their financial position for the fiscal years then ended, in conformity with generally accepted accounting principles applied on a consistent basis.

Haskins + Sells

NEW HAVEN, CONNECTICUT
February 9, 1978

them. If they are dissatisfied with some aspect of the statements, however, they will ask the company to change the statements. If management refuses to make the change, the auditors will describe this disagreement in the opinion itself.

The opinion in Exhibit 1–13 is typical of a so-called "clean" opinion, in which the auditors express no reservations about the financial statements. Although couched in technical language, this opinion is intended to assure the reader that the auditors have done their job. They have used professionally recognized methods to verify that the financial statements are consistent with the available factual evidence and that when the company's accountants have had to use their judgment, they have followed accounting principles that are widely accepted by the accounting profession. The auditors will also submit a longer letter to management, commenting on the perceived strengths and shortcomings of the company's recordkeeping and control procedures.

SUMMARY

Accounting is the primary means of organizing and reporting information, mostly in financial terms, for the use of an organization's management and outsiders. Accounting designed for outsiders is known as financial accounting; measurement and reporting for internal consumption is the domain of managerial accounting.

From an accounting standpoint, an organization can be viewed as a set of resources assembled and used to carry out one or more activities to achieve one or more objectives. Accounting summaries of an organization's resources, generally known as statements of financial position or balance sheets, do not pretend to measure the organization's economic value. Instead, they list as assets the resources which can be measured readily in monetary terms. They also show the sources of these assets, divided into two categories—liabilities and owners' equities. Since the list of assets and the list of liabilities and owners' equities merely measure two aspects of the same set of resources, the two lists have identical totals. This equality is the basis of the accounting equation.

Accountants also report on the economic productivity of an organization's resources. In the business firm, the accountant's measure of productivity is known as net income. In general, net income is the difference between the value of the resources the firm receives for its goods and services and the costs of the resources it consumes in the process.

Accounting measurements for external financial reporting must follow the prescriptions laid down in financial accounting standards. Many of these standards provide only very broad guidelines, and the accountants must use their judgment in applying them. Even so, the standards underlying published financial statements are intended to apply to all companies in like situations, and the certified public accountants who audit the statements must see that they have been followed.

The company's accountants are subject to no such external constraints for internal managerial accounting. Accounting measurements for managerial use can take any form as long as they give management the information it wants at a price it is willing to pay.

KEY TERMS

Accounting equation
Asset
Audit
Auditors
Balance sheet
Control
Current asset
Current liability
Expense
Financial accounting
Financial accounting standards
Financial statements
Historical cost
Income statement

Independent public accountants
Liability
Managerial accounting
Monetary asset
Net income/net loss
Operating cycle
Owners' equity
Planning
Revenue
Statement of changes in
   financial position
Statement of financial position
Working capital

INDEPENDENT STUDY PROBLEMS (Solutions in Appendix B)

1. Organizing a balance sheet and an income statement.   Prepare an income statement and balance sheet from the following (no owner investments or withdrawals were made during the period):

Accounts payable	$ 250
Accounts receivable	300
Cash	100
Cost of goods sold	700
Furniture	600
Inventories	380
Note payable	350
Prepaid rent	40
R. A. Copake, Capital	To be derived
Revenue from sales	1,000
Salaries and wages expense	120
Sundry expenses	60
Taxes expense	20
Taxes payable	5
Wages payable	50

2. Preparing balance sheet; interpreting financial data.   On January 21, 19x4, three young bachelors, Mr. Robinson, Mr. Griffiths, and Mr. Thorndike, formed a partnership to operate a small bar. Each partner contributed $1,500 cash, for a total of $4,500. On the day the partnership was formed, the Dingy Dive Bar was purchased for $14,500. This price included land valued at $2,000, improvements to land at $2,000, buildings at $9,500, and bar equipment at $1,000. The partnership made a down payment of $3,000 (from its $4,500 cash) and signed a note for the balance of the $14,500.

After operating the bar for one month, the partners found that despite withdrawing $200 each in cash from the business, $1,000 in cash remained; in addition, there was inventory on hand amounting to $300 and accounts receivable of $150. They still owed $11,500 on the note, and now had accounts payable of $200. They also owed $50 in wages to one of their bartenders.

a. Draw up a balance sheet for the Dingy Dive Bar as of January 21, 19x4, taking into account the above data.
b. Draw up a second balance sheet as of February 21, 19x4.
c. From the information given, what can you say of the success of the venture to date?

EXERCISES AND PROBLEMS

3. Concepts of wealth and income. Eugene and Janet Bronson own and operate a farm. Their title to the land includes the rights to any mineral wealth it contains. They have just discovered that a rich oil field that was recently found nearby extends far into their property. Drilling wells and selling the oil from these wells will be very worthwhile.

a. Did the discovery lead to an immediate increase in the known assets of this farm? Is it likely that the farm's market value increased as a result of the discovery? Did the discovery add to the Bronsons' income of the period in which the discovery was made?
b. Would the accountant report an immediate increase in assets on the farm's balance sheet? On the income statement for the period in which the discovery was made?

4. Organizing a balance sheet. The Brandon Company's assets, liabilities, and owners' equity were as follows on December 31, 19x1:

Accounts payable	$13,300
Accounts receivable	8,120
Buildings	35,760
Cash on hand and in bank	6,600
Equipment	4,450
Interest payable	180
Inventory of merchandise	11,200
Land	18,000
Long-term debt	10,200
Notes payable	9,000
Owners' equity	To be derived
Prepaid insurance	2,000
Wages payable	1,770

Prepare a statement of financial position for the Brandon Company as of December 31, 19x1.

5.   *Monetary versus nonmonetary assets.* Which of the assets listed in Problem 4 were monetary assets? For each of these identify the individuals or groups against whom the Brandon Company had monetary claims on that date.

6.   *Identifying income statement elements.* The following list includes all the items that should appear on the income statement for Omega Stores for the year 19x1, together with some items that don't belong on that income statement:

Accounts receivable, beginning of year	$ 200
Accounts receivable, end of year	210
Cash on hand, beginning of year	130
Cash on hand, end of year	100
Cost of the merchandise purchased during 19x1	630
Cost of the merchandise sold during 19x1	600
Merchandise inventory, beginning of year	120
Merchandise inventory, end of year	150
Miscellaneous expenses during 19x1	60
Owners' equity, beginning of year	500
Owners' equity, end of year	520
Rent expense for 19x1	40
Salaries and wages expense for 19x1	110
Sales revenues for 19x1	1,000
Tax expenses for 19x1	140
Accounts payable, beginning of year	70
Accounts payable, end of year	90

a.   Using the relevant figures from this list, prepare an income statement for the year 19x1.
b.   For each item you didn't include in the income statement, explain why you excluded it.

7.   *Funds statement.* The Durham Trading Company buys merchandise from manufacturers, stores this merchandise in a rented warehouse, and sells it to retail stores. During 19x1, the company had revenues of $200,000 and expenses of $170,000. It borrowed $20,000 from a bank and paid dividends of $10,000 to its owners. It bought and paid for a plot of land costing $40,000.

a.   Using only this information, prepare a statement of changes in financial position for the year 19x1.
b.   What does this statement reveal about the company's activities in 19x1? Is this same information also revealed by the income statement for the year?

8.   *Measuring and interpreting financial results.* Stanley Throckmorton, who sells popcorn at public events, has no capital invested in his business other than the cash he keeps in his "business" wallet and a pushcart he bought five years ago for $200. This pushcart contains a corn-popping machine, storage space for materials (unpopped corn, butter, and salt), and a

24924   G

compartment in which the popped corn can be kept warm until a customer buys it.

One morning, Mr. Throckmorton left home with $100 in cash in his business wallet. Contemplating an unusually busy day, he bought materials (corn, butter, and salt) costing $120. Although he usually paid cash for his purchases, this was an exceptionally large one for him. Being a regular customer of his supplier, he was permitted to charge $50 of the total amount and pay cash for the rest.

He then attended a baseball game where he sold three quarters of his purchases for $135, all in cash. At the end of the day, he returned home with his unsold stock, planning to replenish his inventory, pay his bill, and obtain fuel for his corn popper on the following morning. (He normally bought fuel on alternate business days at a cost of about $4. A purchase of this size was enough for two days' operation of the corn popper.)

a. How would you measure the results of Mr. Throckmorton's operations for this day? Quantify your answer as much as possible and list the items, if any, which you found difficult to quantify.

b. Why should Mr. Throckmorton be interested in a measure of his operating results, defined as in (a)? How might knowledge of operating results affect his business actions?

c. What other information might Mr. Throckmorton want to be able to get from his accounting records?

9. Managerial accounting.   Helen and Hilda Haldi, former Olympic downhill skiers, were hired by Haddon Hill Associates to manage the Haddon Hill ski area. Their facilities included restaurants, shops, ski lifts, snowmaking and grooming equipment, and five downhill ski runs. They also ran a full instructional program for children and adults.

The Haldi sisters were expected to decide when to open or close individual lifts, slopes, restaurants and other customer service facilities. They hired and supervised the work of a controller and the heads of Haddon Hill's three operating departments: the restaurant manager, the chief ski instructor, and the maintenance manager. The chief instructor was in charge of all customer service activities except the restaurants, lifts, and ski runs. The maintenance manager was responsible for all maintenance of physical plant and equipment and for the operation of lifts and ski runs. The chief instructor also organized and supervised the ski patrol and first-aid operations.

The department heads determined how many employees they would need in their departments each day, following guidelines the Haldi sisters had established at the beginning of the season. Each department head was expected to control costs, maintain the quality of the services provided, hire and fire employees, and maintain effective employee relations. The restaurant manager and chief instructor were also expected to produce revenues in excess of the costs of operating their departments.

a. Outline the kinds of information the Haldi sisters probably received when they were planning for this year's skiing season and state how they probably used it. In what format (that is, what kinds of items and how much detail) did they probably express their financial plan for the year?

b. What kinds of financial information would management probably require during the skiing season? How often would this information be reported and to whom? What kinds of actions would you expect management to take in response to this information?

c. What part would you expect the controller (chief accounting officer) of the Haddon Hill ski area to play in the planning and control process?

10. *Data for owners' decisions.* Angus MacTavish scratched his head in bewilderment. "I can't figure it out," he said. "I've been running this business for almost a year, and I have more customers by far than I had expected when I started. I have had to hire a new bookkeeper just to get out the bills to my customers and to record their payments when they come in. Yet here I am, just before Christmas, and I don't have enough cash in the bank to pay for that new coat I promised to buy my wife if the business did well. I wonder what has gone wrong."

Mr. MacTavish went into business for himself on January 1, 19x1. He took $30,000 from his savings, rented a store, bought a stock of merchandise from a wholesaler, hired a shop assistant, and opened his doors for business. The store proved to be in an excellent location, and Mr. MacTavish quickly earned a reputation of being an honest merchant with good-quality merchandise and favorable prices. As the year wore on, his store became more and more crowded with customers, and he had to add an extra clerk to handle the business.

During the year, he bought one additional display cabinet to display his stock of a new line of products that a manufacturer's representative offered to him. Other than this, he didn't recall any major purchases of furniture or equipment. It seemed to him, however, that the better his business became, the less cash he had in the bank.

Mr. MacTavish was confident that his December business would bring in enough cash so that he needn't worry about not being able to meet the payroll at the end of December, but, even so, he would have a good deal less cash in the bank at the end of the year than he had when he started in business. This disturbed him because, as he put it, "I have sunk everything I have into this business, given up a good steady job with a strong company, and have worked day and night to make a go of it. If it's not going to pay off, I'd like to know it soon so that I can sell out and go back to work with someone else. I've made a lot of sacrifices this past year to go into business for myself, and I'd like to know whether it was all worthwhile."

This statement was made by Mr. MacTavish to Mr. Thomas Carr, a local public accountant to whom he had turned for advice. Mr. Carr replied that the first thing that he would have to do would be to try to draw up a set of financial statements for the MacTavish store that would summarize the results of the first year's operations to date.

a. To what extent does the decline in Mr. MacTavish's cash balance indicate the success or failure of his business operations during this period? What other explanations can you offer for this change? How would you measure the degree of success achieved by the store during its first year?

b. If you were Mr. MacTavish, what kinds of information would you need before you could decide whether to stay in business or to sell out? How much of this information would you expect Mr. Carr to be able to supply?

c. Assuming that Mr. MacTavish decides to stay in business and decides that he needs a bank loan to provide him with additional cash, what kinds of information do you think that the banker would want to have before approving the loan? Would this necessarily be the same as the information needed by Mr. Carr?

2

Deriving Financial Statements from Transactions Analyses

THE ACCOUNTANT'S USUAL MEASURES of a business firm's income and financial position are based on his or her analysis of the economic effects of individual *transactions*—that is, the actions and events the firm participates in directly. Our task in this chapter is to show how an accountant might analyze a series of typical transactions and summarize the results of these analyses in a set of simple financial statements.

TRANSACTIONS ANALYSIS

Even a small business enterprise engages in a wide variety of transactions. It receives and pays cash, buys and sells merchandise, and participates in many related activities. By examining the accountant's analyses of the transactions arising from the formation and operation of one of these, a small retail store, we can illustrate the fundamentals of accounting transactions analysis generally.

Investment Transactions

In June of 19x0, the sales manager of the Ajax Manufacturing Company offered Charles Erskine the exclusive dealership rights in his community for the Ajax line of refrigerators, radios, and other electrical appliances. Mr. Erskine, a salesman for a wholesale distributor of a competing line of appliances, decided that he had a good chance of succeeding; and so he resigned his job and began to organize his own business, The Erskine Appliance Store.

On June 30, Mr. Erskine entered into his first business transaction. He withdrew $30,000 in cash from a savings account in a bank and deposited it in a new checking account under the name of The Erskine Appliance Store. This was an investment transaction, providing the new business with its first asset, $30,000 in cash. It also gave Mr. Erskine an owner's interest in the firm. Since accounting systems measure owners' equities by the amounts invested by the owners in the business, this transaction can be said to have created an owner's equity of $30,000. The full analysis of the transaction therefore can be written as follows:

(1)

Asset Increase		Accompanied	Owner's Equity Increase	
Cash	$30,000	by	Erskine's Investment	$30,000

Notice that this analysis shows what happened to the assets and equities of the *business*, as something separate and distinct from Mr. Erskine and his other activities. If we were to analyze its immediate effect on Mr. Erskine's personal fortune, the results would be quite different. A $30,000 decrease in one asset (cash in the savings account) would be just offset by a $30,000 increase in another asset (investment in The Erskine Appliance Store).

This illustrates an important point. Financial statements always relate to a specific set of resources. The set of resources being reported on constitute what is sometimes referred to as the *accounting entity*. To avoid confusion, therefore, accountants have to begin with a clear definition of the accounting entity they are working with. They can then exclude any transactions that don't affect this entity. For example, if Mr. Erskine were to take another $5,000 from his personal savings account to buy a new automobile for family use, this transaction would not be reflected in the financial statements of The Erskine Appliance Store.

The result of this investment transaction illustrates another point: *every equity in one accounting entity is an asset in some other accounting entity.* This shows up clearly in Exhibit 2–1. A banker looking at Mr. Erskine as an accounting entity would regard his investment in the store as an asset. The same banker looking at the store as an accounting entity would see this same investment as an owner's equity.

Purchase and Payment Transactions

Immediately after opening the new checking account, Mr. Erskine signed the Ajax franchise agreement and took a two-year lease (starting July 1) on a store containing ample office, storage, and

EXHIBIT 2–1

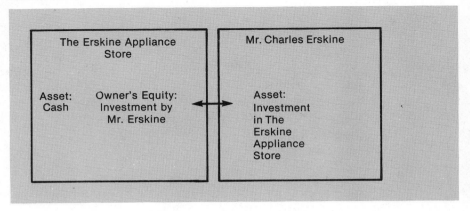

display space. The rent on the store was $1,200 a month, and he paid
the rent for three months in advance by writing a check for $3,600
against the company's checking account. The payment of cash is
known as a *disbursement*.

How did the payment to the landlord affect the company's assets
and its equities? First, we know that the amount in the checking
account was $3,600 smaller than it had been. This means that the
transaction reduced the size of the asset, cash, by $3,600. Second, by
paying the landlord $3,600, the company acquired the right to use
the store for three months. This right was an asset, prepaid rent. It fit
the definition of an asset we provided in Chapter 1—that is, an asset
is an object, a claim, or a right owned by and having value to the
organization.

In this case, the asset was a right; the company owned and clearly
expected to use it to increase the company's value to the owner—
otherwise Mr. Erskine wouldn't have paid $3,600 for the right. In
other words, the transaction was analyzed as follows:

	(2)		
Asset Increase	*Accompanied*	*Asset Decrease*	
Prepaid Rent $3,600	*by*	Cash $3,600	

Since one asset was exchanged for another with no change in the
equities in this transaction, the total assets remained unchanged at
$30,000. The accounting equation showed the following figures after
this transaction was completed.

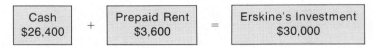

Immediately after the lease was signed, the Ajax Company delivered merchandise to the store, for which Mr. Erskine agreed to pay $12,000 sometime during the next 30 days. By this transaction, the store acquired an asset, merchandise, at a cost of $12,000. No other asset was given up immediately, however, because Ajax agreed to wait a short while for its money. In other words, Ajax made a short-term investment in The Erskine Appliance Store and the store had its first creditor.

Once again we see the two sides of an investment transaction. As a result of this transaction, Ajax had a claim against The Erskine Appliance Store, and it regarded this claim as an asset. To the store, however, this same claim appeared as a liability because it would have to be settled by the payment of cash within 30 days. The store assumed this liability in exchange for the assets received from Ajax, and the transaction was viewed as follows:

(3)

Asset Increase	*Accompanied*	*Liability Increase*
Inventory $12,000	by	Accounts Payable $12,000

This increased the asset total to $42,000.

Next, Mr. Erskine bought secondhand equipment for the store, paying $9,000 in cash from the store's bank account. This transaction was just like the prepayment of rent: one asset, cash, was exchanged for another asset, equipment. The equipment was measured for accounting purposes just as the prepaid rent had been, at its cost—that is, by the amount of cash given up to acquire it. The transaction, therefore, was interpreted in the following way:

(4)

Asset Increase	*Accompanied*	*Asset Decrease*
Equipment $9,000	by	Cash $9,000

This left the total asset figure at $42,000, and the accounting equation remained in balance.

Mr. Erskine's final act on June 30 was to hire Karen Watson to work with him in the store at a salary of $1,000 a month. She was to start work the next morning. This had no effect on the June 30 assets and equities, however. Because Ms. Watson would be paid only if she actually showed up for work, the firm owed her nothing on June 30. No asset was created, either, because the company had no ownership right to Ms. Watson's future services.

Maintaining the Accounting Equation

Transactions analysis is governed by one restriction—the accounting equation must always remain balanced. This means that the accounting analysis of *each* transaction must also be balanced—that is, a change in one item must be accompanied by a change in one or more other items so that the total of the assets remains equal to the total of the liabilities and owners' equity.

These specifications are met by the table in Exhibit 2–2, which shows the effects of The Erskine Appliance Store's first four transac-

EXHIBIT 2–2

THE ERSKINE APPLIANCE STORE
Assets, Liabilities, and Owner's Equity
June 30, 19x0

	Cash	+	Inven-tory	+	Equip-ment	+	Prepaid Rent	=	Ac-counts Payable	+	Erskine's Investment
(1)	+30,000										+30,000
(2)	− 3,600					+	3,600				
Bal.	26,400					+	3,600	=			30,000
(3)			+ 12,000						+12,000		
Bal.	26,400	+	12,000			+	3,600	=	12,000	+	30,000
(4)	− 9,000			+	9,000						
Bal.	17,400	+	12,000	+	9,000	+	3,600	=	12,000	+	30,000

tions. Notice particularly that the accounting equation remained balanced after each transaction was analyzed. The total of the amounts shown for the store's four assets at the end of June was $42,000, and the amounts shown for the liabilities and owner's equity added up to the same total. Of this, $30,000 had been supplied by Mr. Erskine and $12,000 by a creditor, the supplier of merchandise.

Sale Transactions: Revenues and Expenses

Nothing that Mr. Erskine did during June produced measurable income for the firm. When the store opened for business in July, however, Mr. Erskine hoped that the events of that month would produce net income immediately.

We defined net income in Chapter 1 as the excess of total revenue over total expense in a given period. Before seeing how this definition is implemented in the analysis of transactions, we need to look behind the definition. Redrawing the accounting equation in the following form will help us do this:

$$\boxed{\text{Assets}} \quad - \quad \boxed{\text{Liabilities}} \quad = \quad \boxed{\text{Owner's Equity}}$$

In this form, we have simply moved the liabilities from the right to the left side of the equation and changed their sign from plus to minus.

The quantity represented on the left side of this revised equation (assets minus liabilities) is sometimes called the *net assets*. Obviously, anything that increases net assets also increases owner's equity, or vice versa. This is crucial. A business has net income only to the extent that it uses its resources to increase its net assets. If there is no increase in net assets, there is no income. And if the net assets increase, then the owner's equity also increases.

For example, The Erskine Appliance Store sold merchandise to its customers in July for $13,400. Of this, $2,800 was in cash, and the remaining $10,600 was sold on credit.[1] The merchandise covered by these sales was part of the first shipment received from Ajax Manufacturing Company on June 30. The items sold had cost $9,600.

Notice what happened: Mr. Erskine exchanged one group of assets (merchandise) for another (cash and accounts receivable). As a result of these exchanges, his total assets increased by $3,800. Since the liabilities went neither up nor down, the owner's equity must have increased by $3,800 as well. This analysis can be summarized as follows:

(5)

Asset Increases		Accompanied	Asset Decrease	
Cash	$ 2,800	by	Inventory	$9,600
Accounts Receivable	10,600			
			Owner's Equity Increase	
			Erskine's Investment	3,800

This analysis measures the margin between sales revenue and the cost of the merchandise that was sold, usually referred to as the *gross margin*. It doesn't tell us, however, whether this was a large percentage or a small percentage of revenue. Some companies deliberately keep their gross margin percentages low to penetrate mass markets; others, operating in smaller markets, need high margins to cover their marketing and administrative expenses and produce income. For example, the two companies represented by the bars in Exhibit 2–3 have identical total gross margins but very different pricing policies. The one at the left operates in a very small market with high prices relative to the cost of the merchandise it sells. The company at the right is in a large market with a much narrower percentage spread between price and the cost of the merchandise sold.

The total revenue figure is also used in the calculation of other ratios and to measure the company's rate of growth, as we'll see in Chapter 17. To provide the basis for these calculations, accountants

---

[1] The terms *on credit* and *on account* are used interchangeably to mean that payment for goods or services purchased or sold is to be made at some date later than the date of the delivery of the goods or the performance of the service.

EXHIBIT 2–3.   Gross Margin Percentages

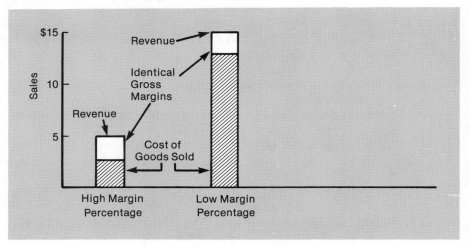

always divide the analysis of sale transactions into two parts, one dealing with the revenue, the other dealing with the expense (cost of goods sold). The analysis of The Erskine Appliance Store's first set of sale transactions therefore showed the following:

(5a)

Asset Increases		Accompanied	Owner's Equity Increase (Revenue)	
Cash	$ 2,800	by	Erskine's Investment	$13,400
Accounts Receivable . . .	10,600			

The items on the left are the assets the store received from its customers during the month; the item on the right shows that assets worth $13,400 were provided to the firm for the owner's benefit. Taken by themselves, in other words, these sale transactions increased the owner's equity by $13,400.

We know, of course, that owner's equity didn't increase by the full $13,400. To obtain this amount, Mr. Erskine had to deliver merchandise which had cost the store $9,600. Since this removed the particular merchandise from the company's inventory, that asset decreased in size and so did the owner's equity. This analysis can be summarized as follows:

(5b)

Owner's Equity Decrease (Expense)		Accompanied	Asset Decrease	
Erskine's Investment	$9,600	by	Inventory	$9,600

Taken together, these two analyses show the same changes in assets and owner's equity as analysis (5) above; the only difference is that two figures, +\$13,400 and −\$9,600, have been substituted for the +\$3,800 figure in analysis (5).

Terminology: Cost and Expense

Two of the terms used in this illustration are often misused in practice, even by experienced analysts of financial statements. The terms are *cost* and *expense*. Cost is the broader term, and Exhibit 2–4 shows how costs flow through organization. First, resources are

EXHIBIT 2–4.   Distinction Between Cost and Expense

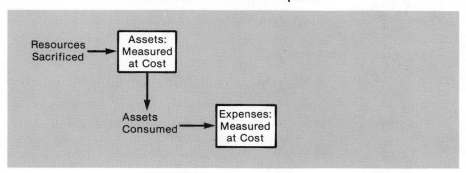

used to acquire assets (for example, inventories). These assets are measured by the amount of resources sacrificed to obtain them (their cost). When the assets are used to produce revenue, their costs are reclassified as expenses.

TERMINOLOGY REMINDER

Cost: the amount of resources sacrificed to obtain something or achieve some objective.

Expense: the cost of resources given up to obtain revenues of the current period; a cost subtracted from revenues on the income statement.

In other words, cost is the basis of measurement: asset and expense are two stages in the life cycle of a cost. Nonmonetary assets are resources the firm still has, measured at their cost; expenses are resources the firm has used up in producing the revenues of a particular time period, measured at their cost.

The term *expense* should also be distinguished from the term *expenditure*. An expenditure is any use of resources. Companies make expenditures when they acquire inventories, when they use inventories, or when they use their employees' services. Some of these expenditures lead to expenses of the current period; others do not.

The key question when a cost is incurred (that is, when resources are committed for a purpose) is when the organization is likely to reap the benefits arising as a result of the cost. If the benefits all materialized in the period in which the cost was incurred, the cost should be classified as an expense. If the benefits are deferred, then the cost should be identified as an asset. The cost of merchandise purchased, for example, should be classified as the cost of an asset until it generates revenue. At that time it becomes an expense because it has produced all the benefit management can reasonably expect from it.

Other Operating Transactions

Subtracting the cost of the merchandise sold from sales revenues doesn't yield the net income figure, of course. Many other goods and services are consumed each period to create the period's revenues. This means that their costs are also expenses of the current period.

For example, The Erskine Appliance Store used Ms. Watson's services during the month of July, at a cost of $1,000. One clear effect of this transaction was to create a liability—by using Ms. Watson's services, the store acquired a legal obligation to pay her for those services.

What else did this transaction (use of Ms. Watson's services) do? Its purpose was to help Mr. Erskine create owner's equity by selling merchandise. Mr. Erskine saw no reason why Ms. Watson's work this month should benefit any period in the future. This means that the entire cost was a cost of generating revenues (increases in owner's equity) in July. Since revenues are increases in owner's equity, the costs incurred to produce them are reductions in owner's equity. In sum, therefore, using Ms. Watson's services had the following effects:

(6)

Owner's Equity Decrease (Expense)	Accompanied	Liability Increase
Erskine's Investment $1,000	by	Salary Payable $1,000

Another group of items had similar effects. Electricity, telephone, and other costs of operating the store and office during the month amounted to $900. Since these costs related to current operations, they had to be regarded as having been consumed in the creation of current revenues—in other words, treated as expense:

(7)

Owner's Equity Decrease (Expense)	Accompanied	Liability Increase
Erskine's Investment $900	by	Accounts Payable $900

Once again, the use of these services reduced the owner's equity while increasing the firm's liabilities.

CARDINAL RULES OF TRANSACTIONS ANALYSIS

1. The accounting equation must remain balanced at all times; the changes resulting from each transaction must also balance each other.
2. Expenses are recognized when resources are used up to create current revenues; *whether cash is paid for these resources at the time they are used, or earlier, or later has no bearing on the question of when expenses take place.*

Other Transactions

A number of other transactions took place during July. First, additional merchandise was purchased on credit at a total cost of $6,400:

	(8)	
Asset Increase	*Accompanied*	*Liability Increase*
Inventory $6,400	*by*	Accounts Payable $6,400

The owner's equity was not affected by this set of transactions. Acquisition of the assets was financed temporarily by an increase in a liability.

Second, collections from customers on credit sales (see transaction 5) totaled $2,500. These were pure exchange-of-asset transactions and had no effect on the owner's equity. The analysis was:

	(9)	
Asset Increase	*Accompanied*	*Asset Decrease*
Cash $2,500	*by*	Accounts Receivable $2,500

Third, the company paid the Ajax Manufacturing Company, the electric company, the telephone company, and other suppliers $12,500, part of the money they were entitled to as a result of transactions (3) and (7). This is known as paying money "on account." In other words, an asset (cash) was surrendered to reduce some of the company's liabilities (accounts payable). These transactions were analyzed in the following terms:

	(10)	
Liability Decrease	*Accompanied*	*Asset Decrease*
Accounts Payable $12,500	*by*	Cash $12,500

Fourth, the store paid Ms. Watson her month's salary. This had exactly the same effects as the payment to suppliers—an asset was used to cancel a liability:

	(11)	
Liability Decrease	*Accompanied*	*Asset Decrease*
Salary Payable $1,000	*by*	Cash $1,000

Payment of the employee's salary canceled the liability we identified in our analysis of transaction (6).

Finally, Mr. Erskine withdrew $1,800 in cash for his personal use. This reduced both the assets and the owner's equity by $1,800 and was analyzed as follows:

	(12)	
Owner's Equity Decrease	*Accompanied*	*Asset Decrease*
Erskine's Investment $1,800	*by*	Cash $1,800

Mr. Erskine was in doubt whether this reduction in owner's equity should be regarded as a salary expense or as a partial repayment of his investment in the business (a "disinvestment"). His accountant promised to discuss this question with him at the end of the month.

Rent Expense

The data for each of the transactions analyses described above were found in documents that were prepared or received by The Erskine Appliance Store as a matter of routine. Data for the analysis of merchandise purchases, for example, came from the bills or *invoices* received from the store's suppliers.

Not all of the facts relevant to the preparation of periodic financial statements were contained in documents of this sort, however. For example, a portion of the asset prepaid rent was consumed during the month, but the landlord had no reason to send Mr. Erskine a document conveying this information. Mr. Erskine's accountant had to be alert to make sure that the cost of the store rental for July was not overlooked.

Going back to the documents underlying transaction (2), the accountant found that the rental payment of $3,600 had covered a period of three months in advance from July 1, at a rental of $1,200 a month. Since one month had gone by, one third of the total prepayment, or $1,200, had been consumed by July 31 as Mr. Erskine used the store premises to conduct his business.

Here is about as clear an example of an expense as we're likely to find. Whatever benefits were to be reaped from use of the store in

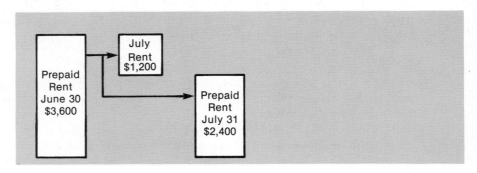

July were obtained in July. Management couldn't reasonably expect to gain any substantial benefit in future periods as a result of the July rental cost. The $1,200, therefore, was an operating expense of the month; both the assets and the owner's equity had been reduced by $1,200. This analysis can be summarized succinctly as follows:

(13)

Owner's Equity Decrease (Expense)	Accompanied	Asset Decrease
Erskine's Investment $1,200	by	Prepaid Rent $1,200

Depreciation

One other resource, the equipment Mr. Erskine had bought on June 30 was used in the business during July. The question was whether any of the $9,000 cost of this equipment had become an expense during the month.

This is a more complicated question than the one we answered in connection with the prepaid rent. As far as Mr. Erskine and Ms. Watson could see, the equipment was in just as good condition at the end of July as at the beginning. They knew it wouldn't last forever, however. It would have to be replaced sometime. Its benefits would be limited to the period between the date of purchase and the date of replacement. The costs, therefore, would be an expense of this long period. The problem was how much of this expense applied to the month of July and how much would apply to the other months the equipment would remain in use.

To resolve this issue, Mr. Erskine asked an equipment dealer how long he could expect to use the equipment in the store. They finally decided that five years (60 months) was a reasonable estimate and that 1/60 of the $9,000 cost ($150) should be considered a cost of producing revenue each month for 60 months.

This is an example of *depreciation*. The accountant defines depreciation as the portion of the cost of an asset, useful for two or more periods, that is attributable to the operations of one of those periods. Depreciation of the equipment in The Erskine Appliance Store in July had the following effects on the company's assets and equities:

(14)

Owner's Equity Decrease (Expense)	Accompanied	Asset Decrease
Erskine's Investment $150	by	Equipment $150

The item on the right says that part of the asset (equipment) was used up during the month; the item on the left says this happened because the equipment was necessary to produce revenues for the store during July—that is, the owner's equity was $150 lower than if no equipment depreciation had taken place.

The process of transferring costs from asset to expense in this way is known as cost *amortization*. Amortization is necessary whenever an asset is expected to produce benefits in two or more periods and will be wholly or partially consumed as it does this. Under most circumstances, land doesn't depreciate because it makes its contribution without losing any of its power to contribute in the future. Equipment depreciates because it loses its usefulness sooner or later. The cost of anything that depreciates must be amortized, that is, assigned in some way to the operations of the periods that intervene between the date the asset is acquired and the date it is disposed of.

THE FINANCIAL STATEMENTS

After these transactions had been analyzed, the assets, liabilities, and owner's equity of The Erskine Appliance Store appeared as in Exhibit 2–5. The numbers in parentheses refers to the transaction

EXHIBIT 2–5

THE ERSKINE APPLIANCE STORE
Assets, Liabilities, and Owner's Equity
For the Month Ended July 31, 19x0

Assets

Cash

Bal. 7/1	17,400
(5a)	+ 2,800
(9)	+ 2,500
(10)	− 1,000
(11)	−12,500
(12)	− 1,800
Bal. 7/31	7,400

Accounts Receivable

Bal. 7/1	—
(5a)	+10,600
(9)	− 2,500
Bal. 7/31	8,100

Inventory

Bal. 7/1	12,000
(5b)	− 9,600
(8)	+ 6,400
Bal. 7/31	8,800

Prepaid Rent

Bal. 7/1	3,600
(13)	−1,200
Bal. 7/31	2,400

Equipment

Bal. 7/1	9,000
(14)	− 150
Bal. 7/31	8,850

Liabilities

Accounts Payable

Ba. 7/1	12,000
(7)	+ 900
(8)	+ 6,400
(11)	−12,500
Bal. 7/31	6,800

Salary Payable

(6)	+1,000
(10)	−1,000
Bal. 7/31	—

Owner's Equity

Erskine's Investment

Bal.	7/1	30,000
(5a)	Sales revenue	+13,400
(5b)	Cost of goods sold expense	− 9,600
(6)	Salary expense	− 1,000
(7)	Misc. expense	− 900
(12)	Withdrawal	− 1,800
(13)	Rent expense	− 1,200
(14)	Depreciation expense	− 150
Bal.	7/31	28,750

numbers in the discussion above. The plus and minus signs alongside the various owner's equity elements identify them as positive or negative components of the total owner's equity.

Mr. Erskine's accountant prepared four financial statements from this exhibit: an income statement, a statement of changes in owner's equity, a statement of financial position, and a statement of cash receipts and disbursements. The cash statement was prepared instead of the statement of changes in financial position (funds statement) we described in Chapter 1, for reasons we'll explain in a moment.

THE TRANSACTIONS EQUATION

Those who understand transactions analysis thoroughly will have little difficulty in tracing the relationships among the various elements in the financial statements. A key relationship is the transaction equation for any statement element:

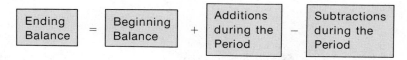

$$\boxed{\text{Ending Balance}} = \boxed{\text{Beginning Balance}} + \boxed{\text{Additions during the Period}} - \boxed{\text{Subtractions during the Period}}$$

Any of the four elements in this equation can be calculated if the other three are known.

The Income Statement

Mr. Erskine's accountant arranged the month's revenues and expenses in the income statement shown in Exhibit 2–6.

EXHIBIT 2–6

THE ERSKINE APPLIANCE STORE
Income Statement
For the Month Ended July 31, 19x0

Sales revenue		$13,400
Expenses:		
Cost of goods sold	$9,600	
Salary	1,000	
Rent	1,200	
Depreciation	150	
Miscellaneous	900	
Total Expense		12,850
Net Income		$ 550

We've gone over the elements in the income statement before, so the structure should be no surprise. In this case the revenues exceeded the expenses by $550, and this was the store's net income for the month.[2]

Statement of Changes in Owner's Equity

The $1,800 Mr. Erskine withdrew from the business during July didn't appear on the income statement. It showed up instead on the statement of changes in owner's equity, reproduced in Exhibit 2–7.

EXHIBIT 2–7

THE ERSKINE APPLIANCE STORE
Statement of Changes in Owner's Equity
For the Month Ended July 31, 19x0

Owner's equity, July 1, 19x0	$30,000
Add: Net income for the month	550
	$30,550
Less: Withdrawals	1,800
Owner's equity, July 31, 19x0	$28,750

This shows the owner's equity at the beginning of the month, the amount added to it during the month (in this case entirely the result of income-producing transactions), the amount subtracted (the withdrawals), and the amount of Mr. Erskine's equity in the business at the end of July.

Mr. Erskine objected to putting the $1,800 withdrawal into this statement. He felt it should be regarded as an expense, just as much as the rent or Ms. Watson's salary. He had given up a job in which he had been earning about $1,500 a month. Furthermore, the securities he had sold to get the $30,000 he had invested in the store had been bringing him earnings of close to $300 a month. While acknowledging that the first month's operations were a poor test of the store's profitability, he knew he couldn't afford to keep the store going indefinitely if it continued to show a loss after his personal salary and interest on his investment were deducted.[3]

Withdrawals of this sort can't be classified as expenses. Treating them as expenses would allow Mr. Erskine to manipulate the net income figure. He's the one who decided to withdraw $1,800, not

---

[2] Mr. Erskine included the income from the store with his income from other sources in calculating his income taxes for the year. The store itself had no income tax. In Chapter 3 we'll see how to account for taxes levied specifically on business income.

[3] Measurements of this kind are sometimes made by economists for statistical or analytical purposes. Starting with accounting net income, economists deduct "imputed wages" for any managerial services provided by owner-managers and "imputed interest" on the owners' invested capital, leaving a residual they call profit.

some larger or smaller amount. If withdrawals were classified as expenses, Mr. Erskine could increase or decrease the net income figure by increasing or decreasing the size of his withdrawals. To avoid this possibility, accountants have excluded owners' withdrawals from the income statement.[4]

Statement of Financial Position

The third financial statement was a comparative statement of financial position (balance sheet), reproduced in Exhibit 2–8. This

EXHIBIT 2–8

THE ERSKINE APPLIANCE STORE
Comparative Statements of Financial Position
July 31 and June 30, 19x0

Assets

	July 31	June 30
Current Assets:		
Cash	$ 7,400	$17,400
Accounts receivable	8,100	—
Inventory	8,800	12,000
Prepaid rent	2,400	3,600
Total current assets	$26,700	$33,000
Equipment	8,850	9,000
Total Assets	$35,550	$42,000

Liabilities and Owner's Equity

Current Liabilities:		
Accounts payable	$ 6,800	$12,000
Owner's Equity:		
Erskine, proprietor	28,750	30,000
Total Liabilities and Owner's Equity	$35,550	$42,000

shows statements for both the beginning and the end of the month. The beginning figures came from the last line of Exhibit 2–2; the July 31 amounts came from Exhibit 2–5.

These balance sheets are just like the ones we saw in Chapter 1, except that one new asset, prepaid rent, is included. Prepaid rent is classified as a current asset because it will be used up during the next operating cycle.

---

[4] Though technically correct, this conclusion is much less important than it used to be. If the business is organized as a corporation, or if the statements are prepared as if the organization is incorporated, salaries of owner-managers are listed as expenses. This treatment is described in Chapter 3.

Statement of Cash Flows

The income and owner's equity statements are *flow* statements, summarizing the effects of transactions that took place during a specified *period*. The balance sheet, on the other hand, is a *status* report, showing the company's position on a specified *date*. Taken together, the two flow statements connect the owner's equity sections of the balance sheets at the beginning and end of the period.

A similar flow statement can be constructed for any balance-sheet item. Mr. Erskine's accountant prepared only one of these, however, the statement of cash flows reproduced in Exhibit 2–9. This state-

EXHIBIT 2–9

THE ERSKINE APPLIANCE STORE
Statement of Cash Flows
For the Month Ended July 31, 19x0

Uses of Cash:
Cash flow from operations:

Cash sales	$ 2,800	
Collections from credit customers	2,500	
Total Receipts from Customers		$ 5,300
Less: Payments to suppliers	$12,500	
Payments to employees	1,000	13,500
Net Cash Outflow from Operations		$ 8,200
Withdrawals by owner		1,800
Total Uses of Cash		$10,000

Sources of Cash:

Cash provided by reducing cash balance (from $17,400 on July 1 to $7,400 on July 31)	$10,000
Total Sources of Cash	$10,000

ment was drawn directly from the summary of cash transactions in the upper left-hand corner of Exhibit 2–5.

This statement differs from the funds statement illustrated in Chapter 1 in that it shows only movements of *cash*. The funds statement, as we shall see more clearly in Chapter 16, shows movements of *working capital*. The accountant in this case, noting how rapidly the company's cash balance was shrinking, prepared this statement to alert Mr. Erskine to the need to manage the store's cash flows for the next few months. Operations in July actually increased the working capital, but increases in receivables and decreases in accounts payable put a heavy drain on cash. An increase in working capital is small solace if the company can't pay its bills when they come due.

The cash-flow statement is in no sense a substitute for the income statement, although a series of them over a relatively long period of time might do the job. The cash-flow statement doesn't show how many resources have been *used;* it shows the resources *paid for* during the period. Payments may be a good deal greater than usage, as in this case, or a good deal less. By the same token, cash receipts from customers in any period may be either greater or less than the value of the claims against customers created by the firm's operations in that period (revenues). In any short period of time, the income statement is likely to be a much better index of the firm's ability to cover its costs and remain in business.

OMISSIONS FROM FINANCIAL STATEMENTS

As our earlier discussion of basic accounting measurement concepts showed, the balance sheet doesn't list all of the resources at the firm's disposal, nor does the income statement list all of the changes that take place in the values of these resources.

Mr. Erskine was particularly aware of some of these omissions because he planned to approach the bank for a loan and was anxious that his balance sheet present every justifiable evidence of financial strength. With this objective in mind, he was concerned that his statements ascribed no value to what he considered his most important assets: his dealership franchise and his customer following in the trade.

There is no question that items such as these are important. Mr. Erskine certainly should have emphasized them in his discussions with the bank's lending officers. Accountants exclude them from the balance sheet, however, because they can't verify the evidence on which measurements of these quantities as assets would have to be based. This kind of asset appears on the balance sheet only if the company buys a franchise or access to a group of customers. In such cases the asset is measured at its cost because the purchase price can be verified fairly easily.

The statements also ignored the two-year lease on the store Mr. Erskine had signed. Signing this lease gave the company the right to use the store building for two years at a fixed rental; it also committed the company to a fixed series of payments to the landlord. This agreement was an important factor, one that would be favorable if property values went up and unfavorable in they went down. Even so, the accounting profession doesn't regard the signing of this sort of lease as an exchange of resources that should be recognized in the statements.[5] The leased property enters the accounting system only as the property is used or as payments are made.

---

[5] Lease accounting is discussed briefly in Chapter 13.

ACCRUAL ACCOUNTING

Just as Moliere's bourgeois gentleman was delighted to learn that he had been speaking prose all his life, it may be a pleasure to discover that while we have been learning the fundamentals of transactions analysis, we have been practicing accrual accounting. Accrual accounting is any accounting system in which changes in assets, liabilities, and owners' equity are measured by flows of resources of all kinds rather than by flows of cash alone. The alternative to accrual accounting is *cash-basis accounting.*

For example, John Appleby operates a small management consulting business under the name of Appleby Associates. On January 2, he agreed to carry out an assignment for the Jones Company. On January 22 he purchased and received materials costing $1,000 for use on this assignment. He paid for the materials on February 9 and started to work on the assignment on March 5. The project was completed on March 28, and the Jones Company was billed for the contract price of $12,000 on that date. Salaries of employees who worked on the assignment during March totaled $4,000 and this amount was paid on March 31.

This series of transactions is summarized in Exhibit 2–10. An expenditure in January was followed by a cash disbursement of $1,000 in February, another disbursement of $4,000 in March, and a cash receipt of $12,000 in April. Cash-basis accounting would indicate that the company lost $1,000 in February, lost $4,000 in March,

EXHIBIT 2–10.   Appleby Associates: Timing of Events

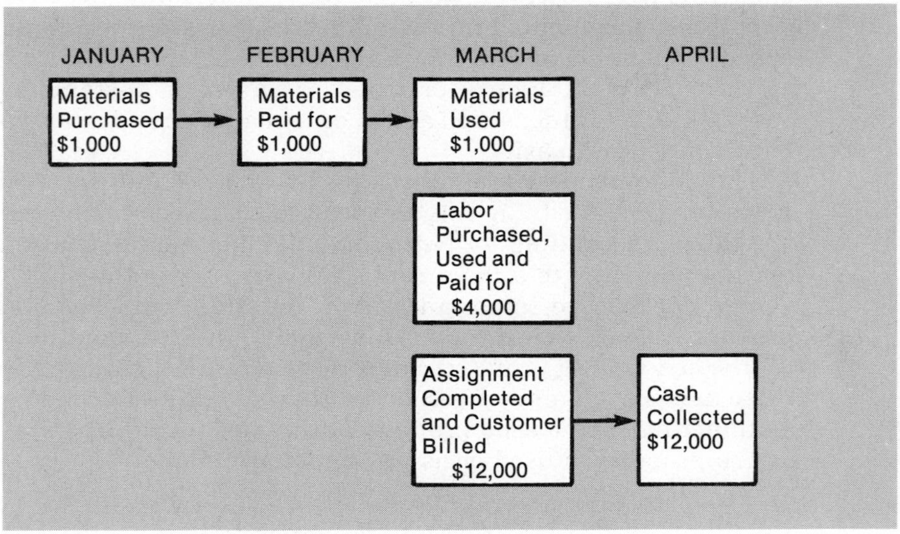

JANUARY	FEBRUARY	MARCH	APRIL
Materials Purchased $1,000	Materials Paid for $1,000	Materials Used $1,000	
		Labor Purchased, Used and Paid for $4,000	
		Assignment Completed and Customer Billed $12,000	Cash Collected $12,000

and earned $12,000 in April, when cash was finally received from the client.

Anyone who has mastered these first two chapters will recognize very quickly that the cash basis ignores many significant resource flows. Accrual accounting would bring all of these figures together in the income statement for March, when all of the work was done. Income of $7,000 on this contract would be recognized in March, even though the company had a $5,000 cash deficiency at the end of the month.

SUMMARY

Accounting measures of income and financial position are based on summaries of the accountants' analyses of individual transactions. The analysis of a transaction consists of the identification of its effects on the firm's assets, liabilities, and owners' equities.

Each transaction affects at least two kinds of assets, liabilities, or owners' equities. For each transaction the sum of the asset changes must equal the sum of the changes in liabilities and the owners' equities, as in the box on this page. As a result, the accounting equation always remains balanced.

> ### BALANCED TRANSACTIONS ANALYSES
>
> An asset increases, another asset decreases.
> An asset increases, a liability increases.
> An asset increases, owners' equity increases.
> An asset decreases, a liability decreases.
> An asset decreases, owners' equity decreases.
> A liability increases, another liability decreases.
> A liability increases, owners' equity decreases.
> A liability decreases, owners' equity increases.
> One part of owners' equity increases, another part decreases.

Various kinds of transactions can be drawn from the summaries of transactions analyses. A statement of cash flows can be a very useful indicator of where the firm is getting its cash, how it is being used, and how adequate the cash inflows are. The balance sheet shows how many resources have been invested in the business up to a given date, where they have come from, and how they have been used. The income statement shows how productive these resources were during a particular period of time.

The income statement and balance sheet don't necessarily reflect all of the available information about the financial status and productivity of the firm, because the accountant is generally unwilling to use estimates that can't be verified readily. This means that both management and outsiders must be alert, ready to recognize situations in which information on unmeasured quantities is vital to an understanding of the firm and its operations.

KEY TERMS

Accounting entity	Disbursement
Accrual accounting	Expenditure
Amortization	Gross margin
Cash-flow statement	Net assets
Depreciation	Transaction

INDEPENDENT STUDY PROBLEMS (Solutions in Appendix B)

1. Analyzing transactions.   A furniture store opened for business on January 1, 19x1. The store's transactions in 19x3, its third year of operations, included the following, among others:

1. The company purchased office furniture on July 1, 19x3, $4,200. The supplier was paid on October 1, 19x3. Office furniture in this company has a 12-year life.
2. Management hired a sales representative on October 1 at a salary of $700 a month. The representative started work immediately and remained in the company's employ until January 31, 19x4. Sales representatives' salaries are paid on the 15th of each month, covering work done in the preceding month.
3. The company sold merchandise on account for $300,000. This merchandise had been placed in inventory in 19x2. It had cost $220,000 at that time.
4. The company paid a supplier $24,000 for merchandise received in 19x2.
5. The company paid $22,500 on November 1, 19x3, for store rental covering the period from October 1, 19x3, through March 31, 19x4.

a. How much expense should have been recognized in the company's 19x3 income statement as a result of each of these events in 19x3?
b. Identify the effects of each of the events in 19x3 on the company's assets, liabilities, and owners' equity.

2. Transactions equation.   For each of the following, apply the transactions equation and calculate and identify the missing figure or figures:

a. Accounts receivable: beginning balance, $100; sales on account, $500; ending balance, $80.
b. Accounts payable: beginning balance, $50; payments to suppliers, $250; ending balance, $40.

c. Wages payable: beginning balance, $20; wages earned by employees, $300; wages paid to employees, $295.

d. Merchandise inventory: ending balance, $90; cost of goods purchased, $240; cost of goods sold, $265.

3. Effects of transactions on income and financial position. Earl Holt decided to operate a hot dog stand near a football stadium during the football season. The following transactions describe the financial effects of his activities in setting up the business and operating it for one week:

1. He deposited $300 in the Second National Bank.

2. He rented a site, paying $45 for the right to use the location on the following three Saturdays.

3. A tent and other equipment were purchased for $110 from a bankrupt concern; a check was issued in payment.

4. Merchandise was purchased from the Hill Wholesale Company, $305; Holt paid $100 down (by check) and promised to pay the balance on Monday after the first game.

5. All of the merchandise was sold for cash on the first Saturday, and Mr. Holt deposited the total receipts, $650 in his bank account.

6. Holt decided that one third of the rent payment was applicable to the business done at the first game and that the tent and equipment would have a cash value of $47 at the end of the third Saturday, the last game of the season. After that game Mr. Holt intended to go out of this business.

7. On Monday, Mr. Holt paid the balance due the Hill Wholesale Company in full.

a. Summarize the effects of these transactions on the assets, liabilities, and owner's equity of Mr. Holt's hot dog business, using the format illustrated in Exhibit 2–2. Be sure to indicate clearly which are the assets, which are the liabilities, and which are the owner's equities.

b. Prepare a balance sheet as of Monday night, after all the above information has been collected.

c. Prepare an income statement for the period that ended Monday night.

4. Transactions analysis; cash-flow statement. A store had the following transactions in 19x1:

1. It bought merchandise on account for $1 million.

2. It sold merchandise on account for $1.5 million.

3. It used the services of its employees; these employees earned $300,000 by providing these services.

4. It received invoices totaling $100,000 from the electric company, the telephone company, and other outside firms for services it used during 19x1.

5. It paid $1,050,000 to merchandise suppliers, utility companies, and other outside service companies.

6. It paid its employees $280,000.

7. It collected $1.6 million in cash from its customers.

8. It bought display cabinets and other store equipment for $40,000, paying $25,000 in cash and promising to pay the balance early in 19x2.

9. It counted the merchandise on hand on December 31, 19x1. The cost of that merchandise was $200,000. (A similar count on December 31, 19x0, had identified merchandise on hand at that time with a cost of $140,000.

10. It estimated that depreciation of store fixtures and equipment during the year amounted to $18,000.

11. The owners withdrew $10,000 in cash for their own use.

a. Identify the effects of each of these transactions and other events on the company's assets, liabilities, and owners' equity. For each change, state both the amount in dollars and the direction of the change (+ or −).

b. Prepare an income statement for the year.

c. Prepare a statement of cash flows for the year.

EXERCISES AND PROBLEMS

5. Net assets and owners' equity.   "Although the accountant chooses to derive the net income figure by measuring changes in the owners' equity, net income in reality consists of an increase in the firm's net assets (total assets minus total liabilities)."

Does this statement add anything to your understanding of accounting? Is it true? Describe a transaction that increases net assets without producing income. Does this disprove the statement quoted above?

6. Measuring expense.   Andrew Jenkins worked 100 hours in the Acme Hardware Store during June. He was paid $450 during July for these services. How much of this amount was an expense of the store in June? How much was an expense in July? Explain.

7. True or false.   State whether each of the following is true, false, or doubtful. Give reasons.

a. The total assets of a business are increased by the purchase of goods on credit.

b. Cash and owners' equity are the same.

c. The total of a firm's assets occasionally may exceed the total of its liabilities and owners' equities.

d. Since long-term debt and owners' investments are both sources of assets, they may be considered as essentially identical.

e. Income is a source of assets.

f. When a firm owes taxes to a governmental body, that governmental body is, in effect, providing some of the resources used by the firm.

8. Analyzing a sale transaction.   Merchandise costing $4,000 is sold for $5,200.

a. Analyze the effects of this transaction on the assets, liabilities, and owners' equity.

b. What expenses connected with this transaction are known at the time the sale takes place? What expenses are not known?

c. How and when will the profit or loss resulting from this transaction be determined?

9. Supplying missing information. From the following financial data for four business firms, determine the amount of each item for which the amount is not given:

	A	B	C	D
Assets 1/1/x0	$ 60,000	$100,000	$ 80,000	$ —
Liabilities 1/1/x0	25,000	—	20,000	100,000
Assets 12/31/x0	70,000	—	—	600,000
Liabilities 12/31/x0	26,000	29,000	16,000	—
Owners' equity 1/1/x0	—	70,000	—	400,000
Owners' equity 12/31/x0	—	74,000	—	420,000
Revenue 19x0	350,000	500,000	400,000	—
Expense 19x0	337,000	—	380,000	1,500,000
Withdrawals 19x0	—	5,000	8,000	15,000

10. Preparing financial statements from account balances. The financial records of Charles Fox's automobile shop showed the following amounts on December 31, 19x6:

Accounts payable	$ 2,210
Accounts receivable	4,100
Buildings	12,000
Cash	640
Equipment	12,130
C. Fox, cash withdrawn for personal use during 19x6	6,000
C. Fox, owner's equity	?
General expenses	3,140
Inventory of repair parts	4,250
Repair parts used during 19x6	3,560
Revenues	28,940
Wages expense	15,090
Wages payable	380

a. Prepare an income statement for 19x6 and a balance sheet as of December 31, 19x6.

b. Explain why the amounts shown for wages expense and wages payable are not identical.

c. Mr. Fox invested no money in the business during 19x6. Calculate his equity in the business on January 1, 19x6 (the beginning of the year).

11. Transactions analysis. Indicate the effects, if any, of each of the following events on the assets, liabilities, and owners' equity of a hardware store. Each of these events took place this month. (Assume that all transactions of previous months were analyzed correctly and that no transactions analyses have been made this month.)

1. Perform services and bill customer for $700.
2. Order an electric typewriter for the office, to be delivered two months from now, price $420 to be paid at delivery.
3. Purchase and pay for a two-year supply of office stationery, price $380.
4. Repay the $1,000 borrowed from a bank on the last day of last month, plus $9 interest.
5. Hire a new secretary on the last day of this month, salary $600 a month.
6. Pay a salesman $750 for services performed last month.
7. Pay the owner's salary for this month, $1,200 (the business is organized as an individual proprietorship).

8.   Collect cash from customer, $1,500, for services performed last year.
9.   Depreciation for this month was $360.

12. Supplying missing information.   The owners of the M Wholesale Company prepared the following lists of their company's assets and liabilities:

	December 31	
	19x8	19x9
Cash	$ 2,000	$ 4,200
Merchandise inventory	12,300	15,000
Accounts receivable	7,000	5,000
Accounts payable for merchandise	8,000	10,100
Furniture and fixtures (net after deduction of depreciation)	3,000	2,600

Expenses for 19x9 consisted of the cost of goods sold, depreciation, and miscellaneous selling and administrative expenses. The goods and services classified as miscellaneous selling and administrative expenses were all bought and paid for in cash during 19x9.

A further analysis of the company's checkbook for 19x9 shows two more groups of transactions: (1) deposits of all amounts received from customers during the year, $50,000 and (2) payments to suppliers for merchandise amounting to $33,000. No other receipts or payments occurred during 19x9.

For 19x9, what were the:

a.   Sales revenues?   e.   Net income?
b.   Purchases of merchandise?   f.   Owners' equity (12/31/x8)?
c.   Cost of merchandise sold?   g.   Owners' equity (12/31/x9)?
d.   Other expenses?

13. Actions not classified as accounting transactions.   The McIntyre Company is engaged in a variety of wholesaling operations. The following are just a few of the many events that took place in this company last year:

1.   A fork life truck was bought from the Warehouse Machinery Company; payment was deferred until this year, but the machine was delivered and placed in service in one of McIntyre's warehouses last year.
2.   The company borrowed $10 million from a life insurance company at the end of last year. Interest payments on this loan will amount to $800,000 a year for 20 years; the amount borrowed will be repaid at the end of that time.
3.   A bookkeeper was hired, employment to begin on January 2 of this year. One month's salary was paid in December of last year to help the book-keeper pay off some outstanding personal debts; the advance will be deducted from this year's salary payments.
4.   The market value of the owners' equity in this company increased by 20 percent last year.
5.   Completion of a highway interchange last year doubled the market value of a parcel of land owned by the company.
6.   A routine audit revealed that the company's cash balance at the end of last year was $250,000 less than the amount shown in the company's records, and that no insurance was carried against such cash shortages.

7. An office machine was leased from the Rothwell Service Company at the end of last year; payments are to be made annually for five years, the first payment to be made this year. At the end of the five-year period, the machine will be returned to Rothwell where it will be scrapped.

8. One of the company's research engineers was finally able to solve a difficult repackaging problem, after several weeks of work on McIntyre Company time. McIntyre patented the solution last year and is now preparing to offer it commercially in exchange for annual royalty payments. A substantial number of royalty agreements are anticipated.

What immediate effect, if any, did each of these events have on the accountant's measurements of the company's assets, liabilities, and owners' equity last year? If the event had no such effect, explain why.

14. Transactions analysis. The S&R Auto Parts Company operates an automobile supplies store. It had the following assets, liabilities, and owner's equity on January 1, 19x1:

Cash	$ 3,200	Accounts payable	$ 3,700
Accounts receivable	1,400	Bank loan payable	10,000
Inventory	22,000	Owner's equity	15,700
Prepaid rent	800		
Equipment	2,000		
Total	$29,400	Total	$29,400

The company had the following transactions in January, 19x1:

1. Bought merchandise on account, $3,300.
2. Sold merchandise to customers: for cash, $6,100; on account, $2,300.
3. Collected $850 cash from customers, on account.
4. Used store clerks' services costing $1,600.
5. Made payments, as follows:
   To store clerks, $1,450.
   To merchandise suppliers, on account, $3,500.
   To landlord, for rent for February, March, and April 19x1, $2,400.
   To insurance company, $720 for three-year insurance policy, coverage to begin on January 1, 19x1.
   To owner, as a salary, $1,500.
   To electric and telephone companies, for services in January, $200.
   To local newspaper, for advertising space used in January, $150.
6. Calculated the cost of the merchandise sold during January, $4,200.
7. Calculated the month's depreciation on the equipment, $50.
8. Remembered that the bank charged interest of $1,200 a year on the $10,000 bank loan, payable $600 on June 30 and December 31 each year.

a. For each transaction or other event, identify the effects on the company's assets, liabilities, and owner's equity, using the format illustrated in Exhibit 2–2.

b. Prepare an income statement for the month and a statement of financial position as of January 31, 19x1. (The bank loan and prepayments should be classified as current items.)

c.   C. Rowe, the owner, claims that the change in the cash balance each month is a better measure of the company's income than the net income figure you calculated in (*b*). Using figures from this problem, prepare an answer to this argument.

15.   Transactions and financial statements.   Jane Doe formed a merchandising company on January 1. It had the following transactions during its first month:

1.   Ms. Doe made a cash investment of $90,000 in the business.
2.   Land, $30,000, a building, $60,000, and equipment, $24,000, were purchased on January 1. Cash in the amount of $89,000 was paid for these items. The balance is owed on a five-year note payable.
3.   Merchandise costing $40,000 was purchased on credit.
4.   Merchandise costing $30,000 was sold for $50,000. Of this latter amount, $21,000 was for cash and the balance was sold on credit.
5.   Salaries and wages totaled $13,500 for the month. This entire amount was paid in cash.
6.   Miscellaneous expenses amounted to $4,200. Of this amount, $3,300 was paid in cash; the rest will be paid in February.
7.   The depreciation for the month was $150 on the building and $200 on the equipment.
8.   The company will have to pay interest on the note payable in the amount of $200 a month. The first interest payment will be made on April 1.

a.   Analyze each of these transactions, identifying their effects on the following assets, liabilities, and owners' equities, using the format illustrated in Exhibit 2–2:

Cash   Land
Accounts receivable   Equipment
Inventory   Accounts payable
Buildings   Notes and interest payable
                               J. Doe, Owner

Label each of these to identify it as either an asset (*A*), a liability (*L*), or an owners equity (*OE*).
b.   Prepare an income statement for the month.
c.   Prepare a statement of financial position as of January 31.

16.   Transactions and financial statements.   On December 31, Grace Harvey completed her first year as proprietor of a sportswear store. The following data summarize the first year's transactions of this business:

1.   She invested $14,000 cash in the business.
2.   In January she borrowed $6,000 cash from a bank.
3.   In January she secured a five-year lease on shop space, rental charges to be based on sales volume in the store. Rent for the 12 months that ended on December 31 amounted to $2,292, paid entirely in cash.
4.   She bought furniture and store equipment for $7,500 cash.
5.   She bought merchandise on credit for $28,585.
6.   During the year she sold some of the merchandise described in (5). The

cost of the merchandise sold was $21,690. She sold this merchandise for $32,200, of which $17,100 was cash and $15,100 was on credit.

7. She paid herself a "salary" of $6,000, paid $642 as wages to part-time employees, and paid $2,022 for other expenses, all in cash.

8. She returned defective merchandise to a supplier for full credit, $881. Payment for this merchandise had not been made to the supplier.

9. She collected $4,426 owed her by customers who had bought merchandise on credit.

10. During the year, she made payments to suppliers on account, totaling $21,520.

11. A shoplifter stole merchandise which had cost $82.

12. On December 31, Ms. Harvey repaid $300 of the amount borrowed plus an additional $480, representing one year's interest on the amount borrowed.

13. She decided to depreciate the cost of the furniture and equipment evenly over a five-year period. She did not believe that any salvage value would be left at the end of that time.

a. Analyze the effects of the above transactions on the assets, liabilities, and owner's equity of Ms. Harvey's business, using the format illustrated in Exhibit 2–2.

b. Prepare an income statement for the year and a year-end balance sheet. What further information would you want to have before you could tell Ms. Harvey whether her business venture was a success from a financial viewpoint?

17. Transactions analysis; financial statements. James Westbridge buys and sells iron pipe. On January 1, his business had the following assets, liabilities, and owner's equity:

Cash, $3,000; receivables, $50,000; inventories, $136,000; prepaid insurance, $816; store equipment, $74,800; accounts payable, $33,800; wages payable, $0; taxes payable, $9,300; note payable, $0; J. Westbridge, owner's equity, $221,516.

The following transactions took place during January:

1. Merchandise costing $78,800 was purchased on account.

2. Merchandise with a cost of $82,100 was sold on account for $106,300.

3. Mr. Westbridge's employees earned $5,000.

4. The costs of telephone service, electricity, and other supporting services provided by outside suppliers and bought on account amounted to $11,200.

5. Tax expense applicable to the month of January was estimated to be $2,000, but no taxes were paid during the month.

6. Customers paid bills amounting to $125,100.

7. Mr. Westbridge paid $5,000 to his employees, $109,700 to his suppliers of merchandise, and $9,700 to suppliers of supporting services.

8. Depreciation of store equipment amounted to $300.

9. Mr. Westbridge purchased and received new store equipment costing $20,000; payment for this equipment was to be made in March.

10. $790 of insurance premiums remained prepaid at the end of January.
11. On January 31, Mr. Westbridge borrowed $6,000 from a bank and deposited this amount in his business bank account. He signed a note promising to repay this amount to the bank, plus interest, at the end of April. He regarded this note as a business debt rather than as a personal debt.

a. List the January 1 figures for the various assets, liabilities, and owner's equity, using the format illustrated in Exhibit 2–2. Then show the financial effects of the month's transactions, using only the 10 categories listed at the beginning of this problem.
b. Prepare an income statement for the month of January and a balance sheet as of January 31.

18. Transactions analysis; financial statements; cash flows. In January, Alan Bucknell opened a retail grocery store. The following list summarizes the transactions of his first year of business:

1. He invested $25,000 in cash.
2. He bought a store building and equipment for $9,000, paying $8,000 cash and borrowing the remaining $1,000 from a bank.
3. He bought on account merchandise costing $22,125.
4. He sold merchandise which had cost him $18,910 for $23,725, of which $12,550 was for cash and the balance on credit.
5. He paid his employees' wages in cash, $4,245.
6. He paid $1,575 cash for other operating expenses.
7. He received $150 cash for rent of storage space in his store loft during the year.
8. He suffered an uninsured loss by fire of merchandise costing $1,000 and equipment which had cost him $520.
9. He paid $19,750 of his accounts payable, $17,250 with cash and $2,500 with notes payable.
10. His customers paid him $10,750 of the amounts they owed him.
11. At the end of the year he owed an employee $50 for wages earned by the employee during the last few days of December.
12. During the year he withdrew for his own use $1,200 in cash and merchandise which had cost $525.
13. Bills for expenses incurred in December but unpaid on December 31 amounted to $110.
14. The depreciation of building and equipment during the period was estimated to be $200.
15. On December 31 he paid the bank $90 interest on the bank loan, covering the period from the time of the loan to the end of the year.

a. Analyze the effects of the above transactions on the assets, liabilities, and owner's equity of Mr. Bucknell's business, using the format illustrated in Exhibit 2–2.
b. Prepare an income statement for the year and a balance sheet as of December 31.
c. Prepare a statement of cash flows for the year.

3

The Mechanics
of Transactions Analysis

IN ANY FIRM which enters into a significant number of transactions, the accountant has to develop a set of formal procedures to translate the analyses of these transactions into financial statements and other usable information. The purpose of this chapter is to describe the basic elements of the methods used for this purpose. In the process, we shall try to explain a number of technical terms that the accountant uses to communicate with others.

THE BOOKKEEPING PROCESS

The means by which the accounting analyses of transactions are recorded in a formal way is known as *bookkeeping*. We shall discuss the following five aspects or components of bookkeeping systems:

1. Accounts.
2. Documents, journals, and ledgers.
3. Double-entry bookkeeping.
4. Debit/credit notation.
5. Closing entries.

Accounts

An account is simply a place in which to record the effects of the firm's transactions on one of its assets, liabilities, or elements of owners' equity. The *balance* in an account on any date is the

cumulative difference between the increases and the decreases that
have been recorded in the account since it was created.

For example, The Erskine Appliance Store's *Cash* account was
used to accumulate the effects on the company's cash position of all
cash receipt and cash payment transactions. The following figures
appeared in this account as a result of the first three transactions
affecting cash, as described in Chapter 2:

Cash

Date	Description	Increase	Decrease	Balance
June 30	Investment by owner	30,000		30,000
30	Prepayment of rent		3,600	26,400
30	Equipment		9,000	17,400

The $17,400 balance in this account at the end of June showed how
much of Mr. Erskine's original bank deposit was still on hand when
the store opened for business on July 1.

Each company is free to decide what accounts are to be set up.
These decisions depend on the information management wants to or
must obtain from the accounting records for various purposes. For
this reason, different companies in the same line of business are
likely to have very different sets of accounts.

For example, suppose management wants to know the cost of
telephone service each month. If telephone costs are included with
the costs of water and electric power in an account titled "Utilities
Expense," the accountant may have to review all the transactions
affecting that account to isolate the telephone service component. To
avoid that chore, the accountant will probably set up three separate
accounts, one for each kind of utility service. The balances in these
accounts can then be used to give management the information it
wants, with little waste motion. In another company, however, management may not need separate information on telephone costs and a
single utilities expense account will be used.

A list of the titles of a company's accounts is known as its *chart of
accounts*. Exhibit 3–1, for example, shows the chart of accounts
Charles Erskine set up to record the transactions we described in
Chapter 2. This was a very short chart of accounts because Mr.
Erskine's business was quite small, and his information needs were
very simple. Large companies, in contrast, may have thousands of
accounts, each with its own identifying number. Account numbers
with 12 or more digits are very common in large organizations.

We'll use most of the account titles in Exhibit 3–1 in the illustrations in this chapter, adding others when we need them. The im-

EXHIBIT 3–1. The Erskine Appliance Store: Initial Chart of Accounts

Assets	Cash Accounts receivable Inventory Prepaid rent Equipment
Liabilities	Accounts payable Salary payable
Owner's Equity	Erskine, Investment Sales revenue Cost of goods sold Salary expense Rent expense Depreciation expense Miscellaneous expense Erskine, Withdrawals

portant point is to remember to use titles that describe the asset, liability, or owners' equity item clearly and then use these account titles consistently.

The accounts that are used to implement the concepts we have been developing may take many forms, but they can all be represented schematically by accounts drawn in the shape of the letter T. A *T-account* representing the Cash account, for example, looks like this:

Cash

(+)		(−)	
Beginning balance	$$$	Disbursements	$$$
Receipts	$$$		

The left side of this account is used to show the balance of cash on hand at any time and to record cash receipts; the right side of the T is used to record cash disbursements.

By tradition and common agreement, T-accounts representing asset accounts show positive balances on the left side; T-accounts for liabilities and owners' equities are just the reverse, with positive balances on the right side, negative balances on the left.

Documents, Journals, and Ledgers

Data usually enter the accounting system on documents that are prepared or received at the time the transactions take place. Analysis of these documents reveals which assets and equities have been affected and which accounts should be used to record these effects.

These analyses are typically assembled ("entered") first in a *journal,* a chronological record of the transactions represented by the documents. A journal is a book, file of papers, reel of magnetic tape, or other medium in which the accounting analysis of each transaction is recorded *in its entirety.* In some cases, a file of the documents themselves may serve as a journal. The record of a transaction in a journal is known as a *journal entry.*

Each figure in a journal eventually must be transferred or *posted* to the accounts in the *ledger.* The ledger is simply the file containing the accounts, one on each page or computer storage section. Since every transaction affects at least two categories of asset, liability, or owners' equity, each journal entry of necessity leads to two or more entries in the ledger. In the ledger, the individual transaction no longer appears as a complete entity; instead, its component parts are scattered among the accounts. The sequence of these data flows is summarized in the following diagram:

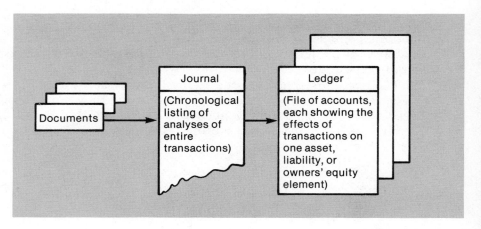

Actually, a company is likely to have more than one ledger. The main file of accounts is known as the *general ledger.* Many of the accounts in the general ledger are likely to be *control accounts,* however—that is, they represent a whole class of assets, liabilities, or owners' equity for which the detailed listing is contained in a separate file, known as a *subsidiary ledger.*

For example, if the general ledger has a single Accounts Receivable account, it will undoubtedly be supported by a subsidiary ledger showing the amounts owed by individual customers. This ledger may take the form of a file of cards, one for each supplier, or a file of unpaid invoices, or perhaps a reel or reels of magnetic tape or other kinds of computer memory.

Double-Entry Bookkeeping

The bookkeeping system that is implicit in the transactions analyses we discussed in Chapter 2 is known as double-entry bookkeeping. Rather than repeat that entire series, let us illustrate the double-entry approach by examining the first four transactions that a new business entered into during its first month of operations:

1. The owners invested $20,000 cash in the business.
2. The firm bought merchandise on credit at a total cost of $10,000.
3. The firm paid its trade creditors $8,000 in cash.
4. The firm exchanged merchandise that had cost $4,000 for $6,000 in cash.

To start with, the business had just four accounts: cash, inventory, accounts payable, and owners' equity. Accounts showing the record of the first four transactions in plus-and-minus form are presented in Exhibit 3–2.

EXHIBIT 3–2. Transactions Analyses in Plus-and-Minus Format

	Cash	+	Inventory	=	Accounts Payable	+	Owners' Equity
(1)	+20,000						+20,000
(2)			+10,000		+10,000		
(3)	− 8,000				− 8,000		
(4)	+ 6,000		− 4,000				{+ 6,000 − 4,000
Ending Balance	18,000	+	6,000	=	2,000	+	22,000

The same accounts and transactions in T-account form are shown in Exhibit 3–3. Notice that each transaction is recorded by an entry on the left side of one account and an entry, equal in amount, on the right side of another. This is the essence of double-entry bookkeeping: the accounting record of each transaction has at least one left-side entry and one right-side entry, and the total of the amounts entered on the left side must equal the total of the amounts entered on the right.

Since positive balances in asset accounts appear on the left, then entries recording increases in assets should also appear on the left. Conversely, an entry recording a decrease in an asset should be placed in the right side of the T-account for that asset. Just the reverse holds true for the liabilities and the owners' equities—an increase is entered on the right, a decrease on the left. The balance in

EXHIBIT 3–3.   Transactions Analyses in T-Account Format

Cash				Accounts Payable			
(+)		(−)		(−)		(+)	
(1)	20,000	(3)	8,000	(3)	8,000	(2)	10,000
(4)	6,000						
	26,000						
Bal. 18,000						Bal. 2,000	

Inventory				Owners' Equity			
(+)		(−)		(−)		(+)	
(2)	10,000	(4)	4,000	(4)	4,000	(1)	20,000
						(4)	6,000
							26,000
Bal. 6,000						Bal. 22,000	

any account at the end of the period can be calculated by subtracting the total of the figures shown in one side of the account from the total of the amounts shown in the other side.

These conventional rules governing the use of T-accounts may be summarized as follows:

1. An *increase* in an *asset* is entered on the *left* side of the T, as is the balance in the asset account.
2. A *decrease* in an *asset* is entered on the *right* side of the T.
3. An *increase* in an *equity* is entered on the *right* side of the T, as is the balance in the equity account.
4. A *decrease* in an *equity* is entered on the left side of the T.

The main advantage of this right-left arrangement is that the nature of account balances and the effects of transactions are indicated clearly by the *positions* of the figures, without need for further verbal description. When we list the final account balances, for example, we find that the total of the left-side balances equals the total of the right-side balances:

	Left	Right
Cash	$18,000	
Inventory	6,000	
Accounts payable		$ 2,000
Owners' equity		22,000
Total	$24,000	$24,000

This equality is simply another expression of the accounting equation. Positive balances in liability and owners' equity accounts are on the right side; positive balances in asset accounts are on the left. Since total assets must equal the total of the liabilities and the owners' equity, the left-side total must equal the right-side total.

Debit and Credit Notation

Just as it is not precise to use the terms *plus* and *minus* without also specifying the kind of account, so is it also a bit cumbersome to use the terms *left side* and *right side* repeatedly. A more concise and general notation has had to be found. The accountant says:

> *Debit* (abbreviated as *Dr.*) for an entry on the *left* side, meaning by this an increase in an asset *or* a decrease in a liability or owners' equity; and *Credit* (abbreviated as *Cr.*) for an entry on the *right* side, meaning by this an increase in a liability or owners' equity *or* a decrease in an asset.

Thus, increase in cash is the event that is recorded by a debit to Cash. Similarly, to credit Cash means to record a cash disbursement.

All this can be summarized in schematic terms very simply, as in the following diagram:

Asset		Liability		Owners' Equity	
+	−	−	+	−	+
Dr.	Cr.	Dr.	Cr.	Dr.	Cr.

The format that was used to represent the analysis of transactions in earlier chapters can now be replaced by a more compact form of notation. For example, the analysis of a $10,000 purchase of merchandise on credit can be presented in the following way:

Accounts	Debit	Credit
Inventory	10,000	
Accounts Payable		10,000

In this form, debits are invariably written first; credits are written underneath, with both the account titles and amounts *indented to the right*. This is a journal entry, written in what is called *general journal form*.

Revenue and Expense Accounts

The Owners' Equity account in our illustration showed two additions to owners' equity and one subtraction:

Owners' Equity			
(−)		(+)	
(4)	4,000	(1)	20,000
		(4)	6,000

As we pointed out in Chapter 2, to prepare income statements the accountant has to separate the revenues and expenses from other elements of the owners' equity. In this case, three accounts would be used to record the three figures shown in the T-account above: one for the initial investment, one for the revenues, and one for the cost of goods sold.

These three accounts can be pictured as subdivisions of the owners' equity, as in the following diagram:

Owners' Equity					
(−)			**(+)**		
Cost of Goods Sold			**Owners' Investment**		
Dr.		Cr.	Dr.		Cr.
(4)	4,000			(1)	20,000
			Revenue from Sales		
			Dr.		Cr.
				(4)	6,000

The two accounts at the right are designed to accumulate the amounts *added* to the owners' equity: the Owners' Investment account accumulates the increases resulting from the owners' investments of funds in the firm; the Revenue from Sales account accumulates the gross increases in owners' equity that result from sales of goods and services during the period. As additions to owners' equity, the amounts are shown in the right-hand column.

Cost of Goods Sold is an expense account. Expenses *reduce* the owners' equity. Therefore, a positive balance in an expense account is a subtraction from owners' equity. Since subtractions from owners' equity are shown by debits, entered on the left side of owners' equity accounts, expenses are entered in the left side of expense accounts. Expense accounts have debit balances.

Transaction (4) can now be written in debit/credit form. The first entry records the increases in cash and owners' equity resulting from the month's sales:

(4a)

Cash	6,000	
Revenue from Sales		6,000

A second entry is necessary to record the cost of securing these revenues:

(4b)

Cost of Goods Sold	4,000	
Inventory		4,000

The debit to Cost of Goods Sold records the expense (decrease in owners' equity); the credit to Inventory records the accompanying decrease in assets.

Debits are also referred to in some cases as *charges*. For example, the $4,000 debit to Cost of Goods Sold is a charge to that account. Similarly, to charge an account is to debit it—for example, we charge $4,000 to Cost of Goods Sold. A charge usually describes a use of resources—that is, charging an account means that resources have been used for the purpose described by the account title. The term is frequently used in managerial accounting to identify the responsibility of individual executives for resources committed to their operations.

Inventory Cost Records

The sale of merchandise requires the removal of the cost of this merchandise from the Inventory account. The amount to be removed can be determined either by the *perpetual inventory method* or by the *periodic inventory method*.

Periodic inventory method. Under the periodic inventory method, no entry is made to record the cost of goods sold until the end of the accounting period. At that time, the remaining inventories are counted and their costs are determined. The cost of goods sold is then measured by subtracting the costs of the ending inventory from the total cost of the beginning inventory and the costs of the goods received in inventory during the period:

$$\boxed{\begin{array}{c}\text{Cost of}\\\text{Goods Sold}\end{array}} = \boxed{\begin{array}{c}\text{Opening}\\\text{Inventory}\end{array}} + \boxed{\text{Purchases}} - \boxed{\begin{array}{c}\text{Ending}\\\text{Inventory}\end{array}}$$

This is shown more clearly in the diagram in the left side of Exhibit 3–4. The height of the large column represents the cost of all the

EXHIBIT 3–4.   Calculating the Cost of Goods Sold

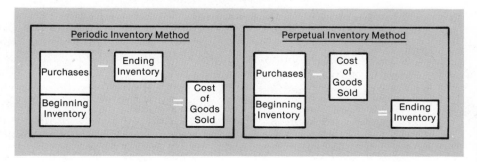

goods available for sale during the period. Once the ending inventory has been counted and subtracted from the total, what's left is the cost of goods sold.

Perpetual inventory method.   The perpetual inventory method, in contrast, requires that the cost of purchased goods be added (debited) to the Inventory account at the time they are received. Each time an item is sold, its cost is identified and an entry like the one in entry (4b) is made. The cost of the ending inventory is determined indirectly, as in the right side of Exhibit 3–4. Barring error, theft, or delay, the balance in the Inventory account should always equal the cost of the goods on hand. Once a year a physical count is taken; the difference between the cost of the inventory actually on hand at that time and the amount shown in the Inventory account is either the cost of lost, stolen, or spoiled goods or the result of bookkeeping errors.

Perpetual inventory records offer substantial advantages. First, they allow the preparation of financial statements quarterly or more often without the burden of taking a physical count each time. Second, they provide an independent check of the reliability of the company's system for protecting the inventory against theft and damage. In periodic inventory systems, the figure labeled "cost of goods sold" actually is a mixture of the cost of goods sold and the cost of goods spoiled or stolen. Management has no way of separating the costs of lost inventory from the costs of the goods that actually have been sold. Perpetual inventory systems provide this information.

Closing Entries

Revenue and expense accounts are temporary owners' equity accounts, used to accumulate the results of operations *for one year only*. Before the next year's transactions can be posted, the existing balances in these accounts must be removed.

This is accomplished by closing entries. A closing entry is an entry designed to transfer the balance in one account to another account. It consists of two parts: (1) an amount equal to the balance in the account, debited to the account if the account has a credit balance, credited if the account has a debit balance, and (2) an identical amount with the opposite sign, credited or debited to the account to which the transfer is to be made.

In our simplified example, we had only two temporary accounts, Revenue from Sales and Cost of Goods Sold. We assumed that other expenses and owners' withdrawals were zero. The credit balance in the Revenue from Sales account is canceled by debiting that account for an amount equal to the account balance. The entry is:

(5)

| Revenue from Sales .... | 6,000 | |
| Owners' Investment .... | | 6,000 |

This simply transfers the credit balance from one owners' equity account (Revenue from Sales) to another (Owners' Investment). The Revenue from Sales account is now ready to receive the next year's transactions.

Similarly, the debit balance in Cost of Goods Sold is eliminated by crediting that account for an amount equal to the account balance:

(6)

| Owners' Investment..................... | 4,000 | |
| Cost of Goods Sold .... | | 4,000 |

Again, all this does is transfer the debit balance from one owners' equity account (Cost of Goods Sold) to another (Owners' Investment). Taken together, these two entries show that the owners' equity in the business has been increased by $2,000 by the operations of this period. The owners' equity accounts now show the following:

Cost of Goods Sold				Revenue from Sales				Owners' Investment			
(4)	4,000	(6)	4,000	(5)	6,000	(4)	6,000	(6)	4,000	(1)	20,000
										(5)	6,000
											26,000
Bal.	0			Bal.	0					Bal.	22,000

This, of course, is exactly where we ended up before we complicated the example by adding revenue and expense accounts.

ACCOUNTING FOR DEPRECIABLE ASSETS: CONTRA ACCOUNTS

Land, buildings, equipment, and other physical assets that provide operating capacity for a number of accounting periods are usually called *fixed assets, long-lived assets,* or *property.* Those that lose their usefulness due to deterioration or obsolescence are known as *depreciable assets.* We need to see how the accountant might use accounts to record the following:

1. Property acquisition and depreciation.
2. Sale of depreciable assets.

Property Acquisition and Depreciation

When an organization buys a piece of equipment, it acquires an asset. Suppose, for example, a company paid $8,000 in cash for a large piece of office equipment it expected to use for eight years. This transaction increased one asset (equipment) and decreased another (cash). The entry to record the purchase was:

Equipment	8,000	
Cash		8,000

The debit to the Equipment account recorded the increase in the asset; the credit to Cash recorded the decrease in that asset.

The company estimated that depreciation on this equipment would amount to $1,000 a year. At the end of the first year, therefore, the company's accountants made the following analysis:

Decrease in owners' equity $1,000	*Accompanied by*	Decrease in asset (Equipment) $1,000

This translates in debit and credit terms into an entry of the following form:

Depreciation Expense	1,000	
Equipment		1,000

If the entries recording depreciation were actually made in this way, the accounts would show the following figures before the closing entries were made at the end of the third year:

Equipment

Original cost of equipment purchased	8,000	Depreciation, year 1	1,000
		Depreciation, year 2	1,000
		Depreciation, year 3	1,000
Bal. 5,000			3,000

Depreciation Expense

Depreciation, year 3	1,000

The $5,000 balance in the Equipment account would show the portion of original cost that had not yet been charged to expense—in other words, *unexpired cost.* The balance shown in the Depreciation Expense account for the third year would be only the cost expiring during that year, of course, because expense accounts accumulate costs for one accounting period only and are closed out at the end of each period.

Although this method in no way violates accounting theory, it makes it impossible to identify the original cost of equipment without complete access to the company's records, and then only after a good deal of work. Because this kind of information is generally thought to be useful (and is often required by law), a more common treatment is to use a separate account in which to accumulate the figures reflecting the expired portion of original cost. This account is called *Accumulated Depreciation, Allowance for Depreciation,* or

Depreciation to Date and is really a subdivision of the related property account:

Furniture and Equipment		Accumulated Depreciation	
Original cost of equipment pur- chased $8,000		Depreciation, year 1	1,000
		Depreciation, year 2	1,000
		Depreciation, year 3	1,000
		Bal. $3,000	

The entry to record depreciation for the third year would be:

Depreciation Expense 1,000
    Accumulated Depreciation 1,000

As before, the debit serves to record the reduction in the owners' equity, while the credit to Accumulated Depreciation records the consumption of the asset.

The Accumulated Depreciation account is our first example of a *contra account*. A contra account is always paired with some other account and serves to accumulate some or all of the negative effects of transactions on the asset or equity item to which it is coupled. For example, the Accumulated Depreciation account is a deduction-from-asset contra account, or *contra-asset* account. Since the parent asset account has a debit balance, the contra account has a credit balance. In financial reporting, the balance in the contra account should always be deducted from the balance in its parent account, as follows:

Equipment, at original cost $8,000
    Less: Accumulated depreciation 3,000
Equipment, net $5,000

The net figure is the asset's *unamortized cost*—that is, the amount that hasn't yet been amortized. It is usually referred to as the asset's *book value.*

It should be emphasized that although the Accumulated Depreciation account normally carries a credit balance, it is neither a liability nor an owners' equity account. As we have just seen, it is inseparable from the account in which the asset's original cost is recorded. As such, it belongs in the asset section of the chart of accounts.

The amount shown in the Accumulated Depreciation account can be used as a rough index of the age of the company's equipment—the older the equipment, the higher the ratio of accumulated depreciation to original cost. An increase in this ratio usually means that the company is riding on its past investments in facilities; a reduction in the ratio is likely to signal a modernization or expansion program.

Sale of Depreciable Assets

When depreciable assets are *retired* (in most cases, this means when they are sold), their original cost and accumulated depreciation must be removed from the accounts. Such sales lead to the recognition of gains or losses, measured by the difference between the assets' unamortized cost (their "book value") and the value of the resources received in exchange for them.

For example, the machine recorded in the Equipment account above was sold for $2,300 in cash at the beginning of year 4. This machine had cost $8,000 originally and depreciation of $3,000 had been accumulated on it during the first three years. The unamortized cost of this machine therefore was $5,000 (8,000 minus $3,000) and the company suffered a $2,700 loss on the sale, calculated as follows:

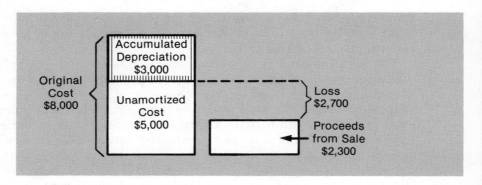

In this case, the loss resulted from an incorrect estimate of life at the time the equipment was acquired. If life had been forecasted correctly, a total of $5,700 would have been charged as depreciation during the first three years, just enough to bring the book value down to the ultimate $2,300 sale price at the beginning of the fourth year:

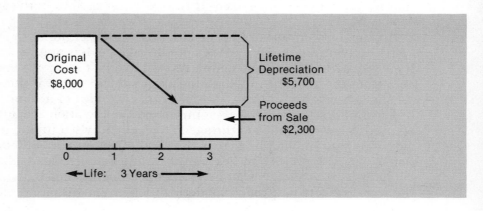

It can be argued that the proper treatment of the loss would be to go back and restate the company's earnings for the first three years. Unfortunately, the income statements of prior years are past history, and repeated correction of prior years' earnings figures could be very confusing. In conformance with common practice, therefore, the company would report the entire loss on its income statement for year 4, with no attempt to prorate any portion of it to earlier years.

The entry to record a sale like this is straightforward. Because the machine was no longer owned by the company, its balances in both the asset and the contra-asset accounts had to be removed. The entry to accomplish this was:

Cash	2,300	
Accumulated Depreciation	3,000	
Loss on Sale of Equipment	2,700	
Equipment		8,000

In this entry, the credit of $8,000 removed the original cost of the machine from the accounts, while the debit of $3,000 did the same for the accumulated depreciation applicable to it. The debit to cash recorded the inflow of this asset, and the debit to the loss account recorded the decrease in the owners' equity that was recognized at the time of the sale.

CORPORATE OWNERS' EQUITY ACCOUNTS

It will be recalled from Chapter 2 that when Charles Erskine opened The Erskine Appliance Store he did so with as few formalities as possible. The legal form of organization he selected was the *individual proprietorship*, an organization that can be created by anyone as one of his or her rights under the common law. No official permission need to be obtained; from a legal point of view, the activities of the business unit are regarded as simply one portion of the activities of the proprietor, or owner.[1]

The Corporation

Most business activity is carried out by corporations, however. A corporation is established by the issuance of a corporate charter by a state government. The property of the corporation is legally separate from that of its owner(s); if an owner dies, the corporation lives on. Furthermore, the corporation, not its owner(s), is liable for the corporation's debts. This *limited liability* feature means that once the

---

[1] Another form of organization that can be formed under the common law is the general partnership, created by pooling the resources of two or more persons under a formal agreement or contract among the partners.

owners of the corporation have made their investment, they have no further obligation to the corporation's creditors. If the corporation fails to pay its bills, the creditors can't demand that the owners pay these bills with their other assets.

Limited liability makes investment in the business feasible for many people who have confidence in its future but don't wish to become active in its management and wish to limit their risks. In fact, the development of large-scale industry in the Western world was made possible only because the corporate form of organization was available.

In exchange for their investment, the owners of a corporation receive shares of capital stock and are called stockholders, shareholders, or shareowners. Stock ownership entitles the shareholder to vote on such questions as the election of members of the board of directors and the appointment of the company's auditors. The board appoints the company's top managers, establishes the basic policies that management is expected to observe in operating the business, and reviews management's performance on the stockholders' behalf.

Paid-In Capital Accounts

The owners' equity section of a corporation's chart of accounts includes two classes of permanent owners' equity accounts. The first of these measures the amounts contributed to the corporation by shareowners in exchange for their shares of stock. These amounts are sometimes referred to as the corporation's *paid-in capital,* or *contributed capital.*

For example, suppose a company issued 10,000 shares of its stock to investors in exchange for $350,000 in cash. An appropriate entry would be:

(1)

Cash	350,000	
Capital Stock		350,000

The debit records the increase in the corporation's assets; the credit to Capital Stock records the increase in the shareowners' equity.

Dividends and Retained Earnings

The second class of permanent owners' equity accounts measures the amounts by which the company's income has exceeded the amounts distributed to the shareholders since the date of incorporation. For example, our illustrative company had net income of $10,000 in its first year and $30,000 in its second year but made no payments to its shareholders in either year. At the beginning of the third year, its Retained Earnings account had a positive (credit) balance of $40,000:

Retained Earnings

	Bal., begin. year 1	0
	+ Net income, year 1	10,000
	= Bal., begin. year 2	10,000
	+ Net income, year 2	30,000
	= Bal., begin. year 3	40,000

The credits to this account were made at the end of each year as the revenue and expense accounts were closed into it.

Revenues and expenses in the third year were $500,000 and $450,000. Assuming for simplicity that only one revenue account and one expense account were used, the closing entry for the third year would be:

(2)

Revenues	500,000	
Expenses...........................		450,000
Retained Earnings		50,000

Something new was added in the third year, however. The board of directors decided that the company's cash position was strong enough to justify paying $15,000 to the shareholders.[2] Payments of this sort are known as *cash dividends*.

Once the directors voted to pay the dividend, it became a legal obligation of the corporation. The stockholders thereby became creditors of the corporation to the tune of $15,000. At the same time, their owners' equity in the corporation dropped by $15,000. A simple way to record this would be to make the following entry:

(3)

Retained Earnings	15,000	
Dividends Payable		15,000

This shows the reduction of the owners' equity and the creation of a new corporate liability.

Notice that the debit was not made to an expense account. Like withdrawals made by the owners of individual proprietorships,

---

[2] In the United States, the power to declare dividends is vested in the board of directors. The directors of companies in which shares are owned by the general public ordinarily meet to declare dividends four times a year. In Europe and in much of the rest of the world, dividends are declared once each year by a formal vote of the shareholders at the annual shareholders' meeting. The vote is usually on a dividend proposal formulated by the directors, however.

corporate dividends aren't expenses. Instead, they are distributions of funds earned by corporate operations. For this reason, they aren't deducted from revenues in the calculation of net income. Exhibit 3–5 shows the Retained Earnings account after entries (2) and (3) were posted.

EXHIBIT 3–5. The Retained Earnings Account

	Retained Earnings		
		Begin. bal.	40,000
Dividends—(3) →15,000		(2)	50,000 ←—Net income
		Ending bal.	75,000

To make it easier to prepare financial statements, the accountants in this company decided to make entry (3) in a slightly different way. They set up a new account, Dividends Declared, to serve as a temporary contra account to Retained Earnings. When the dividend was declared, they made the following entry:

(3a)

Dividends Declared   15,000
      Dividends Payable   15,000

The debit to Dividends Declared recognized the decrease in the owners' equity; the credit to Dividends Payable recognized the liability.

Since the Dividends Declared account was a temporary account, it had to be closed once the financial statements for the year were prepared. The entry in this case was:

(3b)

Retained Earnings   15,000
      Dividends Declared   15,000

This transferred the debit balance in one owners' equity account (Dividends Declared) to another (Retained Earnings). The total effect of entries (3a) and (3b) was the same as in entry (3) above.

After these entries were made, the owners' equity section of the corporate balance sheet appeared as follows:

Capital stock	$350,000
Retained earnings	75,000
Total Shareowners' Equity	$425,000

SUMMARY

Accountants have developed a concise form of notation to discuss the results of transactions analyses with each other. The term *debit* is used to describe an increase in an asset or a decrease in a liability or in an element of owners' equity. The term *credit* describes a decrease in an asset or an increase in a liability or owners' equity. To summarize a transactions analysis in written form, the accountant merely has to write the names and amounts of the items affected in a table, with the debits first and the credits below them and indented to the right.

Consistent with this notation, accounts are generally represented schematically by diagrams in the shape of the letter T. Debits are entered on the left side of the T, credits on the right. When the amounts credited to an account exceed the amounts debited to it, the account is said to have a credit balance; an excess of debits over credits produces a debit balance.

This system provides a basis for subdividing some accounts into positive and negative components. If the account normally has a debit balance, then its companion, known as a contra account, will have a credit balance. The Accumulated Depreciation account, for example, is a contra-asset account with a credit balance, representing the portion of the cost of depreciable assets that has been charged to operations since the asset was originally acquired.

The system also makes it feasible to divide any asset or equity into two or more categories. The permanent owners' equity accounts of corporations, for example, are usually divided into two groups: paid-in capital (amounts paid to the corporation by the owners for their shares of stock) and retained earnings (cumulative net income minus cumulative dividends).

KEY TERMS

Account	Double-entry bookkeeping
Accumulated depreciation	Entry
Board of directors	Fixed assets
Book value	Individual proprietorship
Capital stock	Journal
Cash dividend	Ledger
Chart of accounts	Paid-in capital
Closing entry	Periodic inventory method
Contra account	Perpetual inventory method
Corporation	T-account
Debit and credit	

APPENDIX: THE PLACE OF DEBIT/CREDIT NOTATION

The relationship between transactions analysis and accounting notations is illustrated in Exhibit 3–6. The basic fact in accounting is an *event* that has taken place. In this case the event is the ownership

EXHIBIT 3–6. Events, Analyses of Effects, and Debit/Credit Notation

The Transaction	Analysis of the Transaction	Record of the Transaction
Ownership of a company-operated store for a year; depreciation was $50,000	Asset decreased by $50,000 — Owners' equity decreased by $50,000	Credit the Accumulated Depreciation account, $50,000 — Debit the Depreciation Expense account, $50,000

of a building for a year, during which $50,000 in depreciation took place. The *analysis* of this event shows that an asset (the remaining usefulness of the building) decreased and the owners' equity also decreased.

The *accounts* to be debited and credited to reflect this analysis are specified by the chart of accounts. We have to remember, however, that the credit to Accumulated Depreciation is designed to record a decrease in an asset. It is wrong to say it records an increase in a contra asset because there is no such thing as a contra asset. *Contra asset* is a term used to describe a certain kind of *account*. The balance in that account must be regarded as part of the description of the asset the contra account is attached to. It has no separate existence apart from that asset.

INDEPENDENT STUDY PROBLEMS (Solutions in Appendix B)

1. Income, dividends, and balance sheet changes. Two sisters formed a corporation on January 1, 19x1, each of them investing $10,000 and receiving 1,000 shares of the corporation's capital stock in exchange. The corporation issued no more shares of capital stock during the next four years, and on January 1, 19x4, the company had total assets of $120,000 and total liabilities of $64,000.

During 19x4, the corporation issued 100 additional shares of its capital stock to a friend of the two sisters, receiving in exchange $6,000 in cash. Cash dividends amounting to $24,000 were declared and paid during the year. On December 31, 19x4, the company had assets amounting to $140,000 and liabilities of $68,000.

a.   Calculate net income for 19x4.
b.   Present the owners' equity section of the company's balance sheet on December 31, 19x4.

   2.   *Depreciable assets; journal entries.*   The Alpha Company bought a truck on January 1, 19x7, for $4,000 in cash. Management decided to charge depreciation on the basis of a five-year life and salvage value of $800 at the end of five years, equal amounts to be charged as depreciation expense for each of the five years. The truck was placed in service immediately and used for three years, at the end of which time it was sold for $1,100 cash.

   Using only the following accounts—Cash, Trucks, Accumulated Depreciation, Depreciation Expense, Gain or Loss on Truck Retirements—prepare journal entries to record:

a.   The purchase of the truck.
b.   Depreciation for 19x7.
c.   Sale of the truck.

   3.   *Transactions analyses; journal entries.*   The Harrel Corporation owns and operates a retail store. The following events were among those that took place last month:

1.   The company purchased merchandise for $5,000; the supplier accepted, as payment for this purchase, the company's written promise (its *note*) to pay this amount next month.
2.   The company received $4,000 from customers to pay for goods purchased by them in transactions recorded during the previous month.
3.   The company paid previously recorded accounts payable of $6,000.
4.   Store employees earned salaries of $1,000 during the month.
5.   Store employees were paid $900 of the amounts they had earned.
6.   The company borrowed $50,000 on a long-term note.
7.   The company sold merchandise on account for $8,000; the cost of this merchandise, purchased in a previous period, was $6,000.
8.   The company purchased a piece of land at a cost of $7,000, cash.
9.   The board of directors declared a dividend of $3,000, to be paid in cash to its shareholders next month. (The company uses a Dividends Declared account.)
10.   Office stationery costing $60 was purchased on credit for current use.
11.   Someone stole $100 in cash from the company. The loss is fully covered by insurance, but nothing has yet been received from the insurance company.

   Prepare journal entries in conventional debit-and-credit notation, using account titles similar to those used in this chapter, including appropriately titled revenue and expense accounts. For each debit or credit, indicate whether it represented an increase (+) or a decrease (−) in an asset (*A*), a liability (*L*), or the owners' equity (*OE*). You may assume that all transactions of previous months were recorded correctly.

4. Journal entries; financial statements; closing entries. The Handyman Tool Shop is an incorporated retailer of hardware supplies. Its balance sheet on December 31, 19x1, showed the following:

HANDYMAN TOOL SHOP, INC.
Statement of Financial Position
December 31, 19x1

Assets			Liabilities and Shareowners' Equity		
Current Assets:			Current Liabilities:		
Cash		$ 12,510	Accounts payable		$ 35,180
Accounts receivable		23,060	Salaries payable		1,400
Merchandise inventory ...		67,200	Total Current		
Total Current			Liabilities		$ 36,580
Assets		$102,770	Shareowners' Equity:		
Equipment	$36,140		Capital stock	$50,000	
Accumulated			Retained earnings	35,210	
depreciation	17,120	19,020	Total Shareowners'		
			Equity		85,210
			Total Liabilities		
			and Share-		
			owners'		
Total Assets ...		$121,790	Equity		$121,790

The store's transactions for the year 19x2 are summarized in the following items:

1. Sold merchandise at a total selling price of $301,000. The cost of the merchandise sold was $181,000.
2. Collected $296,000 in cash from customers.
3. Purchased merchandise from suppliers on account at a cost of $246,300.
4. Bought a secondhand delivery truck on account, $3,800.
5. Occupied the store for the entire year at an agreed monthly rental of $1,250.
6. Used telephone, electricity, and other miscellaneous services costing $21,000.
7. Made cash salary payments to employees, $44,400. The company owed nothing to its employees at the end of 19x2.
8. Made other cash payments totaling $248,850, as follows:
   To suppliers of merchandise, $209,000.
   To seller of secondhand delivery truck, $3,800.
   To landlord, for use of the store, $13,750.
   To suppliers of electricity and other miscellaneous services, $22,300.
9. Calculated the year's depreciation on the equipment, $4,800.
10. Issued 1,000 additional shares of capital stock to local investors in exchange for $60,000 in cash.
11. Declared a cash dividend of $25,000, to be paid to shareowners on January 20, 19x3.

The chart of accounts included accounts with the titles listed on the December 31, 19x1, balance sheet, plus the following: Dividends Payable, Sales Revenues, Rental Expense, Salaries Expense, Depreciation Expense, Cost of Goods Sold, Miscellaneous Expenses.

a. Prepare journal entries to record these transactions, using debit-and-credit notation and using only the accounts listed above.
b. Establish T-accounts, enter the December 31, 19x1, balances, and post the amounts from your journal entries.
c. Prepare an income statement for the year and a balance sheet as of December 31, 19x2.
d. Prepare a closing entry or entries in general journal form to prepare the accounts for the next year's transactions.

EXERCISES AND PROBLEMS

5. Equipment retirement. A company uses an Accumulated Depreciation account. One of its machines was scrapped last month. This machine cost $1,000 initially and had a book value of $200 at the time it was scrapped. The company gave the machine to a scrap dealer, who paid the costs of removing it. Someone has suggested that the following entry be made to record the disposition of the machine:

Loss on Equipment Retirement	200	
Equipment		200

a. Why would this be wrong?
b. What entry would be correct?

6. Equipment accounts. The opening balance in an Equipment account was $300, with accumulated depreciation totaling $100 shown in a separate account.

Depreciation for the year is $50, equipment purchases during the year amount to $250, and items originally costing $75 are sold for $20, resulting in a retirement loss of $40.

a. What is the correct ending balance in the Accumulated Depreciation account?
b. Prepare journal entries to record the events described above. You may assume that all purchases and sales of equipment were cash transactions.

7. Calculating net income from balance-sheet changes. The XYZ Company balance sheet on January 1, 19x1, listed assets of $1.1 million, liabilities of $100,000, and capital stock for which the company had received $300,000.

During the year, $140,000 was received from the sale of additional capital stock, and dividends of $40,000 were declared and paid. The balance sheet on December 31, 19x1, showed assets of $1.5 million and liabilities of $350,000.

Calculate the following (label all your calculations):

a. Retained earnings, January 1, 19x1.
b. Retained earnings, December 31, 19x1.
c. Net income for the year 19x1.

8. *Interpreting year-end owners' equity-account balances.* After all transactions for the year had been recorded, the following balances were found in the owners' equity accounts of a small corporation (the sequence of the accounts in the list below is alphabetical and has no other significance):

	Debit	Credit
Capital stock		$ 20,000
Cost of goods sold :..............	$70,000	
Dividends declared	6,000	
Other expenses	21,000	
Retained earnings................		1,000
Sales revenue		100,000

a. What does the $6,000 figure opposite "dividends declared" mean? Were these dividends paid in cash during the year?
b. What does the $1,000 figure opposite "retained earnings" mean?
c. What balance would you show opposite "retained earnings" on the year-end balance sheet?

9. *Equipment accounts; journal entries.* The statement of financial position in a company's annual report for the year ended December 31, 19x1, showed the following figures for plant and equipment:

	January 1	December 31
Plant and equipment	$400,000	$440,000
Less: accumulated depreciation	180,000	190,000
Plant and equipment (net)	$220,000	$250,000

The income statement for the year showed depreciation expenses of $30,000 and a gain of $10,000 on the sale of equipment. This equipment had a book value of $40,000, and it was sold for cash.

a. Calculate the cost of plant and equipment purchased during the year.
b. Prepare an appropriate set of journal entries to record the purchase of plant and equipment, the sale of equipment, and depreciation expense for the year. All plant and equipment purchases were cash transactions.

10. *Transactions analyses: debits and credits.* Prepare journal entries in debit and credit form for each of the following transactions. For each debit and each credit, indicate (1) whether it represents an increase or a decrease in assets, liabilities, or ownership and (2) whether the amount would appear in full on the income statement for the current year. The business is organized as a corporation. These transactions are completely independent of each other and do not represent all the year's transactions of this company.

1. Purchase of merchandise on account, $450.
2. Payment to supplier for goods received and recorded in previous year, $884.

3. Issue of additional shares of capital to Mr. T. O. Pitt, principal stockholder, in exchange for $8,500 cash.
4. Receipt of $10,000 cash as a loan from a bank.
5. One month's salary earned by Mr. T. O. Pitt for his services as company president during December of this year, $2,000, paid in cash on December 31.
6. Sale of merchandise on credit: sale price $1,200, cost $920.
7. Store clerks' wages earned during the year but not yet paid, $2,800.
8. Receipt of bill for electricity used in store and office during the year, $87.
9. Collection of $1,106 on accounts receivable.
10. Expiration of prepaid rent on store, $500.

11. Equipment accounts; journal entries.   On January 2, 19x1, Company X bought an electric typewriter for office use, paying $540 in cash. The company expected to sell this typewriter for $90 after using it for six years. Depreciation was to be charged in equal amounts each year.

a. Assuming that all journal entries for the year have been made correctly but that no closing entries have been made:

1. What balance would you expect to find in the Allowance for Depreciation account as of December 31, 19x3?
2. What balance would you expect to find in the Depreciation Expense account as of December 31, 19x3?
3. What was the "book value" of the typewriter as of December 31, 19x3?

b. What entry would be required on December 31, 19x6, if the typewriter were sold on that date for $90, cash?
c. What entry would be required on December 31, 19x4, if the typewriter were sold on that date for $80, cash?

12. Identifying fixed-asset transactions from financial statement data.
Two successive balance sheets showed the following amounts:

	End of Year 1	End of Year 2
Property, plant, and equipment (cost)	$10,000	$11,200
Less: Accumulated depreciation	4,000	4,500
Property, Plant, and Equipment (net)	$ 6,000	$ 6,700

The income statements for the two years included the following items:

	Year 1	Year 2
Depreciation	$1,000	$ 900
Gain (loss) on the sale of property, plant and equipment	100	(200)

The notes to the financial statements reported that the original cost of property, plant, and equipment retired amounted to $800 in year 1 and $700 in year 2.

Describe the transactions that led to changes in the Property, Plant and Equipment and Accumulated Depreciation accounts *during year* 2. Quantify the effects of these transactions on the company's accounts. (If you decide to do this by means of journal entries, give a brief verbal explanation of the meaning of each entry line.)

13.   Supplying missing data.   You have the following balance sheets for last year for a small retail store:

	January 1	December 31
Cash	$ 10	$ 14
Accounts receivable from customers	20	25
Merchandise inventory	30	32
Current Assets	$ 60	$ 71
Plant and equipment, net	50	52
Total Assets	$110	$123
Accounts payable to suppliers of merchandise	$ 15	$ 22
Dividends payable	—	2
Current Liabilities	$ 15	$ 24
Shareowners' equity:		
Capital stock	60	60
Retained earnings	35	39
Total Liabilities and Owners' Equity	$110	$123

You are given the following additional data on the year's transactions:

1.   Collections from customers, $145.
2.   Payments to suppliers of merchandise, $95.
3.   Purchases of equipment (all paid in cash) $6.
4.   Dividends declared, $5.
5.   Plant and equipment retired or sold, none.

a.   Compute sales revenues for the year.
b.   Compute the cost of merchandise sold during the year.
c.   Compute depreciation for the year.
d.   Compute net income for the year.

14.   T-accounts and journal entries.   Enter the January 1 Balances from Problem 13 in T-accounts. An Accumulated Depreciation account should be used, with a January 1 balance of $25. Then prepare and post entries to record the year's transactions, including a year-end closing entry or entries. Four revenue and expense accounts should be used: Sales Revenues, Cost of Goods Sold, Depreciation Expense, Other Expenses.

15.   Transactions analyses; journal entries.   A retail business owned by Mr. N. R. Gee is organized as an individual proprietorship. The owners' equity section of the ledger contains one revenue account (Sales Revenue), several expense accounts, and one balance sheet account (N. R. Gee, Owner).

This business engaged in the following transactions, among others, this year (each transaction was completely independent of the others in this list):

1.   Purchase of merchandise on an extended-payment contract, $2,100; one third of price paid at time of purchase, the remainder to be paid in installments after the first of next year.

2. Payment of $15,000 to suppliers of merchandise on account.
3. A three-year insurance policy was taken out last year, and the three-year premium of $1,800 was paid in cash at that time. Record the amount applicable to the current year.
4. Sale of merchandise, $8,300 for cash and $13,700 on account; cost of merchandise sold, $16,400.
5. Purchase of land and building, $12,000 for the land and $40,000 for the building; $30,000 was paid in cash and the remainder in the form of a 20-year mortgage payable.
6. Collection of $18,300 on customers' accounts.
7. Use of office supplies, $800; these supplies had been debited to the Office Supplies Inventory account at the time of purchase.
8. Depreciation on delivery equipment, $1,550.
9. Employee's salary for one month this year, $700, to be paid next year.
10. Withdrawal of $560 cash by Mr. N. R. Gee, owner.

a. Prepare a journal entry or entries in debit and credit form for each of these transactions.
b. For each debit and each credit, indicate (1) whether it represents an increase or a decrease in an asset, a liability, or the owner's equity and (2) whether the amount would appear in full on the income statement for this year.

16. Transactions analysis; journal entries. The Woods Company is organized as a corporation and is engaged in retail trade. The owners' equity section of the ledger contains one revenue account (Sales Revenue), a number of expense accounts, and two balance-sheet accounts (Capital Stock and Retained Earnings).

The Woods Company had the following transactions, among others, this month (each transaction was completely independent of the others in this list):

1. Purchased office equipment on account, $4,700.
2. Received bill from plumbing contractor for repairs performed this month, $225.
3. Sold merchandise on account, $22,400; cost of this merchandise was $16,700.
4. Issued 100 shares of the company's capital stock for $5,000 cash.
5. Hired clerk to start work the first of next month, salary $560 a month.
6. Collected $26,200 from customers on account.
7. Borrowed $1,000 cash from bank.
8. Ordered carload of bagged charcoal for sale to customers, $24,000.
9. Recorded $1,400 depreciation and $2,200 expiration of prepaid rent.
10. Recognized $1,500 salary earned this month by Mr. N. A. Woods, president of the company and owner of 75 percent of the corporation's capital stock.
11. Received bills, as follows:
    For new delivery truck, $2,600.
    For insurance policy to be effective the first of next month, $220.
    For this month's telephone service, $85.

These bills will be paid next month. The dealer will not deliver the new delivery truck until it has been paid for.

a. Prepare a journal entry or entries in debit and credit form for each transaction to be reflected in the accounts.

b. For each debit and each credit, indicate (1) whether it represents an increase or a decrease in an asset, a liability, or the owners' equity and (2) whether the amount would appear in full on the income statement for this month.

17. *T-accounts, journal entries, statements, closing entries.* Freemont Hardware Store, Inc., had the following balance sheet as of March 31, 19x1:

FREEMONT HARDWARE STORE, INC.
Balance Sheet
As of March 31, 19x1

Assets			Liabilities and Owners' Equity		
Current Assets:			Liabilities:		
Cash		$11,000	Accounts payable		$15,800
Accounts receivable		24,100	Notes payable		3,000
Merchandise inventory		21,700	Total Current Liabilities		$18,800
Total Current Assets		$56,800	Long-term debt		12,000
Building	$30,000		Total Liabilities		$30,800
Equipment	10,800		Shareholders' Equity:		
Total	$40,800		Capital stock		$40,000
Less Depreciation			Retained earnings		17,800
to date	9,000	31,800	Total Shareholders' Equity		$57,800
			Total Liabilities and		
Total Assets		$88,600	Owners' Equity		$88,600

The following items summarize the company's transactions for the month of April:

1. Purchased merchandise on account from suppliers at a total cost of $13,500.
2. Purchased on account an electric warehouse truck at a cost of $800.
3. Sold on account for $18,200 merchandise costing $11,500.
4. Collected $15,000 on accounts receivable.
5. Received invoices covering telephone service, electricity, and other services bought and used during April, $1,140 (credit Accounts Payable).
6. Accrued employees' salaries for the month of April, $2,800.
7. Purchased, on April 1, a two-year, general coverage insurance policy to cover the period from April 1, 19x1, through March 31, 19x3. Paid the entire two-year premium on this policy, $120 in cash.
8. Rented a small storeroom in a nearby building for 12 months, beginning April 1, 19x1, at a monthly rental of $110. Paid six months' rent in cash.

9. Paid $18,340 on accounts payable, $2,800 in salaries to employees, and $75 to holders of the company's notes payable and long-term debt, covering interest for the use of their money during April.
10. Calculated depreciation for the month of April: office and warehouse equipment, $70; delivery equipment, $80; building $50.
11. The board of directors declared a dividend in the amount of $500, to be paid to shareholders in cash on May 15, 19x1.

a. Set up T-accounts for the items shown on the balance sheet and enter the March 31 balances. Use one account for the building, one for the equipment, and one for the accumulated depreciation.
b. Analyze each transaction and prepare journal entries in debit and credit form, using the account titles you adopted in (*a*) plus any others required by your analyses.
c. Set up additional T-accounts, as required, and post your entries from (*b*).
d. Determine the April 30 balance in each account. Using these balances, prepare an income statement for the month of April and a balance sheet as of April 30. (Ignore income taxes.)
e. Prepare an appropriate closing entry or entries as of April 30.

18. Comprehensive problem. Wentworth Petroleum Company provides fuel oil and oil burner maintenance services to retail customers. Its "fiscal year" begins on July 1 each year, after the end of the heating season, and ends the following June 30. The company's account balances at the start of business on July 1, 19x1, were as follows:

	Debit	Credit
Cash	$50,000	
Accounts receivable	10,000	
Inventory	40,000	
Prepaid rent	12,000	
Equipment	60,000	
Accumulated depreciation		$25,000
Accounts payable		30,000
Salaries payable		5,000
Dividends payable		2,000
Capital stock		75,000
Retained earnings		35,000

The following information relates to the 12-month period that began on July 1, 19x1, and ended on June 30, 19x2:

1. Sales of fuel oil on account, $500,000.
2. Maintenance services provided to customers on account, $50,000.
3. Salaries earned by employees: delivery employees, $30,000; maintenance service employees, $22,000; executive and office employees, $48,000.
4. Purchases on account: fuel oil, $400,000; repair parts for maintenance service work, $5,000; office supplies and postage, $2,500; maintenance of delivery vehicles, $4,000; gasoline and oil for delivery vehicles, $15,000; new delivery truck, $10,000; telephone, electricity, and other miscellaneous services, $3,000.
5. Dividends declared, $20,000.

6. Payments on account: to suppliers, $415,000; to employees for salaries, $103,000; to landlord for 12 months' rent from January 1, 19x2, to December 31, 19x2, $27,000; to shareholders for dividends, $22,000.
7. Cash collections from customers, $540,000.
8. Cash received from sale of old delivery truck, $1,500; this truck had been bought for $8,000 many years earlier and was fully depreciated at the time it was sold.
9. Cash received from the issuance of additional shares of capital stock, $18,000.
10. Depreciation for the year, $12,000.
11. The cost of the fuel oil in inventory on June 30, 19x2, was $90,000; the company maintains no inventories of office supplies or repair parts for maintenance services.

a. Draw up a chart of accounts for Wentworth Petroleum Company, Inc., including appropriate revenue and expense accounts. Wentworth is not subject to an income tax.

b. Set up T-accounts and enter the July 1, 19x1, balances.

c. Prepare journal entries to record your analyses of the information provided above. For each debit and each credit, indicate whether it represents an increase or a decrease in an asset, a liability, or the owners' equity.

d. Post your entries to the T-accounts and calculate the June 30, 19x2, balances.

e. Prepare an income statement and a statement of changes in retained earnings for the year and a statement of financial position at June 30, 19x2.

f. Prepare a closing entry or entries to prepare the accounts to receive entries recording transactions in the 19x2–x3 fiscal year.

19. *Comprehensive problem; incorporated school.* The Greeley School, a private preparatory day school, accepted its first students and held its first classes in September, 19x1. The school was founded by Jonathan Greeley, the former senior tutor of a large eastern preparatory school.

Mr. Greeley was anxious to try out a new system of instruction and had persuaded a group of wealthy businesspeople to supply most of the capital he needed to finance the new venture. He intended to operate the school for profit, partly to demonstrate that it could be done, and partly because this seemed to him the best basis on which to attract the required capital.

As expected, enrollment was below capacity during the first year, but by May 19x2, applications for September enrollment were so numerous that Mr. Greeley believed his classes would be filled during the second year.

His backers were impressed by the file of admission applications and pleased by the competence Mr. Greeley seemed to have shown in administering the school, but they were anxious to find out how much money the school had lost during its initial year of operations. As one of the shareholders said, "The enrollment figures are impressive, but so are those at the university, and they have to tap us alumni every year just to meet the payroll. I don't expect we'll show a profit at Greeley this year, but if the loss is much larger than we had expected we ought to think seriously of closing up shop or selling our shares for whatever we can get for them."

The school started its formal existence on July 1, 19x1, with the issuance of a corporate charter. The following transactions took place during its first 12 months:

1. Two hundred shares of capital stock were issued on July 1, 19x1, for $30,000, cash.

2. At the same time, the shareholders deposited an additional $10,000 in the corporation's bank account, receiving, in exchange, notes payable in this amount.

3. A two-year lease was signed, giving the school the right to use a large mansion and its grounds from July 1, 19x1, to June 30, 19x3. The monthly rental was $2,000. An initial cash payment of $6,000 was made on July 1, 19x1, and cash payments of $2,000 each were made on the first of each succeeding month, through June 1, 19x2.

4. A set of classroom blackboards was purchased on credit for $3,600. Other private schools in the area estimated that, on the average, blackboards could be used for 12 years before replacement became necessary.

5. Classroom furniture costing $9,000 was purchased from the Tower Seating Company, which accepted a down payment of $4,000 in cash and a note payable for the balance. Classroom furniture was expected to have an eight-year life, on the average.

6. Equipment of various kinds, with an expected average life of five years, was purchased for $7,000, cash.

7. Students' tuition and other fees amounted to $78,000. Of this amount, $6,000 had not yet been collected by June 30, 19x2, but Mr. Greeley was confident that this amount would be received before the new school year began in September.

8. Salaries were paid in cash:
   Teaching staff, $54,000.
   Office staff, $11,000.

9. On June 15, 19x2, two parents paid tuition for the 19x2–x3 school year, amounting to $3,400.

10. Various school supplies were bought on credit for $4,100. Of these, $200 were still in the school's storeroom, unused, on June 30, 19x2.

11. Utility bills and other miscellaneous operating costs applicable to the year ending June 30, 19x2, were paid in cash, $3,800.

12. Payments amounting to $4,500 were made on account to suppliers of items referred to in items 4 and 10 above.

13. The holders of the school's notes were paid interest of $900. In addition, the Tower Seating Company was paid $1,500 of the amount borrowed (item 5, above).

a. Prepare a list of account titles that you think would be useful for recording these transactions, including revenue and expense accounts and an allowance for depreciation account. Then analyze the above transactions in debit and credit form. For each debit and each credit, indicate (1) whether the effect is to increase or to decrease an asset (*A*), a liability (*L*), or the shareholders' equity (*OE*) and (2) whether the amount would appear in full on the income statement for the current year. For example:

Cash   xxx
    Capital Stock   xxx
(Increase A; increase OE; no effect on current income.)

Do not forget to record depreciation for the year.

b.   Post these amounts to T-accounts.

c.   Prepare an income statement for the year and a balance sheet as of June 30, 19x2.

d.   Upon seeing your figures, Mr. Greeley objected to the depreciation charge. "We just can't afford to write off any of those costs this year," he said. "Next year our tuition will be up, and we can start recovering depreciation." Do you agree with Mr. Greeley, or do you have a different concept of depreciation? Defend your position.

e.   If you were a shareholder, how would you use the financial statements in your evaluation of the financial success or failure of this new enterprise? Assuming that your decision to retain your shares or sell them would be based on your forecast of future financial statements, would the financial statements of a period already in the past be of any relevance to you?

4

Sales, Purchases, and Payrolls

THE MOST COMMON KINDS of transactions we have discussed so far are purchases, sales, and payroll transactions. The purpose of this chapter is to look more closely at the problems of measuring revenues from sales, the costs of purchased merchandise, and the costs of employees' services.

REVENUES FROM SALES

The price quoted on a sales invoice to a customer may be an imperfect measure of the amount of revenue generated by the sale. Three kinds of differences between invoice price and revenue need to be explained:

1. Customer defaults.
2. Cash discounts.
3. Returns of merchandise.

Customer Defaults

Some businesses wait until they have actually collected cash from their customers before they recognize revenue—that is, they report that a sale has taken place only when the cash is in the company's possession. Other businesses recognize revenues much earlier, while they are doing work for their customers. In Chapter 8, we'll see what criteria should be used in deciding when each of these approaches is appropriate.

Most businesses recognize revenues at the time merchandise is shipped or delivered to customers and invoices are prepared. At that time, however, management isn't sure that every customer will actually pay the amount shown on the invoice. In fact, most businesses *know* that some of their customers won't pay for the goods or services they have received. These unpaid amounts are known as *bad debts, uncollectible accounts,* or *customer defaults.*

This means that the revenue from a credit sale is less than the invoice price. It also means that the value of the company's receivables is less than the total amount due from its customers. Something has to be done to reflect these differences in the financial statements.

Remember that when revenue is recognized, the accountants record an increase in assets (accounts receivable) and an increase in owners' equity (revenue from sales). If the total of the invoice prices in a given year is $1 million, and the company has only one account for sales revenues and one account for accounts receivable, the entry will be:

(1)

Accounts Receivable 1,000,000
    Sales Revenues.......................   1,000,000

We know that both of these figures are overstated because we know that some customers will default. If the company knew which customers would default, the solution would be simple. Management would take these customers' accounts out of the active file and subtract their balances from the amounts shown in the ledger for accounts receivable and sales revenues. Assuming $10,000 in customer defaults arising out of this year's sales, the entry would be:

(2)

Sales Revenues 10,000
    Accounts Receivable   10,000

The debit to Sales Revenues corrects the overstatement in owners' equity; the credit to Accounts Receivable corrects the overstatement in this asset arising from the original entry. The correct revenue figure is $990,000; the correct receivable is also $990,000 at this time because this is the amount management will collect.

The $10,000 debit to Sales Revenues in this entry measures a *sales deduction.* Sales deductions are amounts to be subtracted from some figure representing gross sales, to reflect the fact that the amount to be collected from customers will be less than the gross sales figure. Customer defaults is the first of four of these to be identified in this section. Sales deductions must be subtracted from gross revenues to avoid overstating net income, but they are very different from the other deductions from revenues we have met before, the expenses. Expenses are the costs of resources used up to obtain revenues; sales deductions reduce the amounts obtainable from customers.

In describing entry (2), we said that $10,000 of the receivables arising from this year's sales eventually turned out to be uncollectible. Unfortunately, the company can't wait to prepare financial statements until it knows which customers will default. The figures shown for revenues and receivables will have to reflect *estimates* of the amounts customers won't pay in the future. Luckily, most businesses can predict, usually with great accuracy, the *percentage* of credit sales that will be uncollectible. These predictions can be used to restate revenues and receivables at their correct levels.[1]

For example, suppose our company's past experience indicates that 1 percent of the receivables arising from an average year's credit sales will prove to be uncollectible. On sales of $1 million, this would amount to $10,000. We don't usually reflect this in an entry like entry (2), for two reasons:

1. To provide a check on the accuracy of the ledger, the balance in the Accounts Receivable *account* should equal the total of the balances of the individual accounts outstanding.
2. Because many financial ratios are expressed as percentages of gross revenues (before deducting uncollectible amounts), most companies want the balances in the Sales Revenue account to measure gross revenues.

We can meet both of these needs by using two contra accounts—Allowance for Uncollectible Accounts and Estimated Customer Defaults. The entry would be:

(2a)

Estimated Customer Defaults	10,000	
Allowance for Uncollectible Accounts		10,000

TERMINOLOGY REMINDER: CONTRA ACCOUNT

A contra account is an account established to accumulate a specified class of deductions from the gross amount of some asset, liability, owners' equity, revenue, or expense. For financial statement presentation, the balance in the contra account should always be deducted from the gross amount with which it is paired.

---

[1] A different percentage may be used each year, derived by a method known as "aging the receivables." This will be discussed in Chapter 5.

The Estimated Customer Defaults account is a deduction-from-revenues contra account. It represents a negative component of sales revenue. The debit to this account in entry (2a) is necessary because the credit to Sales Revenues overstated the increase in owners' equity resulting from sales to customers. Those two accounts now show the following:

Sales Revenues			Estimated Customer Defaults		
	(1)	1,000,000	(2a)	10,000	

The income statement should show the following:

Gross sales	$1,000,000
Less: estimated customer defaults	10,000
Net sales	$ 990,000

The Allowance for Uncollectible Accounts is a deduction-from-assets contra account.[2] The purpose of the credit to this account is to recognize the fact that the amounts entered in the Accounts Receivable account overstate the value of that asset. The credit can't be made directly to Accounts Receivable, however, because the company doesn't know which specific customers won't pay their bills. The allowance account normally has a credit balance, which is shown on the balance sheet as a deduction from gross receivables:

Accounts receivable, gross	$1,000,000
Less: allowance for uncollectibles	10,000
Accounts receivable, net	$ 990,000

Accounts receivable are reduced when customers pay their bills. Our company collected $800,000 during the year, and the entries made to record these collections are summarized in entry (3):

(3)

Cash	800,000	
Accounts Receivable		800,000

This shows an increase in the amount of cash in the company's possession and a decrease in the amount of its claims against its customers; in other words, one asset was exchanged for another.

---

[2] Using the word *accounts* in the title of this contra account may lead to some confusion. The reason is that the word is used in two senses: (1) to refer to a space in the company's ledger (the Allowance for Uncollectible Accounts is an account, in this sense) and (2) as the amount due from a specific customer (the ABC Company's account with the XYZ Company now amounts to $14,000, in this sense). The intended sense of the term is almost always clear from the context in which it is used.

The balance sheet figures at the end of the year now are as follows:

Accounts receivable, gross...........................	$200,000
Less: allowance for uncollectibles.................	10,000
Accounts receivable, net	$190,000

This tells us that although estimated customer defaults arose from the $1 million sales of the current month, they now attach to the $200,000 in gross receivables outstanding at the end of the year. The company is now much closer to identifying which specific accounts will prove to be uncollectible. By collecting from some customers, management knows that these aren't the customers who won't pay—the problems lie somewhere in the $200,000 of receivables still outstanding.

At some point management will begin to identify specific customers as likely to default. When management finally decides that a particular receivable is, in fact, uncollectible, it should be removed from the file of current receivables. In addition, since the amounts in the Allowance for Uncollectible Accounts have been put there specifically because some receivables will eventually prove uncollectible, the balance in this account should be reduced whenever the receivables themselves are written off.

In our example, the entry to record the write-off of a $1,000 account would be as follows:

Allowance for Uncollectible Accounts	1,000	
Accounts Receivable		1,000

The credit to Accounts Receivable reduces the balance in this account, and the debit to the allowance reduces its balance by the same amount. The entry does not record a reduction in the asset, however, because the value of the receivables as a whole has not fallen. The only event was management's discovery that an asset previously considered uncollectible proved, in fact, to be uncollectible. The balance sheet will now show the following:

Accounts receivable, gross...........................	$199,000
Less: allowance for uncollectibles.................	9,000
Accounts receivable, net	$190,000

All the entry has done is to identify the *specific* accounts for which a *general* allowance was made when revenues were recorded and the probable defaults were recognized.

Recoveries of overdue amounts.   Writing an amount off against the Allowance for Uncollectible Accounts account doesn't necessarily mean the customer's debt is forgiven. The company may still pursue the debtor quite actively, and substantial amounts may be collected long after they have been written off.

In concept, the estimate of customer defaults should be a net amount, the amount that never will be collected. If this approach is taken, the recovery of $100 previously written off should be recorded as a correction of the previous write-off. First, the gross receivable should be restored to the Accounts Receivable account:

Accounts Receivable   100
   Allowance for Uncollectible Accounts   100

Once this is done, the collection can be recorded just like any other collection:

Cash   100
   Accounts Receivable   100

To emphasize that recoveries really constitute realization of revenues the company has earned, we prefer to make entries with the following net results:

Cash   100
   Recovery of Overdue Accounts   100

The Recovery of Overdue Accounts account is a revenue account representing a class of additions to the owners' equity. The credit to this account indicates that the amount recovered is, in fact, an addition to net revenue. Recording it this way rather than by a credit to Estimated Customer Defaults gives management a running record of the success of its collection efforts. The balance in this account can then be compared with the costs incurred to collect overdue amounts.

Adjustments.   Estimates of customer defaults are bound to be imprecise, and the balance in the Allowance for Uncollectible Accounts account should be examined from time to time to make sure it is neither too high nor too low. We'll describe one technique for making these adjustments in Chapter 5.

Managerial implications.   While customer defaults in most businesses are inevitable, management has a great deal to say about how large they will be. Its main instrument for this purpose is credit policy—that is, the criteria on which decisions to extend credit are based. Credit policy is, to some extent, dictated by the customary practice in individual industries or markets, but all sellers have some leeway in deciding how much credit risk they will bear.

A liberal credit policy usually leads to larger sales volumes but greater collection costs and more customer defaults. A tight credit policy, implemented by careful investigation of the credit-worthiness of prospective customers and refusal to deal with any but the best credit risks, can reduce customer defaults and collection costs, but at the cost of lower sales volume and increased costs of credit investigation. Management must decide how far to go in trading increased customer defaults for greater sales, and different companies in the same line of business will find different answers to this question.

Sales Discounts

The invoice price may also overstate revenues from sales for another reason. Companies in some industries allow their customers to deduct a small percentage from the invoice price if they pay within a specified time period. This is known as a *cash discount*.

For example, a company may give its customers 30 days in which to pay their bills, with a 2 percent discount if they pay within ten days after the invoice date. (These are the "terms of sale," abbreviated in this case as 2/10, n/30, which is read as, two ten, net 30.) The invoice price is known as the *gross price* of the merchandise; the amount due after deducting the discount is the *net price*.

Suppose goods with a gross price of $100,000 are sold on these terms. Sales revenues in this case are really $98,000 rather than $100,000. The reason: the 2 percent discount is so large that most customers can't afford to pass it up. In this case, it is equivalent to an annual interest rate of 36.7 percent on borrowed money, as the calculations in Exhibit 4–1 demonstrate. Except in a highly inflationary

EXHIBIT 4–1. Calculation of Interest Rate in 2/10, n/30 Terms of Sale

1. If customers pay on the tenth day, they will pay $98 for every $100 shown on their invoice. If they don't pay on this date, they are borrowing the $98 from their suppliers.
2. Customers who don't pay within the ten-day period have 20 additional days to pay before the invoices become overdue and their credit ratings become impaired. In other words, by not paying promptly, customers pay $2 for the use of $98 for 20 days, about 1/18 of a year.
3. By doing this 18 times, customers can have the $98 to use for a whole year. The penalty will be 18 × $2 = $36.
4. This is equivalent to an annual interest rate of 36.7 percent:

$$\text{Interest rate} = \frac{\text{Interest for the year}}{\text{Amount borrowed}} = \frac{\$36}{\$98} = 36.7\%.$$

economy, this is an extremely high interest rate. Only very careless or very weak customers will pay it.

The significance of this is that the real price of the merchandise is $98, the amount the seller expects the customer to pay. The other $2 is seldom received. When it is received, it should be interpreted as a form of interest revenue arising from a short-term loan to a customer.

This being the case, management might expect the accountants to record the sale of merchandise with a gross price of $100,000 and a 2 percent cash discount as follows:

Accounts Receivable	98,000	
Sales Revenue		98,000

This isn't done, however, mainly because recording the gross price is the simplest and cheapest way of keeping track of the gross amounts owed by customers. The usual entry would be:

Accounts Receivable	100,000	
Sales Revenues		100,000

This entry records the gross revenues from these sales and the gross receivables.

When sales revenues are recorded in this way, the sales deduction for cash discounts is recorded when collections are recorded. Collection of $88,200 during the discount period on gross receivables of $90,000 would be recorded in an entry like the following:

Cash	88,200	
Sales Discounts	1,800	
Accounts Receivable		90,000

The Sales Discounts account is another sales deductions account, appearing in the chart of accounts as a contra account to Sales Revenues.

Sales Returns and Allowances

The third reason why the total invoice price of merchandise delivered to customers is likely to be greater than the amount of revenue from sales is that customers either return some of the merchandise or keep it on the condition that the seller give them partial allowances—that is, reduce the price.

Sales allowances. Sales allowances usually arise because merchandise has been damaged or because it doesn't meet the customer's specifications perfectly. The customer is willing to keep the merchandise, but only if the price is reduced. The effect of an allowance is to reduce the amount receivable from the customer. The entry to record a $100 allowance is:

Sales Allowances	100	
Accounts Receivable		100

Sales allowances are another kind of sales deduction, and the Sales Allowances account is a deduction-from-revenue contra account. A debit entry to this account records the reduction in owners' equity resulting from the allowance.

Sales returns. Sales returns reduce both revenues and the amounts receivable from customers. To collect data on the magnitude of these returns, companies often use another deduction-from-revenue contra account, with a title such as Sales Returns. The following entry would record a return of merchandise originally billed to a customer at $200:

Sales Returns	200	
Accounts Receivable		200

If management doesn't need separate data on sales returns, the debits can be to a sales revenue account.

If the returned merchandise is in first-class, salable condition, it usually will be put back in inventory. If a perpetual inventory system is used, an entry like the following must be made:

Inventory	120	
Cost of Goods Sold		120

This shows that goods that had cost $120 are now back on the shelves and that the cost of goods sold is $120 less than it had been before the return. The net reduction in assets and owners' equity resulting from this return is $200 − $120 = $80.

If the returned merchandise is unsalable, the accountants have two options. First, if they want to call attention to the damage, they may transfer the cost of the merchandise from the Cost of Goods Sold to a separate expense account, with a title such as Loss on Damaged Merchandise. The entry would be:

Loss on Damaged Merchandise	120	
Cost of Goods Sold		120

This merely moves the cost from one expense category to another; it has no net effect on owners' equity. For this reason, management may choose the second option—leave the cost of the damaged merchandise in the cost of goods sold and make no entry at all.

Revenue Summary

A company with estimated customer defaults, discounts, returns, and allowances will have a sales revenue section like the following:

Gross revenues		$1,000,000
Less: Estimated customer defaults	$10,000	
Sales discounts taken	1,800	
Sales returns	200	
Sales allowances granted	100	
Total Deductions from Gross Sales		12,100
Net Sales		$ 987,900

The customer default figure is based on an estimate; the other three deductions were recorded as part of the analysis of transactions actually completed during the period. In concept, the amounts of the sales discounts, returns, and allowances arising from receivables outstanding at the end of the period should be estimated and subtracted from accounts receivable and sales revenues; these estimates are seldom made, however, because the amounts involved are very small.

In practice, sales deductions are often listed with the expenses, and customer defaults are often even called expenses ("bad debt expense"). Our treatment is the only one consistent with the definition of expense, however. Expense is a cost of a resource used to produce revenues of the current period. Customer defaults, sales discounts, sales returns, and sales allowances don't fit this definition. They represent nonrevenues, portions of the gross sales amount the company will never receive in cash. Net income, of course, will be the same no matter what we call them.

Receivables Summary

Receivables are not an accounting abstraction. They are real claims against real customers. The deductions we have been describing are made because these claims are worth less than some gross amount stated on the invoices or elsewhere. The statement of financial position, therefore, should show the receivables at their net amount, the amount they are worth to the company.

THE COST OF GOODS PURCHASED

The cost of anything bought from an outside supplier consists of all the resources sacrificed to get that item to the buyer—in other words, a *net delivered price*. For example, suppose goods with an invoice price of $10,000 and freight charges of $800 are delivered to the company. The entry to record this purchase should be:

Inventory	10,800	
Accounts Payable		10,800

This shows an asset of $10,800, accompanied by a similar increase in the company's liabilities.

Technically correct though this treatment may be, it would be inconvenient to use. The goods and the freight charges are likely to be covered by separate invoices, received at different times. To record the cost of a purchased item at its net delivered price, the company would have to wait until both invoices arrived. This would be very awkward. As a result, the accountant is likely to record each invoice as it comes in, without attempting to include the cost of freight in the cost of the specific goods purchased. The two entries in this case would be:

```
Inventory .............................      10,000
     Accounts Payable ....................              10,000

Freight In ...............................         800
     Accounts Payable ....................                 800
```

If the amounts are small, the accountant will treat freight in as a current expense. This will lead to a slight understatement of the inventory and an equal understatement of owners' equity.

Cash discounts on purchased goods also affect net delivered cost. For example, suppose a company buys a number of items at an invoice price of $50,000, subject to a 3 percent discount for prompt payment. The cost of the goods is $50,000 less 3 percent, or $48,500. The purchase probably would be recorded at the full invoice price, however, on the grounds that this is simpler and less confusing to clerical employees. The entry to record these purchases would be:

```
Inventory .............................      50,000
     Accounts Payable ....................              50,000
```

Under this approach, the discount is recognized when it is taken, at the time the invoice is paid. If the payment is made on time, the entry to record it will be:

```
Accounts Payable ......................      50,000
     Purchases Discounts ................               1,500
     Cash ...............................              48,500
```

The debit to Accounts Payable records the reduction in the liability; the credit to Cash records the decrease in this asset. The credit to Purchases Discounts is more difficult to interpret. Since the cost of the merchandise is $48,500, the Purchases Discounts account logically should be classified as a deduction-from-assets contra account, attached to the Inventory account. Because this is a cumbersome procedure, however, companies using this method generally report purchases discounts as a form of revenue. This leads to some overstatement of inventory cost, but the amounts are usually quite small.

PAYROLL TRANSACTIONS

A major cost item in the typical company is the cost of its payrolls. A payroll consists of the amounts a specific group of employees earned from the company in a specified period. The cost of a payroll is divided into two parts: (1) the amounts earned by individual employees during the period (their *gross pay*) and (2) payroll taxes and other payroll-related costs.

Gross Pay

Payrolls today are often quite complex. First, management may wish to divide the costs into two or more categories. For example, in evaluating the performance of the people on the sales force, management will want to compare their salaries and other expenses with the gross margins (net revenues minus cost of goods sold) they produce. To provide this information, the accountants will use one or more salary expense accounts to accumulate the salaries of employees on the sales force (e.g., $50,000) and another to record the salaries of office employees (e.g., $30,000).

Second, the company "withholds" part of the employees' pay, for later payment to others. Each employee's pay check is accompanied by a statement showing the amount of the gross pay, the deductions, and the net pay. The withholdings from an $80,000 payroll might be as follows:

F.I.C.A. tax[3]	$ 4,800
Federal income tax	12,000
State income tax	3,200
Total Taxes	$20,000
Pensions	4,000
Medical insurance	1,000
Total Withholdings	$25,000

The taxes will be paid to the various taxing authorities, the amounts withheld for pensions and medical insurance will be paid to insurance companies, and only the net pay will be paid to the individual employees.

To reflect these complexities in this illustration, the accountant might recognize two categories of expenses and three categories of liabilities. If so, the entry will be:

Sales Salaries Expense	50,000	
Office Salaries Expense	30,000	
Taxes Payable		20,000
Accounts Payable		5,000
Salaries Payable		55,000

---

[3] F.I.C.A. stands for Federal Insurance Contributions Act. The tax is popularly referred to as the social security tax, although it is actually only one of a number of taxes supporting social security benefits in the United States. The F.I.C.A. tax is levied on the wages and salaries of all employees in occupations covered by the law. The amount of an individual's wages or salary that is subject to this tax and the tax rate are set by Congress and are likely to change from year to year. To keep the arithmetic simple in this illustration, we are using an arbitrary rate of 6 percent of gross pay to calculate the amounts deductible from an employee's gross pay.

Payment of the net pay to the employees then would be recorded as follows:

Salaries Payable........................	55,000	
Cash		55,000

Payroll Taxes on Employers

Employers in the United States and in most other countries must hand over to governmental agencies not only the amounts withheld from their employees' gross pay but other amounts as well. For example, an employer whose employees are subject to F.I.C.A. taxes is required to match the amounts deducted for this purpose from the employees' gross pay.

In our example, the company had to pay $9,600 to the government for F.I.C.A. taxes, just twice the amount deducted from the employees' paychecks. The additional $4,800 was an operating expense, just as it would have been if it had been paid to the employees directly. The departmental amounts were:

Sales department	$3,000
Office	1,800

Companies also have other payroll taxes, most notably unemployment insurance taxes. In our example, these were levied at a rate of 3 percent of gross pay, and the amounts were:

Sales department	$1,500
Office	900

It should be clear that these additional payroll taxes are really part of the cost of using employees' services. The same is true of the cost of any payroll-related *fringe benefits,* such as employer-paid vacations, holidays, and health and retirement plans. Logically, therefore, the amounts should be added to the gross pay and classified as part of salary expense. Sales salary costs, for example, were $50,000 + $3,000 + $1,500 = $54,500, and office salary costs were $30,000 + $1,500 + $900 = $32,700. These are the amounts that resulted from management's decisions to employ and use these people.

A more typical solution, however, is to report payroll taxes as a separate category. The summary entry to record the month's payroll taxes would be:

Payroll Tax Expense—Sales	4,500	
Payroll Tax Expense—Office	2,700	
Taxes Payable		7,200

Total department payroll expenses are still $54,500 and $32,700, but these totals are split into two parts. Management needs to remember that these two expenses arise from the same managerial actions.

SUMMARY

Invoice prices, salaries, and wage rates are unlikely to measure the impact of revenue, purchase, and payroll transactions on the organization's assets, liabilities, and owners' equity. The major differences between the total invoice amounts and the amounts of resources actually generated by the sales of a period are due to defaults by customers, discounts and allowances granted customers, and returns of merchandise by customers. The costs of goods purchased are subject to similar influences. Payroll costs are affected by payroll taxes and the fringe benefits provided to employees.

Many accounting systems treat the nominal amount and the accompanying variations (discounts, payroll taxes, and so forth) as separate sets of transactions. The main reason is that this makes routine recordkeeping easier. In preparing the financial statements, however, the accountants have to bring these elements back together. Both revenues and receivables, for example, should be reported at their net values if the differences are material in amount.

KEY TERMS

Cash discount	Net pay
Customer defaults	Net price
Delivered price	Payroll taxes
Freight in	Sales deductions
Fringe benefits	Sales returns and allowances
Gross pay	Uncollectible accounts
Gross price	Withholdings

INDEPENDENT STUDY PROBLEMS (Solutions in Appendix B)

1. Customer defaults. The Reilly Company recognizes revenues at the time it delivers its products to its customers. Customer defaults average 1 percent of gross sales. You have the following information for the month of June:

1. Opening balances:
   Accounts receivable, $950,000.
   Allowance for Uncollectible Accounts, $25,000.
2. Gross sales, $500,000.
3. Collections from customers, $510,000.
4. Write-offs of specific uncollectibles, $8,000.

a. Analyze the effects of items (2), (3), and (4) on the company's assets, liabilities, and owners' equity. (Use +/− notation.)
b. Prepare journal entries to reflect your analyses in (a).

c. What amount should be reported to the shareholders as the amount of the accounts receivable at the end of June?
d. What amount should be shown for customer defaults on the income statement for the month of June?

2. Sales discounts and allowances. The Pacific Company purchased, on February 12, 20 radios at $50 each from the Amsterdam Company, terms: 2 percent, 10 days; net, 30 days. On February 14, it sold ten of these radios to the Jones Electric Company for $60 each, terms: 2 percent, 10 days; net, 30 days.

Jones sold five of the radios during February at a price of $100 each, terms: net, 30 days. It returned the other five radios to Pacific on February 16 because the cases were scarred. Pacific gave Jones Electric full credit for the radios it returned. It appraised the returned radios at $30 each, wholesale value, and offered them for sale at a price of $36 each. On February 21, the Amsterdam Company agreed to deduct the difference between the original gross price and the appraised wholesale value from the gross amount due from Pacific. Pacific sold none of the returned radios in February.

Pacific paid Amsterdam $882 on February 21. Jones Electric paid Pacific $300 on March 13.

a. Calculate the following amounts: (1) the net cost of the goods sold by Pacific; (2) Pacific's net revenue from sales to Jones Electric; and (3) Pacific's income from discounts lost by Jones Electric.
b. Analyze each of the transactions that took place during February and prepare journal entries appropriate for (1) Pacific and (2) Jones Electric. Each company accounts for its inventories by the perpetual inventory method.
c. In what way or ways would the methods used by these two companies to record these transactions provide misleading income statements for February or incorrect balance sheets as of February 28?

3. Payroll costs and liabilities. The Northumberland Company is a distributor of textiles in southern New England. You have the following information for the month of March:

1. Taxes payable, March 1: $13,015.
2. Accounts payable, March 1: $49,000 (including $1,800 payable to insurance companies).
3. Salaries payable, March 1: zero.
4. Data from the payroll records for the month of March:

	Office Department	Sales Department	Warehouse Department	Total
Employees' net pay	$7,590	$14,688	$9,836	$32,114
Income tax withheld	1,500	3,500	1,200	6,200
F.I.C.A. tax withheld	650	1,300	780	2,730
Insurance premiums withheld	260	512	184	956
Employer's share of F.I.C.A. taxes	650	1,300	780	2,730
Employer's unemployment taxes	300	600	360	1,260

5.   Payments during March:
      Salary payments to employees, $32,114.
      Taxes paid: employees' income taxes, $6,000; F.I.C.A. taxes, $4,800;
      unemployment taxes, $2,215.
      Employee insurance premiums paid, $585.

a.   Calculate the "gross pay" of the employees in each department during
       the month and the total cost to the company attributable to each de-
       partment's payrolls for the month.
b.   Analyze the effects of the various payroll-related transactions during the
       month and prepare journal entries to reflect these analyses. Each de-
       partment has its own Salaries Expense account. Taxes levied on the
       employer are recorded in departmental Tax Expense accounts.

EXERCISES AND PROBLEMS

4. *Calculating net accounts receivable.*   A company expects that 1 percent of the receivables arising from credit sales eventually will prove uncollectible. The total amount owed the company by its credit customers was
$300,000 on August 1 and $400,000 on August 31, after all write-offs were
made. The allowance for uncollectible accounts on August 1 amounted to
$15,000.
     The company collected $347,000 from its credit customers during Au-
gust. A customer owing the company $3,000 filed a bankruptcy petition on
August 22, and the company's accountants wrote this account off as
uncollectible.

a.   How large should the allowance for uncollectible accounts have been on
       August 31?
b.   What amount of accounts receivable should have been reported on the
       August 31 balance sheet?

5. *Calculating losses from customer defaults.*   Dorothy Warren, controller
of Croton Enterprises, Inc., is concerned by recent increases in the amount
of customer defaults. They are now averaging more than 3 percent of gross
sales, far more than anyone else in the industry is experiencing.
     Lew Jones, the marketing vice president, admits the rate is high but
claims that this is an unavoidable result of the company's effort to expand
sales and net income. Furthermore, he says the amount of customer defaults
is unimportant; the important figures are the costs of merchandise or services provided to defaulting customers, less any amounts received from
these customers.
     Gross receivables outstanding amounted to $100,000 on January 1, 19x1;
a $15,000 allowance for uncollectible accounts had been provided for these.
The company had merchandise revenues of $550,000 during 19x1. It col-
lected $520,000 from its customers and wrote off $16,000 in specific accounts receivable as uncollectible. The correct balance in the allowance for
uncollectible accounts on December 31, 19x1, was $18,000. The cost of
goods sold for the year was $440,000; defaulting customers bought approxi-
mately the same mix of merchandise as other customers.

a. Calculate estimated customer defaults for 19x1.
b. Calculate estimated defaults arising from 19x1 sales, measured on a cost basis.
c. Which of these figures would you use in evaluating Mr. Jones's claim that the company had profited from the new, looser credit policy? Explain your reasons.
d. If the company's financial statements were to reflect Mr. Jones's suggestion, would the allowance for uncollectible accounts be calculated on a cost basis or on a selling price basis? Would estimated customer defaults still be calculated on a selling-price basis? State the reasons for your answers to these questions.

6. Recording payrolls. The Farnsworth Company has two sales representatives, Green and Harris. Green is on a salary of $10,000 a year and gets a 1.5 percent commission on the sales she brings in. Harris's annual salary is $9,000 plus a 2 percent commission. The costs of commissions and salaries are recorded in separate accounts. A single account, Tax Expense, is used to accumulate all tax expenses arising from salaries and commissions.

Green achieved sales of $200,000 last year, while Harris sold $150,000. Income taxes withheld amounted to 20 percent of total salaries and commissions, and the F.I.C.A. tax was 14 percent, half levied directly on the company and half to be deducted from employees' gross pay. In addition, the company had to pay unemployment taxes of 2 percent of the gross payroll. Farnsworth paid both employees the full amount of their net pay. It also paid the government the full amount required by the year's payrolls.

a. Calculate the year's gross pay for each sales representative.
b. Prepare journal entries to record (1) the accrual of the payrolls and (2) the payments of cash to employees and government agencies.

7. Recording payrolls. The Chadwick Company had the following liabilities on August 31:

Wages payable	$ 5,000
Taxes payable	48,000
Accounts payable	65,000

It had the following payroll-related transactions in September:

1. Gross pay earned by employees:

Warehouse	$40,000
Sales	10,000
Administration	12,000

2. Amounts withheld from gross pay:

Federal income taxes	9,000
F.I.C.A. taxes	4,650
Medical insurance premiums	1,750

3. Amounts paid:

To employees	45,000
To government agencies:	
For income taxes withheld	8,200
For F.I.C.A. taxes	9,000
For unemployment compensation insurance taxes ...	1,800
To medical insurance company	1,850

4. Unemployment compensation insurance tax: 2.5 percent of gross pay.

a. Calculate (1) the total cost of employees' services in each of the three departments for the month of September and (2) the amount of taxes payable as of September 30. (Taxes on Chadwick Company's income do not enter into this problem.)

b. Draw up an appropriate set of T-accounts, enter the September 1 balances in the liability accounts, prepare journal entries to record all payroll-related accruals and payments for the month, and post these entries to the T-accounts.

8. Purchases and sales discounts, returns, and allowances. On January 18 the Sanford Plumbers Supply Corporation purchased six laundry tubs on credit from the Stone Manufacturing Company at a gross price of $27 each. The terms were 2/10, n/30.

The tubs arrived on January 25, and three of them were immediately reshipped, in the original crates, to the Lowe Plumbing Company at a gross price of $36 each. The terms of sale were 1/10, n/30.

The following day, Lowe Plumbing notified Sanford that the tubs were defective. Sanford agreed to allow Lowe to deduct $6 a tub, or a total of $18, from the net amount payable to Sanford. Sanford inspected the three tubs that remained in its own inventory and found that they were undamaged. Sanford then contacted the Stone Manufacturing Company, which agreed to deduct $18 from the sum due from Sanford.

On February 4, Lowe paid Sanford $88.92 for the tubs. On February 20, Sanford paid Stone $144.

a. Calculate, for Sanford Plumbers Supply Corporation (1) gross sales, (2) net sales, and (3) the net cost of the goods sold.

b. Sanford uses a perpetual inventory system and records inventories, purchases, and sales at gross prices. To what extent would its net sales and cost of goods sold differ from the amounts you calculated in answer to (a)?

c. Using Sanford's system as described in (b), prepare journal entries to record the transactions described in this problem. At what total amount would the three tubs remaining in inventory be shown on Sanford's balance sheet at the end of January?

9. Purchase costs; managerial implications. The Bartoli Company buys some of its merchandise subject to discounts for prompt payment. Merchandise inventories on March 31 had cost $75,000 less cash discounts of $900, and accounts payable on that date amounted to $40,000 at gross prices, against which cash discounts of $600 were still applicable.

During April, the company bought merchandise on account at a gross price of $50,000, subject to a 2 percent discount for prompt payment. A portion of the month's purchases, with a gross price of $2,500, was returned to suppliers for credit.

During the month the company paid all of its April 1 accounts payable plus $12,000 of the April purchases (measured at gross prices). The company took all available cash discounts on the April purchases but lost $100 of the discounts available to it on the April 1 accounts payable because it failed to pay some of these accounts within the discount period: All discounts on the rest of the April purchases would be taken early in May.

The gross price of the merchandise inventory on hand on April 30 was $45,000. All of this inventory can be assumed to have consisted of goods purchased during April.

a. If you were the sales manager of the Bartoli Company and were interested in measuring the profitability of the month's sales, what figure representing the cost of goods sold would you use? Show your calculations and explain your reasoning.

b. At what amount should accounts payable be listed on the April 30 balance sheet?

c. How much was actually paid on account to suppliers during the month?

10. Revenues, receivables, and customer defaults.   Last year the Carillon Shovel Company sold 40,000 snow shovels on credit at a price of $5 each. Its customers owed Carillon $10,000 at the beginning of the year and $18,000 at the end of the year. In the middle of the year, one of its customers, the Fairweather Hardware Store, went bankrupt, owing Carillon $1,100. Carillon received $300 from Fairweather in final settlement of this account.

Carillon had a $1,000 allowance for uncollectibles at the beginning of last year. Its management expects 0.5 percent of its credit sales to prove uncollectible. Fairweather Hardware Store's bankruptcy was consistent with this expectation.

a. Prepare journal entries to record last year's transactions.

b. Identify the amounts from these transactions that appeared on Carillon's income statement for last year. Indicate whether each of these amounts is a positive or a negative determinant of net income.

11. Customer defaults.   Marcus Electric Company prepares a set of interim financial statements each month and an annual financial report once a year. Its fiscal year ends on December 31. On November 30, after all entries for the month had been made, the following balances were found in the accounts relating to credit sales and accounts receivable:

	Debit	Credit
Accounts receivable	500,000	
Allowance for uncollectible accounts		15,000
Estimated customer defaults	12,800	
Recovery of overdue accounts		300
Revenues from credit sales		2,560,000

Bookkeeping entries during the first 11 months of the year had been based on the assumption that customer defaults would average 0.5 percent of credit sales.

During December, credit sales totaled $250,000, specific accounts receivable in the amount of $1,700 were recognized as uncollectible, and $1,000 of accounts previously written off as uncollectible were collected. Collections of other accounts receivable during the month totaled $270,000. An examination of the accounts receivable outstanding at the end of the year indicated that $11,000 of these accounts would eventually prove uncollectible.

Recoveries of overdue accounts in this company are treated as miscellaneous income of the period in which recovery is made—no attempt being made to adjust the estimate of customer defaults to reflect these recoveries.

a. Explain briefly what each of the five November 30 account balances represented.
b. Calculate total customer defaults applicable to this year's revenues. Was the company's experience with customer defaults normal, high, or low? If high or low, by how much?
c. Present journal entries to record the December transactions.
d. Show the accounts receivable section of the December 31 balance sheet in good form and with the correct account balances.

12. Revenues and receivables: missing data. You have the following partial data on two companies' revenues in a recent year and their receivables at the beginning and end of that year. Neither company offers a cash discount to its customers. Supply the figures missing from this table.

	Company A	Company B
Allowance for uncollectible accounts:		
January 1	$ 4	$ 10
December 31	5	—
Collections from customers	—	545
Customer defaults applicable to the year's gross sales	—	6
Gross accounts receivable:		
January 1	50	—
December 31	—	90
Gross Sales	400	—
Net accounts receivable:		
January 1	—	70
December 31	35	79
Net sales	—	—
Sales allowances	10	17
Sales returns	20	14
Write-offs of specific uncollectibles	6	—

13. Gross price versus net revenue and net cost. The Foundation Retail Company issues monthly financial statements and uses perpetual inventory records. Some of the company's transactions for the month of February were as follows (the numbers at the left are the dates on which the transactions took place):

3   Purchase of goods on account from A&M Company for $50,000, terms 2/5, n/30.
7   Payrolls for the week ended February 7: gross pay, $2,000; income taxes withheld, $300; F.I.C.A. taxes withheld, 6.5 percent; remainder paid in cash.
8   Sale of goods to L. Ward on account for $1,000, terms 2/5, n/10. Foundation Retail always sells at a 25 percent markup on cost.
10   Sale of goods to G. Rankin for $5,000, terms 2/5, n/10. Markup is 25 percent on cost.

11 Payment of $3,000 to government agencies, covering income taxes withheld, F.I.C.A. taxes, and unemployment compensation insurance taxes on January payrolls.

12 Receipt of check for $1,000 from L. Ward in payment for goods purchased on the 8th of the month.

13 Receipt of check from G. Rankin for $4,458 in payment for goods purchased on February 10. He explains that he is returning goods from this shipment with a gross invoice price of $400. Some of these items were damaged in shipment and some were not the items he had ordered. He also says that he has paid a trucking company $50 to return the merchandise to Foundation Retail. He asks for a credit of $450 against the gross balance in his account.

14 Payrolls for the week ended February 14: same amounts as on February 7.

18 Payment of $50,000 is made to A&M Company for the purchase of February 3.

20 L. Ward writes that he forgot to deduct his discount from his payment of February 12. He asks Foundation Retail to credit his account.

21 Payrolls for the week ended February 21: same amounts as on February 7.

24 The goods sent by Rankin are received. (See February 13.) Upon inspection, it is found that goods with a gross sale price of $300 were spoiled through faulty packing by Foundation Retail and must be thrown away; the remainder are in good condition and are placed back on the stockroom shelves. Full credit is extended to Mr. Rankin.

28 Payrolls for the week ended February 28: same amounts as on February 7.

28 Accrual of employers' share of the month's payroll taxes: F.I.C.A. tax, matching employees' share; unemployment compensation, 3 percent of gross payrolls.

a. Assuming that the company records both purchases and sales at their gross prices, using one inventory account, one salaries expense account, one tax expense account, and separate accounts for sales discounts, sales allowances, and purchases discounts, prepare journal entries to record these transactions.

b. Using numbers from this problem to illustrate your answer, in what ways does the company's practice of recording purchases and sales at gross prices affect the amounts shown as inventories, receivables, and net income? What arguments can you advance to support the company's practice?

5

Preparing the Financial Statements

THE ACCOUNTANTS have four kinds of work to do at the end of the accounting period. First, they prepare a *trial balance*, or list of the balances in the general ledger accounts. Second, they make a number of *adjusting* entries, reflecting the results of transactions analyses that haven't been recorded as part of the clerical routine. Third, they prepare the financial statements for the period. Finally, they prepare and post a set of closing entries to make the accounts ready to accumulate the record of the next period's transactions.

The purpose of this chapter is to see what the accountants have to do at each of these four stages. It will also serve as a means of reviewing the main ideas of accrual accounting.

TRIAL BALANCE

Erskine Stores, Inc., is a corporation formed by Charles Erskine to own and operate a local chain of appliance stores. Its trial balance at December 31, 19x7, is shown in Exhibit 5–1.

The account balances shown on the trial balance were taken from the ledger after all entries made as part of the normal bookkeeping routine had been posted to the ledger. Notice that the trial balance shows both balance-sheet and income-statement accounts, balance-sheet items first. The only aspects of an account that have any relevance at this point are the amount of its balance and whether this is a debit or a credit balance.

EXHIBIT 5–1

ERSKINE STORES, INC.
Unadjusted Trial Balance
December 31, 19x7

Account	Debit	Credit
Cash	$ 64,000	
Accounts receivable	319,000	
Notes receivable	95,000	
Allowance for uncollectible accounts		$ 14,000
Merchandise inventory	180,000	
Prepaid insurance	6,000	
Furniture and equipment	144,000	
Accumulated depreciation		39,000
Accounts payable		112,000
Salaries and wages payable		—
Taxes payable		5,000
Advances from customers		12,000
Interest payable		—
Dividends payable		4,000
Notes payable		30,000
Liability for service warranty		1,900
Capital stock		385,000
Retained earnings		50,000
Sales revenue		1,830,000
Interest revenue		—
Customer defaults	9,100	
Cost of goods sold	945,000	
Salaries and wages expense	470,000	
Payroll tax expense	42,300	
Rent expense	70,000	
Office supplies expense	17,000	
Utilities expense	13,000	
Warranty expense	—	
Advertising expense	62,300	
Insurance expense	—	
Depreciation expense	—	
Inventory shrinkage expense	—	
Miscellaneous operating expense	25,000	
Interest expense	1,200	
Purchases discounts lost	1,000	
Loss on retirement of equipment	3,000	
Income tax expense	—	
Dividends declared	16,000	
Total	$2,482,900	$2,482,900

ADJUSTING ENTRIES

Financial statements drawn directly from the account balances at this stage would be incomplete. Certain kinds of information haven't yet been reflected in the accounts because they don't relate directly to events that call for routine clerical action. The entries reflecting this additional information are known as adjusting entries. The accountants for Erskine Stores had to make ten adjusting entries at the end of 19x7:

1. To correct a bookkeeping error.
2. To amortize prepaid insurance costs.
3. To amortize furniture and equipment costs.
4. To adjust the allowance for uncollectible accounts.
5. To accrue interest expense.
6. To accrue interest revenue.
7. To provide for future warranty costs.
8. To accrue payroll expenses.
9. To record inventory shrinkage.
10. To accrue income taxes.

Correcting Bookkeeping Errors

Clerical employees are no less likely to make mistakes than anyone else, and one of the auditor's jobs is to look for various kinds of bookkeeping errors. Common errors are incorrect transcription of dollar amounts, incorrect classifications leading to debits or credits to the wrong accounts, and failure to record transactions.

The auditors for Erskine Stores found only one error large enough to require correction at the end of 19x7. A $10,000 payment had been received in advance from a customer, covering merchandise that had not yet been delivered by the end of 19x7. By accepting the customer's money without doing anything in exchange for it, Erskine Stores accepted a liability, measured by the amount of money received. The entry that should have been made at that time was:

```
Cash ....................................   10,000
     Advances from Customers ...........               10,000
```

The Advances from Customers account is included in the liability section of the chart of accounts for just this purpose.

Unfortunately, when the payment was received, a new bookkeeper recorded it as a cash sale, in the following entry:

```
Cash ....................................   10,000
     Sales Revenue ......................               10,000
```

Obviously, the year-end balance in Sales Revenue was $10,000 too large, while the balance in Advances from Customers was $10,000 too small. To correct this error and to avoid overstating sales revenues and understating the firm's liabilities, the following adjusting entry was made:

(a)

```
Sales Revenue ..........................   10,000
     Advances from Customers ...........               10,000
```

The liability in this case is sometimes called a *deferred revenue,*
unearned revenue, or *deferred credit.* No matter what it is called,
however, it is a liability the company must meet, either by delivering
goods as promised or by returning the customer's money.

Amortizing Prepaid Insurance Costs

The balance in Erskine Stores' Prepaid Insurance account was
$6,000 at the end of 19x7. A review of the insurance-policy file re-
vealed that this amount could be traced back to five insurance policies that had been in force for all or part of 19x7. This information is
summarized in Exhibit 5-2.

EXHIBIT 5-2. Data for Insurance Expense Adjustment

(1)	(2)	(3)	(4)	(5)	(6)	(7)	(8)
Policy No.	Effective Date	Expiration Date	Un-adjusted Balance	Monthly Premium Cost	Months this Year	Premiums Expired (5) × (6)	Un-expired Premiums (4) − (7)
AB 406–721	1/1/x4	12/31/x7	$ 540	$ 45	12	$ 540	—
CD 492–881	4/1/x6	3/31/x7	60	20	3	60	—
XL 172–008	7/1/x5	12/31/x8	2,400	100	12	1,200	$1,200
CD 712–654	4/1/x7	3/31/x8	300	25	9	225	75
PL 202–903	1/1/x7	12/31/x9	2,700	75	12	900	1,800
Total			$6,000			$2,925	$3,075

The total at the bottom of column (4) is the amount shown on
the trial balance. Column (5) shows the monthly premium for each
of these policies, taken from information in the policies themselves.
Column (6) shows how many months each policy was in force between January 1 and December 31, 19x7. The cost of insurance coverage for the year [column (7)] was then calculated by multiplying
the monthly premium by the number of months. The total of these
amounts, $2,925, had to be transferred from the Prepaid Insurance
account to an expense account or accounts. The adjusting entry was:

(b)

Insurance Expense.....................	2,925	
Prepaid Insurance....................		2,925

This entry reduced the balance in the Prepaid Insurance account
to $3,075, the total shown at the bottom of column (8). This rep-
resented the unexpired premiums on the three policies still in force
on January 1, 19x8.

Amortizing Furniture and Equipment Costs

The trial balance showed furniture and equipment on hand at the end of 19x7 with a total original cost of $144,000, of which $39,000 had been amortized in previous years. The company's property records showed the location and annual depreciation rate on each asset. From these records, the accountants found that depreciation amounted to $6,000 in 19x7 on the furniture and equipment in the stores, and $3,000 on office furniture and equipment, a total of $9,000. They made the following entry:

(c)

Depreciation Expense	9,000	
Accumulated Depreciation		9,000

The debit served to recognize the decrease in owners' equity resulting from the effect of the passage of time on the company's furniture and equipment. The credit to Accumulated Depreciation measured an asset reduction, reflecting the reduction in the remaining usefulness of this group of assets.

Allowing for Uncollectible Receivables

Erskine Stores' bookkeepers made a routine entry each month to allow for expected customer defaults at a rate of 0.5 percent of sales. These entries were reflected in the balances of Customer Defaults and Allowance for Uncollectible Accounts, shown in the trial balance. These balances were:

Customer Defaults	Allowance for Uncollectible Accounts
Bal. 12/31 9,100	Bal. 12/31 14,000

Percentage estimates like these are subject to error and have to be checked periodically. Some companies even keep the percentage estimates out of the formal accounts altogether, preferring to record estimates of customer defaults only at the end of the year.

The technique used to check the percentage estimates once a year or to take their place entirely is known as *aging the accounts*. This technique is based on the premise that the older the claim, the less likely it is to be collected. The analysis is performed in five steps:

1. All amounts that seem likely to be uncollectible are identified, and entries are made to remove them from the ledger balances, crediting Accounts Receivable and debiting Allowance for Uncollectible Accounts.
2. All remaining customer account balances are classified by age—length of time since invoice date.

3. An estimated loss percentage is developed for each age group, partly from historical experience, partly from a qualitative examination of a sample of accounts in the group.
4. These loss percentages are multiplied by the amounts receivable in their respective age brackets.
5. The products of these calculations are added together, and an entry is made to bring the balance in the Allowance for Uncollectible Accounts to equal the total.

The accountants for Erskine Stores performed the first stage in this analysis and identified specific receivables with gross balances of $8,000 that seemed very likely to be worthless. These customers' accounts were removed from the active file, and the following entry was made:

(d)

Allowance for Uncollectible Accounts	8,000	
Accounts Receivable		8,000

As we saw in Chapter 4, this reduced the balances in the Accounts Receivable account and in the contra-asset account, leaving the book value of the receivables unchanged.

The accountant's next step was to age the remaining receivables. The aging analysis in this case showed the following:

(1) Number of Days since Invoice Date	(2) Amount Receivable	(3) Estimated Percentage Uncollectible	(4) Estimated Amount Uncollectible (2) × (3)
0–30 days	$150,000	0.2%	$ 300
31–60 days	80,000	1.0	800
61–90 days	50,000	3.6	1,800
91 days and older	31,000	30.0	9,300
Total	$311,000		$12,200

After entry (d) had been posted, the account balance was only $6,000. The table, however, shows that the balance in the allowance at the end of the year should have been $12,200. The following entry therefore was necessary to restore the account balance to its proper level:

(e)

Customer Defaults	6,200	
Allowance for Uncollectible Accounts		6,200

The Customer Defaults account, it will be remembered, is a sales-deduction account. The debit to this account recorded a reduction in the owners' equity. The credit to the Allowance for Uncollectible Accounts recorded a diminution in the company's assets. After entry (*e*) was made, therefore, the balance in the allowance account was $12,200, indicating that current receivables were actually worth $12,200 less than their face value as a result of expected collection difficulties.

Accruing Interest Expense

For many business concerns, an important source of funds, particularly to finance seasonal peaks of activity, is short-term borrowing from commercial banks. The instrument most commonly used for this purpose is called a *promissory note*, and it is a promise to pay a specified amount on a specified date, known as the *maturity date*. The amount borrowed is termed the *proceeds;* the amount paid for the use of the proceeds is called *interest;* and the amount to be repaid to the lender on the maturity date is known as the *maturity value*.

Erskine Stores' trial balance at the end of 19x7 listed notes payable amounting to $30,000. This amount was the proceeds of a bank loan the company had taken out on December 1, 19x7, giving in exchange a 90-day, 8 percent promissory note. The period between the borrowing and maturity dates, in this case 90 days, is the *life* or *term* of the loan. The 8 percent figure is the *interest rate*. Unless some other period is explicitly specified, interest rates are always stated as *annual* rates, regardless of the term of the loan.

It is accepted financial practice to compute interest on short-term loans on the basis of a 360-day year. Therefore, a 90-day note would require interest at 90/360, or one fourth of the annual rate. Erskine Stores, in other words, agreed to pay the bank $30,000 plus interest of $600 ($\frac{1}{4}$ × 8 percent × $30,000) on March 1, 19x8, exactly 90 days from the date of the loan.[1]

The next part of this transaction to be recorded in the normal bookkeeping routine would be the repayment of the loan, plus interest, on March 1, 19x8. No entry would be made until that date. The company used the bank's money for 30 days in 19x7, however, and the cost of using it for this period was a cost of doing business in 19x7:

---

[1] The maturity date is computed on the basis of actual elapsed days, not on the basis of the 360-day year. In computing the maturity date, the day the loan is made is not counted. Thus a loan made on November 15 gives rise to interest for 15 days during November, starting with November 16. Debts maturing on a day on which the banks are closed are payable on the next banking day. In this case, the term of the loan covered 30 days in December, 31 days in January, 28 days in February, and one day in March, for a maturity date of March 1.

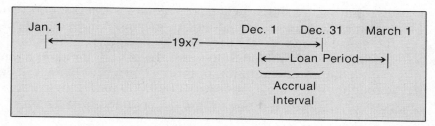

Recognizing the cost of the loan from December 1 through December 31 is an essential feature of the system of accrual accounting we have been describing in these first five chapters. As we saw earlier, accrual accounting differs from cash-basis accounting in that the accounting statements reflect transfers of resources other than cash. In this case the company has received services, the use of the lender's money, without any current outlay of cash. The entry recognizing this is known, appropriately enough, as an *accrual*. An accrual is an entry made to recognize a revenue or expense, together with its related asset or liability, when the accounting period ends before the asset or liability is recorded as part of the ordinary recordkeeping routine.

In this case, 30/90 of the $600 total interest cost, or $200, was a 19x7 expense. The adjusting entry was:

(f)

Interest Expense	200	
Interest Payable		200

The debit to the expense account recorded the reduction in the owners' equity; the credit to Interest Payable recorded the liability for future payment of this amount.

Accruing Interest Revenue

Business firms occasionally accept promissory notes from their customers if payment is to be deferred beyond the normal credit period. For example, Erskine Stores supplied all the major appliances for a new block of apartments completed in 19x7. The price agreed upon was $110,000, but when the end of the normal credit period arrived on November 16, 19x7, the contractor was unable to pay the full amount in cash. Instead, the contractor offered to pay $15,000 in cash and give a 180-day promissory note with a maturity value of $100,000, including interest, to cover the $95,000 balance of the invoice price. The Erskine management agreed, and the note was signed.

Taking a note for a larger amount ($100,000) than the amount exchanged for it ($95,000) is known as *discounting* the note. In discounting a note, the lender calculates the amount due at the maturity date and then deducts interest on this amount to determine the sum to be made available to the borrower.

In this case, Erskine Stores and the contractor agreed that $5,000 was an appropriate amount of interest on $95,000 for 180 days. This is roughly the same as interest of $10,000 for a full year, or about 10 percent.[2] The entry to record this exchange of assets was[3]:

Notes Receivable.........................	95,000	
Accounts Receivable		95,000

Erskine Stores, Inc., now had a note receivable instead of an account receivable. This is the amount shown for notes receivable in the trial balance at the end of the year.

Erskine earned interest on this note for 45 days in 19x7 (14 days in November and 31 days in December). This was 45/180 = one fourth of the full period before the note was to mature. Interest for the 45 days therefore was one fourth of the interest for 180 days:

$$\text{Interest revenue} = \tfrac{1}{4} \times \$5,000 = \$1,250.$$

The adjusting entry to accrue this interest was as follows:

(g)

Notes Receivable.........................	1,250	
Interest Revenue		1,250

The debit in this case was made to Notes Receivable to emphasize the fact that the amount lent to the contractor now included both the invoice price of the merchandise covered by the note ($95,000) and the interest due for the use of Erskine's money for 45 days ($1,250). If Erskine had had an Interest Receivable account in its chart of accounts, we could just as well have debited that one instead.

Interest Revenue is an owners' equity account, of course. Interest revenue is more commonly referred to as "interest income," but, for the sake of clarity, we prefer to reserve the word *income* for measures of differences between revenues and expenses for the firm as a whole.

---

[2] In discounting transactions, the interest rate is applied to the maturity value rather than to the amount actually borrowed. Since the contractor paid $5,000 for the use of $95,000 for six months, the *effective* rate of interest was approximately 2 × $5,000/$95,000, or slightly more than 10 percent a year.

[3] An equivalent alternative is to record the note at its face value, with an accompanying entry to a contra-asset account:

Notes Receivable	100,000	
Unearned Interest on Notes Receivable		5,000
Accounts Receivable		95,000

Providing for Product Warranties

Some costs arising from the sale of merchandise may not be incurred until after the merchandise is delivered to customers. A prime example of this kind of cost is the cost of doing work under the terms of a product warranty. This cost is part of the cost of securing revenues. Therefore, it should be recognized as an expense in the period in which revenues are recorded. Exhibit 5–3 shows how ex-

EXHIBIT 5–3. Classifying Costs as Expenses: Revenues Recognized at Delivery

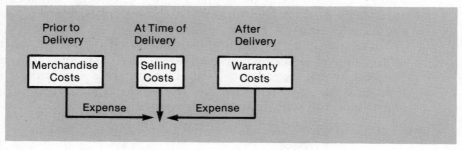

pense in the delivery period includes these costs as well as costs incurred both currently and in previous periods.

Erskine Stores, for example, stands ready to repair or replace defective appliances it has sold to its customers, even after the manufacturers' warranty periods have expired. The costs of providing these services enter the accounting system in two stages:

1. When deliveries are made to customers, Erskine Stores recognizes the future costs of service on these products as current expenses. It also recognizes this amount as a liability, to be eliminated by providing necessary service to its customers.
2. When warranty service is actually provided, the costs reduce the liability.

On January 1, 19x7, the balance in the Liability for Service Warranty account was $17,200. During the year, the costs of providing warranty services amounted to $15,300. The entries to record these costs had the following effects:

Liability for Service Warranty   15,300
    Cash   15,300

This brought the balance in the liability account down to $1,900, the amount shown in the trial balance:

Liability for Service Warranty

Expenditures during 19x7	15,300	Bal. 1/1	17,200
		Bal. 12/31	1,900

No entry was made in 19x7, however, to reflect the future warranty costs on merchandise sold in 19x7. The best estimates of these costs can be based on a technique similar to the account-aging technique we described earlier for accounts receivable. Management can draw up a set of repair experience curves by looking at the past history of each kind of appliance. By checking the ages of the appliances under warranty against these curves, management can estimate its future warranty costs.

Erskine Stores did this, and estimated that its warranties in force at the end of 19x7 would lead to future costs of approximately $18,400. In other words, this was the company's warranty liability at that time. To get this figure into the financial statements, the company made the following adjusting entry:

(h)

Warranty Expense	16,500	
Liability for Service Warranty		16,500

This brought the liability balance up from $1,900 to $18,400, and identified $16,500 as the warranty expense applicable to the revenues for 19x7.

This is a different kind of liability from any we have seen up to now. For one thing, this liability is discharged by performing services, not by paying cash to the creditor. Advances from customers was the closest to this among the liabilities we studied earlier.

Second, the amount of the liability is uncertain. If the appliances turn out to be less reliable than the company has estimated, the company will have to pay more than it has recorded as a liability. This additional amount will have to be reported as an expense of the period in which the work is done. If the amount of repair work is less than the amount predicted, however, then income in the period of delivery will have been understated. This is usually corrected by reducing the expense estimate for the period in which the forecasting error is discovered.

Accruing Wages and Salaries

Another kind of accrual, the accrual of payrolls, also arises because completion of the regular bookkeeping cycle doesn't always take place on the final day of the accounting period. Salaries and wages are often paid weekly, while the accounting period is a year or a month.

For example, Erskine Stores' last weekly payroll period of 19x7 ended on December 28. Monday and Tuesday, December 30 and 31, were full working days, which means that some wages were *earned by employees in 19x7 but were not recorded* in the accounts as part of the normal bookkeeping routine until the next year. These amounts were paid as part of the first weekly wage payroll of 19x8, but part of that payroll was really a cost applicable to 19x7.

Employees in the company's stores and offices earned $5,000 and $1,000, respectively, on the two working days between the end of the last weekly payroll period and the end of the year. The entry to accrue these costs was:

(i)

Salaries and Wages Expense..............	6,000	
Salaries and Wages Payable		6,000

The credit to Salaries and Wages Payable recognized the company's liability on December 31, 19x7, to pay its employees in 19x8 for work done in 19x7.

Notice that the payroll liability was not classified into the amounts that would eventually be paid to the employees and the amounts that would be paid on their behalf to others. It was the *amount* of the liability rather than its distribution that was significant at this point.

Liability for wages also creates a liability for the employer's share of payroll taxes. Payroll taxes applicable to the wages accrued for the last two working days of 19x7 were at a combined rate of 9 percent. The accrual was calculated by multiplying this rate by the figures in entry (i) above:

(j)

Payroll Tax Expense......................	540	
Taxes Payable		540

Inventory Shrinkage

Erskine Stores used the perpetual inventory method to record transfers from the inventory account to Cost of Goods Sold, as described in Chapter 3. This produced the $180,000 year-end balance shown on the merchandise inventory line in the trial balance.

Inventory balances in perpetual inventory systems should be verified periodically by a physical count of the items on hand. Any discrepancy between the book value of the inventory and the cost of the actual quantity on hand on the inventory date has to be taken to the income statement, either as a separate item or as an adjustment to the cost of goods sold figure.

To reduce the clerical load and minimize interference with every-day operations, most companies count only part of their inventory at any one time. Erskine's inventories consisted mainly of a few large items, however, making it feasible to count the entire inventory at one time. The tally on December 31, 19x7, located merchandise with a total cost of only $173,400. The $6,600 difference between this and the $180,000 book value was attributable to theft, carelessness, errors in cost bookkeeping, or even errors in the annual count. Lacking any way of separating the amounts due to these various causes, Erskine's accountants charged off the entire amount by means of the following entry:

(k)

Inventory Shrinkage Expense	6,600	
Merchandise Inventory		6,600

The credit to Merchandise Inventory recognized the reduction in this asset revealed by the annual count; the debit to Inventory Shrinkage Expense recorded the accompanying reduction in owners' equity. If the count had exceeded the book value of the merchandise on hand, the account would have been credited. In published statements, the balance in this account is ordinarily reported as part of the cost of goods sold.

If Erskine Stores had been using a periodic inventory system, the amount shown as inventory on the trial balance would have been either the January 1, 19x7, balance (if the cost of all purchases had been accumulated in a separate Purchases account) or the opening balance plus the cost of the purchases for the year. The Cost of Goods Sold account would have had a zero balance until the end of the year. The adjusting entry then would have closed out the Purchases account, if any, brought the Merchandise Inventory account to its correct year-end balance, and transferred the remaining merchandise costs to the Cost of Goods Sold account.

Accruing Income Taxes

One more accrual remained to be made, the accrual of the income tax on the year's income. This entry had to be made last, because many of the earlier accruals affected the amount of taxable income.

To estimate the tax, the accountants computed revised balances in all of the income statement accounts, and from these, the before-tax earnings for the year. The amounts shown in the company's tax return differed to some extent from those in the accounts, but the overall difference in this case was not great. The estimated tax for the year amounted to $48,000. These figures were summarized in the following entry:

(l)

Income Tax Expense   48,000
    Taxes Payable   48,000

The first figure in this entry recorded the impact of income taxes on the owners' equity; the credit to Taxes Payable recorded the liability.

STATEMENT PREPARATION AND PRESENTATION

Once the adjusting entries have been figured out, the accountants can prepare the financial statements. The basic data for the statements themselves are the balances in the accounts after all adjusting entries have been made. We could summarize these in an *adjusted trial balance,* but the T-accounts in Exhibit 5–4 are more useful for our purposes because they also summarize the adjusting entries we have just finished describing.

The Income Statement

The income statements of U.S. business firms consist of three parts: ordinary income from continuing operations, income from discontinued operations, and income from extraordinary events. Most companies have only the first of these in most years.

Erskine Stores, for example, prepared the income statement shown in Exhibit 5–5 to cover its operations for the year. This is known as a single-step statement in that all revenue items are grouped together at the top and net income is determined by subtracting the expenses from this total in one single step.

Some companies use a different format, preferring to segment the ordinary income portion of their income statements. A simple segmented structure would show the following (including hypothetical figures to illustrate the concept):

Sales revenue	$100
Less: Cost of goods sold	60
Gross margin	$ 40
Less: Operating expenses	28
Income before income taxes	$ 12
Less: provision for income taxes	5
Net Income	$ 7

The purpose of segmentation is to highlight key relationships, such as the relationship between gross margin and sales revenues. We prefer the single-step statement because it is simpler to read. It

EXHIBIT 5–4

ERSKINE STORE, INC.
Ledger Accounts Including Adjusting Entries
December 31, 19x7

Cash

Bal. 64,000	

Accounts Receivable

Bal. 319,000	(d) 8,000
Bal. 311,000	

Allowance for Uncollectible Accounts

(d) 8,000	Bal. 14,000
	(c) 6,200
	Bal. 12,200

Notes Receivable

Bal. 95,000	
(g) 1,250	
Bal. 96,250	

Merchandise Inventory

Bal. 180,000	(k) 6,600
Bal. 173,400	

Prepaid Insurance

Bal. 6,000	(b) 2,925
Bal. 3,075	

Furniture and Equipment

Bal. 144,000	

Accumulated Depreciation

	Bal. 39,000
	(b) 9,000
	Bal. 48,000

Notes Payable

	Bal. 30,000

Interest Payable

	(f) 200

Accounts Payable

	Bal. 112,000

Salaries and Wages Payable

	(h) 6,000

Taxes Payable

	Bal. 5,000
	(j) 540
	(l) 48,000
	Bal. 53,540

Advances from Customers

	Bal. 12,000
	(k) 10,000
	Bal. 22,000

Dividends Payable

	Bal. 4,000

Liability for Service Warranty

	Bal. 1,900
	(h) 16,500
	Bal. 18,400

Capital Stock

	Bal. 385,000

Retained Earnings

	Bal. 50,000

Dividends Declared

Bal. 16,000	

Sales Revenue

(a)	10,000	Bal. 1,830,000
		Bal. 1,820,000

Customer Defaults

Bal.	9,100	
(c)	6,200	
Bal. 15,300		

Interest Revenue

		(g) 1,250

Cost of Goods Sold

Bal. 945,000	

Inventory Shrinkage Expense

(k) 6,600	

Salaries and Wages Expense

Bal. 470,000	
(i) 6,000	
Bal. 476,000	

Payroll Tax Expense

Bal. 42,300	
(j) 540	
Bal. 42,840	

Rent Expense

Bal. 70,000	

Office Supplies Expense

Bal. 17,000	

Utilities Expense

Bal. 13,000	

Warranty Expense

(h) 16,500	

Advertising Expense

Bal. 62,300	

Insurance Expense

(b) 2,925	

Depreciation Expense

(c) 9,000	

Miscellaneous Operating Expense

Bal. 25,000	

Purchases Discount Lost

Bal. 1,000	

Interest Expense

Bal. 1,200	
(f) 200	
Bal. 1,400	

Income Tax Expense

(l) 48,000	

Loss on Retirement of Equipment

Bal. 3,000	

EXHIBIT 5–5

ERSKINE STORES, INC.
Income Statement
For the Year Ended December 31, 19x7

Gross revenue from sales		$1,820,000
Less: Customer defaults		15,300
Net revenue from sales		$1,804,700
Interest revenues		1,250
Total Revenues		$1,805,950
Expenses:		
Cost of merchandise sold	$945,000	
Salaries and wages expense	476,000	
Payroll tax expense	42,840	
Rent expense	70,000	
Office supplies expense	17,000	
Utilities expense	13,000	
Warranty expense	16,500	
Advertising expense	62,300	
Insurance expense	2,925	
Depreciation expense	9,000	
Inventory shrinkage expense	6,600	
Miscellaneous operating expense	25,000	
Interest expense	1,400	
Purchases discounts lost	1,000	
Loss on retirement of equipment	3,000	
Income tax expense	48,000	
Total Expense		1,739,565
Net Income		$ 66,385

leaves it to the readers to select the relationships they wish to emphasize and study.

Income from Discontinued Operations and Extraordinary Events

The income statement of a U.S. business firm may also include gains or losses from two sources other than ordinary, continuing business operations:

1. Major business operations which have been discontinued during the year.
2. Events which are clearly unusual and unexpected; gains and losses from these events are referred to as *extraordinary items*.

This means that the income statement of a company with both discontinued operations and extraordinary items will show the following segmentation at the bottom of the statement (with hypothetical numbers inserted for illustrative purposes):

Income from continuing operations		$ 7
Discontinued operations:		
Income (loss) from operations of discontinued Division X		
(less applicable income taxes of $3)	$(5)	
Gain on disposal of Division X, including provision of		
$1 for operating losses during phase-out period (less		
applicable income taxes of $2)	2	(3)
Income before extraordinary items		$ 4
Extraordinary item: earthquake damage (less applicable		
income taxes of $1)		(1)
Net Income		$3

To qualify for recognition as an extraordinary item, a gain or loss must be of a type that occurs infrequently and is unusual in the circumstances in which the company operates. Thus losses due to strikes would not be classified as extraordinary; they may be infrequent, but they are not really unusual. Gains and losses on the sale of plant and equipment are specifically classified as ordinary income, and only three items are specifically accepted as extraordinary—major casualties (such as earthquakes), expropriations, or prohibitions under newly enacted laws or regulations.[4]

Statement of Changes in Retained Earnings

Changes in retained earnings are summarized each year in the retained earnings statement, illustrated in Exhibit 5–6. As this

EXHIBIT 5–6

ERSKINE STORES, INC.
Statement of Changes in Retained Earnings
For the Year Ended December 31, 19x7

Retained earnings, beginning of year	$ 50,000
Add: Net income	66,385
	$116,385
Less: Cash dividends declared	16,000
Retained earnings, end of year	$100,385

shows, the only changes in Erskine Stores' retained earnings in 19x7 were the net income for the year and the dividends declared during the year. This may seem strange at first glance. As we have already seen, many of the figures on the income statement represent estimates of amounts the company doesn't know with certainty. The

---

[4] AICPA, "Accounting Principles Board Opinion 30," in *Professional Standards—Accounting, Current Text* (New York: Commerce Clearing House, Inc., 1978), sec. 2012.23.

amount of income tax is a good example. When the actual amounts are determined, the financial statements for the period have already been issued, and since the net income of that period has been closed into retained earnings, it may seem logical to add or subtract any differences between the actual and estimated amounts to or from retained earnings.

The accountants don't do this, preferring to pass these corrections through the income statement of the period in which they are identified. By doing this, they hope to make the series of net income figures a more complete history of the company's income. They fear that charges or credits to retained earnings may be overlooked; putting them on the income statement, in a separate section at the bottom of the statement, makes them much more visible. Accountants

EXHIBIT 5–7

ERSKINE STORES, INC.
Statement of Financial Position
December 31, 19x7

Assets

Current Assets:		
Cash		$ 64,000
Notes receivable		96,250
Accounts receivable	$311,000	
Less: Allowance for uncollectible accounts	(12,200)	298,800
Merchandise inventory		173,400
Prepaid insurance		3,075
Total Current Assets		$635,525
Furniture and equipment	$144,000	
Less: Accumulated depreciation	48,000	96,000
Total Assets		$731,525

Liabilities and Shareowners' Equity

Current Liabilities:		
Notes and interest payable		$ 30,200
Accounts payable		112,000
Salaries and wages payable		6,000
Taxes payable		53,540
Dividends payable		4,000
Advances from customers		22,000
Liability for service warranty		18,400
Total Current Liabilities		$246,140
Shareowners' Equity:		
Capital stock	$385,000	
Retained earnings	100,385	
Total Shareowners' Equity		485,385
Total Liabilities and Shareowners' Equity		$731,525

do adjust the retained earnings figure directly in some situations, but these arise too infrequently to detain us here.

Statement of Financial Position

The third financial statement is the statement of financial position, or balance sheet. Erskine Stores' year-end balance sheet is shown in Exhibit 5–7. The asset and liability balances in this statement were copied from the T-accounts in Exhibit 5–4. They were divided between current and noncurrent items, as defined in Chapter 1. In this case, the company had no noncurrent liabilities.

The retained earnings figure on this balance sheet differs from the balance in the Retained Earnings account in the trial balance. The latter figure, it will be remembered, was the balance in this account at the *beginning* of the year. The year-end balance was obtained by adding the net income for the year and subtracting the dividends—in other words, the figures summarized in the statement of changes in retained earnings (Exhibit 5–6).

Cash-Flow Statement and Funds Statement

Two other statements can be prepared from the account balances in the adjusted trial balance, the statement of cash flows, and the statement of changes in financial position, or funds statement. The techniques used to prepare these statements are complicated enough to require more explanation than we have space for here. For this reason, we'll postpone any further discussion of these statements to Chapter 16.

CLOSING ENTRIES

Once the adjusting entries have been posted to the ledger and the statements have been prepared, the only remaining step is to close the various temporary owners' equity accounts and make sure the balance-sheet accounts have the correct beginning-of-year balances. (The new year is well under way before this is done, but routine bookkeeping can proceed before the closing entries are made.) When these bookkeeping tasks have been finished, the so-called *accounting cycle* can be said to be completed. The accounting cycle is summarized in Exhibit 5–8.

Erskine Stores made two closing entries at the end of 19x7, one to transfer the balances in revenue and expense accounts to retained

EXHIBIT 5–8.   The Accounting Cycle

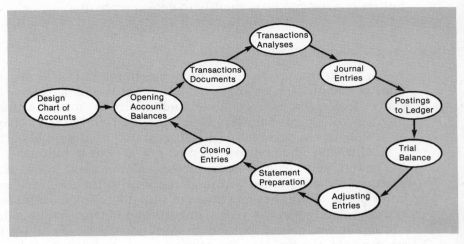

earnings, the other to close the Dividends Declared account. The first of these was as follows:

(m)

Sales Revenue	1,820,000	
Interest Revenue	1,250	
Customer Defaults		15,300
Cost of Goods Sold		945,000
Salaries and Wages Expense		476,000
Payroll Tax Expense		42,840
Rent Expense		70,000
Office Supplies Expense		17,000
Utilities Expense		13,000
Warranty Expense		16,500
Advertising Expense		62,300
Inventory Shrinkage Expense		6,600
Insurance Expense		2,925
Depreciation Expense		9,000
Miscellaneous Operating Expense		25,000
Interest Expense		1,400
Purchases Discounts Lost		1,000
Loss on Retirement of Equipment		3,000
Income Tax Expense		48,000
Retained Earnings		66,385

Because the Sales Revenues and Interest Revenue accounts had credit balances prior to closing, the debit entries had the effect of reducing the balances in these accounts to zero. Similarly, the credits to the contra-revenue and expense accounts restored the balances in those accounts to zero. The final credit entry, to Retained Earnings, was the net income for the year.

Finally, the balance in Dividends Declared was closed into Retained Earnings:

(n)

Retained Earnings	16,000	
Dividends Declared		16,000

The debit to Retained Earnings recognized that the distribution of dividends reduced the owners' equity permanently. The credit to Dividends Declared restored this account to a zero balance so that it could start 19x8 with a clean slate, ready to accumulate the 19x8 dividend information.

Once the closing entries were posted, the accountant could prepare a *post-closing trial balance*. If the closing entries have been recorded properly, the only accounts with nonzero balances will be the permanent balance sheet accounts, as in Exhibit 5–9. All of the temporary accounts will have zero balances.

EXHIBIT 5–9

ERSKINE STORES, INC.
Post-Closing Trial Balance
December 31, 19x7

	Debits	Credits
Cash	$ 64,000	
Accounts receivable	311,000	
Notes receivable	96,250	
Allowance for uncollectible accounts		$ 12,200
Merchandise inventory	173,400	
Prepaid insurance	3,075	
Furniture and equipment	144,000	
Accumulated depreciation		48,000
Accounts payable		112,000
Salaries and wages payable		6,000
Taxes payable		53,540
Advances from customers		22,000
Dividends payable		4,000
Notes payable		30,000
Interest payable		200
Liability for service warranty		18,400
Capital stock		385,000
Retained earnings		100,385
Total	$791,725	$791,725

SUMMARY

Most bookkeeping is designed not to facilitate the preparation of financial statements but to prepare such action documents as payrolls, customer invoices, and materials requisitions. Data for information purposes is derived as a by-product of these important but routine activities.

In this situation it is probably not surprising that the bookkeeping routine fails to take account of all of the data that have a bearing on accrual-basis financial statements. These data must be reflected in end-of-period adjusting entries, initiated by the accountant for the sole purpose of deriving financial statements. This chapter has illustrated a number of the more common types of adjusting entries.

Once the adjusting entries have been made, the accountants can translate the adjusted account balances into income statements, balance sheets, and statements of changes in retained earnings. After they have finished preparing these statements, the accountants can then close the temporary owners' equity accounts, setting the stage for the next accounting cycle.

KEY TERMS

Accounting cycle	Interest
Accrual	Post-closing trial balance
Adjusted trial balance	Prior-period adjustment
Adjusting entry	Promissory note
Aging the accounts	Trial balance
Deferred revenue	Warranty expense
Discounting notes	Worksheet
Extraordinary item	

APPENDIX: THE COLUMNAR WORKSHEET

Accountants often use *worksheets* to bring the trial balance and adjusting entries together in a convenient format. A six-column worksheet for Erskine Stores, Inc., is shown in Exhibit 5–10. The first two columns contain the unadjusted trial balance, the next two have the adjusting entries, and the third two columns show the adjusted account balances.

This is less formidable than it looks. Look at the fourth line, for example. The $14,000 in the second column shows that the Allowance for Uncollectible Accounts account had a $14,000 credit bal-

EXHIBIT 5–10

ERSKINE STORES, INC.
Columnar Worksheet
For the Year Ended December 31, 19x7

	Trial Balance Dr.	Cr.	Adjustments Dr.	Cr.	Adjusted Account Balances Dr.	Cr.
Cash	64000				64000	
Accounts receivable	319000			(l) 8000	311000	
Notes receivable	95000		(g) 1250		96250	
Allowance for uncollectible accounts		14000	(d) 8000	(e) 6200		12200
Merchandise inventory	180000			(k) 6600	173400	
Prepaid insurance	6000			(b) 2925	3075	
Furniture and equipment	144000				144000	
Accumulated depreciation		39000		(c) 9000		48000
Accounts payable		112000				112000
Salaries and wages payable		—		(i) 6000		6000
Taxes payable		5000		(j) 540		53540
				(l) 48000		
Advances from customers		12000		(a) 10000		22000
Interest payable		—		(f) 200		200
Dividends payable		4000				4000
Notes payable		30000				30000
Liability for service warranty		1900		(h) 16500		18400
Capital stock		385000				385000
Retained earnings		50000				50000
Sales revenue		1830000	(a) 10000			1820000
Interest revenue		—		(g) 1250		1250
Customer defaults	9100		(e) 6200		15300	
Cost of goods sold	945000				945000	
Salaries and wages expense	470000		(i) 6000		476000	
Payroll tax expense	42300		(j) 540		42840	
Rent expense	70000				70000	
Office supplies expense	17000				17000	
Utilities expense	13000				13000	
Warranty expense	—		(h) 16500		16500	
Advertising expense	62300				62300	
Inventory shrinkage expense	—		(k) 6600		6600	
Insurance expense	—		(b) 2925		2925	
Depreciation expense	—		(c) 9000		9000	
Miscellaneous operating expense	25000				25000	
Interest expense	1200		(f) 200		1400	
Purchases discounts lost	1000				1000	
Loss on retirement of equipment	3000				3000	
Income tax expense	—		(l) 48000		48000	
Dividends declared	16000				16000	
	2482900	2482900	115215	115215	2562590	2562590

ance after all routine bookkeeping work was done. The two adjustments to this account are shown in the next two columns (one for the debit adjustment, the other for the credit adjustment). The $12,200 in the sixth column is the adjusted balance in this account, the amount that will appear on the year-end balance sheet.

The worksheet can be expanded to eight columns by replacing the Adjusted Account Balances columns with two sets of columns, one for balance-sheet items and one for income-statement items and changes in retained earnings. Changes in retained earnings can be identified in separate columns of their own if they are numerous, bringing the total number of columns up to ten. In most cases, however, the six- or eight-column format will be adequate.

INDEPENDENT STUDY PROBLEMS (Solutions in Appendix B)

1. *Interest accrual.* On September 15, Calhoun Company borrowed $6,000 from the bank, promising to pay the bank $6,000 plus accrued interest at 8 percent 60 days from the date of the note. On November 14 the company paid the accrued interest and renewed the note for an additional 30 days. At the second maturity, on December 14, Calhoun paid $4,000 in cash and gave a new 30-day, 8 percent note for the remaining amount due. This last note was paid in full when due.

a. Calculate Calhoun's interest expense for the year that ended on December 31.
b. Prepare a journal entry to record the December 31 accrual.
c. Assuming that no additional entry was made between the accrual entry and the repayment date in January, prepare a journal entry to record the January payment.

2. *Warranty accrual.* For many years Philox Corporation has given each of its customers a two-year warranty on all their purchases of Philox products. Management estimated that it would cost $55,000 to carry out its future obligations under the warranties in force on December 31, 19x0, and this amount was reflected in the company's ledger.

Although warranty costs fluctuate slightly, past experience has shown that they will average very close to 3 percent of gross sales revenues.

The company had gross revenues of $1 million in 19x1 and paid $38,000 for warranty work. As far as management could judge at the time, warranty experience was normal in 19x1.

a. Calculate the amount of warranty expense to be shown on the company's income statement for 19x1.
b. Using whatever accounts are appropriate, prepare journal entries to record warranty expenses and other warranty-related transactions in 19x1.

3. *Adjusting entries; financial statements.* The December 31, 19x3, trial balance of the Guyton Company is as follows:

THE GUYTON COMPANY
Trial Balance
As of December 31, 19x3

	Debit	Credit
Cash	$ 28,800	
Notes receivable	17,700	
Accounts receivable	91,600	
Allowance for uncollectible accounts		$ 1,500
Inventory of merchandise, January 1, 19x3	89,000	
Prepaid insurance	1,900	
Other prepayments	1,340	
Land	16,000	
Building and equipment	45,800	
Allowance for depreciation		8,100
Accounts payable		18,800
Mortgage payable		45,000
Capital stock		150,000
Retained earnings		53,720
Sales revenues		412,000
Sales discounts, returns, and allowances	12,000	
Customer defaults	2,100	
Interest income		480
Purchases	344,500	
Advertising expense	1,200	
Salaries and wages expense	16,400	
Miscellaneous selling expense	5,800	
Property tax expense	3,300	
Insurance expense	525	
Miscellaneous general expenses	8,435	
Interest expense	3,200	
Total	$689,600	$689,600

The following information had not yet been recorded in the accounts when the trial-balance was taken:

1. A customer's account amounting to $165 was 18 months overdue, with little chance it would ever be collected; management decided to write it off.
2. Aging of the accounts receivable remaining on the books after the write-off in (1) indicated that receivables amounting to $89,315, measured at gross invoice prices, probably were collectible.
3. The cost of the merchandise in the inventory on December 31, 19x3, was $86,440.
4. Merchandise costing $975 was received on December 31, 19x3, but was still in the receiving room and therefore wasn't included in the inventory count [item (3)]. The invoice covering this shipment wasn't reflected in the trial balance.
5. $1,725 of the insurance premiums paid before December 31, 19x3, were for insurance coverage in 19x4.
6. Depreciation for the year was $1,240.
7. Unrecorded interest accruing on the mortgage payable since the last interest payment amounted to $400.
8. Unrecorded wages earned by employees between the end of the last payroll period of 19x3 and the end of the year amounted to $240.

9. Cash discounts still available to customers on December 31, 19x3, on credit sales made to them in 19x3 amounted to $890. (Use an Allowance for Sales Discounts account.)
10. The income tax rate was 40 percent in 19x3.

a. Set up T-accounts or a columnar worksheet, enter the figures from the trial balance, and make the necessary adjusting entries.
b. Prepare a balance sheet as of December 31, 19x3, and an income statement for the year ended December 31, 19x3.
c. Prepare a journal entry or entries to close the accounts for 19x3 and prepare the ledger for 19x4. You should assume that the adjusting entries have been posted.

EXERCISES AND PROBLEMS

4. *Interest accrual; discounted note.* A company borrowed money from a bank on November 16, 19x1. It gave the bank a 60-day promissory note, promising to pay $10,000 to the bank 60 days after the date of the note. The bank discounted the note at an interest rate of 9 percent a year, giving the company $9,850 in exchange for the note.

a. Calculate interest expense for 19x1.
b. Prepare entries to record (1) the initial borrowing, (2) the year-end adjustment, and (3) the payment of the amount due on January 15, 19x2.

5. *Interest accrual.* The Peterson Company borrowed $20,000 from a bank on January 21, giving in exchange a 90-day, 9 percent note.

a. Prepare an entry to record the borrowing.
b. Prepare whatever entry this transaction would make necessary on January 31 if the Peterson Company wished to prepare a set of accrual-basis financial statements as of the close of business on that date.
c. What entry would be necessary on January 31 if the Peterson Company prepared financial statements quarterly instead of monthly, the first quarter of the year ending on March 31? What entry would be made on February 28? On March 31?

6. *Record-keeping errors.* The Crown Company uses the periodic inventory method. The annual inventory count was made at the end of 19x1 and was reflected in the ledger at that time. Subsequently, the following record-keeping errors were discovered:

1. A purchase of merchandise for $4,200 was incorrectly debited to Furniture and Fixtures.
2. Cash of $1,300 received from a customer on account was incorrectly credited to Sales.
3. A $400 payment to a vendor on account was incorrectly debited to Merchandise Inventories.
4. A sales invoice for $400 was not recorded; payment was not received from the customer before the end of the year, but Crown's management anticipated no difficulty in collecting it early in 19x2.

5. A $100 telephone bill was incorrectly charged to Entertainment Expense instead of to Telephone Expense.

a. For each of these, construct the adjusting entry that would have been made if the error had been discovered before the financial statements were prepared and before the year-end closing entries were made.

b. How would your answer to (a) differ if these errors had been discovered after the closing entries had been made and the financial statements for the year had been published?

7. Interpreting account entries; adjusting entry.   The following figures appeared in the Prepaid Rent account of a motion picture theater during 19x1:

Prepaid Rent

Bal. 1/1	10	(2)	55
(1)	55		
Bal. 12/31	10		

The debit and the credit shown here summarize the many debits and the many credits that were actually entered in this account during the year.

Investigation shows that the balance in this account on December 31, 19x1, should have been $5.

a. How much money was paid to the landlord in 19x1?
b. What was the rent expense for 19x1?
c. What adjusting entry had to be made before the books could be closed at the end of 19x1?
d. How did the credits to this account arise during the year?

8. Interpreting accounting entries; adjusting entry.   The following figures appeared in the Accrued Salaries Payable account of an advertising firm during 19x2:

Accrued Salaries Payable

(2)	1,360	Bal. 1/1	50
		(1)	1,400
		Bal. 12/31	90

The debit and the credit shown here represent the many debits and the many credits that were actually entered in this account during the year.

All of these figures were correct, and no further adjustments were necessary. Payroll taxes were zero, and all salary costs passed through this account.

a. Calculate salary expense for the year.
b. How much of the salaries earned by employees in 19x2 were paid in cash during the year?
c. How much was paid to employees during 19x2 for work done in 19x1?
d. How much will be paid to employees in 19x3 for work done in 19x2?

9. Aging accounts receivable.   The following is a summary of the "aged" schedule of accounts receivable of Billerica Trading Company as of the end of the fiscal year:

Total	0–30 Days	31–45 Days	46–60 Days	Over 60 Days
$348,788	$283,615	$52,110	$12,552	$511

According to past experience, bills more than 60 days old were likely to be completely uncollectible, those in the third category about 4 percent uncollectible, those in the second category about 1 percent uncollectible, and those in the first category about 0.2 percent uncollectible.

The trial balance listed the Allowance for Uncollectible Accounts account with a credit balance of $1,816 and the Customer Defaults account with a $3,216 debit balance.

a. Calculate estimated customer defaults for the year.
b. Prepare an adjusting entry to reflect this information.

10. Customer defaults; aging the accounts. The Flintop Company was organized and commenced business on January 1. Management decided to recognize revenue at the time of delivery. Although it had no prior experience as to the collectibility of its receivables, it decided to use 1.5 percent of sales as its estimate of customer defaults until better information became available.

During the year the company delivered products to customers at an aggregate selling price of $200,000, and collected $150,596 on account from these customers.

a. Prepare journal entries to record your analyses of the effects of these transactions on the company's assets, liabilities, and owners' equity.
b. On December 1, the Elk Products Company, one of Flintop's customers, was declared bankrupt, with no assets to satisfy creditors' claims. At that time Elk Products owed Flintop $404. Prepare the necessary entry.
c. On December 31, an analysis of accounts receivable showed the following:

Age of Accounts	Amount Receivable
0–30 days	$30,000
31–60 days	11,000
61–120 days	6,000
More than 120 days	2,000

The Company's auditors suggested that the following percentages be used to compute the amounts that would probably prove uncollectible: 0–30 days, 0.25 percent; 31–60 days, 1 percent; 61–120 days, 10 percent; more than 120 days, 50 percent. Prepare a journal entry to implement this suggestion.

11. Product warranty. The Joplin Manufacturing Company guarantees its products against product defects that are detected during the first year after the products are delivered to customers. Past experience indicates that the cost of correcting any such defects will average 2 percent of Joplin's selling prices. Revenues are recognized at the time of delivery. You have the following information for the year 19x1:

1. Opening balance in Liability under Product Guarantees account, $25,000.

2. Gross sales revenue for the year, $3 million, all on credit; collections from customers, $2.8 million.
3. Expenditures made to correct defects discovered and reported by customers during the year, $53,000, all paid in cash.

a. Analyze the effects of these transactions on the firm's assets, liabilities, and owners' equity. Then prepare journal entries in general journal form to record your analyses.
b. Set up a T-account for the Liability under Product Guarantees account, enter the opening balance, post the entry or entries that you assigned to this account as a result of your analyses in (a), and compute the balance in this account at the end of the year. What does this balance measure?

12. Corrections; adjusting entries. The data in the paragraphs that follow were collected by the companies' accountants before their companies' financial statements for the year 19x1 were prepared and before the closing entries for the year were made. Each company was engaged in wholesaling, with a fiscal year ending on December 31, 19x1.

For each company, prepare the journal entry necessary to adjust the accounts as of the end of the fiscal year. If no entry is necessary, write "no entry."

a. In Company A, local property taxes covering the period October 1, 19x1, through September 30, 19x2, were expected to amount to $30,000. These would be paid in July, 19x2.
b. Company B received invoices on January 10, 19x2, covering telephone and electric service for the month of December, 19x1, totaling $1,000.
c. Company C's perpetual inventory records and Inventory account balance indicated that the cost of merchandise on hand on December 31, 19x1, was $50,500. A physical count revealed that the amount actually on hand had cost $48,500.
d. Company D's last weekly payroll period of 19x1 ended on December 27. The next weekly payroll covered the period December 27, 19x1, through January 2, 19x2. This included three working days in 19x1 and two working days in 19x2, holidays being counted as "working days" for this purpose. The total January 2 payroll was $25,000, of which $5,000 was for office employees and $20,000 was for store employees. The company uses a separate salary expense account for each department. Employer payroll taxes may be ignored.
e. In 19x0 Company E bought merchandise for inventory amounting to $10,000, but at the time of acquisition the purchase was incorrectly debited to Office Supplies Expense. The merchandise itself was placed in the storeroom, however, and was counted properly in the annual physical inventory taken at the end of 19x0. In reviewing certain records now, just after the end of 19x1, the earlier error has been discovered.
f. A machine that had cost Company F $11,000 when new, was sold during 19x1 for $5,000. At the time of the sale, its book value was $3,000. To record the sale, an accounting clerk debited Cash and credited Other Income $5,000.
g. Company G records sales revenues at the gross price of the merchandise sold. On December 31, 19x1, the balance in Accounts Receivable was

$40,000. The company grants a 2 percent cash discount for prompt payment, and it was expected that all of the amounts receivable on December 31, 19x1, would be paid during the cash discount period. (Use an Allowance for Sales Discounts account.)

13. Supplying missing information.   The Tabor Supply Company sells scientific instruments to the trade. After all entries in the company's journals for 19x0 had been posted to the ledger accounts, the journals were destroyed by fire. The company's accountants have been able to reconstruct most of the journal entries from the basic documents, but in each of the following accounts *one* entry is still unexplained.

In each case, reconstruct the complete journal entry that was *most probably* made during the year and which will account for the unexplained portion of the change in the account balance. Each problem is independent of the other problems. You should assume that the balances are correct and, therefore, that no correcting entries are required:

Example:

Given: Capital Stock account:

Beginning balance	$ 40,000
Ending balance	65,000

Answer:

Cash	25,000	
Capital Stock		25,000

   a. Retained Earnings account:

Beginning balance	$ 95,000
Ending balance	100,000
Net income for year, transferred by closing	12,000

   b. Prepaid Insurance account:

Beginning balance	$ 2,400
Expired during period	2,600
Ending balance	1,900

   c. Wages Payable account:

Beginning balance	$ 1,100
Wages paid	10,500
Ending balance	1,400

   d. Accounts Receivable account (at gross):

Beginning balance	$100,000
Written off as bad	2,000
Cash received	200,000
Discounts allowed	4,000
Ending balance	110,000

   e. Patents account:

Ending balance	$ 20,000
Purchased for cash	10,000
Beginning balance	14,500

f. Accounts Payable account:

Beginning balance	$ 50,000
Ending balance	70,000
Purchases	90,000
Returns	2,000

g. Buildings account:

Beginning balance	$200,000
New building purchased	50,000
Ending balance	230,000

Building—Accumulated Depreciation account:

Net increase in account balance	$ 35,000
Depreciation expense	42,000

Note: There were no cash receipts from sale of buildings.

14. *Product warranty; income statement and journal entries.* Ward Sales, Inc., sells and installs air conditioning equipment. As soon as equipment is installed on a customer's premises, an invoice is prepared and the full price of the equipment is recorded in the Accounts Receivable account.

Although Ward's installers try to install the equipment to meet the needs of those who will be living or working in the air conditioned space, adjustments often have to be made after the equipment has been in operation for some time. Ward recognizes an obligation to make these adjustments without charge to the customer.

The following data have been derived from the company's records for the month of June:

1. Beginning balances in selected accounts:

Cash	$ 50,000
Accounts receivable	88,000
Air conditioner inventories	125,000
Accounts payable (to air conditioner manufacturers)	110,000
Wages payable to equipment installers	500
Wages payable to equipment adjusters	300
Liability for product adjustments	2,500

2. Cash collected from customers ... 135,000
3. Payments to air conditioner manufacturers, on account ... 85,000
4. The cost of making post-installation adjustments of customers' air conditioners is expected to average 3 percent of the selling price of the equipment.
5. Wage payments to employees:

To installers	8,500
To equipment adjusters	1,400
To sales and administrative employees	11,000

6. Other operating costs, all paid in cash:

Installation of air conditioning equipment	800
Adjustment of air conditioning equipment	100
Selling and administrative activities	3,700

7. Ending balances in selected accounts:

Accounts receivable	103,000
Air conditioner inventories	105,000
Accounts payable	95,000
Wages payable to equipment installers	1,000
Wages payable to equipment adjusters	300

a. Compute sales revenues for the month.
b. Calculate the cost of air conditioners purchased during the month.
c. Determine the expenses for the month and calculate net income.
d. What should be the June 30 balance in the Liability for Product Adjustments account?
e. Prepare journal entries to record your analyses of all of the above transactions.

15. Comprehensive statement preparation problem. The preliminary trial balance of the Blackstone Machine Company taken on December 31 is shown below:

BLACKSTONE MACHINE COMPANY
Preliminary Trial Balance
December 31

Debit		Credit	
Cash	$ 60,000	Accounts payable	$ 50,000
Accounts receivable	197,500	Notes payable	140,000
Inventories	370,000	Accrued payroll	3,000
Land	40,000	Accrued interest	2,000
Buildings	150,000	Accrued taxes	5,000
Machinery and equipment ...	400,000	Mortgage on real estate	100,000
Dividends declared	36,000	Allowance for depreciation:	
Sales returns and allowances	26,000	Buildings	30,000
Discounts allowed customers	17,000	Machinery and equipment .	90,000
Cost of goods sold	785,000	Capital stock	600,000
Administrative expense	45,000	Retained earnings	165,000
Interest expense	14,000	Sales	1,080,000
Selling expense	132,000	Interest income	500
		Discounts received	7,000
Total	$2,272,500	Total	$2,272,500

The auditors' investigation has disclosed the following facts:

1. The physical inventory count, taken on December 31, was accurate. The balance in the Inventories account has already been corrected to reflect the quantities revealed by this count.
2. $1,500 should be added to the Accrued Taxes account because a dispute as to the proper income tax for a previous year was settled in favor of the government.
3. Merchandise shipped back for credit by a customer on December 29 has not been recorded. This merchandise cost $1,400 and had been sold to the customer at a price of $2,100. The merchandise is in salable condition and will be placed back in the merchandise stockroom as soon as it is received.
4. A purchase of equipment for $2,000 was debited to the Inventories account at the time of purchase.
5. On December 1 the company gave its bank a 60-day note with a face value of $140,000. The bank discounted this note at 9 percent and the company debited the interest of $2,100 to Discounts Allowed Customers.

6. The cash amount shown on the trial balance is the sum of the balances in three accounts: Cash on Hand, Cash in Bank, and Petty Cash. Petty Cash includes $2,600 advanced to the company's sales representatives for travel and entertainment expenses. December expense statements received from sales representatives early in January amounted to $1,700.

7. Machinery costing $17,000 was sold and the proceeds of $2,000 were debited to cash and credited to Sales, no other record being made. The book value of these assets at the time of sale was $4,800.

8. An invoice for raw materials received on December 29 was recorded at $5,290 instead of $5,920, a clerk having transposed the 9 and the 2.

9. No provision was made for the 2 percent discounts offered for payment within ten days on $100,000 of sales made subsequent to December 21.

10. The board of directors on December 15 declared a quarterly dividend to shareholders, amounting to $12,000, payable on the following January 5. This action was not recorded.

a. Prepare any journal entries necessary to reflect this additional information.

b. Prepare an income statement for the year, together with a statement of changes in retained earnings.

c. Prepare a statement of financial position at the end of the year.

d. Prepare all entries necessary to close the accounts at the end of the year.

16. Comprehensive statement preparation problem; departmental operations. The Caron Corporation operates an appliance store and repair shop. It has four kinds of inventory: merchandise, store supplies, office supplies, and repair supplies. Purchases of merchandise are charged initially to the Purchases of Merchandise account; purchases of store, office, and repair supplies are entered directly in inventory accounts. The company keeps perpetual inventory records for none of these inventories, however; instead it counts the inventories on hand at the end of each quarter.

The fiscal year begins each year on January 1. The company's trial balance on March 31, 19x4, was as follows:

	Debit	Credit
Cash	$ 22,372	
Accounts receivable	67,840	
Allowance for uncollectible accounts		$ 1,830
Merchandise inventory	61,180	
Repair supplies inventory	800	
Store supplies inventory	330	
Office supplies inventory	1,260	
Prepaid insurance	2,000	
Store equipment	28,600	
Allowance for depreciation—store equipment		8,150
Office equipment	10,200	
Allowance for depreciation—office equipment		3,870
Repair equipment	20,400	
Allowance for depreciation—repair equipment		7,010
Accounts payable		49,700
Notes payable		20,000
Capital stock		80,000

	Debit	Credit
Retained earnings		29,840
Revenue from sale of merchandise		185,130
Repair department revenues		17,440
Purchases of merchandise	97,330	
Salaries, store employees	40,100	
Payroll taxes, store	2,807	
Sundry store expenses	7,600	
Salaries and wages, repair employees	11,900	
Payroll taxes, repair department	833	
Sundry repair department expenses	2,030	
Salaries, office employees	18,400	
Payroll taxes, office	1,288	
Sundry office expenses	5,700	
Total	$402,970	$402,970

The following additional information is available:

1. An inventory at the end of March revealed the following balances: merchandise, $58,920; store supplies, $140; office supplies, $660; repair supplies, $350. The cost of repair supplies used should be charged to the Repair Supplies Expense account; the costs of office and store supplies used should be charged to the departmental sundry expense accounts.
2. The balance in Notes Payable on the trial balance represents a 90-day, 9 percent promissory note dated March 16, 19x4, and due on June 14, 19x4. Interest on this note had not yet been recorded in the accounts; it was to be paid along with the face value of the note on June 14, 19x4.
3. Depreciation is calculated at the following rates: store equipment, 10 percent of original cost per year; office equipment, 20 percent per year; and repair equipment, 8 percent per year. No purchases or sales of equipment were made between January 1 and March 31. Departmental depreciation expense accounts should be used.
4. Wages earned during March but unpaid as of March 31 were as follows: store, $1,500; office, $600; repair department, $400. These wages were subject to employer payroll taxes totaling 10 percent.
5. Uncollectible accounts in this company average 0.5 percent of merchandise sales.
6. The balance in Prepaid Insurance reflects the January 1 unexpired premiums on the following three policies: (a) a three-year fire insurance policy expiring March 31, 19x5, three-year premium, $2,160; (b) a one-year workmen's compensation policy, expiring December 31, 19x4, annual premium, $800; and (c) a one-year comprehensive liability policy, expiring June 30, 19x4, annual premium, $600.
7. Dividends amounting to $1,500 were declared on March 20, payable on April 15, 19x4.
8. Property taxes amount to $6,000 a year; taxes for the calendar year 19x4 were payable on August 1, 19x4.

a. Establish T-accounts or a columnar worksheet, enter the account balances from the trial balance, and make all necessary adjustments. You will need to set up a number of accounts in addition to those in the trial balance.

   b. Prepare an income statement for the three months that ended on March 31, 19x4. The income statement should consist of three columns. The first two columns should measure the operating results of the sales and repair departments, insofar as this is possible. The third column should contain the totals of the amounts in the first two columns, plus any items not identifiable specifically either with the sales department or with the repair department.

   c. Prepare a statement of financial position as of March 31, 19x4.

   17. *Comprehensive review problem; forecasted transactions; statement interpretation.* The income statement for Crestmore Stores, Inc., for last year and the company's statement of financial position as of the end of the year were as follows:

CRESTMORE STORES, INC.
Statement of Financial Position
At the End of Last Year
(000 omitted)

Assets

Current Assets:

Cash		$ 321
Accounts receivable ($235 gross, less allowance for uncollectible amounts, $21)		214
Merchandise inventory		578
Prepaid rent		14
Total Current Assets		$1,127
Furniture and equipment	$660	
Less: Accumulated depreciation	279	381
Total Assets		$1,508

Liabilities and Shareowners' Equity

Current Liabilities:

Accounts payable		$ 64
Accrued salaries and wages		16
Accrued income taxes payable		87
Total Current Liabilities		$ 167
Shareowners' Equity:		
Capital stock (480,000 shares)	$460	
Retained earnings	881	
Total Shareowners' Equity		1,341
Total Liabilities and Shareowners' Equity		$1,508

CRESTMORE STORES, INC.
Income Statement
For Last Year

Gross sales		$2,776
Less: Cash discounts	$ 53	
Estimated customer defaults	22	75
Net sales		$2,701
Expenses:		
Cost of goods sold	$1,221	
Salaries and wages	920	

Rent	122
Depreciation	46
Lost and stolen merchandise	12
Other operating expenses	133
Interest	7
Income taxes	96
Total Expenses	2,557
Net income	$ 144

You have the following figures from the company's operating budget for the current year (in thousands of dollars):

1. Gross sales, $3,595.
2. Cash discounts taken by customers, $68.
3. Estimated customer defaults, $18 (0.5 percent of gross sales).
4. Write-offs of specific customer accounts as uncollectible, $14.
5. Accounts receivable (gross) at end of year (after write-offs of specific uncollectible accounts), $350.
6. Purchases of merchandise for resale, $1,857.
7. Payments to suppliers of merchandise, $1,612.
8. Cost of merchandise lost or stolen, $20.
9. Merchandise inventory at end of year (as determined by physical count), $1,040.
10. Salaries and wages paid, $1,199.
11. Accrued salaries and wages at end of year, $30.
12. Rental payments, $171.
13. Prepaid rent, balance at year-end, $26.
14. Other operating expenses, paid in cash, $201.
15. Depreciation on furniture and equipment, $78.
16. Income tax payments, $103.
17. Income tax expense, $163. (The company will benefit for one final year from special tax advantages, and for this reason the tax rate is lower than the normal rate.)

The following additional information is available from the capital expenditure and finance budgets for the year (in thousands of dollars):

18. Quarterly dividends to be declared March 20, June 20, September 20, and December 20, for cash payment 60 days later, $12 each quarter.
19. Proceeds of bank loan, carrying interest at 9 percent, to be received on July 1, $400. Interest will be payable to the bank semiannually, the first payment falling due on January 1 of next year. Management does not intend to borrow any other money during the year.
20. Proceeds from sale of additional shares of common stock to be issued on December 24 to company officers under stock option plan, 10,000 shares, $27 ($2.70 a share).
21. Purchases of store and office furniture and equipment for cash, $628.
22. Retirement and disposal of worn and obsolete furniture and store equipment: original cost, $235, accumulated depreciation, $146, cash proceeds from sale, $76.

a. Prepare an estimated income statement for the current year and an estimated end-of-year balance sheet. (Probably the most efficient way to proceed is to set up accounts, enter the year-beginning balances, and then enter the information provided above.)

b. Prepare a statement of the estimated cash flows for the year, consisting of three sections: (1) the net cash flow (receipts minus disbursements) from ordinary operations; (2) other cash receipts; and (3) other cash disbursements.

c. Be ready to comment briefly on the apparent profitability, liquidity, and financial policies of Crestmore Stores, Inc., insofar as you can determine them from the information provided above.

d. Prepare a rough estimate of the effects that achieving a sales level of only 90 percent of the budgeted amount would have on net income and cash. What assumptions did you make in preparing this estimate? How might management use this additional information?

6

Income and Cash Flow from Manufacturing

ALL OF THE PREVIOUS CHAPTERS were concerned with the operations of merchandising businesses. The purpose of this chapter is to see how accountants apply the same set of concepts in their analyses of manufacturing transactions for financial accounting purposes and how income and cash flow are likely to differ in manufacturing firms.

MANUFACTURING PROCESSES AND COSTS

Manufacturing firms buy goods which they then use to make other goods. The goods they start with we call *materials;* the goods they make are *finished products*. Factory employees, usually using equipment located in factory buildings supplied with electric power and other supporting services, perform the production operations necessary to convert materials into finished products.

The accountant's interest in manufacturing operations for financial accounting purposes focuses on the relationships between manufacturing costs and the production of finished goods. To understand the accountant's methods of accounting for these relationships we need to examine three preliminary questions:

1. How accountants classify manufacturing systems.
2. What the manufacturing cycle consists of.
3. How manufacturing costs relate to the manufacturing cycle.

Kinds of Manufacturing Systems

Manufacturing systems take many forms, depending on the technology used to produce finished products. All of these systems can be classified for accounting purposes into two broad classes: job order production and process production.

Job order production. In job order production, products are manufactured in separate batches or *job lots*. The same people and equipment will be used at different times to make different products. In some cases, the batch may consist of only one unit. The manufacture of a yacht to compete for the America's Cup is an example of a job lot of this sort. In most cases, however, the lots contain many units; once the required number of units has been manufactured. the job is finished and the employees can turn to other jobs.

Process production. In process production, a given set of people and equipment is used exclusively to manufacture one particular product for a long period of time. Flour milling, bread baking, sugar refining, and cement making are all process production systems. Materials typically enter the factory at one location and then move systematically from location to location, a separate operation or operations being performed in each location until the product is finished.

The Manufacturing Cycle

The sequence of events from the purchase of materials to the completion of finished products is known as the *manufacturing cycle*. The first step in the cycle is the purchase of materials. These are generally placed in storerooms or stockpiles when they are received. The quantities in these locations are known as *materials inventories*. When some of them are needed in the factory, they are transferred from the storeroom or stockpile to appropriate locations in the factory. When this happens, we say that materials have been *issued*. They then become part of *work in process inventory*. This sequence of events is diagrammed in Exhibit 6–1.

Work in process is a form of inventory, an inventory of partly processed products. This inventory doesn't consist of materials alone, however. It also embodies the other factory resources that have been

EXHIBIT 6–1. Flows of Manufacturing Materials

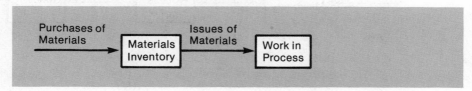

used to convert the materials into their present partly processed state. The most obvious of these other factory resources is *labor time*, the amount of time factory employees have spent working on the materials. These are just as much a part of work in process inventory as the materials because they are just as necessary to bring the items in process to their partly processed state.

The manufacturing cycle comes to an end when the last operations have been performed on the product and it is placed in a warehouse or other location, ready for delivery to a customer. The product then becomes part of the *finished goods inventory*. Like materials and work in process, finished goods are assets. They remain assets until they are shipped to customers.

Manufacturing Cost Flows

Costs flow through the accounting records as products flow through the manufacturing cycle. When materials are purchased, their costs are assigned to the materials inventory. When materials are issued, their costs are assigned to the work in process. The costs of labor time ("labor cost") and the costs of other factory resources consumed in the manufacturing process are also assigned to the work in process inventory.

This flow of manufacturing costs is diagrammed in the central portion of Exhibit 6–2. As this shows, three groups of costs merge to form the costs of the work in process inventory: labor costs, materials costs, and the costs of other factory resources used in production.

Costs continue to be assigned to the work in process inventory as work is performed, bringing the products closer to completion. When

EXHIBIT 6–2.   Costs of Factory Inventories

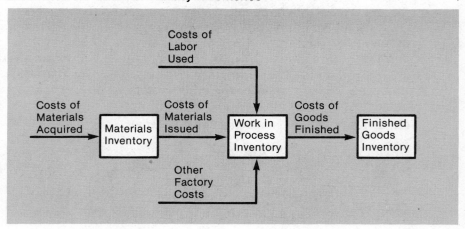

the manufacturing cycle comes to an end, the costs of the completed products are transferred from the work in process category to the finished goods category, as shown in the right side of Exhibit 6–2.

The inventories of finished goods in a manufacturing firm are exactly the same as the merchandise inventories of a retail store. The only remaining step in each case is to deliver them to customers. Notice how we have stretched out the chain between the acquisition of resources and the point at which the firm has something ready for delivery, however. For a retailer, all inventories are one step removed from the customer; manufacturers, on the other hand, are likely to have inventories at all three of the stages shown in Exhibit 6–2.

ANALYSIS OF MANUFACTURING COST FLOWS

The accounting systems used in practice to trace the flows of manufacturing costs through the organization are known as *cost accounting systems*. They are likely to be fairly complex, mainly because they must meet management's needs for information. The simplified model we'll describe in the next few pages has only the elements necessary to help us understand how accountants analyze manufacturing cost transactions for company financial reporting. We'll provide more details on these questions in Chapter 20, and we'll also focus on the managerial implications of these systems at that time.

The Manufacturing Operation

Strong Cabinets, Inc., was founded by David Strong on July 1, 19x1, to manufacture bookshelves, cabinets, and other kinds of wooden furniture. Some of the furniture was made in standard designs, to be sold to retail stores; the rest was of very high quality, manufactured to fill the orders of specific customers. Production was on a *job-order* basis. The cost accounting system, therefore, was a job-order costing system.

Preproduction Transactions

The company began operations with $20,000 in cash, provided by Mr. Strong in exchange for shares of capital stock. The entry was:

(1)

Cash	20,000	
Capital Stock		20,000

Mr. Strong hired a skilled cabinetmaker, a carpenter, and a part-time secretary. The company expended no resources in hiring these employees, however, and acquired no property rights. Nor did the company incur a liability—the liability would be created only as the employees did their work, providing their services to the company. As a result, no entry was made in the accounts to record the hiring of these employees.

Three other transactions took place before manufacturing operations began: (1) prepayment of rent, (2) purchase of factory equipment, and (3) purchase of materials. The accounting treatment of each of these is familiar to us from previous chapters, so we'll describe them very briefly.

The rental on the factory space amounted to $8,400 a year, payable in advance. The entry to record this on July 1, 19x1, showed the acquisition of one asset in exchange for another:

(2)

Prepaid Rent	8,400	
Cash		8,400

The tools and equipment were bought on account for $10,000, and their cost was entered in a new asset account, Factory Equipment. The accompanying liability was also recognized at this time by an entry in the Accounts Payable account. The record of this transaction therefore showed the following changes:

(3)

Factory Equipment......................	10,000	
Accounts Payable		10,000

Most of a retailer's or wholesaler's purchases are of merchandise bought for resale to the company's customers. A manufacturer's purchases, in contrast, consist mainly of materials and parts that are to be used in the manufacturing process. Strong Cabinets, for instance, purchased lumber and other materials for use in the factory but had no intention of selling those materials without converting them into finished products.

The materials purchased during 19x1 were obtained from suppliers on credit, at a total cost of $22,000. The entries recording these purchases showed that both assets and liabilities had increased:

(4)

Materials Inventory	22,000	
Accounts Payable		22,000

The only difference between this and other inventory purchases we discussed in previous chapters is that these are materials rather than merchandise. The asset account title reflects this difference.

Recording Materials Costs

Production in a job-order factory ("job shop") begins when some-one in authority issues a production order or job order calling for the manufacture of a specified quantity of one of the company's products or component parts. The next step is to issue *direct materials* for that job. Direct materials are materials that can be traced readily to individual jobs.

For example, Job No. 1 in Strong Cabinets' factory was an order for 50 36-inch bookcases. The cabinetmaker took lumber from the storeroom to be cut into lengths for finishing and assembly into book-cases. The cost of this lumber was $212. This was recorded in the left-hand column of the simplified job cost sheet shown in Exhibit 6–3. (An actual job cost sheet would have more columns and would

EXHIBIT 6–3. Job Cost Sheet

Job No. 1	Description 36″ bookcases	
	Quantity 50	
Direct Materials	Direct Labor	Overhead
$212		

contain more descriptive detail, of no concern to us here.) A similar job cost sheet was set up for each job started during the rest of the year.

The cost of each batch of direct materials issued during the next six months was entered on the appropriate job cost sheet. Job cost sheets are supplementary records rather than accounts, however. They are represented in Strong Cabinets' ledger by a single account, Work in Process Inventory. The direct materials costs entered in the job cost sheets were also entered in this inventory account. The total cost of direct materials for the last six months of 19x1 was $13,000. The entries to record this amount had the following effects on the accounts:

(5)

Work in Process Inventory................   13,000
    Materials Inventory   13,000

The materials merely moved from one asset class to another.

A few other materials were issued during the year, not for use on any specific job but to support factory operations generally. Exam-ples are lubricants for power equipment, cleaning compounds, glue, and nails. These are referred to as *indirect materials* or *supplies,* defined as the costs of any materials that are not readily traceable to individual jobs. The costs of glue and nails are included in this category, even though they are used directly in furniture manufacture. The reason: the amounts used on any one job are too small to justify the cost of tracing them to jobs. The others couldn't have been traced to individual jobs, no matter how hard the accountants tried.

Indirect materials costs are our first example of *factory overhead costs.* Factory overhead costs in job-order costing are all factory costs not directly assigned to individual job orders. Indirect materials costs, like other factory overhead costs, increase the cost of work in process as they are incurred: they are just as necessary as direct materials costs to the production of finished products. They can't be assigned directly to the Work in Process Inventory account, however. The reason: the Work in Process Inventory account is a *control account,* representing the job cost sheets in the ledger. Since indirect materials costs aren't traced to individual jobs, they can't be assigned directly to individual job cost sheets. And since they can't be assigned directly to individual job cost sheets, they can't be assigned directly to the Work in Process Inventory account. The balance in that account on any date must equal the total of the costs assigned to the individual job cost sheets for jobs in process on that date.

For this reason, indirect materials and other factory overhead costs are assigned to a *temporary* asset account or accounts when they are incurred. Strong Cabinets, for example, used a temporary asset account titled *Factory Overhead.* The total cost of indirect materials issued in 19x1 was $1,000, and this amount was charged to the Factory Overhead account by means of the following entry:

(6)

Factory Overhead   1,000
    Materials Inventory   1,000

This entry recorded the shift of assets (materials) to the production floor for use in the production of other assets (finished goods). "Factory overhead" doesn't describe any asset the company has, of course, but the amount assigned to the Factory Overhead account is the portion of the cost of the work in process inventory that hasn't yet been transferred to specific items of inventory. We'll explain in a moment how this transfer is made.

The amounts classified as factory overhead costs have to be subdivided for various purposes. One way to do this is to use a number of overhead accounts instead of just one. Each of these accounts will be used to provide a record of the amounts of a particular kind of overhead cost, and may also relate solely to one particular part of the factory. The costs of glue, for example, might be charged to the account, "Indirect Materials—Assembly Department." Because we want to emphasize the flows of costs into the financial statements with a minimum of distractions, however, we'll ignore this greater detail in this simple example.

The distribution of the $22,000 cost of materials acquired during the company's first six months is illustrated in Exhibit 6–4. The

EXHIBIT 6–4. Distribution of Materials Costs

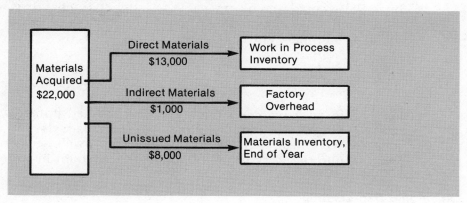

$13,000 in direct materials costs went directly into the work in process, while the $1,000 in indirect materials was classified as factory overhead, leaving $8,000 in the materials inventory at the end of the year.

Labor Costs

Payroll costs for factory employees are recorded just as for office and store employees, with one difference: the costs are charged to factory cost accounts rather than to expense accounts. Shop labor is used to create assets, the work in process. The costs of this labor don't become expense until the revenues from furniture sales appear on the income statement.

The costs of the time employees spend working on individual job orders are known as *direct labor costs*. They, too, are entered in the job cost sheets, and summary entries are made in the general ledger to assign these costs to the Work in Process Inventory account. These costs amounted to $18,000 in 19x1, and the entry was:

(7)

Work in Process Inventory...............	18,000	
Wages Payable		18,000

(Crediting the entire amount to Wages Payable shows that we are ignoring payroll taxes and other withholdings in this illustration. Our focus is the *cost* of manufacturing operations; how the accompanying liability is divided has no bearing on this question.)

Some labor time is spent on work that can't be traced to any one job. This kind of work is known as *indirect labor*. Cleaning floors and maintaining equipment are good examples of indirect labor activities. Strong Cabinets had $2,000 in indirect labor costs in 19x1. Since these costs weren't traceable to individual jobs, they weren't entered on the job cost sheets. Instead, they were recorded by the following summary entry:

(8)

Factory Overhead 2,000
    Wages Payable 2,000

Once again we have costs that can't be classified immediately as expenses yet can't be assigned directly to specific assets. The charge to Factory Overhead was a temporary expedient; we'll see how these costs got into the Work in Process Inventory account in a moment.

Recording Depreciation

Depreciation is a cost that is ordinarily treated as a current expense when it relates to facilities used for administrative or marketing activities. When it relates to manufacturing facilities, however, it is a cost of producing an asset—work in process inventory in the first instance and finished goods later on.

The argument for this treatment is that the asset has merely been converted from one form to another—the services formerly embodied in a machine have now been embodied in the goods manufactured during the period. Thus factory depreciation doesn't become an expense until revenues from the goods to which it has been charged are recognized on the income statement. Because it can't be identified with specific jobs, however, it has to be charged initially to one or more factory overhead accounts.

Depreciation on shop facilities in the cabinet shop during the second half of 19x1 amounted to $800; the entry to record this treated it as a conversion of one asset (equipment) into another (inventory):

(9)

Factory Overhead 800
    Accumulated Depreciation 800

The credit to Accumulated Depreciation served to record the decrease in the company's equipment assets. This account was a contra-asset account, as explained in Chapter 3. The balance in this account appeared on the balance sheet as a deduction from the original cost of the equipment.

Other Factory Costs

Running a factory calls for the use of many more resources than materials, labor, and equipment. Factories have to pay for electricity, telephone calls, taxes, and many other services. These are just as much part of the cost of production as direct labor and materials. They aren't traceable to individual jobs, however, and therefore are part of factory overhead.

The costs of these services used by Strong Cabinets during the second half of 19x1 amounted to $7,000. The entries to record these transactions had the following effects on the account balances:

(10)

Factory Overhead	7,000	
Accounts Payable		7,000

As this shows, the costs that were incurred to help create salable goods were added to a temporary asset account; the liability to pay for the cost-originating services was recognized by the addition to the Accounts Payable account.

Finally, six months' rent on the cabinet shop itself had to be charged to shop operations. Rent of $8,400 was paid on July 1, 19x1, (entry [2] above) covering the next 12 months. Six months' rent, therefore, had to be treated as a cost of factory operations for the last six months of 19x1. The accountant's analysis showed the following asset changes:

(11)

Factory Overhead	4,200	
Prepaid Rent		4,200

This means that the asset Prepaid Rent decreased, the temporary asset Factory Overhead increased.

Factory Overhead Applied

We still haven't resolved the issue of how factory overhead costs get assigned to the various products manufactured in the factory. They can't be traced to products, yet they are part of the cost of production. The solution is to include them in product cost on the basis of an *average*. The averages used for this purpose in cost accounting are known by names such as *burden rates, overhead rates,* or *indirect costing rates*.

Averages are always relationships between two quantities. In this case, we need to relate overhead cost to some other quantity that represents the amount of production in the factory. Sometimes we can measure the amount of production by the number of units manufactured. Strong Cabinets couldn't do this, however, because the factory made so many different products. A bookcase isn't the same thing as an end table or a kitchen chair, and we can't add the number of units of each to get anything that makes any sense.

In situations like this, the accountants usually look for some other characteristic of individual products they can measure. This may be the number of direct labor-hours used to make them, the amount of direct labor cost, or the amount of raw material used, to mention just a few of the possibilities. Ideally, we'd like to find a measure of volume that is most closely related to changes in the amount of overhead cost. If we can't find one measure that does this noticeably better than some other, we'll probably choose the one that's easiest to measure.

Strong Cabinets, for example, calculated its overhead rate as the ratio of factory overhead costs to the number of direct labor hours used in the factory. Statistics on the number of direct labor hours were readily available, and changes in the amounts of many kinds of overhead costs could be predicted fairly accurately on the basis of estimated changes in the number of direct labor hours. Choosing direct labor hours as the measure of volume meant that the factory overhead rate was the ratio of total factory overhead cost to the total number of direct labor hours used.

Factory overhead costs in Strong Cabinets' factory in 19x1 consisted of the following:

Indirect materials	$ 1,000
Indirect labor	2,000
Depreciation	800
Rent	4,200
Other factory overhead	7,000
Total	$15,000

In all, 2,500 direct labor-hours were used during the second half of 19x1. The overhead rate therefore was:

$$\text{Overhead rate} = \frac{\$15,000}{2,500} = \$6 \text{ per direct labor-hour.}$$

This rate was used to fill in the third column of each job cost sheet. Exhibit 6–5, for example, shows the same job cost sheet we saw in Exhibit 6–3, but with all three columns filled in. The $60 shown in the overhead column was calculated by multiplying the overhead

EXHIBIT 6-5. Job Cost Sheet Revisited

Job No. 1		Description 36" bookcases
		Quantity 50
Direct Materials	*Direct Labor*	*Overhead*
$212	10 hours $72	10 hours $60

rate ($6 per direct labor-hour) by the number of direct labor-hours used on this job (ten hours).

The amount of factory overhead cost assigned to a job order is known as the amount of *factory overhead applied* to the job or the amount of *factory overhead absorbed* by the job. The total amount charged to all jobs in the last half of 19x1 was $15,000, and the entry to record overhead absorption was:

(12)

Work in Process Inventory...............   15,000
    Factory Overhead   15,000

With this entry, the costs of factory overhead were finally assigned to an asset account, Work in Process Inventory. The Factory Overhead account was reduced to a zero balance:

Factory Overhead

Overhead	(6)	1,000	(12)	15,000	→ to work in process
costs	(8)	2,000			
incurred →	(9)	800			
	(10)	4,200			
	(11)	7,000			
		15,000			

In practice, the overhead rate is often established before the period begins. This means that the amount assigned to products is likely to differ from the amount of overhead actually incurred, and a balance of some sort will remain in the Factory Overhead account. We'll deal with this complication in Chapter 20.

The Cost of Goods Finished

Some of the job orders begun during 19x1 were still unfinished at the end of the year. The job cost sheets for these jobs were still in the work in process file at that time. Other jobs were finished during the year, however, and the finished products were placed in Strong Cabinets' shipping room. Job No. 1 was one of these. The job cost sheet for that job was taken out of the file and the amounts that had been entered on that sheet for direct materials, direct labor, and factory overhead were totaled ($212 + $72 + $60 = $344).   This amount was transferred from the Work in Process Inventory account to the Finished Goods Inventory account.

The total of these transfers during 19x1 amounted to $36,000. The summary entry to record the completion of these job orders was:

(13)

Finished Goods Inventory	36,000	
Work in Process Inventory		36,000

Both of these were asset accounts; the entry merely indicated the change in the inventory from an unfinished to a finished form. The Work in Process Inventory account showed the following after this entry was made:

Work in Process Inventory

(5)	13,000	(13)	36,000
(7)	18,000		
(12)	15,000		
	46,000		
Bal.	10,000		

In other words, the cost of the unfinished furniture still in process on December 31, 19x1, was $10,000.

The Cost of Goods Sold

The Finished Goods Inventory account plays the same role in a manufacturing organization as the Merchandise Inventory account does for a wholesaler or retailer. It keeps the costs of salable products on the balance sheet until the goods themselves are sold.

Strong Cabinets, Inc., had perpetual inventory records for its inventory of finished products. A separate card was prepared for each finished product. When a job order was finished, the total cost and unit cost of that job were entered on the card. When a shipment was made to a customer, a share of the costs proportionate to the number of units shipped was subtracted from the balance on the card and identified as the cost of goods sold.

The file of inventory cards is an example of a subsidiary ledger. It stands in the same relationship to the Finished Goods Inventory account as the file of job-order sheets for unfinished jobs bears to the Work in Process Inventory account. A similar subsidiary ledger is maintained for materials inventories. This parallel is diagrammed in

EXHIBIT 6–6. Control Accounts and Subsidiary Ledgers

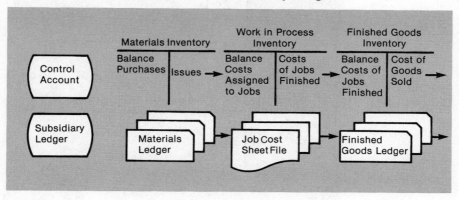

Exhibit 6–6. The balance in the control account will be equal in each case to the sum of the balances in the subsidiary ledger, barring bookkeeping errors.

The sum of the factory costs of the individual items Strong Cabinets sold in 19x1 was $28,000. The delivery of these items to the company's customers reduced both the inventory asset and the owners' equity. The entries to record these changes can be summarized as follows:

(14)

Cost of Goods Sold	28,000	
Finished Goods Inventory		28,000

This left a balance of $8,000 in the Finished Goods Inventory account, the cost of the finished cabinets still on the storeroom shelves at the end of 19x1:

Finished Goods Inventory

(13)	36,000	(14)	28,000
Bal. 12/31	8,000		

The Manufacturing Cost Statement

This completes the operating cycle of a manufacturing company. This cycle consists of purchasing materials, processing them into finished goods, and selling them to customers. The flow of manufacturing costs through the accounts is diagrammed in Exhibit 6–7. Notice that inventories are found at three stages—unprocessed,

EXHIBIT 6–7. Manufacturing Cost Flows for Income Reporting

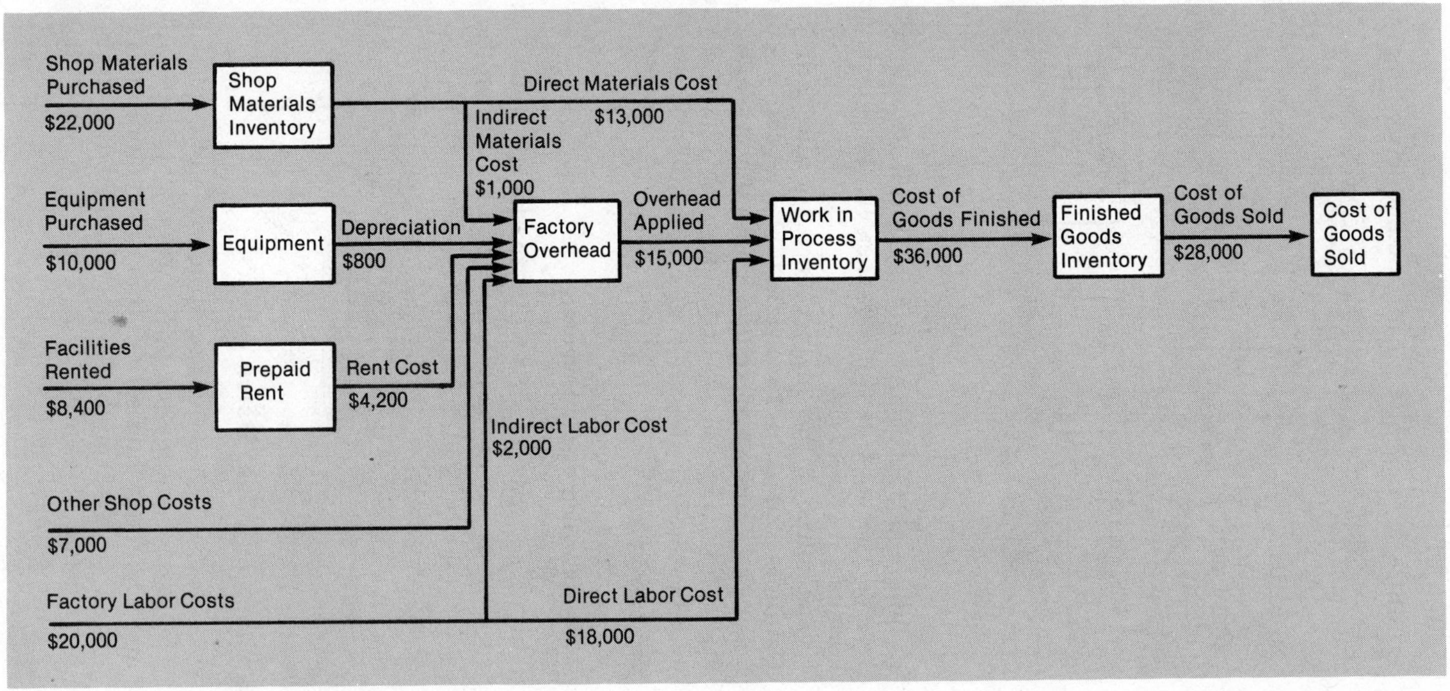

partly processed, and finished. Each of the dollar amounts identified with a cost flow in this diagram came from one of the ten entries that we used in the illustration.

The diagram can be converted very simply to T-account form by inserting a large T in place of each of the rectangular boxes. Costs flowing into an account would be represented by debits at the left; costs leaving an account would be shown as credits, at the right of the account.

These cost flows can also be summarized in tabular form, as in the manufacturing cost statement in Exhibit 6–8. This shows that of the

EXHIBIT 6–8

STRONG CABINETS, INC.
Statement of Manufacturing Costs and Cost of Goods Sold
For the Six Months Ended December 31, 19x1

Direct Materials Cost:			
Materials purchased			$22,000
Less: Indirect materials issued		$1,000	
Materials on hand, December 31, 19x1		8,000	9,000
Direct Materials Cost			$13,000
Direct labor cost			18,000
Factory Overhead Cost:			
Indirect materials		$1,000	
Indirect labor		2,000	
Rent		4,200	
Depreciation		800	
Other		7,000	15,000
Total Factory Cost			$46,000
Less: Work in process, December 31, 19x1			10,000
Cost of goods finished			$36,000
Less: Finished goods inventory, December 31, 19x1			8,000
Cost of Goods Sold			$28,000

$46,000 in costs actually applicable to factory operations during 19x1, only $28,000 was transferred to expense on the income statement for the year. The remaining $18,000 was divided between the work in process inventory and finished goods inventory. In addition, materials inventories showed a year-end balance of $8,000, factory equipment costs of $9,200 remained on the balance sheet, and rent prepayments amounted to $4,200 at the end of the year.

Notice that nowhere in this illustration was reference made to the payment of cash. The timing of cash payment has no bearing on the apportionment of costs among the various categories of assets and expenses. Eliminating cash transactions from the illustration interfered in no way with our ability to trace the manufacturing costs through the accounts.

Nonmanufacturing Costs and the Income Statement

Every manufacturer incurs many costs for activities other than manufacturing. Advertising costs, the president's salary, and expenditures on research and development are only a few examples of costs that are incurred for purposes other than the conversion of raw materials into finished products.

All such costs are accounted for just as they would be in a retailing or wholesaling concern. Sales office rental costs and advertising costs are recognized as expense when the space and advertising services are provided, whether products have been sold or not. They aren't part of the cost of manufacturing products and therefore they don't enter the factory cost accounts in any way. They go directly to expense without passing through the Work in Process Inventory and Finished Goods Inventory accounts along the way.

Mr. Strong and a part-time clerical assistant constituted the entire selling and administrative work force at Strong Cabinets during 19x1. Their salaries for this period amounted to $17,000. The entries to accrue these payrolls can be summarized as follows:

(15)

Selling and Administrative Salary Expense	17,000	
Wages and Salaries Payable		17,000

The effect of these transactions, in other words, was to decrease the owners' equity and increase the company's liabilities.

Transactions giving rise to other selling and administrative costs had similar effects. They amounted to $3,100 and can be summarized as follows:

(16)

Other Selling and Administrative Expenses	3,100	
Accounts Payable		3,100

To complete the illustration of the operating cycle, we need to identify the revenues of the period and show what accounts they affected. Finished furniture was sold on account in 19x1 for a total of $50,000, thereby increasing the company's assets and its owners' equity:

(17)

Accounts Receivable	50,000	
Sales Revenue		50,000

The income statement derived from the revenue and expense accounts appears in Exhibit 6–9.

EXHIBIT 6–9

STRONG CABINETS, INC.
Income Statement
For the Six Months Ended December 31, 19x1

Sales revenue		$50,000
Expenses:		
Cost of goods sold	$28,000	
Selling and administrative salaries	17,000	
Other selling and administrative expenses	3,100	
Total Expenses		48,100
Net income		$ 1,900

INCOME VERSUS CASH FLOW

As we pointed out earlier, the net income figure doesn't necessarily measure the net flow of cash into the company as a result of the period's operations. Strong Cabinets, for example, had many more cash transactions than the two we included in our example of manufacturing costs. In brief, they were as follows:

Cash Receipts		Cash Disbursements	
Investments by Mr. Strong	$20,000	Payment of rent	$ 8,400
Collections from		Payment for equipment	8,000
customers	44,000	Payments to suppliers	25,000
Loan received from bank	15,000	Payments to employees	36,500
Total	$79,000	Total	$77,900

The cash balance at the end of the year was $79,000 − $77,900 = $1,100.

These cash flows have been rearranged in Exhibit 6–10 to distinguish between those that arose in connection with the routine operation of the business and those that arose in other ways. Although the operations for the period generated a *net income* of $1,900, they also resulted in a *cash outflow* of $25,900. The purchase of equipment consumed another $8,000. The company was able to meet these demands for cash only as a consequence of Mr. Strong's investment and the bank loan.

The size of the spread between operating cash flow and net income depends on several factors. One of these is the *rate of growth*. In companies that don't grow, net cash flow will tend to equal net income, if price levels are relatively stable. For example, the amount of materials paid for in one period will be roughly equal to the amount bought, the amount used, and the amount incorporated in the goods

EXHIBIT 6–10

STRONG CABINETS, INC.
Statement of Cash Flows
For the Six Months Ended December 31, 19x1

Cash Outflows:
For operations:

Received from customers		$44,000
Less: Paid to suppliers	$25,000	
Paid to employees	36,500	
Paid to landlord	8,400	69,900
Net Cash Outflow for Operations		$25,900
For equipment		8,000
Total Cash Outflows		$33,900
Cash Inflows:		
From initial investment	$20,000	
From bank loan	15,000	
Total Cash Inflows		35,000
Increase in Cash Balance		$ 1,100

sold in that period. As a result, the materials component of the cost of goods sold will be the same as the amounts paid to materials suppliers in an average period. The amounts paid to suppliers of plant and equipment will fluctuate more, but, in the absence of inflation, a nongrowing company will pay out about the same amount it identifies as depreciation. Cash payments, in other words, will be about the same as current expenses.

The same equality is true on the revenue side of a nongrowing company. The amounts collected from customers will equal the revenues of some previous period. Since revenues are constant from period to period, the amount collected will equal the current period's revenues. Since expenses equal payments and revenues equal receipts, net income will equal net cash flow.

This equality is diagrammed in the left side of Exhibit 6–11. The situation diagrammed at the right is very different. In a growing company, revenues will be greater than collections because collections are based on the smaller revenues of a previous period. Payments, on the other hand, are determined by purchases of goods and services, and the purchases of one period are determined by the larger expenses of a later period. Other things being equal, payments for goods and services in a growing company will exceed the amounts reported as expenses.[1] Since revenues exceed receipts and

---

[1] This statement may not be true if depreciation is a large element of operating cost and if the company's depreciable facilities are relatively new. Under these conditions, purchases of depreciable assets will be smaller than the amount of depreciation recognized as an expense of the current period. The difference between these two amounts may be great enough to offset opposite expense/cash flow spreads in other expense elements.

EXHIBIT 6–11. Comparison of Income and Cash Flow

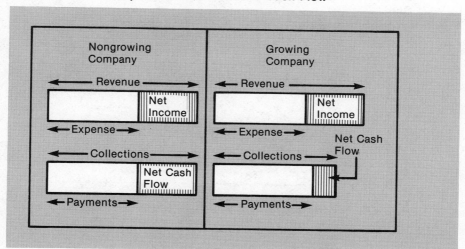

expenses are smaller than payments, net income will exceed net cash inflow.

Strong Cabinets' experience in 19x1 is an extreme example of the impact of growth. Starting from zero, Strong Cabinets had to build all three kinds of inventories, totaling $26,000. In addition, its sales ($50,000) exceeded its collections ($44,000) by $6,000. Accounts payable and wages payable financed only a small percentage of these needs.

The second major determinant of the gap between net income and net cash flow is the length of the operating cycle. Other things being equal, a growing company which buys materials six months before it delivers finished products to its customers will have a greater income/cash gap than a company with the same growth rate but a one-month operating cycle. The growth rates in operating costs are the same in both sides of Exhibit 6–12, for example, but the operating cycle is much longer in the right-hand diagram, creating a much greater gap between current expenditures and current expenses.

Whether this will be translated into an income/cash flow gap depends on a third pair of factors, the terms of purchase and sale. Any delay from expenditure to payment reduces the income/cash flow gap; any delay from revenue recognition to collection increases it. If payments for goods and services aren't made until the goods are sold, then expenses will equal cash disbursements. And if customers pay at the time of delivery, revenues will equal operating cash receipts and the income/cash flow gap will disappear.

The income/cash flow gap in a very young company is likely to be relatively greater than in a larger, more established company be-

EXHIBIT 6–12.   Effect of Operating Cycle Length on Expenditure/Expense Gap

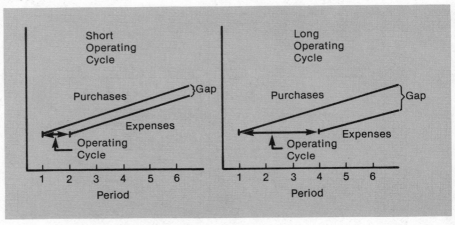

cause the new company has to build and pay for its initial plant and equipment. This was a serious problem for Strong Cabinets in 19x1. Fortunately, however, many of the factors leading to the great demand for cash in 19x1 would not be present in 19x2. No further expenditures for equipment would be necessary. Further increases in the amount of work in process were unlikely, and increases in materials inventories could be covered by increase in accounts payable.

The major pressure on cash would come from the increase in receivables resulting from increases in sales. Mr. Strong's strategy, therefore, had to be to keep the rate of growth at a level low enough to be sustained by the rate of collections from customers.

SUMMARY

Manufacturing costs provide an excellent illustration of the application of the accrual concept. Accounting views manufacturing as a process of adding the costs of manufacturing labor and other manufacturing services to the cost of purchased materials. The costs of manufacturing follow the flow of the goods themselves, from raw materials inventory to work in process to finished goods and finally to goods sold.

The costs of the goods at all of these stages except the last are regarded as costs of assets and thus rest appropriately in the inventory section of the balance sheet. Only when the goods are sold do these costs become expenses as the cost of goods sold. Costs of administering the company and of selling and distributing its products, of course, are taken directly to expense, just as in a wholesaling or retailing concern.

The size of the gap between income and cash flow depends largely on the rate of growth and the length of the operating cycle. If production, sales, and collections are the same from period to period, income and cash flow will be identical. If sales are growing, however, the excess of cash receipts over cash disbursements (net cash flow) is likely to be less than the excess of revenues over expenses (net income) and may even be negative. At a given growth rate, the size of the gap between income and net cash receipts will be greater if the operating cycle is long than if it is short.

The cash/income gap may force management to limit the rate of growth. How serious a threat this is depends on the length of the operating, collection, and payment cycles, on the income/revenue ratio, and on the availability of funds from outside investors. Firms with long operating cycles and low income ratios find it very difficult to finance growth from internal sources and may have difficulty finding outside funds as well.

KEY TERMS

Cost accounting systems	Indirect materials (supplies)
Direct labor	Job cost sheet
Direct materials	Job-order production
Factory overhead	Overhead rate
Finished goods	Work in process
Indirect labor	

INDEPENDENT STUDY PROBLEMS (Solutions in Appendix B)

1. Unit cost and journal entries. The Basic Foundry prepares metal castings for specific orders, using a job-order costing system. The following information about Job No. 103 is available:

1. Direct materials issued: 21,000 pounds at 66 cents a pound.
2. Direct labor: 2,000 hours at $6.68 an hour.
3. Factory overhead rate: $4 a direct labor-hour.
4. Unused direct material returned to storeroom: 800 pounds.
5. Castings started: 10,000.
6. Castings completed: 9,800.
7. Castings sold: 4,900.

a. Calculate unit cost of production to the nearest cent.
b. Prepare journal entries to record these transactions.

2. Manufacturing cost flows; income statement. The King Appliance Company had the following inventories on October 1:

Materials	$11,650
Work in process	8,320
Finished goods	11,100

The following transactions took place during the month:

1. Purchased materials on account at a cost of $4,500.
2. Issued direct material, $6,320; indirect material, $930.
3. Accrued payrolls: direct labor, $3,300; indirect labor, $1,800; selling and administrative salaries, $2,600.
4. Depreciation on manufacturing facilities, $400.
5. Miscellaneous goods and services purchased on account for immediate use in the factory, $1,820.
6. Manufacturing overhead applied: 150 percent of direct labor cost.
7. Goods completed during the month cost $12,650.
8. Ending inventory, finished goods, $9,250.
9. Depreciation on administrative office equipment, $100.
10. Miscellaneous goods and services purchased on account for immediate use by sales and administrative personnel, $1,735.
11. Sales revenue from goods sold on credit, $19,350.

a. Account for the above transactions, using T-accounts, and establish the closing balances in the inventory accounts. Use a Factory Overhead account and a single account for selling and administrative expenses.

b. Prepare an income statement for the month. Ignore income taxes.

3.   Deriving cash flows from income statement and balance sheet data.
The Beecham Manufacturing Company's annual report for 19x1 included the following income statement for the year:

Sales		$500,000
Less: Cost of goods sold	$320,000*	
Other expenses	100,000	420,000*
Net Income		$ 80,000

* Includes depreciation, $20,000.

The company's assets, liabilities, and owners' equity were as follows at the beginning and end of 19x1:

	January 1		December 31	
Cash		$ 40,000		$ 50,000
Accounts receivable		80,000		100,000
Inventory		60,000		70,000
Plant and equipment:				
Original cost	$200,000		$260,000	
Accumulated depreciation	70,000	130,000	90,000	170,000
Total Assets		$310,000		$390,000
Accounts payable		$ 50,000		$ 30,000
Capital stock		110,000		140,000
Retained earnings		150,000		220,000
Total Liabilities and Owners' Equity		$310,000		$390,000

All accounts payable arose out of the purchase of materials or the purchase of other goods and services for immediate consumption. All accounts receivable arose out of sales of merchandise to customers.

a. How much cash was received from customers during the year?
b. What was the total cost of goods purchased during the year?
c. How much cash was paid to suppliers, employees, and others during the year for goods or current services?
d. How much cash was provided by the company's operations during the year?
e. What were the company's other sources and uses of cash during the year?
f. Summarize this information in a statement of cash flows for the year. List the sources of cash first, distinguishing between cash flow from operations and cash flows from other sources.

EXERCISES AND PROBLEMS

4. Supplying missing information. The following data were taken from the ledger accounts of the Abcess Manufacturing Company for the most recent month:

Factory materials inventory, beginning of month	$ 0
Work in process inventory, beginning of month	0
Finished goods inventory, beginning of month	5,000
Purchases of factory materials	360,000
Depreciation on factory and factory equipment	15,000
Factory materials placed in production	290,000
Depreciation on office equipment	2,000
Sales and administrative salaries	59,000
Factory labor	140,000
Sundry selling and administrative expense	29,000
Sundry production costs for the month	135,000
Revenue from sales	525,000
Income taxes on taxable income for the month	24,000
Dividends declared during the month	35,000
Work in process inventory, end of month	115,000
Finished goods inventory, end of month	85,000
Retained earnings, beginning of month	40,000

Compute the following figures:

a. Total production costs for the month.
b. Total cost of goods finished during the month.
c. Cost of goods sold during the month.
d. Net income for the month.
e. Retained earnings, end of month.
f. Raw materials inventory, end of month.

5. Supplying missing information. The following data are available for a manufacturing operation:

Balance-sheet data:

	December 31, 19x1	December 31, 19x2
Raw materials inventory	$240	$285
Work in process inventory	128	271
Finished goods inventory	87	172
Factory plant and equipment (net)	492	476

Totals for the year 19x2:

1. Purchases of raw materials, $1,250.
2. Purchases of factory plant and equipment, $23.
3. Wages earned by factory employees, $566.
4. Production costs other than raw materials, labor, and depreciation, $2,418.
5. Factory plant and equipment sold, none.

a. Calculate the cost of raw materials used during the year.
b. Calculate factory depreciation for the year.
c. Calculate the cost of goods finished during the year.
d. Calculate the cost of goods sold during the year.

(*Prepared by Charles Boynton*)

6. Statement of manufacturing costs. The Albatross Corporation is engaged in the manufacture and sale of plastic water toys. Its inventories were as follows:

	January 1	June 30
Raw materials	$10,000	$16,000
Work in process	40,000	50,000
Finished goods	20,000	10,000

The following costs were incurred between these two dates:

Factory raw materials purchased	$90,000
Factory labor	40,000
Factory depreciation	7,000
Factory utilities and other costs	13,000
Sales salaries	5,000
Office salaries	8,000
Other selling and office costs	4,000

Included in the above costs of this six-month period were direct materials, $80,000, and direct labor, $30,000.

Prepare a statement of the cost of goods manufactured and sold during the six months ended June 30.

7. Job-order costs. A factory uses a job-order costing system. You have the following information about the factory's operations last week:

1. Direct labor and direct materials used:

Job Order	Direct Materials	Direct Labor-Hours
878................	$ 250	46
882................	412	32
891................	346	18
905................	1,215	81
906................	811	20
910................	1,440	62
912................	196	10
Total	$4,670	269

2. The direct labor wage rate was $8 an hour.
3. Actual factory overhead costs for the week totaled $1,345. They were applied to jobs at a rate of $5 a direct labor-hour.
4. Jobs completed: Nos. 878, 882, and 905.
5. The factory had no work in process at the beginning of the week.

a. Prepare a summary table that will show all the costs assigned to each job.
b. Calculate the cost of the work in process at the end of the week.

8. Manufacturing transactions. The Goodhue Chemical Company buys chemicals in bulk and packages them for sale to small local customers. The company's activities last month included the following, among others:

1. Ordered from a supplier 30 55-gallon drums of chemicals. The price of the chemicals was $60 a drum, plus a $5 returnable deposit on the drum. In addition, Goodhue was responsible for paying freight and delivery charges on these chemicals.
2. Received 27 of the drums ordered above.
3. Paid freight charges of $108 for delivery of the 27 drums.
4. Returned two drums of chemicals to the supplier for full credit as defective merchandise; supplier agreed to reimburse Goodhue for freight costs on original shipment of these drums.
5. Paid the bill due to the supplier after deducting the amount paid for incoming freight charges on the two defective drums.
6. Bought 5,500 empty quart tins on credit at a total cost of $475, delivered and labeled.
7. Paid five temporary employees $40 each per day for two days' work to fill the tins with chemicals and put them on the shelves.
8. Returned 24 empty drums to the supplier for credit against the next purchase. The remaining drum had been lost from the pile at the rear of the store.
9. Sold 4,400 tins of chemicals on account at a price of 80 cents each.

a. Calculate the effects, if any, of each of these events on the company's assets, liabilities, and owners' equity.
b. Prepare journal entries, using suitable account titles, to reflect your analyses in (a).

9. Transactions analysis; use of idle time. The Central Department Store purchased a large quantity of unfinished and unassembled wooden kitchen cabinets at a bankruptcy sale with the intention of retailing these units "as is" at a very low price. The management soon discovered, however, that the units were too complicated for the average householder to assemble without great difficulty. The company then decided to assemble and finish the cabinets and offer them at a price sufficiently above that originally intended to cover the costs of these operations. The following transactions took place:

1. Purchase of 2,100 unassembled units for cash at $10 each.
2. Sale of 100 unassembled units on credit at a unit price of $16.
3. Payment of one month's wages to employees for assembling and finishing the remaining 2,000 units: four carpenters at $900 each and six painters at $750 each.
4. Payment of one month's wages to two regularly employed warehouse workers who acted as material handlers, $660 each. Because this activity occurred during a slack period, this actually entailed no extra cost to the company. For the same reason, adequate work space was available in the company's warehouse.
5. Purchase of paint and other supplies on credit, $900. When the operation was finished, supplies estimated to have cost $60 remained on hand. These could all be used in the company's normal maintenance operations.

a. Analyze these transactions in debit and credit form.
b. In line with the company's original objective of increasing the retail price just enough to cover assembly and finishing costs, what would you set as the new selling price? Support your conclusion.
c. Assuming that the company has set the price at the figure you selected in (b), prepare all of the journal entries that would be necessary to record the changes in the assets, liabilities, and owners' equity resulting from a credit sale of 200 finished cabinets.

10. Forecasting the cost of goods sold. The Velting Corporation manufactures and sells only one product. Management estimates that the company will sell 200,000 units of this product next year. You have been asked to estimate the cost of goods sold at this volume, based on the following information:

1. Each unit of the product requires approximately four pounds of material A and 0.1 pounds of material B.
2. The company has no inventory of material A, which is highly perishable and is delivered to the factory daily in quantities sufficient for the day's production. Purchase prices during the coming year are expected to average 60 cents a pound.
3. The company will have 25,000 pounds of material B on hand at the beginning of the year and will buy no more until this stock has been exhausted. The material now in stock was purchased at a cost of $4 a pound. The market price of material B is now $4.50 a pound and is expected to hold constant at that level throughout the coming year.
4. It is estimated that two hours of direct labor at $8 an hour will be required to produce each finished unit.

5. Annual depreciation on factory buildings and equipment will be $136,000.
6. Other factory costs are expected to total $40,000 plus an additional $2,000 for every 10,000 units finished.
7. Production is of such a nature that there will be no opening or closing inventories of goods in process.
8. The company will have 20,000 units of finished products in inventory at the beginning of the year, at a cost of $19 each.
9. A partially completed inventory study by an operations research team leads you to feel that the final inventory at the close of the year should consist of 40,000 finished units.
10. Due to a design change, the units produced during the year will be slightly different from those in stock at the beginning of the year. For this reason, the units in the opening inventory will be sold before any units produced during the coming year are placed on sale.

You have decided to perform the calculations in the sequence listed below. To help management understand these calculations, identify the steps you take and label each figure clearly.

a. Calculate the number of finished units to be produced next year.
b. Calculate the estimated cost of the raw materials to be used for the desired production.
c. Calculate the estimated cost of goods to be manufactured next year.
d. Calculate the estimated cost of goods to be sold next year.
e. Calculate the estimated cost of all materials and finished goods that will remain in inventory at the end of the coming year.

11. Journal entries; net income; cash-flow statement. The Poirot Manufacturing Company has a very simple accounting system. It uses only 19 accounts, which had the following balances at the start of business on September 1, 19x1, the start of the company's fiscal year:

Cash	$ 20,000	
Accounts receivable	95,000	
Materials inventory	62,000	
Factory overhead	—	
Work in process	28,000	
Finished goods inventory	122,000	
Machinery and equipment	100,000	
Accumulated depreciation		$ 32,000
Accounts payable		38,000
Wages and salaries payable		—
Dividends payable		—
Notes payable		—
Capital stock		200,000
Retained earnings		157,000
Sales revenues		—
Cost of goods sold	—	
Selling and administrative expenses	—	
Nonoperating gains and losses	—	
Dividends declared	—	

The company completed the following transactions during the month of September:

1. Materials purchased on account and placed in the storeroom, $34,000.
2. Materials issued to factory production departments: direct materials, $32,500; indirect materials, $3,500.
3. Wages and salaries accrued: factory direct labor, $14,000; factory indirect labor, $6,000; selling and administrative salaries, $4,000.
4. Depreciation: factory machinery, $500; administrative office equipment, $300.
5. Costs of other goods and services acquired on account and used immediately: manufacturing, $8,000; selling and administrative, $3,800.
6. Factory overhead costs applied to work in process, $18,000.
7. Products completed and transferred to finished goods inventories, $62,000.
8. Sales on account, $78,000.
9. The balance in the Finished Goods Inventory account was $1,000 greater on September 30 than on September 1, after all appropriate entries for September were recorded.
10. Cash dividends declared, $20,000.
11. Collections from customers on account, $65,000.
12. Cash payments: to employees, $23,700; to suppliers on account, $69,600; to shareowners (dividends), $20,000.
13. Borrowed from bank on September 30, $5,000.
14. Cost of factory equipment purchased on account and installed on September 30, $30,000.
15. Equipment sold for cash, $500. This equipment had an original cost of $9,000 and accumulated depreciation of $7,000.
16. Additional shares of capital stock issued in exchange for $50,000 cash.

a. Prepare journal entries to record these transactions, using only the 19 account titles listed above.
b. Calculate net income for the month of September. Ignore income taxes.
c. Calculate the amount of cash flow from operations during the month and prepare a statement of cash flows. For this purpose you should assume that the equipment purchased during the month was paid for in cash a few days later.

12. Transactions analysis; financial statements. On February 1, 19x1, the Paltry Corporation's accounts showed the following balances (all accounts not shown had zero balances):

Cash	9,200	
Accounts receivable	13,000	
Raw materials	3,500	
Work in process	5,000	
Finished goods	6,200	
Prepaid insurance	1,000	
Plant and equipment	62,000	
Allowance for depreciation		22,000
Accounts payable		13,900
Capital stock		34,000
Retained earnings		30,000

The following transactions took place during February:

1. Purchased raw materials on account, $42,000.
2. Issued raw materials to factory for use on month's production: direct materials, $35,000; indirect materials, $3,500.
3. Sold merchandise: for cash, $10,000; on credit, $90,000.
4. Collected $93,000 on accounts receivable.
5. Paid rent on office equipment for February, March, and April, $900.
6. Purchased factory equipment on account, $9,000.
7. Purchased office furniture on account, $1,000.
8. Accrued employees' wages and salaries for the month: factory direct labor, $16,000; factory indirect labor, $4,000; office and sales force, $8,000.
9. Received invoices for various goods and services bought on account and used during the month: factory, $25,200; office and sales departments, $15,000.
10. Recognized depreciation for February: factory, $300; office, $100.
11. Paid sales representatives and executives: for travel and entertainment expenses during month, $2,000; as advances against March expenses, $1,050.
12. Paid employees (for wages and salaries), $27,300.
13. Paid suppliers on account, $75,200.
14. Sold a piece of factory equipment for $500 cash; its original cost was $3,000, and it had accumulated depreciation of $2,100 at the date of sale.
15. Noted expiration of insurance premiums: on office, $50; on factory, $250.
16. Applied factory overhead to jobs in process, $33,250.
17. Finished and transferred to warehouse goods costing $68,000.
18. Declared cash dividend to shareholders, $2,000, payable on March 15.
19. Counted inventories on February 28; cost of finished goods on hand was $5,800.

a. Prepare journal entries to record all of the above information.
b. Enter the February 1 account balances in T-accounts and post the journal entries to these accounts.
c. Prepare an income statement for February and a balance sheet as of February 28.

13. Transactions analysis; financial statements. On May 1, 19x1, the Deppe Company's accounts had the following balances (all accounts not listed had zero balances):

Cash	25,600	
Accounts receivable	11,800	
Materials and supplies	7,200	
Work in process	6,500	
Finished goods	12,900	
Prepaid insurance	1,200	
Plant and equipment	156,000	
Accumulated depreciation		76,000
Accounts payable		15,400
Capital stock		80,000
Retained earnings		49,800

The following transactions took place during May:

1. Materials and supplies purchased on account, $30,300.
2. Wages and salaries earned by employees during month: factory direct labor, $27,000; factory indirect labor, $2,700; factory supervision, $4,900; sales and office salaries, $23,400. (Note: Cash payments occasioned by employee payrolls are described in item [14] below.)
3. Direct materials put into production, $18,800.
4. Equipment purchased on contract, $10,000, payments to be made in four quarterly installments of $2,500 each.
5. Goods sold on account for $110,000.
6. Supplies issued from storeroom and used: factory, $3,200; office, $2,700.
7. Costs of miscellaneous goods and services bought on account and used during May:
   Office rental, $2,300.
   Repairs of factory equipment, $600.
   Electricity and other utilities: factory, $3,600; office, $500.
   Newspaper advertising, $300.
   Other: factory, $11,860; office, $13,740.
8. Invoice received for taxes on factory, May 1 through October 31, 19x1, $1,200.
9. Insurance premiums expired: factory, $200; office, $100.
10. Depreciation: factory, $800; office, $160.
11. Factory overhead applied to work in process, $28,060.
12. Collections from customers, $106,000.
13. Sale of capital stock for cash, $10,000.
14. Payments made:
    To suppliers of materials and other goods and services, on account, $61,260.
    To equipment manufacturer, on contract (see [4] above), $2,500.
    To employees, $57,740.
    To collector of taxes, on factory, $1,200.
15. Equipment sold, $300 cash (original cost, $5,000; book value, $800).
16. Dividends declared, $3,000, to be paid on June 15.
17. Work in process, May 31, $16,160.
18. Finished goods on hand, May 31, $11,800.

a. Prepare journal entries to record all of the above information in accrual-basis accounts. You will need to open accounts in addition to those listed at the beginning of this problem.
b. Set up T-accounts, enter the May 1 account balances, and post your journal entries to these accounts.
c. Prepare an income statement for May and a balance sheet as of May 31. Ignore any income taxes that might be levied on the Deppe Company's income for the month.

14. Cash flows in growth company.   John Q. Wixon, sole owner and chief executive of the Wixon Widget Company, operated a very simple business. He made widgets at a cost of 80 cents each and sold them for $1. He had no other expenses, and the Wixon Widget Company's income therefore amounted to 20 cents for each widget he sold.

All production costs were paid in cash; suppliers in this industry were unwilling to provide credit to their customers. Mr. Wixon tried to keep his inventory at the end of each month equal to the number of units sold during that month. Inventory turnover, therefore, was 12 times a year when sales were constant; this was better than any of Mr. Wixon's competitors had been able to achieve.

All sales were made on 30-day credit—that is, customers were required to pay cash one month after receiving their widgets. These terms were strictly enforced, even though Mr. Wixon's competitors granted more liberal terms.

The Wixon Widget Company had no liabilities on January 1, 19x1. It had the following assets on that date:

Cash	$1,075
Accounts receivable	1,000
Inventory	800

During January, Mr. Wixon produced 1,000 widgets, sold 1,000 widgets, and collected $1,000 in cash from his customers. The company's net income for January was $200 and its assets on January 31, 19x1, were:

Cash	$1,275
Accounts receivable	1,000
Inventory	800

In February, sales increased to 1,500 widgets (500 widgets more than in January). The company produced 2,000 widgets during the month and collected $1,000 from customers. Net income was $300.

Mr. Wixon sold 2,000 widgets in March, produced 2,500 widgets, and collected $1,500. The company's net income jumped to $400.

Sales continued to increase in April and seemed likely to continue to increase by 500 units a month indefinitely. In fact, the sales picture looked so good that Mr. Wixon went on vacation on April 20. On May 1 he received a telegram from home: "Return immediately. We're overdrawn at the bank." Returning to the office, he found that production, sales, and collections had gone according to plan but that the company's bank account was overdrawn by $225. Extremely puzzled, he rushed to the bank, asking for a loan and an explanation of what had gone wrong.

a. Prepare a table showing revenues, expenses, and net income for each month, January through December, assuming no further action is taken.
b. Prepare a table showing cash receipts, cash disbursements, and net cash flow for each month.
c. Prepare a list of the firm's assets as of the end of each month. (The firm had no liabilities at the beginning of the year. If your figures indicate that cash disbursements will reduce the cash balance to less than zero, show the deficiency as a negative amount on the "Cash" line rather than as a liability. Ignore interest costs on any such amounts.)
d. Using the figures in the tables above, prepare an answer to Mr. Wixon's question. What were the factors that determined the size of the monthly cash flows?
e. What actions could Mr. Wixon take to solve the problem that had arisen? (Suggestion: examine the effects on cash flows of actions that might be taken to influence each of the factors that you have identified as a determinant of cash flow.)

7

Measuring and Reporting Economic Values

ASSETS, as we pointed out in Chapter 1, are objects, claims, and other rights owned by and having value to a specific organization. In deciding whether an object, claim, or other right is an asset, therefore, we must ask whether it has value. And to answer that question, we must know what we mean by value.

This chapter has two objectives: (1) to explain the concept of value as it relates to accounting and (2) to see why company financial statements list most assets at their costs rather than at their values.

THE VALUE OF AN ASSET

An organization's assets are valuable because it can use them to benefit the organization in the future. Some business assets produce benefits as they are sold to outside customers (bottled soft drinks, for example). Others (bottling machines, for instance) are valuable because they can be used to produce other assets that can be sold to outsiders. Still others generate benefits by reducing the cost of the company's operations or by helping management do a better job of managing the business (electronic computers are examples here). In this section we'll see what form these benefits take and how estimates of benefits can be translated into estimates of values.

Benefits Measured by Cash Flows

An asset's benefits to a business firm take the form of net cash inflows—that is, they increase the amount of cash the firm can use to buy other assets or distribute to lenders and the owners. Cash is the only asset that can always be used for these purposes.

One possibility, therefore, would be to measure the value of an asset by adding up all the additional cash flows it is expected to generate while it is in the company's control. Unfortunately, this total wouldn't mean much in many cases. For many assets, the benefits come in installments, some now, some next year, and some five, ten, or even more years in the future. Spreading the cash flows out in this way affects the asset's value. To see why this is so, we need to study two possible measures of value: (1) future value and (2) present value.

Future Value

The future value of a sum of cash is the amount to which that sum will grow if it is invested at a specified interest rate for a specified period of time. Suppose, for example, that a bank will pay $1,050 one year from now in return for a $1,000 deposit today. We say that this bank is paying interest at the rate of 5 percent a year. This relationship can be expressed mathematically in the following expression:

$$F_1 = P(1 + r) \qquad (1)$$

in which P = the present outlay or deposit in the bank, r = the rate of interest, and F_1 = future value. If p = $1,000 and r = 0.05, then F_1 = $1,050.

Continuing the example, if the $1,050 is left in the bank for a second year, it will build up by the end of the two years to a balance of $1,050 + ($1,050 × 0.05) = $1,102.50. Interest in this second year amounts to $52.50 and is greater than the first year's interest because the bank is now paying interest not only on the original investment but also on the interest earned during the first year. The mathematical formula for computing the future value of a present sum two years later is:

$$F_2 = F_1(1 + r) = P(1 + r)(1 + r) = P(1 + r)^2 \qquad (2)$$

If r = 0.05, $(1 + r)^2$ will be 1.1025 and the future value of $1,000 now will be $1,012.50.

Extending these calculations beyond two years reveals the relationships shown graphically in Exhibit 7–1. Starting with $1,000, the depositor's account will build at 5 percent to $1,050 in one year, $1,102.50 in two years, and so on, up to $2,653.30 at the end of 20 years.

This form of interest calculation, in which interest is earned on previously earned interest, is known as *compounding*. In this case interest has been compounded annually, meaning that interest is

EXHIBIT 7–1.   Future Values Equivalent to a Present Value of $1,000 (annual compounding at 5 percent a year)

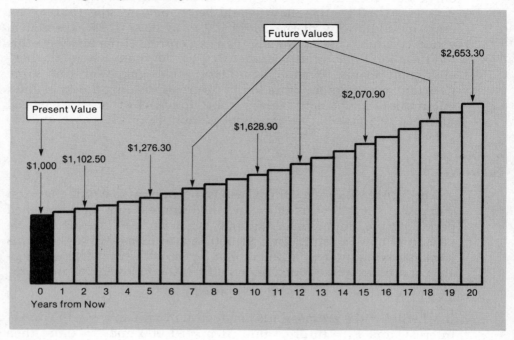

added to the bank balance only once a year. In general, it can be shown that if an amount P is put out at interest of r percent a year, compounded annually, at the end of n years it will have grown to a future value (F_n) of the following amount:

$$F_n = P(1 + r)^n \qquad (3)$$

Present Value

This relationship can also be inverted to focus attention on the *present value* of a future amount. The present value of a future sum of cash is the amount which, if invested now at compound interest at the specified rate, will grow to an amount equal to the future sum at the specified future date. Present value and future value, in other words, are just two ends of the same relationship. Since all of the bars in Exhibit 7–1 are future values of $1,000, it follows that each of them has the same present value, $1,000. An investor who considers 5 percent annual compound interest as a satisfactory return on money should regard each of these amounts as fully equivalent to each of the others.

We can draw a fundamental conclusion from this: *the longer we have to wait for our money, the more we'll have to receive to give us a specified present value.* If we only have to wait two years, $1,102.50 will give us a $1,000 present value. If we have to wait 20 years, however, we'll have to ask for $2,653.30 if we want to have the same present value.

The formula for computing present value from known or estimated future values can be found by turning equation (3) around. Since $F_n = P(1 + r)^n$, then

$$P = \frac{F_n}{(1 + r)^n} \tag{4}$$

This shows that the present value of any future sum can be determined by multiplying the latter by $(1 + r)^{-n}$ or by dividing it by $(1 + r)^n$. If n is two years, r is 5 percent, and an asset is expected to yield a cash inflow of $1,000 two years from now, then the present value of this asset today is:

$$P = \$1,000/(1.05)^2 = \$1,000/1.1025 = \$907.03.$$

In other words, $907.03 will grow to $1,000 in two years if it is invested now at 5 percent interest, compounded annually; it is therefore the present value of that future amount.

Suppose, however, the $1,000 won't be received until five years from now. The present value of this $1,000 is:

$$P = \$1,000/(1.05)^5 = \$1,000/1.2763 = \$783.51.$$

That is, we'll have to invest only $783.51 now if the $1,000 cash receipt won't come in until five years from now. Again we have a fundamental conclusion: dollars available in the near future are worth more than the same number of dollars in the more distant future. The sooner the cash is available, the sooner it can be invested to earn more cash; this makes it more valuable.

The process of finding the present value of a future amount is known as *discounting*. In our illustration we discounted $1,000 to be received two years from now by dividing it by 1.1025. The more common technique is to multiply it by the reciprocal of this figure: $1/1.1025 = 0.90703$. The end result is the same, but multiplication is usually easier than division.

The Value of a Series of Cash Receipts

While some assets derive all of their value from the expectation of a single cash receipt, the value of others is based on not one but a series of future cash receipts. The value of an asset of this kind is the sum of the values of the various cash flows.

EXHIBIT 7–2.   Value of a Series of Cash Flows

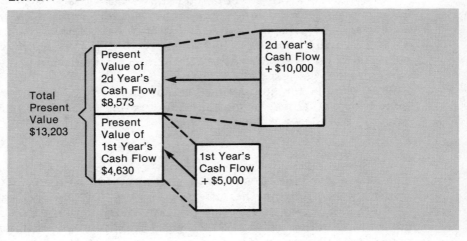

This idea is illustrated in Exhibit 7–2. The two blocks at the right represent two cash sums a company expects to receive from a creditor. The first of these, $5,000, will come in a year from now; the other, $10,000 in amount, will be received two years from now. The two blocks joined together in the left-hand side of the diagram are the present values of these two cash flows, calculated on the basis of an 8 percent interest rate. Since the company's ownership of this asset gives it the right to receive both of these future amounts, the value of the asset must be the sum of the values of the two amounts.

The calculations behind this exhibit are quite simple. Since $1 now is equivalent to $1.08 a year from now, the present value of the first $5,000 can be derived by substituting these figures in equation (4):

$$\text{Present value} = \$5,000 \times \frac{1}{1.08} = \$4,630.$$

Similarly, the present value of $10,000 to be received two years from now can be calculated by dividing $10,000 by $(1.08)^2$, or 1.1664. The results of these calculations are summarized in the following table:

(1) Years from Now	(2) Cash Receipt	(3) Multiplier	(4) Present Value at 8% (2) × (3)
1......................	$ 5,000	1/1.0800 = .9259	$ 4,630
2......................	10,000	1/1.1664 = .8573	8,573
Total			$13,203

The multipliers in column (3) are generally known as *discount factors* because they are used to discount future sums to their present values.

Varying the Discount Rate

As this example shows, the value of an asset depends on three factors: the amounts of the future cash flows, their timing, and the interest rate used to discount them. If we hold the first two of these constant while varying the third, we find that the greater the interest rate the smaller the value.

The reason is simple. Present value is the amount which, if invested at the specified rate of interest, will produce the expected future cash flows. If the rate of interest is increased, the future cash flows will have to be greater to produce the required interest. If the cash flows don't increase, the investment will have to be smaller if it is to yield the higher interest rate.

For example, an investment of $13,203 now will produce future cash flows of $5,000 one year from now and $10,000 two years from now. These cash flows are big enough to yield an 8 percent rate of return on the $13,203 investment. We can prove this by calculating interest at 8 percent, deducting this amount from the cash flow, and using the amount left over to pay off part of the debt to the lender. If the final payment is just big enough to pay interest at 8 percent and pay off the lender, then we know the investment produces an 8 percent rate of return.

The amount invested in the first year is $13,203. A year's interest on this amount at 8 percent is .08 × $13,203 = $1,056. This means that the remaining $3,944 of the first year's $5,000 cash receipt is available to repay part of the initial investment. This leaves $13,203 − $3,944 = $9,259 still invested at the start of the second year. Interest in the second year is 8 percent of this, or $741, leaving $10,000 − $741 = $9,259 of the second year's cash receipt to repay the remainder of the original investment. At that point the entire investment has been repaid and the investor has received interest at the rate of 8 percent on the amounts invested. These calculations are summarized in the following table:

Year	(1) Amount Invested, Beginning of Year	(2) Interest (1) × 8%	(3) Amount Available to Repay Investors Cash Flow − (2)	(4) Amount Invested, End of Year (1) − (3)
1	$13,203	$1,056	$3,944	$9,259
2	9,259	741	9,259	0

Suppose the interest rate is 10 percent, however. Now the cash flows aren't large enough to support an investment of $13,203. This is shown in the following table:

Year	(1) Amount Invested, Beginning of Year	(2) Interest (1) × 10%	(3) Amount Available to Repay Investors Cash Flow − (2)	(4) Amount Invested, End of year (1) − (3)
1	$13,203	$1,320	$3,670	$9,533
2	9,533	953	9,047	486

As this shows, $486 of the original investment would remain unrecovered at the end of the second year. The asset must be worth less than $13,203 because it isn't good enough to return 10 percent, the rate the investors expect.

Interest Tables

The calculation of multipliers (for example, $1/1.1664 = .8573$) is time consuming. Fortunately, we don't have to make these calculations by hand. We can use an electronic computer, if we have one, or a calculator containing a present-value program. If we don't have ready access to either of these, we can consult published interest tables which contain the values of $(1 + r)^{-n}$ for all important values of r and n.

Although the remainder of this chapter can be read and understood without the aid of computers or interest tables, something of this sort must be used to solve the problems and exercises at the end of the chapter. To meet this need, we have provided an abbreviated set of interest tables in Appendix A at the end of the book, together with instructions for using them.

CALCULATING PRESENT VALUE

1. Estimate the amount of each future cash flow and the date or period when it will take place.
2. Enter these amounts in a cash-flow timetable.
3. Choose an appropriate discount rate.
4. Identify the discount factor at this rate for each amount in the timetable and enter these factors in the next column of the timetable.
5. Multiply each cash-flow amount by the appropriate discount factor and enter these amounts in the last column of the timetable.
6. Add the amounts in the last column to obtain the asset's total present value.

FINANCIAL STATEMENTS BASED ON PRESENT VALUE

The concept of present value provides us with a possible alternative basis for financial reporting: the balance sheet might reflect the present values of the company's estimated future cash flows, and the income statement might report the changes occurring in present value during the year.

To examine this alternative, we need to answer four questions:

1. What determines the value of a going concern?
2. What accounts for the difference between present value and the total reported net tangible assets?
3. What would appear on a present value-based balance sheet?
4. How would income be measured on a present value basis?

Valuation of a Going Concern

Value-based financial statements can be understood best if they are developed for a company some investor is thinking of buying as a "going concern"—that is, buying in its entirety. Precision Instrument Company was in this position in 19x8. The company had been formed in 19x0 by four young people to market a simple but revolutionary measuring instrument one of them had invented. The company prospered, and by 19x7, sales had grown to $1.4 million, and net income amounted to $114,000 a year.

The company's latest balance sheet, shown in Exhibit 7–3, listed a total owners' equity of $280,000. Annual earnings therefore represented an after-tax rate of return of $114,000/$280,000 = 40.7 percent of the reported owners' equity. This high return was due mainly to the increasing value of the company's patents and the scientific and managerial skill of the company's officers.

Early in 19x8, the Walden Corporation offered to buy all the shares of Precision Instrument Company at what seemed like a good price. Precision's four owners asked for a few weeks to consider the offer and make their own appraisal of the company's value. As they saw it, they had established a small but solid position in the industry. They served a portion of the market their larger competitors were poorly equipped to handle, and their relationships with their customers were very good. They had no doubt they would be able to maintain this position, but they felt that the potential for further growth was very small. They drew good salaries, but they would continue to earn as much if they sold out to Walden.

Calculating the present value of ten-year ownership. At this point the owners decided to calculate value two ways. First, they made what they thought was a conservative estimate: if they didn't sell in

EXHIBIT 7–3

PRECISION INSTRUMENT COMPANY
Statement of Financial Position
December 31, 19x7

Assets

Current Assets:

Cash	$ 25,000
Receivables	160,000
Inventories	120,000
Current Assets	$305,000
Equipment	80,000
Total Assets	$385,000

Liabilities and Owners' Equity

Current Liabilities:

Taxes payable	$ 15,000
Accounts payable	90,000
Current Liabilities	$105,000
Owners' equity	280,000
Total Liabilities and Owners' Equity	$385,000

19x8 they would hold their shares for ten years and then sell them, at an estimated price of $400,000. They also estimated that Precision's net income would be approximately $114,000 a year for the next ten years. Equipment replacement expenditures would be just about equal to the annual depreciation charges, and working capital requirements wouldn't change.

If these assumptions were valid, the annual cash flow would equal the annual net income, $114,000, and the cash flows from continued ownership would be as follows:

Year	Receipts
1 to 10	$114,000 a year
10	400,000

The next step was to calculate the present value of these cash flows. Precision's owners estimated that 12 percent after taxes was a satisfactory return on investment for the type of business in which Precision was engaged. The question was how much the anticipated cash flows were worth at this rate.[1]

---

[1] An alternative approach favored by many scholars is to adjust each year's anticipated cash flow downward to allow for the risk that the actual cash flow will be smaller than the anticipated amount. These adjusted cash flows are then discounted at the rate of interest on a "risk-free" investment, presumably in government securities. The approach described here is simpler and fully adequate for our purposes.

Present value can be calculated quite simply with the aid of figures from Appendix A. Because the cash flows were expected to be constant throughout the ten-year period, Table 4 can be used. The multiplier for ten equal annual receipts, discounted at the desired earnings rate of 12 percent, is 5.650. The $400,000 figure, in contrast, is a single lump-sum receipt, and Table 3 must be used. The multiplier for a receipt at the end of ten years is 0.322.

The calculation of present value can now be summarized as follows:

Year	Receipts	Multiplier	Present Value
1 to 10	$114,000 a year	5.650	$644,100
10	400,000	0.322	128,800
Total Present Value			$772,900

In other words, if these assumptions were right, the owners should have accepted nothing less than $772,900 for their shares of the capital stock of Precision Instrument Company.

Calculating present value with constant resale value. Precision's owners' second estimate was based on a more optimistic view of the future. They saw no reason why the market value of their shares should decrease as long as they kept the research and marketing staffs on their toes and continued to sell high-quality products of modern design and usefulness.

Letting P stand for the present value of the future cash flows, then, they made the following calculations:

Year	Receipts	Multiplier	Present Value
1 to 10	+$114,000 a year	5.650	$644,100
10	+P	.322	.322P

They then calculated the estimated value of their shares by solving the following equation:

$$P = \$644,100 + .322P$$

$$P = \$644,100/.678 = \$950,000$$

This same figure can be obtained by applying a widely used *capitalization formula* to the anticipated annual cash flows. A capitalization formula is an equation used to determine the amount of capital a given set of cash flows will support. The simplest of these capitalization formulas is:

$$\text{Present Value} = \frac{\text{Average Annual Cash Flow}}{\text{Rate of Return}}$$

Applying this formula to Precision Instrument, we get the following:

$$\text{Present Value} = \frac{\$114,000}{.12} = \$950,000.$$

This capitalization formula is based on two interrelated assumptions:

1. Annual expenditures to modernize or replace existing assets will be enough to maintain the value of the rights to future net cash flows at a constant level forever, and, therefore, the entire net cash flow can be distributed as dividends.
2. The owners can sell their rights at any time for an amount equal to their present value.

These assumptions state that investors can buy Precision Instrument today for $950,000 and sell it at any time in the future for the same amount. None of the $114,000 of annual cash flows will be offset by a reduction in the value of the investment; in other words, the entire $114,000 is income to the investors. Their rate of return is:

$$\text{Rate of Return} = \frac{\text{Annual Cash Flow}}{\text{Investment}} = \frac{\$114,000}{\$950,000} = 12\%$$

The capitalization formula is simply this rate of return formula with the amount of the investment rather than the rate of return as the unknown quantity.

Goodwill and Other Intangible Assets

The net tangible assets reported on Precision Instrument's balance sheet amounted to $280,000, calculated as follows:

Net Tangible Assets		Total Tangible Assets		Total Liabilities
$280,000	=	$385,000	−	$105,000

The estimated value of Precision Instrument's shares to their owners was much greater than this, $950,000. The $670,000 difference between these two figures arose because Precision Instrument had *intangible assets*. An intangible asset is any attribute enabling a business to generate more cash flows and, therefore, more income than the business's tangible assets would normally be expected to generate.

For example, if 12 percent was regarded as the normal rate of return on investments in the markets Precision Instrument was serving, then the normal income on the $280,000 of net tangible assets was:

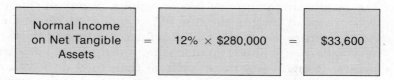

Normal Income on Net Tangible Assets = 12% × $280,000 = $33,600

Since the company expected to have total income of $114,000 a year from all sources, its expected income from its intangible assets must have been $114,000 − $33,600 = $80,400. Using the capitalization formula, we find that this is enough to provide the required interest on an investment of $80,400/.12 = $670,000, the amount we ascribed to the company's intangible assets in the first place.

A company's intangible assets sometimes can be given specific names. For example, the company's high earning power may be clearly ascribable to ownership of a well-known trademark or a particularly valuable patent. Most of the time, however, high earning power is the *joint* result of many factors, such as superior product design, marketing and managerial skills, and a reputation for providing prompt, careful attention to customers' needs. In these cases, we generally use a single term, *goodwill*, to describe the entire package of intangible assets. Goodwill is the set of attributes which gives an ongoing business enterprise a total value in excess of the amounts ascribed specifically to other assets.

Goodwill can be measured in various ways. One way is to subtract the *book value* of the net tangible assets from the total present value of the entire organization:

Goodwill = Present Value of Future Cash Flows − Book Value of Net Tangible Assets

Another measure of goodwill is the difference between present value and the *appraised value* of the net tangible assets:

$$\text{Goodwill} = \frac{\text{Present Value}}{\text{of Future Cash Flows}} - \frac{\text{Appraised Value}}{\text{of Net Tangible Assets}}$$

For this purpose, the appraised value of an asset is an expert's estimate of the amount the company would have to pay to acquire a comparable asset in an arm's-length market transaction under current conditions.[2]

In estimating the goodwill of a company to be acquired, the purchasing company should measure the tangible assets at their appraised values rather than at their book values. The reason is that the purchasing company has an option of buying the entire going concern or of buying the tangible assets (and separable intangible assets) separately. If it buys the going concern, and if the concern has no goodwill, it will pay no more than the appraised value of the other assets. It might pay more (or less) than total book value, however, because book values reflect transactions that took place in the past, when conditions were very different from those of today. The fact that a company bought land 50 years ago for $1 an acre is irrelevant—if it buys land as part of a package today, it is paying current prices for the land, not the prices of 50 years ago.

In our illustration, both Walden's management and Precision's owners agreed that the amounts shown for inventories and equipment were reasonably close to their current appraised values. Any value in excess of the reported net assets, therefore, had to be ascribed to the intangibles.

Companies list intangible assets on their balance sheets only if they have bought them from outsiders. A company buying a patent or a trademark or a copyright, for example, would list it as an asset, measured at its cost. Even goodwill may be listed if the company has bought it—that is, if it has bought an ongoing business at a price greater than the current appraised value of its net tangible assets.

Most intangible assets are built, not bought, however. The typical company builds its goodwill gradually by patient and skillful development of its organization, its product lines, and its markets. The accountants classify the costs of the activities producing this result as expenses as they take place. No portion of the current marketing cost, for example, is treated as the cost of acquiring an intangible asset. As a result, intangible assets acquired in this way don't appear on conventional balance sheets. To identify them, we must make calculations like those Precision Instrument's owners made in 19x8.

---

[2] Appraisals can also measure the estimated selling prices of the company's assets. We don't use appraisals of this sort in these calculations because our calculations assume that the company is a *going concern,* one that will continue to use its assets rather than sell them.

A Balance Sheet Based on Present Value

Having estimated the value of the company as a whole and the appraised value of its individual tangible assets, management was able to prepare a value-based statement of financial position. The statement for Precision Instrument Company as of December 31, 19x7, is presented in Exhibit 7–4.

EXHIBIT 7–4

PRECISION INSTRUMENT COMPANY
Adjusted Statement of Financial Position
December 31, 19x7

Assets

Current Assets:
Cash	$ 25,000
Receivables	160,000
Inventories	120,000
Current Assets	$ 305,000
Equipment	80,000
Tangible Assets	$ 385,000
Goodwill	670,000
Total Assets	$1,055,000

Liabilities and Owners' Equity

Current Liabilities:
Taxes payable	$ 15,000
Accounts payable	90,000
Current Liabilities	$ 105,000
Owners' equity	950,000
Total Liabilities and Owners' Equity	$1,055,000

Statements of this kind differ from conventional cost-based statements in three ways. First, assets that are usually measured on a cost basis are reported, instead, at their appraised values. For Precision Instrument, cost and appraised value were identical, but in the usual situation, differences are likely to be significant. Second, liabilities are also shown at their appraised values, the amounts lenders would be willing to give the company in the current market in exchange for the company's present notes payable and other debt instruments. We'll discuss liability measurement in some detail in Chapter 13; for the moment, we have to simplify, and the balance sheet in Exhibit 7–4 reflects the assumption that the conventionally measured liability figures were a good approximation to appraised value on December 31, 19x7. Finally, the assets include an estimate of the value of goodwill. In this case the amount attributed to goodwill was almost two thirds of the total value of all the assets combined.

Income Measurement on a Present-Value Basis

Income statements also can be constructed on a present-value basis. A proponent of measuring income in this way would say that the owners' income from their ownership of a business has two components:

1. The cash dividends they receive during the period.
2. The increase or decrease in the value of their ownership rights between the beginning and the end of the period.

If we measure the value of the ownership rights by the present value of the future cash flows they will generate, then we'll measure income by the method diagrammed in Exhibit 7–5. If the value is the

EXHIBIT 7–5.   Income on a Present-Value Basis

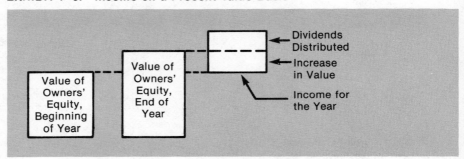

same at the end of the year as it was at the beginning, then income is equal to the amount of the dividend distributed. If value decreases, however, then the dividend must be regarded to that extent as a repayment of the owners' investment in the company, not as income. Income, in other words, is the amount the company could distribute to its owners without decreasing the present value of the business to them.

To illustrate, suppose that during 19x8 Precision Instrument Company developed a new device which permitted greater automation of a wide variety of chemical processes. New orders increased rapidly in the final quarter of 19x8, and earnings in 19x9 and later years were expected to amount to $144,000. This amount of cash would be paid out to the owners each year because further growth of the company would not be feasible. Using the same capitalization rate and the same assumptions as in the previous example, the value of the enterprise at the end of 19x8 would be:

$$\frac{\$144,000}{0.12} = \$1,200,000.$$

This represents an increase of $250,000 over the comparable beginning-of-year figure. The shareholders were that much better off as a result of the events of 19x8; this amount would be recognized as income in an income statement based on present value. In addition, the owners' wealth increased as a result of the dividends distributed to them in 19x8 ($114,000), and this amount is also income attributable to their ownership of the business in 19x8. Income, in other words, would be calculated as follows:

Net assets at end of year:	
Present value of net future payments to owners	$1,200,000
Net assets at start of year:	
Present value of net future payments to owners	950,000
Net increase in value	$ 250,000
Add back: Owners' cash withdrawals during the year	114,000
Value-Based Income	$ 364,000

The easiest way to embody these figures in an income statement is to reproduce the conventional income statement, with a balancing figure at the bottom to bring the net income into agreement with the calculated amount. The upper part of Exhibit 7–6, for example, con-

EXHIBIT 7–6

PRECISION INSTRUMENT COMPANY
Adjusted Income Statement
For the Year Ended December 31, 19x8

Sales revenues		$1,400,000
Cost of goods sold		840,000
Gross margin		$ 560,000
Less: Operating expenses	$334,000	
Income taxes.......................................	112,000	446,000
Realized net income		$ 114,000
Unrealized increase in the present value of future cash flows ..		250,000
Net Value Change		$ 364,000

sists of Precision Instrument's conventional income statement. Net income calculated on this basis is labeled *realized net income*. The remainder of the change in present value was "unrealized," and is shown separately on the next line.

Market Value of the Going Concern

The financial statements in this section have reflected the notion that the total value of a going concern is measured by the present value of the concern's future cash flows. An alternative is to use the amount the business could be sold for on the open market—that is, its *market value*. Goodwill would be measured as follows:

$$\text{Goodwill} = \begin{array}{c}\text{Market Value}\\\text{of the Firm}\end{array} - \begin{array}{c}\text{Appraised Value}\\\text{of the Net}\\\text{Tangible Assets}\end{array}$$

For example, suppose the directors of Walden Corporation offered $800,000 for Precision Instrument's shares on December 31, 19x7. Using this figure, we find that Walden's implicit valuation of Precision's goodwill was $520,000, calculated as follows:

$$\text{Goodwill} = \$800,000 - (\$385,000 - \$105,000) = \$520,000$$

The appraised value of the net tangible assets in this case was $385,000 − $105,000 = $280,000, the difference between the appraised value of the tangible assets and the appraised value of the liabilities.

Precision's management rejected the offer and operated the company for another year, as we described earlier. It declared and paid cash dividends of $114,000 during the year, and, at the end of the year, Walden made another offer, this time for $1,250,000. Net tangible assets again amounted to $280,000 at the end of the year. The goodwill valuation implicit in Walden's new offer therefore was $1,250,000 − $280,000 = $970,000.

The firm's income on a market-value basis is measured by the change in its market value plus the amount of dividends distributed during the year. In this case, the calculation is:

$$\text{Net Income} = (\$1,250,000 - \$800,000) + \$114,000 = \$564,000$$

This is a much larger figure than the one we calculated earlier, using present-value estimates, but it could have gone the other way. What made it so large in this case is that, in the eyes of Precision's owners, Walden undervalued the firm in 19x7 and then recognized its mistake in 19x8, bringing in a new offer that reflected Precision's goodwill in full.

The Case against Present Value

Because present value is generally recognized as directly relevant to managerial and investor decisions, it probably would be used as a major element in financial reporting if measurement problems could be overcome. Two factors probably explain why it isn't used for this purpose.[3]

1. The cash-flow estimates in most cases can't be verified satisfactorily.
2. The appropriate discounting rate isn't known with certainty and varies from individual to individual.

The future cash flows of a business are highly uncertain. Accountants can verify management's past estimates of future cash flows to some extent, but their ability to verify current estimates is much more limited. Present-value financial statements, therefore, would summarize management's estimates of future cash flows. The most the accountants could do would be to test the assumptions on which management based its estimates, using available information on the economic and political climate.

The second obstacle to financial reporting on a present-value basis is that estimates of the appropriate rate at which the estimated future cash flows are to be discounted are far from precise and can't be verified adequately. Errors in these estimates have a very large effect on estimates of present value, as we can see if we use different interest rates in the capitalization formula applied to Precision Instrument Company's future cash flows:

Interest Rate	Present Value December 31, 19x7 (Based on $114,000 Annual Cash Flow)	Present Value December 31, 19x8 (Based on $144,000 Annual Cash Flow)	Income for 19x8 (Including $114,000 in Dividends)
6%	$1,900,000	$2,400,000	$614,000
8	1,425,000	1,800,000	489,000
12	**950,000**	**1,200,000**	**364,000**
15	760,000	960,000	314,000
20	570,000	720,000	264,000

The choice of the discount rate would also affect the relevance of the statements to individual investors. Some investors may wish to capitalize future cash flows at 8 percent, some may wish to use 12 percent, and others may prefer to adjust for perceived differences in the future cash flows by discounting different portions of the cash-flow stream at different discount rates. No matter what rate or set of rates is chosen, it won't meet everyone's needs.

---

[3] The present-value concept is used directly in the measurement of certain monetary assets and liabilities, as we shall see in some detail in Chapter 13.

Alternatives to Present-Value Reporting

Despite these problems, many accountants and financial analysts are convinced that some form of value-based reporting would be appropriate. Most of these authorities suggest that any information of this sort should be published as supplementary information, issued in addition to the financial statements based mainly on historical data.

One possibility for supplementary disclosure is to publish management's cash-flow forecasts, letting the readers make their adjustments and apply their own discount rates. This is done to a limited extent in Great Britain.

Another possibility is to present supplementary present value information for some assets only. U.S. oil and gas producing companies, for example, are now required to disclose the physical quantities of their proved underground reserves of oil and gas, and the Securities and Exchange Commission is asking for estimates of the present values of these reserves as well.[4]

We'll return in Chapter 11 to explore a number of other ways companies might include additional value-related information in their income statements and statements of financial position.

SUMMARY

The assets of a business firm are valuable to it insofar as they are expected to produce future cash flows, either through their use in the business or through selling them to outsiders. Cash flows expected to take place in the distant future are worth less than those expected to take place in the near future, however, mainly because cash received earlier can be reinvested sooner. Before estimates of cash flows can be added together, therefore, each one has to be discounted to its present value at an appropriate interest rate.

Conventional business balance sheets don't pretend to measure either the organization's market value or the present value of its future cash flows; income statements don't pretend to measure either the increase in market value or the increase in present value. The present-value concept is used directly only in the measurement of some monetary assets and liabilities and by management in evaluating proposals to invest the company's funds.

Suggestions have been made to attach forecasts of future cash flows to the historically based financial statements and to publish certain kinds of value information in addition to the conventional

---

[4] Financial Accounting Standards Board, "Statement No. 19," in American Institute of Certified Public Accountants, *Professional Standards—Accounting, Current Text* (New York: Commerce Clearing House, Inc., 1978), Section 6021; Securities and Exchange Commission, "Accounting Series Release No. 253," August 31, 1978.

statements. We'll return in Chapter 11 to look at some of the forms this additional disclosure might take.

KEY TERMS

Annuity	Future value
Capitalization formula	Goodwill
Compound interest	Intangible assets
Discount factors (multipliers)	Interest tables
Discount rate	Present value

INDEPENDENT STUDY PROBLEMS (Solutions in Appendix B)

1. Present-value exercises. Calculate the value on January 1, 1980, of assets that have the following cash flows, with interest at 12 percent compounded annually:

a. Outlay: $35,000 on January 1, 1980.
   Receipt: $100,000 on January 1, 1990.
b. Outlays: $80,000 on January 1, 1980, $20,000 on January 1, 1985.
   Receipts: $10,000 on each January 1, 1981 through 1986,
            $20,000 on each January 1, 1987 through 1996.
c. Outlays: $20,000 on each January 1, 1980 through 1990.
   Receipt: $250,000 on January 1, 1992.

2. Future-value exercises. For each of the three assets in Question 1, calculate the future value at 12 percent, compounded annually, as of the date of the final cash receipt. In each case check to make sure your answer is consistent with your answer to Question 1.

3. Calculating an equivalent annuity. The Future Company has just borrowed $1 million. Interest on this amount will be paid to the lender each year for ten years. In addition, the $1 million will have to be repaid to the lender at the end of ten years. How much will the Future Company have to deposit in the bank at the end of each of the next ten years to enable it to repay the $1 million at the end of the ten years if the bank compounds interest annually at a rate of 8 percent? An identical amount is to be deposited each year.

4. Calculating the annuity equivalent to a different annuity. You will need $4,000 a year for five years, starting exactly four years from today. You wish to purchase this annuity by making a series of seven annual payments of equal size. The first of these payments will be made immediately. Interest will accrue at a rate of 8 percent, compounded annually. Calculate the size of the annual payment.

5. Calculating the annuity equivalent to a given future value. Mr. Provident is 30 years old. He desires to have, at age 50, a savings fund of $100,000. He expects to earn 6 percent compounded annually on what he saves. How much must he set aside out of his earnings at the end of each year for the 20 years to accumulate his $100,000?

6. Calculating income on a present-value basis. William Appersham operates a ferry service across Deepwater Bay. A bridge is now being built across the bay. When it is completed two years from now, Mr. Appersham will close the ferry service and retire to his plantation in the Virgin Islands. He expects the following cash flows from the ferry operation:

Year	Cash Receipts	Cash Disbursements	Net Cash Receipts
1	$300,000	$200,000	$100,000
2	350,000	220,000	130,000

At the end of each year he will withdraw the year's net cash receipts and invest them in highway bonds where they will earn interest at an annual rate of 6 percent, compounded annually. In addition, at the end of year 2, he will be able to withdraw the $50,000 he now must maintain as a working cash fund to keep his ferry service going.

The sale value of his ferry boats two years from now will be virtually zero.

a. What is the present value of the ferry service to Mr. Appersham now?

b. Assuming that all forecasts are correct, what will be the present value of the assets of the ferry service a year from now, before Mr. Appersham withdraws the net cash receipts of the first year's operations?

c. Compute the net income of the ferry service for the first year on a present-value basis, assuming that all forecasts are correct.

d. Compute the ferry service's income for the second year on a present-value basis, again assuming that all forecasts are correct.

e. Mr. Appersham has just discovered that he can invest his available cash at 8 percent, compounded annually, instead of at 6 percent. How would this affect your analysis?

EXERCISES AND PROBLEMS

7. Valuation differences. The management of the Gupta Corporation has recently been cited by a national society of industrial engineers for its efficiency in organizing and controlling the company's affairs. The aggregate market value of the company's stock, based on the current market price per share, is $10 million; book value is only $4 million. Management's own forecast of future cash flows, discounted at an interest rate that seems appropriate for a company of its size and class, is $9 million.

The board of directors of the Marshall Company has just made a cash offer of $12 million for the outstanding stock in the Gupta Corporation. What might account for the premium valuation placed by Marshall on the Gupta Corporation?

8. Calculating present value without interest tables. Without using the interest tables, calculate the present value at 10 percent of a single sum of $100 to be received six years from now. Then verify your figure by using the appropriate table in Appendix A.

9. Present-value exercise. Using Table 4 in Appendix A, determine the present value of a series of payments of $100 a year for each of the next six years. Assume that the first payment is received one year from now and that the interest rate is 12 percent, compounded annually.

10. Present-value exercise. Check your answer to Question 9 by using Table 3.

11. Calculating present value. You are considering the purchase of six noninterest-bearing notes. Three of them have face values of $100 and will come due one each at the end of years 3, 4, and 5. The other three have face values of $150 and come due one each at the end of years 6, 7, and 8. If your interest rate is 15 percent, what will you be willing to pay for these now? (Use Table 3 in Appendix A.)

12. Verifying present-value calculation. Use Table 4 to solve Question 11. You should get the same answer.

13. Present-value exercises. Calculate the present value of each of the following at 10 percent, using the interest tables in Appendix A:

a. $100,000 to be received ten years from now. Interest is compounded annually.
b. $10,000 to be received at the end of each of the next ten years. Interest is compounded annually.
c. $5,000 to be received at the end of each of the next five years, plus $15,000 to be received at the end of each of the five years after that. Interest is compounded annually.
d. $15,000 to be received at the end of each of the next five years, plus $5,000 to be received at the end of each of the five years after that. Interest is compounded annually.
e. $5,000 to be received at the end of each of the next 20 six-month periods. Interest is compounded semiannually at 5 percent each six month period.

14. Future-value exercises. For each of the cash-flow streams described in Question 13, calculate the net future value ten years from now at an interest rate of 10 percent. In each case, check to make sure your answer is consistent with your answer to Question 13.

15. Calculating annuity equivalent to present value. A pension fund not subject to income taxes plans to buy a piece of equipment for $10,000 and lease it to a manufacturer. The equipment has an estimated useful life of ten years and is to be leased to the manufacturer for that period of time. Annual rentals are to be paid at the beginning of each year. If the desired earnings rate is 8 percent, what is the lowest annual rental the pension fund should accept?

(Prepared by Professor Carl L. Nelson)

16. Value of asset to buyer and seller. A house can be bought for $21,000, payable in cash immediately. Alternatively, the seller will accept a series of cash payments, starting with $10,000 immediately and then $2,000 at the end of each of the next eight years.

a. If buyers can always invest their money at 10 percent, compounded annually, which of these alternatives should they prefer?

b. Assuming that sellers can invest their money at 8 percent, what is the series of payments worth to them?

17. Comparability of values at different times.   You have three assets for which you forecast the following cash flows:

Years from Now	Asset A	Asset B	Asset C
1	+$1,000		
2	+ 1,000		
3	+ 1,000	+$1,700	
4	+ 1,000	+ 1,700	
5	+ 1,000	+ 1,700	+$2,000
6			+ 2,000
7			+ 2,000

Each of these assets is being managed by one of your firm's trainees. You have asked them to calculate the values of these assets, assuming that money is worth 10 percent. They have given you the following figures:

Asset A: present value today, $3,791.
Asset B: present value three years from now, $4,650.
Asset C: future value seven years from now, $6,620.

Which of these assets is the most valuable? Which is the least valuable? Show your calculations.

18. Calculating income from investment.   Sarah Jones leased a store for three years. She paid rent of $2,000 each year and sublet it to someone else for $3,000 a year, both payable yearly in advance. If she invested the difference at 8 percent, how much did she gain in the first three years?

19. Calculating annuity equivalent to future value.   A firm that owns a gravel pit is obligated to pay the cost of leveling the terrain at the time the gravel deposit is exhausted. It is estimated that this payment will be made seven years from now and that the amount will be $20,000. The firm wishes to build up a fund to be used to meet this obligation at the end of seven years. It will make seven equal annual payments into the fund, one at the end of each year; the seventh payment is to be made at the time the gravel deposit is exhausted.

If the fund earns interest at the rate of 6 percent, compounded annually, how much must each annual payment be?

(Prepared by Professor Carl L. Nelson)

20. Annuity equivalent to an annuity.   On January 1, 1975, Meridian Products entered into an employment agreement with its president. As part of that agreement, the firm agreed to pay the president $10,000 each year for ten years after his retirement. The payments were scheduled to start on July 1, 1985, and to terminate on July 1, 1994.

The firm wished to make these payments out of a fund. This fund was to be built up by equal annual payments starting July 1, 1975, and ending July

1, 1985. It was anticipated that the fund would earn 5 percent a year, compounded annually. How much was each payment?

(Prepared by Professor Carl L. Nelson)

21. Calculating residual amount. A firm borrowed $100,000 on October 1, 1975. The interest rate was 8 percent. The firm agreed to pay $15,000 a year for ten years starting October 1, 1978, to cover interest and a portion of the principal each year. No amounts were to be paid on October 1, 1976, or October 1, 1977.

A "balloon" payment to repay the indebtedness remaining on October 1, 1988, was to be made on that date. How large a payment should the company have planned to make on that date?

(Prepared by Professor Carl L. Nelson)

22. Calculating the value of an asset. Thomas Peterson is an investor who expects to earn at least 8 percent a year on his investment. He estimates that an investment in a new mine will bring him $10,000 in cash at the end of each of the next 15 years. At the end of that time, the mine will be worthless.

a. How much is the mine worth to Mr. Peterson?
b. How much would the mine be worth to Mr. Peterson if it were to produce $10,000 a year for 25 years? For 40 years? For 50 years?
c. Prepare a diagram with "values" on the vertical scale and the number of years on the horizontal scale. Enter your answers to (a) and (b) on this diagram. From the diagram, try to estimate how much the mine would be worth if it were to be productive at the present rate for 100 years. What other method or methods could you have used to calculate this figure?

23. Goodwill. The book value of Company A's net tangible assets is $100,000. Their current appraised value is $125,000.

Net income before extraordinary items has averaged $15,000 a year for the last five years, and capital expenditures each year have equalled the annual depreciation of $15,000. Present forecasts are that net income and capital expenditures will continue at this level indefinitely.

a. Calculate the amount of goodwill, using book value as the base and assuming the normal rate of return in this industry is 10 percent.
b. Company B has just bought Company A's net assets for $145,000. How much goodwill should it recognize in its balance sheet?

24. Discussion question: effects of purchase and sale on income. On July 1, 19x1, Ruth Norris bought 500 shares of stock in the Parkway Corporation at a price of $20 a share. She estimated that the present value of these shares to her was $22 a share at that time.

Ms. Norris received cash dividends of 50 cents a share on December 30, 19x1. On December 31, 19x1, she estimated the present value of these shares at $24 a share. She sold the shares on that date at a price of $25 a share.

a. If Ms. Norris were to measure her income on a present-value basis and ignore income taxes, how much income would she say she had earned from this investment (1) on July 1, 19x1, and (2) between July 1, 19x1, and January 1, 19x2?

b. How, if at all, would your answer to (a) change if Ms. Norris hadn't sold her stock on December 31, 19x1? Discuss the differences between this situation and the situation addressed in (a) and the arguments for and against treating the two situations differently.

25. Effect of timing of cash flows on asset value. Cole Hammerlowe, the famous author-composer of Broadway musicals in the 1940s, bequeathed the rights to all of his literary and musical works to the Hammerlowe Foundation, a newly established charitable organization. Some of these rights were due to expire in a few years, but others would be valid for 30 years.

Mr. Hammerlowe's work had a small but loyal band of admirers, and a steady stream of royalty payments could be counted on for a number of years. In addition, the trustees of the foundation expected that Mr. Hammerlowe's works would have several years of renewed popularity as a new generation of theater critics rediscovered them, a phenomenon that had been observed for every other author-composer of Mr. Hammerlowe's stature in the past. Accordingly, the trustees prepared the following estimates of the cash flows the foundation would be likely to receive:

Year	Annual Cash Receipts
1– 5	$ 50,000
6–10	200,000
11–15	100,000
16–20	50,000
21–30	20,000

The trustees expect to be able to invest any funds that become available to them to yield an annual rate of return of 10 percent. The foundation is not subject to income taxes.

a. Compute the value of Mr. Hammerlowe's gift to the foundation.

b. The anticipated cash flows in this case average $70,000 a year for 30 years. Suppose that a long-established, respectable commercial publisher were to offer to pay the foundation $70,000 a year *forever* in exchange for the rights to Mr. Hammerlowe's works. Should the trustees accept this offer? Explain briefly.

26. Calculating equivalent annuity; effect of interest rate. William Lazere wished to provide for the college education of his three children. He estimated that he would need the following amounts:

August 31, 1980	$ 5,000
August 31, 1981	10,000
August 31, 1982	15,000
August 31, 1983	15,000
August 31, 1984	10,000
August 31, 1985	5,000

On September 1, 1973, he asked the representative of an insurance company to draw up an endowment policy that would provide these amounts. The insurance representative said that his company compounded interest annually at 6 percent.

a. What is the amount of the *annuity* that Mr. Lazere had to pay each September 1 from 1973 to 1984, inclusive, to obtain the funds needed for his children's education? Show your calculations.

b. Recompute your answer to (*a*) on the basis of a 7 percent interest rate.

27. Goodwill. Company X is interested in acquiring Company Y. The book value of Company Y's assets is $750,000, and its liabilities amount to $250,000. The assets have a total appraised fair value of $800,000; the liabilities are appraised at $250,000.

Company Y's net income has been $52,000 a year for the last five years. Annual expenditures on plant and equipment have equalled the depreciation each year, $20,000.

Company Y's shareholders have offered to sell Company Y's assets for $600,000; Company X would also accept responsibility for Company Y's liabilities.

a. Calculate Company Y's goodwill, using book value as the base and assuming that the normal rate of return in this industry is 8 percent and that income and capital expenditures will continue at their current levels forever.

b. Given the assumptions in (*a*), will goodwill appear on either company's balance sheet (1) if Company X buys Company Y's assets and (2) if the sale doesn't go through? If so, at what amount would it appear?

28. Value of shares of stock. The Carrington Corporation has been in operation for three years. It markets a new kind of plastic foam for sale to industrial customers. The company has reported a net loss each year since it was founded, but sales are now increasing, and management expects to report a small net income this year.

To finance the company's growth and broaden its ownership base, the owner-managers have decided to "go public" and have offered to sell shares of the company's common stock at a price of $10 a share. Book value per share is now $4.

You have $25,000 which you wish to invest in a growth situation of this sort, and you are willing to buy this stock if you think that it will yield you an annual return of 12 percent before taxes.

You forecast that the Carrington Corporation will report earnings and pay dividends as follows:

Years from Now	Earnings per Share	Dividends per Share
1	$0.10	—
2	0.75	$0.50
3	1.00	0.50
4	1.25	0.50
5	1.50	0.50
6	1.75	0.50
7	2.00	1.00
8	2.00	1.00
9	2.00	1.00
10	2.00	1.00

(For simplicity, you should assume that dividends will be paid once each year, at the end of the year.)

You believe that the market price of this stock ten years from now will probably be about $16 a share.

What is this stock worth to you? Show the calculations which support your answer. Ignore income taxes.

29. Calculating the value of goodwill. The Loralèe Corporation's sole asset is a 100-percent stock ownership of the New York, Chicago, and Pacific Railway Company. The latter's only asset is 200 miles of mainline railroad track which it has leased on a 99-year lease to the Pennsylvania and Chesapeake Railroad at a semiannual rental of $50,000. This lease still has 25 years to run, and the P&C is one of the strongest railway companies in the country.

The book value of the ownership equity in the New York, Chicago, and Pacific on its own books is $1,200,000. The Loralee Corporation carries its investment on its books at an original cost of $900,000. Loralee Corporation stockholders are satisfied with a 12 percent before-tax return on their investment. Loralee stock is now selling at $800,000.

a.   What is the value of the Loralee Corporation's goodwill if it is assumed that cash flows after the end of 25 years will be zero? (Interest should be compounded semiannually.)

b.   What is the value of the goodwill if it is assumed that the semiannual rental will remain at its present level forever?

c.   Should the stockholders keep or sell their Loralee stock? State any assumptions you have made and show all your computations.

30. Calculating income on a present-value basis. The city of Hicksville has decided to sponsor an international exposition promoting the values of rural living. The exposition will operate for a period of four years. The city will provide a site for the exposition in Bucolic Park, rent free.

Turning to experts, the city has asked the International Corporation for Expositions (ICE) to construct the buildings and to operate the exposition. ICE has prepared the following estimates of operating cash receipts and cash disbursements:

Year	Receipts	Disbursements
1	$2,000,000	$1,300,000
2	3,000,000	1,500,000
3	2,000,000	800,000
4	1,350,000	350,000

Construction costs, all to be paid at the beginning of year 1, are estimated to be $4 million. An additional investment of $300,000 will be necessary at that time to provide a working cash fund; the need for this will continue throughout the four-year period. The exposition buildings will be sold to the city at the end of year 4 for $1 million.

ICE has enough confidence in the predictions to participate in the venture if it will earn a return of 10 percent before income taxes. If it decides to do so, it will form a subsidiary, the Hicksville Exposition Corporation. This subsidiary will issue common stock to ICE for $1,000 and will borrow the remaining $4,299,000 from ICE, giving noninterest-bearing notes as evidence of its indebtedness. The subsidiary will repay the notes as rapidly as possible, keeping only a cash balance of $300,000. ICE assumes in all of its calculations that all cash receipts and disbursements take place at the end of the year.

The subsidiary will be liquidated at the end of year 4, and its remaining cash assets will be paid back to ICE at that time.

a. Assuming that ICE agrees to undertake this project and that all the forecasts are correct, compute the subsidiary's income for each year if assets are measured by the present value approach. Ignore income taxes.

b. If the historical cost approach is used instead of present value, what will be the income for each year? Historical cost depreciation will be the same for each of the four years. Ignore income taxes.

31. *Financial statements on a present value basis.* On January 1, 1973, the Vista Hotel opened its doors. The hotel had just been completed at a cost of $6 million, and it had an expected life of 30 years. The hotel had been built by the Vista Realty Corporation on land acquired on a 30-year, nonrenewable lease at a rental of $75,000 per year. Vista Realty, in turn, leased the hotel on a 30-year lease to the Vista Operating Company, which was to operate the hotel and pay all operating expenses. The annual rental to be paid by Vista Operating to Vista Realty was to be 40 percent of the hotel's revenue with a minimum rental of $400,000 a year.

Realty's management estimated that the hotel would gross an annual revenue of $1.8 million. It was not ordinarily willing to undertake projects of this kind unless the anticipated rate of return on investment was at least 10 percent before income taxes.

In 1973, the Hotel earned revenue of $1.6 million. Toward the end of 1973, the city began building an auditorium and related facilities for conventions, indoor sports, and so forth. The management of Vista Realty believed this would increase annual hotel revenue to about $2 million a year starting in 1975. The projection for 1974 remained at $1.8 million.

a. Assuming that the hotel was the sole asset of Vista Realty and that its entire cost was financed by stockholder investment, present balance sheets as of January 1, 1973, under (1) the historical-cost basis and (2) the present-value basis of measurement.

b. Mr. Jones, a wealthy investor, had the opportunity to buy a 10 percent interest in Vista Realty on December 31, 1973. Calculate the maximum price he should have been willing to pay for the stock if he required a 10 percent return on his investment.

c. Present financial statements as of December 31, 1973, under the two bases of measurement. Ignore income taxes.

8

The Timing of Revenue and Expense Recognition

CHANGES IN THE VALUE OF A BUSINESS are recognized, for the most part, only as revenues are recognized. The income statement reports the difference between the sum of a set of current values (revenues) and the sum of another set of past values and current values (expenses). For example, Exhibit 8–1 shows the amount invested in an asset (inventory) increasing gradually as costs are incurred to bring it to the point of revenue recognition. At that point the accounting measurement increases because the value of the asset—that is, the inventory or the cash or receivable exchanged for it—exceeds the cost that has been incurred up to that point.

This chapter has two goals: (1) to explain the criteria accountants use in deciding when the value of marketable goods and services is measurable enough to justify the recognition of revenue and (2) to see how the choice of a revenue-recognition point will affect the figures shown in the financial statements.

CRITERIA FOR REVENUE RECOGNITION

At least six distinct events can be found in the operating cycle of a manufacturing company:

1. Acquisition of resources.
2. Receipt of customer orders.
3. Production.

EXHIBIT 8–1. Accounting Measurement of Value Changes

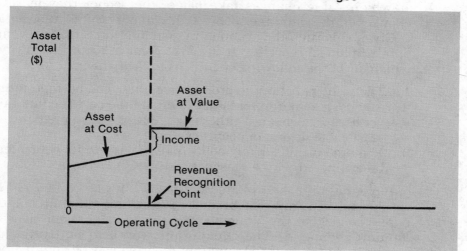

4. Delivery of goods or performance of services.
5. Collection of cash.
6. Completion of all contractual obligations.

In the illustrations we used in the first six chapters, revenues were always recognized at the time of delivery, and our task was to decide what costs were to be reported as the expenses of generating those revenues. The time of delivery isn't the only possible choice, however. Any of the six events in our list might conceivably be taken as the signal that revenues have been earned—that is, it is conceivable that each might be adopted under certain circumstances as the *revenue-recognition basis*. Our first problem, therefore, is to see what criteria accountants use in choosing among these six possibilities.

We should point out at the outset that *each* of these is a productive activity that adds value in some measure to the goods or merchandise purchased. On these grounds, a portion of the ultimate sale price ought to be recognized as revenue as each activity is performed. The difficulty is that the ultimate sale price is the *joint* product of *all* activities and it is impossible to say with certainty how much is attributable to any one of them. *For this reason, the accountant selects one event as the signal for revenue recognition and ignores the others.*

In choosing a basis for revenue recognition, the accountant follows a simple rule: the investor's interests call for recognizing revenue just as soon as the value change it represents can be measured reliably. Investors' decisions presumably are influenced by the rate at which value changes take place; the sooner they learn about changes in this rate, the sooner they can act on this information.

Given this rule, the accountant generally recognizes revenue for public financial reporting at the *first* point in the operating cycle at which *all* of the following conditions are satisfied:

1. The principal revenue-producing service has been performed.
2. Any costs that are necessary to create the revenue but have not yet been incurred are either negligible or can be predicted with a reasonable degree of accuracy.
3. The amount ultimately collectible in cash or its equivalent can be estimated with a reasonable degree of accuracy.

Revenues and their related expenses can't be recognized before these conditions are met because, before this time, no one can be sure enough that the value change has actually taken place in the amount indicated. The accountant wants to notify the public promptly, but only if the amounts reported can be counted on as a reasonable measure of what has actually happened. In other words, there is a trade-off between promptness and reliability—the accountant's job is to locate the point beyond which more promptness can be had only by too great a sacrifice in reliability.

THE DELIVERY BASIS

We'll look at the delivery basis first because it is the basis most frequently used in practice. Specifically, we'll try to answer four questions:

1. What is the delivery basis?
2. Why is the delivery basis used so widely?
3. What estimates have to be made if this basis is used?
4. How will assets, income, and expenses be measured?

The Nature of the Delivery Basis

The delivery basis probably should be called the *shipment basis*. When the delivery basis is used, revenues and their associated expenses are usually recognized at the time merchandise is shipped to customers and invoices are prepared, even though delivery takes place a few days or weeks later. The time lag is usually short, however, and the distinction between shipment time and delivery usually has no practical importance.

We might also have referred to this as the *sale basis* of revenue recognition, the term most accountants use. We don't use this term because we find it ambiguous. The sales force "makes a sale" when it persuades a customer to place a purchase order. This may be days, weeks, or even months before delivery takes place. Since accountants identify the time of delivery as the time of sale, we find it simpler to refer to this revenue-recognition basis as the delivery basis.

Reasons for the Use of the Delivery Basis

The delivery basis is widely used because, in most cases, it's the first point in the operating cycle at which all three revenue-recognition criteria are met:

1. The seller's economic role has been performed, for the most part, when the goods are delivered or the services are performed.
2. Few, if any, costs remain to be incurred in the future, and those that remain can be predicted accurately.
3. While the amount that eventually will be collected from customers is unknown, it is usually predictable. Defaults, customer discounts, and other future leakages from the stated price of the goods delivered are generally small and predictable.

A second reason for the prevalence of the delivery basis is that it permits the company to reduce its record-keeping costs. Invoices have to be prepared to notify customers that certain payments are due. These invoices are usually prepared when the merchandise is shipped or when services are performed for customers. Using these invoices as the source of revenue-recognition data avoids the need to perform these same calculations at some other time. Although recognition of revenue at some other time might provide better information, the added cost of providing that information might outweigh the added benefits.

Estimates Required: Cash Collections

In any basis of revenue recognition, the key figures to estimate are (1) the amount to be collected from the customer and the date it will be collected and (2) the costs still to be incurred after the recognition point. As to the first of these, the total amount collected from customers is almost always less than the total invoice price, for one or more of the following reasons:

1. The company grants cash *discounts* to its customers.
2. The company grants *sales allowances* (price reductions) to customers who agree to accept merchandise not meeting their specifications.

3. The company cancels all or part of the invoice price of merchandise returned by customers (*sales returns*).
4. Customers fail to pay the full amounts they owe the company (*customer defaults* or *bad debts*).
5. The company accepts an *asset other than cash or a short-term receivable* in exchange for the merchandise.

The only one of these we didn't discuss in Chapter 4 is the acceptance of assets other than cash or short-term receivables. Sometimes this is a way of giving a customer a concealed discount; sometimes it is a way of settling an account that otherwise would be uncollectible; and sometimes it is a way of making a sale to a customer who is short of cash but rich in longer-term assets.

Regardless of the reason, the company's problem is to determine the amount at which to record the asset it receives in exchange for its goods and services and the gain or loss on the exchange. Sometimes the asset is a long-term receivable, meaning that the company is lending money to the customer. Part of the face value of the receivable, therefore, is interest on this loan. For example, an exchange of merchandise for a $10,000 one-year promissory note when the appropriate lending rate is 10 percent, compounded annually, should lead to the recognition of $9,091 in revenues, the present value of the $10,000 future amount.[1] The remaining $909 represents a year's interest on the $9,091 loan. (The $9,091 would appear on the balance sheet as a note receivable, perhaps at the face value of the note less $909 in unearned interest.)

In other cases, the company may exchange goods or services for some asset the customer owns, not for cash or the customer's promise to pay. The customer, for example, may transfer shares of stock in other companies or corporate bonds or even equipment or real estate. Again the problem is to determine the current value of the asset received. Value in such cases is measured either by the estimated market value of the asset given up or by the estimated market value of the asset received, whichever is more clearly evident.[2] For example, if the company accepts 100 shares of stock in exchange for merchandise with a list price of $10,000, the revenue should be measured by the market value of the stock at the time of the settlement, whether this is $11,000 or $9,000. The stock's market value is likely to be more readily determinable than the market value of unsold inventories.

---

[1] AICPA, "Accounting Principles Board Opinion 21," para. 11, in *Professional Standards—Accounting, Current Text* (New York: Commerce Clearing House, Inc., 1978), sec. 4111.11.

[2] Ibid., "Opinion 29," para. 18, in *Professional Standards—Accounting*, sec. 1041.18.

Establishing value in this way has two effects. First, if revenues have already been recognized in the usual way, accepting the new asset in exchange for the previously recognized receivable is likely to give rise to a gain or a loss. If our company accepts stock worth $9,000 to settle a $10,000 account, the loss is $1,000.

Second, this estimate of *value* is accounted for as the *cost* of the asset received when it is used or sold later. Suppose the stock is worth $9,000 at the exchange but is sold later for $7,000. The $2,000 difference is a loss resulting from management's decision to hold onto the stock instead of selling it right away. After all, a decision not to sell an asset is economically equivalent to a decision to buy it. Any change in the value of an asset held for investment is a gain or loss on the act of investment—it doesn't matter how the asset was acquired in the first place.

Estimates Required: Future Costs

If revenues are recognized at the time of delivery, the costs associated with those revenues should also be recognized as expenses at that time. For example, suppose a company sells merchandise at an invoice price of $100. It offers no sales discounts, expects to receive payment promptly (within 30 days), has negligible sales returns and allowances, and expects customer defaults to average 2 percent of the average invoice price. The net revenue from an average shipment of merchandise with an invoice price of $100, therefore, is $100 − $2 = $98.

The diagram in Exhibit 8–2 shows the costs our illustrative company incurs at each stage in its operating cycle. It spends $20 to buy the materials for a unit of product, $10 a unit to a sales representative to secure an order from a customer, $40 to process the materials into a unit of finished product, $6 to deliver it to the customer, $4 a unit to collect the amount due from the customer, and $5 to provide service under the terms of the warranty attached to the product. These costs add up to $85.

If the sequence in Exhibit 8–2 is followed, the costs assignable to an average $100 customer order will grow along the path traced by the solid line in Exhibit 8–3. The dashed line is obtained by adding the $13 income on the average $100 order ($98 expected value of the order, less $85 average total cost) to the accumulated cost at each stage from delivery on.

The main accounting question is how much cost should be classified as expense of each phase of the operating cycle. Strictly speaking, the entire $85 in costs should be expensed, and the full $13 in income should be recognized when the goods are delivered. If

EXHIBIT 8-2.   Costs Incurred in a Manufacturer's Operating Cycle

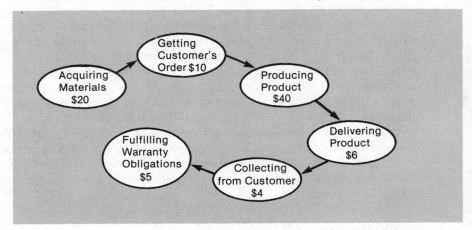

order-getting costs are incurred before the time of delivery, they should be capitalized at that time. And if collection and warranty costs are incurred later, they should be estimated, and the estimated amounts should be expensed at the time of delivery.

TERMINOLOGY REMINDER

A cost is said to be **capitalized** when it is recorded as a cost of an asset.

A cost is said to be **expensed** when it is classified as a deduction from revenues on the income statement.

EXHIBIT 8-3.   Delivery Basis: Cumulative Total Cost and Income

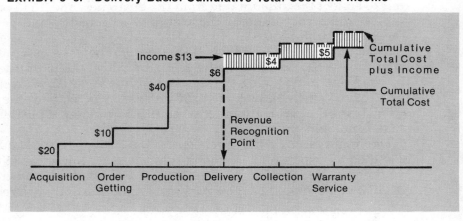

EXHIBIT 8–4. Expenses Associated with a $100 Order from an Average Customer

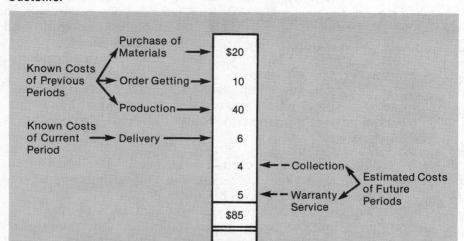

Expenses calculated on this basis are summarized in Exhibit 8–4. The costs of the first four elements are known at the time of delivery; the costs of the other two are estimated.

Measuring Inventories, Receivables, and Income

The balance-sheet figures consistent with this approach would show that the undelivered inventory associated with a $100 customer order has a cumulative cost of $70 ($20 in materials costs, $10 in order-getting costs, and $40 in production costs). The $10 in order-getting costs might be capitalized separately from the costs of the physical inventory as a "deferred charge" against future revenues.

Delivery of an average $100 order would then have the following effects:

Increase in receivables		$94
Gross amount	$100	
Less: anticipated customer defaults	2	
Net Amount Collectible	$ 98	
Less: anticipated collection costs	4	
Net Value of the Receivable	$ 94	
Decrease in inventory and capitalized order-getting costs.................		70
Decrease in cash (delivery costs)		6
Increase in liability for warranty service		5

The net result of these changes is a $13 increase in owners' equity. The anticipated collection costs could be accumulated in an account such as Allowance for Future Collection Costs, and the amount could be shown along with the allowance for uncollectible accounts as a deduction from the face value of the receivable.

Actual practice is likely to differ from this prescription to some extent. Order-getting costs and collection costs are usually recognized as expenses when they are incurred, not when delivery is made. Warranty costs, too, are sometimes expensed as they are incurred rather than when goods are delivered. Three factors account for these practices:

1.   The amounts may be small enough to be classified as immaterial.
2.   The amounts may be very difficult to attribute to individual customer orders or groups of orders.
3.   Companies can reduce their clerical costs by adopting income tax definitions for financial reporting, and income tax regulations encourage or require expensing these items at the time of expenditure.

Materiality is an important accounting concept we haven't mentioned before. Materiality is an attribute of the difference between two alternative accounting treatments or modes of presentation, measured by the likelihood that this difference will affect the meaning readers of the financial statements will attribute to the figures in the statements. A difference is immaterial if it is highly unlikely to change the interpretation of the statements. Immateriality is probably the main reason why collection costs are expensed when they incurred. It may also explain the failure to accrue warranty service liabilities in many cases.

The *difficulty of attributing costs* to individual orders applies particularly to order-getting costs. Management incurs costs, such as advertising and sales salaries, not to obtain a specific order, but in the hope and expectation of securing an uncertain number of orders. The company may spend millions of dollars and never receive an order from a customer. And when the orders do come in, management seldom knows whether they resulted from the current period's order-getting activities or from those of one or more previous periods. Lacking any clear basis for associating the current period's costs of order getting with specific present or future orders, accountants ordinarily classify them as expenses as they occur.

In the United States, *tax considerations* merely reinforce the first two reasons for expensing the costs of order getting, collection, and warranty fulfillment as they are incurred. If the costs are material in amount and readily identifiable with specific revenues, generally accepted accounting principles require that they be recognized as expenses when the related revenues are recognized, no matter what the tax regulations require or allow. Tax considerations, therefore, affect the financial accounting treatment only in borderline cases, when materiality or ease of association is in doubt.

ACQUISITION BASIS

We'll argue in Part III that management should base its decisions to acquire inventories and equipment on estimates of the difference between the present values of the cash flows they will generate and their present cost. For decision purposes, in other words, management should recognize revenues at the time resources are acquired.

The acquisition basis is never used for public financial reporting, however, because some (usually all) of the three revenue-recognition criteria haven't been met at that time. The company hasn't performed all of its major value-creating functions, costs subsequent to acquisition are large and uncertain, and the amounts of cash to be received from customers are usually even more uncertain. This means that the income numbers measured under this basis would be too unreliable for use by outsiders.

SALES ORDER BASIS

Another possible point for revenue recognition is the point at which the sales order is received. The order is a highly significant event in the operating cycle. Most companies which experience significant lags between the date of the order and the date of the shipment will keep track of the orders received so that the amount of orders on hand for future delivery (the backlog) can be reported periodically to management. In these circumstances, the performance of the sales force probably should be judged more on the basis of orders received than on goods shipped.

Order and backlog information is sometimes also reported to creditors and stockholders to guide them in their appraisals of the company's future prospects, but revenues and receivables are never recognized in externally published reports on the basis of orders received during the period. The reason is simply that the criteria for revenue recognition are not met at the time the order is received— the goods have not yet been produced, the costs of producing them are not adequately predictable, or order cancellations are frequent and variable.

PRODUCTION BASIS

The third of our potential alternatives to the delivery basis—that is, the production basis—is used occasionally, when no significant amount of services is required subsequent to production, when the amount of ultimate collection is reasonably certain and collection costs are immaterial, and when the timing of deliveries is more volatile than the timing of production. Application of this method is most common in shipbuilding and other industries in which the production cycle is very long and production is initiated only on receipt of a firm order.

Measuring Inventories, Receivables, and Expenses

Applying the production basis strictly to our previous example, we would recognize income of $13 at the time of production. Exhibit 8–5 describes the bases on which the various components of expense

EXHIBIT 8–5.   Expenses Associated with a $100 Order from an Average Customer: Production Basis

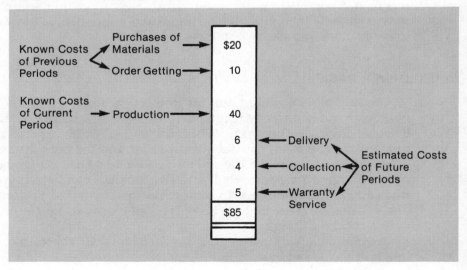

would be recognized. This exhibit is like Exhibit 8–4, except that delivery costs have been moved from the known costs to the estimated costs associated with the order.

When the production basis is used, the company will state its inventories of manufactured goods at their net realizable value. In other words, these inventories will be measured as if they were receivables. In our illustration, the inventory should be measured at the $100 invoice price, less allowances for the anticipated customer defaults ($2) and the costs still to be incurred for delivery, collection, and warranty service ($6, $4, and $5). In other words, the balance sheet should show an $83 inventory of undelivered goods instead of an inventory measured by the $70 in costs already incurred:

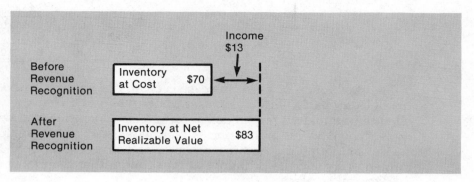

When the production basis is used in practice, allowances for delivery and collection costs are seldom made. Furthermore, order-getting costs may not be capitalized, and provisions for warranty liabilities may not be accrued. The reasons are the same as those we listed in discussing probable departures from the strict application of the delivery basis: (1) future costs are immaterial in amount or (2) no clear basis can be found for attributing costs to individual production orders. The second of these reasons is particularly applicable to order-getting and collection costs, but it may apply to the others as well.

Advantages of the Production Basis

Using the production basis when the recognition criteria are met serves investors by notifying them more promptly of owners' equity increases or decreases arising from operations. This is particularly important whenever production precedes delivery by a substantial or widely varying time interval and production is the last major value-creating activity.

For example, consider a mining company that produces ore and sells it under a long-term contract at $12 a ton, the buyer to pay all delivery costs. During the first three quarters of 19x1 it produced and delivered 600,000 tons at a total cost of $6.3 million. It mined an additional 180,000 tons of ore during the final quarter of the year at a cost of $1.8 million, but a transportation strike prevented the delivery of this ore until 19x2. If the company used the production basis, it would recognize $360,000 more income than if it used the delivery basis, as the following table shows:

	Delivery Basis	Production Basis
Revenues:		
First three quarters (600 tons × $12)	$7,200,000	$7,200,000
Fourth quarter (180 tons × $12)	—	2,160,000
Total Revenues	$7,200,000	$9,360,000
Expenses	6,300,000	8,100,000
Income Before Taxes	$ 900,000	$1,260,000

The production basis in this case is clearly more informative than the delivery basis. With a contract under which the customer takes all of the company's production at an agreed-upon price, and with all costs known when production is completed, the act of production really completes the earning process, and investors should be informed of its success or failure at that time rather than later, when delivery takes place.

Percentage-of-Completion Accounting

The most widely used version of the production basis is the percentage-of-completion method of revenue recognition. Percentage-of-completion accounting has four main features:

1. Costs are accumulated job by job.
2. The ratio of the amount of work done on each job to the total amount of work required by that job is estimated at the end of each period.
3. Revenue from each job is recognized in proportion to progress on the job, as measured by the ratio of work done to total work required.
4. Job costs are classified as expenses as revenues are recognized.

For example, Marsden-Brown, Inc., decided to adopt the production basis for recognizing revenues. Marsden-Brown is an engineering firm specializing in the design and installation of lighting systems. In mid-19xl the firm obtained a contract to install the lighting for the Arkwright County Sports Arena, a job that was to take six months. The contract price was $200,000, and the estimated total cost was $160,000. Marsden-Brown was to bill the customer at the end of each quarter for 80 percent of the sales value of the work done to date.

Work began on October 18, 19xl, and the actual costs charged to the job prior to December 31, 19xl, amounted to $80,000. Progress on the contract was reviewed at the end of the year, and the job was found to be 45 percent completed. Production-basis accounting, therefore, required recognition of revenue of $90,000 for 19xl (45 percent of the $200,000 contract price). The customer was billed for *progress payments* of $72,000 (80 percent of $90,000).

In practice, the account structure to record this information would be relatively complex. In essence, however, Marsden-Brown's income statement showed a gross margin of $10,000:

Contract Revenue	$90,000
Less: Cost of Work Performed	80,000
Gross Margin on Contract Work Performed	$10,000

The balance sheet showed:

Accounts receivable		$72,000
Inventory (market value of contract work performed to date)	$90,000	
Less: Progress billings	72,000	
Inventory (Net)		18,000

The only novel element here is the method used to measure the inventory. The inventory is measured not at cost, but at the value of the work done. Furthermore, since a portion of this value has already been billed to customers, only the unbilled portion is shown as an inventory amount. The inventory, in other words, can be interpreted as a longer-term receivable.

We should also emphasize that the amount billed in 19xl had no effect on the amount of revenue recognized during the period. When the job was completed in 19x2, the revenue for that year was $110,000—that is, the full contract price ($200,000) minus the $90,000 recognized in 19x1.

The percentage-of-completion method is most often used when the production cycle is long, the work is done under contracts with specific clients or customers, and adequate data on progress are available. The contracts provide a basis on which to estimate the amount of cash to be collected after all production work has been completed; if the progress percentage data are valid, they provide assurance that the work done to date will ultimately lead to the collection of cash. Since the cost of the work done to date is readily measurable, the three revenue-recognition criteria are satisfied at the time of production as long as valid progress percentage data are available.

Use of the percentage-of-completion method when the production cycle is long has two effects. First, it leads to an earlier recognition of revenue and expense than the delivery basis would yield. Investors, therefore, will be informed more promptly of changes in the volume of activity or in the profit rate.

Second, this method is likely to report a smoother income stream in long-cycle operations than delivery-basis accounting. Suppose Marsden-Brown completed four contracts in 19x1, eight contracts in 19x2, and two contracts in 19x3. Its reported income on a delivery basis might follow the path traced by the solid line in Exhibit 8–6.

EXHIBIT 8–6.   Income Smoothing Effect of Production Basis

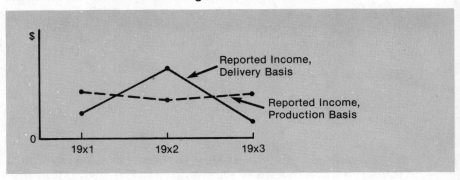

The work done was approximately constant through the three years, however, and revenue recognition on a production (percentage-of-completion) basis might lead to the income pattern traced by the dashed line in the exhibit. Although the number of deliveries declined drastically in 19x3, production-basis income rose because the company was able to work more efficiently in 19x3 than in 19x2.

Estimating the Percentage of Completion

Estimating the percentage of completion isn't easy. Most authorities agree that it should be based on the amount of progress achieved rather than the amount of cost actually incurred, but how to measure progress is not at all clear. For example, should the purchase of materials to be used on the job be regarded as progress?

Probably the best solution is to decide in advance how much of the contract price is to be assigned to each phase of the contract, with most if not all of the weight assigned to labor and other services that are intended to add value to purchased materials. If the available evidence points to the probability of substantial cost overruns on remaining portions of the contract, however, the profit margin on the contract as a whole should be reestimated and a new allocation prepared. In practice, if the anticipated overrun is large enough to produce a loss on the contract, the entire amount of the anticipated loss will be reported immediately.

COLLECTION BASIS

In most situations, as we have already said, revenue is recognized at the time products or services are delivered to customers. We have also pointed out that the revenue-recognition criteria are sometimes met earlier, when goods are produced or work is done. When this is true, revenues are recognized at the time of production.

Still one more set of circumstances must be recognized, however. If the amount of cash to be collected or the amount of cost yet to be incurred isn't readily predictable at the time of production or delivery, revenue recognition must be delayed until cash or its equivalent is collected from the customer. This is the collection basis of revenue recognition.

Measuring Inventories, Receivables, and Expenses

A strict application of the collection basis would require the accountant to capitalize all the costs related to particular products and customer orders until the customers have actually paid for the goods. At the time of delivery, the asset would become a receivable rather than an inventory, but it would continue to be measured at cost until the time of collection. No allowance for customer defaults would be made; instead, the costs of goods delivered to defaulting customers would be written off when the defaults were recognized.

On 100 orders like those described in our previous example, the company should capitalize $7,600 in costs prior to the collection point:

Materials	$20
Order getting	10
Production	40
Delivery	6
Total	$76 × 100 = $7,600

At the time of collection the company would:

Collect and Recognize Revenue	98 × $100 = $9,800 in Cash

Recognize as Expense	100 × $ 5 = $	500 in Warranty Liability[3]
Spend and Expense	100 × $ 4 =	400 in Collection Costs
Expense	98 × $ 76 =	7,448 in Previously Capitalized Costs
Expense	2 × $ 76 =	152 as the Cost of Defaulted Accounts

Recognize Income	= $1,300

In other words, the collection of cash would be the signal to the accountant to remove costs of $7,448 + $152 = $7,600 from the receivables and recognize income of $1,300 ($9,800 − $500 − $400 − $7,448 − $152).

In practice, the order-getting and delivery costs might not be capitalized, for the reasons we cited earlier.

Use of the Collection Basis[4]

The collection basis is used very sparingly. Very few types of receivables are so uncertain of collection that customer defaults can't be forecasted accurately enough to satisfy the revenue criteria earlier than the time of collection. The collection basis is now encountered mainly in small businesses which sell services rather than goods.

The best-known application of the collection basis is in the *installment method*, used to account for certain types of installment sales. Under the installment method, revenues and expenses are recognized when customers make their installment payments, not before. Land development companies, for example, use the installment method because they can't predict collections and future costs reliably enough at the time of delivery or production. This method shouldn't be used for most installment sales of merchandise, however, because customer defaults ordinarily can be predicted quite accurately.

---

[3] We assume, for simplicity, that deliveries are made to dealers, some of whom default, but warranty service is provided to ultimate consumers who don't lose their warranty rights because the dealers default.

[4] The collection basis of revenue and expense recognition should not be confused with the so-called *cash basis* of accounting, the alternative to the accrual basis system we are describing in this book. In cash-basis accounting, the expenses of a period are measured by the cash disbursements of that period; under the collection basis of revenue and expense recognition in accrual accounting, expenses may be recognized either before or after cash disbursements are made.

Before leaving this topic, we should point out that collection doesn't always *follow* the delivery of goods and services. In many cases the two events coincide, and sometimes customers even pay cash *before* delivery is made. Magazine subscribers, for example, usually pay cash before the publisher begins producing and delivering the magazines covered by the subscriptions. In such cases, revenues are recognized as magazines are published and mailed to the subscribers. Revenues can't be recognized earlier, when cash is received, because the first criterion of revenue recognition—completion of all significant revenue-producing activities—hasn't been met at that time. Instead, the receipt of cash gives rise to a liability.

COMPLETED OBLIGATIONS BASIS

In most cases, the final stage in the operating cycle is the completion of all obligations to the purchasers of the company's products or services. For companies with warranty obligations, this stage is being reached later than it used to be, and the revenue-recognition criteria are becoming harder to meet before the obligations have been completed than they used to be. Consumer groups and government agencies in the United States are more active in demanding product reliability, and individual consumers are more preconditioned to demand service, even beyond the end of formal warranty periods. This means that income measured at earlier stages is somewhat less predictable than it used to be in like circumstances.

Even so, accountants never use the completed-obligations basis. The main reason is that waiting for the last obligation to be liquidated would deprive investors of timely information and thereby presumably reduce the quality of their decisions. Fortunately, the costs of warranty service are seldom a large percentage of the selling price, and the inaccuracies in estimates of warranty liabilities are relatively small. In other words, we can still use other methods even though product-warranty costs are larger than they used to be.

IMPACT ON THE FINANCIAL STATEMENTS

Only one revenue-recognition basis is appropriate in any given situation. The three recognition criteria we discussed earlier must be used, and they will point to only one method in each situation. The financial statements of a production-basis company don't have quite the same meaning as the statements of a collection-basis firm, however, and the reader should be aware of these differences.

We have already seen that one effect of the production basis may be to reduce or "smooth" the fluctuations in reported income because the rate of production is likely to be more stable than the rate of delivery or the collection rate. The basis selected has other effects, however, even if the delivery pattern is stable. These effects depend on four factors:

1. The volume of business done.
2. The width of the profit margin.
3. The length of the operating cycle.
4. The rate of growth.

The No-Growth Case

To illustrate the effects of these factors, we'll use the net realization and manufacturing cost figures we've been using right along, $98 and $60 a unit. To simplify the discussion, we'll assume that the costs of order getting, delivery, collection, and warranty service are expensed as the expenditures for these purposes are made. We'll also assume a stable volume of production, deliveries, and collections of 160 units a year. The interval from production to delivery is three months; delivery and collection are separated by the same interval.

Income statement effects.   At a zero growth rate, the number of units sold in an average period equals the number of units delivered and also the number of units on which collections are made. In other words, each of the three revenue-recognition bases will lead to the same total revenue and, therefore, the same net income. In this case, net revenue will be $160 \times \$98 = \$15,680$ a year, no matter which revenue-recognition basis is used. The gross margin will be $160 \times (\$98 - \$60) = \$6,080$.

Balance-sheet effects.   The choice of the revenue-recognition basis will affect the balance sheet, even if business volume remains steady from period to period. Given our assumptions of three-month intervals between production and delivery and between delivery and collection, the company will always have three months of produced but undelivered production and three months of receivables from products already delivered to customers. The inventory at any time, therefore, will be 3/12 of 160 or 40 units. The receivables will represent another 40 units. At a cost of $60 a unit, the inventory or receivable will amount to $40 \times \$60 = \$2,400$; at $98, the net realizable value of 40 units will add up to $40 \times \$98 = \$3,920$.

If these assumptions hold, the following figures will appear on the balance sheets of production-basis, delivery-basis, and collection-basis companies:

	Production Basis	Delivery Basis	Collection Basis
Accounts receivable	$3,920	$3,920	$2,400
Inventory	3,920	2,400	2,400
Total	$7,840	$6,320	$4,800

Since income is the same in all three cases, the apparent rate of return on investment for the collection-basis company is much higher than for the other two companies.

Changing the assumptions.   What happens if we change the assumptions on which these calculations were based? The first three factors—profit margin, volume, and cycle length—determine the relative size of the differences between different bases:

1. Increasing the profit margin from $38 a unit will increase the balance-sheet differences.
2. Increasing the physical volume of business done from 160 units to some larger quantity will increase the balance-sheet differences.
3. Lengthening the interval between production and delivery will increase the balance-sheet differences between the production and delivery basis; lengthening the interval between delivery and collection will increase the balance-sheet differences between the delivery and collection bases.

Decreasing the size of any one of these variables will decrease the balance-sheet differences between bases. Changes in the first two variables will change the amount of income reported each year, but the amount will be identical, no matter which basis is used.

The Impact of Growth

The illustration so far has reflected a no-growth assumption in which production, deliveries, and collections are all at the same level. Suppose, however, the business is growing by 32 units a year. Now we'll see differences in reported income as well as differences in balance-sheet totals. The reason: collections in one period arise from deliveries in an earlier period, when volume was lower, and from production in a still earlier period, when volume was lower yet.

The 32-unit annual growth in our revised example is achieved by increasing production by two units each quarter. This means that production each quarter is eight units larger than production in the comparable period a year earlier. Production figures for two years are shown in the upper panel of Exhibit 8–7. If revenues are recognized at the time of production, revenues and gross margins for 19x1 will reflect the production of the four quarters of 19x1—the top bar in the lower panel of the exhibit. If the delivery basis is used, however, revenues and gross margins will be recognized with a one quarter lag.

The second bar in this panel is slightly smaller. Since production in the fourth quarter of 19x0 was eight units smaller than production in the fourth quarter of 19x1, delivery-basis revenues are eight units smaller than production-basis revenues in this growth situation. The

EXHIBIT 8-7. Revenue Recognized on Different Bases in 19x1

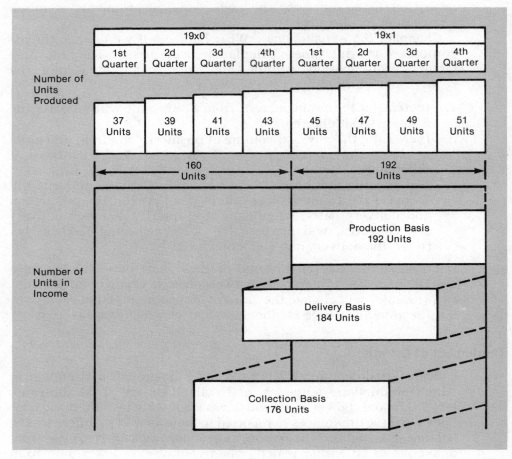

bar at the bottom of the lower panel is the smallest of them all be-cause the collection basis takes units into revenue with a two-quarter lag—that is, it brings in two quarters of 19x0 production instead of only one.

These figures translate into the following gross margin figures for 19x1:

	Production Basis	Delivery Basis	Collection Basis
Revenues (at $98)	$18,816	$18,032	$17,248
Directly related expenses (at $60)	11,520	11,040	10,560
Gross Margin (at $38)	$ 7,296	$ 6,992	$ 6,688

Using the production basis, in other words, increases revenues and gross margins by 4.3 percent over those yielded by the delivery basis and by 9.1 percent over those yielded by the collection basis.

The choice of a recognition basis also has an effect on the asset figures. Remember that both inventories and receivables are measured at cost under the collection basis; both are measured at value under the production basis. The comparison is:

	Production Basis	Delivery Basis	Collection Basis
Accounts Receivable (49 Units):			
At $98 value	$4,802	$4,802	
At $60 cost			$2,940
Inventory (51 units):			
At $98 value	4,998		
At $60 cost		3,060	3,060
Total	$9,800	$7,862	$6,000

The differences are substantial and are slightly larger than they were in the no-growth case we started with.

SUMMARY

In most companies, revenues are recognized at the time goods are delivered or services are performed for outside customers or clients. This is known as the sale basis or delivery basis of revenue recognition. The justification for this rule is that delivery is the first point in the operating cycle at which the revenue is both earned and quantifiable with a sufficient degree of accuracy. Earlier revenue recognition would delay the transmission of information unnecessarily.

Under the delivery basis, the reported revenue is the selling price of the goods or services delivered less discounts, returns, allowances, and any anticipated customer defaults arising from these transactions. If the goods or services are exchanged for an asset other than a short-term receivable, the revenue is measured by the current market value of the goods and services delivered or by the market value of the asset received from the customer, whichever is more clearly evident.

The costs of producing the delivered goods or services are subtracted, when the delivery basis is used, as expenses of the period in which delivery is made, along with the order-getting costs, delivery costs, and collection costs actually incurred during that period. If the costs of fulfilling the company's warranty obligations to its customers are likely to be substantial, estimates of these amounts are recognized as expenses when delivery is made; if the amounts are small, they will be expensed as they are incurred.

In most companies, then, inventories are measured at the cost of production (including the costs of raw materials). Receivables are measured at the amount billed less the estimated customer defaults included in these amounts. A liability for warranty service is recognized if the future cost of discharging present warranty obligations is substantial.

The delivery basis is not always used. Revenues should be and are recognized prior to delivery if they are both earned and quantifiable earlier. They should be and are deferred to a later point if quantification is subject to too great a degree of uncertainty at the time of delivery. On these grounds, revenues are sometimes recognized as production takes place (production basis) or as cash is collected (collection basis). In each case, the expenses deducted from the revenues of a given period are the costs attributable to those revenues, to the extent that a ready basis can be found for linking costs with specific revenues. Until the point of revenue recognition, the inventory or account receivable is measured at cost.

KEY TERMS

Collection basis	Percentage-of-completion
Decision profit	accounting
Delivery basis	Production basis
Materiality	Revenue-recognition criteria
	Revenue-recognition point

INDEPENDENT STUDY PROBLEMS (Solutions in Appendix B)

1. Effect of recognition basis on assets and owners' equity. The Burfran Manufacturing Company has just been formed to produce a new product at a cost of $12 a unit, which will be paid in cash at the time of production. It will cost $6 a unit to sell the product, and this amount will be paid for at the time of shipment. The sale price is to be $25 a unit; all sales will be on credit. No collection costs are incurred.

The following results are expected during the first two years of the company's operations:

	Units Produced	Units Shipped	Cash Collected from Customers
First year	100,000	70,000	$1,500,000
Second year	80,000	90,000	1,875,000

a. State the effect on the various assets and owners' equities of producing one unit, shipping one unit, and collecting $25, if revenue is recognized at the time of production.

b. What total income would the company report in each year if revenue were recognized at the time that cash is collected from the customer? (For this purpose, assume that general administrative expenses amount to $200,000 a year and that income taxes are zero.)

2. Production basis versus delivery basis. The Gilbert Company recognizes revenue at the time of production and classifies selling costs as expenses as they are incurred. You have the following information about the Gilbert Company's operations for 19x1:

1. The company produced 100,000 units of product in 19x1 at a total production cost of $350,000. It sold and delivered 90,000 units at a price of $5 a unit.
2. Payments to factory employees and suppliers of raw materials and other goods and services for use in the factory [as described in item (1)] totaled $330,000.
3. Factory depreciation [included in the production costs listed in (1)] amounted to $10,000.
4. Customer defaults were expected to average 2 percent of gross sales.
5. Selling costs for the year, all paid in cash, totaled $80,000.
6. Administrative costs for the year, including collection costs, amounted to $50,000, all paid in cash.
7. Collections from customers totaled $420,000; write-offs of specific accounts as uncollectible totaled $8,500.
8. The company's liability under its product warranties was negligible.

a. Prepare an income statement for the Gilbert Company for the year 19x1. (Ignore income taxes.)
b. The company had no inventories at the beginning of 19x1. At what amount was the finished goods inventory reported on the company's December 31, 19x1, balance sheet?
c. Recompute net income on the assumption that the company recognizes revenue at the time of delivery.
d. What effect, if any, would changing to a delivery basis of revenue recognition have on the reported finished goods inventory figure?

EXERCISES AND PROBLEMS

3. Cash-basis accounting versus collection basis of revenue recognition.
Joan and Samuel Marx, doing business as Marx Enterprises, design and make fine wooden furniture. They have always kept their records on a cash basis, meaning that they have recognized revenues when customers have paid their bills and have measured the expenses each year by the amounts of cash paid to employees, suppliers, and government agencies in that year.

The business has grown, and the Marx family has been advised to move from the cash basis to accrual accounting. Because the company sells mainly to individuals whose credit ratings are difficult to establish, they have decided to recognize revenues on the collection basis once the changeover to accrual accounting is made.

a.   What changes will have to be made immediately in the balance sheet of Marx Enterprises to reflect the changeover to accrual accounting?

b.   In what respects will the income statement on the collection basis differ from a cash basis income statement?

4. Measuring revenue.   On January 1, 19x1, Arleigh Equipment Company sold and delivered ten earth movers to Denby Contractors, Inc., at a list price of $20,000 each. To secure this order, Arleigh agreed to let Denby pay for this equipment on the following schedule:

Immediately	$ 50,000
One year later	50,000
Two years later	100,000

Arleigh recognizes revenues at the time of delivery. Denby made its payments on schedule. The applicable interest rate was 8 percent, compounded annually.

a.   How much revenue did Arleigh Equipment Company report at the time of delivery?

b.   How much revenue originating in the transaction with Denby did Arleigh include in income for the year 19x1? What caption would you assign to the figure representing the difference between this amount and your answer to (a)?

5. Effects of transactions: different recognition bases.   Quantify the effects on the assets, liabilities, and owners' equity of the events described in each of the following:

a.   The firm recognizes revenue at the time of production. *Events:* The firm produced goods at a cost of $10,000 and paid cash in this amount. The estimated selling price was $16,000, estimated selling costs were $4,000, and collection costs and uncollectible accounts were insignificant.

b.   The firm recognizes revenue at the time of delivery. *Events:* Goods which had cost $10,000 in a previous period were sold on account for $16,000. Selling costs, paid in cash, were $4,000. Estimated collection costs were $500. Of the $16,000, $300 was expected to be uncollectible.

c.   The firm recognizes revenue at the time of collection. *Events:* Goods which had cost $12,000 in a previous period were sold on account for $19,000. Selling costs, paid in cash, were $3,500. Estimated collection costs were $200. Of the $19,000, $1,500 was expected to be uncollectible.

6. Measuring revenue.   The Herklion Company purchased a large quantity of used industrial equipment and shipped it to a foreign country for use in the government's industrialization program. Herklion paid $800,000 for the equipment and an additional $30,000 to transport it to the foreign country.

By the time the equipment arrived at its destination, the customer government had no foreign exchange to pay for it. Instead, it offered to give Herklion $100 of its own 7 percent bonds for every $95 due on the shipment of equipment. At that time, these bonds had a market value of $91 for every $100 of bonds.

Herklion accepted the offer and received $1 million in bonds which it kept for two years and then sold at a price of $90 for every $100 of bonds. During this two-year period, the foreign government paid interest promptly and regularly on these bonds at the prescribed interest rate of 7 percent a year.

a. Did the contractor make a profit or a loss on the equipment transaction? When and how much?

b. How, if at all, would your answer to (a) have differed if the bonds had been sold immediately?

c. How, if at all, would your answer have differed if the bonds had been held until their maturity date and then collected in full?

7. Delivery basis.   A company recognizes revenue at the time it ships merchandise to its customers. The beginning-of-year balance sheet showed gross accounts receivable of $20,000 and an allowance for uncollectible accounts of $1,000.

During the year, goods which cost $100,000 were shipped to customers on account for $160,000. Selling and administrative costs amounting to $40,000 were paid in cash.

Collections on accounts receivable amounted to $155,000 during the year. A bill-collecting agency was paid $5,000 for its services in helping the company collect a portion of this, representing part of the beginning-of-year balance in accounts receivable. Collection costs of this kind ordinarily amount to 3 percent of credit sales, but collection costs are expensed only when they are incurred.

Accounts with a face value of $1,200 were recognized as uncollectible during the year.

The company expects that 1 percent of its credit sales will eventually prove uncollectible and a year-end aging of accounts has confirmed that estimate for this year.

a. Prepare an income statement for the year, ignoring income taxes.

b. Show how the accounts receivable would be presented on the year-end balance sheet.

c. Is the company's method of accounting for collection costs consistent with the shipment basis of revenue recognition? Explain.

8. Choosing a recognition basis.   Sam Stephens operates a pig farm. Each year his sows give birth to piglets, which he raises for eventual sale to meat packers. Each year he buys feed for the pigs and pays a hired man to feed them. Some years when pig prices are high, he sells more pigs than are born; in other years, he sells fewer pigs than are born, resulting in an increase in the total number and weight of his herd. Sales are always for cash, and quotations of prices from hog auctions are published daily in the newspapers.

a. What basis of revenue and expense recognition would be most meaningful to Mr. Stephens in this case? Explain your reasoning.

b.   Assume that feed and labor costs average $2 per pig per month. A pig born on July 1 weighs 80 pounds in December when hog prices are 30 cents a pound. It is sold the following March for $40. Using the method of revenue recognition you selected in (a) above, compute the cumulative effect of these transactions on the figures shown as total assets and total owners' equity on the December 31 and March 31 balance sheets.

9.   Comparing recognition bases.   The Saranac Company produces a single product at a cost of $6 each, all of which is paid in cash when the unit is produced. Selling expenses of $3 a unit are paid at the time of shipment. The sale price is $10 a unit; all sales are on account. No customer defaults are expected, and no costs are incurred at the time of collection.

During 19x1, the company produced 100,000 units, shipped 76,000 units, and collected $600,000 from customers. During 19x2, it produced 80,000 units, shipped 90,000 units, and collected $950,000 from customers.

a.   Determine the amount of net income that would be reported for each of these two years:
   1.   If revenue and expense are recognized at the time of production.
   2.   If revenue and expense are recognized at the time of shipment.
   3.   If revenue and expense are recognized at the time of collection.
b.   Would the asset total shown on the December 31, 19x2, balance sheet be affected by the choice among the three recognition bases used in (a)? What would be the amount of any such difference?

10.   Effect of recognition basis on income; managerial aspects.   The XYZ Manufacturing Company was in a declining industry. Each year its sales decreased; each year it reduced its inventories; each year the accounts-receivable balance decreased. Bad debts, fortunately, were insignificant.

In 19x1 the company delivered products to its customers with a total sales value of $1,050,000. It manufactured 10,000 units of product at a total manufacturing cost of $700,000, an average of $70 a unit. Its inventories of manufactured products, measured at their manufacturing cost, decreased in 19x1 by $35,000, to $210,000. The amounts due from customers decreased by $15,000, to $150,000. Selling and administrative costs totaled $200,000, none of them readily attributable to specific deliveries or collections.

Management expected deliveries to fall by 10 percent in 19x2. Selling and administrative costs would amount to $190,000; increasing them wouldn't increase deliveries by an amount large enough to justify the expenditure. Production volume would also be reduced by 10 percent, but average manufacturing cost would remain at $70 a unit. The amount due from customers would be $15,000 smaller at the end of 19x2 than at the beginning. Selling prices were the same in 19x2 as in 19x1.

a.   Calculate total revenue, gross margin, and income before taxes for 19x1: (1) on a production basis, (2) on a delivery basis, and (3) on a collection basis. You should assume that the ratio of manufacturing cost applicable to revenue was the same for all three bases. (Suggestion: Start with the delivery basis and then redo the calculation on the other two bases.

b. Make the same calculations for 19x2.

c. In these circumstances, would you suggest that reports to management reflect the production basis for revenue recognition even though the company uses the delivery basis for public financial reporting? Why might management even consider doing this—that is, what purpose would it be intended to serve? In particular, consider whether this practice would be likely to do a better job than other methods of achieving the purpose you have ascribed to it.

11. Collection basis. From the time of its founding, The Wagner Company deferred recognizing revenues until the time of collection on the grounds that bad debts were too unpredictable to permit recognition at the time of delivery. The following information relates to the year 19x3:

1. Amounts due from customers on January 1 for goods shipped by the Wagner Company prior to that date, $300,000; the cost of the goods represented by these receivables was $180,000. The cost of the company's merchandise inventory on January 1, 19x3, was $210,000.
2. Goods shipped: price, $800,000; merchandise cost, $600,000.
3. Collections, $900,000; merchandise costs applicable to amounts collected, $650,000.
4. Specific customer defaults, $18,000; merchandise costs applicable to these amounts, $11,000; the affected merchandise could not be repossessed or otherwise recovered.
5. One customer who had defaulted early in 19x2 and whose account had been written off at that time paid the overdue account in full, $1,200. At the time of the default, Wagner had recognized a loss of $950, which was the cost of the merchandise shipped to this customer.
6. Selling and administrative expenses, paid in cash, $182,000.
7. Merchandise purchased on account, $630,000.
8. Payments to suppliers of merchandise, $660,000.

a. At what amount did the Wagner Company report its receivables in its balance sheet at the *beginning* of the year? Set up a T-account and enter this figure.

b. Analyze the transactions for the year, using the collection basis of revenue recognition, and state these analyses in general journal form.

c. Prepare an income statement for the year, based on your analyses of the year's transactions and reflecting the collection basis of revenue recognition.

12. Conversion to the delivery basis. The Wagner Company (Problem 11) was 100 percent owned by members of the Wagner family until December 30, 19x2, when a few hundred shares of stock were sold to outsiders. To meet its responsibilities to the new shareholders, the company's board of directors engaged the firm of Wachum and Krey, independent public accountants, to audit the company's financial statements and review the company's accounting procedures. Wachum and Krey completed its audit early in 19x4. One of its findings was that the company's financial statements didn't conform to generally accepted accounting principles because use of the delivery basis of revenue recognition was fully warranted. The company set to work to prepare its 19x3 financial statements on that basis.

To supplement the information available in Problem 11, the accountants made the following additional estimates:

1. $30,000 of the accounts receivable on January 1, 19x3, would never be collected. (In other words, a delivery-basis balance sheet as of January 1, 19x3, would include a $30,000 allowance for uncollectible accounts.)
2. Uncollectible amounts had averaged 3 percent of sales.

a. Calculate the adjustments necessary to restate the January 1, 19x3, inventory and receivables balances at the levels appropriate to the delivery basis.
b. Prepare an income statement for the year 19x3, reflecting the delivery basis of revenue recognition. The adjustment of the beginning-of-year inventory and receivables balances should be shown on the income statement as a single item entitled, "Cumulative effect on prior years of changing to a different revenue-recognition basis," to be included as the final figure in the determination of net income for 19x3.
c. Is the delivery basis likely to give management and investors a better or poorer indication of the firm's current performance than the collection basis? Illustrate your answer with figures from this problem and Problem 11.

13. Effect of recognition basis.   The Naive Manufacturing Company produces a product at a cost of $7.50 a unit, all of which is paid at the time of production. It costs $2 a unit to sell the product, all of which is paid at the time the product is shipped to the customer. The sale price is $10 a unit. All sales are on account. Collection costs are 2 percent of the amount collected, all paid during the period of collection. No customer defaults are expected, and the income tax rate is zero.

During the first year of operation, the company expects to produce 20,000 units, to ship 18,000 units, and to collect $170,000 from its customers.

During the second year it expects to produce 30,000 units, to ship 29,000 units, and to collect $280,000 from its customers.

a. Suppose that the company recognizes revenue and all related expenses at the time of production:
1. State the effect on the various assets and equities of producing one unit and incurring the related production costs.
2. State the effect on the various assets and equities of shipping one unit and incurring the related selling costs.
3. State the effect on the various assets and equities of collecting $10 and incurring the related collection costs.
4. What net income will be reported for the first year?
5. What net income will be reported for the second year?
b. Repeat the calculations called for in (a), but on the assumption that the company recognizes revenue and all related expenses at the time of shipment.

c. Repeat the calculations called for in (b), but on the assumption that the company recognizes revenue and all related expenses at the time of collection.

d. Companies that recognize revenue at the time of shipment ordinarily treat collection costs as an expense of the period of collection. Using this procedure, what is the net income for each year?

e. Companies that recognize revenue at the time of collection ordinarily treat selling costs as an expense of the period in which they are incurred. Using this procedure, what is the net income for each year?

(Prepared by Professor Carl L. Nelson)

14. Usefulness as a criterion in choosing a recognition basis.* Smith & Wells, Ltd., manufactures a variety of machined parts which it sells to customers in the automotive and transportation industries. About half of the company's sales are of products listed in the company's regular catalog. The remainder of the annual sales is in custom items. Sales revenues for both types of products are recognized at the time the goods are shipped to the customers.

Deliveries of catalog items, except for very large orders, are made from warehouse inventories, which are allowed to fluctuate from month to month to help stabilize production levels.

Custom items, often designed to the customer's own specifications, are manufactured only upon receipt of a firm order. Cancellations of orders on which production operations have commenced are extremely rare, and Smith & Wells, Ltd., can always recover its costs on any such cancelled orders.

During 1976 the company's sales force turned in a gratifying 20 percent increase in new orders over their 1975 level, almost all of the increase being for custom products. To meet this increased demand, the rate of production in the company's factory was increased twice during the year, once in July and once again in October. Because the production cycle for custom items averages four to six months, however, the increase in the rate of production did not lead to any marked rise in revenue.

In mid-January of 1977, Mr. T. E. S. Evans, the managing director of Smith & Wells, Ltd., received a preliminary set of financial statements for 1976 from his chief accountant, Mr. J. B. Burke. Excerpts from these statements are shown in Exhibit 1.

Mr. Evans understood that income was recognized at the time of delivery, but he asked Mr. Burke whether something could be done to reflect the increase in customer orders in the income figures. Mr. Burke replied that the company's auditors would never accept customer orders as evidence that revenue had been earned.

a. Could the revenue-recognition criteria be met for either product line under an order basis for revenue recognition? Under a production basis?

b. Reconstruct the income statements for 1975 and 1976 with revenues from custom products recognized at the time of production.

---

* Copyright 1967, 1977 by l'Institut pour l'Etude des Méthodes de Direction de l'Entreprise, (IMEDE), Lausanne, Switzerland. Reproduced by permission.

c. Do the income figures you derived in answer to (b) provide a better measure of management's operating performance than those stated at the top of Exhibit 1? Would they meet Mr. Evans' objections to the existing reporting basis? Would you recommend a shift to the production basis?

EXHIBIT 1

SMITH & WELLS, LTD.
Selected Financial Data for 1974–76
(000 omitted)

	1974	1975	1976
Net revenue from goods shipped:			
Catalog items	£xxx	£ 960	£ 970
Custom products	xxx	990	1,030
Total	£xxx	£1,950	£2,000
Cost of goods shipped	£xxx	£1,170	£1,240
Selling and administrative expenses	xxx	600	620
Net operating income before taxes and special charges	£xxx	£ 180	£ 140
New orders received, net of cancellations (at sale prices):			
Catalog items	£xxx	£ 980	£1,000
Custom products	xxx	1,020	1,400
Total	£xxx	£2,000	£2,400
Inventories on 31 December (at cost):			
Materials.......................................	£100	£ 100	£ 150
Work in process:			
Catalog items	45	50	50
Custom products	148	155	230
Finished goods (catalog items only)	470	500	480
Details of custom products work in process on 31 December:			
Total contract sale prices	£480	£ 500	£ 625
Estimated total production cost	290	300	375
Production costs incurred to date	148	155	230
% of work completed to date	50%	50%	60%
Orders on hand but not yet put into production on 31 December, custom products (at contract sale prices)	£790	£ 800	£1,045

xxx—Data not available.

part II

EXTERNAL FINANCIAL REPORTING

9

Inventory Costing

NONMONETARY ASSETS and expenses representing the use of the services of these assets are usually measured in financial statements on the basis of the historical costs of the resources they represent. The purpose of this chapter is to see how accountants quantify the historical costs of goods in inventory or issued from inventory. We'll also discuss how, in some cases, accountants use market value instead of cost to state the inventory in dollars. The chapter has four main parts:

1. A description of three frequently used historical costing methods.
2. A discussion of their effects on net income and cash flow.
3. A discussion of the criteria companies use in choosing among these methods.
4. An explanation of the cost or market rule, which requires inventories to be restated at their market values if market values are lower than historical costs.

HISTORICAL COSTING METHODS

When inventory accounting is tied to the historical costs of the goods entering and leaving the inventory, the accountants' job is to identify and distribute the costs of goods available for use or sale in any period. In this section we'll discuss the composition of the cost of goods available and describe three commonly used methods of distributing those costs:

1.   First-in, first-out (Fifo) costing.
2.   Last-in, first-out (Lifo) costing.
3.   Average costing.[1]

For convenience, all of the illustrations will relate to the merchandise inventories of companies engaged in retailing or wholesaling businesses. The same methods can be applied to manufacturing firms' inventories of raw material or finished goods, and even to work in process.

The Cost of Goods Available

The total of the number of physical units sold and the number of units in the ending inventory must equal the total number of units available for sale during the period. By the same token, the total of the *costs* of the goods sold and the *costs* of the ending inventory must equal the total of the *costs* of the goods available for sale during the period.

This equality is illustrated in Exhibit 9–1. The numbers in this diagram may refer either to physical quantities—pounds, kilograms, and so on—or to costs. Goods available for sale in any period come from two sources: the quantity in inventory at the beginning of the period and the quantity acquired during the period. These quantities are represented by the two blocks at the left of the diagram. The total of these two quantities is the quantity of goods available, represented by the large block in the center. This block can also represent the total *cost* of the goods available for sale.

Two things can happen to the goods available for sale in any period: they will either be sold (or stolen, damaged, evaporated, or lost in other ways) or remain in inventory at the end of the period.[2] If an item isn't sold or lost, it will be in the inventory at the end of the period. These quantities are represented by the two blocks in the right-hand section of the exhibit.

These last two blocks can also represent the dollar cost of goods sold and the cost of the ending inventory. The cost of goods available will either be deducted from revenues on the income statement as the cost of goods sold or assigned to the goods that remain in inven-

---

[1] A fourth method, *specific-lot costing,* is used whenever each product unit or lot is unique, as in automobile dealers' vehicle inventories. It presents a flow of costs to the income statement similar to that emerging from Fifo costing and needn't be discussed separately here.

[2] For inventories of materials destined for use in manufacturing, the words "goods issued" should be substituted for "goods sold" in this discussion.

EXHIBIT 9–1. Goods Acquired, Available, and Sold during a Period

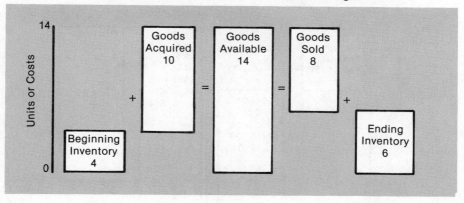

tory at the end of the period. From Exhibit 9–1, for example, we see that the cost of goods sold was $8. If these goods were sold for $12.50, the income statement would show the following:

Revenue from sale of goods	$12.50
Cost of goods sold	8.00
Gross Margin	$ 4.50

The $6 cost assigned to the ending inventory becomes the cost of the beginning inventory in the next period, and the cycle is repeated.

First-in, First-out (Fifo) Costing

The Fifo method assigns the oldest costs in the inventory records to the items that are transferred out of the stockroom first; the ending inventory is measured at the cost of the units most recently acquired.

For example, suppose a company started 19x1 with an inventory of four units that had cost $1 each in the preceding year, a total of $4. It bought eight units at $1.25 each and sold ten units during the year, leaving two units in inventory at the end of the year. The Fifo costing method would divide the cost of the available goods as shown in Exhibit 9–2. The first four units to be sold would be assigned a unit cost of $1, the cost of the *first* units that were available during the year ($4). The other six units sold would be assigned a unit cost of $1.25 each, the cost of the *next* units to become available during the year ($7.50). The cost of goods sold would be the sum of these two figures. The two units in inventory at the end of the year would be assigned the costs of the *last* two units to enter the inventory during

EXHIBIT 9–2.   First-in, First-out (Fifo) Costing

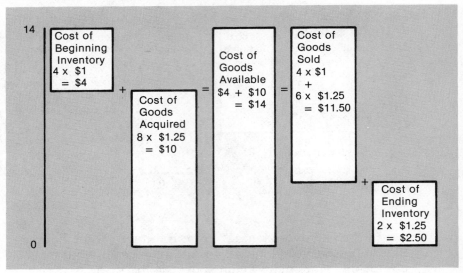

the year, $1.25 \times 2 = 2.50. (The first-in, first-out method can also be called the "last-in, still-here" method.)

Another way to calculate the Fifo cost of goods sold is to calculate the cost of the ending inventory and then subtract that from the total cost of the goods available:

Beginning inventory	$ 4.00
Purchases	10.00
Cost of Goods Available	$14,00
Less: ending inventory	2.50
Cost of Goods Sold	$11.50

The division of costs between the goods that were sold and the goods remaining in inventory under the Fifo method is entirely arbitrary. The units accumulating in the stockroom and available for sale are identical, both physically and economically (unless their value is affected by the passage of time, such as perishable goods). Physically, they are identical because they have the same physical properties and characteristics; economically they are identical, since they would be used identically by those who buy them. In other words, the user will obtain the same satisfaction (or utility) no matter which units are used—hence the market prices of all units will be identical at any given time.

The Fifo method distinguishes among the costs it assigns to these identical units on the basis of an artificial analogy between the flow of costs and the physical flow of the units themselves. The Fifo physical flow assumption is that goods flow out of the stockroom in the same order they enter it. That is, the first unit entering the stockroom is the first to leave it, the second unit in is the second unit out, and so on. The Fifo method uses this sequence to measure the cost of goods sold. This analogy with physical flows also leads to the assumption that the units remaining in inventory at any time are those that last entered the stockroom—that is, the last units in are the units still there.

This analogy has two defects. First, the order of departure has no necessary relationship to the order in which the units enter the stockroom. Units may actually leave in reverse order, in random order, or in some other order chosen to please the stockroom clerk.

Second, even if goods always flow into and out of inventory in a given sequence, costs needn't flow out of inventory in that same sequence. The accountant's objective is to choose measures of the cost of goods sold and the cost of the ending inventory that have the greatest *information value*—that is, the greatest assistance to those who use these figures in making decisions.[3] This objective may be served by assuming a flow of costs that is different from the flow of physical units. In any case, physical flow has nothing to do with information value and therefore should be ignored. If we want to argue for the Fifo method, we need to find something other than the physical flow of goods to justify our choice.

Last-in, First-out (Lifo) Costing

The second method of dividing the total historical cost of goods available between the income statement and balance sheet is the last-in, first-out method, or Lifo. Under Lifo, the units in the ending inventory are measured by the oldest unit costs in the inventory records; the cost of goods sold is quantified by the unit costs of the most recent purchases. To illustrate the Lifo method, we'll examine two different situations:

1. Case I: the physical inventory is larger at the end of the year than it was at the beginning.
2. Case II: the physical inventory is smaller at the end of the year than it was at the beginning.

[3] For discussion of this concept, see AICPA, "Report of the Study Group on the Objectives of Financial Statements," *Objectives of Financial Statements* (New York: 1973 [vol. 1] and 1974 [vol. II]).

Case I: inventory increase.   Suppose a company had a beginning inventory of four units on January 1, 19x1, with a cost of $1 a unit. The company bought eight units during the year, three of them on April 3 at $1.20 each and the other five on July 17 at $1.50 each. The costs of the goods available were as follows:

Beginning inventory	4 units × $1.00	$ 4.00
Purchases:		
April 3	3 units × $1.20	3.60
July 17	5 units × $1.50	7.50
Cost of Goods Available		$15.10

Only six units were sold during the year, leaving six units in inventory at the end of the year.

The Lifo measurements are diagrammed in Exhibit 9–3. Under Lifo, we calculate the cost of goods sold by working backward from

EXHIBIT 9–3.   Last-in, First-out (Lifo) Costing—Case I

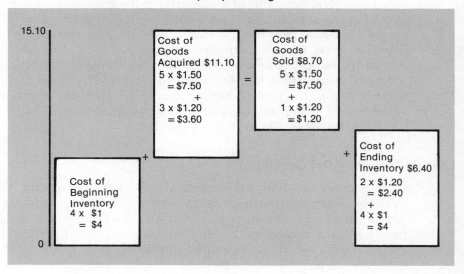

the most recent purchases. The *first* five units sold are assigned the unit costs of the *last five* units bought (5 × $1.50 = $7.50). The cost of the other unit sold is measured at the unit cost of the *next most recent* purchase, $1.20. The total cost of goods sold is $8.70.

The Lifo cost of the ending inventory is measured by starting with the *oldest* unit cost and working forward. The costs assigned to the first four units in the ending inventory, therefore, are the costs of the four units in the beginning inventory, $1 each. The next oldest unit cost is the cost of the first lot purchased during the year, $1.20 a unit, and this is the cost assigned to the other two units in the ending inventory. These two units are known as the *inventory increment* for the year; the $2 \times \$1.20 = \$2.40$ added to the inventory is known as the 19x1 *layer* in the inventory. The total Lifo inventory is $4 \times \$1 + 2 \times \$1.20 = \$6.40$.

Once again, the total of the cost of goods sold and the cost of the ending inventory equals the cost of goods available:

$$\$8.70 + \$6.40 = \$15.10.$$

Case II: inventory decrease.   Our second example forces us to go back into history. Remember that in historical costing systems the cost assigned to the beginning inventory of one year is the cost that was assigned to the ending inventory of the preceding year. Now suppose a company first adopted Lifo as of January 1, 19x1. At that time it had four units in inventory, at a unit cost of $1 (determined by the company's previous measurement method). This is known as the *base quantity*.

In 19x1, the quantity sold equalled the quantity purchased—in other words, all the costs of the last units in (the 19x1 purchases) were taken out to the income statement, leaving the costs of the base quantity untouched. In 19x2 the company bought 13 units at a cost of $1.50 each, but sold only ten units, thereby adding three units to the inventory and a 19x2 layer of $3 \times \$1.50 = \$4.50$. On January 1, 19x3, therefore, the company had the following inventory, on a Lifo basis:

	No. of Units	Unit Cost	Total Cost
Base quantity (19x0 prices)	4	$1.00	$4.00
19x2 layer	3	1.50	4.50
Total Lifo Inventory	7		$8.50

In 19x3 the company bought 15 units at a price of $1.60 each; it sold 17 units. The Lifo cost of goods sold is once again determined by working back, starting with the most recent purchases. The cost assigned to the first 15 units sold, therefore, is $15 \times \$1.60 = \$24$. The cost of the other two units sold comes from the beginning inventory. Since the first costs to go out of the inventory are the last costs to go into it, they must come, in this case, from the 19x2 layer: $2 \times \$1.50 = \$3$. This transfer from the inventory is known as an *inventory decrement* or *Lifo liquidation*.

EXHIBIT 9–4. Last-in, First-out (Lifo) Costing for the Year 19x3—Case II

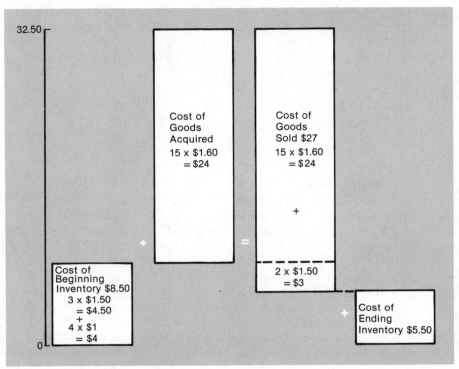

These calculations are illustrated in Exhibit 9–4. The ending inventory now consists of four units, measured at the unit cost of the base quantity, and one unit, measured at the $1.50 cost of the 19x2 layer.

The physical flow assumption.   Like Fifo, the Lifo method has an implicit physical flow assumption, that the last units entering the stockroom are the first to leave when sales occur. Consequently, it is assumed that the first unit to enter the stockroom is the last to leave it, as if the stockroom clerk always takes items from the front of the shelf, restocking it from the front and leaving the units at the back of the shelf untouched. The ending inventory is, therefore, measured at the costs of the original base quantity, plus the cost of any later increments and less any decrements, the decrements being costed at the unit costs of the most recent increment or increments.

This physical flow assumption is as arbitrary as the Fifo flow assumption. The actual physical flow in any particular company need be neither the former nor the latter, and, in fact, has no relevance to the quantification method choice.

Year-end adjustments. One feature of the Lifo method should be emphasized: *inventory fluctuations during a year do not affect the end-of-year Lifo inventory calculation.* Even if the inventory quantity drops to zero at one or more points during the year, the unit costs in the beginning inventory will carry over to the year-end inventory if inventory quantities have been restored before the end of the year. For example, suppose we have the following data for 19x3:

	No. of Units	Unit Cost	Total Cost
Beginning Inventory:			
Base quantity	4	$1.00	$ 4.00
19x2 layer	3	1.50	4.50
Total	7		8.50
Sales, April 3	5	?	?
Purchases, July 17	5	1.80	9.00

Because the number of units sold was just equal to the number of units bought during the year, the Lifo cost of goods sold is measured at the prices of the units bought during the year ($5 \times \$1.80 = \$9.00$); that is, the cost of goods sold equals the cost of purchases. The company hadn't made the July 17 purchase at the time it made its sales on April 3, however. To keep its perpetual inventory records up to date, it transferred the costs of five units from the beginning inventory to the cost of goods sold:

From the 19x2 layer (the "last in" at that time)	$3 \times \$1.50 = \$4.50$
From the base quantity (the next most recent batch)	$2 \times \$1.00 = \underline{2.00}$
Total	$\underline{\underline{\$6.50}}$

This was $2.50 less than the Lifo cost of goods sold, so the company had to make the following year-end adjusting entry:

Cost of Goods Sold	2.50	
Inventory		2.50

A similar adjustment would have to be made if routine inventory recordkeeping were based on Fifo or some other method.[4]

---

[4] Companies which keep their routine inventory cost records on a Fifo or average costing basis use an inventory "reserve" or allowance account or accounts to reconcile these records with the Lifo figures on the balance sheet date. For example:

Inventory, at Fifo cost	$12.60
Less: Lifo adjustment	4.10
Inventory, at Lifo cost	$ 8.50

Average Costing

The procedures necessary to maintain perpetual Fifo inventory cost records are somewhat cumbersome. The quantity and unit cost of each purchase lot have to be tracked through the system sepa-

EXHIBIT 9–5. Moving Average Costing

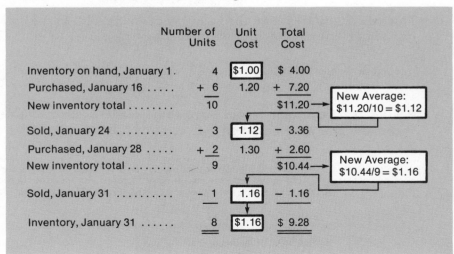

rately. To avoid this, many companies use a method known as the average-costing or weighted-average method.

Under average costing, all units in inventory on any date are measured at the same cost per unit, representing the average historical cost of the units in inventory at that time. One variant of this method is illustrated in Exhibit 9–5. The procedure is to recalculate the average cost after each purchase. This average is then used to measure inventory quantities and quantities sold until the next purchase is recorded. When the next purchase is made, a new average is calculated and the cycle is repeated.

Notice that the average in this illustration rose as additional purchases were made, but not as rapidly as the purchase prices themselves. Unless price changes are extreme, however, as they are in the exhibit, or the inventory turns over very slowly, the average cost at the end of the year will be reasonably close to the average cost of the most recent purchases.

EFFECTS OF INVENTORY COSTING ON INCOME AND CASH FLOW

The choice of one inventory costing method rather than another is likely to affect the company's net income, its cash flow, or both. It affects cash flows because the choice of Fifo precludes the use of Lifo for tax purposes—therefore, companies generally use the same inventory method for tax and financial reporting. The direction and magnitude of these effects depend on three sets of factors:

1. The direction (increase or decrease) and size of the change in the purchase price of the inventoried item.
2. The direction and size of the change in the physical inventory between the beginning and the end of the year.
3. The length of the period covered by the analysis.

We'll use five different hypothetical situations to study the effects of the first two of these; we'll discuss the third factor separately at the end of this section. In this discussion, we'll limit ourselves to Fifo and Lifo—average costing produces inventory costs and costs of goods sold very similar to those emerging from Fifo.

Situation A: Inventory Increases; Price Increases

The XYZ Company started the year 19x1 with a beginning inventory of four units, acquired earlier at a cost of $1 each. The company bought eight units at $1.25 each in 19x1 and sold seven units at a selling price of $2.25 each. In other words, the purchases were made at a price higher than the unit cost of the beginning inventory, and the inventory increased from four units at the beginning of the year to five units at the end of the year.

Exhibit 9–6 shows how the choice between Fifo and Lifo made in 19x1 would affect the company's income and cash flow for that year.

EXHIBIT 9–6.   Fifo versus Lifo: Inventory Increases; Purchase Price Increases

	Fifo	Lifo
Income:		
Sales revenues	$15.75	$15.75
Cost of goods sold:		
Beginning inventory	$ 4.00	$ 4.00
Purchases	10.00	10.00
Goods Available for Sale	$14.00	$14.00
Ending inventory*	6.25	5.25
Cost of goods sold	$ 7.75	$ 8.75
Income before taxes	$ 8.00	$ 7.00
Income tax at 50%	4.00	3.50
Net Income	$ 4.00	$ 3.50
Cash Flow:		
Cash flow before taxes:		
Receipts from sales	$15.75	$15.75
Payments for goods	10.00	10.00
Cash Flow before Taxes	$ 5.75	$ 5.75
Income tax	4.00	3.50
Net Cash Flow	$ 1.75	$ 2.25

* *Fifo:* ending inventory consists of the last five units purchased at $1.25 each.
   Lifo: ending inventory consists of the beginning inventory ($4.00) plus the first unit purchased at $1.25.

For simplicity, we have assumed that all expenses other than income taxes and the cost of goods sold were zero and that the income tax rate was a flat 50 percent. We have also assumed that all sales and purchases were on a cash basis and that taxes were paid immediately.

In this case we can see that the choice between Fifo and Lifo had the following effects:

1.   Fifo produced a *greater income before taxes* and a greater *net income* than Lifo.
2.   The choice of method didn't affect the amount of the *cash flow before taxes*.
3.   Fifo produced a smaller *net cash flow* (after taxes) than Lifo.

The differences arose because the Fifo cost of goods sold was $1.00 smaller than the Lifo cost of goods sold:

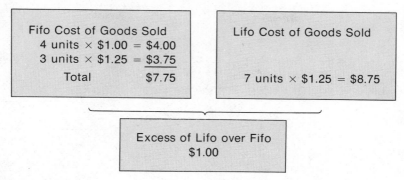

Since the Lifo cost of goods sold was greater, it provided a smaller taxable income than Fifo and the company's tax obligation was smaller. The tax reduction increased the amount of cash available for investment in equipment and other productive purposes.

Situation B: Inventory Increases; Price Doesn't Change

In 19x2 the company again bought eight units and sold seven. The purchase price was $1.25, the same as in 19x1, but the selling price moved up to $2.50. Assuming the company made its choice between Fifo and Lifo in 19x1, Exhibit 9–7 shows how this choice affected income and cash flow in 19x2. In this case, each method produced the same cost of goods sold figure, the same income, and the same cash flow. The main reason is that purchase prices had remained stable for two years, so that unit costs coming out of the beginning Fifo inventory were the same as the current purchase prices at which the entire Lifo cost of goods sold was measured.[5]

In other words, if prices remain stable for long periods of time and inventory quantities don't decline, it doesn't matter which method is used.

Situation C: Inventory Decreases; Price Increases

The purchase price jumped sharply at the beginning of 19x3, to $1.75 a unit. The company sold nine units in 19x3 at a price of $2.75

---

[5] If the company had started 19x1 with an inventory of nine units at a cost of $1.00 each, the beginning inventory in 19x2 would have included two units at $1.00, and the Fifo cost of goods sold would have been smaller than Lifo cost. Few inventories are this large, however, and introducing this additional feature into the illustration would add much complexity and little benefit. Our illustrations assume that the beginning inventory quantity is always smaller than the quantity sold during the year.

EXHIBIT 9–7. Fifo versus Lifo: Inventory Increases; Purchase Price Remains Unchanged

	Fifo	Lifo
Income:		
Sales revenues	$17.50	$17.50
Cost of goods sold:		
Beginning inventory	$ 6.25	$ 5.25
Purchases	10.00	10.00
Goods available for sale	$16.25	$15.25
Ending inventory*	7.50	6.50
Cost of goods sold	$ 8.75	$ 8.75
Income before taxes	$ 8.75	$ 8.75
Income tax at 50%	4.37	4.37
Net Income	$ 4.38	$ 4.38
Cash Flow:		
Cash flow before taxes:		
Receipts from sales	$17.50	$17.50
Payments for goods	10.00	10.00
Cash flow before taxes	$ 7.50	$ 7.50
Income tax	4.37	4.37
Net Cash Flow	$ 3.13	$ 3.13

Fifo: ending inventory consists of the last six units purchased at $1.25 each.

Lifo: ending inventory consists of the beginning inventory ($5.25) plus the first unit purchased in 19x2 at $1.25.

each, but bought only eight units at the $1.75 purchase price. Exhibit 9–8 summarizes the impact of the 19x1 choice between Fifo and Lifo on 19x3 income and cash flow.

The impact was basically the same as in Situation A: Fifo produced higher income figures and a smaller net cash flow than Lifo. This situation differs from Situation A only in that the Lifo cost of goods sold includes one unit at the unit cost of a previous period, reflecting the decrease in the quantity of inventory on hand. If this decrease hadn't taken place, the differences between Fifo and Lifo would have been even greater. We'll return to this point in a moment.

Situation D: Inventory Remains Unchanged; Price Decreases

In 19x4 the purchase price fell to $1.50. The company bought eight units at this price and sold eight units at a price of $2.50 each. The company had the same number of units in inventory at the end of the year as it had had at the beginning. Exhibit 9–9 shows how the 19x1 choice of inventory costing method affected the 19x4 results.

EXHIBIT 9-8.   Fifo versus Lifo: Inventory Decreases; Purchase Price Increases

	Fifo	Lifo
Income:		
Sales revenues	$24.75	$24.75
Cost of goods sold:		
Beginning inventory	$ 7.50	$ 6.50
Purchases	14.00	14.00
Goods Available for sale	$21.50	$20.50
Ending inventory*	8.75	5.25
Cost of goods sold	$12.75	$15.25
Income before taxes	$12.00	$ 9.50
Income tax at 50%	6.00	4.75
Net Income	$ 6.00	$ 4.75
Cash Flow:		
Cash flow before taxes:		
Receipts from sales	$24.75	$24.75
Payments for goods	14.00	14.00
Cash flow before taxes	$10.75	$10.75
Income tax	6.00	4.75
Net Cash Flow	$ 4.75	$ 6.00

Fifo: ending inventory consists of the last five units purchased at $1.75 each.
    Lifo: ending inventory consists of the beginning inventory ($6.50) less the last unit added to the Lifo inventory in 19x2 ($1.25).

Five units entered the Fifo cost of goods sold at the higher 19x3 price, whereas all units entered the Lifo cost of goods sold at the lower 19x4 price. (If the physical inventory doesn't decrease, Lifo measures the cost of all units sold by their current purchase prices.) The Fifo cost of goods sold, therefore, was greater than the Lifo cost and Fifo income was smaller. Fifo's higher cost of goods sold figure reduced current income taxes, however, and the after-tax cash flow was larger under Fifo than under Lifo.

Situation E: Inventory Decreases Substantially: Price Increases Slightly

The purchase price increased to $1.60 a unit in 19x5, and the selling price went up to $2.60. The company bought eight units during the year and sold ten units, thereby reducing the inventory from five units at the beginning of the year to three units at the end.

Exhibit 9-10 shows how the 19x1 choice between Fifo and Lifo affected the company's income and cash flows in 19x5. This situa-

EXHIBIT 9–9. Fifo versus Lifo: Inventory Remains Unchanged; Purchase Price Decreases

	Fifo	Lifo
Income:		
Sales revenues	$20.00	$20.00
Cost of goods sold:		
Beginning inventory	$ 8.75	$ 5.25
Purchases	12.00	12.00
Goods available for sale	$20.75	$17.25
Ending inventory*	7.50	5.25
Cost of goods sold	$13.25	$12.00
Income before taxes	$ 6.75	$ 8.00
Income tax at 50%	3.37	4.00
Net Income	$ 3.38	$ 4.00
Cash Flow:		
Cash flow before taxes:		
Receipts from sales	$20.00	$20.00
Payments for goods	12.00	12.00
Cash flow before taxes	$ 8.00	$ 8.00
Income tax	3.37	4.00
Net Cash Flow	$ 4.63	$ 4.00

* *Fifo:* ending inventory consists of the last five units purchased at $1.50 each.
    Lifo: ending inventory consists of the beginning inventory ($5.25).

tion is like Situation C except that the inventory reduction was larger (40 percent) and the increase in unit cost was much smaller (7 percent). In this case, the inventory liquidation was large enough to bring a substantial amount of older, lower unit costs into the Lifo income statement:

Fifo Cost of Goods Sold		Lifo Cost of Goods Sold	
5 units × $1.50 = $ 7.50		8 units × $1.60 = $12.80	
5 units × $1.60 = 8.00		1 unit × $1.25 = 1.25	
		1 unit × $1.00 = 1.00	
Total	$15.50	Total	$15.05

If the inventory liquidation had been smaller or the price increment larger, the Lifo cost of goods sold probably would have been greater than the Fifo cost, as in Situation C.

The result here is that Fifo income was smaller than Lifo income, while Fifo cash flow was larger than the Lifo cash flow.

**EXHIBIT 9-10.   Fifo versus Lifo: Inventory Decreases
Substantially Purchase Price Increases**

	Fifo	Lifo
Income:		
Sales revenue	$26.00	$26.00
Cost of goods sold:		
Beginning inventory	$ 7.50	$ 5.25
Purchases	12.80	12.80
Goods available for sale	$20.30	$18.05
Ending inventory*	4.80	3.00
Cost of goods sold	$15.50	$15.05
Income before taxes	$10.50	$10.95
Income tax at 50%	5.25	5.47
Net Income	$ 5.25	$ 5.48
Cash Flow:		
Cash flow before taxes:		
Receipts from sales	$26.00	$26.00
Payments for goods	12.80	12.80
Cash flow before taxes	$13.20	$13.20
Income tax	5.25	5.47
Net Cash Flow	$ 7.95	$ 7.73

Fifo: ending inventory consists of the last three units purchased at
$1.60 each.
   Lifo: ending inventory consists of three units from the Lifo base
quantity.

The Effect of the Age of Lifo Inventories

The comparisons we made in the preceding example all reflected
the effects of a choice between Fifo and Lifo in 19x1. The reason for
taking this cumulative approach is that the company can't change its
method easily once it has made its initial choice. The company has to
explain and justify any changes of this type,[6] and management is
reluctant to make such changes unless the arguments for change are
very strong.

The cumulative nature of the comparison shows up most strongly
when we consider the impact of an inventory decrement. If the decrement takes place the year after Lifo is adopted, the Lifo cost of
goods sold will be greater than under Fifo, if purchase prices have
fallen, and smaller than Fifo, if prices have risen. But if the liquidation takes place several years after Lifo was adopted, the unit cost
transferred from the inventory may be greater than, less than, or

---

[6] AICPA, "Accounting Principles Board Opinion 20," para. 16, in *Professional
Standards—Accounting, Current Text* (New York: Commerce Clearing House, Inc.,
1978), sec. 1051.16.

equal to the unit costs entering the income statement under Fifo, regardless of the direction prices have taken during the latest year.

Exhibit 9–11 diagrams the cumulative effect of the decision to use Lifo. The company has had an inventory of four units at the end of

EXHIBIT 9–11.   Cumulative Effect of Lifo on Inventory Cost

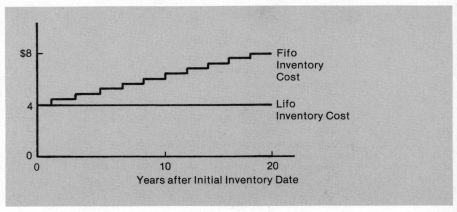

each year for the past 20 years. Unit cost was $1 at the beginning of this 20-year period, and the company adopted Lifo at that time. Since the year-end inventory always consisted of four units, the Lifo cost of the inventory remained at $4 throughout the period. This is represented by the height of the horizontal line in the diagram.

Prices rose five cents each year for 20 years, so that the purchase price is now $2 a unit. Under Fifo, the ending inventory each year would have been measured at the current year's price, and the Fifo cost of the ending inventory would have moved up the stepped line in the diagram. As this shows, although Lifo kept only $4 \times \$.05 = \$.20$ out of income before taxes each year, it has kept a total of $4 \times \$1 = \$4$ out of income during the entire 20-year period. If an inventory liquidation takes place now, the impact on income and cash flow will be much greater than it would have been 5, 10, or 15 years earlier.

Summary: Income and Cash Flow Effects

The conclusions we can reach from these illustrations are summarized in Exhibit 9–12. As long as the year-end inventory quantity is as large as or larger than the beginning quantity, the impact of the difference between the two methods is predictable. If an inventory decrement has taken place, however, we need information on the

EXHIBIT 9–12.   Fifo versus Lifo: Impact on Income and Cash Flow

If Purchase Price is: / And the Ending Inventory is:	Higher than in the Previous Year	The Same as in the Previous Year	Lower than in the Previous Year
Greater than the beginning inventory	Lifo income is smaller, Lifo cash flow larger	Lifo and Fifo have the same effects	Lifo income is larger, Lifo cash flow smaller
The same as the beginning inventory	Lifo income is smaller, Lifo cash flow larger	Lifo and Fifo have the same effects	Lifo income is larger, Lifo cash flow smaller
Less than the beginning inventory	Effects depend on size of price change, size of inventory change, and age of costs in the Lifo inventory.		

size of the decrement and the size of the gap between the current purchase price and the unit cost of the Lifo layers that were affected. Whether this year's price is higher or lower than last year's has no bearing on the question.

CHOOSING BETWEEN FIFO AND LIFO

Fifo and Lifo, despite their different effects on income and cash flow, are equally acceptable inventory costing methods in the United States. Management, therefore, is free to choose between them, subject to the requirements that the method chosen must be used consistently year after year and any changes must be justified. This being the case, we need to try to answer two questions:

1.   Which method is more likely to meet management's objectives?
2.   Which method is more likely to meet the needs of outside users of the financial statements?

Management's Criteria

Management's choice of an inventory method is likely to be based on its evaluation of the relative desirability of the impact the different methods will have on the company's cash flows and on its income. One issue is whether bigger cash flows are more desirable than smaller cash flows; the other issue is whether a bigger income figure is more desirable than a smaller figure.

If cash flow were the only variable, management would be expected to choose the method that maximized the company's cash flows—or, more accurately, the present value of those cash flows. A large cash flow gives management the ability to make the company grow, to pay its employees well, to pay dividends, and to reward management itself. The more cash management can generate, the faster the company can grow and the greater the prestige and monetary rewards the managers can reap for themselves.

Lifo generally meets the cash flow criterion better than Fifo. The reason is that the prices of most products and commodities have been and still are on a long-term upward trend. And because most successful businesses continue to grow, their needs for inventory also grow. From our illustrations in the preceding section, we saw that a combination of increasing prices and inventory growth produces a situation in which Lifo produces greater cash flows than Fifo because it leads to smaller income tax payments.

Lifo doesn't always provide tax advantages, of course. If inventories consist mainly of products without pronounced upward price trends, management has little incentive to use it. One reason for this reluctance is that the aspect of Lifo that produces the tax advantage also reduces reported net income. Other things being equal, management would rather report a higher income figure to the shareholders than a smaller one.

This preference may be due in part to executive compensation agreements that tie managerial bonuses and other rewards to reported income. Another reason may be that the company's creditors have imposed restrictions on managerial actions if reported income or retained earnings falls below a specified level.

A third possible explanation of management's preference for higher income figures is management's assumption that higher income figures can induce higher market prices for the company's stocks. Recent research seems to indicate that this effect is unlikely to occur unless the higher income figure represents a larger positive cash flow,[7] but informal surveys of managers reveal widespread doubts that these research findings are valid. Tax advantages, in other words, have to be truly substantial to induce managers to take the initiative to adopt Lifo.

---

[7] For a summary of evidence on this point, see Nicholas J. Gonedes and Nicholas Dopuch, "Capital Market Equilibrium, Information Production, and Selecting Accounting Techniques: Theoretical Framework and Review of Empirical Work," *Studies in Financial Accounting Objectives: Supplement to the Journal of Accounting Research*, 1974, pp. 48–161.

Outsiders' Criteria

Another question is whether, given the power to choose the inventory method, outside users of financial statements would choose the same method management has chosen. It can be argued that the best method is the one that gives outside users the greatest amount of help in predicting the amount and timing of the company's future cash flows and the uncertainty surrounding them—that is, the greatest information value.

Although it is not entirely clear how this requirement can be implemented, we suggest it might mean that the preferable method is the one that comes closest to providing investors and other outsiders with the following:

1. The dollar cost assigned to the goods sold should help the investor identify the *sustainable profit margin*—the rate of profit the company can sustain on a continuing basis.
2. The inventory figure should bear a normal relationship to the amount recoverable from customers.

Both of these needs for information are derived from a normative view of the objectives of financial statements: to help users predict and evaluate the company's future cash flows so as to make sound investment decisions.

Sustainable profit margin. The sustainable profit margin in a competitive industry is the spread between the market price and the current cost of obtaining the goods being sold. As the cost of buying goods goes up, their selling price is also likely to rise. If it doesn't rise enough, the company's ability to generate cash and distribute dividends will decline. Furthermore, the company won't be able to continue to replace the goods that have been sold or to maintain its marketing capacity at the same level as before, let alone expand it. When this happens, investors might reasonably conclude that the company will have to shrink its capacity to serve the market and its market share as well.

For example, suppose a retailer buys merchandise from a wholesaler at a price of $1 a unit and sells it to retail customers at a price of $1.50. If the replacement price has risen to $1.20 at the time of the sale, only 30 cents a unit will be available to contribute toward the costs of running the company and producing a profit. If the retailer wishes to restore the inventory to its former physical level, the remaining $1.20 will have to be used for that purpose.

An investor who wishes to calculate the sustainable profit margin should measure the cost of goods sold at the current replacement cost rather than at the historical cost of the goods sold to customers.

If the reported cost of goods sold is lower than the current replacement cost of these goods, then a portion of the net income can't be counted on to continue in the future. This portion results from the company's skill or good fortune in buying goods when prices were lower. We refer to this portion as an *inventory profit*. If prices have declined, the difference will be an *inventory loss*. In our example, if the cost of the units sold is measured at the historical price of $1, then $1.20 − $1.00 = $.20 of the reported gross margin is an inventory profit. This adjustment is illustrated in Exhibit 9–13.

EXHIBIT 9–13.   Inventory Profit Adjustment

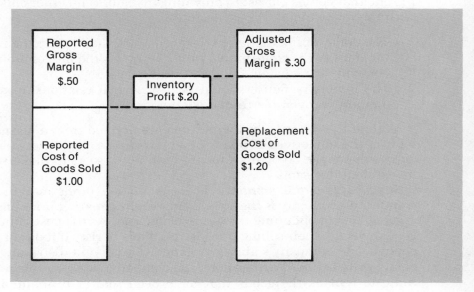

Inventory profits and losses, in other words, are measured by differences between the current replacement cost of the goods sold and the reported historical cost of goods sold. Since the Lifo cost of goods sold is ordinarily closer than Fifo to the current cost of the goods being sold, it ordinarily includes fewer inventory profits in reported income. Only if a company has substantial inventory liquidations will Lifo include large inventory profits in reported income.

Inventory measurement.   In a strict sense, inventories are measured at their historical cost because this shows the amount of resources that have been used to acquire them. Cost can also be interpreted, however, as a surrogate for the value of the inventory to a going concern. This value is an important figure to investors who wish to predict the company's cash flows, based on the assumption that cost is a reasonable approximation to the amount that will be left over from the ultimate selling price after deducting such factors as customer defaults, selling costs, interest on investment, and a normal merchandising profit.

This assumption, if it is valid at all, is valid only if unit cost is stated at or near current levels. Prices paid for inventory in the distant past have no relevance to the question of how much can be recovered from them today. The only prices that come near to answering this question are the prices that could be obtained for the inventory when sold in an orderly way, less selling cost, customer defaults, and interest on the investment in the inventory in the interim. Alternatively, under certain conditions, current replacement costs could serve as surrogates for the recoverable amounts.

Fifo certainly does a better job of approximating the current replacement cost of inventories than Lifo does. The unit costs in a Fifo inventory are seldom more than a few months old; Lifo inventories, in contrast, may be measured at the unit costs of 10, 20, or even more years in the past. The difference between the unit cost in the inventory figures and the current replacement cost at the inventory date is the *cumulative* inventory profit. As we saw in Exhibit 9–11, this is likely to be substantial for Lifo inventories, small for Fifo.

COST OR MARKET, WHICHEVER IS LOWER

No matter which costing method is used, generally accepted accounting principles require that the end-of-year inventory be restated at its market value whenever the market value of the ending inventory is less than the cost assigned to it. This is known as the *cost or market rule*, and the amount reported as inventory is known as the *lower of cost or market*.

For example, suppose a company has an ending inventory of five units at a Fifo cost of $1.50 a unit; the market value of these units dropped sharply just before the end of the year, to $1.30 a unit. The inventory would be written down by 20 cents a unit, a total of $1. The adjusting entry would have the following effect:

```
Cost of Goods Sold ......................        1
    Inventory ...........................                 1
```

In other words, the inventory write-down is added to the other costs included in the cost of goods sold.

Notice that the cost or market rule is applied to the ending inventory quantity, not to the quantities sold during the year. The cost of goods sold is measured at cost, not at market. The $1 we just added to the cost of goods sold is simply that portion of the cost of the ending inventory the decline in market value presumably has made unrecoverable in the future.

Evaluation of the Cost or Market Rule

The argument for the cost or market rule is that no asset should be listed on a company's balance sheet at an amount greater than it is likely to be able to recover from the use or sale of that asset in the normal course of events. Unrecoverable amounts have no value and, therefore, aren't assets.

The main objection to this rule is that it treats value increases and value decreases inconsistently. For example, if the market value of the inventory is greater than its cost, the company is not allowed to restate the inventory at this higher figure, even though the value increase is no less clear than a decline in market value.

The failure to recognize increases as well as decreases in market value can be regarded as a weakness of the historical cost basis of accounting. An increase in market value means that the company is better off because its future cash flows have increased. Since the financial statements are supposed to help investors predict the company's future cash flows, failure to recognize the increased market value reduces the statements' usefulness in the prediction process.

The cost or market rule is often defended on the grounds that it is "conservative" accounting. By writing an asset down to its market value, however, the accountant sets the stage for reporting a smaller cost of goods sold and more income in a future period. After all, the cost or market figure is treated as the *cost* of the next year's opening inventory, and this eventually gets into the cost of goods sold.

Application to Lifo Inventories

Although the cost or market rule is applicable no matter which method is used to establish the cost of the ending inventory, in practice it is seldom applied to Lifo inventories. The reason is that Lifo measures inventory costs at the costs prevailing when the inventories were built up, and in most cases these were lower than costs and market values are now. Market values would have to drop catastrophically in most cases to bring them down to the level of Lifo costs. A market adjustment to a Lifo inventory is therefore rare.

SUMMARY

Accountants base their measures of the historical cost of goods sold and the cost of the ending inventory on an assumed sequence of cost flows through the inventory system. The main alternative assumptions are first-in, first-out (Fifo), last-in, first-out (Lifo), and moving average.

Any of these methods can be used by any company; no criteria have been accepted to govern the choice among them as far as investors' needs are concerned. If Lifo is used for tax purposes in the United States, however, it must also be used for financial reporting; tax considerations, therefore, have a strong impact on the choice of an inventory measurement method.

In periods of rising prices, Lifo tends to produce higher cost of goods sold figures than either Fifo or average costing. This is likely to produce substantial income tax benefits, but the lower income figures Lifo produces may not be palatable to management. Lifo is also seen as a way of removing most so-called inventory profits and losses from reported income, however, and this has the effect of bringing the net income figure closer to the company's sustainable profit margin. At the same time, it takes the inventory figure farther away from the current replacement cost of the goods sold, a figure that may be relevant to the reader of the balance sheet.

Generally accepted accounting principles require the year-end inventory to be adjusted to the lower of their historical cost or their market value. In practice, because Lifo cost almost never exceeds market value, this cost or market adjustment ordinarily comes into play only in connection with inventories measured on a Fifo or average costing basis.

KEY TERMS

Average costing	Last-in, first-out (Lifo)
Cost or market rule	Lifo base quantity
Current replacement cost	Lifo inventory layer
First-in, first-out (Fifo)	Lifo liquidation
Inventory profit or loss	Sustainable profit margin

INDEPENDENT STUDY PROBLEMS (Solutions in Appendix B)

1. Inventory profits and losses. The Higby Company had 10,000 pounds of product in inventory on January 1, 19x1, at a Fifo cost of $30,000. Management decided to switch to the Lifo method, beginning in 19x1. Purchases and sales for the next eight years were as follows:

Year	Purchases	Sales (Pounds)
19x1	60,000 × $3.10 = $186,000	55,000
19x2	70,000 × $3.50 = 245,000	68,000
19x3	90,000 × $3.75 = 337,500	80,000
19x4	70,000 × $3.80 = 266,000	72,000
19x5	80,000 × $4.00 = 320,000	75,000
19x6	70,000 × $4.25 = 297,500	80,000
19x7	100,000 × $4.40 = 440,000	85,000
19x8	95,000 × $4.50 = 427,500	95,000

a.   Calculate the Lifo cost of goods sold for each year and the Lifo cost of the inventory at the end of each year.

b.   Calculate the Fifo cost of goods sold for each year and the Fifo cost of the inventory at the end of each year.

c.   Calculate the amount of inventory profit or loss for each year under each method.

2.   Lifo: effect of inventory liquidation and replenishment.   The Franklin Steel Warehouse Company adopted Lifo on January 1, 1972, and its 15,000-ton inventory was costed at its Fifo cost of $125 a ton on that date, a total of $1,875,000.

During 1972, the company purchased 100,000 tons at an average price of $130 a ton, and sold 95,000 tons. The last 20,000 tons purchased during December, 1972, cost $135 a ton.

Sales in 1973 amounted to 105,000 tons, but purchases totaled only 90,000 tons at an average cost of $140 a ton. (The last 5,000 tons purchased during 1973 also cost $140 a ton.) The inventory was down to 5,000 tons at the end of 1973 because a steel strike had cut off supplies. The company expected to rebuild its inventories to 15,000 tons as soon as steel became available again in 1974.

The Franklin Steel Warehouse Company measures the annual increments to its Lifo inventory at the average of all purchase prices paid during the year.

a.   Provide the figures necessary to complete the following table, showing inventories and cost of goods sold on both a Fifo and a Lifo basis:

	Inventory Cost		Cost of Goods Sold	
	Fifo	Lifo		Fifo	Lifo
January 1, 1972	$1,875,000	$1,875,000			
			1972 _____	_____
December 31, 1972	_____	_____		
			1973 _____	_____
December 31, 1973	_____	_____		

b.   Assuming that 15,000 tons is the normal inventory quantity and that the company intended to rebuild its inventories to this level as soon as possible, what was the effect of the "involuntary liquidation" of inventory on income before taxes for 1973?

c.   Assuming that inventories were increased to 15,000 tons by the end of 1974, with 1974 purchases at a cost of $145 a ton, what was the net

effect of the 1973 involuntary liquidation on Lifo inventory cost as of
December 31, 1974?

d. Assuming an income tax rate of 50 percent, calculate the effect of the
choice between Fifo and Lifo on the company's cash flows in 1972, 1973,
and 1974. The company purchased 100,000 tons of steel in 1974.

EXERCISES AND PROBLEMS

3. *Fifo and Lifo exercise.* New York Corporation made the following purchases during its first year of operation:

January 10, 1977	1,000 Units @ $3.00
March 20,1977	2,000 Units @ 3.25
May 12, 1977	2,500 Units @ 3.30
November 10, 1977	1,200 Units @ 4.00
December 20, 1977	1,800 Units @ 4.05

The company sold 6,000 units during 1977 at a price of $5 a unit. It had
pretax operating expenses of $5,000 and was subject to income taxes at a
rate of 25 percent.

a. Calculate the cost of goods sold, the cost of the ending inventory, and the
gross margin, all on a Fifo basis.
b. Perform the same calculations, using Lifo costing.
c. Discuss the impact of the choice between the two inventory costing
methods on the company's income and cash flows.

4. *Cost or market rule.* Apex Corporation has four products in inventory
at year-end:

Product	No. of Units	Cost/Unit	Market price/Unit
A	10,000	$10	$ 8
B	20,000	15	16
C	30,000	20	23
D	40,000	10	8

a. Calculate the ending inventory by applying the cost or market rule (1)
item by item and (2) to the inventory as a whole.
b. Calculate the effects on the cost of goods sold and gross margin of using
one version of the cost or market rule instead of the other.
c. Which of these ways of applying the cost or market rule do you prefer?
State your arguments.

5. *Lifo costing exercise.* A company had 60,000 units in inventory on
January 1, 19x8, at the following Lifo cost:

	No. of Units	Unit Cost	Total Cost
Base quantity	30,000	$ 5	$150,000
19x1 layer	15,000	6	90,000
19x4 layer	10,000	8	80,000
19x6 layer	5,000	10	50,000
Total	60,000		$370,000

It made the following purchases and sales during 19x8 and 19x9:

January 1—June 30, 19x8	Sales, 40,000 units
July 1, 19x8	Purchase, 100,000 units @ $12
July 1—December 31, 19x8	Sales, 50,000 units
January 1—June 30, 19x9	Sales, 60,000 units
July 1, 19x9	Purchase, 100,000 units @ $13
July 1—December 31, 19x9	Sales, 70,000 units

a.   Calculate the Lifo cost of goods sold and the Lifo cost of the ending inventory for each year.

b.   Calculate the inventory profit or loss for each year. State your assumptions.

6.   *Fifo costing exercise.* A company had 60,000 units in inventory on January 1, 19x8, at a Fifo cost of $11 a unit. It made the purchases and sales in 19x8 and 19x9 described in Exercise 5 above. The market value of the company's inventories was determined to be $11.50 a unit at the beginning of 19x8, $12.50 at the end of 19x8, and $12.40 at the end of 19x9.

a.   Calculate the Fifo cost of goods sold and the Fifo cost of the ending inventory for each year.

b.   Apply the cost or market rule to determine the inventory and cost of goods sold for each year.

c.   Given your answer to (*b*), calculate the inventory profit or loss for each year. State your assumptions.

7.   *Average costing exercise.* A company had 60,000 units in inventory on January 1, 19x8, at an average cost of $10.90 a unit. It made the purchases and sales in 19x8 and 19x9 described in Exercise 5 above.

a.   Calculate the cost of goods sold and the cost of the ending inventory for each year on an average costing basis.

b.   Comment on the numerical differences between your answer to (*a*) and the answers to Exercises 5 and 6.

8.   *Meaning of published replacement cost data.* The balance sheet in a company's annual report described the company's inventories as follows:

Inventories—substantially all stated at cost on "last-in, first-out" basis
with current replacement cost approximately $28,100,000 in excess
of stated cost.. $53,334,933

A year earlier, the corresponding inventory figure was $56,047,919, and current replacement cost was approximately $24,200,000 in excess of stated cost.

What information about the financial position and operations of the company do the figures on excess of replacement cost over stated cost provide?

9.   *Discussion question: excerpt from annual report.* The Mead Corporation listed inventories of $152,442,000 in its 1971 annual report. The following note was included in the report:

Accounting principles: Inventory—The inventories are stated at cost, determined principally on the last-in, first-out (Lifo) basis, which is less than market value. The Lifo inventory method results in a conservative inventory valuation during inflationary times. At December 31, 1971, the Lifo reserve was $26,016,000. In 1971, this reserve increased by $5,208,000 which, after taxes, decreased earnings by 16 cents per common share.

a.   What is this "Lifo reserve"? Why did it increase? Why did this increase lead to a decrease in earnings per share?
b.   Were the prices paid by the Mead Corporation rising or falling in 1971? In general, how would you expect rising purchase prices to affect the size of the Lifo reserve?

10. Discussion question: excerpt from annual report.   The notes to the 1971 financial statements of The Budd Company included the following paragraph:

Effective January 1, 1971 the company changed its method of pricing that portion of its inventories previously stated on the last-in, first-out cost basis (Lifo) to the lower of average cost or market. As a result of this change net earnings in 1971 were increased by approximately $450,000 (7 cents per share). The use of the Lifo inventory method was discontinued because (*a*) the Lifo values were not used in determining product selling prices or in measuring divisional operating results and (*b*) fourth-quarter earnings were distorted since adjustments to the Lifo reserve for the year normally had been provided in that quarter. The financial statements for 1970 have been restated for the resultant increase in 1970 inventories of $2,438,000; the effect on the loss for 1970 was negligible.

a.   Why did the company have to make adjustments to the "Lifo reserve" in the fourth quarter of each year? What effect did these adjustments probably have? Why did the company regard this as an argument for dropping Lifo?
b.   Why did the $2,438,000 inventory adjustment in 1970 have only a negligible effect on net income for that year? Why did the change increase the 1971 net income by $450,000?
c.   Do you think that the company's reasons for switching from Lifo were valid?

11. Change from Fifo to Lifo; recommendation to management.   The Weeks Woolen Company had always used the Fifo method of inventory costing. For the calendar years 19x7 and 19x8, its reported net income or loss before deducting income taxes was as follows:

19x7 . . . . $234,690 profit
19x8 . . . .   60,140 loss

Early in 19x9, the company's management was considering shifting to a last-in, first-out basis. Investigation revealed that the inventory figures for the three years were or would have been as follows:

	Pounds	Fifo Amount	Lifo Amount
December 31, 19x6	500,000	$225,000	$225,000
December 31, 19x7	475,000	403,000	210,000
December 31, 19x8	513,000	338,000	235,000

The cost of goods purchased amounted to $400,000 in 19x7 and $350,000 in 19x8.

a. Compute the net income before income taxes the company would have reported each year if it had adopted the Lifo method of inventory costing as of January 1, 19x7.

b. Would adoption of Lifo as of that date have led to more informative income statements for the two years? Explain your reasoning.

c. By the beginning of 19x9, management no longer had the option of adopting Lifo as of January 1, 19x7, but it could adopt it as of January 1, 19x8. Write a brief report to management, recommending for or against adoption of Lifo as of that date, giving your reasons for your recommendation.

12. *Lifo costing; inventory recordkeeping.* The XYZ Company uses Fifo for inventory recordkeeping in its perpetual inventory system and Lifo for external financial reporting. The inventory accounts showed the following balances on January 1, 19x1:

> Inventories (50,000 units) .... $50,000 dr.
> Lifo Inventory Adjustment ....   20,000 cr.

The balance in the Lifo Inventory Adjustment account measured the difference between Lifo and Fifo inventory cost on that date.

Purchases and sales during the year were as follows:

Quarter	Purchases	Sales
1	50,000 units × $1.10	45,000 units
2	40,000 × 1.15	50,000
3	60,000 × 1.12	55,000
4	70,000 × 1.25	60,000

Annual increments to the Lifo inventory were measured at the prices paid for the first units purchased during the year.

a. Calculate the Fifo cost of goods sold for each quarter and for the year as a whole.

b. Calculate the Lifo cost of goods sold for the year.

c. Set up a T-account to represent the Inventories account, enter the opening balance, record the purchases and cost of goods sold as the company would record them each quarter on a Fifo basis, and calculate the ending balance in this account.

d. Prepare the entry that should be made to adjust the balance in the Lifo Inventory Adjustment account at the end of the year.

e. Management told the shareholders that inventory losses in the fourth quarter erased most of the net income reported on the interim financial statements for the first three quarters of the year, despite record fourth-quarter sales. Explain what happened.

13. Effect of inventory method on inventory profits. A company had an inventory of 15,000 pounds of product on January 1, 19x9. This was shown on the balance sheet in the following way:

Inventory, at Fifo cost	$30,000
Less: Adjustment to reduce inventory to a Lifo basis	15,200
Inventory, at Lifo Cost	$14,800

The supporting data showed the following:

Base quantity	8,000 lbs. × $0.80	$ 6,400
19x0 layer	4,000 lbs. × $1.00	4,000
19x3 layer	2,000 lbs. × $1.40	2,800
19x6 layer	1,000 lbs. × $1.60	1,600
Total Inventory, at Lifo Cost		$14,800

The company bought 25,000 pounds of material during 19x9 and sold 29,000 pounds. Each unit purchased cost $2.50, and the purchase price remained constant at this level throughout the year. On December 31, 19x9, however, the company's supplier announced that the price of the material had been raised to $3, effective immediately.

a. Compute the December 31, 19x9, inventory on a Lifo basis.
b. Suppose this company had always used Fifo instead of Lifo. By what amount would Fifo income before taxes in 19x9 have differed from Lifo income in that year?
c. What was the total effect of the company's shift to Lifo on income before taxes in all years since the adoption of Lifo, taken together?
d. Calculate the amount of inventory profit or loss, if any, that was included in 19x9 net income under Lifo.
e. Would the use of Fifo have increased or decreased the amount of inventory profit or loss included in reported income before taxes for 19x9? Quantify and explain.

14. Relationship of inventory growth to effects of inventory method. A company started in business on January 1, 19x0, by purchasing 10,000 units of merchandise at a cost of $10 each. Sales amounted to 50,000 units in 19x0, and the company had 10,000 units in inventory at the end of 19x0.

The purchase price of the merchandise increased by $1 a unit on January 1 of each year for the next four years. For example, all purchases in 19x0 were made at a price of $10, all purchases in 19x1 cost $11, and all purchases in 19x4 cost $14. The income tax rate was 40 percent for the entire five-year period, and the company had taxable income each year.

a. Calculate the cost of the ending inventory for each of the five years on the assumption that the inventory quantity remained at its 19x0 level: (1) on a Fifo basis and (2) on a Lifo basis.
b. Repeat the calculations called for in (a) on the assumption that year-end

inventory quantities increased by 2,000 units each year, beginning in 19x1.

c. Repeat the calculations for the situation described in (b), except that the year-end inventory quantity fell to 4,000 units in 19x3 and then returned to 18,000 units at the end of 19x4.

d. Given these calculations, describe briefly how growth influences the effects of the inventory costing method choice on income and cash flow.

15. *Effect of inventory method on managerial decision.* "We'd be foolish to buy now," Helen Hunt, the Carthage Company's purchasing agent said. "The price can't be any higher next spring than it is now, and I expect it to be much lower. We can make $7,000 by keeping our inventory down to 80,000 pounds until the new crop comes in next year."

"You forget," replied Dave Jones, the company's controller, "that if we don't replace these inventories before the end of the year we'll lose our favorable Lifo base. Not only that, but if you aim at an 80,000-pound inventory, you'll be buying in uneconomically small lots. You'll probably have to pay premiums on rush orders, too."

The Carthage Company is a large, wholesale distributor of food products. One of these products is made from citrus fruits. The annual price is determined largely by the size of the winter crop in Florida. A very severe winter in 1977–78 caused heavy damage to the Florida citrus crop. The purchase price went up to 32 cents a pound in January of 1978 and remained at this level throughout the year.

In 1972, the company had adopted the Lifo method of inventory costing for all of its products, both for tax purposes and for financial reporting. The balances in the company's inventory accounts on January 1, 1972, became the costs of the Lifo base quantities.

Separate accounts were established at that time for the materials cost and processing cost components of the Lifo inventories. The company's inventories of its citrus-based product on January 1, 1972, contained materials with a purchase weight of 100,000 pounds, at an inventory cost of 20 cents a pound, a total of $20,000. Increments to inventories in subsequent years were priced at the prices paid for the first purchases during the year cumulating to the incremental quantity.

The following table shows purchases and inventory data for the materials content of this product for the years 1972 through 1978:

Year	Beginning-of-Year Inventory (Pounds)	Price Paid for First Purchases (per Pound)	Total Cost of Materials Purchased
1972	100,000	$0.20	$ 60,000
1973	100,000	0.22	74,000
1974	110,000	0.23	92,000
1975	150,000	0.24	96,000
1976	180,000	0.30	88,000
1977	130,000	0.26	112,000
1978	200,000	0.32	?

Because of the high purchase prices, Ms. Hunt deliberately bought less citrus fruit in 1978 than the company was using. As a result, the inventory had dropped to 80,000 pounds by the end of October, 1978, the quantity referred to in the conversation quoted earlier. Her recommendation was to maintain inventories of this product at this level until the new crop was processed in the spring of 1979.

Mr. Jones opposed this and recommended that inventories be rebuilt to 200,000 pounds by the end of 1978, at a purchase price of about 32 cents a pound. He estimated that if this were not done, the lower inventory levels would increase purchasing and handling costs by $2,000 in 1978 and $400 in 1979.

Both executives were agreed that an inventory of 200,000 pounds of this product represented an optimum inventory level. If her proposal was accepted, Ms. Hunt planned to rebuild inventories to this level as soon as the 1979 crop was processed. An average crop in 1979 would lead to a price of about 26 cents a pound.

The income tax in both years was 55 percent of taxable income.

a. Calculate the materials cost component of the cost of goods sold and the materials cost component of the end-of-year inventory of this product for each year, 1972–77.
b. By how much would 1978 reported income before taxes have been increased or decreased if the purchasing agent's proposal had been accepted?
c. Assuming that all purchases are paid for immediately in cash, would the purchasing agent's proposal or the controller's alternative have led to a larger cash balance after inventories were replenished in 1979? What would have been the amount of the difference? Ignore interest costs.
d. Should the purchasing agent's proposal have been accepted? Would your conclusion be different if the company's inventory had been on Fifo? How, if at all, does the inventory costing method influence decisions of this kind?

10

Depreciation

INVENTORIES CONSIST OF ITEMS that will provide their services all at once, when the individual items are used or sold. A depreciable asset, in contrast, is a bundle of services to be used by during the asset's lifetime. This bundle of services is known as the asset's *service potential*. The accountant's problem is to estimate the percentage of this service potential that is likely to be used each year, and place a dollar figure on this percentage. This dollar amount is the depreciation for that year.

The purpose of this chapter is to explore the factors the accountant might consider in calculating depreciation:

1. The nature of depreciation.
2. The length of the asset's life.
3. The time pattern of the asset's usefulness.
4. Recognizing gains and losses from asset retirements.
5. Changes in the underlying assumptions.
6. Depreciation for nonaccounting purposes.

THE NATURE OF DEPRECIATION

The use of the services of an asset is expected to result in future net cash flows to the company in excess of the net cash flows that would have been generated in the absence of that asset. These excess net cash flows are known as the *incremental cash flows* attributable to the asset. As we saw in Chapter 7, the present value of these incremental cash flows measures the value of this asset to the company. Because management has no reason to buy an asset that isn't worth its cost, we can assume the present value of these cash flows is at least equal to the asset's cost at the time it is acquired.

This means that two figures can be identified or estimated for every asset starting its life in the company: (1) its economic value, based on its estimated incremental cash flows and (2) its acquisition cost. Each of these can be a starting point for a depreciation calculation.

One possibility is to base depreciation on the change in value occurring each year. As the asset's services are used during a given year, the incremental cash flows attributable to it and arising in that year are realized. This leaves fewer services available for the future and fewer future cash flows; the asset's value, therefore, will be smaller at the end of the year than it was at the beginning unless some of the estimates have changed. *An economist would use this decline in value as the estimated depreciation for the year*—that is, "economic depreciation."

Exhibit 10–1 shows how this would work. It represents an asset that management expects will generate cash flows for ten years. The height of each bar shows the present value of the cash flows the asset is expected to generate after that date. Depreciation each year is measured by the difference between the height of the bar at the end of that year and the height of the preceding bar.

EXHIBIT 10–1. Economic Depreciation Measured by the Estimated Decline in Present Value

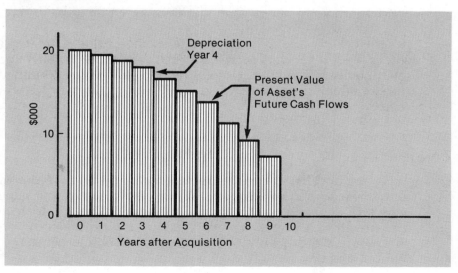

Calculated in this way, total depreciation during the asset's life will add up to its full present value at the time of acquisition. For the reasons outlined in Chapter 7, however, accountants start with a different total amount to be depreciated. Instead of value, they base their depreciation charge each year on the asset's cost. In other words, they use *cost* to represent the asset's total lifetime service potential; the asset's depreciation in any year is the cost of the services of that asset the company used up during the year.

Why may cost be unequal to the present value of the asset's estimated incremental cash flows at the time of acquisition? The seller and the buyer are likely to have different expectations regarding the magnitude and timing of the incremental cash flows. If the seller assigns a higher present value to these cash flows than the buyer, the buyer won't buy. The purchase is evidence that the purchase price is either equal to *or less than* the present value of the incremental cash flows expected by the buyer. In other words, cost may be less than the asset's value.

In a conventional accounting system in which expenses are measured by the historical cost of the resources used to generate current revenues, the total cost applicable to a depreciable asset's usable service potential is the difference between the asset's original cost and its ultimate resale or salvage value. This difference is known as the *depreciable cost:*

$$\begin{array}{ccc} \text{Depreciable} \\ \text{Cost} \end{array} = \begin{array}{c} \text{Original} \\ \text{Cost} \end{array} - \begin{array}{c} \text{Estimated End-of-Life} \\ \text{Salvage Value} \end{array}$$

In other words, the asset's ultimate salvage value is treated as the cost of the services this company doesn't expect to use but expects to sell to someone else. In practice, salvage value is often assumed to be zero, in which case the entire original cost becomes the depreciable cost.

ECONOMIC LIFE

Having decided to base depreciation charges on cost, the accountant's next step is to estimate the period of time during which the asset will be useful to this firm. This period is known as the asset's economic life. It comes to an end and the asset is replaced or retired as a result of either physical deterioration or obsolescence.

Physical Deterioration

Physical deterioration arises through asset use, the passage of time, or accidental damage. Its consequence is a decline in the quantity or quality of the asset's output or a rise in its unit cost.

The effect of wear and tear and age on output quantity or quality often can be offset or at least reduced by maintenance expenditures. At some point, however, the maintenance outlays needed to accomplish this may increase, and eventually they may become so large that replacement or retirement will become preferable to continued operation. The length of the period before this is expected to happen is the asset's estimated physical life.

Obsolescence

In a dynamic economy, obsolescence is sometimes more important than wear and tear and age in impairing and eventually terminating the useful lives of plant and equipment.

Obsolescence sometimes results from a revolutionary development such as a sudden shift in market demand. When this happens, the asset's life is likely to come to a sudden end if it is highly specialized and incapable of being converted to other uses. For example, the diaper industry experienced a dramatic market-demand shift from cloth to plastic, which had a devastating obsolescence effect on the industry's capital assets.

Evolutionary obsolescence takes place more gradually, through developments that lower the cost or increase the output of the latest available equipment. As this happens, the incremental cash flows attributable to newly available assets will exceed those of the old assets. When the difference between these two streams of cash flows gets large enough, replacement will become desirable and the old asset's life will come to an end. This is becoming increasingly true due to new technological advances in many products such as computers and with the increasing governmental pressure on companies to conform to tighter environmental protection standards.

For example, a company may have purchased an electric adding machine ten years ago. Though still usable, modern technology has made it obsolete. An electronic calculator can do multiplication, division, percentage calculations, and many other operations and is even capable of being programmed for more complex operations the firm now needs to perform. Furthermore, the time, effort, space, and repair cost of the adding machine compared with those of an electronic calculator are so much greater that replacement is profitable. This is how evolutionary obsolescence works.

If obsolescence strikes before the asset reaches the end of its physical life, its profitability to the company will come to an end then. In
other words, economic life is the shorter of physical life and obsoles-
cent life.

DEPRECIATION TIME PATTERNS

Once life has been estimated, the next problem is to decide what
percentage of the asset's total lifetime service potential is likely to be
used up each year. This is an important part of accrual accounting,
which requires the matching of current revenues with the costs of
the resources used up in producing them. Accountants sometimes
refer to this accrual requirement as the *matching principle*.

The amount of depreciation to be recognized each year is calculated in advance, when the asset is first placed in service. A number
of well-known formulas are available for this purpose, each designed
to construct predetermined *depreciation schedules* conforming to a
specific year-by-year pattern of service consumption. We'll discuss
four of these:

1.   Straight-line depreciation.
2.   Accelerated (diminishing-charge) depreciation.
3.   Production-unit depreciation.
4.   Implicit-interest depreciation.

We'll finish the section with a brief discussion of the criteria used to
choose among these methods for public financial reporting.

Straight-Line Depreciation

In straight-line depreciation, the depreciation amount is the same
each year, no matter how lightly or heavily the asset is used. If a new
machine, costing $36,000, is expected to last 12 years with a $1,500
end-of-life salvage value, the straight-line annual depreciation will
be:

$$\frac{\$36,000 - \$1,500}{12} = \$2,875.$$

For convenience, the straight-line formula is usually expressed as
a *depreciation rate,* equal to the reciprocal of the number of years
the asset is assumed or expected to be useful. A 10 percent rate
represents a ten-year life, a 4 percent rate represents a 25-year life,
and so on. In our example, the rate is $1/12$, or 8.33 percent. This rate is
then multiplied by the depreciable cost—original cost less anticipated end-of-life salvage value.

Accelerated (Diminishing-Charge) Depreciation

As the term implies, accelerated-depreciation formulas produce periodic depreciation charges that are greater in the early years of the asset's life than the straight-line formula. The most widely used accelerated formulas in the United States are the *sum-of-the-years'-digits* and *double-rate, declining-balance* formulas.

Sum-of-the-Years'-Digits Depreciation. The first step in the sum-of-the-years'-digits method is to number each year of the asset's anticipated life, starting with the number 1 for the first year, 2 for the second and so on. Thus if n represents the asset's life in years, each year from 1 to n can be represented by a digit 1, 2, 3, . . . , n.

The next step is to add these digits together to get their sum. For example, if $n = 12$, the sum of the digits is $1 + 2 + . . . + 12 = 78$. This figure can also be derived from the following equation:

$$\text{Sum-of-the-Years' Digits} = n(n + 1)/2.$$

In this case, since $n = 12$, the sum is $12 \times 13/2 = 78$.

The third step is to calculate a *separate* depreciation rate for each year by dividing the sum of the digits (78) into the individual digits arranged in *reverse* order. In other words, the digit 12 is assigned to year 1, the digit 11 to year 2, and so on. The depreciation rates are 12/78 for the first year, 11/78 for the second, and so on, down to 1/78 for the 12th year.

The final step is to multiply these rates by the depreciable cost to determine the annual depreciation amounts. The sum of these depreciation figures will reduce the asset's book value to its estimated salvage value at the end of its estimated life.

In the example, total depreciable cost is $36,000 - $1,500 = $34,500. The first year's depreciation is 12/78 × $34,500 = $5,308. This figure is shown in the first line of the second column of Exhibit 10–2. The rest of this column lists the depreciation charges for subsequent years, computed in this way. Book value at the end of 12 years is $1,500, the estimated resale value at that time.

Double-rate, declining-balance depreciation. Double-rate, declining-balance depreciation is calculated by multiplying a *fixed rate* by the asset's *book value* at the beginning of each year. Since book value declines each year, the depreciation charge also declines. (Book value equals original cost minus accumulated depreciation.)

The depreciation rate specified in this method is twice the straight-line depreciation rate. For our machine with a life of 12 years the rate is $2 \times 8\frac{1}{3}$ percent $= 16\frac{2}{3}$ percent. The depreciation amounts determined by this method are shown in the fourth column

EXHIBIT 10–2.   Comparison of Depreciation Schedules

Year	Sum-of-the-Years' Digits Beginning Book Value	Annual Charge	Double Rate, Declining Balance Beginning Book Value	Annual Charge	Straight Line Beginning Book Value	Annual Charge
1	$36,000	$ 5,308	$36,000	$ 6,000	$36,000	$ 2,875
2	30,692	4,865	30,000	5,000	33,125	2,875
3	25,827	4,423	25,000	4,167	30,250	2,875
4	21,404	3,981	20,833	3,472	27,375	2,875
5	17,423	3,538	17,361	2,894	24,500	2,875
6	13,885	3,096	14,467	2,411	21,625	2,875
7	10,789	2,654	12,056	2,009	18,750	2,875
8	8,135	2,211	10,047	1,674	15,875	2,875
9	5,924	1,769	8,373	1,395	13,000	2,875
10	4,155	1,327	6,978	1,163	10,125	2,875
11	2,828	885	5,815	969	7,250	2,875
12	1,943	443	4,846	807	4,375	2,875
13	1,500	—	4,039	2,539	1,500	—
Total		$34,500		$34,500		$34,500

of Exhibit 10–2. For example, the amount for the first year is $0.167 \times \$36,000 = \$6,000$. This reduces the asset's book value from $36,000 to $30,000 at the end of the year. Depreciation for the second year, therefore, is $0.167 \times \$30,000 = \$5,000$.

Notice that this formula fails to reduce the book value to the salvage-value level at the end of the asset's life. Book value at the end of 12 years is $4,039, or $2,539 more than the estimated salvage value. This $2,539 would have to be recognized as a loss when the asset was retired at the beginning of the 13th year.

To avoid this, most companies use a modified form of the double-rate, declining-balance (DDB) method, in which they switch to straight-line depreciation of the *remaining depreciable cost* in the year in which the DDB depreciation figure would be less than the straight-line amount. In our illustration, this switchover point comes in the eighth year, when the remaining depreciable cost is $10,047 - $1,500 = $8,547$ and the asset still has five years' life left. The comparison for that year is:

Straight-Line Depreciation of Remaining Depreciation Cost	Double-Rate, Declining-Balance Depreciation
$8,547/5 = \$1,709$	$0.167 \times \$10,047 = \$1,674$

Depreciation for the eighth year and each of the four years after that would be set at $1,709, and this would bring the book value down to $1,500 at the end of the 12th year.[1]

Comparing the results. Both sum-of-the-years'-digits and double-rate, declining-balance depreciation methods will produce depreciation amounts greater than straight-line depreciation in the early years of an asset's life and smaller in the later years. Book values under either of the diminishing-charge methods will be smaller in all years than book values under straight-line depreciation.

To make these relationships stand out as clearly as possible, we have drawn the diagrams in Exhibit 10–3 to reflect depreciation and

EXHIBIT 10–3. Graphic Comparisons of Annual Depreciation and Book Value

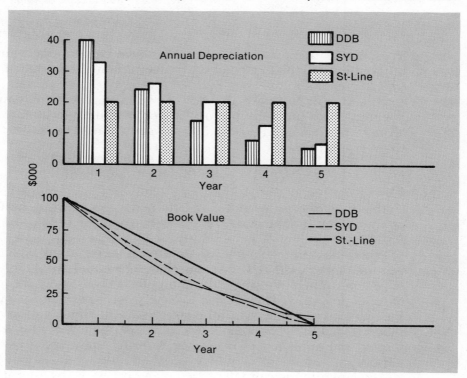

---

[1] In the absence of strong opposing evidence, business firms tend to estimate zero salvage value in establishing their depreciation schedules. In such cases, the switchover is made at the midpoint in the asset's life. In the illustration, the switchover would be made in the seventh year and the annual depreciation for the final six years would be one sixth of the declining-balance book value at the beginning of the seventh year ($12,056, from Exhibit 10–2), or $2,009 a year.

book values of an asset with a five-year estimated life and zero estimated salvage value. The upper diagram shows the annual depreciation schedules under the three methods we have described so far; the lines in the lower diagram trace the paths the asset's book value would take.

Production-Unit Depreciation

Some companies use a depreciation method known as production-unit depreciation. The depreciation rate is calculated as follows:

$$\text{Depreciation/Unit} = \frac{\text{Original Cost} - \text{Estimated Salvage Value}}{\text{Lifetime Production Capacity (Units)}}$$

The depreciation charge in any year is then equal to the number of units of output (pounds, gallons, or usage hours) multiplied by the unit depreciation rate.

For example, suppose abrasion of certain high-cost moving parts is expected to limit the life of the new machine to 20,000 hours, after which it will have a $1,500 salvage value. The rate reflecting these assumptions is:

$$\frac{\$36,000 - \$1,500}{20,000 \text{ hours}} = \$1.725 \text{ an hour.}$$

If the machine is used for 1,000 hours during the first year, production-unit depreciation for that year will be 1,000 × $1.725 = $1,725.

Production-unit depreciation is almost never used for ordinary commercial or industrial assets because economic life is more likely to be determined by rising costs or obsolescence than by the number of units produced. The method is widely used, however, to quantify the *depletion* of such natural resources as oil and gas reserves and mineral deposits and the depreciation of the costs of the wells, mines, and other assets necessary to bring these resources to the surface.

Accountants measure depletion on a cost basis, by allocating the cost of the natural resources to the units removed in any time period. For example, if a company buys an oil field for $1 million with an estimated reserve of 1 million barrels of oil, the cost per barrel is $1 million/1 million = $1. If 50,000 barrels of oil are removed during the first year, depletion of $50,000 (50,000 barrels × $1 a barrel) will be recognized for financial reporting purposes.

The entries to record cost depletion are identical in form to those used to record estimated depreciation:

Depletion   50,000
    Accumulated Depletion—Oil Field ...   50,000

The debit records depletion as an operating cost for the year, assignable to the oil produced; the credit records the reduction in the asset.

Implicit-Interest Depreciation

We pointed out at the beginning of this chapter that a decision to acquire an asset is evidence of management's judgment that the prsent value of this asset's incremental cash flows is at least equal to its cost. As time goes by, the asset generates cash flows, leaving fewer cash flows for the future. This means the value of the remaining cash flows declines from year to year, if the original estimates remain unchanged. For management to justify holding an asset for one more year, the cash flows have to be large enough to cover interest on the asset's value at the beginning of the year plus this decline in value. Phrased differently, this says the cost of using the asset's services for a year is the sum of a year's interest and the year's depreciation.

This idea is the basis of the *implicit-interest method* of depreciation. We'll illustrate this method by applying it to a machine which has an estimated life of only five years with no salvage value at the end of that time. The machine costs $6,000, and management expects it will generate incremental cash flows of $1,503 at the end of each of the five years. These cash flows are equivalent to an annual rate of return of 8 percent every year during the asset's life. (We'll explain this calculation in more detail in Chapter 22, but, in essence, what we've done is find the rate of interest at which the present value of the future cash flows is equal to the machine's $6,000 initial cost.)

Column 5 in Exhibit 10–4 shows a depreciation schedule calculated to enable the company to report an 8 percent rate of return on the asset's book value each year, if the cash flows are as predicted. For example, income for the first year must be $6,000 \times 0.08 = $480 if the asset is to earn 8 percent on the asset's $6,000 beginning book value. This $480, referred to as *implicit interest,* is the first figure in column 4 of the exhibit. This leaves $1,023 of the $1,503 cash flow to cover amortization of the asset's cost, and this amount is entered in the first line of column 5.

Depreciation of $1,023 in the first year reduces the asset's book value from $6,000 to $4,977 at the beginning of the second year. An

EXHIBIT 10–4. Implicit-Interest Depreciation: Level Cash Flow Stream

(1) Year	(2) Book Value (= Present Value), Beginning of Year [Line above: (2) − (5)]	(3) Anticipated Cash Flow	(4) Income (2) × 8%	(5) Implicit-Interest Depreciation ("Economic Depreciation") (3) − (4)
1	$6,000	$1,503	$480	$1,023
2	4,977	1,503	398	1,105
3	3,875	1,503	310	1,193
4	2,682	1,503	214	1,289
5	1,393	1,503	111	1,392

8 percent return on this amount would be $398, the amount shown in the second line of column 4. If the company reports this income in the second year, its reported rate of return on book value will be just 8 percent:

> Rate of Return = $398/$4,977 = 8 Percent.

Depreciation for the second year, therefore, must be $1,503 − $398 = $1,105, the amount shown in the second line of column 5. Repeating this process for the other three years produces the figures shown in the last three lines of column 5. The $1 difference between the depreciation charge for the fifth year and the asset's book value at the beginning of the year is a rounding error and has no other significance.

Notice that each book value figure in column 2 equals the present value of the machine's anticipated future cash flows, discounted at 8 percent. For example, the book value at the beginning of the second year is the present value of four annual receipts of $1,503 each. ($1,503 times 3.3121, the four-year factor in Table 4 of Appendix A, equals $4,978, which differs from the figure in column 2 by a $1 rounding error only.) Similarly, the present value of three annual $1,503 receipts is $3,875, the book value at the beginning of the third year, and so on.

Moreover, the implicit-interest depreciation figures in column 5 are also "economic-depreciation" figures, if interest is calculated at 8 percent. In other words, we could have derived the depreciation schedule in column 5 by computing the present values of the machine in succeeding years (as in column 2) and subtracting. Depreciation for the first year thus is $6,000 − $4,977 = $1,023.

To summarize, if the company calculates present value at the interest rate that is implicit in the acquisition decision—that is, if acquisition cost equals present value at the time of acquisition—then the periodic cash flows produced by an asset are exactly equal to economic depreciation plus interest.

The time pattern of depreciation in the implicit-interest method depends on the pattern of the anticipated cash flows. Some of the possible relationships are:

If the Cash Flow Is	Implicit-Interest Depreciation Will Be
Constant from year to year	Small at first and then rise more and more rapidly
Increasing from year to year	Small or negative at first and then rise more and more rapidly
Decreasing from year to year	Roughly constant from year to year or large at first and then fall

To round out our illustration, we need to consider two situations in which the cash flows are expected to decrease from year to year:

Situation A: The decrease is such that implicit-interest depreciation is equivalent to straight-line depreciation.

Situation B: The decrease is such that implicit-interest depreciation is equal to sum-of-the-years'-digits depreciation.

Situation A: equivalent to straight line.   Suppose everything is the same as in our last illustration except that the anticipated cash flows are those shown in column 3 of Exhibit 10–5. Depreciation is calculated in exactly the same way as in Exhibit 10–4. Income in the first year is 8 percent of $6,000, or $480. This leaves $1,680 − $480 = $1,200 as depreciation for the first year, the

EXHIBIT 10–5. Implicit-Interest Depreciation: Situation Equivalent to Straight-Line Depreciation

(1) Year	(2) Book Value (= Present Value) Beginning of Year [Line above: (2) − (5)]	(3) Anticipated Cash Flow	(4) Income (2) × 8%	(5) Implicit- Interest- Depreciation ("Economic Depreciation") (3) − (4)
1	$6,000	$1,680	$480	$1,200
2	4,800	1,584	384	1,200
3	3,600	1,488	288	1,200
4	2,400	1,392	192	1,200
5	1,200	1,296	96	1,200

amount shown in the first line of column 5. Depreciation in the second year is also $1,200, as it is in the third, fourth, and fifth. That is, depreciation each year is exactly 20 percent of the asset's original cost. It is also equal to the difference between the asset's present value at the beginning of the year and its present value at the end of the year.

In other words, if cash flows are expected to decline each year by a modest amount, the straight-line and implicit-interest depreciation methods will produce similar depreciation schedules.

Situation B: equivalent to sum-of-the-years' digits. Our final illustration is summarized in Exhibit 10–6. Everything is the same as

EXHIBIT 10–6. Implicit-Interest Depreciation: Situation Equivalent to Sum-of-the-Years'-Digits Depreciation

(1) Year	(2) Book Value (= Present Value) Beginning of Year [Line above: (2) − (5)]	(3) Anticipated Cash Flow	(4) Income (2) × 8%	(5) Implicit-Interest Depreciation ("Economic Depreciation") (3) − (4)
1	$6,000	$2,480	$480	$2,000
2	4,000	1,920	320	1,600
3	2,400	1,392	192	1,200
4	1,200	896	96	800
5	400	432	32	400

in the two previous illustrations except that the cash flows are those shown in column 3. These cash flows decrease very sharply, year after year, and the resulting depreciation schedule is the same as the sum-of-the-years'-digits method would have produced. (The sum of the digits for a five-year life is 15; depreciation is 5/15 of $6,000 = $2,000 in the first year, 4/15 of $6,000 = $1,600 in the second year, and so on.)

The Choice of a Depreciation Method

As we have emphasized repeatedly, the best accounting method from the standpoint of the users of financial statements is the one which best helps them predict the company's cash flows, the timing of these flows, and the uncertainty surrounding them. This criterion is difficult to apply directly to the selection of a depreciation method. Depreciation doesn't represent a cash flow, although it represents a resource use that will result in a cash flow later.

One possibility is to measure depreciation as the economist would, by the decline in the present value of the company's depreciable assets. This can't be done under generally accepted accounting principles, however, because they require that depreciation be based on the original cost of the asset, rather than its present value.

Implicit interest depreciation is the closest approximation to present value depreciation that bases depreciation on historical cost. The only difference is that implicit interest depreciation is calculated so as to report a constant rate of return on the unamortized cost at the beginning of each period rather than on the present value of the asset at that time.

Implicit-interest depreciation is never or almost never used in external financial reporting. One possible explanation is that management assumes that most cash-flow streams are like those described earlier as *Situation A* and *Situation B*. If so, the simpler straight-line or diminishing-charge depreciation formulas will approximate implicit-interest depreciation. A certain amount of clerical effort can be avoided by taking the simpler route, and the accountants won't have to make the extra effort to explain the more complicated implicit-interest method.

The other explanation of the virtually universal preference for straight-line and accelerated-depreciation formulas is that few practitioners regard implicit interest as a factor that should influence the determination of current expense. In this view, the users of financial statements will be better served if only interest payable in connection with specific borrowing and lending transactions is allowed to enter into the determination of periodic income. The cost of a depreciable asset presumably should be amortized, therefore, in proportion to the realized undiscounted cash flows. If 10 percent of the asset's lifetime cash flows are expected to come in during the first year, then 10 percent of the depreciable amount should be recognized as depreciation for that year.

If this second explanation is the correct one, then accountants and managers will support straight-line depreciation, if the anticipated cash-flow stream is a level stream from year to year, or some form of accelerated depreciation, if the anticipated cash flow stream diminishes from year to year.

These explanations have one common element: they both start with the idea that the depreciable cost should be amortized on the basis of each asset's expected benefits to the company, benefit being defined to reflect the asset's anticipated cash flows. A benefit standard of this sort is difficult to enforce, however, because clear evidence to support or refute management's expectations of the cash flows attributable to an asset is almost never obtainable.

This being the case, management's choice is likely to be based either on the ease of implementing the various methods or on the effect of the choice on reported income.[2] The cheapest (most easily implementable) solution is to base depreciation for public reporting on the method used for income tax purposes, and this generally means using one of the diminishing-charge formulas. Diminishing-charge depreciation generally has advantages over straight-line depreciation for income tax purposes because it shifts tax deductions to earlier years, thereby reducing taxable income and income taxes in those years. Reducing income taxes increases the company's cash flows in the early years of assets' lives, and these cash flows, therefore, have greater present values than they would have if they came later.

For example, sum-of-the-years'-digits depreciation of an asset with a five-year tax life and a depreciable cost of $100,000 for tax purposes would generate tax reductions with a present value of $46,167 in a company subject to a 55 percent tax rate which discounts cash flows at 8 percent; straight-line depreciation would generate tax reductions with a present value of $43,920.[3]

	Sum-of-the-Years' Digits			Straight Line		
Year	Deprecia-tion	Tax @ 55%	Pres. Value	Deprecia-tion	Tax @ 55%	Pres. Value
1	$33,333	$18,333	$16,975	$20,000	$11,000	
2	26,667	14,667	12,574	20,000	11,000	
3	20,000	11,000	8,732	20,000	11,000	$43,920
4	13,333	7,333	5,390	20,000	11,000	
5	6,667	3,667	2,496	20,000	11,000	
Total ..			$46,167			$43,920

The income effect of the choice of depreciation method depends on the rate of growth. If a company isn't growing but has a stable mix of assets of different ages, total depreciation will be the same no matter what method is chosen. Some assets will be in the early parts of their lives, some will be in the middle, and some will be in their final years. The book value of the company's assets will be affected, however. If accelerated methods are used, book value will be smaller than if straight-line depreciation is used. A straight-line company, therefore, will report a smaller rate of return on its assets than a diminishing-charge company.

The situation is different if the company is growing. Because growing companies have proportionally more young assets than old as-

---

[2] Income tax considerations have no bearing on this choice because income tax regulations permit companies to use methods for tax purposes that differ from those used for financial reporting.

[3] The present value factors used in these calculations were taken from Tables 3 and 4 of Appendix B, reflecting the assumption that the tax impact would fall at the end of each year.

sets, they'll have more assets subject to the larger depreciation charges accelerated methods assign to the early years of assets' lives. Total diminishing-charge depreciation, therefore, will exceed total straight-line depreciation.

This relationship is illustrated in Exhibit 10–7, which shows two methods of calculating depreciation and book value for a new com-

EXHIBIT 10–7. Comparison of Depreciation Schedules for a Growing Company

Year	Cost of Equipment Purchased	Straight-Line Depreciation		Double-Rate, Declining-Balance Depreciation*	
		Book Value, Beginning of Year	Deprecia-tion	Book Value, Beginning of Year	Deprecia-tion
1	$100,000	$100,000	$ 10,000	$100,000	$ 20,000
2	100,000	190,000	20,000	180,000	36,000
3	100,000	270,000	30,000	244,000	48,000
4	100,000	340,000	40,000	295,200	59,040
5	100,000	400,000	50,000	336,160	67,232
6	100,000	450,000	60,000	368,928	73,786
7	100,000	490,000	70,000	395,142	80,338
8	100,000	520,000	80,000	414,804	86,891
9	100,000	540,000	90,000	427,913	93,444
10	100,000	550,000	100,000	434,469	100,000
Total			$550,000		$665,531

* The cost of each year's purchases is depreciated by the double-rate, declining-balance method for the first five years, followed by five years of straight-line depreciation of the book value remaining at the end of five years.

pany which is growing by buying new equipment costing $100,000 each year for ten years. The equipment has a ten-year useful life and no salvage value. Straight-line depreciation, for example, is 10 percent of the accumulated original cost of the equipment, the sum of the figures in the first column. Accelerated depreciation is calculated by the double-rate, declining-balance method with a shift to straight-line depreciation of the remaining book value of each year's purchases in the sixth year of their life. The first year's declining-balance depreciation is $100,000 \times 0.2 = $20,000$; depreciation for the second year is calculated as follows:

Year of Purchase	Book Value, Beginning of Year	Factor	Depreciation
2	$100,000	0.2	$20,000
1	80,000	0.2	16,000
Total			$36,000

Depreciation for the seventh year is $80,338, calculated as follows:

Year of Purchase	Book Value, Beginning of Year	Factor	Depreciation
7	$100,000	0.2	$20,000
6	80,000	0.2	16,000
5	64,000	0.2	12,800
4	51,200	0.2	10,240
3	40,960	0.2	8,192
2	32,768	32,768/5	6,553
1	26,215	32,768/5	6,553
Total			$80,338

Repeating these calculations for all ten years gives us the depreciation schedule in the right-hand column of Exhibit 10–8. As this

EXHIBIT 10–8.   Effects of Choice Between Straight-Line and Accelerated Depreciation on Reported Income and on Income Taxes

Reporting Basis	Tax Basis	Effect on Net Income	Effect on Income Taxes
Straight line	Straight line	Greater income	Greater taxes
Straight line	Accelerated	Greater income	Smaller taxes
Accelerated	Straight line	Smaller income	Greater taxes
Accelerated	Accelerated	Smaller income	Smaller taxes

shows, straight-line depreciation is smaller than declining-balance depreciation, and straight-line book value is larger than declining-balance book value in all ten years.

Exhibit 10–8 summarizes the effects of the major alternatives available to a growing company. If straight-line methods are used for both tax and investor reporting (the first line in the exhibit), both income and income taxes will be greater than under accelerated depreciation. If accelerated depreciation is used for both purposes (line 4 in the table), both taxes and income will be reduced.

The most popular combination for large, publicly owned corporations is the second one in Exhibit 10–8—straight-line depreciation for investor reporting and accelerated depreciation for income taxation. In this connection, it is interesting to note that a number of companies changed their depreciation methods for investor reporting during the business recession of the early 1970s. Most of these changes substituted straight-line depreciation for accelerated methods, and the effect was to increase reported income.[4]

The third combination in the exhibit is generally considered the worst of both worlds in that it gives investors negative profitability

[4] Charles W. Lamden and Dale L. Gerboth, "Depreciation: The Incantation and the Reality," *PMM & Co. World*, Autumn 1972, pp. 6–13.

signals while giving the government more taxes. It might be chosen if management predicted higher tax rates in the future and preferred to transmit less-favorable income signals so as to reduce demands for increased dividends, wages, and so forth. This latter preference might also lead to a choice of the fourth combination in the table.

> ### REVIEW
>
> Depreciation charges are a systematic method of allocating the *depreciable cost* of tangible assets among the time periods in which they will benefit the business. Fundamental to this allocation are the concepts of original cost, useful life, depreciation method, and salvage value.

DEPRECIATION ADJUSTMENTS

The depreciation charge in each year of an asset's life is determined by the asset's cost and estimated life at the time it is acquired and by the depreciation method selected at that time. Two final issues need to be resolved, however:

1. Why can't the depreciation schedule be changed from time to time as conditions change?
2. How and under what conditions can the original depreciation schedule be modified?

We'll consider three different situations under this second heading: (a) an asset's service potential appears to be smaller than was originally anticipated, (b) the depreciation method has to be changed, and (c) the estimate of economic life has to be revised.

Rationale for Predetermined Depreciation Schedules

The employment of an asset and its profitability fluctuate from one year to the next with business conditions and other factors. Since these fluctuations can't be forecast when the depreciation schedules are drawn up, these schedules are bound to get out of date. It can be argued, therefore, that management should be allowed to adjust the schedules from year to year to provide signals to the market about asset utilization.

Any such changes should reflect changes in management's estimates of the assets' present and future cash flows. Increasing the current depreciation charge would imply that the current period's share of the assets' remaining cash flows has increased; reducing the charge would have the opposite meaning.

Unfortunately, in most cases, the company's independent accountants wouldn't be able to verify changes of this sort. Since wide fluctuations in reported income are inconsistent with the image of stable, orderly, profitable growth management prefers, management might be tempted to use any latitude it has to smooth the fluctuations in net income. It could do this by reducing depreciation charges in poor years and increasing them when profit margins are high.

Faced with these conflicting arguments for and against flexible depreciation schedules, the accounting profession has decided to forgo the possible advantages of flexibility until better safeguards against manipulation can be devised. Companies can make changes as described in the remainder of this section, but only if reasonable evidence to support these changes can be found.

Asset Write-Downs

One means by which changes in depreciation schedules are effected is the asset *write-down*. A write-down of a depreciable asset is an action to recognize a portion of the asset's undepreciated cost as a current expense before it is scheduled to be amortized. Write-downs are made when it becomes inescapably clear that the economic value of the asset's remaining service potential has fallen materially below its book value. Upward adjustments of the book values of plant and equipment are not acceptable accounting practices except in connection with the methods changes described in the next subsection.

A write-down recognizes both the decline in the asset and the accompanying decline in the owners' equity. For example, suppose an asset costing $10,000 has been depreciated on a straight-line basis for three years at $1,000 a year. It has been used mainly to manufacture a product the company has withdrawn from the market, and it will be used only intermittently in the future, probably for another seven years. For this purpose it is worth only $2,800, 40 percent of its present book value. The entry to recognize this fact is:

```
Write-Down of Equipment ...............    4,200
    Accumulated Depreciation ...........            4,200
```

The debit in this entry records the write-down as a current expense; the entry to Accumulated Depreciation records the reduction in the asset's remaining potential for useful service.

Once a write-down has taken place, the remaining portion of the depreciation schedule has to be redrawn so as to amortize the remaining depreciable cost over the remaining life. With seven years to go, an adjusted book value of $3,500, and zero estimated salvage value, this machine would have annual depreciation charges of $3,500/7 = $500 for the remaining seven years of its life.

Changes in Depreciation Method

The second occasion for a departure from the originally established depreciation schedule is a decision that the benefit pattern is
different from the pattern expected when the original schedule was
drawn up. For example, management may have chosen straight-line
depreciation because it expected a level year-to-year benefit pattern;
the evidence now reveals that benefits are declining from year to
year and diminishing-charge depreciation is appropriate.

A change from one depreciation method to another is classified by
the accounting profession as a "change in accounting principle." As
such, it may be made only if evidence is available that the new
method is preferable.[5] To illustrate how the change would be made,
let's suppose a company decided to use sum-of-the-years'-digits depreciation for a machine costing $36,000 with an estimated life of 12
years and a $1,500 salvage value (the illustration in Exhibit 10–2,
above). The depreciation schedule for the first four years was as
follows:

Year	Sum-of-the-Years'- Digits Depreciation	Accumulated Depreciation, End of Year
1	$5,308	$ 5,308
2	4,865	10,173
3	4,423	14,596
4	3,981	18,577

The company followed this schedule for the first four years, but, in
the fifth year, management decided that straight-line depreciation
would have been more appropriate for this asset. The company's
independent public accountants agreed, and the change was made.

The annual depreciation on a straight-line basis would have been
$2,875 (Exhibit 10–2), adding up to $11,500 for the first four years.
To effect the change in method, therefore, the company had to reduce the beginning balance in Accumulated Depreciation by
$18,577 − $11,500 = $7,077.

One question is how this $7,077 should be reflected in the com-
pany's financial statements. When we make an adjustment of this
sort, we are saying that depreciation in the first four years was overstated by this amount. Income before taxes, therefore, was understated by the same amount. Rather than correct past statements,
however, we call investors' attention to the earlier understatements
of income by putting the adjustment on the current income statement. It isn't part of the recurring income stream, however, so it has

---

[5] AICPA, "Accounting Principles Board Opinion 20," para. 16, in *Professional Standards—Accounting, Current Text* (New York: Commerce Clearing House, 1978), sec. 1051.16.

to be reported separately at the bottom of the income statement, along with the extraordinary items.[6]

The entry to record the restatement of the asset and equity accounts takes the following form:

Accumulated Depreciation	7,077	
Change in Depreciation Method		7,077

The Change in Depreciation Method account is a temporary owners' equity account. Crediting this account restores to owners' equity the amounts that shouldn't have been deducted from it in the past. Accumulated Depreciation now has the following balance:

Accumulated Depreciation

Adjustment 7,077	Year 1	5,308
	Year 2	4,865
	Year 3	4,423
	Year 4	3,981
	Bal. 11,500	

This sets the stage for depreciation in the fifth year and later to be recorded at the straight-line rate of $2,875 a year.

As we'll see in more detail in Chapter 13, reported income tax expense is based on the revenues and expenses shown on the income statement rather than the figures on the income tax return. This means that the reported income tax effects of depreciation are based on the depreciation expenses shown on the income statement. Any revision of past depreciation expense, therefore, requires a cumulative adjustment of past income tax expense.

In this case, our adjustment is to *reduce* past depreciation expense by $7,077, as we saw a moment ago. If the income tax rate is 55 percent, we should also *increase* past income tax expense by 55 percent of $7,077, or $3,892. The after-tax adjustment, therefore, is $7,077 − $3,892 = $3,185. In other words, the balance in Retained Earnings would have been $3,185 greater if straight-line depreciation had been used from the outset.[7]

Revisions of Life Estimates

The third situation in which a revision in the original depreciation schedule is necessary arises when evidence is found that a life estimate is seriously wrong. An error in an estimate of useful life results in an overstatement or understatement of depreciation during the years before the error is discovered. For reasons too subtle to detain

---

[6] Ibid., para. 20, sec. 1051.20.

[7] Ibid., para. 22, sec. 1051.22.

us here, the accounting profession has decided that no adjustments of current income are to be made to correct errors of this sort. Instead, the remaining depreciable amount is spread over the remaining years of useful life reflected in the new estimate.[8]

For example, suppose an asset's book value is $150,000 and the remaining life estimate has been shortened from five years to three, with no salvage value. Under straight-line depreciation, the annual depreciation charge would be raised from $30,000 to $50,000 a year. The accumulated depreciation from prior years would not be changed to reflect the new estimate.

A related issue is how to account for major overhauls that extend an asset's total economic life. This is really a question of whether to capitalize the cost of the overhaul, and we'll deal with it when we consider questions of this sort in Chapter 12.

SUMMARY

Reporting annual depreciation charges and the book value of depreciated assets serves no purpose unless these figures affect decisions. The accounting model presumes that income and asset figures will influence investors' decisions to buy or sell shares in the company and a wide variety of managerial decisions as well.

For these purposes, the accountant must estimate the amount of each asset's service potential that is consumed during each period and the amount that remains at the end of the period. Because patterns of depreciation are difficult to identify, the accountant has generally used some simple formula as an approximation. The most widely used formulas are straight-line (uniform annual amounts) and accelerated (diminishing-charge) methods (smaller amounts in each succeeding year).

Forecasting errors occur, of course, and the accountant must be prepared to revise depreciation rates, methods or lives, whenever substantial evidence is found that the pattern-of-service-potential consumption differs from the forecasted pattern.

KEY TERMS

Accelerated (diminishing-charge) depreciation
Depletion
Depreciable cost

Depreciation schedule
Double-rate, declining-balance
Economic depreciation
Economic life

---

[8] Ibid., para. 31, sec. 1051.31.

Implicit-interest depreciation   Straight-line depreciation
Matching principle   Sum-of-the-years' digits
Obsolescence   Write-downs
Production-unit depreciation
Service potential

INDEPENDENT STUDY PROBLEMS (Solutions in Appendix B)

1. Depreciation methods exercises. Fast Buck, Inc., has just bought a sophisticated copying machine for $30,000. It is expected to last five years and has an estimated salvage value of $1,500. The annual cash flow from ownership and use of this machine is expected to be $7,668, and this will produce a rate of return on investment of 10 percent. Calculate depreciation for each of the five years by:

a. The straight-line method.
b. The double-rate, declining-balance method.
c. The sum-of-the-years'-digits method.
d. The implicit-interest method.

2. Change in depreciation method. T. Best, Inc., has been amortizing the cost of a machine for three years by the sum-of-the-years'-digits method. The machine cost $16,500 and had an estimated life of ten years and a zero estimated salvage value. In the fourth year, the company's management decided that straight-line depreciation would have been more appropriate for this machine.

a. Establish the original sum-of-the-years'-digits depreciation schedule for the first three years.
b. Calculate the amount of any adjustment that you think should have been made as of the beginning of the fourth year. (Ignore income taxes.) How would this adjustment be shown on the financial statements for the fourth year?

3. Choosing a depreciation method. Book publishers spend substantial sums to edit textbook manuscripts and to prepare the photographic plates from which the books themselves are printed. Textbook A is expected to remain in print for about five years. Up-to-date competing textbooks will be published each year by other publishing companies. The longer a textbook has been in print, the more out of date it is likely to be, making it more and more difficult to compete with the newer textbooks on the market.

a. What depreciation method should be adopted for textbook A?
b. What effects would your choice have on the publisher's financial statements?

EXERCISES AND PROBLEMS

4. Discussion question: comparability of methods. Company X depreciates its equipment on a straight-line basis, while Company Y uses a declining-charge method. Are the depreciation charges of these two companies necessarily noncomparable?

5. Discussion question: choice of depreciation method. The Pilot Company has just purchased a piece of equipment. This equipment is expected to produce approximately the same number of units of product each year until it is retired, and the company sees no reason why the prices of the products sold will either increase or decrease during the machine's lifetime. Operating and repair costs per year are expected to increase each year, however, and economic life is expected to come to an end seven years from now when the cost savings from a new machine will be adequate to justify replacement.

What method would you use to calculate annual depreciation charges on this machine? State your reasons.

6. Discussion question: effects of subsequent events. A company purchased a large piece of equipment 15 years ago at a cost of $300,000. At that time it estimated that the economic life of the equipment would be 20 years and its ultimate scrap value would be $30,000.

Assuming the company uses straight-line depreciation, study the following events and state whether each one necessitates a revision of the original depreciation rate, with reasons for your answer.

a. Due to recent price increases, the present replacement cost of the same type of equipment is $500,000.

b. For the same reason as in (*a*), end-of-life scrap value is now estimated at $50,000.

c. The company could sell the equipment now at the sale price of $100,000.

d. At the end of the last year, a major breakdown impaired the efficiency of this equipment. After stopgap repairs, the equipment now has a productive capacity of 5,000 units a month instead of the initial capacity of 10,000 units a month. The company still expects to use the equipment for five more years, retiring it when it is 20 years old, with a scrap value of $15,000.

7. Exercise: different depreciation methods. Allied Manufacturing Corporation bought three machines on January 1, 19x0, each costing $50,000 with a ten-year useful life and no salvage value. One machine was depreciated on a straight-line basis, the second by the double-rate, declining-balance method, and the third by the sum-of-the-years'-digits method.

a. Calculate depreciation for each machine in its first, fifth, and tenth years.

b. Calculate each machine's book value at the end of ten years.

8. Exercise: different depreciation methods. Shakey Corporation bought a building on January 1, 19x1, together with title to the land on which the building was located. The building and land cost $1 million, and the land was appraised at $300,000. The building was assumed to have a 35-year useful life, with zero net salvage value.

Calculate depreciation for the second year (19x2) appropriate to:

a.   Straight-line depreciation.

b.   Sum-of-the-years'-digits depreciation.

9.   *Exercise: depletion.*   Excavating Coal Company bought a mine for $1.3 million. A geological surveyor estimated that 2.6 million tons of coal could be mined. In the first year the company mined 130,000 tons of coal from this mine.

a.   Using production-unit depletion accounting, calculate depletion for the first year.

b.   Would straight-line depletion be likely to produce a more level stream of net income figures than production-unit depletion? Explain your answer.

10.   *Exercise: different depreciation methods.*   A company has just bought four assets for which you have the following data:

Asset	Cost	Life	Salvage	Method
Truck..................	$ 11,000	200,000 miles	$ 1,000	Production unit
Machine	300,000	12 years	25,000	Double rate, declining balance
Typewriter	660	3 years	—	Sum-of-the-years' digits
Furniture	3,500	8 years	500	Straight line

The truck was driven 50,000 miles the first year and 40,000 miles in its second year.

Calculate depreciation for each asset for each of the first two years.

11.   *Calculating depreciation schedules; justifying the choice.*   F. Coons, Inc., bought a dump truck for $10,450. This truck was delivered on January 2, 19x1, and was placed in service immediately hauling salt for the local highway department. The company's past experience led management to believe the costs of maintaining and operating the truck would increase as it grew older, but the truck would be used about the same number of weeks each year and carry about the same number of loads.

Management decided to depreciate this truck by the sum-of-the-years'-digits method, based on a six-year life and a $1,000 estimated end-of-life salvage value.

a.   Prepare a depreciation schedule for this truck.

b.   Recompute depreciation by the double-rate, declining-balance method.

c.   Do the company's estimates justify the use of one of these accelerated methods instead of straight-line depreciation?

12.   *Choosing a depreciation method.*   A company has just bought a new electric typewriter for $750. The manufacturer of the typewriter will provide service on this typewriter for eight years at an annual cost of $100. With this service contract, the typewriter will be inoperative, awaiting service, for approximately five days each year.

After eight years, the manufacturer will provide service only on a time-and-parts basis. This arrangement is likely to be so expensive that the company will sell the typewriter at the end of eight years. In the past, used electric typewriters have been sold to employees for about 20 percent of their original cost.

a. Which depreciation method would you recommend for this typewriter? Give your reasons.
b. Calculate the annual depreciation charge for each of the next eight years.

13. *Implicit-interest depreciation.* On January 1, 19x1, the Lubberdink Company purchased a machine for $56,910. The machine was expected to produce cash savings at the rate of $15,000 a year for a period of five years and to have a salvage value of $5,000 at the end of that time.

a. Calculate annual depreciation by the straight-line method. For each year, compute the ratio of the machine's earnings after depreciation to its book value as of January 1 of that year.
b. Recompute annual depreciation by the implicit-interest method such that the annual rate of return on the machine's January 1 book value is 12 percent each year.
c. Is the rate of 12 percent an appropriate one to use in this case? Could the implicit-interest method have been applied with a rate such as 15 percent? Support your conclusion with appropriate calculations.
d. Calculate economic depreciation as the difference between successive present values, using the same discount rate (12 percent).

14. *Changing depreciation methods; revised life estimate.* A company bought a machine costing $44,000 and placed it in service on January 2, 19x1. Depreciation was calculated by the sum-of-the-years'-digits method, with an estimated life of 12 years and an estimated end-of-life salvage value of $5,000.

In the fourth year, management decided that depreciation should have been calculated on a straight-line basis, and the accountants made the adjustment that was necessary to reflect this change.

In the ninth year, it became clear that technological change in the machinery industry was progressing more slowly than had been originally anticipated and that, therefore, the machine would probably remain in service for 15 years instead of 12. The end-of-life salvage value was revised downward to $4,000. The accountants made the necessary adjustments to reflect this additional information.

The machine was sold for $2,000 at the end of the 15th year.

a. Calculate depreciation for each of the first three years.
b. Determine and describe the adjustment, if any, to be made in the fourth year to reflect the change in the depreciation method.
c. Calculate depreciation for each year from the fourth through the eighth year.
d. Determine and describe the adjustment, if any, to be made in the ninth year to reflect the changes in the estimates.
e. Calculate depreciation for each year from the ninth through the 15th year.

    f.   Prepare a journal entry to record the retirement and sale of the machine at the end of the 15th year.

    15.   Effects of changes in estimates.   A company has been using an annual depreciation rate of 20 percent of original cost for a certain type of office equipment. Now, after several years of experience, a study of actual equipment mortality rates indicates that the rate should have been based on a life of six years and an end-of-life resale value of 16 percent of original cost. The original cost of the equipment now on hand was $200,000, and its age is two years. Straight-line depreciation has been used.

    a.   If the company had known at the outset what it knows now, how much more or less would it have charged as depreciation in the past two years?

    b.   What adjustment, if any, should be made in the accounts at this time?

    c.   Calculate depreciation on this equipment for each of the next four years.

    16.   Change of depreciation method; journal entries.   The Prometheus Bindery installed a new binding machine at the beginning of January, 19x1, to take the place of an old machine which had become obsolete. The old machine was sold to a salvage firm for $2,000 cash. Its original cost was $19,000, and depreciation of $12,000 had been accumulated prior to the retirement date.

    The new machine was to be depreciated by the double-rate, declining-balance method. The following data were available at the time it was installed:

Invoice price	$32,000
Installation cost	1,600
Cash discount	600
Estimated end-of-life scrap value	3,100
Estimated economic life	15 years

    At the beginning of the year 19x2, while the plant was temporarily closed for stock taking, a conveyor attachment was built onto the machine at a total cost of $2,900. This was capitalized as part of the cost of the machine.

    After the books had been closed and the statements prepared for the year 19x1, the management decided, on the basis of the plant engineer's recommendation, that the depreciation on this machine should have been computed (and should be computed in the future) on a *production basis*, using a *machine-hour rate*. The following additional data were available as of January 1, 19x2:

Estimated total life of machine from date of installation, January 1, 19x1	30,000 machine-hours
Production time for the year 19x1	3,000 " "
New estimated scrap value of machine, including the conveyor	$ 3,200

    a.   Prepare journal entries to record the retirement of the old machine and the purchase and installation of the new machine on January 1, 19x1. The company uses a single account, Equipment, for all its equipment and a single Accumulated Depreciation account.

b. . Calculate and prepare a journal entry to record the depreciation for 19x1. Prometheus Bindery had no work in process or finished goods inventories at the end of 19x1.

c. Prepare a journal entry to record the installation of the conveyor.

d. Prepare a journal entry to record the correction of the asset accounts when the machine-hour rate was established. (Ignore any income tax adjustments that may have been necessary.) Indicate clearly how your adjustments would affect the financial statements for 19x2.

e. Calculate the depreciation charge for 19x2. The machine operated 2,700 machine-hours during the year.

17.* _Choosing a depreciation method._ The Alexander Cargo Service was started in 1967 to carry freight from a coastal seaport in the United States to several inland locations. By the beginning of 1976, the company had three small cargo vessels capable of operating in the small river which flowed into the port.

A fourth ship was purchased for $110,000 and placed in service on July 1, 1976. The public accountant who prepared the company's annual tax returns ascertained that a life of 20 years has been accepted by the income tax authorities for similar vessels in the past. For tax purposes, depreciation could only be by the straight-line method, but no estimated salvage value had to be entered into the tax-depreciation calculations.

Mr. Alexander could not agree that the estimated life of this new vessel would be as long as 20 years. He had seen so many changes in the transportation pattern in his area just since he started in business that he felt that a ten-year life would be much more likely. From experience that he had had in buying and selling second-hand ships, he also concluded that he could sell the ship for at least $10,000 at the end of ten years even if economic conditions did not permit its use for containerized service locally after that time.

By the time the ship went into service on July 1, 1976, it was clear to Mr. Alexander that his original estimates were sound, at least for the first few years of the new ship's life. Contracts had been signed with several shippers. Bookings for space on the new vessel continued near capacity throughout the first six months of its operation. Mr. Alexander felt that he might gradually lose some of this business from year to year as the pattern of local cargo operation changed, but he saw no reason why he could not continue to operate the vessel for at least ten years before the volume of business declined so far that he would find it necessary to take the new vessel out of service and sell it.

Sales revenues of the Alexander Cargo Service amounted to $1 million in 1976 and were expected to reach $1.2 million in 1977. Net income, before taxes and before deducting depreciation on the new ship amounted to $50,000 in 1976 and was expected to total $100,000 in 1977. The book value of all assets other than this new vessel totaled $250,000 and was expected to remain constant at this level. The income tax rate was 40 percent of taxable income.

---

* Abstracted from an original case, copyright 1967, 1977 by l'Institut pour l'Etude des Méthodes de Direction de l'Entreprise (IMEDE), Lausanne, Switzerland. Published by permission.

The company had, in the past, sometimes used the tax basis for capitalizing and depreciating costs when this seemed to fit the facts of the case. At other times, it felt justified in using some basis other than the tax basis for the financial statements that it issued to its shareholders and to its bank creditors and which its management also used.

For its published statements, the Alexander Cargo Service used only straight-line depreciation or the double-rate, declining-balance method.

a.   What depreciation method should have been used for this new ship in the company's financial reports? Explain your reasoning.
b.   Using this method, calculate depreciation for 1976. (Only one-half-year's depreciation should be charged for the year.)
c.   How important was the decision called for in (a)? Support your answer by giving figures from the problem.

18.   A pencil pusher: effect of depreciation method and growth.   The Marple Company has established a strong but stable position in its industry. Management has no interest in expanding the company; the company now has all the business management can handle.

Marple now has equipment with an original cost of $500,000 and a book value of $230,000. Each year it has purchased equipment costing $100,000 a year. This equipment has a useful life of five years, and salvage values average 10 percent of the original cost of the equipment retired. Depreciation has been by the straight-line method. All purchases and retirements are assumed to take place on the first of the year.

a.   Assuming that five-year-old equipment with an original cost of $100,000 and salvage value of $10,000 is retired each year and that new equipment costing $100,000 is bought each year, calculate total depreciation and the year-end book value of the company's equipment on a straight-line basis for each of the next seven years. You should take a full year's depreciation on each item bought during a year. (You may assume that each year's purchase is of a single item.)
b.   Using the same assumptions, make the same calculations as in (a), applying double-rate, declining-balance depreciation to all new equipment purchased from this year on. Straight-line depreciation will continue to be used for the present stock of equipment until it is all retired.
c.   Repeat the calculations in (a) and (b), assuming that purchases this year will amount to $110,000 and purchases each year hereafter will exceed purchases in the preceding year by 10 percent. Retirements will continue to take place exactly five years after the items are purchased.
d.   What conclusions can you draw from the results of these calculations?

11

Adjusting for Changes in Resource Prices and for Inflation

FINANCIAL STATEMENTS drawn up on the basis we have been describing measure the company's purchased resources—inventories, buildings, labor services, equipment, and so forth—at the prices they were acquired for. Since different resources are acquired at different times, both the balance sheet and the income statement will contain costs measured at the prices that prevailed in many different periods. The expenses of a period, for example, will include some resources measured at current prices (labor), some measured at prices of relatively recent periods (materials and merchandise from Fifo inventories), and some measured at prices of many periods in the past (depreciation on well-seasoned equipment).

Furthermore, if the general level of prices changes from period to period, the dollars used to acquire resources in one period have an amount of purchasing power different from that of the same number of dollars used in a different period.

Our objectives in this chapter are to explain why price changes of various kinds affect the meaning of traditional financial statements and to explain two techniques accountants and others have developed to adjust traditional accounting figures. One technique, known as current costing, deals with the measurement problems arising from changes in the purchase prices of individual resources from period to period. The second technique, known as general price-level adjustments, tackles the problems raised by changes in the general level of prices.

IMPACT OF CHANGES IN REPLACEMENT PRICES

Changes in the prices a business has to pay for the resources it uses don't affect the meaning of the accounting numbers unless the business has some of these resources among its assets. Ownership of these resources means that their historical costs remain in the accounting records after the periods in which those costs were current.

For example, if the purchase price of merchandise goes up by $10, the cost of goods sold may still be measured at the old price if costs flow to the income statement on a Fifo basis. The effect of this time lag is illustrated in Exhibit 11–1. When purchase prices and selling

EXHIBIT 11–1.   Lag in Expense Reporting After Purchase Price Change

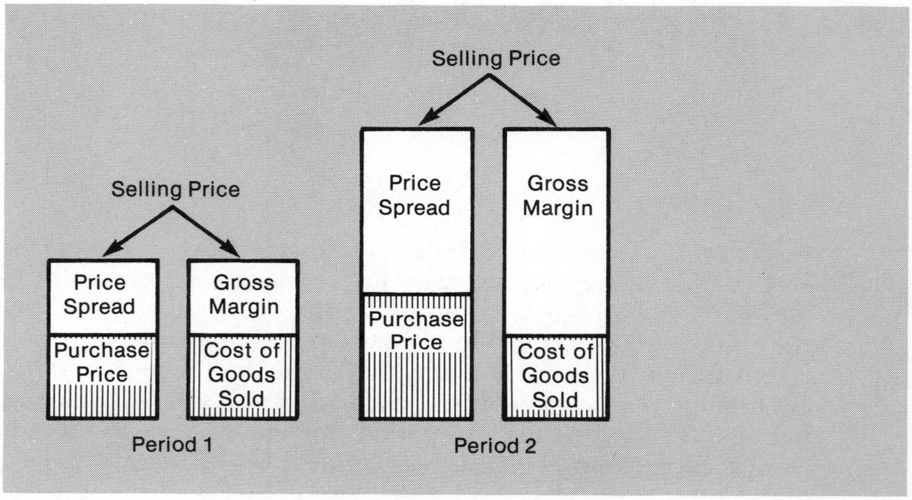

prices go up in Period 2, the lag in getting the new purchase prices into the income statement produces a gross margin figure that overstates the current margin over the current cost of the merchandise.

This lag effect is even more pronounced in connection with changes in the prices of buildings and equipment. Buildings and equipment last for many years, and the 1980 income statement may include some depreciation charges based on the much lower building construction prices of 1950 and equipment prices of 1970. Historical cost lags can continue to affect the net income figure long after the cost changes have taken place.

These lags have four effects on the meaning of the financial statements:

1.   They lead to measures of net income that overstate or understate the income level the company can sustain on a continuing basis.

2. They lead to overstatement or understatement of taxable income.
3. They distort comparisons of the rates of return on investment achieved by companies with different asset structures.
4. They lead to net income figures that fail to measure management's skills in using the company's resources.

Over- and Understatement of Sustainable Income

Conventional net income figures will overstate or understate the income level the company can sustain on a continuing basis. The reason is that current expense charges for depreciation and for some portions of materials or merchandise costs are likely to be different from the amounts the company will have to spend for these resources each year, on the average, to maintain the physical operating volume at its current level.

Although this argument applies whether prices have risen or fallen, in practice most prices are more likely to rise than to fall. Those supporting this argument contend, for example, that the inventory profits we described in Chapter 9 represent portions of the company's cash flows that must be used to finance the purchase of goods to replace those being sold. The company's ownership of inventory, plant and equipment purchased when prices were lower allows it to report income it wouldn't have reported if all inputs had had to be paid for at current prices.

Over- and Understatement of Taxable Income

A second argument is that measuring expense by the historical costs of the resources used in generating revenues leads to misstatements of taxable income. Again the argument is usually related to resources that have risen in price because they are far more numerous. Business firms have to pay tax on portions of their revenue streams that will have to be reinvested simply to replace the resources they are using up.

The argument for reform of financial reporting is based on the assumption that changes in the way income is measured for public financial reporting will sooner or later affect the figures entered on the company's income tax returns. Meaningful tax reform will be impossible unless business financial reporting is reformed first.

Distortion of Rate-of-Return Comparisons

The third argument for a reform in accounting measurement is based on the assumption that the rate of return on investment tends to be overstated when resource prices are rising, both because income is overstated for the reasons described above and because investments in fixed assets and perhaps in inventory as well are understated. This overstatement of the rate of return is greater for companies with extensive investments in inventories and equipment than for those with more rapid asset-turnover ratios. It is also greater for older companies, whose equipment is older and whose inventories, if on Lifo, will be much more understated than those of younger companies.

The main problem is that the degree of overstatement (or possibly of understatement) is uneven. To the extent accounting rates of return influence investors' decisions, this factor will influence them to favor companies with larger percentages of their funds invested in nonmonetary assets, if resource prices are rising in general.

Distortion of Managerial Performance

The fourth argument for change is that present measurement methods measure managerial performance incorrectly. Because some changes in purchase prices enter the income statement only after a time lag, the net income figure includes a component that results almost exclusively from the increase in purchase prices rather than from management's skill in managing the company's resources. Furthermore, this component of net income is reported neither separately nor consistently. Investors, therefore, find it difficult to appraise management's ability to anticipate and respond to changes in resource prices.

CURRENT (REPLACEMENT) COSTING

One approach that has been suggested as a possible means of remedying some of the defects of historical costing is to substitute *current costs* for the historical costs of inventories and plant and equipment in both the balance sheet and the income statement. The current cost of a company's inventories on any date is the amount the company would have to spend to replace them at the prices prevailing on that date. The current cost of the goods that are sold is their replacement cost on the date of the sale. Accounting systems that measure resources by their current costs are known as *current costing systems*.

In this section we'll study five aspects of an accounting measurement system based on current costing:

1. Inventory costing on a current-costing basis.
2. Comparison of current costing with Fifo costing.
3. Comparison of current costing with Lifo costing.

4. Application of current costing to fixed assets.
5. Difficulties encountered in current costing.

Current Cost Margins and Inventory Holding Gains

In a current costing system, the inventory would always be stated at its current replacement cost, and income would have two components: (1) the current operating margin and (2) holding gains and losses.[1] To see how such a system would work, we need to construct a simple hypothetical example. The Plastics Supply Company buys and sells plastic sheeting. Its purchase and selling prices in 19x4 were as follows:

Period	Selling Price per Yard	Purchase Price of Replacement Merchandise
January 1–June 28	$0.35	$0.25
June 29–December 28	0.40	0.30
December 29–December 31	0.50	0.40

The spread between the current selling price and the current purchase price of replacement merchandise on any date can be referred to as the current cost margin. In this case, it remained steady at ten cents a yard throughout 19x4. If the company could buy and sell sheeting simultaneously, thereby eliminating the need to carry inventory, and if it also chose not to carry any inventory, the current gross margin would be its sole source of income.

Plastics Supply Company did have an inventory, of course, so it could fill customers' orders promptly. It started the year 19x4 with 100,000 yards of plastic sheeting on hand. Its purchases and sales during the year were:

Period	Yards Purchased	Yards Sold	Yards in Ending Inventory
January 1–June 28	170,000	200,000	70,000
July 1–December 28	170,000	200,000	40,000

No purchases or sales were made on the last two days of June or the last three days of December, immediately after the announcements of price changes in plastic sheeting.

A company that holds inventories when prices change will have holding gains and losses as well as operating income. A *holding gain* results from the holding of a nonmonetary asset at the time the price

---

[1] Current costing is not now acceptable as a basis for public financial reporting. The Securities and Exchange Commission does require certain large corporations to disclose the replacement costs of inventories, production capacity, and related income statement items, but only as supplementary information, not as integral components of the financial statements.

of that asset increases; a *holding loss* results from the holding of a nonmonetary asset at the time the price of that asset decreases.

We measure the holding gains and losses from the holding of inventories by the changes in the *purchase* prices of the items in inventory. The idea is that a purchase before the date of a price change is a substitute for a purchase after that date. By buying early, the company gets the benefit or incurs the penalty of buying at the old price.

As we saw earlier, the prices of plastic sheeting changed twice during 19x4, both times in an upward direction. The holding gains for the year are calculated in Exhibit 11–2.

EXHIBIT 11–2. PLASTICS SUPPLY COMPANY: Calculation of Holding Gains, 19x4

(1) Date of Price Change	(2) Yards in Inventory at Time of Price Change	(3) Amount of Price Change	(4) Holding Gain or (Loss) (2) — (3)
June 29, 19x4	70,000	+$0.05	$3,500
December 29, 19x4	40,000	+ 0.10	4,000
Total			$7,500

If current costing were used in the preparation of financial statements, the cost of goods sold would be measured at replacement price *on the date of each sale*, and inventories would be measured at the replacement price *on the date of the statement*. The income statement would be divided into two sections, one representing the results of manufacturing and trading operations, the other reporting the holding gains and losses.

Exhibit 11–3 presents income calculations for Plastics Supply Company on a current costing basis. (To simplify the exhibit, we have assumed that selling and administrative expenses were zero.)

EXHIBIT 11–3

PLASTICS SUPPLY COMPANY
Current Costing Income Calculations
For the Six-Month Periods Ended
June 30, 19x4, and December 31, 19x4

	First Half	Second Half
Sales revenues	$70,000	$80,000
Cost of goods sold	50,000	60,000
Current gross margin	$20,000	$20,000
Holding gain (loss)	3,500	4,000
Net Income	$23,500	$24,000

Sales revenues in the first six months, for example, amounted to 200,000 yards at 35 cents a yard, a total of $70,000. The $50,000 current cost of goods sold is the same quantity at 25 cents a yard, the price that prevailed while all of the sales of this six-month period took place. Subtracting this figure from the revenues produces the current gross margin figure on the third line of the exhibit. Adding the holding gain from Exhibit 11–2 produces the net income figure shown on the bottom line.

The main argument for an income statement structured in this way is that operating and holding gains measure two different aspects of the enterprise's performance. A surgeon making $80,000 a year from his or her professional practice can be very badly off if his or her investments consistently turn out to be losers, and business firms have the same kind of problem. Poor operating performance may be masked by holding gains during a period of rising prices, and good operating performance may be offset by holding losses during a period of falling prices. The segregation of the two elements, therefore, ought to provide a more effective basis for interpretations and predictions by the users of financial statements.

Comparison with Fifo Costing

While current costing isn't used for external financial reporting, it is analytically useful because it lets us estimate how much of the reported income in historical costing systems is the result of inventory holding gains and losses.

Under Fifo, for example, the ending inventory is measured at the historical cost of the most recent purchases which add up to the quantity on hand. The average Fifo cost of the ending inventory typically will be somewhere between the last purchase price and the average purchase price for the year.

The table in Exhibit 11–4 shows the result of applying Fifo costing to the Plastics Supply Company's inventories of plastic sheeting in 19x4. The company started the year 19x4 with an inventory of 100,000 yards of sheeting. Under Fifo, these units were assigned the cost of the last 100,000 yards purchased in 19x3, or 20 cents a yard and $20,000 in all. This is the first figure shown in the first column of the exhibit.

Plastics Supply Company purchased 170,000 yards of sheeting during the first half of 19x4 for $42,500 (25 cents a yard) and another 170,000 yards for $51,000 (30 cents a yard) during the second half. The Fifo cost of the ending inventory, therefore, was $17,500 at the end of the first half year (70,000 yards × $0.25) and $12,000 at the end of the year (40,000 yards × $0.30).

EXHIBIT 11–4

PLASTICS SUPPLY COMPANY
Fifo-Based Income Calculations for 19x4

	First Half	Second Half
Initial inventory	$20,000	$17,500
Purchases	42,500	51,000
Goods available	$62,500	$68,500
Ending inventory	17,500	12,000
Fifo cost of goods sold	$45,000	$56,500
Sales revenues	70,000	80,000
Net Income	$25,000	$23,500

The relationship between Fifo net income and net income on a current costing basis (ignoring income taxes and selling and administrative expenses) is summarized in the following table:

Period	Current Costing Net Income	Fifo Net Income	Difference
First half, 19x4	$23,500	$25,000	$1,500
Second half, 19x4	24,000	23,500	(500)
Total	$47,500	$48,500	$1,000

The differences in the right-hand column arose because Fifo and current costing recognize inventory holding gains and losses at different times. In the first half of 19x4, for example, the Fifo gross margin included $5,000 in holding gains which current costing would have included in reported income for 19x3. This time lag arose because the Fifo cost of the first 100,000 yards sold in 19x4 was the Fifo cost of the opening inventory, 100,000 yards × $0.20 = $20,000, whereas current cost was 25 cents a yard, or $25,000. In other words, $5,000 of the Fifo gross margin for 19x4 represented holding gains that had taken place during 19x3, when the replacement cost of the inventory rose by five cents a yard.

Accountants would say that this $5,000 was *realized* through the sale of plastic sheeting in the first half of 19x4. In contrast, the 70,000 yards of sheeting in the ending inventory carried an *unrealized* holding gain of five cents a yard because their Fifo cost was 25 cents, or five cents less than their current replacement cost at that time. The realized inventory holding gains and losses—that is, the amounts included in reported income for the year—are the amounts we referred to in Chapter 9 as *inventory profits and losses.*

The inventory profits and losses under Fifo can be summarized as follows:

Period	(1) Opening Inventory Quantity (Yards)	(2) Difference between Fifo Cost and Current Cost per Yard at Time of Sale	(3) Fifo Inventory Profit or (Loss) (1) × (2)
First half, 19x4	100,000	$0.05	$5,000
Second half, 19x4	70,000	0.05	3,500
Total			$8,500

These figures contrast with the holding gains the company would report under current costing (from Exhibit 11–2):

Period	Fifo Inventory Profit	Current Costing Holding Gain
First half, 19x4....................	$5,000	$3,500
Second half, 19x4	3,500	4,000
Total	$8,500	$7,500

As this shows, Fifo in this instance put the holding gains into reported income one period after they would have been recognized under current costing.

The main shortcoming of the Fifo method is its failure to separate inventory profits and losses from merchandising gains and losses. Plastics Supply Company's Fifo gross margin, for example, would be more meaningful if it were subdivided as follows:

Period	Merchandising Income	Inventory Profit/(Loss)	Fifo Gross Margin
First half, 19x4	$20,000	$5,000	$25,000
Second half, 19x4	20,000	3,500	23,500
Total	$40,000	$8,500	$48,500

CHECK FIGURE

Inventory profits and holding gains can be reconciled by the following calculation:

Unrealized holding gains (losses), beginning of period	$ 5,000
Add: Holding gains (losses) arising during the period	7,500
	$12,500
Less: Unrealized holding gains (losses), end of period	4,000
Holding gains (losses) realized during the period [inventory profits (losses)]	$ 8,500

Comparison with Lifo Costing

To compare Lifo costing with current costing, we need to take our illustration back one more year, to 19x3. Exhibit 11–5 presents the Lifo income calculations for 19x3 and 19x4, using the same format we used for Fifo in Exhibit 11–4. Because the Lifo cost of goods sold is determined annually, only the annual totals are shown here. To make the statements easier to follow, the cost structure of the Lifo inventories is shown at the bottom of the exhibit.

In 19x3 the ending inventory quantity was exactly equal to the

EXHIBIT 11–5

PLASTICS SUPPLY COMPANY
Lifo Income Calculations for 19x3 and 19x4

	19x3	19x4
Initial inventory*	$ 16,700	$ 16,700
Add: Purchases	80,000	93,500
Cost of goods available	$ 96,700	$110,200
Less: Ending inventory*	16,700	5,200
Lifo cost of goods sold	$ 80,000	$105,000
Sales revenues	120,000	150,000
Net Income	$ 40,000	$ 45,000

* Composition of Lifo Inventory:

	Basis	December 31, 19x2	December 31, 19x3	December 31, 19x4
Base quantity	20,000 yds @ 11¢	$ 2,200	$ 2,200	$2,200
19x1 layer	30,000 yds @ 15¢ (20,000 yds in 19x4)	4,500	4,500	3,000
19x2 layer	50,000 yds @ 20¢ (no yds in 19x4)	10,000	10,000	—
Total		$16,700	$16,700	$5,200

Lifo cost has to be estimated quarterly for interim reporting, but the annual figures are determinant, so no purpose would be served by showing the quarterly or semiannual breakdown here.

beginning quantity. This meant that, based on the measurement rules that we described earlier, the Lifo cost of the ending inventory was the same as the Lifo cost of the inventory at the beginning of the year. The cost of goods sold was equal to the total cost of goods purchased during the year.

Under these circumstances, the cost of goods sold in 19x3 was all measured at 19x3 replacement prices. Holding gains or losses would be included in the Lifo gross margin only if inventories fluctuated during the year, with purchases made at one price and sales made at times when replacement prices were different. For example, if goods were bought for 15 cents in January and sold in August when replacement prices were 21 cents, the Lifo gross margin would include a six-cent holding gain.

The situation was very different in 19x4. Sales exceeded purchases by 60,000 yards. The costs removed from the inventory as a result of this inventory liquidation were as follows:

19x2 layer	50,000 yards × $0.20	$10,000
19x1 layer	10,000 yards × 0.15	1,500
Total		$11,500

The Lifo cost of goods sold, in other words, was a combination of 19x1, 19x2, and 19x4 purchase prices.

To avoid these liquidations, the company would have had to buy an additional 30,000 yards of sheeting in the first half of the year and another 30,000 yards in the second half, at the following cost:

1st 6 months	30,000 yards × $0.25	$ 7,500
2nd 6 months	30,000 yards × 0.30	9,000
Total		$16,500

This amount would have appeared in the cost of goods sold. The difference between this sum and the $11,500 that actually was transferred from the Lifo inventory account was the realized holding gain for the year, reported as part of the Lifo cost margin:

Reported cost of units liquidated	$11,500
Replacement cost at time of sale	16,500
Holding Gain Included in Reported Income	$ 5,000

In other words, reported income before taxes included $5,000 which would not have been reported if inventories had not been reduced during the year. As we saw in Chapter 9, this is called a *liquidation profit*. It is the realized holding gain on the 60,000 yards of sheeting from the opening inventory. Most of this holding gain actually arose in previous years, but was unrealized until 19x4.

Unrealized holding gains are likely to be much larger if Lifo is used than if the company uses Fifo. The reason is that Lifo always keeps its oldest prices in inventory. After a number of years of rising prices, the spread between these old prices and current replacement prices is likely to be quite large.

The main case for Lifo is that in most years it produces net income figures that are closer to current cost *operating* income than any other historical costing method. In our example, the current cost operating income was $20,000 every six months, or $40,000 a year. Lifo net income was identical to this, except in 19x4 when an inventory liquidation took place. Since the current cost operating income is the best available index of the product's ability to support the costs of marketing it, this has to be chalked up as an advantage of Lifo costing.

Lifo can be criticized on three grounds. First, except in years of large inventory liquidations, Lifo excludes holding gains and losses from the income statement. Investors, therefore, are deprived of information on this portion of the overall earnings stream.

Second, the exclusion of holding gains and losses from reported income is not achieved consistently every year. Whereas realized holding gains and losses that arise as a result of differential timing of purchases and sales within individual years are a more or less regular feature of Lifo systems, those arising from inventory liquidations are highly erratic. Furthermore, since a long time can elapse between the acquisition of an inventory layer and its liquidation, the holding gain included in income can be very large and unrelated to the holding gain or loss that actually took place during the year.

Third, Lifo inventory cost is a varying and often small percentage of the current cost of the items in inventory. For some companies, the total may be close to current replacement cost; for others a large gap will arise. The outsider has no way of judging the extent of these unrealized inventory holding gains and losses and no meaning can be attached to the inventory figure.

Application of Current Costing to Fixed Assets

The arguments for measuring the inventory and the cost of goods sold at current cost can also be used to support the measurement of fixed assets—plant and equipment—at current cost. Historical costs are likely to understate both the current cost of the company's plant and equipment and the annual depreciation charge.

Current costing of fixed assets is much more difficult than current costing of inventories. Before considering these difficulties, however, let's see how it would work. Suppose a machine having a useful life of 20 years was bought at the end of 19x0 for $20,000. It was depreciated at a straight-line rate of $1,000 a year.

The manufacturer of this machine went out of business in 19x2, but other companies continued to make roughly comparable machines. Because specific replacement prices aren't available, we have to approximate them by constructing a series of *index numbers*. An index number is the ratio of a figure in one period or at one time to the comparable figure in another period or at another time that has been chosen as the reference point or *base period*. Index numbers are used in current costing of plant and equipment, as in this illustration, because comparable sets of specific prices are seldom available for long periods of time.

Based on the quoted prices of active manufacturers of this type of equipment, we have developed the following partial price index series for machines of this type:

End of 19x0 120
End of 19x8 180
End of 19x9 204

This says that machinery prices were 120 percent of the base-period level at the end of 19x0 and 204 percent of the base-period level at the end of 19x9. By dividing these two figures, we can find that prices at the end of 19x9 were 204/120 = 170 percent of the prices prevailing at the end of 19x0, an increase of 70 percent.

In other words, if the company had wanted to replace the machine at the end of 19x9 with a comparable asset, it would have had to pay approximately 170 percent of the amount it had paid in 19x0. The calculation is:

$$\begin{aligned}\text{Estimated 19x9 Replacement Cost} &= \frac{\text{19x9 Index}}{\text{19x0 Index}} \times \text{19x0 Cost} \\ &= \frac{204}{120} \times \$20,000 = \$34,000\end{aligned}$$

To calculate accumulated depreciation on a current costing basis, we need to estimate the percentage of its total service potential that had already expired at the end of 19x9. We know the machine was used from the beginning of 19x1 to the end of 19x9, a nine-year period, and we also know depreciation is accounted for on a straight-line basis. The machine, therefore, was 9/20 = 45 percent depreciated, and accumulated depreciation at the end of 19x9 was 45 percent × $34,000 = $15,300 on a current costing basis.

We can now compare the historical cost of this asset with its replacement cost:

	Historical Cost Basis	Current Cost Basis
Cost, new	$20,000	$34,000
Accumulated depreciation	9,000	15,300
Undepreciated Cost	$11,000	18,700

The $7,700 difference between the two undepreciated cost figures is the unrealized holding gain associated with this machine at the end of 19x9.

The same kind of calculation can be applied to the depreciation charge for 19x9. The replacement cost index was 180 at the beginning of the year and 204 at the end of the year, an average of 192 for the year. This means that the average price level in 19x9 was 192/120 = 160 percent of the price level prevailing at the end of 19x0, when the machine was bought. We can use this percentage to adjust the historical cost depreciation figure to a current costing basis:

$$\text{Current Cost Depreciation} = 160\% \times \$1{,}000 = \$1{,}600$$

The difference between $1,600 and the $1,000 historical cost depreciation is the *realized holding gain* for the year.

The depreciation element makes the calculation of the holding gain more difficult than it was for inventory. To begin with, we have to calculate undepreciated cost on a current costing basis as of the beginning of the year:

	Historical Cost Basis	Current Cost Ratio	Current Cost Basis
Cost, new	$20,000	180/120	$30,000
Accumulated depreciation	8,000	180/120	12,000
Undepreciated Cost	$12,000		$18,000

Unrealized Holding Gain, Beginning of Year $6,000

We know the replacement cost went up from 180 to 204 during the year, but we didn't have the same asset all year long. The machine used 1/20 of its lifetime service potential during the year, and this portion of the asset, therefore, had the benefit of only half of the price increase that took place. To make the calculation easier, we can divide the undepreciated cost (at 19x8 prices) into two parts, the 1/20 applicable to 19x9 and the 11/20 applicable to the next 11 years:

	Current Cost, 19x8	Adjustment Factor	Current Cost, 19x9	Holding Gain, 19x9
Applicable to 19x9	$ 1,500	192/180	$ 1,600	$ 100
Applicable to next 11 years	16,500	204/180	18,700	2,200
Total	$18,000		$20,300	$2,300

The holding gain for 19x8, therefore, was $2,300. This can be verified by applying our check formula:

| Unrealized Holding Gain at Beginning $6,000 | + | Holding Gain for the Year $2,300 | − | Holding Gain Realized this Year $600 | = | Unrealized Holding Gain at End $7,700 |

The impact of these calculations on the income statement can be seen in Exhibit 11–6. We start by assuming a $9,000 income before

EXHIBIT 11–6.   Income Calculated on Historical Costing and Current Costing Bases

	Historical Cost Basis	Current Cost Basis	Modified Historical Cost Basis
Income before depreciation	$9,000	$9,000	$9,000
Depreciation	1,000	1,600	1,600
Operating Income		$7,400	$7,400
Holding gain		2,300	600
Net Income	$8,000	$9,700	$8,000

depreciation and no income taxes. The first column shows the conventional historical costing figures. The second column shows an income statement reflecting both the operating income and the full holding gain for the year. The third column is a compromise, in which the conventional income figure remains undisturbed but the portion represented by the realized holding gain is segregated.

Problems of Implementing and Interpreting Current Costing

The adoption of current costing, either as the primary basis for business financial reporting or as supplementary information, would require each company to develop an extensive set of replacement cost figures. Objections to current costing fall into two classes: (1) measurement difficulties and (2) interpretation difficulties.

Measurement difficulties.   Replacement cost can be defined in either of two ways:

1. The amount which would have to be expended to acquire an asset either identical or equivalent in all respects to an existing asset.
2. The amount necessary to replace the productive capacity of existing assets.

The first definition is the easier one to use as long as identical assets remain available for purchase. Even so, we face some problems. First, quoted prices may not be the actual prices at which goods change hands. Second, the company may have so many different kinds of materials, merchandise, and plant and equipment that individual pricing isn't feasible and index numbers must be used. Index numbers trace average price movements, and the items making up the average are seldom identical to those to which the index is applied.

These problems are compounded if technological changes have taken place since the assets were acquired. Technological change forces a shift to the second definition of replacement cost, the amount necessary to maintain productive capacity. Measuring this quantity calls for the exercise of judgment. For example, if the new equipment available is 10 percent more expensive, produces 15 percent more units per hour, and costs 2 percent more to operate each hour, it's not clear whether replacement costs have gone up or down.

Difficulties of another sort arise because identical assets aren't available for purchase. Some assets are unique, for example, and no price quotations are ever available. Land and special-purpose equipment are good examples here; reserves of natural resources also generally fall into this category. Engineering estimates or appraisals might be sought for some of these; in other cases, suitable index numbers may be available.

All these difficulties come together in an obstacle of still another sort. Development of comprehensive replacement costing figures would add to the costs of companies' data-gathering systems. These costs would be smaller once the measurement systems were operating smoothly, but they wouldn't be negligible even then. More evidence on this point is likely to emerge from the experiences of companies which are now providing replacement cost data to the Securities and Exchange Commission.

Interpretation difficulties.   Objections to current costing are also raised on the grounds that the replacement cost figures, even if accurate, are difficult to interpret. First, changes in the relative prices of different assets may lead to changes in the mix of assets used. Therefore, when replacements are made, they won't be made in the same proportions as existing assets. This would make current replacement cost totals less meaningful as predictors of future cash flows.

Second, replacement cost may not be a good measure of the amounts the company will actually pay to replace its present inventory and physical capacity sometime in the future, when conditions are very different from those prevailing today. Again, replacement cost may not be a useful predictor of a future cash flow.

Third, market conditions may prevent the company from passing along increases in purchase prices; therefore, holding gains may be more illusory than real. Conversely, the current cost margin may understate the company's ability to generate cash flows in the future if the company operates in markets in which increases in selling prices occur later than purchase-price increases. In other words, the holding gains are real, but the current cost margin is misleading.

Each of these arguments can also be applied to historical costing. The question is whether they are stronger or weaker with respect to current costing than to historical costing.

THE IMPACT OF INFLATION ON ACCOUNTING MEASUREMENT

So far we have made no mention of *inflation*, defined as the average rate of increase in the prices of a broad range of goods and services. *Current costing is a means of adjusting for changes in the prices of individual resources, not a means of adjusting for changes in the average level of prices in general.* To see why this is so, let's examine two topics:

1. The nature of general price-level indexes.
2. The impact of inflation on assets and liabilities.

An understanding of these two topics is also necessary if we are to understand the various methods of adjusting financial statements for the effects of inflation, some of which we'll discuss in the section beginning on page 326.

The General Price-Level Index

Purchasing power is the power of money to enable its owner to acquire goods and services. The purchasing power of a given quantity of money, therefore, should be measured by the quantity of goods and services a particular holder of money can acquire with that quantity of money. As prices rise, each dollar will buy fewer goods and services. When this happens, we say the purchasing power of the dollar has fallen.

A common way of measuring purchasing power is to trace the total cost of a specific collection of goods, the so-called *market basket*. For example, the prices of a basket of food products suitable for a family of four may be tabulated on July 1, again on August 1, again on September 1, and so forth. These totals may then be published to show how food costs are changing—$100 on July 1, $101.50 on August 1, $102.90 on September 1, and so on.

We can also state these figures in index-number form. For example, if we choose August 1 as the base period, we get the following:

	Market Basket Price	Price Index Relative to August 1
July 1	$100.00	98.5
August 1	101.50	100.0
September 1	102.90	101.4

Price indexes of this type have two major defects. First, they are averages of the price movements of a number of goods and services, and prices of these goods and services won't all change at the same time, at the same rate, or even in the same direction. Second, they reflect the average consumption patterns of many different individuals and businesses—these individuals and businesses don't all buy goods and services at the same place or in the same proportions. For example, Jones may buy one pound of meat for every pound of cheese, while Smith buys ten pounds of meat for every pound of cheese. If meat prices rise faster than cheese prices, Smith's purchasing power will fall more rapidly than Jones's. And if Smith lives in a city in which relative meat prices are rising more sharply than in Jones's city, the purchasing-power differences will be even stronger.

By grouping individuals with similar purchasing patterns, we can get an index for each group that is a reasonable measure of the purchasing power of a dollar held by any member of that group. The broadest price indexes, however, known as general price-level indexes, average the price movements and purchasing patterns for all the people in all sections of an entire country. The number of people they fit exactly will be a small percentage of the total.[2]

This means that any adjustments made with general price-level indexes will be very imprecise. The question is whether this imprecision is so serious that adjusted financial statements will be worse than the unadjusted statements they supplement or replace.

The Impact of Inflation on Assets and Liabilities

Inflation affects both the value of a firm's assets and the burden of its liabilities. It affects different assets and different liabilities in different ways, however. Holders of monetary assets suffer losses during periods of inflation because the fixed amounts of money their assets represent will buy progressively fewer goods and services. Conversely, those who owe monetary liabilities gain during a period of inflation because their debts will be repaid with money having less purchasing power than the money they borrowed.

---

[2] Most general price-level indexes aren't based on changes in the cost of a fixed market basket of goods and services. Instead, as individual consumption patterns change, the weights assigned to individual goods and services change, too.

TERMINOLOGY REMINDER

Monetary assets consist of cash and the rights to receive specified amounts of cash, usually at specified times. Accounts and notes receivable and short-term government securities are monetary assets.

Monetary liabilities consist of obligations to pay specified amounts of cash, usually at specified times. Accounts and notes payable are monetary liabilities; warranty obligations are nonmonetary obligations because they are liquidated by the performance of services and the passage of time rather than by the payment of specified quantities of cash.

Nonmonetary assets don't actually have purchasing power. A company owning nonmonetary assets can use their services without a current outlay of money, however, and this gives them something equivalent to purchasing power. The money value of nonmonetary assets may increase while their *real value* (the number of units of purchasing power they represent) may remain constant or even decline.

Exhibit 11–7, for example, shows the differences between money-value changes and purchasing-power changes for a plot of

EXHIBIT 11–7. Changes in Money Value and in Real Value of Land

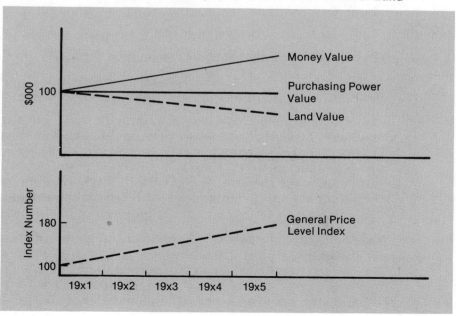

land. The land had a money value of $100,000 on January 1, 19x1, and $150,000 on December 31, 19x5. This movement is traced by the solid line at the top of the diagram. Prices in general rose more rapidly than that, from an index of 100 at the beginning of the period to 180 at the end, as shown by the dotted line in the lower half of the diagram. Dividing the money prices by the index numbers measures the value of the land in units of *constant purchasing power,* the purchasing power of a dollar on January 1, 19x1. Measured in this way, the land value moved along the path traced by the dashed line in Exhibit 11–7.

This shows that an investment in this land was an inadequate hedge against the effects of inflation. If the price index had gone up only to 130, however, the owners of this land would have experienced an increase in their purchasing power.

GENERAL PRICE-LEVEL ADJUSTMENTS

In recognition of these effects of inflation, a number of proposals have been made to adjust accounting figures for changes in the general price level. We'll look briefly at two possible ways of making general price-level adjustments:

1. By applying general price-level indexes to conventionally measured accounting figures.
2. By applying general price-level indexes to current-costing figures.

Applying Index Numbers to Conventional Accounting Figures

A pure general price-level adjustment technique, ignoring the current-costing concept completely, has two main features:

1. It adjusts nonmonetary assets in exactly the same way as in current costing, except that it uses a single general price-level index to make the adjustments rather than specific replacement prices or indexes specific to individual classes of assets.
2. It includes the increase or decrease in the purchasing power of the company's net monetary assets (monetary assets—monetary liabilities) as a component of net purchasing-power income.

Balance-sheet adjustments.   Suppose a company had the balance sheet shown in Exhibit 11–8 on December 31, 19x9. Our first step is to decide whether the balance sheet is to be stated in units with the purchasing power dollars had on December 31, 19x9, or on some other date. The usual answer is to use the balance-sheet date.

EXHIBIT 11–8

A COMPANY
Statement of Financial Position
December 31, 19x9

Assets		Liabilities and Shareowners' Equity	
Cash	$100	Accounts payable	$ 80
Inventory	210	Warranty liability	30
Plant and equipment	290	Total Liabilities	$110
		Capital stock	250
		Retained earnings	240
		Total Liabilities and	
Total Assets	$600	Shareowners' Equity	$600

The next step is to obtain a list of general price-level index numbers for various dates or time periods up to and including the balance-sheet date. Let's assume we find the following:

Date or Period	Index
January 1, 19x0	100
January–February, 19x2	120
Average for 19x8	150
January 1, 19x9	150
Average for 19x9	155
December 31, 19x9	160

Restating monetary assets and liabilities is a simple task. Each of these represents a fixed number of dollars, and each of these dollars is equal to one unit of purchasing power on the balance-sheet date. The monetary liabilities could be liquidated by paying them off with dollars of that amount of purchasing power; the monetary assets could be used to buy that many units of purchasing power on December 31, 19x9. This takes care of the following items from the year-end balance sheet:

	Monetary Assets and Liabilities from Conventional Balance Sheet of December 31, 19x9	Restated Monetary Assets and Liabilities in Units of 19x9 Purchasing Power
Cash	$100	$100
Accounts payable	80	80

Adjusting nonmonetary assets and liabilities isn't this simple. We have to find out how many purchasing-power units (of December 31, 19x9, size) were used to acquire these assets and liabilities, and this depends on the relationship between the price level when the acquisition was made and the price level on the date we are using as a reference. For example, suppose we find that our company's inventory is measured on a Lifo basis and the December 31, 19x9, quantity was costed at 19x2 prices, when the general price-level index was 120. This would be equivalent to a much larger number of 19x9 dollars. The adjustment is to multiply the Lifo cost by the ratio of the December 31, 19x9, index number to the index number for 19x2, when the inventory costs were established. The adjustment is:

Inventory Cost in Units of 19x2 Purchasing Power	Adjustment Factor	Inventory Cost in Units of 19x9 Purchasing Power
$210	160/120	$280

The adjustment for plant and equipment is very similar to the inventory adjustment. Suppose we find that all of our company's plant and equipment was bought in 19x0, when the general price-level index was 100. The adjustment is:

Original Cost, Less Accumulated Depreciation	Adjustment Factor	Cost in Units of 19x9 Purchasing Power
$290	160/100	$464

A similar adjustment has to be made to nonmonetary liabilities such as warranty liabilities. These liabilities are to be liquidated by the performance of services, not by the payment of a fixed amount of cash established when the liability was created. For example, a liability created when the general price level is 120 will have to be honored later, when the price level may be 130 or 140. This calls for an upward adjustment of the liability figure. In our example, the liability was created in 19x8, when the index was 150, and the adjustment is:

Warranty Liability in Units of 19x8 Purchasing Power	Adjustment Factor	Cost in Units of 19x9 Purchasing Power
$30	160/150	$32

Finally, we need to adjust the owners' equity figures. Although more elaborate approaches are sometimes justified, we'll limit ourselves here to a simple adjustment, applying the same procedure to contributed capital we used for nonmonetary assets and liabilities. In this case, the paid-in capital all dated back to 19x0, when the index was 100:

Capital Stock in Units of 19x0 Purchasing Power	Adjustment Factor	Restatement in Units of 19x9 Purchasing Power
$250	160/100	$400

The adjusted retained earnings then can be calculated as a residual, the difference between the adjusted paid-in capital and the adjusted net assets, determined by subtracting the adjusted liability figures from the total of the adjusted asset figures:

```
Cash ............................    $100
Inventory .......................      280
Plant and equipment .............      464
    Total Assets.................    $844
Accounts payable .............  $80
Warranty liability ...........    32   112
    Adjusted Net Assets .........    $732
```

```
                        Common              Retained
                         Stock              Earnings
                         $400                 $332
```

The procedure for restating balance-sheet amounts at their current purchasing-power equivalents can be summarized quickly:

1. All items are to be stated in units with the purchasing power dollars have *on the balance-sheet date*.
2. Monetary assets and liabilities are stated at the amounts at which they are reported on the conventional balance sheet.
3. Each nonmonetary item is restated to reflect the change in general purchasing power that occurred between the time it first entered the company's financial structure and the balance-sheet date.
4. If an inventory is written down to its market value which is lower than historical cost, this market value will be used to quantify the inventory on the purchasing-power balance sheet.

We simplified our illustration to eliminate any market value adjustments, since they would have added no really new element to the procedure.

The results of our application of this restatement procedure are summarized in Exhibit 11–9. As this shows, the greatest adjustments are made in the oldest items. The more recent the nonmonetary item, the less chance inflation has had to act.

Income statement adjustments. Income statements reflecting general purchasing-power adjustments have two components: (1) conventional income, adjusted for purchasing power changes, and (2) losses or gains in the purchasing power of monetary assets and liabilities.

For example, our company's conventional income statement for 19x9 showed the following revenues and expenses:

```
Revenues .........................    $500
Expenses:
    Cost of goods sold ...........  $280
    Salaries .....................    80
    Depreciation .................    30
    Income taxes .................    50
        Total expenses ...........          440
    Net income ...................         $ 60
```

EXHIBIT 11–9.   Adjusted versus Unadjusted Balance-Sheet Figures

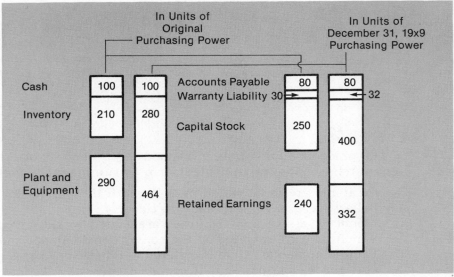

We have decided to restate the income statement in units with the purchasing power dollars had at the end of 19x9, to be consistent with the figures in our adjusted balance sheet. To do this, we have to restate each element in the income statement by an index number calculated as follows:

$$\frac{\text{Year-end price index}}{\text{Price index at the time the income element arose}}$$

As we saw earlier, the year-end index number was 160, and the average index number for the year 19x9 was 155. Since the year-end price index was greater than the average for the year, we know that a dollar received during the year had a greater amount of purchasing power than a dollar received at year's end. If we assume that revenues arose at a uniform rate during the year, we can say that each $155 of these revenues were equivalent to 160 purchasing-power units, each one having the purchasing power a dollar had at the end of 19x9. To get the year-end purchasing power equivalent of the year's revenues, in other words, we must multiply them by 160/155. A similar adjustment applies to salaries and income taxes, if we assume they too arose at a uniform rate during the year.

Different adjustments were required for the cost of goods sold and for depreciation expense, because the resources these figures represent were acquired, in whole or in part, at earlier dates when the purchasing power of the dollar was greater. For example, our company's $280 historical cost of goods sold in 19x9 was calculated on a Lifo basis. This figure was dominated by the costs of goods purchased during 19x9, but a Lifo liquidation that year brought a few older costs into the income statement. When we bring these into the calculation, we find that the ratio of the year-end general price level to the average price level prevailing when the goods sold were acquired was 160/150. The cost of goods sold in purchasing power units therefore was $280 × 160/150 = $299.

Depreciation charges, on the other hand, reflected costs incurred in 19x0, when the purchasing power of a dollar was much greater than at the end of 19x9. The price index at that time was 100; therefore, to restate the depreciation charge in units with the purchasing power dollars had at the end of 19x9, we have to multiply the historical cost figure by 160/100.

The net effect of these adjustments is to reduce the ordinary income figure from $60, the amount shown on the conventional income statement, to 34 year-end purchasing power units, the figure at the bottom of the right-hand column of the following table:

	Unadjusted	Factor	Adjusted
Revenues	$500	160/155	$516
Expenses:			
Cost of goods sold	$280	160/150	$299
Salaries	80	160/155	83
Depreciation	30	160/100	48
Income taxes	50	160/155	52
Ordinary Income	$ 60		$ 34

The total result was a substantial reduction in the income figure because more purchasing-power units than dollars were used to acquire the revenues of 19x9.

The second element of purchasing-power income for the year is the effect of inflation on the value of the company's holdings of monetary assets and monetary liabilities. Gains and losses from the holding of monetary items are calculated by restating the opening balances of, and transactions in, monetary assets and liabilities at the purchasing power of these amounts at the balance sheet date.

At the beginning of the year, this company had cash of $105 and accounts payable of $96. These were the company's only monetary assets and monetary liabilities at that time. The *net monetary position* (monetary assets minus monetary liabilities), therefore, was only $9 at the beginning of the year. Since the purchasing-power index was 150 at the beginning of the year and 160 at the end, this beginning-of-year balance was equivalent to $9 × 160/150 = 9.6 year-end purchasing-power units.

The year-end net monetary position was $20 (cash of $100 minus $80 in accounts payable, from Exhibit 11–9 above). This means the company added $11 to its net monetary position during the year. If we assume these additions took place gradually during the year, the average price index of 155 is applicable. The year-end purchasing power equivalent of the $11 increase in net monetary position is $11 × 160/155 = 11.4 purchasing-power units. These figures are combined in the following table:

	Unadjusted Amount	Adjustment Factor	Adjusted Amount
Beginning balance	$ 9	160/150	$ 9.6
Year's transactions	11	160/155	11.4
Total	$20		$21.0

Since the actual number of purchasing-power units on hand at the end of the year was only $20, a $1 loss in purchasing power must have taken place. Net income, therefore, was $34 from ordinary operations less $1 in purchasing-power losses, a net income of $33 purchasing-power units.

Applying Index Numbers to Current-Costing Figures

A major criticism of the current-costing approach to income measurement is that most holding gains aren't "real"—that is, they represent increases in the *apparent* dollar value of the company's holdings (value being measured at replacement cost) but these increases are usually offset by decreases in the purchasing power of the measuring unit.

As a result, many authorities have recommended either (*a*) ignoring the holding gains, or (*b*) restating the converted dollar figures in units of *constant* purchasing power. To illustrate this second procedure, let's consider one final, highly simplified example. On January 1, 19x1, an investor exchanged $200 in cash and land with a market value of $300 for all the shares in Investments, Inc. The company's January 1 balance sheet therefore showed the following:

Cash	$200	Capital stock	$500
Land	300		
Total Assets	$500	Total Owners' Equity	$500

The company had no activity at all during 19x1, but the replacement cost of the land increased by 20 percent by the end of the year. The year-end balance sheet on a current-costing basis, therefore, showed the following:

Cash	$200	Capital stock	$500
Land	360	Unrealized holding gain	60
Total Assets	$560	Total Owners' Equity	$560

The current costing income statement would show only the $60 unrealized holding gain. (A conventional income statement, of course, would show no revenues and no expenses.)

To determine the purchasing-power gain or loss for the year, we have to restate the beginning-of-year amounts at the amounts they would have reached if their purchasing power had remained constant. The general price level rose only 10 percent during this period, from an index number of 100 at the beginning of the year to 110 at the end. This means we multiply each beginning balance by 110/100, the ratio of the ending to the beginning general price-level index. The restatement would be:

Cash	$220
Land	330
Total	$550

The actual total was $560, on a current-costing basis. Therefore, the company experienced a $10 gain in purchasing power during the year. This gain arose because the value of land increased by $30 more than the value of money declined, while the purchasing power of the company's cash holdings fell by $20, measured in dollars of end-of-year purchasing power.

Comparison of the Methods

Two differences between these two approaches are worth noting:

1. The adjusted current-cost method recognizes purchasing-power gains and losses on both the net monetary position and on nonmonetary assets and liabilities, whereas the straight general price level adjustment recognizes price-level gains and losses on the net monetary position only.

2. The year-end figures in the straight general price-level approach don't recognize differences in the price behavior of different kinds of nonmonetary assets and liabilities—an asset's measurement will be increased to conform to the rise in the general price level even if its own replacement cost hasn't risen.

Much ink has been spilled in the dispute over the merits of these two approaches in comparison with each other and with current costing. We can't hope to resolve these questions here. Our main objective is to describe the problem and outline possible solutions to it.

The current-costing route has been adopted for income measurement by corporations headquartered in the Netherlands, with unrealized holding gains omitted from the income statement. In Brazil, on the other hand, a general price-level index has been adopted to restate nonmonetary assets and expense figures. The accounting profession in the United States has taken neither of these routes, however. As this edition goes to press, the Financial Accounting Standards Board is considering and seems likely to adopt a proposal to require publicly-owned corporations in the United States to *supplement* their conventional financial statements with statements reflecting *either* current costing or general price level adjustments. The principal statements will continue to be based on historical cost.

SUMMARY

The historical costs of the resources used in any period reflect a mixture of current and past resource prices. Historical costing systems, in other words, reflect movements in resource prices only with a lag, and this lag may be either long or short, depending on the company's asset structure. The result is to lead the income statement to overstate or understate the amount of resources the company can distribute or pay in taxes without reducing its operating capacity. It also reduces the value of the income statement as a measure of managerial and company performance.

Measuring resources used and on hand at their current replacement costs has been proposed as a way of remedying these defects of historical costing figures. Under current costing, the company would recognize holding gains and losses when replacement prices change rather than later when resources are used. The operating profit margin would measure the difference between revenues and current replacement costs at the time of revenue recognition. The income statement, therefore, would include both realized and unrealized holding gains and losses.

Current costing deals only with changes in specific prices, not with the effects of changes in the general price level. The holding gains and losses measured for nonmonetary assets under current costing may not be real if the general price level has moved even farther than the prices of the company's specific assets. Furthermore, current-costing statements ignore changes in the purchasing power of the company's net monetary position.

Restating financial statements in units of purchasing power has been proposed as a means of adjusting for changes in the purchasing power of the monetary unit. Broad general price-level indexes would be used for this purpose, applied either to the conventional account-ing figures or to the current-costing figures.

Neither current costing nor general price-level adjustments are acceptable in the United States as the primary basis for financial reporting. Current costing and general price level adjustments seem likely to be restricted to supplementary statements and schedules for many years to come.

KEY TERMS

Current cost	Index numbers
Current cost margin	Inflation
Current costing	Net monetary position
General price-level adjustments	Purchasing power
Holding gains and losses	Replacement cost

INDEPENDENT STUDY PROBLEMS (Solutions in Appendix B)

1. Calculating inventory holding gains and losses. Company A had 50,000 units of merchandise in inventory on January 1, 19x1. The replace-ment cost of these units at that time was $2 a unit.

The company bought 40,000 units between January 1, 19x1, and May 15, 19x1, at a cost of $2 each. It sold 55,000 units during this period at a price of $3 each.

On May 16, 19x1, Company A's supplier increased the wholesale price of this merchandise from $2 to $2.20. The company bought 60,000 units at this price between May 16 and the end of the year, and sold 35,000 units at an average price of $3.10. Replacement cost remained at $2.20 a unit through the end of 19x1. The company's inventory on December 31, 19x1, amounted to 60,000 units.

a. Calculate the current cost of goods sold in 19x1 and the current cost of the inventory on December 31, 19x1.
b. Calculate the holding gain or loss for the year.
c. Calculate the current cost margin for the year.

2. Company without inventories. Company B is in the same business as Company A (see Problem 1) but carries no inventories. Between January 1, 19x1, and May 15, 19x1, it bought 55,000 units merchandise at a cost of $2 each; it sold 55,000 units during this period at a price of $3 each. Between May 16, 19x1, and December 31, 19x1, it bought 35,000 units at $2.20 a unit and sold 35,000 units at a price of $3.10 each.

a. Calculate the current cost of goods sold, the inventory holding gain or loss, and the current cost margin for the year.
b. What conclusion can you draw from a comparison of Company B's per-formance with that of Company A?

3.   *Realized inventory holding gains and losses.* Company A (see Problem 1) uses the Fifo method to cost inventories and the merchandise it sells. On January 1, 19x1, the Fifo cost of its inventory was $1.95 a unit.

a.   Calculate the Fifo cost of goods sold during 19x1, and the Fifo cost of the December 31, 19x1, inventory.

b.   Calculate the unrealized inventory holding gain or loss on January 1, 19x1, and on December 31, 19x1.

c.   Calculate the amount of inventory holding gain or loss that was included in pretax income for 19x1. How would this amount be reported to the shareholders?

4.   *Equipment holding gains and losses.* Company C had the following equipment in its factory on January 1, 19x9:

Year of Purchase	Original Cost	Accumulated Depreciation, January 1	Depreciation for 19x9
19x0	$150,000	$90,000	$10,000
19x2	45,000	21,000	3,000
19x5	60,000	16,000	4,000

The replacement cost index for equipment of this kind traced the following path?

Year	Index
19x0	100
19x2	110
19x5	150
19x9:	
Beginning of year	180
Average for year	190
End of year	200

No equipment was purchased or retired during 19x9.

a.   Calculate the unrealized equipment holding gain or loss as of January 1, 19x9.

b.   Calculate depreciation for 19x9 on a current-costing basis.

c.   Calculate the realized equipment holding gain or loss for 19x9. Where and in what manner would this be reported to investors?

d.   Calculate the unrealized equipment holding gain or loss as of December 31, 19x9.

e.   Calculate the total equipment holding gain or loss arising during the year 19x9 (including both the realized and unrealized portions).

f.   If the general price-level index went from 225 on January 1, 19x9, to 250 on December 31, 19x9, and averaged 237.5 for the year, how much of the holding gain or loss represented a gain or loss in purchasing power?

5.   *General price-level adjustments.* The Gregory Company presented the following balance sheets, prepared in the conventional manner, in its annual financial report for 19x9:

	January 1	December 31
Current Assets:		
Cash	$ 10	$ 15
Accounts receivable	20	40
Inventory	30	35
Total Current Assets	$ 60	$ 90
Plant and equipment	200	220
Less: Accumulated depreciation	(80)	(83)
Total Assets	$180	$227
Current Liabilities:		
Accounts payable	$ 5	$ 7
Notes payable	10	30
Total Current Liabilities	$ 15	$ 37
Bonds payable	10	10
Total Liabilities	$ 25	$ 47
Common stock	100	100
Retained earnings	55	80
Total Liabilities and Shareowners' Equity	$180	$227

Gregory's income statement for the year 19x9 showed the following results:

Sales revenues	$320
Expenses	285
Net Income	$ 35

Of the expenses, $20 was depreciation and $30 was the cost of the beginning inventory. (Fifo costing was used for all inventories.) All other expenses can be assumed to have been incurred evenly throughout the year.

Equipment was purchased during 19x9 at a cost of $40; depreciation of $5 on this equipment was recognized in 19x9. Equipment with an original cost of $20 and a book value of $3 was retired in 19x9 and sold for $3, cash. Gregory had purchased this equipment in 19x0. All purchases and sales can be assumed to have taken place at midyear.

The following information is available to describe the plant and equipment in place on January 1, 19x9:

Year of Purchase	Original Cost	Accumulated Depreciation, January 1	Depreciation for 19x9
19x0	$120	$60	$8
19x3	50	18	4
19x8	30	2	3

The January 1, 19x9, inventory was all purchased or manufactured in the final quarter of 19x8; the December 31, 19x9, inventory was all purchased or manufactured in the final quarter of 19x9.

The general price-level index traced the following path during the decade:

Period	Index
19x0	110
19x3	130
19x8:	
Average for the year	170
Final quarter	175
19x9:	
Beginning of the year................	180
Average for the year	190
Final quarter	195
End of the year.....................	200

a. Restate the income statement in units with the purchasing power of dollars at the end of 19x9.

b. Calculate the purchasing-power gain or loss on the company's net monetary position during 19x9.

c. Restate the December 31, 19x9, balance sheet in units with the purchasing power of dollars at the end of 19x9. You may assume the common stock was issued in 19x0 and restate the retained earnings as a residual.

EXERCISES AND PROBLEMS

6. Calculating inventory holding gains and losses.   Company X started the year 19x8 with an inventory of 50,000 units of merchandise. The replacement cost of this merchandise was $2 a unit on January 1; it rose to $2.50 on March 22, to $2.80 on July 1, and to $3.00 on September 16. It remained at $3.00 to the end of the year.

The following purchases and sales were made during 19x8:

Period	Purchases	Sales
1/1–3/21	60,000 × $2.00	45,000 × $2.70
3/22–6/30	70,000 × 2.50	65,000 × 3.20
7/1–9/15	50,000 × 2.80	65,000 × 3.40
9/16–12/31	40,000 × 3.00	60,000 × 3.50
Total	220,000	235,000

The company had 35,000 units in inventory at the end of 19x8.

a. Calculate the current cost of goods sold in 19x1 and the current cost of the inventory on December 31, 19x8.

b. Calculate the holding gain or loss for the year.

c. Calculate the current cost margin for the year.

7. Realized inventory holding gains and losses.   Company X (see Problem 6) used Lifo to account for its inventories and the cost of goods sold. The Lifo cost of its January 1, 19x8, inventories was:

Base quantity	30,000 units × $1.00	$30,000
19x2 layer	16,000 units × 1.40	22,400
19x5 layer	4,000 units × 1.60	6,400
Total	50,000 units	$58,800

a. Calculate the Lifo cost of goods sold during 19x8 and the Lifo cost of the December 31, 19x8, inventory.

 b. Calculate the unrealized inventory holding gain or loss (1) on January 1, 19x8, and (2) on December 31, 19x8.

 c. Calculate the amount of inventory-holding gain or loss that was included in pretax income for 19x8. How would this amount be reported to the shareholders?

 8. **Replacement cost depreciation: discussion question.** Miller Enterprises, Inc., is incorporated in a country in which corporations aren't required to base their financial statements on generally accepted accounting principles. In view of the steadily rising costs of equipment and building construction in that country, Miller's controller has suggested basing depreciation each year on replacement cost. Depreciation each year would be reflected in a journal entry of the following form:

```
Depreciation . . . . . . . . . . . . . . . . . . . . . . . . . . . . . . . . .   X
     Accumulated Depreciation  . . . . . . . . . . . . . . .        Y
     Reserve for Replacement . . . . . . . . . . . . . . . . .      Z
```

in which X is the depreciation charge based on replacement cost and Y is the depreciation charge based on acquisition cost.

 a. What effect would the proposed method have on net income during a period of rising equipment costs? Would this effect continue after equipment costs stopped rising? Explain.

 b. If the controller's proposal were accepted, how would you interpret the "reserve for replacement"? Would it appear on the income statement for the year or would it go directly to the year-end balance sheet? In which section of the statement should it appear? State your reasons.

 c. If a machine is replaced at the end of its anticipated useful life by an identical machine with a higher replacement cost, will the reserve for replacement equal the difference between the original cost of the first machine and the cost of its replacement? Explain.

 9. **Current costing.** Company Y had 10,000 pounds of product in inventory on January 1, 19x2. The replacement cost of that inventory on that date was $10 a pound. The following events took place during 19x2:

January 30:	Supplier announced a price increase to $11 a pound.
February 20:	Company sold 3,000 pounds at a price of $15 a pound.
May 15:	Supplier announced a price increase to $12 a pound.
June 6:	Company sold 4,000 pounds at a price of $15 a pound.
September 15:	Company bought 5,000 pounds at a price of $12 a pound.
December 10:	Supplier announced a price decrease to $11.50 a pound.

 a. Calculate the cost of goods sold and the cost of the ending inventory on a current costing basis.

 b. Calculate the inventory holding gain or loss arising during the year.

 10. **Realized inventory holding gains and losses.** Company Y (see Problem 9) used Fifo to account for its inventories and the cost of goods sold in 19x2. The Fifo inventory cost on January 1, 19x2, was $9.80 a pound. The market value of the year-end inventory was greater than its cost.

a. Calculate the Fifo cost of goods sold for 19x2.

b. Calculate the amount of the unrealized holding gain, if any, (1) at the beginning of 19x2 and (2) at the end of 19x2.

c. How much of the Fifo gross margin consisted of realized holding gains and losses?

11.   Realized inventory holding gains and losses (Lifo).   Suppose Company Y (see Problem 9) used Lifo to cost its inventory and the cost of goods sold in 19x2. The Lifo cost of the January 1, 19x2, inventory was as follows:

Base quantity	6,000 pounds	$6.00	$36,000
19x0 layer	3,000 pounds	8.50	25,500
19x1 layer	1,000 pounds	9.50	9,500
Total	10,000 pounds		$71,000

a. Calculate the Lifo cost of goods sold for 19x2.

b. Calculate the amount of the unrealized holding gain, if any, (1) at the beginning of 19x2 and (2) at the end of 19x2.

c. How much of the Lifo gross margin consisted of realized holding gains and losses?

12.   Supplying missing figures.   You have the following information from three companies for a recent year:

	Company A	Company B	Company C
Current cost, beginning inventory	$100	$ ___	$ 50
Current cost, ending inventory	110	150	65
Current cost of goods sold	315	650	___
Historical cost, beginning inventory	___	120	45
Historical cost, ending inventory	65	110	
Historical cost of goods sold	320	___	285
Holding gain (loss) arising during the year	___	20	___
Holding gain (loss) realized during the year	___	___	(5)
Unrealized holding gain, beginning of year	40	80	___
Unrealized holding gain, end of year	___	___	0

a. Make the calculations necessary to supply the missing data.

b. Identify each company as a probable user of Fifo or a probable user of Lifo. Explain how you reached your conclusion in each case.

13.   Interpreting published data.   A corporation's financial statements for 1977 included the following footnote:

The last-in, first-out (Lifo) method of inventory measurement is utilized for the majority of inventories at manufacturing facilities, while the average cost method is used for all other inventories, as summarized below:

	1977	1976
Average cost	$294,000	$269,000
Lifo	155,000	154,000
Total	$449,000	$423,000

If Lifo inventories had been measured at their replacement costs, these inventories would have been $40,000, $34,000, and $30,000 greater than those reported at December 31, 1977, 1976, and 1975, respectively.

a. Did this company's unrealized inventory-holding gains on its Lifo inventories increase or decrease in 1976 and 1977? By how much?
b. Can you determine whether this company included a realized inventory-holding gain or loss on its Lifo inventories in its pretax income for 1977? If so, was this amount a gain or a loss? If you can't determine this precisely, state whatever you can determine and explain why you are unable to be more precise.

14. General price-level adjustments. Company M presented the following information on its assets and liabilities in its 19x1 annual report:

	January 1	December 31
Cash	$ 20	$ 20
Accounts receivable	40	40
Inventory (Lifo)	50	50
Plant and equipment (net)	100	100
Accounts payable	10	10
Notes payable.............................	20	20

The general price-level index at the end of the year was 150. It was 125 at the beginning of the year and 100 when the inventory was acquired. The average general price-level index on the purchase dates of the plant and equipment owned on January 1 was 90; the average index on the purchase dates of the plant and equipment owned on December 31 was 95.

a. Restate the December 31 assets and liabilities in units with the purchasing power dollars had on that date.
b. Calculate the purchasing-power gain or loss on the company's holdings of net monetary assets.

15. Using Lifo to keep holding gains off the income statement. The Ethereal Spirits Company is a wholesale distributor of wines and liquors. It measures all of its inventories on a Lifo basis. Increments to the Lifo inventories in any year are measured at the prices paid for the first units purchased during the year.

One of Ethereal's products is Sonoma Mountain Red, produced and bottled by the Carson Brothers Winery in California. Ethereal's inventory of this product on January 1, 19x9, was as follows:

	No. of Gallons	Lifo Cost Per Unit	Lifo Cost Total
Base quantity	1,000	$1.50	$1,500
19x2 layer	200	2.00	400
19x7 layer	100	2.20	220
Total	1,300		$2,120

The price charged by Carson Brothers was $2.50 a gallon on January 1, 19x9, and remained at that level until October 15, 19x9, when it was increased to $2.75. Ethereal's purchases and sales during 19x9 were as follows:

	Gallons Purchased	Gallons Sold
Prior to October 15	8,000	6,000
From October 15 to December 31	3,000	4,000
Total	11,000	10,000

a. Calculate the current cost of goods sold in 19x9 and the current cost of the December 31, 19x9, inventory.

b. Calculate the Lifo cost of goods sold for 19x9 and the Lifo cost of the December 31, 19x9, inventory.

c. Calculate the total inventory-holding gain or loss arising during 19x9, including both the realized and the unrealized components.

d. Using data from this problem, comment on the proposition that Lifo keeps inventory-holding gains and losses out of the income statement as long as the number of units purchased in any year equals or exceeds the number of units sold.

16. Applying current costing to plant and equipment. Regal Duds, Ltd., was incorporated in the mythical republic of Bellerivia on January 1, 19x1. The first four years of the company's life were a period of relative price stability, and replacement costs were equal to historical costs on December 31, 19x4. Early in 19x5, however, the government of Bellerivia launched a large-scale rearmament and social welfare program, financed mainly by government borrowing from the Bellerivian central bank. Taking prices at January 1, 19x5, as 100, price indexes in Bellerivia traced the following path in 19x5:

	Plant and Equipment Replacement Costs	General Price Level
January 1, 19x5	100	100
Average during 19x5	150	160
December 31, 19x5	200	220

The historical costs of the company's plant and equipment were as follows:

	Original Cost	Accumulated Depreciation
January 1, 19x5	$2,000,000	$400,000
Additions	0	100,000
Retirements	0	0
December 31, 19x5	2,000,000	500,000

The average annual rate of depreciation on the plant and equipment the company owned on January 1, 19x5, was 5 percent.

The company's pretax income for 19x5, measured on an historical costing basis, was $400,000.

a. Restate the December 31, 19x5, plant and equipment at its replacement cost on that date.

    b. Restate depreciation for the year on an average replacement-cost basis.

    c. Calculate the total holding gain arising from the company's ownership of plant and equipment during 19x5.

    d. To what extent did this holding gain represent an increase in the purchasing power of the company's resources? Cite evidence to support your answer.

    e. Calculate the realized holding gain on plant and equipment for the year. Where would this appear on the company's income statement? What problems of analysis and interpretation does it create?

    17. *General price-level adjustments.* Horton Holdings, Ltd., had the following balance sheets in its 19x9 annual report:

	January 1	December 31
Current Assets:		
Cash	$ 500	$ 600
Accounts receivable	800	1,100
Inventories (Lifo)	1,400	1,400
Total Current Assets	$ 2,700	$ 3,100
Plant and equipment (cost)	12,100	12,500
Accumulated Depreciation	(6,800)	(7,100)
Total Assets	$ 8,000	$ 8,500
Current Liabilities:		
Accounts payable	$ 1,100	$ 1,400
Notes payable	100	100
Total Current Liabilities	$ 1,200	$ 1,500
Common stock	3,700	3,700
Retained earnings	3,100	3,300
Total Liabilities and Shareowners' Equity	$ 8,000	$ 8,500

Horton's income statement for 19x9 showed the following components:

Sales revenues		$9,600
Expenses:		
Depreciation	$ 600	
Other	8,600	
Total Expenses		9,200
Net Income		$ 400

Cash dividends of $200 were declared and paid during the year.

    The company's plant and equipment underwent the following changes in 19x9, measured on an historical cost basis:

	Original Cost	Accumulated Depreciation
January 1	$12,100	$6,800
Additions	800	600
Retirements	(400)	(300)
December 31	$12,500	$7,100

The age distribution of the original cost of the plant and equipment was as follows:

Year of Purchase	January 1	December 31	19x9 Depreciation
19x0	$ 6,000	$ 5,800	$200
19x2	1,000	1,000	60
19x3	800	600	50
19x5	2,500	2,500	150
19x8	1,800	1,800	90
19x9	—	800	50
Total	$12,100	$12,500	$600

The common stock was issued in 19x0; the Lifo inventory quantities were acquired in 19x2.

The general price-level indexes applicable to these figures were as follows:

19x0	110
19x2	120
19x3	130
19x5	150
19x8	180
19x9:	
January 1	200
Average	220
December 31	240

Except for the 19x9 indexes, each index represents an average for its year.

a. Calculate the purchasing-power gain or loss on the company's ownership of net monetary assets during 19x9.

b. Restate the income statement in units with the purchasing power dollars had at the end of 19x9.

c. Restate the December 31, 19x9, balance sheet in units with the purchasing power dollars had at the end of 19x9.

18. *Interpreting adjusted data.* Upon its formation on January 1, the Nuovo Company bought inventories at a cost of $2,000 and equipment at a cost of $4,000. The balance sheet at that point was as follows:

Assets		Liabilities and Owners' Equity	
Cash	$1,000	Liabilities	$1,500
Inventory	2,000	Capital stock	5,500
Equipment	4,000	Retained earnings	0
Total	$7,000	Total	$7,000

On that date, of course, the figures for inventory and equipment represented not only original cost but current cost as well. (The Nuovo Company operated in a country which had no income taxes. Its monetary unit was the dollar.)

The income statement for the first year of operations was computed both on a conventional historical cost basis and on a replacement cost basis, using *average* replacement costs for the year. This produced the following figures:

	Historical Cost Basis	Replacement Cost Basis
Sales	$6,000	$6,000
Cost of goods sold	$4,100	$4,400
Depreciation	600	612
Other expenses	900	900
Net Income	$ 400	$ 88

The year-end balance sheet was also stated on an historical cost basis and on a replacement cost basis, using *year-end* replacement prices to restate Inventory and Equipment account balances. The figures were:

		Historical Cost Basis	Replacement Cost Basis
Assets			
Cash		$2,100	$2,100
Inventory		2,300	2,400
Equipment	$4,000		$4,160
Less: Allowance for depreciation	600		624
Equipment, net		3,400	3,536
Total Assets		$7,800	$8,036
Liabilities and Owners' Equity			
Liabilities		$1,900	$1,900
Common stock		5,500	5,500
Retained earnings		400	88
Accumulated holding gains		—	548
Total Liabilities and Owners' Equity		$7,800	$8,036

The "accumulated holding gains" figure in the right-hand column was obtained as a residual by subtracting the sum of the liabilities, capital stock, and retained earnings from the adjusted asset total.

Further investigation revealed that the general price level on December 31 had reached 110 percent of the January 1 level. The average for the year was 105 percent of the January 1 figure.

After examining these figures, the company's purchasing agent commented that although operating income on a replacement cost basis was not satisfactory, the holding gains experienced during the period were very gratifying. The marketing vice president, on the other hand, rejected the replacement cost figures, saying the marketing people had done a good job selling the company's products at a good margin over their cost. No bookkeeper was going to take that achievement away from them.

In the treasurer's view, the holding gain wasn't a real gain because the purchasing power of the dollar had fallen during the year. Working quickly on the back of an envelope, the treasurer produced the following calculation:

1. Assets, January 1 .... $7,000
2. Liabilities, January 1 1,500
3. Net assets, January 1 ([1] − [2]) $5,500
4. Purchasing power index, December 31 .... 110%
5. Adjusted net assets, January 1, at end-of-year prices ([3] × [4]) $6,050
6. Adjusted net assets, December 31 (from balance sheet) 5,900
7. Loss in Purchasing Power during the Year ([5] − [6]) .... $ 150

a. Whose side would you take in this argument? Prepare a short statement that you might use to try to convince the others that you were right.
b. If accounting reports had been stated in units of stable purchasing power, would this company have reported a profit or a loss on its ordinary operations (exclusive of holding gains and losses)? Explain.
c. What changes in management policies would you recommend for the future if events during the next several years seem likely to follow the pattern set this year?
d. What is the explanation of the gap between the treasurer's income figure and income on a replacement cost basis? Do you agree with the treasurer's method of computing a purchasing power loss?

12

Capitalization of Costs

EVERY COST IS INCURRED to obtain something. This something may be a physical object, a property right, or a service. In a business firm, the purpose of expenditures for each and all of these is to create income at some time, either by producing revenues in excess of the cost (revenue-producing expenditures) or by reducing other costs (cost-saving expenditures). These income effects may be expected to occur in the current period, in some single future period, or in a number of periods.

These distinctions are reflected in the definitions of asset and expense:

1. The cost of any resource that has been consumed in obtaining the *current* period's revenues is an *expense*.
2. The cost of any resource that will be used to obtain revenues or reduce operating costs in *future* accounting periods is the cost of an *asset*.

These definitions are not always easy to apply in practice, and the accountants have to exercise their judgments. Our purpose in this chapter is to examine the factors that affect capitalization decisions on the following three kinds of expenditures:

1. Ancillary expenditures made in connection with the acquisition of long-lived tangible assets.
2. Expenditures for intangible assets.
3. Expenditures in which outlay costs must be approximated.

ANCILLARY EXPENDITURES: BASIC PRINCIPLES

An expenditure to acquire an asset is often accompanied by one or more ancillary expenditures, more or less related to the acquisition. In principle, the cost of an asset consists of all outlays necessary to render the asset suitable for its intended use. The question is whether all of the costs that meet this definition should be capitalized and, if so, whether they should be capitalized as part of the asset or separately.

An example will help us discuss these questions. Some time ago, the Camden Company decided to install a conveyer system to transport materials, work in process, and finished products between work stations in its two-story plant. The following outlays were direct consequences of this decision:

1.	Price of conveyor components	$26,500
2.	Freight charges on conveyor components	800
3.	Installation of conveyor	3,600
4.	Compensation for injuries to an employee of the contractor engaged for conveyor installation	10,000
5.	Architect's fee for redesigning conveyor housing to avoid future injuries like those suffered by contractor's employee	1,000
6.	Alterations to building to accommodate conveyor	4,200
7.	Payments to factory employees during period of shutdown for conveyor installation:	
	a. For rearranging machines	1,600
	b. For idle time	1,200
8.	Training of one employee in conveyor maintenance	300
	Total	$49,200

In deciding which of these costs should be capitalized, we need to answer three questions:

1. Was the expenditure necessary to render the asset suitable for its intended use?
2. Did it maintain or expand the previously anticipated service capacity of some other asset?
3. Did it bring the total cost of the asset to an amount in excess of some specified maximum amount?

Identifying Necessary Expenditures

The only item associated with Camden's new conveyor that might be classified as unnecessary is the injury compensation cost (item 4). Had ordinary caution been exercised, the Camden Company would have either engaged an insured contractor or itself secured the requisite coverage at a nominal charge. In either case, the insurance premium would have been part of the reasonably necessary cost of the asset and therefore capitalizable.

But what about the rest of this cost—should it be capitalized, too? If the cost of buying insurance measures the amount of cost that was *necessary* to the installation of the conveyor, it follows that any cost in excess of this amount was unnecessary and, therefore, wasted. Highlighting this waste as a loss in the income statement rather than burying it in the acquisition cost of the asset would alert the readers of the financial statements to management's error in failing to provide insurance coverage. This is another application of the value of information criterion we introduced in Chapter 9.

Capitalizing an amount equivalent to the insurance premium the company would have paid if it had carried insurance is an example of a practice known as *self-insurance*. A company with a self-insurance plan measures the insurance costs of any period by the actuarially estimated average loss due to the events being insured against, rather than by the loss actually experienced during that particular period.

Self-insurance accounting can't be used for external financial reporting, however, because the accounting profession has taken the position that no asset has been reduced and no liability has arisen until the self-insured loss actually takes place.[1] For this reason, the Camden Company wouldn't be allowed to capitalize the appropriate insurance premium. The entire $10,000 would have to be capitalized if the basic rule were followed.

A question may also be raised about the architect's fee (item 5). Management clearly didn't anticipate this when it decided to install the conveyor. Even so, it clearly meets our first capitalization test— that is, it was necessary to render the conveyor suitable for its intended use. The cost was incurred to provide future benefits (from the use of the conveyor), not to support the operations of the current period alone. Although this cost wasn't anticipated, therefore, it should be capitalized as part of the installed cost of the conveyor.

One important cost item didn't appear in the Camden Company's list—the cost of the money the company tied up between the time it bought the conveyor components and the time the conveyor was installed and ready to use. Although tying up capital during the installation period is clearly necessary to make the asset ready to use, neither the amount of capital tied up nor the cost of providing this capital is easy to measure. Partly because of these difficulties, except

---

[1] Financial Accounting Standards Board, "Statement of Financial Accounting Standards No. 5," in AICPA, *Professional Standards—Accounting, Current Text* (New York: Commerce Clearing House, Inc., 1978), sec. 4311.30.

in some specialized circumstances, the accounting profession has generally treated interest on borrowed money as an expense of the period in which the money is used. This position is now being debated, however, and may be changed while this edition is in print.

Maintenance versus Betterments

Our second question is whether the expenditures maintained or expanded the previously anticipated service capacity of some other asset. For example, the Camden Company's expenditures for building alterations and machinery rearrangement (items 6 and 7a) affected two assets the company had already identified, the building and its machinery. This raises the question of whether these costs are incurred not to "render the conveyor suitable for its intended use" but to preserve the previously existing suitability of other assets under changed operating conditions.

Accountants treat this as a problem of distinguishing between *betterments,* connoting some form of progressive change, and *maintenance,* meaning the prevention or retardation of retrogressive change. Costs of betterments are subject to capitalization; maintenance costs are properly chargeable to current operations.

This problem can be solved if we recognize that the *total productive capacity* of a long-lived asset, or any interrelated set of these assets, is a joint function of their rate of output per unit of time and the length of time over which satisfactory output is achieved (economic life). Both of these variables are more or less dependent on the level of maintenance provided. At the time of acquisition, therefore, each asset has an *expected lifetime capacity* reflecting an *intended maintenance policy.* This leads to the following definitions:

1. Any cost incurred to obtain the service initially expected of an asset is a maintenance cost.
2. Any cost incurred to increase lifetime productive capacity by raising the output rate or by extending the economic life or by reducing operating cost to less than its originally anticipated level is a capitalizable betterment.

Whether the building alteration and rearrangement costs should be classified as maintenance or as betterments is still a matter of judgment. For example, developments in conveyor technology or movements in operating costs may not have been anticipated correctly when the depreciation rates on the building and on the machinery were established. As a result, the entire conveyor installation may be necessary to achieve the previously anticipated lives of those assets. This position is difficult to maintain because we have decided the conveyor itself is a betterment—that is, it is an asset separate from the building and the other machinery already in place.

It might also be argued that the building alteration costs should be added to the costs of the building itself and the costs of machinery rearrangement should be assigned to the individual machines. This would be appropriate only if these expenditures increased the total lifetime productive capacity of those assets. Otherwise, the only place left for these expenditures is as part of the cost of the new conveyor.

Maximum Capitalization

All of these capitalization decisions are subject to one further test. If the total cost identifiable with an asset is so large it clearly can't be recovered from the anticipated use of the asset during its life, the excess should be transferred immediately to the income statement as a loss of the current period. Our measurement basis, in other words, could be characterized as "cost or recoverable cost, whichever is lower."

Separate Capitalization

Deciding to capitalize these costs is only part of the capitalization decision. A second issue must be resolved: whether to recognize a single asset or more than one in recording the costs arising out of a related set of transactions. Answers to this question are based on the application of two criteria:

1. Do the objects acquired have different life expectancies?
2. Do the objects acquired have different perceived identities?

An affirmative answer to *either* of these questions is a sufficient reason for separate capitalization. For example, few accountants would include item 8, training costs, as part of the cost of the conveyor even if the life expectancies of the conveyor and the training were identical; the reason is that training and conveyors are perceived to be in different asset categories. By the same token, the movable treads on the conveyor might be classified separately if their life expectancy is shorter than that of the conveyor frame and motor, even though few would perceive these as two separate kinds of assets.

Finally, if the alterations to the building are expected to produce benefits after the conveyor's life has come to an end, the expenditures of $4,200 for this purpose should be capitalized separately from those for the conveyor, perhaps as additions to the cost of the building itself.

Maintenance versus Replacement

The results of the application of the two criteria for separate capitalization are often likely to seem arbitrary. For example, although most people would regard an entire airplane as a single asset, an airline might capitalize the costs of the airframe, engines, and interior fittings in three separate asset categories. The company may do this partly because it reports its costs this way for income tax purposes or because it believes separate capitalization will produce better financial-statement information. We'll examine the impact of income tax considerations in the next section.

The issue here is whether *subsequent* expenditures are to be treated as maintenance (a current expense) or as replacement costs (capitalized as asset costs). Replacement of an entire asset requires removal of that asset from the accounts and the capitalization of the cost of the replacement. The cost of replacing a *part* of an asset, however, is usually treated as a maintenance cost unless it is expected to increase the asset's service potential or extend its useful life.

In other words, the definitions of maintenance and replacement depend on what has been chosen as the unit of account. For example, if the conveyor is the unit of account and if its estimated useful life is based on the assumption that the treads will be replaced periodically, then later expenditures on replacement treads will be treated as maintenance costs. If the treads are capitalized separately, then the costs of the original treads must be removed from the account when they are replaced and the cost of the replacement treads will be capitalized in their place. If the unit of account is made small enough, even a routine lubrication can be treated as a replacement, and no room will be left for the concept of maintenance.

Separate capitalization is likely to have a slight smoothing effect on year-to-year movements in operating costs. For example, suppose the conveyor is expected to last for 20 years, with treads costing $8,000 to be replaced every five years. If the cost of the first set of treads is capitalized as part of the cost of the conveyor, it will be depreciated over 20 years, at an average of $400 a year. Depreciation and maintenance cost, therefore, will be $400 in all years except years 6, 11, and 16, when replacements take place. In those three years, the depreciation and maintenance cost will total $8,400. This cost pattern is traced by the solid line in Exhibit 12–1. The dashed line, on the other hand, shows the annual cost if the treads are capitalized separately. In that case they will be depreciated over five years, at $1,600 a year. The replacements at the end of five, ten, and 15 years will also be capitalized and depreciated at these same amounts, thereby smoothing the annual cost.

EXHIBIT 12–1. Effect of Separate Capitalization on Reported Annual Cost

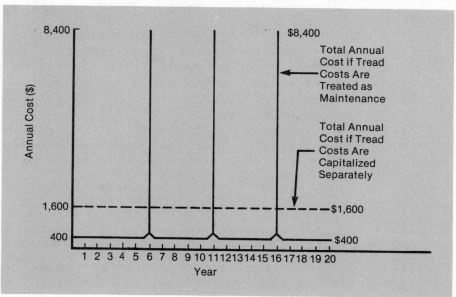

Major Overhauls

A very similar set of questions arises in connection with expenditures made to effect major overhauls of existing facilities. If the overhaul is made to restore to the facilities the service potential that was anticipated when the depreciation schedule was originally established, the cost of the overhaul is a maintenance cost. If the overhaul extends an asset's remaining lifetime service potential beyond the amount originally anticipated, however, the cost of achieving any such extension should be capitalized and the depreciation schedule recalculated.

Eighteen years ago, for example, the Puhlan Waite Railway purchased a group of freight cars and began depreciating their cost by the item method at a straight-line rate of 5 percent a year. Ten of these cars were still in service until a few months ago, when they were reconditioned at a cost of $62,000. Their combined book value prior to reconditioning was:

Original cost	$100,000
Less: Accumulated depreciation	90,000
Undepreciated Cost	$ 10,000

The original depreciation rate in this case was based on an assumed life of 20 years, with zero salvage value. The reconditioning is expected to extend the life to ten years from the date of the reconditioning. Salvage value is expected to be negligible at the end of that time.

It should be clear from this description that this expenditure should be capitalized because the future benefit it was incurred to obtain was a *new* benefit, not the service the cars were initially expected to provide. The cost to be depreciated during the next ten years, therefore, is the $10,000 undepreciated cost of the cars plus the $62,000 renovation cost, a total of $72,000.

The only other issue is how the $62,000 should be identified with the asset. One possibility would be to add the $62,000 to the original cost of the cars. This would produce the following figures:

Freight Cars	Accumulated Depreciation—Freight Cars
Orig. cost . 100,000 Overhaul . . 62,000 162,000	Sum of annual amounts 90,000

This would be appropriate if the purpose of the expenditure was to provide the cars with characteristics they had never possessed. In this instance, however, the reconditioning consisted mainly of *replacing* various component parts. The original cost of these parts, therefore, should be removed from the Freight Cars account (and from the allowance for depreciation), to be replaced by the cost of reconditioning the cars.

In practice, the accountants usually cannot identify clearly the original cost of replaced parts. Their solution is to deduct the expenditure from accumulated depreciation:

Allowance for Depreciation—Freight Cars   62,000
    Accounts Payable, etc.   62,000

This increases the book value of the asset by $62,000 without including both the original cost and the replacement cost in the Freight Cars account. The overhaul is thus seen as a partial restoration of the service potential that expired in previous years, and the $72,000 book value is depreciated over the ten-year remaining life.

ANCILLARY EXPENDITURES: PRAGMATIC CRITERIA

In practice, the facts are often less clear-cut than a textbook description may make them appear. Although the Financial Accounting Standards Board is making an effort to reduce management's freedom of choice on these questions, the company still has a good deal of latitude in applying the general measurement principles stated above. In exercising their judgment, the company's managers and their accountants are influenced by a number of pragmatic considerations, most of which generally lead to an earlier recognition of expense than the basic principles would suggest.

Recordkeeping Convenience

Among the least impressive but by no means least important of such influences is that of recordkeeping convenience. Although the Camden Company did, in fact, isolate the cost of equipment rearrangement by its own work force, the firm's accounting system might have been so organized that this portion of factory payroll costs could not be readily distinguished. This is often the case when equipment installation, remodeling, and the like are accomplished by regular employees. Under these conditions, management may understandably adopt the view that it is more interested in making money than in measuring precisely how much money it has made. Where the cost to be isolated is relatively small and the cost of isolating it relatively large, this argument is quite persuasive.

A similar argument is often used to justify expensing the cost of hand tools and other high-volume, low-unit-cost items that should be useful for more than one year. The total cost of these items may run into millions of dollars a year in large corporations, but they are expensed to avoid the cost of maintaining detailed property records for them.

Tax Advantage

A more compelling and entirely rational cause for expensing costs which might otherwise be capitalized is the tax advantage to be gained thereby. So long as a firm has current taxable income, increasing the amount of current expense will have the effect of reducing current tax payments. Transferring cost to expense currently rather than deferring it to future periods generally will inflate future taxable income, but this fact is a deterrent only when an increase in the tax rate is expected. The dollar saved this year is unquestionably worth more than the dollar that may be saved in some future year.

Since taxable income is not necessarily the same as reported income, a cost may be capitalized for public reporting while being expensed for tax purposes. However, the taxpayer has a very understandable tendency to buttress the case for current tax deductibility of borderline items by expensing them for both purposes. Thus, tax matters do undoubtedly exert an influence on accounting policy.

Conservatism

When a legitimate question exists as to whether a cost ought to be capitalized or expensed and the decision will have no impact on tax treatment, the general tendency is to expense the cost on the grounds that it is the conservative thing to do.

For example, as we pointed out earlier, the employee training cost shown as item 8 in the example above was incurred to obtain a future benefit. Although the trained employees can leave the company whenever they wish, taking their skill with them, the initial training cost is like the priming of a pump—once the water is flowing, very little effort is required to keep it flowing. An argument could be made, in other words, for depreciating the initial training cost over the expected useful life of the conveyor system. Most practicing accountants would invoke the notion of conservatism, however, and charge the entire cost to expense, either immediately or over some short future period.

The major consequences of conservatism are (1) the understatement of assets and owners' equity, (2) the understatement of current income, and (3) the overstatement of future income, other things being equal. Probably the main reason for the widespread support of conservatism in the face of these obvious defects is psychological. Large fluctuations in earnings create great expectations on the part of the stockholders one year and bitter disappointment the next. Application of the idea of conservatism tends to limit this. In good years, earnings are reduced, and in bad years, earnings are raised, since large expenditures that benefit future years and may be expensed currently tend to be made in years when income is otherwise high.

Income Control

All three of the factors we have just discussed introduce a bias toward expensing expenditures that might on theoretical grounds be capitalized. The fourth factor, income control, can work in either direction.

Management has a substantial interest in controlling the net income figure. Net income, expressed as earnings per share, is widely regarded as a primary index of corporate and management success. If earnings per share exceed the amounts predicted by stock market analysts, the market price of the shares is likely to rise; if the earnings per share figure is disappointing, market price will fall.

Net income is also widely regarded as a measure of managerial skill. Even if management's compensation isn't tied directly to reported income, managers who have been able to generate income and higher share prices for their companies are likely to share in the rewards. Altogether, management has powerful incentives to influence the net income figure by varying its capitalization policy from year to year, changes that may be difficult for outsiders to identify. In some years the incentive is to increase reported income; in others, when the market's expectations are low, heavy write-offs that reduce reported income may seem desirable.

This is not to suggest that income manipulation is rampant or, even, that management has a great deal of leeway in most years. Still, to the extent that expenditures fall in the grey area between obvious capitalization and obvious expensing, the objective of income control may exert an influence on practice.

Consistency and Disclosure

Probably the most serious problem posed by the application of these pragmatic criteria is that they give management a great deal of power to affect reported income. To limit management's ability to use this power in ways that might distort net income, the accounting profession requires the firm to be *consistent* from year to year in its treatment of specific types of cost.

For example, once a firm decides to expense employee training costs, it must do so consistently, year in and year out, regardless of current conditions. This requirement is based on the proposition that a bias consistently followed impairs the usefulness of information less seriously than a bias that depends on what management wants the stockholders to believe.

The consistency doctrine doesn't lock the company into a single set of accounting practices forever. Conditions change, and companies do change the ways they account for some of their assets, liabilities, and shareowners' equities from time to time. As accounting changes are made, however, the company must provide full explanations of their nature, the reasons for making them, and their effects on the financial statements. In addition, the Securities and Exchange Commission now requires the independent auditors to endorse any such changes in reports filed with the Commission, stating their conclusion that the new practices are preferable to the old under current conditions.[2]

As one might imagine, consistency is not an unmixed blessing. For example, partly because the amount is not *material* (that is, not large enough to be significant), a company may decide to expense the cost

---

[2] Accounting Principles Board, "Opinion No. 20," in AICPA, *Professional Standards—Accounting*, sec. 1051; Securities and Exchange Commission, *Accounting Series Release No. 177* (Washington, D.C.: Securities and Exchange Commission, 1975).

of alterations to equipment and find this accounting practice to be satisfactory for a number of years. Sooner or later, however, it may come to a year in which the cost is large because of a large-scale plant modernization effort. Under these circumstances, the firm's accountants may well insist that this cost should be capitalized and amortized over the expected remaining life of the equipment. This departure from consistent reporting is justified by the materiality of the amount. The corporation, however, must disclose in its published financial statements the departure from previous practice and its quantitative implications.

Enforcing year-to-year consistency in the capitalization of ancillary expenditures is extremely difficult. Simple changes in the bookkeeping routine can lead to substantial changes in the percentage of ancillary expenditures that will be capitalized, even though the stated capitalization policy remains unchanged. The independent public accountant is alert to this possibility, but these changes are often difficult to detect.

INTANGIBLE ASSETS

Perhaps the most important reason offered for expensing items that might in theory be capitalized is neither convenience nor tax deferral nor conservatism, but the uncertainty of the future benefits. This difficulty is thought to be most pronounced in connection with the so-called "intangible" assets such as those which arise from sales promotion and research and development expenditures. To illustrate the problems of accounting for intangibles, we'll discuss three of these situations:

1. Purchases of specific intangibles.
2. Sales promotion expenditures.
3. Research and development expenditures.

Purchases of Specific Intangibles

Patents, franchises, copyrights, and trademarks are sometimes acquired by purchase. Purchases of this kind present no unique problems, and the purchase prices are fully capitalized.

Amortization of these costs may also be a simple matter, if clear bases can be found for estimating the anticipated life and productivity patterns. Publishers, for example, can predict the useful life of most textbooks quite accurately and can even predict what proportion of textbook revenues will materialize each year. The useful lives of patents, on the other hand, may be much more difficult to estimate even though they represent exclusive legal rights for a fixed period,

17 years. If the anticipated useful life of a purchased patent is shorter than 17 years, its cost should be amortized over that shorter period.

Other intangibles are more difficult to identify with specific benefits. A trademark, for example, may live forever or may fade away gradually. When these uncertainties are great, some accountants maintain that the entire cost of the intangible should be charged to expense immediately. Others go to the opposite extreme and oppose any amortization at all whenever the benefits to be derived from the intangible seem likely to continue perpetually.

The methods used in practice represent a compromise between these two viewpoints. When benefit periods and patterns can be predicted well enough, the costs of purchased intangibles are amortized on the basis of these predictions. When no such basis can be found, the cost is amortized over a period not to exceed forty years. The argument for setting an upper limit of this sort is that all intangibles lose their value at some time, meaning that their cost should be deducted from the revenues of the years in which the assets are expected to be productive.[3]

Sales Promotion Expenditures

Most intangibles are probably created by internal expenditures rather than by external purchases. Perhaps the commonest example of this is the development of customer goodwill through sales promotional activities.

Although the bulk of the firm's promotional activity is ordinarily intended to produce current sales, a significant portion is designed to enhance the general reputation of the firm and increase its future sales. Costs in this latter category, plus numerous others less easily identified but likewise aimed at building goodwill, are at least partially applicable to *future* revenues. Nevertheless, it is universal practice to expense all selling and promotional costs as incurred.

The main reason for treating the costs of internally created intangibles as current expenses is that the current and probable future effects of sales promotion and other similar expenditures are very difficult to identify separately and quantify. It is also difficult to assign specific cost flows to specific future benefits. While the salespeople confidently expect that some of today's efforts will produce subsequent orders, they have no clear idea when these will materialize.

Even if current efforts are directed specifically to the future with every prospect of beneficial results, it may be impossible to establish

---

[3] APB, "Opinion No. 17," in AICPA, *Professional Standards—Accounting*, Sec. 5141.29.

the periods in which these benefits will be realized. Consequently, it will be impossible to establish a valid basis for systematic cost amortization.

Although this approach will often understate the firm's assets, it may not distort the annual expense totals. Sales promotion costs tend to be relatively stable from year to year, either constant or gradually growing, and consistent expensing probably yields significant errors in reported income only in periods in which expenditure rates change abruptly.

Research and Development Expenditures

The case for capitalizing research and development costs is stronger than it was for sales promotion. *All* of the intended benefits are future benefits; therefore, expensing will lead to a greater distortion of reported income than will expensing of sales promotion outlays, most of which have current as well as future benefits.

A second argument for capitalization is that expensing research and development expenditures may encourage managers to shortchange the future to meet short-term income objectives. Although a stable rate of expenditure is often essential to the success of these programs, management ordinarily can increase current net income by cutting back on research and development costs that would otherwise be expensed immediately, in full. If the costs are capitalized, on the other hand, research cutbacks will have little effect on current net income. This may shield the function to some extent from the impact of short-term business recessions.

The major objection to capitalizing research and development is that at the time an expenditure is made, management is generally uncertain as to what future periods, if any, will be benefited. It is quite possible that the knowledge obtained on any particular project will prove worthless to the firm. The concept of conservatism, therefore, argues that all outlays be expensed at the time they are made. On these grounds, despite the clear evidence that a firm undertakes research and development because the benefits from the work *in the aggregate* are expected to justify the costs, research and development costs are expensed immediately.[4]

Accounting for research and development expenditures for internal management use should be guided by entirely different considerations. Management needs to keep track of the costs of each project, regardless of the period in which the expenditure is made. These costs can be compared with the rate of progress of the research to assist management in judging whether to keep on with the project.

---

[4] FASB, Statement No. 2, *Professional Standards—Accounting,* sec. 4211.12.

Also, after the project is completed, an analysis of its costs and benefits can be useful in the evaluation of subsequent research proposals.

ACQUISITION COST APPROXIMATIONS

Even if the measurement criteria described above are clearly understood and fully accepted, measurement of the acquisition cost of an asset is not always simple. Three problems deserve brief comment here:

1. Allocation of joint-acquisition cost.
2. Noncash acquisitions.
3. Purchase in advance of use.

Allocation of Joint Acquisition Cost

Two or more assets are sometimes acquired at a single purchase price, known as their *joint cost*. The method usually used for joint-cost allocation is the *relative market value* method. This presumes that the anticipated values of the individual assets to the purchaser, and, therefore, the amounts that the purchaser was willing to pay for the various assets, were proportional to the prices they would have commanded if purchased separately. For example, if an independent appraiser says that comparable land could have been bought on the market for $1 million and a comparable building would have cost $4 million, then 20 percent of the total purchase price will be assigned to the land and 80 percent to the building.

This method should not be applied when a group of assets is acquired to obtain one of them. For example, a company may buy an old loft building together with the land on which it is located, intending to raze the building and erect a new one. In this case, the entire purchase price clearly relates to the land. What distinguishes this situation from the one in the preceding paragraph is that we don't have two joint products. The land is the asset desired and being purchased. The building, unwanted by the purchaser, is incidental to the land acquisition, and any costs that otherwise would be assigned to it are treated as part of the cost of the land, along with the costs of razing the building. This is just another illustration of the general principle that outlays necessary to render an asset suitable for its intended use should be capitalized as part of the cost of that asset.

Noncash Acquisitions

Companies sometimes pay for assets with shares of their own stock or with nonmonetary assets, such as securities of other companies. In these cases acquisition cost has to be estimated.

When an asset is acquired in exchange for cash, the amount of cash paid is a perfect measure of the value of the resources sacrificed—that is, the acquisition cost. Similarly, when nonmonetary assets are used to pay for newly acquired assets, their market value is a good measure of the amount of resources sacrificed to effect the purchase. When good evidence of the market value of the assets given up is available, therefore, the accountant should use this figure to measure acquisition cost. If this kind of evidence is not available, then the market value of the assets being acquired should be used to measure acquisition cost. Presumably the seller will not accept anything less than the market value of the assets given up. If neither of these figures is available, an outside independent appraiser should be called in to establish the values of the resources exchanged.

Market value in these cases is clearly superior to the book value of the assets given up as a measure of acquisition cost. Book values get out of date very rapidly and may be far from the current sacrifice made to acquire the new assets. Market price of the goods given up can be taken as the measure of current sacrifice if it can be assumed that the buying company could get this much from some other source.

The accounting profession in the United States treats exchanges of nonmonetary assets in two different ways. If the transaction is the "culmination of an earning process," and if the fair values of the assets exchanged are determinable within reasonable limits, the transaction will be regarded as a combination of a purchase and a sale and a gain or loss will be reported if market value is different from the book value of the asset given up in the exchange. An example would be the exchange of merchandise inventory for shares of stock in a publicly traded company.

If the exchange isn't the end of an earning process or if fair value can't be determined clearly enough, the cost of the new asset will be measured by the book value of the old asset and no gain or loss will be reported.[5] An example is an exchange of an old delivery vehicle for a new one. If the trade-in allowance is greater than the book value of the old vehicle, then the cost of the new vehicle will be measured by the book value of the old plus any other amounts given to the seller of the new vehicle. If the trade-in allowance is less than book value, however, then the company will report a loss.[6]

The reason for this apparent inconsistency is that trade-in allowances often include implicit price concessions to the buyer. Rather

---

[5] APB, "Opinion No. 29," para. 21, in AICPA, *Professional Standards—Accounting*, Sec. 1041.21.

[6] Ibid., para. 22 and Sec. 1041.22.

than attempt to estimate these, the accountants assume the entire excess is a price concession. Unwillingness of the seller to allow the full book value as an allowance against the price of the new vehicle, on the other hand, is reasonable evidence that the market value of the old asset has a market value less than its book value—therefore, a loss has occurred and should be recognized.

A somewhat similar problem arises when an asset is paid for with shares of the firm's own capital stock. Once again the accountant must make an effort to establish the cost of these assets. Except for a special class of acquisitions we'll discuss in Chapter 15, the accountant measures cost by the current market value of the stock issued or of the assets acquired, whichever is more clearly evident. In the absence of such evidence, an outside appraisal must be sought.

SUMMARY

The use of historical cost as the basis of asset measurement at the time of acquisition raises a number of difficult questions. Some of these result from uncertainty—for example, will the expenditure lead to a commensurate future benefit? Others are definitional—for example, did the expenditure increase the firm's total productive capacity or merely prevent it from deteriorating? All are alike, however, in that they require the exercise of accounting judgment.

Lacking precise answers to these questions, the accountant needs a conceptual framework on which to build a capitalization policy. The basic concept calls for capitalization of all costs that are incurred in anticipation of a benefit or benefits after the end of the current accounting period. An apparent exception is maintenance cost, but here the future benefit is one that was already assumed in the decision to capitalize the costs of the asset to which the maintenance is applied.

Rigid application of this concept is unlikely, partly due to demands that capitalization policy be conservative, clerically convenient, and tax sensitive. For expenditures that are designed to create intangibles, the situation is even worse, in that the anticipated future benefits are so uncertain. The result is that accountants typically expense far more costs than a strict application of the basic concept would permit.

The balance sheets that reflect these departures from an ideal capitalization policy are likely to understate the historical cost of the firm's assets. Because the company must follow its policy consistently, year after year, the effects on the income statement will be much weaker than the balance-sheet effects, as long as total expenditures in borderline categories are relatively constant from year to year. Even if such expenditures fluctuate, however, or rise or fall along a trend line, consistency will lead to financial statements that are more reliable than those that would result if management were free to change its asset-measurement practices at will, depending on its needs of the moment.

KEY TERMS

Ancillary expenditure   Maintenance
Betterment   Replacement
Joint cost

INDEPENDENT STUDY PROBLEMS (Solutions in Appendix B)

1. *Exchange of assets.* In 1952, the Experimental Company bought 21,600 shares of the capital stock of Respirator, Inc., at a price of $15 a share. On January 1, 1977, this stock was given to Ordway, Inc., in exchange for an office building. The appraised value of the building on that date was $2 million, while the stock was being traded on the market at a price of $105 a share.

The Experimental Company capitalized the new asset (building) at the original cost of the old asset (stock). Do you agree with this treatment? What further information, if any, would you like to have before reaching a final decision on this question?

2. *Ancillary expenditures.* An automobile manufacturer bought six heavy stamping machines at a price of $16,250 each. When they were delivered, the purchaser paid freight charges of $4,200 and handling fees of $1,200. Four employees, each earning $10 an hour, worked three 40-hour weeks setting up and testing the machines. Special wiring and other materials applicable to the new machines cost $600.

How much of these costs should be capitalized as costs of these machines?

3. *Major overhaul.* In January 1964, Abercrombie Mills, Inc., bought and placed in service a new paper machine costing $50,000. Its estimated useful life was 20 years, with no major overhauls planned for that period. Depreciation was to be calculated on a straight-line basis, with a zero estimated salvage value.

In December, 1967, certain improvements were added to this machine at a cost of $6,000. Twelve years later, in the fall of 1979, the machine was thoroughly overhauled and rebuilt at a cost of $12,000. It was estimated that the overhaul would extend the machine's useful life by five years, or until the end of 1988. Depreciation charges for 1979 were unaffected by the overhaul.

a. Calculate the machine's book value at the end of 1967, after depreciation for the year was recorded but before the improvements were accounted for.

    b. Show the journal entry required to record the improvements added in December, 1967.

    c. Compute depreciation for 1968 on a straight-line basis.

    d. Show the journal entry required to record the overhauling of the machine in the fall of 1979.

    e. Compute depreciation for 1980 on a straight-line basis.

EXERCISES AND PROBLEMS

    4. Consistency versus uniformity. A financial executive recently stated that the only important requirement for a capitalization policy is consistency—in other words, the details of the policy are unimportant so long as it is applied consistently from year to year. Can you identify any possible adverse effects of allowing management to choose its own capitalization policy and apply it consistently? If so, are they likely to be important?

    5. Joint acquisition costs. The Coyle Construction Company paid $21,000 for a house and lot. The house was then torn down at an additional cost of $500 so that Coyle could begin to construct a gasoline service station on the site. At the time of the acquisition, an appraisal of the property placed the value of the land at $18,000 and the value of the house at $9,000.

    What asset(s) did the company acquire? Calculate the cost of each asset that you have identified.

    6. Betterment or maintenance. The Bay Shore Company built an office building ten years ago. It rented space to several tenants, but its major tenants, Gallagher Coal Company, gradually took more and more space so that, by last year, it occupied the entire ten-story building.

    A year ago Gallagher notified Bay Shore that it would not renew its lease on the building unless Bay Shore made extensive alterations to the building to make it suitable for use as the company's headquarters. Since other tenants were unlikely to use as much space as Gallagher or to pay the rentals Gallagher was paying, Bay Shore decided to make the changes.

    The alterations cost $1.4 million. Bay Shore's management estimated the present value of the future cash flows from the renovated building to be $3.2 million.

    Before the renovation took place, the building was listed at its original cost of $2.4 million, less accumulated depreciation of $800,000. The land on which the building was located had cost $400,000. An appraiser estimated that the land and the renovated building had a market value of $3 million but that finding a buyer might take a year or more.

    How should the renovation expenditure be accounted for? List the alternatives you considered and your reasons for choosing the one you are recommending.

    7. Noncash acquisition. The Griffin Company bought a ten-acre plot of land from Gargoyles, Ltd., issuing 20,000 shares of its own capital stock in exchange for this land. The land was to be the site of Griffin's new corporate headquarters.

    Gargoyles had bought this land 15 years earlier for $20,000 and had used it as the site of a drive-in theater. The land was located near the intersection of an interstate highway and the local arterial highway, making it a very attractive location for a number of potential users.

Gargoyles' balance sheet listed the land at $20,000; the theater installations had been destroyed in a storm six months earlier and the company had written their costs off completely. Although the assessed valuation for tax purposes was $100,000, an appraiser estimated that the land was worth twice that amount.

Griffin's stock was traded actively on the New York Stock Exchange at prices ranging from $24 to $26 at the time of the acquisition.

List the alternative bases on which Griffin might have capitalized this property, choose the basis you would have recommended, calculate the capitalized amount, and state the reasons for your choice.

8. Exchange of assets. The Park Wells Company has just purchased all the assets of the Crawford Corporation, giving in exchange government bonds which were purchased two years ago for $1 million. The market price of these bonds was $970,000 on the day when Park Wells purchased the Crawford assets.

On the date of the purchase by Park Wells, Crawford's books showed current assets of $300,000 and plant and equipment with a book value of $200,000. No other assets were listed on the Crawford Corporation's books.

An appraiser hired by Park Wells estimated that the replacement cost of the current assets on the purchase date was $350,000. The replacement cost of the plant and equipment, less an allowance for depreciation, was $400,000.

a. Should the Park Wells Company have recognized $1 million, $970,000, or some other figure as the total cost of the Crawford assets?

b. How should this total amount have been allocated among the various assets acquired? Prepare a journal entry reflecting your allocation and give your reasons for your choice.

9. Ancillary expenditures; joint costs. To obtain a new factory site, the Mosk Manufacturing Company purchased a 12-acre tract of wasteland, paying $13,000 to the former owners. Expenses for searching titles and for drawing and recording deeds amounted to $300. Grading cost $2,800. As only six acres were required for its own factory, it considered two offers for six acres: (1) $12,000 for the north half and (2) $8,000 for the south half. It accepted the offer of $8,000 for the south half and received a certified check in payment.

a. At what amount should the remaining land be carried on the next balance sheet?

b. What gain or loss, if any, should be reported on the income statement for the current period?

10. Capitalization: one asset or two? A machine has cost $21,000 and is expected to be useful for 12 years, with no end-of-life salvage.

A major component of this machine is a heavy-duty air compressor that must be replaced every four years. Replacement compressors cost $6,000 each.

a. Determine for each of the next 12 years the effect on net income of capitalizing the compressor and the other components of the machine in separate accounts instead of in one single account.

b. Which of these two alternatives do you prefer? Give your reasons.

11. Ancillary expenditures. The Caldbec Stationery store has just purchased a photocopying machine and a manual typewriter. The photocopying machine will be used to print copies of documents, manuscripts, and other items for Caldbec customers. The typewriter has been placed on sale in the store. The following data relate to these two acquisitions:

	Copier	Typewriter
Invoice price	$5,000	$100
Discount taken	2%	2%
Freight cost	$ 200	$ 4
Insurance in transit	20	1
Cost of installation and testing:		
Materials	175	xxx
Labor of company employees	250	xxx
Bill from electrician for power connections	75	xxx

a. Ignoring depreciation, at what amount does accounting theory require the copying machine to be shown on the company's year-end balance sheet?

b. Assuming that the typewriter is still unsold at the end of the year, at what amount does accounting theory require it to be shown on the company's year-end balance sheet? (Note: The cost to replace the item at the end of the year is higher than its original cost.)

c. Are the underlying principles the same in each case or different? Explain briefly.

d. In accounting practice, at what amounts might you expect these assets to be shown? Explain your reasons for any differences between these amounts and those given in answer to parts (a) and (b) above.

12. Ancillary expenditures; trade-in value. In January, 19x1, a storekeeper bought a used delivery truck for $2,000. Before putting the vehicle into service, $280 was spent for painting and decorating the body and $520 for a complete engine overhaul. Four new tires were bought for $200. The storekeeper expected to keep the truck in service for three years, at the end of which time it would have a trade-in value of $600.

Gasoline, oil, and similar items were charged to expense as procured. In January 19x2, a new battery ($40) and miscellaneous repairs ($180) were purchased. Straight-line depreciation was used.

Four new tires were bought for $220 in January 19x3, and the body was repainted at a cost of $350. Miscellaneous repairs were made at a cost of $300.

A new truck costing $6,800 was bought in January 19x4. The trade-in allowance on the old vehicle was $860.

a. Which of the outlays made in 19x1 should be capitalized?

b. Which of the outlays made in 19x2 and 19x3 should be capitalized?

c. Calculate depreciation on a straight-line basis for each year, 19x1 through 19x3. (A full year's depreciation should be taken in each year.)

d. Indicate how the replacement of the old truck by a new one would be accounted for in 19x4.

13. Betterment, overhaul, and retirement; journal entries. A barge with an estimated life of 20 years and no end-of-life salvage value was bought in January 19x1 for $200,000. It proved too small to be profitable, and five years later was lengthened at a cost of $30,000, paid in cash.

At the end of 15 years, the barge was thoroughly overhauled and reconditioned at a cost of $40,000, paid in cash. This action was expected to extend the life of the barge to ten years from the date of the reconditioning (that is, to 25 years from the original acquisition date.)

Early in its 22nd year the barge was lost in a storm, and $15,000 insurance was collected. Depreciation was by the straight-line method.

a. Determine the correct balance in the Barge and Accumulated Depreciation accounts at the end of five years.

b. Prepare a journal entry to record the cost of lengthening the barge.

c. Calculate depreciation for the sixth year.

d. Prepare a journal entry to record the cost of reconditioning the barge.

e. Calculate depreciation for the 16th year.

f. Determine the correct balance in the Barge and Accumulated Depreciation accounts at the end of 21 years.

g. Prepare a journal entry to record the loss of the barge and the collection of the insurance.

14. Discussion question: stating and applying an accounting principle. The general ledger of Enter-tane, Inc., a corporation engaged in the development and production of television programs for commercial sponsorship, contains the following accounts before amortization at the end of the current year:

Account	Balance (Debit)
Sealing Wax and Kings	$51,000
The Messenger	36,000
The Desperado	17,500
Shin Bone	8,000
Studio Rearrangement	5,000

An examination of contracts and records has revealed the following information:

1. The balances in the first two accounts represent the total cost of completed programs that were televised during the accounting period just ended. Under the terms of an existing contract, Sealing Wax and Kings will be rerun during the next accounting period at a fee equal to 50 percent of the fee for the first televising of the program. The contract for the first run produced $300,000 of revenue. The contract with the sponsors of The Messenger provides that they may, at their option, rerun the program during the next season at a fee of 75 percent of the fee on the first televising of the program.

2. The balance in The Desperado account is the cost of a new program which has just been completed and is being considered by several companies for commercial sponsorship.
3. The balance in the Shin Bone account represents the cost of a partially completed program for a projected series that has been abandoned.
4. The balance of the Studio Rearrangement account consists of payments made to a firm of engineers which prepared a report recommending a more efficient utilization of existing studio space and equipment.

a. State the general principle or principles by which accountants guide themselves in deciding how much of the balances in the first four accounts should be shown as assets on the company's year-end balance sheet.
b. Applying this principle or principles, how would you report each of these first four accounts in the year-end financial statements? Explain.
c. In what way, if at all, does the Studio Rearrangement account differ from the first four? How would you report this account in the company's financial statements for the period?

15. Small tools; effect of capitalization policy. Asobat, Inc., commenced business operations at the beginning of year 1. At that time its accountants decided, with the approval of management and the company's independent auditors, to expense immediately the costs of all small tools and other long-life items which cost less than $50 apiece. The company's purchases of these items during the first 11 years of operations, together with its reported net income, were as follows:

Year	Purchases	Net Income (Loss) before Taxes
1	$20,000	$(21,000)
2	2,000	400
3	0	5,400
4	6,000	6,600
5	4,000	6,600
6	10,400	1,800
7	11,200	4,200
8	5,600	16,600
9	4,400	21,800
10	7,680	20,920
11	11,280	21,720

Having noticed how large these purchases have been in comparison with net income, the controller asked an assistant to look into the matter. The assistant's inquiry has turned up the following additional information:

1. Purchases seem to have been amply justified by legitimate operating needs.
2. Twenty percent of the items purchased were discarded after four years' use, another 60 percent were discarded after five years' use, and the remaining 20 percent were disposed of at the end of six years.
3. The scrap value of the discarded items was negligible.
4. The company's new computer could be used to calculate annual depreciation charges on these items at a very low cost.

a. Calculate straight-line depreciation, year by year, on the items purchased in the first 11 years of Asobat's existence. Assume that all purchases were made at the beginning of the year and all retirements took
place at the end of the year, after the annual depreciation charge was
calculated. Depreciation on all items should be based on a five-year
life.

b. Restate income before taxes for each of these years as it would have been
reported if these expenditures had been capitalized and depreciated on
the basis described in (a).

c. What conclusions, if any, about the firm's capitalization policy do these
calculations seem to point to?

**16. Self-manufactured   equipment: determining   the   capitalizable
amount.** The Beckman Company late in 19x1 requested bids from several
equipment manufacturers on the construction of a unique piece of special-
purpose equipment to be used in the Beckman factory to replace an out-
moded piece of equipment then in use. Several bids were received, the lowest in the amount of $55,000. The management of the Beckman Company
felt that this was excessive. Instead, the machine was manufactured in the
company's own machine shop which was then operating at substantially less
than full capacity.

The machine was built during the early months of 19x2 and was placed in
service on July 1, 19x2. The machine was capitalized at $55,000, comprising
the following elements:

Raw materials used in construction of new machine	$ 8,000
Direct labor used in construction of new machine	20,000
Amount paid to Ace Machinery Service Company for installation of new machine	1,000
Cost of dismantling old machine	800
Cost of direct labor for trial runs	1,500
Cost of materials for trial runs	500
Costs of special tooling for use in operating the machine	6,000
Savings in construction costs	17,700
Less: Cash proceeds from sale of old machine	(500)
Total Cost of Machine	$55,000

The following additional information is available:

1. Factory costs other than labor and materials averaged 80 percent of direct labor cost. This percentage was used to assign these other costs to
products made in the factory for sale to outside customers.
2. Freight charges on the materials used in construction of the machine
amounted to $250. This amount was debited to the Freight-In account.
3. Cash discounts on the materials used in construction amounted to $50.
This amount was credited to Purchases Discounts.
4. The replaced equipment had an original cost of $25,000 and accumu-
lated depreciation of $21,000 at the time it was dismantled and sold.
5. The new machine had an anticipated useful life of 15 years; the special
tooling would be useful for three years.
6. Savings in construction costs were computed on the basis of the differ-

ence between the lowest outside bid and the net costs charged to the job during construction. These savings were credited to the account, Gain on Construction of Equipment.

7. Products produced during the trial runs were scrapped; scrap value was negligible.

a. At what amount should the new machine have been capitalized in the equipment account on July 1, 19x2? Show the details.

b. Explain how you would have accounted for each of the cost elements in the above list that you would not have capitalized as part of the cost of this piece of equipment.

17. Ancillary expenditures. The Realty Corporation owns a large number of buildings which it rents to commercial and residential tenants. In January 19x1, it bought a building for conversion into quarters suitable for use by a foreign legation. The building was in an advanced state of disrepair, but was structurally sound except for the top (fourth) floor. This floor had been vacated two years earlier on the order of a city building inspector.

The purchase price of this property was $80,000 for the building and $90,000 for the land. Extensive remodeling and interior decorating was begun immediately to adapt the building to its intended use. The following outlays were made during the period January through June, 19x1:

1.	Interior painting and decorating	$ 40,000
2.	Structural alterations including replacement of plumbing fixtures at a cost of $12,000 and landscaping at $8,000	62,000
3.	Replacement and renewal of electric wiring	10,000
4.	Removal of fourth story	50,000
5.	Payment of hospital and medical expenses of passerby injured by falling brick	2,000
6.	Architect's fees, building permits, and so forth	16,000
	Total	$180,000

In addition, property taxes accrued for the period January 1 through June 30 amounted to $3,000.

Late in June, the company was notified that it was being sued for $45,000 for the personal injuries and mental anguish suffered by the passerby who was hit by the falling brick (item 5 above). The suit was scheduled for trial in February 19x2. At the time the remodeling work was done, the Realty Corporation had elected to be its own insurer in matters pertaining to public liability, and, therefore, it was not insured either for the medical expenses or the amount of any payment that might result from the lawsuit. The premium that an insurance company would have charged for liability coverage during the period of remodeling was $1,250.

The building was ready for occupancy on July 1, 19x1, and a ten-year lease, running from July 1, 19x1, was signed with a foreign government.

Indicate how these facts should have been reflected in the company's accounts as of July 1, 19x1. How much should have been capitalized and under what account titles? How much should have been charged to expense for the first half of 19x1? Give your reasons for your treatment of each item.

13

Liabilities and Related Items

A COMPANY'S CAPITAL STRUCTURE has great significance to management and to outsiders alike. The amount and composition of the liabilities can have a great influence on the profitability of the shareholder's investment and on the risks of investment in the company. This chapter will examine the problems encountered in measuring various kinds of liabilities. Because liability measurement is inseparable from asset measurement in some cases and expense measurement in others, our examination will cover some of these related topics, too. The discussion falls under four major headings:

1. Long-term borrowing.
2. Interperiod income tax allocations.
3. Pension plans.
4. Leases in lessees' financial statements.

LONG-TERM BORROWING

Most large corporations obtain at least part of their funds through long-term borrowing. This kind of debt financing permits the shareholders to benefit from using low-cost funds to finance high-yield operations. It also allows the company to grow larger than it could if it had to rely on shareholder capital alone. These benefits are obtained at some sacrifice, however. Increasing long-term borrowing relative to the shareholders' equity also increases the risks the shareholders assume. This happens because the residual earnings that accrue to shareholders become more uncertain as the fixed payments required by the long-term debt increase.

In this section we'll examine the nature of long-term borrowing, the market prices and yields on debt securities, accounting measurements of long-term debt and interest expense, and the refunding or restructuring of long-term debt.

The Nature of Bonds

Corporations often borrow money for long periods from single lenders such as insurance companies. In other cases, they meet their needs by borrowing from many lenders at the same time, each one lending a relatively small percentage of the total. Under these circumstances, a single long-term loan contract is signed by the borrower and a representative of the lenders. The contract is known as an *indenture,* and the lenders' representative is the *trustee.*

Each of the lenders in one of these long-term contractual arrangements receives one or more documents known as bond certificates or *bonds*. These certificates specify the amounts to be paid to the owners of the bonds and the times at which the payments are to be made. The final payment to the bondholder, the amount to be paid on the maturity date (the date on which the contract expires if all its provisions have been met), is called the *maturity value* or *face value* of the bond. Interim interest payments are customarily made semiannually, but they are normally expressed as an annual percentage of the face value. This percentage is called the *coupon rate* or *face rate* of interest. Thus a $1,000, 8 percent, 20-year bond represents an agreement to pay $1,000 at the end of 20 years plus $40 (one half of 8 percent of $1,000) at the end of each half-year for 20 years. Exhibit 13–1 illustrates the lifetime pattern of cash payments to the holder of one of these bonds.

Bond Values

The value of bonds to investors depends on the *yield to maturity* they could earn on other bonds of comparable risk that are now available on the market. Yield to maturity is the rate of interest the investors can earn if they buy bonds at a given price, collect the specified interest payments on schedule, and collect the face value from the borrower on the maturity date.

For example, suppose other comparable bonds now yield 9 percent if held to maturity. If bonds are offered with a coupon rate of 8 percent, the investors have to figure out how much to pay for these bonds so that they will yield 9 percent, the yield the investors can get elsewhere. They do this by calculating the present values of the cash flows they will receive.

EXHIBIT 13–1.   Cash Payments Required for a 20-year, 8%, $1,000 Bond

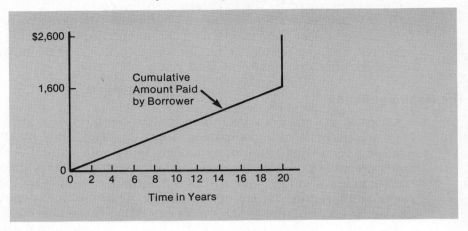

Calculating present value.   Investors who buy the 8 percent bonds when they are issued become entitled to two kinds of payments for each $1,000 bond they hold: (1) a stream of 40 semiannual payments of $40 each and (2) a payment of $1,000 at the end of 40 periods, 20 years from the issue date. The present values of these cash flows can be determined by multiplying them by discount factors taken from Tables 3 and 4 in Appendix A.

Because interest is paid twice a year, the usual technique is to use semiannual compounding. A quoted bond yield of 9 percent means that investors can earn 4.5 percent on their investment every six months.[1] This means using the discount factors in the 4.5 percent columns of the two tables for 40 six-month periods. The calculations are:

Period	Amount	Discount Factor	Present Value
1 to 40	$40 a period	18.4016	$736.06
40	$1,000	0.1719	171.90
Total			$907.96

The value of this 8 percent bond on the issue date is thus $907.96 to an investor whose comparable alternative is an investment yielding

---

[1] The effective *annual* yield is more than twice the six-months' rate because the bondholders can earn interest of 4.5 percent in the second half of the year on the 4.5 percent interest they earned in the first half. If investors can always reinvest the interest they receive at the same rate, the effective annual yield is $(1.04)^2 - 1 = 9.2$ percent. We'll conform to common practice, however, and quote annual yields at twice the six-month rate.

4.5 percent interest every six months. The $92.04 difference between this amount and the $1,000 maturity value serves to bring the yield on the bond up from 8 percent to 9 percent. This difference is referred to as a *discount*.

Use of bond-yield tables.   If investors had to go through the previous calculations every time they considered buying or selling a bond, much time would be wasted unnecessarily. To avoid this, special tables have been prepared for the financial community, based on the kind of calculations just illustrated. A partial set of such tables is included in Appendix A (Tables 5 through 9). The present value of a 20-year, 8 percent bond in a market in which the prevailing yield is 9 percent may be found in Table 8 (the table for a coupon rate of 8 percent) by locating the column for bonds with 20 years to maturity and the row for the 9 percent yield rate. The figure is 90.80, which means that the market price will be $908 for each $1,000 of face value. Except for a four-cent rounding error, this is the same figure we obtained using Tables 3 and 4.

Changes in bond prices as maturity approaches.   The market value of the bond won't remain at $908 forever, of course. The day it matures it will be worth $1,000, because that's how much the company will pay the lender at that time. The lowest line in Exhibit 13–2 shows how the market value of an 8 percent bond will change as it approaches the maturity date, other things being equal. For example, if the bond is still outstanding five years after it is issued (15 years before maturity), and the market yield rate is still 9 percent at that

EXHIBIT 13–2.   Market Value of an 8%, $1,000 Bond for 20 Years with Different Market Yield Rates

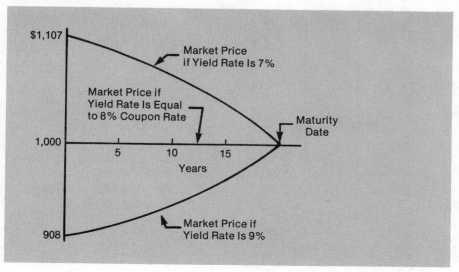

time, Table 8 indicates the bond will have a value of $918.60. The price will be $935 at the end of ten years and $960.40 after 15 years.

The horizontal line in the middle of the diagram shows the market price of a bond for which the market yield always equals the coupon rate. In such cases the present value of the future stream of payments is always $1,000, and buying a bond for $1,000 will always bring a yield equal to the coupon rate, in this case 8 percent ($80/$1,000 = 8 percent every year).

Finally, the top line in Exhibit 13–2 shows how market prices will move if the bond is issued at a *premium*—that is, at a price higher than its face value. A 20-year, 8 percent bond issued in a 7 percent market should sell for $1,106.80. (The 7 percent row of the 20 year column in Table 8 shows a figure of $110.68 for every $100 in face value.) This premium arises because the company is paying $80 a year, or $10 more than the market expects to receive on $1,000 invested in bonds at 7 percent. The $106.80 is the price the market pays for this extra $10 a year. As the bond approaches maturity, of course, the investor has fewer and fewer of these $10 extra payments to look forward to, and the market price will fall. At the maturity date, the market price will equal the face value.

Effects of changes in marketing yields.   Market prices change for other reasons, of course. The market's perception of the risk of owning a particular company's bonds may change, or market yields generally may change. For example, suppose market conditions changed

EXHIBIT 13–3.   Market Value of an 8%, $1,000 Bond with Yield of 9% for Five Years and 7% for the Remaining 15 Years

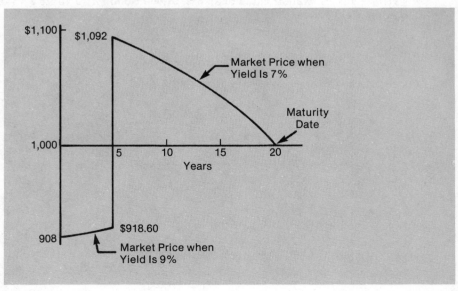

five years after our 8 percent bond was issued, so that newly issued bonds of comparable risk were being sold to yield only 7 percent. The $80 annual interest payments would then command a premium. From Table 8 we find that an 8 percent bond with 15 years to maturity in a 7 percent market would command a price of $1,092 rather than the $918.60 it brought just before the market changed.

The market price path on this bond is traced by the line in Exhibit 13–3. After rising gradually for five years, the market price jumped dramatically as market yields fell. Assuming market yields remain at 7 percent for the next 15 years, this bond's market price will decline gradually until it reaches face value at maturity. In practice, the path would be much more irregular, as market yields move up and down, but it would always be moving toward face value at maturity if the company seemed likely to be able to meet its repayment obligation at that time.

Measuring Bond Liability and Interest Expense

The major accounting problem in connection with bonds is to measure the issuing corporation's liability and annual interest expense. We'll examine three situations:

1. The bonds are sold at their face value.
2. The bonds are sold at a discount.
3. The bonds are sold at a premium.

Bonds sold at face value. Bond accounting is simple when bonds are sold at their face value. The initial liability is measured by the amount received from the lenders and remains at that level until the maturity date. A suitable entry to record the sale of $1 million in 9 percent bonds at their face value would be:

```
Cash.....................................  1,000,000
    Bonds Payable ......................              1,000,000
```

A suitable entry to record the payment at maturity would be:

```
Bonds Payable ..........................  1,000,000
    Cash................................              1,000,000
```

In this case, the payment of face value at maturity just cancels out the amount originally received from the lenders, and the only payments to the bondholders for the use of their money are the $90,000 interest payments made each year. In other words, interest expense is equal to the annual interest payment.

Bonds sold at a discount. The accounting problem isn't quite as simple when bonds are sold at a discount or at a premium. For example, suppose the Reading Company decided late in 1977 to issue $1 million of 9 percent, 20-year mortgage bonds. (Mortgage bonds are bonds "secured" by mortgages on specified company properties, usually land and buildings, meaning that if the company fails to pay the amounts it has promised to pay when they are due, the bondholders can have the property sold and collect the amounts due them from the proceeds of the sale.)

By the time the bonds were issued on January 1, 1978, the going market rate of interest had gone up to 9.5 percent. Therefore, the bonds had to be sold at a discount. The total amount received from the sale was $955,600. The purchasers needed the $44,400 discount from face value to compensate them for accepting annual interest payments of $90,000 (coupon rate times face value) instead of the $95,000 (market rate times face value) they could have obtained by investing their $955,600 somewhere else.

The general rule in accounting for liabilities and owners' equities is to record for each source of funds *the amount the investor has invested in the corporation.* Accordingly, the company's accountants first thought of recording the issue of the bonds on the Reading Company's books as follows:

Cash	955,600	
Bonds Payable		955,600

Although this entry would have been correct, the controller decided to conform to the more usual practice of recording the face value of the bonds and the discount or premium in two separate accounts, as follows:

Cash	955,600	
Discount on Bonds	44,400	
Bonds Payable		1,000,000

Some consider this treatment more informative because it discloses the final lump-sum payment the borrower is obliged to make (the face value). This provides investors with additional information regarding the magnitude and timing of major cash outflows. The same information could be disclosed in footnotes to the financial statements, of course, but the general practice is to put the face value in the balance sheet itself.

The form of the journal entry doesn't affect the amount of the liability, which should have appeared on the January 1, 1978 balance sheet as follows:

Bonds payable (face value) ..... :	$1,000,000
Less: Unamortized discount on bonds	44,400
Liability to bondholders	$ 955,600

If the Reading Company's bonds were to remain outstanding until the January 1, 1998, maturity date, the bondholders would receive the $1 million face value plus $1.8 million in coupon interest payments ($45,000 every six months for 20 years). The difference between this lifetime total of $2.8 million and the $955,600 proceeds of the issue ($1,844,400) represents the price paid by the corporation for the use of the bondholders' money, or *interest expense*. The $44,400 discount is just as much a component of interest expense as the semiannual payment—after all, the company's alternative was to sell the bonds at a higher coupon rate and higher semiannual payments.

The accounting problem is to decide how much of the $1,844,400 lifetime interest to charge to expense each period. The preferred method of doing this is known as the *effective-interest* method. This method amortizes bond discount (or premium) each period by the amount necessary to keep the ratio of each period's interest expense to the beginning-of-period liability constant throughout the life of the bond issue. This ratio is the yield to maturity or *effective interest rate*.[2]

The effective yield on the Reading Company's mortgage bonds was 9.5 percent. We can verify this by going to the 20-year column of Table 9 in Appendix A, where we find that a price of $95.56 for each $100 in face value is on the row corresponding to an annual yield of 9.5 percent. As we mentioned earlier, this means a return on investment of 4.75 percent every six months. It is reasonable, therefore, for the company to calculate interest expense for each six-month period by multiplying 4.75 percent by the amount of the liability at the beginning of the period. The first six months' interest expense, therefore, was $0.0475 \times \$955,600 = \$45,391$.

This interest expense decreased the stockholders' equity by $45,391 and increased the liability to the bondholders by the same amount, from $955,600 to $1,000,991. A portion of the liability (45,000) was current; the remainder (955,991) was a long-term liability. In other words, the long-term liability increased by $391 during the first six-month period. This portion of the interest will be paid when the bond becomes due at maturity:

Interest payable currently		Interest payable at end of 20 years		Interest expense
$45,000	+	$391	=	$45,391

---

[2] The Accounting Principles Board made this method mandatory in 1971. Other methods of amortization such as straight line are allowed only if the results obtained are not materially different from those obtained under the effective-interest method. APB, "Opinion No. 21, para. 14, in AICPA, *Professional Standards—Accounting, Current Text* (New York: Commerce Clearing House, Inc., 1978), sec. 4111.14.

The entry to record interest expense for the first six months and the cash payment at the end of that period was:

Interest Expense	45,391	
Cash		45,000
Discount on Bonds		391

The credit to Discount on Bonds recorded the increase in the long-term liability during the first six months.

The bonds were reported on the company's June 30, 1978 balance sheet as follows:

Bonds payable (face value)	$1,000,000
Less: Unamortized portion of original discount on bonds	44,009
Liability to bondholders	$ 955,991

The interest expense during the second six-month period was 4.75 percent of the liability at the beginning of that period, $955,991. Interest expense was thus $45,410, of which $45,000 was payable currently and $410 was payable at the bonds' maturity date. Interest expense was slightly greater during the second six months because the liability was greater during this period ($955,991 instead of $955,600), and it continued to increase as the liability increased. Eventually, the interest during the final six-month period in 1997 will be 4.75 percent of $997,613, or $47,387. The interest rate underlying the expense charge is the same throughout the life of the bonds.

Calculating interest expense and the accrual of the amount not paid currently (by a credit to Discount on Bonds) for the other 38 six-month periods produces the liability figures diagrammed in Exhibit 13–4. The nearer the company comes to the maturity date, the closer the liability comes to the face value of the bonds.

Bonds sold at a premium.   The effective-interest method is also appropriate when bonds are sold for more than their face value—that is, at a premium. For example, the Craft Company sold $1 million in 20-year, 9 percent debentures in 1977. (Debentures are "unsecured" bonds—that is, they are secured only by the company's ability to generate cash flows, not by special claims against specific pieces of property.) The market yields on other bonds comparable in risk and maturity were 8.5 percent at that time. Craft's bonds, therefore, sold at a premium price of $1,047,700 (see the 8.5 row of the 20-year column of Table 9 in Appendix A). The balance sheet should have shown the following liability at that time:

Bonds payable (face value)	$1,000,000
Add: Unamortized premium on bonds	47,700
Liability to bondholders	$1,047,700

EXHIBIT 13–4. Liability to Holders of $1,000,000 in 20-year, 9% Bonds Yielding 9.5% to Maturity

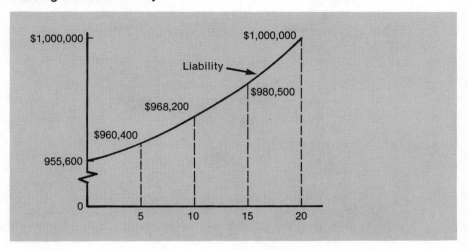

Using the effective-interest method, the company calculated interest expense for the first six months as follows:

$$\$1,047,700 \times 8.5\% \times \tfrac{1}{2} = \$44,527.$$

This was $473 less than the amount of cash paid to the bondholders at the end of the first six months. This $473 represented a payment of a portion of the $1,047,700 the company had borrowed six months earlier:

Cash Payment $45,000	=	Interest Expense $44,527	+	Payment of Liability $473

This company had used a separate account to record the initial premium on the issuance of the bonds. The entry to recognize the interest accrual and the payment of cash at the end of the first six months was:

Interest Expense	44,527	
Premium on Bonds......................	473	
Cash		45,000

The debit to Premium on Bonds decreased the liability by that amount, and a balance sheet prepared immediately after this payment showed the following liability:

Bonds payable (face value)	$1,000,000
Add: Unamortized portion of the initial premium on bonds sold	47,227
Liability to bondholders	$1,047,227

Notice what all this amounts to. In purchasing the bonds, the lenders paid $47,700 for the privilege of receiving $90,000 a year instead of the $85,000 they could have gotten from investing $1 million elsewhere at 8.5 percent. That $47,700 will be repaid to them gradually during the 20 years the bonds will be outstanding. As a result, the liability at maturity will be only $1 million the face value of the bonds.

CALCULATION OF INTEREST AND PRINCIPAL

1. Identify the principal at the beginning of the period.
2. Find the effective yield to maturity when the bonds were first issued.
3. Multiply this yield rate by the beginning-of-period principal— this is the interest expense for the period.
4A. If the interest expense is greater than the payment, add the excess to the beginning-of-period principal to determine the principal at the end of the period.
4B. If the payment is greater than the interest expense, subtract the excess from the beginning-of-period principal to determine the principal at the end of the period.

Retirement and Refunding of Long-Term Debt

When the corporation buys its bonds back from the bondholders, the bonds are said to be *retired*. Bonds are sometimes retired at maturity, but other arrangements are also common. For one thing, bond issues are often very large, and it may be more convenient to retire them gradually rather than all at once. Furthermore, a company may not need all of the borrowed funds continuously until the maturity date or may have an opportunity to obtain substitute financing on more favorable terms prior to that date. In principle, long-term debt will be retired whenever the company can maximize the net present value of future cash flows by doing so. Most bond issues, therefore, provide the issuing corporation with opportunities to retire some or all bonds at early dates.

Debt retirement is sometimes a one-way street—that is, the company pays cash and thereby reduces both its total assets and its total liabilities. In other cases the company merely replaces one bond issue with another. This is known as debt *refunding*. We need to look briefly at each of these situations.

Debt retirement by conversion. Debt retirement may come about in several ways. For example, some bonds are *convertible* into shares of common stock. This means the owners of the bonds have the right to exchange their bonds for a specified number of shares of common stock. Convertible bonds give the bondholders an opportunity to share in the benefits if the company is able to use their funds profitably. For this reason, convertible bonds are easier to sell than nonconvertible bonds carrying the same coupon rate. In some cases, the conversion price (the number of common shares obtainable for each bond) is so favorable that everyone expects all the bonds to be converted within a very few years. Such issues are really indirect means of selling common stock.

Debt retirement by serial redemption.   A second possibility is to provide for the gradual retirement of the bonds outstanding by making the issue subject to *serial redemption*—that is, by staggering the due dates of the component securities. Thus an issue of $100 million of serial bonds may provide for $10 million to mature each year for ten years, the first maturity coming 11 years after the date of original issue. Serial bonds are usually offered at a range of prices, set to provide higher yields for the longer maturities. The accountants treat each series as a separate issue, using the accounting method described earlier.

Debt retirement by sinking fund.   A third device for orderly debt retirement is the *sinking fund*. Each year the corporation sets aside a certain amount of cash for the sinking fund, and this is then used to purchase company bonds. The trustees of the sinking fund will either buy bonds on the market or will require the holders of certain bonds chosen at random to sell them to the sinking fund at specified prices. Bonds the trustees can force bondholders to sell to the company are said to be *callable* for sinking fund purposes.

Companies may also take advantage of changes in market conditions and ample cash balances to purchase the company's bonds on the open market and retire (cancel) them. For example, suppose market yields have gone up to 10 percent by 1983. Consistent with this, the market price of the Reading Company's 9 percent bonds on January 1, 1983, (five years after the issue date, 15 years before maturity) is $92.31. This price can be verified from the 15-year column, 10 percent row of Table 9 in Appendix A.

Suppose the company buys $100,000 of its bonds at this price, $92,310 in all. The book value of these bonds, reflecting the 9.5 percent yield to maturity five years earlier, can be found by looking at the 9.5 row in the 15-year column of Table 9. The figure is $96.04. In other words, the liability has increased from the original $95,560 to $96,040, and the unamortized discount on bonds has decreased from $4,440 to $3,960. The $3,730 difference between the liability ($96,040) and the amount paid ($92,310) would be reported on the income statement for 1983 as an extraordinary item.[3] A suitable entry to record the purchase and retirement would be:

Bonds Payable	100,000	
Discount on Bonds		3,960
Cash		92,310
Gain on Bond Retirement		3,730

Market prices, it should be emphasized, have no effect on the company's accounts unless the firm engages in some market transaction. The company continues to amortize bond discount (or bond premium) on the basis of the original yield rate, on the ground that this represents the cost of the financing.

Debt retirement by self-amortization.   Another method of reducing indebtedness in an orderly fashion is to take out a *self-amortizing loan*. In a self-amortizing loan, the borrower pays the lender(s) a specified amount each period for a specified number of periods. Each payment is identical to each of the others. A portion of the payment is for interest; the remainder is a repayment of a portion of the principal. The debt is completely liquidated by the final payment in the series.

For example, Roscoe Products Company borrowed $61,446 on a ten-year note bearing interest at 10 percent a year.[4] Under the terms of this note, Roscoe was to pay the lender $10,000 a year for ten years, the first payment to be made one year after the date of the borrowing. Interest expense was calculated by the effective-interest method.

Interest expense for the first year was $61,446 × 10 percent = $6,144.60. The difference between this amount and the $10,000 payment was a partial repayment of principal. The company made the following entry:

Notes Payable	3,855.40	
Interest Expense	6,144.60	
Cash		10,000.00

Many self-amortizing loans call for monthly or quarterly payments rather than annual amounts, but the basic principle is the same: the principal of the loan is repaid gradually during the life of the loan, not by a single lump-sum payment at the end of that time.

---

[3] FASB, Statement No. 4, in AICPA, *Professional Standards—Accounting*, sec. 2013.08. Gains and losses from purchases for sinking-fund purposes are reported as part of ordinary income or loss.

[4] If we know the amount of the loan ($61,446), the term of the loan (ten years), and the interest rate (10 percent), we can calculate the required annual payment by dividing the amount of the loan by the discount factor from Table 4 of Appendix A. In this case, the factor from the ten-year row of the 10 percent column is 6.1446, and the annual payment is $61,446/6.1446 = $10,000.

Bond refunding. For most large corporations, debt is a more or less permanent component of the capital structure. Far from wishing to reduce its indebtedness, the corporation seeks to maintain or increase it. When one bond issue matures, it is succeeded by another. Replacing one bond issue with another is known as *refunding*.

Refunding is easier when the bonds are callable. Some bonds are callable for sinking-fund purposes only, but others can be called for other purposes as well. Callability allows the corporation to refund prior to maturity if conditions seem right. The borrowing corporation can take advantage of declines in money rates by calling the old higher-yield bonds, replacing them with bonds at the new lower rates.

To protect the bondholder, the bond contract usually specifies that an amount greater than the face value of the bond will be paid in the event of premature retirement. This *call price* normally varies with the age of the debt, approaching the face value at maturity or at some earlier date.

To illustrate, suppose borrowing conditions improve considerably in 1987. Late in the year, an insurance company offers the Reading Company a $1,070,000 loan at 7 percent interest for ten years. The proceeds would be used to pay off the 9 percent bond issue at its call price of $107 for each $100 of face value. This refunding would have two effects: (1) a reduction in the interest payments each year, from $90,000 to 7 percent of $1,070,000 = $74,900, a saving of $15,100 a year for ten years, and (2) a $70,000 increase in the face value to be paid off at the end of 10 years.

Refunding in this case would be profitable unless even greater savings could be obtained by waiting for the interest rate to fall still farther a year or so later. It would be profitable because the present value of $15,100 a year for ten years (the benefit) is greater than the present value of $70,000 at the end of that time (the cost of obtaining the benefit).

The refunding would present a substantially less favorable picture on the company's financial statements for 1987, however. The book value of the old bond issue on December 31, 1987, would be $968,200 (9.5 row of the ten-year column in Table 9). This is $101,800 less than the $1,070,000 call price. This $101,800 would be reported as an extraordinary loss on the income statement for 1987. The requirements of financial reporting, in other words, are clearly inconsistent with the interests of the corporation and its shareholders, who benefit from the refunding.

Restructuring of Debt

A creditor sometimes grants a borrower a concession when the latter has financial difficulties. The concession agreement may call for the borrower's transfer of receivables or other assets or the granting of an equity interest to the creditor. Alternatively, the terms of the debt may be modified to ease the burden of payment.

For example, the maturity date may be extended or the scheduled amounts payable may be decreased or deferred. Creditors will grant these concessions if they conclude that the present value of their net cash inflows after granting the concessions will be higher than the present value if the concessions aren't granted.

The accounting issue is whether and in what amount gains or losses should be recognized in the income of the period in which debt restructuring occurs. Restructurings don't provide income investors can realize on a regular basis, but they do represent increases in the company's net assets, and investors presumably should be informed of this. The Financial Accounting Standards Board has taken a middle position on this question. When debts are liquidated by the transfer of the company's assets to the lender, the company must recognize as a gain or loss any difference between the amount of the liability and the fair value of the assets transferred. This amount is classified in the income statement as an extraordinary item. If the creditor merely reduces the amounts or delays the due dates of the amounts due, however, no gains or losses are recognized.[5]

INTERPERIOD INCOME TAX ALLOCATIONS

Taxable income, as we have indicated before, may differ substantially from the figures shown in financial statements that are prepared for outside investors. Some of these differences are *permanent*—that is, they lead to tax reductions the company will never have to pay back under any circumstances, or to added taxes the company will never be able to recover. Others arise because of *timing differences*—that is, revenues or expenses appear on the tax return and on the income statement, but in different periods. In this section we'll see how these differences affect the company's financial statements.

Product-Warranty Expense

Some timing differences arise because expenses are reported to shareholders before they are allowable as tax deductions. Product-warranty expenses fall in this category. Expenses and liabilities for product-warranty service are accrued when the related revenues are recognized; warranty expense for income tax purposes is based on

---

[5] FASB, Statement No. 15, "Accounting by Debtors and Creditors for Troubled Debt Restructurings," in AICPA, *Professional Standards—Accounting*, sec. 5363.016. This statement also provides for other treatments under extraordinary circumstances.

expenditures actually made under the terms of the warranty, and these come after the revenues are recognized.

The accepted treatment in such cases is to calculate income tax expense on the basis of the financial-reporting figures. For example, Evans Products Company started selling a line of products in 19x1 with a one-year repair warranty. Sales of these products in 19x1 totaled $1 million, and income before warranty expense and income taxes was $195,000. The income tax rate in 19x1 was 40 percent.

The estimated warranty costs arising from the year's sales amounted to $50,000. This amount was reflected in the following entry:

Warranty Expense...................... 50,000
    Liability for Product Warranty........   50,000

Only $20,000 of warranty-related expenditures were actually made in 19x1, however, leaving a $30,000 liability at the end of the year:

Liability under Product Warranty

Expenditures	20,000	Accruals	50,000
		Bal. 30,000	

For financial reporting, the appropriate warranty expense is $50,000. Only $20,000 was deductible from revenues in calculating taxable income, however. Taxable income, in other words, was $195,000 − $20,000 = $175,000. At the 40 percent tax rate, the current tax liability was $175,000 × 0.4 = $70,000. If this amount had been reported as the income tax expense for the year, the income statement would have shown the following:

Income before warranty expense and income tax	$195,000
Warranty expense	50,000
Income before Taxes	$145,000
Income tax expense	70,000
Net Income	$ 75,000

The apparent income tax rate in this statement is $70,000 ÷ $145,000 = 48 percent, a figure we know is too high. If the $50,000 warranty expense had been allowed as a current tax deduction, taxable income would have been only $175,000 − $30,000 = $145,000, and the tax for the year would have been $58,000.

The accountants recognized the $12,000 difference between the two tax figures as a long-term *prepayment*, using a Deferred Income Taxes account as a prepaid taxes account. The entry to record income taxes for the year was:

Income Tax Expense 58,000
Deferred Income Taxes 12,000
    Income Taxes Payable................   70,000

In other words, the company *deferred* reporting $12,000 of its current income tax payments as income tax expense until some later period.

The situation was reversed in 19x2. The amount accrued for warranty expense in that year was $65,000, but the amounts expended totaled $75,000. This meant that taxable income was $10,000 *less* than pretax reported income. At a 40 percent tax rate, $4,000 was transferred from the Deferred Income Taxes account. The tax return for 19x2 showed a tax of $80,000, and the entry was:

Income Tax Expense	84,000	
Deferred Income Taxes		4,000
Income Taxes Payable		80,000

Income tax expense for the year was $4,000 greater than the tax return showed because warranty expense was $10,000 less than the amount allowed for tax purposes.

These two entries illustrate the process known as *interperiod income tax allocation,* the assignment of income tax expense to the periods in which the related revenues are reported rather than to the periods in which current income tax liabilities are accrued. When this is done, the income tax expense is said to be *normalized.*

The case for the allocation of income taxes to the periods in which the related pretax income is reported is that it is these revenues and expenses which create the tax liability. Congress may decide that these taxes are to be paid earlier or later, but how much is to be paid depends on the profitability of the company's operations. Normalizing the tax is intended to provide a net income figure that is representative of this underlying profitability. If warranty expense is shown at $50,000 but taxes are calculated on the basis of $20,000, the net income figure will be a poor approximation to the company's continuing earning power.

Depreciation

Interperiod income tax allocations arising from warranty expenses and similar items are a relatively small part of the total for most companies. In the typical case, costs appear as income tax deductions *before* they appear as expenses on the income statement.

Depreciation is one of these. Many companies use straight-line depreciation for financial reporting but accelerated depreciation for tax purposes, for the reasons we outlined in Chapter 10. This means that the depreciation figures on the income tax returns of the early years will be greater than on the income statement, and the income tax payments will be smaller than if straight-line depreciation were used for tax purposes. Unless the income tax expense figures are adjusted, net income will reflect both the lower depreciation figure and the lower income tax.

For example, the Brubeck Corporation started business on January 1, 19x1. It bought equipment costing $300,000 and placed it in a rented building. Depreciation for tax purposes was based on the double-rate, declining-balance method and a ten-year life; depreciation for financial reporting was on a straight-line basis with a ten-year estimated life and zero estimated salvage value. Income before depreciation and income taxes was $100,000 in 19x1, and the tax rate was 40 percent.

Tax depreciation for 19x1 was 2×10 percent $\times \$300,000 = \$60,000$, and the tax calculation was as follows:

Income before depreciation and taxes	$100,000
Tax depreciation	60,000
Taxable Income	$ 40,000
Tax at 40 percent	16,000

Using interperiod income tax allocation, however, the income statement showed the following:

Income before depreciation and taxes	$100,000
Depreciation expense	30,000
Income before Taxes	$ 70,000
Income tax at 40 percent	28,000
Net Income	$ 42,000

In other words, income tax allocation led the company to report $12,000 more income tax expense in 19x1 than it was currently obligated to pay.

The explanation of this treatment is that the due date for payment of $12,000 of the current income tax expense was postponed, not cancelled. By postponing the collection of taxes, the government increased the amount of the company's cash flow it could retain and use during the first half of the assets' lives. The government hoped this would encourage businesses to buy more equipment and stimulate the economy. Payment of these taxes was only *deferred*, however; it wasn't avoided. As the assets aged, annual tax depreciation would drop below the straight-line figure and the company would have to start paying these deferred amounts.

The basis for this process of tax deferral and eventual payment is illustrated in Exhibit 13–5. This compares the tax-depreciation schedule on Brubeck Corporation's $300,000 equipment purchase with straight-line depreciation. At first, tax depreciation exceeded straight-line depreciation, reducing the company's taxable income for the first five years. In the sixth year, however, tax depreciation dropped to $19,661, and the company exercised its option to switch to a straight-line amortization of the remaining undepreciated cost at

EXHIBIT 13–5.   Depreciation Expense versus Tax Depreciation for Assets Costing $300,000 with a Ten-Year Life

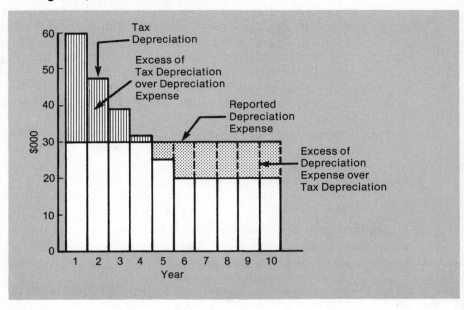

that time. From the sixth year to the tenth, therefore, tax depreciation was $10,339 less than the $30,000 depreciation shown each year on the income statement. This means that the company was paying 0.4 × $10,339 = $4,136 more income taxes each year than it would have paid if it hadn't accelerated its depreciation schedule for tax purposes in the first five years.

EXHIBIT 13–6.   Effect of Income Tax Deferral on Reported Income

	(1) Straight-Line Depreciation Used for Tax and Reporting	(2) Declining-Balance Depreciation Used for Tax; Straight-Line Used for Reporting — Reported Tax Is the Amount Currently Due	(3) Declining-Balance Depreciation Used for Tax; Straight-Line Used for Reporting — Reported Tax Includes Deferred Tax
Income before depreciation	$100,000	$100,000	$100,000
Depreciation expense	30,000	30,000	30,000
Income before tax	$ 70,000	$ 70,000	$ 70,000
Income tax	28,000	16,000	28,000
Net Income	$ 42,000	$ 54,000	$ 42,000

Exhibit 13–6 shows how the tax deferral affected Brubeck's reported income in 19x1. The figures in column 1 would have been reported if the government hadn't allowed accelerated depreciation for tax purposes and if the company believed that straight-line depreciation was the best measure of the decline in the assets' service potential. The figures in column 2 would have been reported if the tax hadn't been normalized, and column 3 is the income statement the company actually presented.

The net income figures in columns 1 and 3 are identical, but the net cash flows are higher under the alternative shown in column 3 than under the alternative in column 1. The company saved $12,000 in current tax payments, even though the net income was the same.

The entry to record the income tax expense for the year under these assumptions might be as follows:

Income Tax Expense	28,000	
Current Taxes Payable		16,000
Liability for Deferred Income Tax		12,000

If, in some future year, the normalized tax expense is, say, $40,000, and the amount currently due is, say, $40,500, the entry for that year will be:

Income Tax Expense	40,000	
Liability for Deferred Income Tax	500	
Current Taxes Payable		40,500

Under this treatment, the deferred portion of the tax is classified as a liability. Many accountants and financial analysts aren't convinced it is really a liability, however. Their argument is that these taxes may never have to be paid, and, if paid, the amounts may be different from the amounts accrued. The liability will never decrease as long as the cumulative difference in tax timing doesn't decrease. And the deferred amounts won't be paid in their entirety unless the corporation is liquidated. Liquidation is highly unlikely, and if it does take place, the deferred taxes may be erased by tax-deductible losses arising in the liquidation process.

The official position of the accounting profession goes in two directions at the same time. The Accounting Principles Board concluded that the amount of the deferral isn't an economic obligation, but it ruled that the deferral must be classified as a liability, anyway, because it is neither an offset against an asset nor part of the owners' equity.[6]

---

[6] APB, Statement No. 4, Chap. 5, para. 19, in AICPA, *Professional Standards — Accounting*, sec. 1025.19.

The Investment Credit

The tax laws of many countries provide for complete forgiveness of a portion of income taxes if the taxpayer satisfies specific requirements. A typical provision of this sort is the so-called *investment credit*, which has been available to taxpayers in the United States at various times since it was first introduced in 1962. The present version allows taxpayers to subtract from their current income taxes (not from taxable income but from the amount of taxes actually due) an amount equal to 10 percent of current outlays for certain depreciable assets, subject to certain maximum limitations.

For example, the Trilby Company's equipment purchases for the year amounted to $1 million. Before reflecting the investment credit, its income statement was as follows:

Sales		$6,180,000
Less: Cost of sales	$4,206,500	
Other expenses	1,386,000	5,592,500
Income before Taxes		$ 587,500
Income taxes		235,000
Net Income		$ 352,500

In this case, the tax credit was 10 percent of $1 million or $100,000, and the net current tax liability was thus reduced to $135,000. As long as the company retained the assets for a stipulated period, it had no liability for any future repayment of this tax reduction. In other words, this is one of the *permanent differences* we referred to at the beginning of this section.

The accounting question is whether the entire tax credit should flow through into the current income statement or be spread over the estimated life of the depreciable assets acquired. In the *flow-through* method, income tax expense is reduced by the full amount of the investment credit and no deferred tax liability is recognized. In the example above, the company's net income would be increased from $352,500 to $452,500, an increase of almost 30 percent.

Under the so-called *deferral* method, in contrast, the amount would be spread over the useful life of the property. Assuming a ten-year life and straight-line depreciation in the financial statements, only $10,000 of the tax credit would flow into the Trilby Company's income statement for the year; the remaining $90,000 would be listed on the balance sheet and amortized during the next nine years.

The case for the flow-through method is that the investment credit is simply a tax reduction that leaves income before taxes unchanged, and, therefore, income after taxes in the current period should be reduced by the full amount of the tax credit. Advocates of the deferral method, on the other hand, argue that the tax credit is conditional on the purchase of equipment, and that, therefore, it represents a reduction in the cost of the equipment. It is also argued that deferral is required to avoid an abnormal increase in after-tax income. The Accounting Principles Board ruled in favor of deferring the tax credit, but its position was undermined when the Securities and Exchange Commission agreed to accept either method.

The main difficulty with the deferral method is in classifying the deferred tax credit on the balance sheet. Since the deferral method is predicated on the assumption that the credit represents a reduction in the assets' cost, it should be classified as contra to the asset figures. Similarly, in calculating depreciation each year, a portion of the investment credit should be offset against the depreciation charges that are based on the purchase price of the equipment.

Most companies report the investment credit either as a liability or as a "deferred credit," listed in the limbo between the liabilities and the owners' equity. This is a way of dodging the issue. It cannot be owners' equity, because this would imply that it reflects a benefit already earned, an assumption that is totally inconsistent with the logic of the deferral method. It can be regarded as a liability, but only if it is assumed to compensate the company for incurring higher operating costs in the future than it would have incurred if it had not purchased the equipment in the first place. The difficulty of verifying this assumption lends further support to our case for listing the deferred investment credit as a reduction of asset cost.

LIABILITIES UNDER PENSION PLANS

Some of the more complex questions in the recognition and measurement of liabilities have arisen in connection with employee pension plans. Legislation in the 1970s solved some of the accounting issues, but others linger on. In this section we'll study three topics:

1. Common attributes of pension plans.
2. Accounting for current-service benefits.
3. Accounting for past-service benefits.

Attributes of Pension Plans

The number of variations in pension plans is virtually limitless, but the most important variations come in a few key elements. First, the plan may be *fully vesting, partially vesting,* or *nonvesting*. Under a fully vesting plan, the employees' rights to retirement benefits accrue periodically and cannot be revoked or withdrawn by the employer. If the employees' rights are not vested, they lose all their retirement benefits if they leave the company prior to retirement. Between these two extremes are a host of intermediate arrangements.

Second, the plan may be *funded* or *nonfunded*. In a fully funded plan, enough cash has been set aside to meet the expected future costs of all retirement benefits earned to date, assuming that these segregated funds are invested at the rates of interest assumed or specified in the plan. In a nonfunded plan, the employees rely on the employer's future solvency; no cash is set aside until actual payments have to be made.

Some plans are *defined-contribution* plans, meaning that the company fulfills its obligations by making specified payments to the pension fund; the employees' pensions then depend on the amounts contributed on their behalf and the effectiveness of the investments of these funds by the fund administrators.

Other plans are *defined-benefit plans,* in which the employees' pensions are determined by a formula, usually based on the employees' length of service and average salary during some part of this period. In such cases the company's obligation is to set aside enough funds at some time to pay the amounts required.

Plans in either of these categories may be *contributory,* meaning that employees pay part of the cost of the plan; others have the employer bear all the costs.

Most pension plans in the United States today must meet the requirements of the Employee Retirement Income Security Act of 1974, more popularly known as ERISA. From an accounting point of view, this very complex piece of legislation is important because it requires rapid vesting of pension rights, immediate full funding of the pension benefits under plans covered by the act and arising from services performed after the act went into effect, and gradual funding of benefits arising from service before that time.

Current-Service Benefits

In defined-benefit plans, pension expense in any year arising out of the services provided by employees in that year are referred to as the costs of *current-service benefits*. They are measured by the present value of the portion of future pension payments attributable to services performed in the current year, discounted at the average rate of interest the assets in the fund will achieve.

The accounting problems of defined-benefit plans are formidable because the company's payments under these plans aren't fixed in advance. Management has to estimate variables such as the employees' average length of service to retirement, average length of life after retirement, average salary during the period on which benefits are based, and the rate of return achieved by any amounts that have been deposited in funds earmarked for the plans. These estimates have to be made by specialists and reviewed frequently. Because of their complexity, we'll go no farther with them here.

Defined-contribution plans are a good deal simpler, but they do offer some problems unless the plan merely requires the employer to make specific payments each year to an insurance company or pension-fund trustee. To illustrate a slightly more complicated plan, let's assume the Genesee Corporation adopted a pension plan for the first time on January 1, 19x1. Under this plan, the company entered into a contract with each of its employees. This contract required the company, when the employee retired at age 65, to deposit with an insurance company an amount equal to 5 percent of the employee's wages from the date of employment to the date of retirement, compounded annually at 4 percent interest. This money was to be used by the insurance company to provide the employee with a pension.

The contracts for employees hired on or after January 1, 19x1, are accounted for easily. At the time it hires new employees, Genesee has no pension liability to them. At the end of their first year of employment, the company's liability amounts to 5 percent of the employees' wages for the year. (Because interest is compounded annually under this agreement, the year-end liability includes no accrued interest at the end of the first year.) At the end of 1, 2, 3, . . . , n years, the company has a liability arising from the employment contract equal to 5 percent of the employees' wages for the 1, 2, 3, . . . n years plus interest on these amounts compounded at 4 percent.

Although this plan is not funded, each year Genessee should credit a pension liability account by an amount equal to 5 percent of the wage payroll for the year, plus 4 percent interest on amounts accrued previously. For example, if the wage payroll for 19x9 is $300,000, and amounts previously accrued for current-service benefits under the pension plan are $500,000, Genesee's 19x1 pension expense arising from these contracts would be the following:

Wage payroll for the year × 5%: $300,000 × 5%	$15,000
Amounts previously accrued × 4%: $500,000 × 4%	20,000
Total Pension Expense for the Year	$35,000

The entry is:

Pension Expense	35,000	
Liability for Pensions		35,000

When payment is made to the insurance company at the time of the employee's retirement, the insurance company takes over the obligation and the entry is:

Liability for Pensions	xxx	
Cash		xxx

Past-Service Benefits

Current pension accruals of the kind we have just described will be adequate to cover the portion of the retirement benefits arising from employees' services from January 1, 19x1, onward. Genesee's plan also provided benefits for services performed before that date. These are known as *past-service benefits*.

The company's contracts with employees who were already on the payroll on January 1, 19x1, provided that the amount to be paid to the insurance company at retirement would equal 5 percent of wages, compounded annually at 4 percent, from the *date of employment*, not from the date of the contracts. Thus on January 1, 19x1, Genesee had a substantial liability for past-service benefits that had never been reflected in the company's financial statements. This liability was measured by the amounts the company would have accrued in previous years if the plan had been in force then. For an employee who had worked for three years at $12,000 a year, the past service liability was:

First year	$0.05 \times \$12,000 \times (1.04)^2 =$	$ 648.96
Second year	$0.05 \times \$12,000 \times 1.04 \quad =$	624.00
Third year	$0.05 \times \$12,000 \qquad\qquad =$	600.00
Total		$1,872.96

In other words, the liability is the future value on January 1, 19x1, of 5 percent of all active employees' earnings in previous years.

The main accounting issue with respect to pension plans is whether the liability for past-service benefits should be recognized immediately or gradually over time. On the one hand, the liability comes into existence at the time the pension plan is adopted. On the other hand, the company assumed this obligation in the expectation that future production costs would be reduced through lower employee turnover, greater company loyalty, and so forth.

Although the old Accounting Principles Board ruled against immediate accrual of the entire past service liability by charges to expense, the basic issue is still unresolved.[7] Most large companies are accruing their past service liabilities gradually, over periods of 30 years or so. The unaccrued amount is reported in a footnote.

LEASES IN LESSEES' FINANCIAL STATEMENTS

In the past, accountants regarded leases as *unfulfilled agreements* to buy the *use* of property. The signing of a lease wasn't re-

---

[7] APB, Opinion No. 8, "Accounting for the Cost of Pension Plans," in AICPA, *Professional Standards—Accounting*, sec. 4063.17.

garded as a transaction; the only recognized transactions were the use of the property, the payment of rent, or the prepayment of rent. Leases are now very common means of acquiring the use of land, buildings, and equipment, however, and these leases often run for many years. As a result, accountants have had to develop a new approach to lease accounting. In this final section, we'll examine some common characteristics of long-term leases and describe situations in which lessees are required to recognize leases in their balance sheets.

Lease Characteristics

Many leases serve the same purposes as purchases of property financed by long-term borrowing and have many similar characteristics. For example, to serve its southeastern market, the Trevett Company has decided to build a new manufacturing plant in a small town about 50 miles from Atlanta, Georgia. The cost of the land and buildings is $1 million, and it is estimated that the facility will be used for 30 to 40 years. The company doesn't have the liquid assets needed to finance the investment. Its financial position is strong, but a firm of investment bankers has advised Trevett against trying to float a bond issue until additional ownership capital has been obtained. Trevett's present owners are unwilling to increase their commitment in the firm and are equally unwilling to endanger their operating control by broadening the ownership base to include new outside owners.

With the conventional avenues to new financing closed off, Trevett has decided to enter into a *sale-leaseback* agreement with the Globe-Wide Insurance Company. This agreement provides that Trevett will have the plant built to its own specifications, after which the insurance company will buy the land and building at Trevett's cost ($1 million) and lease it back to Trevett on a 30-year lease. Trevett will pay Globe-Wide $94,778 at the beginning of each year for 30 years and will also pay property taxes, insurance, maintenance, and all other operating costs. All Globe-Wide will do each year is collect the rent. At the end of the initial 30-year lease term, Trevett can either vacate the property or buy it by meeting the best offer received by Globe-Wide at that time.

A sale-leaseback of this type differs from a purchase financed by borrowing in that the lease entitles Trevett to the use of the property for a specified period of time, but it doesn't convey any title to the rights to any residual values at the end of the lease period. If conventional debt financing had been available at an effective interest rate of 8 percent, and if the estimated market value of the property at the end of 30 years is $300,000, the two alternatives might be described as follows:

1. Purchase (financed by borrowing): Pay $80,000 a year (8 percent of $1 million) for 30 years, the interest portion of the loan; and $1 million at the end of the 30 years, the principal of the loan.
2. Sale-leaseback: Pay $94,778 a year for 30 years, starting immediately at the beginning of the first year (the leasing charge per year); and $300,000 at the end of the 30 years, the sale price of the property at that time, if the continued use of the property is desired.

In other words, the choice of lease financing requires Trevett to pay $14,778 more each year than if it had borrowed the money in a more conventional manner. If it leases, however, it will have to pay out $700,000 less ($1 million minus $300,000) 30 years from now.

The effective cost of each of these methods of financing can be calculated from an analysis of the anticipated cash flows. In this case, the cost of conventional borrowing is 8 percent before taxes and 4 percent after taxes at a 50 percent tax rate. The cost of lease financing is 10 percent before taxes and more than 5.25 percent after taxes.[8]

The popularity of leasing stems from its adaptability to a wide variety of specific circumstances and its availability when conventional borrowing is either not feasible or impossible. In addition, leasing is often a considerably cheaper source of funds than additional ownership investment, when used within limits. Leasing, therefore, affords the stockholder the same kind of leverage that was described earlier in the case of long-term bonds.

Lease Capitalization

The concern here is not with the desirability of lease financing, difficult though it is to keep away from that topic. The main interest is in the representation of the lease on the company's published financial statements. If the plant were financed by conventional borrowing, the Trevett balance sheet would report an increase in fixed assets and in long-term debt. Investors considering the purchase of the company's stock would note the greater risk caused by the increased leverage. Furthermore, they would also include the $1 million cost of the plant in its asset base in calculating return on investment.

The lease imposes no less a debt burden than long-term borrowing. If anything, the burden is heavier because the fixed annual payments include the amortization of the principal as well as the inter-

---

[8] At these rates, the present value of the future cash flows under leasing is $1 million. The method of deriving these rates will be discussed in Chapter 22.

est on the loan. Given this, a strong argument can be made for showing the lessee's rights to use the property and the corresponding liability for future rental payments in the asset and liability sections of the company's balance sheets.

Balance-sheet recognition of this sort is known as *lease capitalization*. Leases can be capitalized in much the same manner as any other liability, at the present value of the future obligatory payments under the lease, discounted at an appropriate rate. If the lease payments were capitalized at an interest rate of 10 percent, compounded annually, their present value would be $982,810, and an appropriate entry would be:

Leased Property	982,810	
Lease Liability		982,810

Once leases have been capitalized, both the asset and the liability must be amortized. For example, suppose Trevett decided to amortize the asset's cost by the straight-line method. The annual depreciation would be $982,810/30 = $32,760. Interest expense, calculated by the effective-interest method, would be $88,803, calculated as follows:

Initial liability	$982,810
First rental payment (paid immediately)	94,778
Principal, first year	$888,032
Interest (10 percent of $888,032)	$ 88,803

Total expense, therefore, would be $32,760 + $88,803 = $121,563, considerably greater than the annual rental. In the later years of the lease, annual expense would be smaller than if the lease were regarded as a simple rental agreement.

Lessees must capitalize leases if they meet *any one* of the following four criteria:

1. The lease transfers ownership of the property to the lessee by the end of the lease term.
2. The lease contains a bargain (less than fair value) purchase option for the lessee.
3. The lease term is equal to 75 percent or more of the estimated economic life of the leased property.
4. The present value at the beginning of the lease term of the minimum lease payments equals 90 percent or more of the net fair value of the leased property at that time.[9]

---

[9] For a more complete statement of these criteria and related matters, see FASB, Statement No. 13, "Accounting for Leases," in AICPA, *Professional Standards—Accounting*, sec. 4053.

SUMMARY

In this chapter, consideration has turned from the *forms* capital takes once it has been injected into the enterprise to an examination of some of the problems encountered in accounting for the funds invested by the company's creditors. In the first part of the chapter we outlined a consistent procedure whereby any long-term liability can be capitalized and illustrated the application of this method to the liability associated with long-term bonds.

We followed this with a discussion of interperiod tax allocation, a practice that is made necessary by differences between the tax and accounting bases for reporting revenues and expenses, gains and losses. Although these allocations occasionally lead to the recognition of assets, in most cases taxes are deferred and a liability is shown on the balance sheet.

The remainder of the chapter was given over to a discussion of the liabilities arising out of company pension plans and leasing arrangements.

KEY TERMS

Bond discount	Income tax allocation
Bond premium	Investment credit
Callable bonds	Lease capitalization
Convertible bonds	Normalization of tax expense
Coupon rate	Past-service benefits
Current-service benefits	Principal
Debt retirement	Refunding
Deferred taxes	Self-amortizing loan
Effective-interest method	Sinking fund
Face value	Yield to maturity

INDEPENDENT STUDY PROBLEMS (Solutions in Appendix B)

1. *Accounting for long-term bonds.* The Mountain Electric Company sells a million-dollar issue of 8 percent bonds on a 9 percent basis.

a. What does this mean?
b. The price is $1,092,000 or $908,000. Which, and why?
c. What is the term of this issue?
d. Calculate interest expense for the first six months. What entry should be made to record the accrual of interest and the payment of the first semiannual coupon?
e. What entry should be made at the second coupon payment?
f. How should this bond issue be shown on the balance sheet one year after it is issued and all interest for the year has been paid?

2. **Income tax allocation.** The Winston Corporation's income before depreciation and taxes in 19x3 was $6 million. Its depreciation for tax purposes was $1.25 million, and the depreciation for financial statement purposes was $850,000.

a. Derive the corporation's income after taxes, assuming a 50 percent tax rate.

b. Present journal entries to account for the year's depreciation and accrual of the income tax liability for the year.

3. **Lease accounting.** Company X has leased a truck from Truck Lessors, Inc., for $2,000 a year, payable at the beginning of each year for five years. Company X is responsible for all taxes, insurance, and maintenance on this truck, and the lease is to be accounted for as a means of borrowing money at 12 percent.

a. Show how this lease would be reflected on a balance sheet prepared immediately after it was signed and the first payment was made.

b. Compute the amount of expense that would be reported on the income statement for the first year of the lease, assuming that depreciation was straight-line with zero salvage value.

c. Compute the book value of the asset and of the liability at the beginning of the second year, immediately after the second lease payment.

EXERCISES AND PROBLEMS

4. **Calculating bond value.** What is the maximum price you would pay for a $1,000, 7 percent bond maturing eight years hence if you required a return of at least 4 percent every six months, compounded semiannually? (Don't use the bond-yield tables except to check your answer.)

5. **Self-amortizing loan.** The Bell Company borrows $100,000 with the understanding that it will pay the interest and principal on the loan in five equal annual payments, the first payment to be a year from the date the money is borrowed.

a. If the interest rate is 8 percent, what will be the amount of each annual payment?

b. Present a schedule showing the interest and the principal components of each of the five payments, assuming an 8 percent interest rate.

c. Prepare journal entries to record the loan and the payment at the end of the first year.

6. **Calculating principal and interest.** Howell Company borrows $2 million. It will repay the loan, with interest, by making ten annual payments of $311,638 each at year-end.

a. What is the interest rate on the loan? (Assume annual compounding.)

b. What is interest expense for the first year? Prepare a journal entry to record the accrual of the first year's interest and the payment to the lender.

c. What is Howell's liability at the end of the first year, after making the first payment?

d. What is interest expense for the second year?

7. Self-amortizing loan; calculating principal amount. Ted Jones purchased a house on January 1, 1940. The cost of the house was $20,000. He paid $2,000 on that date and agreed to pay $1,000 on January 1 of each year, starting in 1941, until the loan was repaid. What was the remaining indebtedness before the payment on January 1, 1980, if the interest rate was 5 percent?

(Prepared by Carl L. Nelson)

8. Self-amortizing loan; calculating number of payments. A company borrowed $20,000 from a bank at an interest rate of 12 percent, compounded annually. It promised to pay the bank $4,000 at the end of each year until the loan was paid off. The final payment would be the amount of the last repayment of principal plus the final year's interest on this amount. This final payment, therefore, would be less than $4,000.

a. How many years will it take to pay off the loan?

b. What will be the amount of the final payment?

(Prepared by Carl L. Nelson)

9. Bond accounting. A corporation issues $10 million in 5 percent, two-year bonds on January 1, 19x5. These bonds are sold to yield 4 percent per half-year. The $250,000 payments are made on each January 1 and July 1; the face value will be paid on January 1, 19x7.

a. How much cash will the company receive?

b. How will the sale affect the borrower's assets, liabilities, and owners' equity?

c. How will the bonds appear on the balance sheet at the time they are sold?

d. How will the bonds appear on the December 31, 19x5, balance sheet?

(Prepared by Carl L. Nelson)

10. Pension accounting: defined benefit plan. A small company has only one employee, Leroy Williams. Mr. Williams started to work for the company 30 years ago, when he was 33 years old. The company established a pension plan at the beginning of this year, when Mr. Williams was 63 years old. According to this plan, Mr. Williams will receive a pension each year equal to $100 times the number of years he has worked for the company by the time he retires. This pension will be given to him every year until his death, the first payment being made one year after the date of his retirement.

The company will amortize and fund the past-service costs during the next two years, and Mr. Williams will retire at the end of that time, when he is 65 years old. Mr. Williams, being in poor health, is expected to live only three years after his retirement. He will receive the payment due him on the day of his death, however.

Each year the company will also fund an amount equal to the current-service cost. The interest rate to be used in these calculations is 8 percent.

a. Calculate the past-service costs at the present time, when Mr. Williams is 63 years old.

b. Calculate the annual amortization amount for the past-service costs.

c. Calculate this year's pension expense.

11. Investment credit. A company uses the same depreciation method for tax and financial-reporting purposes. In 19x1, it purchased facilities with a ten-year estimated life, entitling it to a $35,000 investment credit. Its income before taxes and before reflecting the investment credit was $370,000. The income tax rate was 40 percent. The company had no other differences between income taxes and income tax expense.

a. Calculate net income for 19x1 if the investment credit was accounted for on a flow-through basis.

b. Make the same computations, using the deferral method of accounting for the investment credit.

c. Is the difference between your answers to (*a*) and (*b*) large enough to be regarded as significant?

12. Income tax allocation. The Pelican Corporation has purchased a machine for $10,298, delivered and installed. The service life of the machine is estimated to be six years, at the end of which time it is estimated that the machine can be disposed of for $1,100. The machine is put into service on the first day of the fiscal year. It is the firm's only depreciable asset.

The firm uses the straight-line method in its financial statements, and the sum-of-the-years'-digits method for income tax purposes. It has no other differences between the amounts shown on the income tax return for the year and the amounts shown on the income statement.

Reported net income before taxes on income is $6,000 for the first year in which the machine is used. The amount of income taxes currently due as a result of the firm's operations for that year is $2,452.50. The income tax rate is 50 percent.

a. Calculate the amount of income before deductions for depreciation and income taxes were taken.

b. Calculate the net income (after income taxes) that the company will report for the year.

c. What is the amount of deferred income taxes for the year?

d. Assuming that this is the firm's only asset and that the tax rate does not change, calculate the balance in the deferred income taxes account at the end of each year of the asset's life.

(Adapted from a problem prepared by Charles W. Bastable)

13. Investment credit; depreciation differences. The Lambert Corporation purchased a mill on January 1, 19x0, at a cost of $10 million. A portion of this expenditure was for elements that made the company eligible for an investment credit of $400,000. In addition, the company was allowed to depreciate the full cost of the mill for tax purposes at a straight-line rate of 20 percent of original cost each year for five years.

Management estimated that the mill would be useful for 20 years, with negligible end-of-life salvage value, and that straight-line depreciation would be appropriate for public financial reporting. The mill was the Lambert Corporation's only depreciable asset, and the company's income before depreciation and income taxes was $3 million each year. The income tax rate was 40 percent, and the investment credit was to be accounted for by the deferral method.

a. Derive the corporation's net income in 19x3 and 19x9, as reported to the stockholders.
b. State the balance in the Provision for Deferred Income Taxes at the close of 19x0, 19x2, 19x6, and 19x9.

14. Lease accounting. On January 1, 19x0, the Green Company entered into a noncancelable lease agreement under which the Blatt Company would have the use of one of Green's machines for a period of ten years. This machine was carried on Green's accounting records at $2 million. Payments under the lease agreement, which extended to December 31, 19x9, amounted to $355,080 a year for ten years, the first payment coming due on January, 19x0, when the lease agreement came into effect. Although the form of the agreement was a lease, for accounting purposes this transaction was treated as a sale by Green and as a purchase by Blatt.

The lease agreement stipulated that the cost of the machine to Blatt was $2 million and that the interest rate implicit in the agreement was 10 percent. This was considered fair and adequate compensation to Green for the use of its funds. Blatt expected the machine to have a ten-year life, no salvage value, and a straight-line benefit pattern.

a. Ignoring income taxes, what were Blatt's expenses from this lease in the year ended December 31, 19x0?
b. How much income before income taxes did Green derive from this lease for the year ended December 31, 19x0?

(AICPA adapted)

15. Income tax allocation. A company started business on January 1, 19x1, with the purchase of 20 delivery trucks costing $3,600 each. A full year's depreciation was taken on these trucks in 19x1.

Depreciation for financial-reporting purposes was by the straight-line method. Depreciation for tax purposes was by the sum-of-the-years'-digits method. The estimated life for tax purposes was eight years; the estimated life for financial reporting was ten years. A zero salvage value was assumed for both purposes. Item depreciation was used for each truck.

Two trucks were sold for $2,500 each on December 31, 19x2. A full year's depreciation on these trucks was recorded in the company's accounts before the sale was recorded.

The income tax rate was 40 percent both in 19x1 and in 19x2. This rate was applicable both to ordinary income and to gains and losses on the sale of trucks.

Income before depreciation, taxes, and gains and losses on the sale of trucks amounted to $40,000 each year.

a. Calculate the amount of depreciation that was shown on the income statement for 19x1. (*This has nothing to do with income taxes!*)
b. Calculate net income (after taxes) for 19x1.
c. Calculate the amount of the deferred-tax liability that was shown on the company's balance sheet at December 31, 19x1. Did recognition of this liability have an effect shareholders would have regarded as significant?
d. Calculate the amount of the deferred income tax on December 31, 19x2, before the sale of the two trucks was recorded.
e. Calculate the effect of the sale of the trucks on the deferred income tax account.
f. Calculate the after-tax gain or loss the company would report to its shareholders on the sale of the two trucks.

16. Lease accounting. A firm needs an additional machine and determines that it can acquire the use of a particular machine in two ways:

1. It can buy the machine for $92,442, paying $10,000 in cash on the date of purchase and promising to pay the remainder and 8 percent interest in 14 equal payments of $10,000 a year, starting one year after the date of purchase. Depreciation would be by the straight-line method over the machine's anticipated useful life of 15 years, with no estimated salvage value.
2. It can lease the machine for ten years, paying rent of $10,000 at the beginning of each year. The machine is expected to have a market value of $43,121 at the end of the ten years. The lease contains no purchase or renewal options, and if the firm wanted to continue using the machine after the end of ten years, it would have to negotiate a new lease.

a. Would the balance sheet at the date of acquisition be any different if the asset were purchased rather than leased? If so, how?
b. Calculate income before taxes for the first year under each of these two financing methods, assuming that income before taxes, interest, and depreciation or rent on this machine is $50,000.

17. Bond accounting; refunding. On July 1, 1962, the Vulcan Forge Company sold a $1 million issue of 6 percent, 20-year bonds to an insurance company at a price of $94.45. Interest was payable semiannually, on June 30 and December 31.

The company paid interest regularly for ten years. In 1972, the need for additional capital prompted Vulcan's management to try to borrow another million dollars. The insurance company refused to renegotiate the loan, but Vulcan found a pension trust that was willing to take a $2 million issue of 8 percent, 20-year bonds at a price of $95.23. Vulcan accepted this offer and used part of the proceeds to retire the 1962 bonds on June 30, 1972, at their call price of 102.

a. Indicate how the original bond issue should have been shown on the balance sheet dated July 1, 1962.
b. Calculate interest expense for the six months that ended on December

31, 1962. Prepare a journal entry to record the accrual of interest expense and the payment of the December 31, 1962, coupon.

c. Indicate how the bond issue would have been shown on the balance sheet dated December 31, 1962, after the December 31, 1962, interest payment.

d. Calculate the book value of the original issue at June 30, 1972, after payment of the interest coupon.

e. Prepare a journal entry to record the accrual of interest expense and the payment of the June 30, 1972, coupon.

f. Prepare a journal entry to record the issuance of the 8 percent bonds in 1972.

g. Calculate the gain or loss, if any, from the retirement of the 6 percent bonds. Prepare a journal entry to record the retirement of these bonds.

h. Calculate interest expense for the six-month period ended December 31, 1972, and prepare a journal entry to record the accrual of interest for the period and the payment of the December 31, 1972, coupon.

18. Pension liabilities: discussion question. Uniroyal, Inc., is a manufacturer of automobile and truck tires, chemicals, rubber goods, and plastic products. Its sales revenues in 1977 exceeded $2.5 billion, and its net income was almost $35 million. Accruals for employees' pay and benefits amounted to $877 million in 1977. Retained earnings at the end of 1977 amounted to $472 million, and the shareowners' equity totaled $644 million.

One of the footnotes to the financial statements for 1977 read as follows:

The Company and certain subsidiaries have trusteed retirement plans covering the great majority of their employees. In general, the plans provide for normal retirement at age 65. The domestic plans permit early unreduced retirement at age 55 with 30 years of service. Accounting for the plans is on an accrual basis. Most plans are funded by payments to independent trustees of amounts, computed by independent actuaries, sufficient to provide for current service costs and the amortization of prior service costs over periods not exceeding 30 years.

The total cost for all plans (before reduction for income tax) was $82,209,000 in 1977 and $79,362,000 in 1976.

At January 2, 1977, the date of the most recent actuarial valuation, the actuarially computed value of vested benefits of domestic plans, determined in the manner specified by the Pension Benefit Guaranty Corporation (PBGC), exceeded the pension funds by $515 million; amounts related to foreign subsidiaries are not significant. The decrease of $45 million from that reported in 1976 results from more favorable actuarial assumptions under the PBGC method.

Five years earlier, the company reported that the actuarially computed value of vested pension benefits for employees in the United States exceeded the pension funds and balance sheet accruals by $395 million.

In replying to a question from a securities analyst in 1977, the company's financial vice president made the following statement:

We began funding [the unfunded vested amount] in 1966 and in 1973 went to a 30-year program, which now has 25 more years to go. We are very much aware that this represents a substantial obligation for Uniroyal, but it must be put into perspective. This is not a current liability. It is a projection of the future pension payments we will pay to retired employees, extending from the present through approximately the next 50 years.

a. Since the company began funding its unfunded vested benefits in 1973, what explanation can you offer for the substantial increase in the unfunded amount between 1972 and 1977?

b. The company's treatment of its "prior-service obligation" was in accord with generally accepted accounting principles. Should those principles be modified to require companies such as Uniroyal to recognize the past-service obligation more quickly? State the arguments you considered on both sides of this question.

c. Suppose the Financial Accounting Standards Board had issued a new standard in 1978 requiring Uniroyal to recognize a major portion of the $515 million unfunded past-service obligation in 1978. If you had been empowered to decide how this change was to be implemented, would you have established the pension liability by a deduction from revenues on the 1978 income statement or by some other means? State the reasons for your choice.

14

The Shareowners' Equity

THE OWNERS' EQUITY has two main components, contributed capital and retained earnings. Previous chapters focused on changes in owners' equity resulting from current income and the declaration of cash dividends which affect the retained-earnings component. The purpose of this chapter is to examine a number of other transactions that affect either the contributed-capital component alone or both contributed capital and retained earnings simultaneously. The discussion falls under four major headings:

1. Classes of capital stock.
2. Issuance of additional shares.
3. Treasury stock.
4. Contingency reserves.

CLASSES OF CAPITAL STOCK

Each state in the United States has a general incorporation law. Anyone meeting the requirements of this law is entitled to draw up a set of *articles of incorporation* and receive a corporate charter from the state. The owners of the corporation then receive shares of capital stock in exchange for the resources they contribute to the corporation. Two classes of corporate stock can be distinguished: common stock and preferred stock.

Common Stock

When a corporation has only one class of capital stock, it is usually referred to as *common stock*. In such cases, each share of common stock represents a proportionate share of all of the ownership rights in the corporation.

The articles of incorporation specify the number of shares of common stock the corporation is authorized to issue and the *par value* of each share. In some cases, the articles will specify that the shares are *no-par* shares, in which case either the articles or the directors will designate a portion of the issue price as the *stated value* of the stock. For most corporations, the number of shares issued is smaller than the number of shares authorized in the articles of incorporation.

Par value had its origin in the concept of legal capital. The amount designated as the legal capital is intended to establish a minimum limit on the owners' equity. In concept, this provides a cushion or margin of protection for the creditors. The economic significance of par or stated value today is minimal, however. The issue price of shares of common stock in the United States is frequently a large multiple of the par or stated value, and the total par value of a company's shares is likely to be only a small fraction of the total of its liabilities. The creditor's protection, in other words, comes from the amount and continuity of the company's cash flows rather than from the designation of part of the owners' equity as par value or legal capital.

The spread between the issue price and par or stated value is reported on the balance sheet under some heading such as Additional Paid-In Capital or Capital in Excess of Par Value. The entry to record the issue of 100,000 shares of $1 par common stock in exchange for $1 million in cash would be as follows:

Cash.....................................	1,000,000	
Common Stock		100,000
Additional Paid-In Capital...........		900,000

At any time after the stock is issued and after earnings have been recorded, the owners' equity structure will be as reflected in Exhibit 14–1. In this diagram the left half of the circle represents contributed capital and the right half represents retained earnings. The circle is divided down the middle to emphasize this two-way split; contributed capital isn't necessarily one half of the total.

Preferred Stock

Some corporations have one or more classes of capital stock in addition to the common stock. These other classes of stock are usu-

EXHIBIT 14–1.   Shareowners' Equity: One Class of Stock

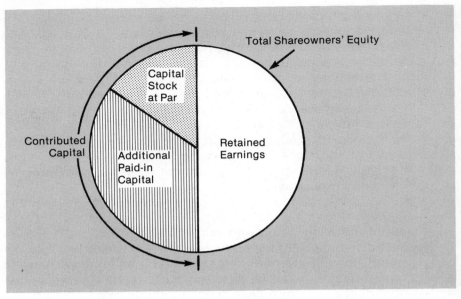

ally called *preferred* or *preference stock*. Exhibit 14–2 shows the shareowners' equity of a corporation with two classes of preferred stock. Three of the wedges of this diagram represent the par or stated values of the three classes of stock; the remainder of the contributed capital is shown as a single wedge, including the amounts originating in the issuance of all classes of stock. The amounts attributable to the preferred shares aren't reported separately on the balance sheet.

The rights of each class of shares are specified in the articles of incorporation and by-laws, but each share of a given class has the same rights as any other share of that class. Thus an owner of 1,000 shares of $5 preferred stock receives twice as much dividend money as a holder of 500 shares of this stock.

Shares of preferred stock usually entitle their owners to dividends of a fixed amount that must be paid before any dividends can be paid on the common stock. The owners of preferred ordinarily also have precedence over the common stockholders in any liquidation of assets, up to a specified maximum amount per share. They may even have voting rights.

The dividend priority is usually *cumulative,* meaning that no distribution can be made to the common shareholders until all current and back dividends have been paid on the preferred. In most cases, shares of preferred stock are also *callable* at a specified price. This means that the company has the right to repurchase the stock if

EXHIBIT 14–2. Shareowners' Equity: Several Classes of Stock

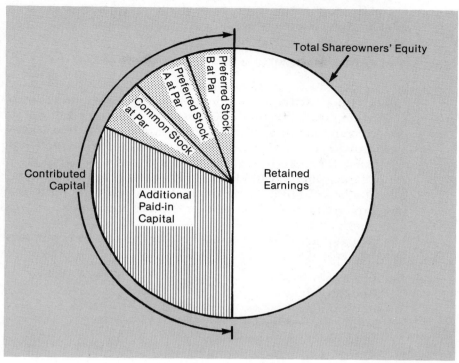

certain conditions are met, even if the owners of the stock don't wish to sell it. All these characteristics of the preferred stock limit the risks of its owners, but at the same time, they limit the owners' return on the amounts they have invested in the stock.

A preferred stock differs from a bond in that the stockholders have no legal right to insist on payment of their dividends on specified dates. Furthermore, the stock has no maturity date. A corporation may omit or pass the dividend on the preferred indefinitely without being declared insolvent, although some preferred stocks provide for the transfer of corporate control to the preferred shareholders when the dividends have fallen a specified amount in arrears. Thus, preferred stock lies somewhere between bonds and common stock on the risk-return spectrum: it typically offers higher risk and a higher return than bonds, but lower risk and a lower return than common stock.

Many preferred stocks issued in recent years have been *converti-ble* into a predetermined number of shares of common stock. The sale of preferred stock and bonds with the conversion privilege or with detachable options to buy common stock is sometimes an indirect way of selling common stock. The interesting features of such securities and the accounting problems they raise will be discussed later in this chapter.

ISSUING ADDITIONAL COMMON SHARES

The initial source of corporate financing is the sale or issuance of capital stock. Without an adequate base of ownership capital, the corporation would be unable to obtain debt financing and would even experience difficulties in obtaining short-term trade credit.

Although companies raise some capital by issuing preferred stock, they raise far more by issuing shares of common stock, both at the time of incorporation and later on. Even some issues of preferred lead eventually to additional common shares when the preferred shares are converted into (exchanged for) shares of common, as we'll see in a moment.

Existing corporations issue additional shares of common stock in at least six ways:

1. Straight-cash sales.
2. Stock dividends.
3. Stock splits.
4. Securities conversions.
5. Exercise of stock options.
6. Acquisitions of other companies.

We'll discuss the first five of these now, leaving the issuance of shares of stock in exchange for the stock or assets of other companies to Chapter 15.

Cash Sales of Additional Shares

Small numbers of shares of capital stock are often sold to employees as part of company employee-savings plans. The most significant kind of straight-cash sales, however, are sales of additional shares either to the company's current shareowners or to other outside investors. The company is likely to do this because it needs more funds to finance its growth than earnings retention can supply.

Registration requirements.   Large corporations wishing to raise capital in this way must register each new issue with the Securities and Exchange Commission and make a detailed prospectus available to any potential purchaser of the shares. The task of the SEC is to insure that the information provided in the registration statement is complete and accurate. SEC approval of a registration statement does not constitute or even imply an endorsement of the shares as a sound investment vehicle.

Preemptive rights. The common shareowners in many companies have the right to purchase any additional shares of common stock the company may offer for sale. Rights of this kind are known as *preemptive rights.* For example, if a company with 1 million shares of common stock outstanding wants to raise capital by selling 100,000 additional shares of stock, each current shareowner will have the right to buy one share of the new issue for every ten shares he or she now owns.

Some shareowners may not wish to exercise this privilege, of course. They may be short of cash or unwilling to increase the percentage of their total assets they have invested in this particular company's common stock. In such cases, they may try to sell the rights to others. If the price at which the new shares are offered is less than the price at which the old shares are being traded, the rights will be valuable.

For example, the market value of the right to buy a tenth of a new share when the market price is $50 a share and the offer price is $40 should be close to $1. This figure is derived in Exhibit 14–3. These

EXHIBIT 14–3. Calculating the Value of a Preemptive Right to Purchase One Tenth of a Share of Common Stock

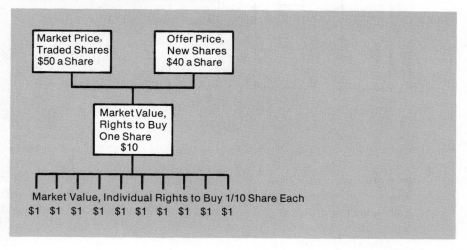

rights are valid only until a specified date, however, and any right that hasn't been exercised by that date becomes worthless.

All new issues aren't offered through rights. The owners of many companies don't have this privilege, and, in other cases, the shareowners may vote to waive their preemptive rights, leaving the company free to offer the shares to the general public. These are known as *public offerings,* as opposed to *rights offerings.*

Dilution of the market value of the equity.   When shares of stock are offered to the general public, the existing shareowners are very interested in the price at which these shares are offered. For example, suppose the XYZ Corporation has 100,000 shares of common stock outstanding with a market value of $30 a share. If the company sells an additional 100,000 shares at $20 a share, a reasonable expectation is that all of the shares will trade at $25 a share. If this happens, the market value of the old shareholders' holdings will fall from $3 million to $2.5 million; the new shareowners will pay $2 million for stock worth $2.5 million ($25 × 100,000 shares).

This transfer of part of the old shareowners' equity to the new shareowners is known as *dilution of the equity*, and is illustrated in Exhibit 14–4. This shows the old shareowners giving $5 of the value

EXHIBIT 14–4.   Dilution of the Equity

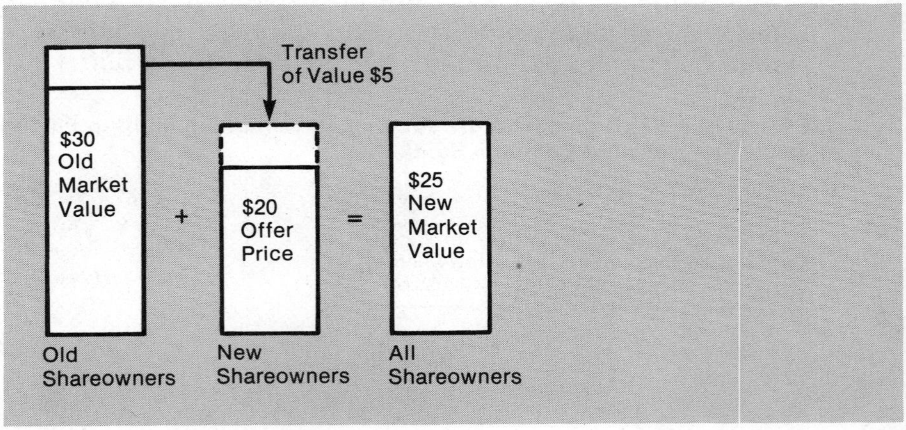

of their stock to new shareowners to induce them to invest their money in the corporation. The dilution is measured by the difference between the market price before the offer was made and the market price after the new shares were issued, adjusted for other influences on the stock's price.

Offering the new shares at a price lower than the current market price is intended to make the new issue attractive to potential buyers. The reason why the existing shareowners may be willing to make this offer may not be quite as clear, however. The answer has to be that *they expect little or no dilution to take place.* In some cases, for example, the old shareowners and the new shareowners are the same people—that is, the new shares are issued through a rights offering. The old shareowners can then protect themselves either by purchasing the new shares they are entitled to or by selling their rights at prices reflecting their values.

A second possible explanation of existing shareowners' willingness to offer new shares at low prices is that they may be convinced management can invest the new capital so effectively that the price of the stock will rise within a reasonable period of time to the level it would have reached without the new capital or even higher.

For example, if the old shareholders had expected the stock to increase in price to $36 within two years and if it actually goes up to that level as a result of management's ability to invest the new $2 million profitably, the long-term dilution of the equity is zero. In fact, the dilution may even be negative if prices rise faster than they would have without the new infusion of capital into the firm. This approach to dilution is illustrated in Exhibit 14–5.

EXHIBIT 14–5. Elimination of Dilution by Effective Investment

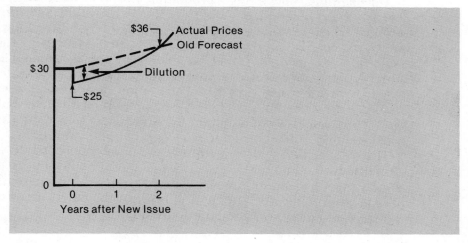

It is difficult to anticipate accurately how new investments will work out, however, let alone document these expectations. To avoid challenges by dissident stockholders, the board of directors generally tries to set the offer price in a public offering very close to the market price prevailing at the time of the offer.

Dilution of earnings. The funds obtained from the sale of additional shares are unlikely to generate enough income in the short run to keep net income per share unchanged. If the shares are issued to allow the company to retire debt, for example, interest expense will fall and total net income will rise. The percentage increase in the number of shares outstanding will probably be larger than the percentage increase in net income, however, and earnings per share will fall. (Net income is often referred to as *earnings* and net income per share as *earnings per share*.)

This reduction in earnings per share is referred to as *dilution of the earnings* due to the stock issue. This doesn't mean that the stock issue was unwise; if future earnings per share are higher than they would have been without the new issue, the financing was worthwhile.

Stock Dividends

Corporations sometimes increase the number of shares of common stock outstanding without increasing the total amount of resources available to the firm. One way of accomplishing this is to issue what is known as a stock dividend.

For example, Space Age Corporation was very successful during its early years of operation, and the balance in retained earnings had reached $715,000 by the end of 19x6. The demand for funds to finance the company's growth was equally strong, however, and, consequently, the company had no money to pay dividends. In this situation, the directors declared a 10 percent *stock dividend*. A stock dividend consists of the distribution of additional shares of stock to the existing stockholders in proportion to their holdings. With 55,000 shares outstanding, the Space Age 10 percent dividend consisted of 5,500 shares, one for every ten outstanding.

This transaction was treated as if the corporation had declared a cash dividend equal to the market value of the 5,500 shares and the stockholders had simultaneously purchased the 5,500 shares at their market price.[1] Because the market price of the stock at the time of the stock dividend was $60, the journal entry was:

Retained Earnings	330,000	
Common Stock		55,000
Additional Paid-In Capital............		275,000

The "dividend" reduced retained earnings, and the "stock sale" increased the paid-in capital by the market value of the number of shares.

The shareowners' equity section of the balance sheet before and

---

[1] Measuring the stock dividend at the market value of the shares is arbitrary. It is simply a convenient basis for determining how much is to be capitalized.

EXHIBIT 14–6. Effect of a Stock Dividend

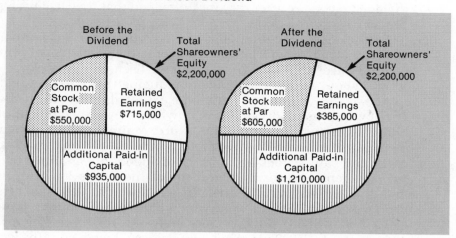

after the stock dividend are shown schematically in Exhibit 14–6. As this shows, the total owners' equity was unaffected by the stock dividend; it was merely divided into a larger number of shares, each one representing a smaller portion of the company than formerly. Book value per share was as follows:

	Before Stock Dividend	After Stock Dividend
Common stock—stated value	$10.00	$10.00
Additional paid-in capital	17.00	20.00
Retained earnings	13.00	6.36
Total	$40.00	$36.36

These figures were obtained by dividing the figures in Exhibit 13–6 by 50,000 and 55,000, the numbers of shares outstanding before and after the stock dividend.

It should be evident that the stock dividend may properly be called a *paper transaction*. After the dividend, each stockholder had 11 shares which conveyed the same rights as the ten shares he or she had owned previously. After the dividend, 11 shares had the same $400 book value (11 × $36.36) the owner's ten shares had had before.

Although the stock dividend does not give the stockholder any new asset, the market in the stock may be slightly more active than formerly because of the increase in the number of shares outstanding.

Many companies also follow the practice of paying the same cash dividend per share after the stock dividend that they had been paying previously.

Furthermore, the market often interprets the declaration of a stock dividend as evidence of management's prediction of continued company growth. Once dividends have been increased, large corporations show a great resistance to reducing them, except under the most extreme conditions.[2] To a large extent, directors avoid dividend cuts by increasing dividends only when they are confident of their ability to maintain them in the future. Maintaining a constant dividend per share, therefore, is likely to increase the total market value of the company's stock because the dividends are assumed to convey management's positive assessment of the firm's long-run earning and dividend-paying potential. In other words, although 11 shares should sell for what ten shares would have brought previously (10 × $60 = $600), in fact, they may sell for more (for example, 11 × $56 = $616). This effect won't persist, however, if the expected cash flows don't materialize.

Stock Splits

A stock split is akin to a stock dividend in that each stockholder is given additional shares in proportion to the number he or she owns. The par or stated value is usually reduced to accompany a stock split, but the main difference is in the number of shares distributed. When an increase of more than about 20 or 25 percent in the number of shares outstanding is to be achieved, the mechanism of the stock split is usually employed.[3]

For example, the market price of Space Age Corporation had risen to $90 by the end of 19x9, and the board of directors decided to declare a 2 for 1 stock split and to reduce the stated value of the stock from $10 to $5. Only the common stock account was affected by this transaction, and no transfers occurred between the various ownership accounts, as shown in Exhibit 14-7.

Stock splits, like stock dividends, are signals to the market about the company's future cash flows. Recent empirical work has estab-

---

[2] See John Lintner, "Distribution of Incomes of Corporations Among Dividends, Retained Earnings and Taxes," *American Economic Review*, May 1956, pp. 97–113; and Jacob B. Michaelsen, "The Determinants of Dividend Policies: A Theoretical and Empirical Study" (Ph.d., diss., Graduate School of Business, University of Chicago, 1961).

[3] This is the dividing line prescribed by the accounting profession. See *Accounting Research, Bulletin No. 43*, chap. 7, sec. B, para. 15, codified in AICPA, *Professional Standards—Accounting, Current Text* (New York: Commerce Clearing House, Inc., 1978), sec. 5561.15.

EXHIBIT 14–7

SPACE AGE CORPORATION
Shareowners' Equity
December 31, 19x9

	Before Stock Split		After Stock Split	
	Total	Per Share	Total	Per Share
Common stock—stated value	$ 605,000	$10	$ 605,000	$ 5
Additional paid-in capital	1,210,000	20	1,210,000	10
Retained Earnings	1,089,000	18	1,089,000	9
Total Shareholders' Equity	$2,904,000	$48	$2,904,000	$24

lished that stock splits are very often associated with substantial cash-dividend increases. The evidence indicates that the market realizes this and uses the announcement of a split to reevaluate the stream of expected cash flows from the shares. Stock splits lead to adjustments in the market price of common stock to the extent they are associated with changes in the anticipated level of future dividends.[4]

Securities Conversions

Corporations often attach conversion privileges to shares of their preferred stock or to their long-term bonds. They do this either to make the securities more attractive to potential investors or to use these *senior securities* (that is, senior to the common stock) as an indirect way of selling common stock to the public. To see how this works, we'll examine a simple issue of convertible preferred stock in some depth and then deal very briefly with convertible debt.

Convertible preferred stock. The convertibility of shares of preferred stock enables their owners to increase the market value of their investments in this company if the market value of its common stock goes up. They can do this by exchanging their preferred shares for shares of common stock whenever the dividend and market price on the common shares have risen above the dividend and market price of the equivalent number of preferred shares.

For example, in 19x1, a corporation issued 1,000 shares of convertible preferred stock at an issue price of $100 a share. The annual dividend on the preferred was $5, and each share was convertible

---

[4] See Eugene F. Fama, Lawrence Fisher, Michael C. Jensen, and Richard Roll, "The Adjustment of Stock Prices to New Information," *International Economic Review*, February 1969, pp. 1–21.

into five shares of common stock at the discretion of the holder. The cash dividend on the common stock was 75 cents a share, and the market price of the common shares was $18 a share.

Given these figures, the preferred stockholders had no incentive to exercise their conversion option. By converting a share of preferred into five shares of common, they would have lost $1.25 in dividends and $10 in market value:

	Dividends	Market Value
1 Preferred share	$5.00	$100
5 Common shares	3.75	90
Difference	$1.25	$ 10

This doesn't mean the conversion option was valueless, however. If earnings and dividends on the common stock continued to rise in the years ahead, the market price of the common would probably rise, too. If that happened, conversion could become very desirable. For example, the cash dividend on the common rose to $1.60 a share in 19x6. The market price of a common share at that time was $40. Conversion of the preferred shares at that time would have given the preferred shareholder $8 in dividends instead of $5, and a market value of $200 (five shares at $40 each). In other words, the conversion privilege clearly has value if the price of the common is expected to rise. In practice, most of the holders of the preferred stock are likely to convert even before the benefits of conversion are as great as this.

Issuing convertible securities also involves a cost to the common shareholders. To retire the 1,000 shares of preferred in 19x6, the company had to issue 5,000 shares of common, worth about $200,000. If the preferred had been callable at $100, however, the company could have retired the entire issue with the payment of $100,000 in cash. This $100,000 could have been obtained by issuing only 2,500 shares at $40 a share. The conversion privilege, in other words, carries with it a potential dilution of the common equity.

Calculations of earnings per share of common stock that ignored these potential conversions could mislead investors. Suppose the company had 20,000 shares of common stock outstanding in 19x5 and net income of $65,000. The total preferred dividend was 1,000 × $5 = $5,000, and the earnings available to the common shareowners was $65,000 − $5,000 = $60,000. Ignoring the potential dilution, earnings per common share would be calculated as follows:

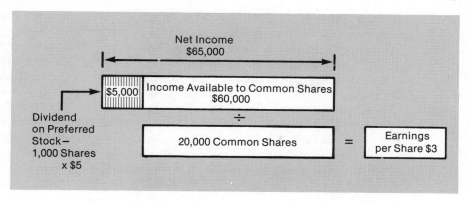

The conversion of all of the preferred, however, would raise the number of common shares outstanding to 25,000 and would make the entire $65,000 net income available to the common shareholders. Earnings per share calculated on this basis would be:

$$\frac{\text{Adjusted income available}}{\text{Adjusted number of shares}} = \frac{\$65,000}{25,000} = \$2.60 \text{ a share.}$$

Accountants reflect this possibility when they calculate earnings per share. They label the result differently, however, depending on how important the conversion feature was when the preferred stock was first issued. If the percentage yield on the preferred stock at the time it was issued was less than two thirds of the *prime rate* (applicable to banks' loans to their lowest-risk customers), the dilution is reflected in *primary earnings per share*.[5] If the yield on the preferred at the time of issuance was greater than two thirds of the prime rate, primary earnings per share is based on the number of shares of common stock actually outstanding, but a second figure, known as *fully diluted earnings per share*, is calculated by the method illustrated above.

For example, if when the $5 convertible preferred was issued the prime rate was more than 7.5 percent, primary earnings per share in 19x5 would be $2.60 and no additional calculations would be necessary. If the prime rate was 6 percent on the issue date, however, two figures would be published:

Primary earnings per share:	$3.00
Fully diluted earnings per share:	2.60

---

[5] This dividing line is highly arbitrary and was adopted as a means of achieving uniformity. See APB "Opinion No. 15," para. 33, in AICPA, *Professional Standards—Accounting*, sec. 2011.33.

Convertible debt.   Bonds are also issued with convertible features, as we saw in Chapter 13. The two-thirds-of-prime-rate rule is applied to these, too, in determining whether primary earnings per share should be adjusted for potential dilution. The only difference is that, because interest is tax deductible, less than the full amount of the interest on the bonds is added back to net income.

For example, suppose instead of preferred stock the company had $100,000 in 5 percent bonds outstanding and its taxable income was subject to a 40 percent tax rate. Net income was $62,000 and 20,000 common shares were outstanding. The first step is to calculate the net income the company would have reported if the debt had been converted into common stock. Without debt, the company would have had no interest to pay. Interest at 5 percent on the debt was $5,000. This was tax deductible, meaning that the after-tax interest cost was $5,000 − 0.4 × $5,000 = $3,000. Without debt, therefore, the company would have reported net income of $62,000 + $3,000 = $65,000.

The $100,000 debt was convertible into 5,000 shares of common stock. Conversion, therefore, would have increased the number of shares outstanding to 25,000. The revised earnings per share would be $65,000/25,000 = $2.60. Whether this would be reported as primary or fully diluted earnings per share depends on how the two-thirds-of-prime-rate test comes out.

Stock Options

Options to buy corporate stock are issued for various reasons. For example, they are sometimes attached to the company's bonds as a means of reducing interest costs and making the bonds more easily marketable.

The most highly publicized stock options are executive stock options, awarded to key corporate executives as part of their compensation. In most option plans, key executives are given options to buy specified numbers of shares at a fixed price, usually the market price at the time the options are granted. If the market price goes up, the executives can exercise some or all of their options and participate in the gain.

The argument for executive stock options is that they provide executives with a strong inducement to perform effectively so that the price of the company's stock will rise. In other words, the executives can't benefit from the options unless the stockholders also benefit.

Because the company receives no direct payment when stock options are granted to employees, no changes in the owners' equity can be recognized. The potential dilution must be recognized in the financial statements, however. This is accomplished by disclosing such information as the number of options outstanding and the option price and by calculating earnings per share on the assumption that all outstanding options have been exercised in full. We'll leave the details of these calculations to more advanced texts.

TREASURY STOCK

Corporations from time to time repurchase shares of their own stock. These repurchased shares are called treasury stock.

Objectives of Treasury-Stock Purchases

Share repurchase may have a number of objectives. Some reacquired shares may be used for distribution to executives in bonus or stock option plans. Others may be used for distribution to shareholders as stock dividends, to employees in stock-purchase plans, or to the company's pension funds for long-term investment. Share repurchasing eliminates the necessity to issue new shares for these purposes and thus helps the company avoid the costs and additional reporting requirements associated with new issues.

Share repurchase may also be viewed as a more profitable use of the company's funds than the available alternatives. If the company has more cash than it can invest profitably internally, stock repurchase may prevent a dilution in earnings per share, particularly when market prices seem unjustifiably low.

The negative aspects of these transactions should not be overlooked, however. For one thing, the purchase and sale of treasury stock in any volume can generate short-term movements in the price of the stock which might be interpreted as the use of the corporation's funds by "insiders" to influence the price of the stock to their advantage. Similar objections can be raised to the use of the corporation's funds to purchase stock to prevent voting control from being concentrated in unfriendly hands.

A third drawback is that the purchase of treasury stock reduces the company's assets and equities. Treasury stock, in other words, represents a reduction of the stockholders' total investment in the firm and may impair the company's ability to discharge its obligations to its creditors. This would hurt not only the creditors but the shareholders and employees as well.

Reporting Treasury Stock at Cost

The customary method of accounting for treasury stock is to carry it as a separate amount, measured at the price paid to acquire it. This is the cost method, used by most companies to record temporary reacquisitions of common shares. Under this method, the cost of treasury shares is shown on the balance sheet as a negative element of owners' equity.

For example, if Space Age Corporation were to repurchase for $46,000 a total of 1,000 shares of its common stock after the stock split on December 31, 19x9, the revised December 31, 19x9, balance sheet would show the following:

Common stock—stated value	$ 605,000
Additional paid-in capital	1,210,000
Earnings retained in the business	1,089,000
Total	$2,904,000
Less: Treasury stock (at cost)	(46,000)
Total Shareholders' Equity	$2,858,000

Treasury stock is not an asset, although it is sometimes reported as one. Shares of stock represent portions of the owners' equity in the firm. When the shares are repurchased, the assets are reduced and so is the owners' equity. To treat treasury stock as an asset would imply that the company has ownership rights in itself, and this is not true. Treasury shares cannot be voted, nor do they participate in cash dividends or carry any other perquisites of ownership. The purchase of treasury shares represents a partial and perhaps temporary liquidation of the enterprise and represents a reduction in both total assets and total owners' equities. Thus, the amount paid for the stock should be deducted from the shareholders' equity. It should not be included among the assets.

Resale of treasury stock at prices different from their acquisition cost is not reported as a gain or loss on the company's income statement. The company cannot make or lose money by buying and selling a portion of itself, although the equity of the surviving shareholders can be increased or decreased by such actions. The accepted accounting treatment is to add positive differences to the additional paid-in capital and, with some exceptions, to subtract negative differences from retained earnings.

CONTINGENCY RESERVES

Businesses operate in an environment of uncertainty. A previously successful company may suffer serious reverses from events it wasn't able to foresee. To provide for these, management may wish to make deductions from revenues in good years to reflect the possibility that unforeseen events in the future may impair the values of the company's resources.

For example, suppose most of a company's facilities are located in an area that is subject to the possibility of earthquakes. Management has decided that outside insurance against earthquake damage is too expensive. Instead, it has decided to show in its financial statements that its investment in plant, equipment, and inventories is subject to the risk of loss due to earthquakes. It has done this by setting up a "reserve for contingencies," a subdivision of the owners' equity calling attention to the *possibility* that a present condition or commitment will lead to a future event that will reduce the firm's assets or increase its liabilities. The company's shareowners' equity, including this subdivision, is shown schematically in Exhibit 14–8. Both of

EXHIBIT 14–8. Shareowners' Equity, Including Contingency Reserve

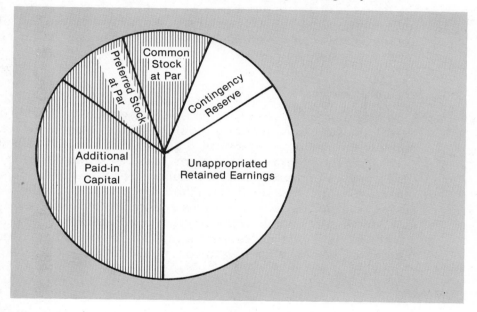

the unshaded segments of this diagram are parts of the retained earnings.

We face two difficulties in attempting to reflect the contingency of an earthquake in the financial statements. First, the probability that an earthquake will occur and that this earthquake will be strong enough to cause damage (that is, will impair the value of assets or give rise to new liabilities) can't be assessed reliably because adequate statistics are unavailable. Earthquakes just don't happen in ways that are predictable enough to support the necessary accounting figures. Second, the amount of the possible loss can't be estimated accurately enough. An earthquake, if it happens, may destroy all of the firm or part of it or none of it.

For these reasons the accounting profession has taken the position that contingency reserves can't be set up by deductions from revenues on the income statement. Revenue deductions (expense charges) are permitted only if it is deemed probable that a loss has *already* occurred and that it can be estimated accurately enough. In such cases, certain assets are written down or a liability (provision for loss) is established.[6]

Appropriations for losses that don't meet these conditions can be created only by transfers from retained earnings, and they must be shown within the shareowners' equity section of the balance sheet and clearly identified as appropriations *of retained earnings*. When the losses actually materialize, they are to be charged against revenues, not against the appropriations. Furthermore, no part of the appropriations can be transferred to the income statement at any time.

Other Types of Reserves

The term *reserve* is very imprecise. For one thing, it may imply that it measures the amount of liquid resources that the firm keeps on hand for use in times of need. This is highly unlikely to be true.

A second problem is that this term may be used to describe three distinct types of amounts: appropriations of retained earnings, discussed above; contra assets or *valuation reserves,* such as the reserves (allowances) for depreciation and uncollectible accounts; and *liability reserves,* such as the reserve (provision) for income taxes. All three are based on estimates and all have credit balances—otherwise, they have nothing in common.

SUMMARY

All corporations have common stock. Some also have one or more classes of preferred stock, with a prior but limited right to dividends. The amounts paid the corporation (contributed capital) are divided into two parts, the par values of the shares and the amounts paid in excess of par.

The initial issue of common stock provides the base for the company's capital structure. Additional shares are issued from time to time, and the proceeds from these issues are also divided between par value and additional paid-in capital. Shareholders are usually given preemptive rights to purchase these additional shares so they can avoid having their equity diluted unduly. They may waive these

---

[6] FASB, Statement No. 5, paras. 8 and 15, in AICPA, *Professional Standards— Accounting,* secs. 5513.08 and 5513.15.

rights, however, to allow the company to issue shares in connection with executive stock options and convertible senior securities and for other purposes. Shares held for conversions and options are included with the number of shares outstanding in certain calculations of earnings per share.

The line between contributed capital and retained earnings is clouded by stock dividends, which require the transfer of amounts from retained earnings to the contributed capital section. Stock dividends and stock splits are generally regarded as signals that the company intends to increase the total cash dividend payment, and the market price of the shares is likely to move to a higher level. It will stay at this higher level, however, only if the cash dividend actually does increase as anticipated.

Corporations in the United States occasionally use funds to repurchase some of their own outstanding shares. These shares are known as treasury stock. They are shown at cost on the balance sheet, deducted from the total of contributed capital and retained earnings to determine the net shareowners' equity.

KEY TERMS

Additional paid-in capital	Preemptive rights
Common stock	Preferred stock
Contingency reserves	Stated value
Convertible securities	Stock dividend
Dilution of earnings	Stock option
Dilution of the equity	Stock split
Par value	Treasury stock

INDEPENDENT STUDY PROBLEMS (Solutions in Appendix B)

1. Issuance of common stock for cash; dilution. Angel Rings, Inc., had the following shareowners' equity on January 1, 19x1:

Common stock, $1 par (authorized, 1,000,000 shares)	$ 800,000
Additional paid-in capital	300,000
Retained earnings	500,000
Total	$1,600,000

On January 2, 19x1, the shareowners were given rights to purchase 160,000 new shares of common stock at a price of $4 a share. The market price of the company's stock immediately prior to the announcement of the rights offering was $5 a share. All rights were exercised, and the new shares were issued on February 18, 19x1.

Net income for the year ended December 31, 19x1, was $441,600. A cash dividend of 20 cents a share was declared on December 15, 19x1, and paid on January 15, 19x2.

a.   Prepare the shareowners' equity section of the company's balance sheet on December 31, 19x1.
b.   Did the issuance of the new shares lead to a dilution of the equity? State the reasons for your answer, including any calculations you find necessary.

2.   Stock dividend.   Company A's board of directors declared and distributed a stock dividend of one share of common stock for each 20 shares outstanding. Prior to the stock dividend, 20,000 shares were outstanding with a par value of $10 a share. The company capitalized the stock dividend at $30 a share.

State the effect of this transaction on the figures shown on the company's balance sheet.

3.   Treasury stock.   On January 1, 19x1, Company B had 100,000 shares of $5 par common stock outstanding. On January 4, 19x1, the company purchased 100 shares of this stock on the market at a price of $30 a share and placed these shares in the treasury. On March 2, 19x1, the company declared a cash dividend on the common stock of 30 cents a share; this dividend was distributed on April 5, 19x1. On May 15, 19x1, the company sold its treasury stock at a price of $40 a share.

State the effects of each of these transactions on the company's assets, liabilities, and shareowners' equity. Be careful to specify which portions of the shareowners' equity were affected.

4.   Dilution: calculating earnings per share.   The Denver Corporation in 19x1 had a net income of $312,000. It had 100,000 shares of common stock outstanding and 10,000 shares of $5 convertible preferred stock. Each share of preferred was convertible into two shares of common.

a.   Calculate primary earnings per common share, ignoring the convertibility of the preferred stock.
b.   Calculate the fully diluted earnings per common share.

EXERCISES AND PROBLEMS

5.   Issuance of stock for cash; book value.   On January 8, 19x0, the Alpine Company started operations by issuing 100,000 shares of common stock, $10 par, at a price of $15 a share. No additional shares of stock were issued between that date and December 31, 19x3. Retained earnings of the company as of December 31, 19x3, totaled $2 million.

a.   How did the issuance of the stock affect the various components of the shareowners' equity?
b.   What was the book value per share of common stock on December 31, 19x3?

6. Purchase of treasury stock. On January 2, 19x4, the Alpine Company (see Problem 5) repurchased 1,000 shares of its stock at the market price of $28 a share. This stock was held as treasury stock.

a. How should this treasury stock have been listed on the company's June 30, 19x4, balance sheet?

b. Did the purchase of this treasury stock increase, decrease, or leave unchanged the book value per share of stock issued and outstanding?

c. Should a gain or loss be shown in the 19x4 income statement as a result of the repurchase of the stock? Why?

7. Sale of treasury stock. On July 1, 19x4, the Alpine Company (see Problem 6) resold its treasury stock at a price of $34 a share.

a. How did the sale of the treasury stock affect the various components of the shareowners' equity?

b. Should a gain or loss be shown on the 19x4 income statement as a result of the resale of stock? Why?

8. Book value per share; treasury stock. A balance sheet showed the following shareowners' equity section on December 31:

Stockholders' Investment:

$5 par value common stock (5,559,500 shares issued)	$27,797,500
Other paid-in capital	10,960,500
Income invested in the business	55,389,500
Cost of shares held by the company (9,500 shares)	(153,500)
Total Stockholders' Investment	$93,994,000

The market price of the stock on December 31 was $25 per share.

a. What was the book value per share of common stock issued and outstanding at the end of the year?

b. Give three alternative explanations as to how the "Other paid-in capital" might have been accumulated. (One phrase or sentence for each will be adequate.)

c. If the corporation decided to cancel and retire the 9,500 "shares held by the company," how would the various components of the shareowners' equity be affected? Why would the accountants analyze this transaction in this way?

9. Stock dividend. Assume the corporation in Problem 8 declared a 10 percent stock dividend on December 31.

a. How would this transaction affect the various components of the shareowners' equity?

b. What would be the new book value per share?

c. What would be the new book value (on the corporation's books) of the shares owned by an investor who had owned ten shares of stock prior to the stock dividend?

10. Stock split. Assume that instead of a stock dividend, the corporation in Problem 8 declared a two-for-one stock split (two new shares exchanged for each old one), and changed the par value to $3 a share.

a. How would this transaction affect the various components of the shareowners' equity?
b. What would be the new book value per share?
c. What would be the new book value (on the corporation's books) of the shares owned by an investor who had owned ten shares of stock prior to the stock split?

11. Calculating earnings per share. The Massena Corporation in 19x1 had a net income of $4,416,000. It had 1 million shares of common stock outstanding and 100,000 shares of $6 convertible preferred. Each share of preferred was convertible into 1.5 shares of common stock.

The company also had $5 million in 5 percent bonds payable, convertible into common shares at a ratio of 16 shares of common for every $1,000 in bonds. The effective tax rate in 19x1 was 40 percent.

a. Calculate primary earnings per common share, ignoring the convertibility of the bonds and the preferred stock.
b. Calculate the fully diluted earnings per common share.

12. Issuance of common shares for cash; dilution. The shareowners' equity in Beehive Industries was as follows on January 1, 19x1:

Common stock, no par, stated value, $5 a share (authorized, 2,000,000 shares, outstanding, 1,800,000 shares)	$ 9,000,000
Additional paid-in capital	6,300,000
Retained earnings	4,500,000
Total	$19,800,000

The company's shareholders voted in April 19x1 to increase the authorized number of shares of common stock from 2 million shares to 5 million shares. In September 19x1, the company gave its common shareholders rights to purchase 450,000 new shares of common stock at a price of $15 a share. All rights were exercised, and the new shares were issued on October 1, 19x1. The market price of Beehive Industries' common stock just prior to the offering was $20 a share.

The company's net income for the year ended December 31, 19x1, was $956,250. Cash dividends of ten cents a share were declared and paid in May and in November, 19x1.

a. Present the shareowners' equity section of the company's balance sheet as of December 31, 19x1.
b. Did the issuance of these shares result in a dilution of the equity? Present figures to support your conclusion.
c. If the earnings per share figure is to be used as an approximation of future earnings per share, should the denominator of the ratio in 19x1 be 1,800,000 shares, 1,912,500 shares, 2,250,000 shares, or some other number? Summarize the reasons for your choice and any assumptions you had to make.

13. Series of transactions. On December 31, 19x5, the stockholders' equity section of the Broadmoor Corporation's balance sheet was as follows:

Common stock, 400,000 shares, par value, $1	$ 400,000
Additional paid-in capital	3,000,000
Retained earnings	2,700,000
Total	$6,100,000

The following events took place during 19x6, in the sequence given:

1. A cash dividend of 50 cents a share was declared.
2. A stock dividend of 5 percent was declared and issued; the stock was capitalized at the market price of $40 a share.
3. Five thousand shares of stock were repurchased to be held as treasury stock; the cost was $42 a share.
4. Three thousand shares of treasury stock were sold at $45 a share.
5. A contingency reserve of $400,000 was set up for possible future losses on overseas investments.
6. Forty thousand new shares of stock were issued at a price of $48 a share.
7. The stock was split two for one without changing the par value. The treasury shares participated in the split.
8. Net income for 19x6 was $900,000.

a. Enter the opening balances and record the above transactions in appropriate T-accounts.

b. Prepare the owners' equity section of the corporation's balance sheet on December 31, 19x6.

c. How many shares were issued as of December 31, 19x6?

d. How many shares were outstanding as of December 31, 19x6?

e. What was the book value per share on December 31, 19x6?

14. *Series of transactions.* The shareowners' equity section of the Corky Company's balance sheet showed the following amounts on January 1:

Preferred stock, 10,000 shares, $100 par	$ 1,000,000
Common stock, 400,000 shares, no par, stated value, $5	2,000,000
Additional paid-in capital	4,000,000
Retained earnings	8,000,000
Total	$15,000,000

The following transactions affecting the shareholders' equity took place during the year:

Jan. 1   Sale of common stock, 100,000 shares at $12 a share—proceeds received in cash.

Jan. 20   Declaration and payment of cash dividend: common stock, 25 cents a share; preferred stock, $1.50 a share.

Mar. 20   Declaration and distribution of stock dividend, one common share for each 20 common shares outstanding—to be capitalized at the stock's current market price of $18.

Apr. 20   Declaration and payment of cash dividends: 25 cents a share on common stock, $1.50 a share on preferred stock.

Apr. 28   Purchase of 2,000 shares of the company's common stock for cash, $20 per share.

June 1   Repurchase and retirement of preferred stock by cash payment of $110 a share. The stock thus reacquired was canceled, not held as treasury stock.

July 20   Declaration and payment of cash dividends on common stock outstanding, 25 cents a share.

Oct. 20   Declaration and payment of cash dividends on common stock outstanding, 50 cents a share.

Nov. 15   Sale of treasury stock, 2,000 shares at $22 a share.

Dec. 1   Stock split two for one; new stated value, $2.50 a share.

a.   Prepare journal entries to record each of the above transactions.
b.   Present the owners' equity section of the balance sheet as it would appear on December 31 after all of the above transactions were recorded. Net income for the year was $1 million.

15. Effect of conversion on earnings per share.   On February 12, 19x1, the Burgoyne Corporation issued 100,000 shares of $3.50, no-par, convertible preferred stock at an issue price of $55 a share. All shares were paid for in cash. These shares were convertible into common stock (par value, $5 a share) at a rate of 2.5 shares of common stock for each share of preferred. The preferred stock was issued when the banks' prime rate of interest was 5 percent, and it was not regarded as equivalent to common stock in the calculation of primary earnings per share.

The company's earnings increased sharply during the next two years, and, during the second quarter of 19x3, all shares of preferred were converted into common shares. If the conversion had not taken place, the company's primary earnings per share for 19x3 would have amounted to $2. Other data were as follows:

	February 12, 19x1	Second Quarter, 19x3
Market prices:		
Burgoyne common stock	$ 20	$ 40
Burgoyne $3.50 preferred stock	55	110
Index of common stock prices	100	109
Book value per Burgoyne common share (before conversion of preferred)	28	32

a.   What was the effect of the conversion on book values and primary earnings per common share? One million common shares were outstanding prior to the conversion. What was the effect of the conversion on fully diluted earnings per share?
b.   Did the conversion of the preferred shares into common stock lead to a dilution of the common shareholders' equity? Explain your reasoning.
c.   Prepare journal entries to record the issuance and conversion of the preferred stock.

16. Executive stock options.   The stockholders of Topper Corporation voted approval of an executive stock option plan at the annual stockholders' meeting on May 14, 19x0. The vote authorized the board of directors to grant purchase options to key executives up to a maximum of 30,000 shares of the company's previously unissued stock.

The first options were granted on September 10, 19x0. Various executives were given rights to purchase a total of 12,000 shares at $22 a share, the market price of the stock at the close of trading on that date. These options would lapse within two years if they were not exercised.

On June 1, 19x2, officers were given three-year options to buy an additional 15,000 shares at $28 a share, the market price on that date.

Options on 8,000 shares at $22 a share were exercised in November, 19x3. The company's stock was then selling at $36 a share.

In 19x4, the stockholders approved the addition of another 20,000 shares to the stock option plan. In September of that year three-year options were granted on 6,000 shares at $43 a share, the market price at that time.

Options on 4,000 shares at $22 a share and 3,000 shares at $28 a share were exercised in 19x4. The stock was selling at $40 a share at the time.

a. Prepare a footnote to be appended to the 19x0 financial statements, giving adequate disclosure of the stock-option plan. The company's fiscal year ends on December 31 each year.

b. Prepare a footnote on the stock-option plan for the 19x4 financial statements. Explain your reasons for disclosing each item that you have included in your footnote. Why is it important to disclose this information?

c. Did the exercise of the options in 19x3 and 19x4 constitute dilution of the equity? Explain.

d. What was the effect of all the above transactions on the stockholders' equity in Topper Corporation?

15

Investments, Business Combinations, and Segment Reporting

CORPORATIONS CAN MAKE two kinds of investments in securities: (1) investments in bonds and other credit instruments and (2) investments in the stocks of other corporations. Each has its own set of accounting problems, and these problems vary, depending on the purpose for which the investments are made and the degree of influence or control they enable the investor to exert on the investee. We'll study these problems in this chapter, under four major headings:

1. Investments in bonds and notes.
2. Noncontrolling investments in stocks.
3. Controlling investments in stocks.
4. Business combinations.

We'll conclude the chapter with a brief description of the information a multisegment business must disclose about each of its segments.

INVESTMENTS IN BONDS AND NOTES

Corporations may hold the bonds issued by other corporations or by various governmental units. They may also hold short-term government notes, bank certificates of deposit, or commercial paper (promissory notes of corporations with the highest credit ratings). Financial corporations (banks, in particular) also hold the promissory notes of other corporations and individuals. In this section we'll discuss investments nonfinancial corporations make in bonds and notes for two purposes:

1.   Short-term marketable securities.
2.   Bonds held for long-term investment.

Short-Term Marketable Securities

Most bonds, government notes, and commercial paper are marketable, in the sense that brokers, dealers, and other intermediaries stand ready to buy them at some price or locate others who are willing to buy. The term *marketable securities* is usually used by nonfinancial corporations, however, to describe the bonds, notes, and commercial paper they have bought with cash temporarily in excess of current operating needs.

The primary consideration in selecting securities for this purpose is the safety and liquidity of the amount invested. The principal should be readily convertible back into cash without substantial loss or delay; the rate of return on the investment is a secondary consideration. Securities in this group, in other words, are usually securities that either will be or can be sold on short notice at prices not significantly lower than current prices. They are reported as current assets and are ordinarily reported at cost. Interest on these notes and bonds should be accrued unless the amounts are too small to be material.

Long-Term Investments in Bonds

Bonds or notes purchased as long-term investments are measured at their amortized cost. For example, suppose the Granite Corporation bought $10,000 of the XYZ Corporation's 9 percent bonds on July 1, 19x1, five years before their maturity date. The price paid was $10,406, and interest was to be received semiannually, on January 1 and July 1 each year. By consulting Table 9 of Appendix A, we find that the quoted annual yield to maturity on a bond costing $10,406 is 8 percent, meaning that investors can earn 4 percent on their investment every six months, compounded semiannually.

REMINDER: FINDING YIELD TO MATURITY

1.   Select the column in the table in Appendix A corresponding to the coupon rate on the bond and the number of years to maturity.
2.   Locate the row in this table showing the price paid for each $100 of face value—the decimal at the left end of this row is the yield to maturity.

In other words, Granite paid a $406 premium for the privilege of receiving $450 interest every six months for five years, $50 more than the market was providing at the time to investors buying 8 percent bonds at their face value. In calculating interest income every six months, Granite Corporation will recognize that a portion of the $450 is a return of part of the $10,406 investment—that is, interest income is less than $450. Using the effective-interest method we described in Chapter 13, we find that the company earned interest income of 4 percent of $10,406, or $416.24, in the first six months. The amount received from XYZ Corporation was $450, however. The $33.76 difference between these two figures was a repayment of part of the $10,406 Granite paid when it bought the bonds. An appropriate entry to accrue the interest income would have been:

Interest Receivable	450.00	
Interest Income.......................		416.24
Investments		33.76

Receipt of the interest the next day converted the receivable into cash.

CALCULATING INTEREST AND PRINCIPAL ON INVESTMENTS IN BONDS

1. Calculate yield to maturity at the time of purchase.
2. Multiply principal amount at beginning of period by half of this yield percentage—this is interest income for six months.
3. Subtract this amount from the semiannual interest payment—the difference represents a partial repayment of or addition to the amount of the investment.
4. Add or subtract this difference to or from the principal at the beginning of the period—this is the principal at the end of the period.

Gains and Losses on Sales of Notes and Bonds

If a company buys bonds or notes and holds them to maturity, the entire difference between the purchase price and the maturity value is interest income. If the securities are sold prior to maturity, however, part of the difference between the purchase price and the selling price may be a gain or a loss.

For example, suppose the Granite Corporation changed its mind about making the XYZ Corporation bonds a long-term investment and sold them on January 1, 19x2, at a price of $10,456. The investment in the bonds was $10,406 − $33.76 = $10,372.24, so the company would recognize an $83.76 gain on the sale ($10,456 − $10,372.24).

NONCONTROLLING INVESTMENTS IN SHARES OF STOCK

Many corporations own shares of stock in other corporations. In this section we'll examine the problems of accounting for investments in stocks that constitute 50 percent or less of the voting rights of their corporations. We'll consider two types of investments:

1. Long-term investments that don't give their owners significant influence on the investees' actions.
2. Long-term investments that give their owners significant influence on the investees' actions.

Stocks held as short-term investments are encountered so rarely we'll ignore them here. Furthermore, to focus the discussion more clearly, we'll also omit any reference to investments in preferred stocks.

Long-Term Noninfluential Investments in Stocks

Any ownership of less than 50 percent of the voting shares of a corporation is a *minority interest* in that corporation. A company may buy a minority interest in another company as an income-producing investment in and of itself. That is, the future dividends and increases in the market value of the shares are expected to be large enough to justify making the investment. In other cases, the shares purchased may be the first stage in an effort to gain control of the company. That, too, would produce income for the purchaser, but by a different route.

In either case, if the number of shares is small enough relative to the total, the company owning them won't be able to influence the management of the investee significantly. The only question is, how small is "small enough"? The answer depends on the circumstances in each case, but accountants have developed a rule of thumb to help them make this judgment. The rule is that ownership of less than 20 percent of the voting stock should lead to a *presumption* that the investor lacks the ability to have a significant amount of influence on the investee.[1] This presumption will carry the day unless the company's independent public accountants have evidence that the investor is able to exert influence on the investee.

---

[1] APB, "Opinion No. 18," para. 17, in AICPA, *Professional Standards—Accounting, Current Text* (New York: Commerce Clearing House, Inc., 1978), sec. 5131.17.

The reason for making this distinction is that accountants use different methods to account for investments, depending on whether the investor is able to exert a significant amount of influence or control. For stock investments classified as noninfluential (generally, those with less than 20 percent of the voting rights), the investment is measured on a *cost or market basis;* income is measured by the investor's share in the *dividends* declared by the investee, plus or minus any gains or losses on sales of investments.

For example, suppose the National Company bought 10,000 shares of the Local Company's common stock on July 1, 19x1. These shares represented 10 percent of the common stock outstanding, and National paid $30 a share for this investment. The purchase was recorded as follows:

Investments	300,000	
Cash.................................		300,000

Local Company earned $3.25 a share during the second half of 19x1. It declared and paid cash dividends of $1.50 a share during this period. National's accountants recorded its share of the dividends as follows:

Cash....................................	15,000	
Revenues from Investments		15,000

National made no entry to reflect its equity in the rest of Local's $3.25 earnings per share.

The argument for this treatment is that because National didn't own enough shares to influence Local's board of directors, it had no way of increasing the dividend or of making sure the rest of the cash flows from Local's operations were invested profitably, to generate a larger stream of cash flows in the future. The only cash flows National's shareowners could count on were the dividends from Local, nothing more. If no dividends were declared, no investment revenue would be reported.

Long-Term Influential Investments in Stocks

The policy of recognizing only dividends as income has been criticized on the grounds that the shareholders do benefit eventually from the accumulation of retained earnings, because the investment will produce future cash flows at a satisfactory rate. According to this reasoning, a corporation should treat as income the *earnings* on the stock it owns and not merely the dividends declared.

The accounting method reflecting this reasoning is known as the *equity method.* It is used for *influential* investments—that is, those that give the investor a significant influence on the affairs of the investee. This is presumed to be the case if the investor owns 20 percent or more of the voting rights in the latter company.

To illustrate this method, let's suppose the National Company bought 30,000 shares of Local stock on July 1, 19x1, not 10,000 shares, at a price of $30 a share. The entry was:

```
Investments ...........................    900,000
     Cash................................              900,000
```

Earnings per share were $3.25, and cash dividends totaled $1.50 a share in the remainder of 19x1. With 100,000 shares outstanding, Local's total net income was $325,000, and its total dividend was $150,000. These amounts are shown in the box at the bottom of Exhibit 15–1. The volume of the *entire* box represents the net income; the volume of the shaded section stands for the dividends.

National's share in Local's earnings was 30,000 × $3.25 = $97,500, or 30 percent of the total. This is represented by the vol-

EXHIBIT 15–1.   National's Share of Local's Earnings and Dividends

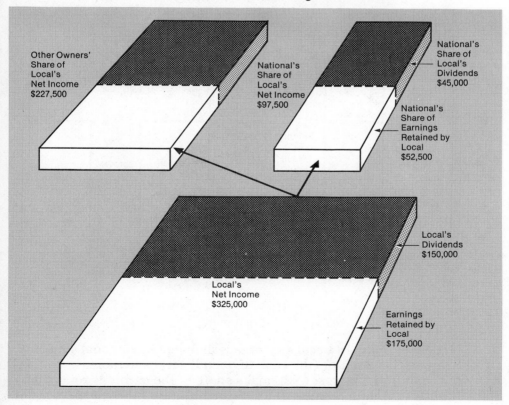

ume of the box in the upper right-hand portion of the exhibit. National's share of the dividends paid by Local was 30,000 × $1.50 = $45,000, represented by the shaded segment of this smaller box.

Under the equity method, National would recognize the following effects on its assets and equities during the final six months of 19x1:

Increase in cash	$45,000
Increase in investments	52,500
Increase in owners' equity as a result of revenues from investments	97,500

In other words, National's equity in the earnings retained by the Local Company (30,000 shares at $1.75 a share) is added to the cost of the investment. The investment at any time thus equals cost at the date of acquisition plus the *subsequent* retained earnings allocable to the shares owned.

The differences between the cost and equity methods are diagrammed in Exhibit 15–2. In the diagram at the left, we see that

EXHIBIT 15–2.   Income and Investment under the Cost and Equity Methods

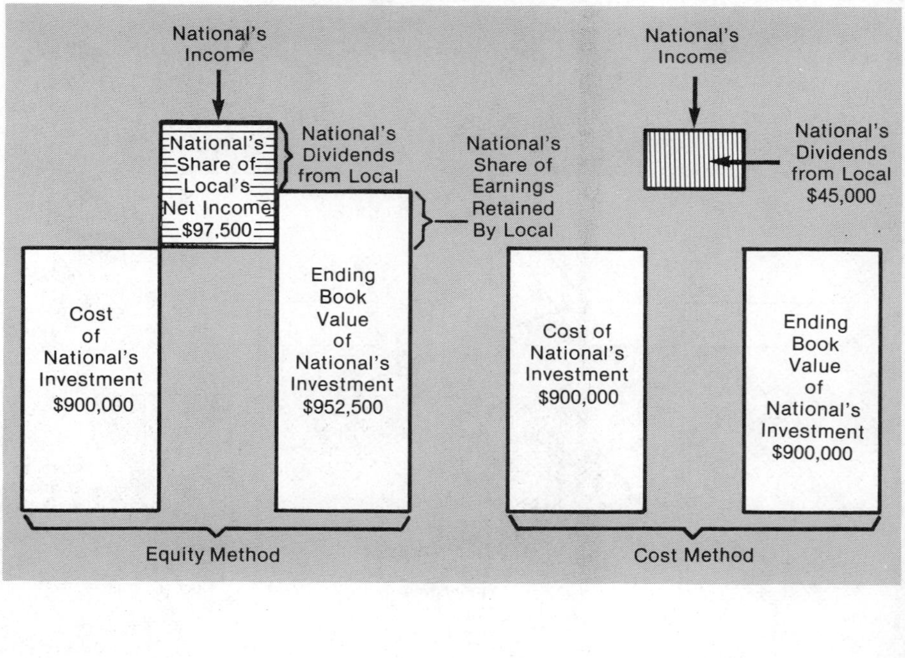

National's share in Local's income is included in National's income. Some of this amount (the cash dividend) serves to increase National's cash flow; the rest (National's share of the earnings retained by Local) is added to National's investment in the block at the right of

this portion of the exhibit.[2] This right-hand block would then appear as the block at the left in a similar diagram drawn for 19x2.

The three blocks at the right of Exhibit 15–2 show how the same data would be treated in the cost method. Only the dividend received would enter National's income for 19x1, and its investment would be carried at cost at the end of the year unless its market value had declined in the interim. The cost method is used for noninfluential investments.

INVESTMENTS IN STOCKS OF SUBSIDIARIES

When a company owns more than 50 percent of the stock in another company, it has a controlling interest in the other company.[3] The former is commonly referred to as the *parent* company, and the controlled company is referred to as its *subsidiary*. In general, the assets, liabilities, and shareowners' equities of the parent and its subsidiaries are combined and reported to the public as a single set of *consolidated* financial statements. In this section we'll try to answer three questions:

1. Why is consolidation appropriate?
2. How do companies decide which of their subsidiaries to include in the consolidation?
3. How can consolidated statements be prepared?

Reasons for Consolidated Statements

A parent company report showing the investment in the subsidiary and the income from it as single figures would be like a company report showing only a total asset figure and a net income figure. In fact, a parent company which is solely a *holding company,* with no direct operations of its own, would present such a report if it reported on a parent-only basis. Its only assets would be its investment in subsidiaries, and its income statement would show merely the subsidiaries' net income figures or the amount of dividends received from them.

Consolidated statements, in contrast, show the income, financial position, and changes in financial position of the group of companies as a whole, as if all transactions had been recorded in a single set of accounts. For example, the consolidated balance sheet will show the

---

[2] If the cost of the shares exceeds the investor's proportionate share of the shareowners' equity in the investee, this difference must be amortized. This amortization process is discussed in the section on business combinations later in this chapter.

[3] Although control often can be exercised with less than a majority ownership, this chapter will identify as subsidiaries only those companies in which the parent owns more than 50 percent of the voting power.

cash balances of the parent and its consolidated subsidiaries as a single figure, representing the sum of the cash balances of the individual companies in the consolidation. Similarly, the sales revenue figure on the consolidated income statement will show the combined sales revenues of all the consolidated companies rather than those of the parent company only.

The argument for preparing consolidated statements is that the investors are placing their trust in the entire group of companies, not just in the parent. The various corporations are separate *legal entities,* but common control serves to merge them into a single *economic entity.* For this economic entity, it is argued, consolidated statements portray overall performance and status more accurately than separate statements for the parent and each subsidiary.

In other words, consolidated statements show the financial relationships of the group of companies as a whole to the outside world; relationships within the group are unimportant for this purpose.

Consolidation Policy

Nonfinancial corporations in the United States sometimes exclude some of their wholly owned subsidiaries from the consolidation. These nonconsolidated subsidiaries fall largely into two categories: (*a*) customer finance companies and (*b*) foreign subsidiaries.

The financial subsidiaries are usually excluded on the ground that their operations are so different from those of the parent that to include them would produce distorted statements. For example, the General Motors Acceptance Corporation (GMAC) was organized to finance consumer purchases of General Motors cars and other products. GMAC assets are almost exclusively the notes of the purchasers of General Motors products, and GMAC finances these assets predominantly by borrowing. Consolidated statements for General Motors and GMAC, therefore, would show a much higher ratio of debt to equity than is typical for a manufacturing firm.

Although a consolidated balance sheet would show a more complete picture of GM's overall financial position, the accounting profession doesn't require consolidation in this case. Instead, General Motors presents separate financial statements for GMAC in its annual report, along with the consolidated statements for the rest of its holdings.

Most companies with foreign operations now consolidate the results of operations and the resources of their foreign subsidiaries with those of the parent for external financial reporting. The main rationale for excluding some foreign subsidiaries is that these subsidiaries' operations are highly regulated, expropriation is a near possibility, or the repatriation of dividends is severely restricted or prohibited.

The exclusion of foreign subsidiaries from the consolidation should be justified by the circumstances of each individual case. A general policy of excluding all foreign subsidiaries may produce misleading financial statements. Corporations with rapidly growing foreign subsidiaries will allow a large fraction of the foreign earnings to remain abroad, while other corporations may be drawing dividends in excess of earnings from their foreign subsidiaries. Hence the dividend is a very poor basis on which to report earnings of most foreign subsidiaries.

The equity method is used to account for a company's investments in any subsidiaries that are not included in the consolidation.

The Consolidated Statement of Financial Position

To consolidate the accounts of parent and subsidiary, the accountant must cancel out the effects of transactions between members of the group. For example, the parent company carries its investment in each subsidiary's common stock in an asset account. The accountant cannot show both the investment and the subsidiary's assets in a consolidated statement because this would count the same set of resources twice.

To show how the accountant avoids this kind of double counting, let us assume that Parent Corporation on January 1, 19x1, purchased 100 percent of the common stock of Subsidiary Corporation (10,000 shares) at a total price of $400,000. At that time Subsidiary had assets with a book value of $500,000 and liabilities of $100,000:

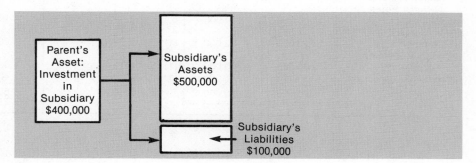

The balance sheet for Subsidiary Corporation, in other words, showed an owners' equity of $400,000, or $40 a share. Since Parent owned all the shares, its equity in Subsidiary was just equal to the amount it paid for the shares ($400,000).

Consolidation in this case is very simple. Subsidiary's $500,000 assets and $100,000 in liabilities are substituted on the consolidated balance sheet for the $400,000 balance in the parent's investment account.

The accountant uses a formal *work sheet* to consolidate the accounts of parent and subsidiaries. No entries are made in the ledger accounts of either parent or subsidiary. One work sheet format lists the accounts of parent and subsidiaries in parallel columns, with all like items (for example, cash in bank) on a single line, followed by two columns for *eliminations*. The amounts entered in the elimination columns are those amounts which should not appear on the consolidated statements. The elimination is performed by crediting the accounts having any unwanted debit balances and debiting accounts with redundant credit balances.

Exhibit 15–3 illustrates this format. Because the consolidated balance sheet should show neither the balance shown in Parent's in-

EXHIBIT 15–3

PARENT CORPORATION AND SUBSIDIARY
Condensed Consolidation Work Sheet
January 1, 19x1

| | Parent | Subsidiary | Eliminations | | Consolidated |
			Debits	Credits	
Assets:					
Investment in					
Subsidiary	400,000	—		(1) 400,000	—
Other assets	5,000,000	500,000			5,500,000
Total	5,400,000	500,000			5,500,000
Liabilities and					
Owners' Equity:					
Liabilities	1,000,000	100,000			1,100,000
Shareholders' equity:					
Common stock	1,200,000	50,000	(1) 50,000		1,200,000
Additional paid-in					
capital	800,000	100,000	(1) 100,000		800,000
Retained earnings	2,400,000	250,000	(1) 250,000		2,400,000
Total	5,400,000	500,000			5,500,000

vestments account nor Subsidiary's shareholders' equity account balances, these amounts must be "eliminated" in the consolidation. The eliminating entry in this exhibit can also be expressed in conventional journal form:

(1)

Common Stock (Subsidiary).............	50,000	
Additional Paid-In Capital (Subsidiary) ...	100,000	
Retained Earnings (Subsidiary)	250,000	
Investment in Subsidiary (Parent) ...		400,000

The net result is to produce a balance sheet representing the combined assets, liabilities, and owners' equities of the economic entity—the resources of the integrated operation under the common control of the owners of the parent company. In this case the total operating assets amount to $5.5 million, not $5.4 million as indicated by the balances in the parent company accounts alone.

Notice that this entry completely eliminates the subsidiary's retained earnings. The consolidated retained earnings at the date of acquisition would be $2.4 million—that is, the retained earnings of Parent Corporation only. This reflects the idea that the retained earnings figure shown on the consolidated balance sheet should represent the earnings accruing to the parent company's shareholders from operations under their control. By purchasing Subsidiary's stock, Parent bought a share of the earnings retained prior to the acquisition, but in no sense did Parent or its shareholders *earn* this amount. Thus consolidated retained earnings represents the retained earnings of the parent company plus the parent's share of any earnings retained by the subsidiary *after* the date of. acquisition.

Minority interests. The foregoing procedure would have to be modified if Parent had purchased less than a 100 percent ownership interest in Subsidiary. For example, suppose Parent had bought only 8,000 shares (an 80 percent interest) for $320,000. A condensed version of its balance sheet immediately after the acquisition is shown in Exhibit 15–4. Parent's total assets are the same as in Exhibit 15–3,

EXHIBIT 15–4

PARENT COMPANY
Statement of Financial Position
January 1, 19x1

Investment in Subsidiary		$ 320,000
Other assets		5,080,000
Total Assets		$5,400,000
Liabilities		$1,000,000
Shareholders' equity:		
Common stock	$1,200,000	
Additional paid-in capital	800,000	
Retained earnings	2,400,000	4,400,000
Total Liabilities and Shareholders' Equity		$5,400,000

but its investment in Subsidiary is smaller, leaving more in other asset categories.

In this situation, the equity of the owners of the 2,000 shares not bought by Parent (the *minority* shareholders) was $80,000—that is, 20 percent of the total owners' equity in Subsidiary, corresponding to their holding of 20 percent of Subsidiary's shares. When the assets, liabilities, and owners' equities of the two companies are consolidated, this amount must be treated as one of the equities.

The consolidation process under these circumstances is illustrated in Exhibit 15–5. First, Parent's investment is offset against its 80

EXHIBIT 15–5

PARENT CORPORATION AND SUBSIDIARY
Condensed Consolidation Work Sheet
January 1, 19x1

	Parent	Subsidiary	Eliminations		Consolidated
			Debits	Credits	
Assets:					
Investment in Subsidiary	320,000	—		(1a) 320,000	—
Other assets	5,080,000	500,000			5,580,000
Total	5,400,000	500,000			5,580,000
Liabilities and Owners' Equity:					
Liabilities	1,000,000	100,000			1,100,000
Shareholders' equity:					
Common stock	1,200,000	50,000	(1a) 40,000 (1b) 10,000		1,200,000
Additional paid-in capital	800,000	100,000	(1a) 80,000 (1b) 20,000		800,000
Retained earnings	2,400,000	250,000	(1a) 200,000 (1b) 50,000		2,400,000
Minority interest	—	—		(1b) 80,000	80,000
Total	5,400,000	500,000			5,580,000

percent equity in Subsidiary:

(1a)

Common Stock	40,000
Additional Paid-In Capital	80,000
Retained Earnings	200,000
Investment in Subsidiary	320,000

An elimination identical to this would be made every time a set of consolidated statements was being prepared, as long as Parent continued to measure its investment in Subsidiary at cost.

The assets, liabilities, and owners' equity could be consolidated at this point without further adjustment, but it is customary to represent the equity of the minority shareholders by a single figure instead of by three figures corresponding to their share of the balances in Subsidiary's three owners' equity accounts. This transfer is made by entry (1b):

(1b)

Common Stock	10,000	
Additional Paid-In Capital................	20,000	
Retained Earnings	50,000	
Minority Interest.....................		80,000

The consolidated balance sheet then would show the figures in the right-hand column of Exhibit 15–5.

Notice that the consolidated list of assets and liabilities includes *all* of the assets and liabilities of Subsidiary, not merely amounts representing Parent's ownership percentage. It does so because Parent's ownership percentage is big enough to give it control over all of Subsidiary's net assets.

Intercompany receivables and payables. Our illustration hasn't provided details on individual assets and liabilities because we wanted to focus attention on the relationships between the parent company's investment and the owners' equity in the subsidiary. These details are important, however, first because they must be used in preparing the consolidated balance sheet and, second, because some of these items are related to each other.

Exhibit 15–6 shows the assets (other than Parent's investment in Subsidiary) and the liabilities of Parent Corporation and its consolidated subsidiary. In general, the consolidated totals can be obtained

EXHIBIT 15–6

PARENT CORPORATION AND SUBSIDIARY CORPORATION
Other Assets and Liabilities
January 1, 19x1

	Parent	Subsidiary
Assets:		
Cash	$ 200,000	$ 90,000
Accounts receivable	500,000	60,000
Notes receivable	60,000	—
Inventory..	940,000	260,000
Investment in nonconsolidated subsidiary	350,000	—
Plant and equipment (cost)	4,480,000	120,000
Less: Accumulated depreciation	(1,450,000)	(30,000)
Total Assets	$5,080,000	$500,000
Liabilities:		
Accounts payable	$ 350,000	$ 40,000
Notes payable	150,000	60,000
Bonds payable	500,000	—
Total Liabilities	$1,000,000	$100,000

by adding across these two columns. Thus the consolidated cash balance was $290,000, the sum of Parent's $200,000 and Subsidiary's $90,000. We have to be careful, however, not to count as assets and liabilities any amounts arising from borrowing/lending transactions between the parent and the subsidiary.

For example, prior to the acquisition of stock, Parent had lent $60,000 to Subsidiary. This amount was included among Parent's assets and among Subsidiary's liabilities. The consolidated group as a whole, however, had neither an asset nor a liability in this amount. The group had no claim on any party outside the group, nor did it have any obligation to make payments to anyone outside the group.

To avoid double counting, in other words, this $60,000 had to be subtracted from both the assets and the liabilities. The eliminating entry was:

Notes Payable (Subsidiary)   60,000
   Notes Receivable (Parent)   60,000

This entry would be entered in the eliminations columns of the work sheet. After this was done, we would have the consolidated balance sheet shown in Exhibit 15–7. Notice that this statement

EXHIBIT 15–7

PARENT CORPORATION AND SUBSIDIARY
Consolidated Statement of Financial Position
January 1, 19x1

Assets:		Liabilities and Owners' Equity:	
Current assets:		Current liabilities:	
Cash	$ 290,000	Accounts payable	$ 390,000
Accounts receivable	560,000	Notes payable	150,000
Inventories	1,200,000		
Total Current Assets ..	$2,050,000	Total Current Liabilities	$ 540,000
Investment in nonconsoli-		Bonds payable	500,000
dated subsidiary	350,000	Total Liabilities ...	$1,040,000
Plant and equipment	4,600,000	Minority interest	80,000
Less: Accumulated		Shareowners' equity:	
depreciation	(1,480,000)	Common stock	1,200,000
		Additional paid-in	
		capital	800,000
		Retained earnings	2,400,000
Total Assets	$5,520,000	Total Liabilities and Owners' Equity .	$5,520,000

shows no notes receivable at all, because the only note receivable in either company was Subsidiary Corporation's $60,000 note to Parent. Similarly, consolidated notes payable amounted to only $150,000, the amount of Parent's note to an outside party.

The only other item we need to mention is Parent's investment in a nonconsolidated subsidiary. As we said before, these are rare, but Parent had a wholly owned subsidiary in a highly unstable foreign country. The assets and liabilities of this company were left out of the consolidation; instead, the investment in the subsidiary was shown on the consolidated balance sheet, measured by the equity method.

The Consolidated Income Statement

Income statement consolidation is based on the same principles. The income statement for the parent company alone may have a separate legal significance, but as long as the earnings of the subsidiaries are subject to the parent's control, it is the total controlled earnings that parent company investors are interested in.

Exhibit 15–8 shows the separate income statements of Parent Corporation and its subsidiary, Subsidiary Corporation, for the year

EXHIBIT 15–8

PARENT CORPORATION AND SUBSIDIARY CORPORATION
Statements of Income and Dividends
For the Year Ended December 31, 19x1

	Parent		Subsidiary	
Revenue from sales		$7,500,000		$700,000
Revenue from dividends		28,000		—
Total Revenue		$7,528,000		$700,000
Cost of goods sold	$4,700,000		$500,000	
Other expenses	1,900,000		150,000	
Total Expense		6,600,000		650,000
Net income		$ 928,000		$ 50,000
Dividends declared		500,000		35,000
Net Addition to Retained Earnings		$ 428,000		$ 15,000

following the acquisition. This exhibit will be the basis for our discussion of three items:

1. Intercorporate dividends.
2. Minority interests in consolidated net income.
3. Intercompany sales.

Intercorporate dividends. The $28,000 shown on Parent's statement as revenue from investments represents dividends received from Subsidiary. To avoid double counting, this amount must be eliminated in the consolidation.[4] In the absence of any other adjustments, therefore, consolidated net income would be as follows:

Parent Corporation income	$928,000
Subsidiary Corporation income	50,000
Less: Parent Corporation's share in Subsidiary Corporation's dividends	(28,000)
Consolidated Income before Minority Interest	$950,000

Minority interest income.   Not all of the consolidated net income was assignable to the equity of Parent's shareholders. The minority shareholders had a 20 percent share in Subsidiary's net income, or $10,000. The net income applicable to Parent's shareholders was thus $950,000 less $10,000, or $940,000. This is reflected in Exhibit 15–9.

EXHIBIT 15–9

PARENT CORPORATION AND SUBSIDIARY
Consolidated Income Statement
For the Year Ended December 31, 19x1

Revenue from sales		$8,200,000
Less: Cost of goods sold	$5,200,000	
Other expenses	2,050,000	
Total Expenses		7,250,000
Income before minority interest		$ 950,000
Less: Equity of minority shareholders in net income of Subsidiary		10,000
Net Income		$ 940,000
Dividends declared		500,000
Net Addition to Retained Earnings		$ 440,000

The consolidated retained earnings at the end of the year, therefore, amounted to the $2.4 million opening balance, plus the $440,000 net addition to retained earnings in 19x1 (from Exhibit 15–9), or $2.84 million. This was the total of Parent's own retained earnings, plus its equity in the earnings of Subsidiary *since the date of the acquisition.*

The minority interest in the consolidated net assets at the end of the year was $83,000, calculated as follows:

Minority interest, beginning of year (Exhibit 15–7)	$80,000
Add: Equity of minority shareholders in net income of Subsidiary	10,000
Less: Dividends paid by Subsidiary to minority shareholders	(7,000)
Minority interest, end of year	$83,000

---

[4] If Parent Corporation took up its full equity in Subsidiary's earnings as its revenue from investments, then the amount shown on its income statement would be 80 percent of $50,000, or $40,000. In that case, this is the amount that would have to be eliminated in the consolidation.

The work sheet entry to concentrate the minority interest in Subsidiary in a single number is the same as at the beginning of the year, except that the minority interest in Subsidiary's retained earnings was $3,000 greater at the end of the year:

Common Stock (Subsidiary)..............	10,000	
Additional Paid-In Capital (Subsidiary) ...	20,000	
Retained Earnings (Subsidiary)	53,000	
Minority Interest.....................		83,000

Intercompany sales. Exhibit 15–9 reflects the assumption that neither company bought any goods or services from the other during the year. All sales were to customers outside the consolidated entity, and consolidated sales revenue, cost of goods sold, and other expenses could be determined simply by adding together the figures for the two companies, without elimination of any kind.

This isn't always the case. For example, suppose a parent company sold merchandise costing $70,000 to its wholly owned subsidiary for $100,000. The parent would recognize a $30,000 gross margin on this transaction. For the group as a whole, however, the transaction created neither income nor loss. No matter how many sales the two companies make to each other, the parent company stockholders gain nothing unless sales are made to outsiders. In other words, to avoid double counting, all intrafirm sales and purchases, like intrafirm receivables and payables, must be netted out.

In this case, the parent company's statements included $100,000 in sales revenues from merchandise that was never sold outside the group. Its cost of goods sold included the $70,000 cost of this merchandise. The subsidiary had an inventory on its books at a recorded cost of $100,000, the amount it had been billed by the parent.

All of these figures have to be corrected. To do this, let's examine only one small portion of the company's consolidation work sheet, using a set of assumed numbers for the unadjusted balances:

	Parent	Subsidiary	Eliminations Debits	Eliminations Credits	Consolidated
Inventory..............	900,000	320,000		30,000	1,190,000
Sales revenues	7,500,000	700,000	100,000		8,100,000
Cost of goods sold	4,700,000	500,000		70,000	5,130,000

This elimination reduced consolidated sales revenues by $100,000, consolidated cost of goods sold by $70,000, and consolidated inventory by $30,000, bringing it back to a cost basis.

Suppose the subsidiary had sold this merchandise before the end of the year, however. The sales were to outside customers, and the price was $120,000. The subsidiary, in other words, recognized a

$20,000 gross margin on the sale. In total, the two companies' records of these two transactions showed the following:

	Parent	Subsidiary	Total
Sales revenues	$100,000	$120,000	$220,000
Cost of goods sold	70,000	100,000	170,000
Gross Margin	$ 30,000	$200,000	$ 50,000

The total gross margin figure in the right-hand column is correct: the total gross margin on these sales is the difference between the revenues from sales to outsiders ($120,000) and the cost of this merchandise to the parent company ($70,000). Total sales revenues, however, amounted to $120,000, not $220,000. Similarly, the cost of goods sold was only $70,000, not $170,000. In this situation, an eliminating entry is required to eliminate the overstatement in both items:

Sales Revenues	100,000	
Cost of Goods Sold		100,000

BUSINESS COMBINATIONS

A special problem arises at the time the assets or stock of one corporation are exchanged for the stock of another. Exchanges of this sort are known generally as *business combinations,* and two different methods are used to account for them, depending on the circumstances: (1) purchase method and (2) pooling-of-interests method.

Purchase Method: Acquisition for Cash

The main characteristic of the purchase method is that it recognizes two separate totals, which may not be equal: (1) the cost incurred by the purchaser to acquire the stock of the acquired company and (2) the purchaser's share of the net assets and shareowners' equity of the acquired company. To see what effect differences in these two totals have, let's study a situation in which the acquiring company uses cash to pay for the stock of the acquired company. The purchase method is always used when one corporation acquires the stock of another corporation in exchange for the acquiring corporation's cash or other assets.

Parent Corporation, the acquiring company in our illustrations in the preceding section, used the purchase method to account for its acquisition of its shares of Subsidiary Corporation's stock. To get a better understanding of the purchase method, however, let's suppose Parent paid $55 a share for 8,000 shares of Subsidiary Corporation stock. This was $15 a share greater than the book value of these shares on Subsidiary's books at the date of acquisition.

The $440,000 Parent paid for its 8,000 shares of Subsidiary's stock was $120,000 more than the book value of the equity acquired (8,000 shares × $15 a share). We'll refer to this temporarily as Parent's share of Subsidiary's goodwill:

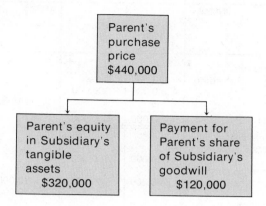

Parent recorded no goodwill in its own books, however. Instead, it recorded the full $440,000 purchase price as the cost of its investment in Subsidiary. Parent Corporation's own balance sheet immediately after the acquisition contained the figures shown in the first column of Exhibit 15–10. The figures in the second column of this exhibit are from Subsidiary Corporation's balance sheet on that date.

We need two eliminating entries this time. The first one is to remove the $440,000 investment and Parent's 80 percent share of Subsidiary's owners' equity:

	Subsidiary's Owners' Equity	Parent's Share (80%)
Common stock	$ 50,000	$ 40,000
Additional paid-in capital	100,000	80,000
Retained earnings	250,000	200,000
Total	$400,000	$320,000

The $120,000 difference between $320,000 and $440,000, as we saw before, is the amount Parent paid for a share in Subsidiary's goodwill. Our elimination entry, therefore, will have to set this up as an asset if we want the balance sheet to reflect the cost of all assets Parent bought. The entry is:

(1)

Goodwill	120,000	
Common Stock (Subsidiary)	40,000	
Additional Paid-In Capital (Subsidiary)	80,000	
Retained Earnings (Subsidiary)	200,000	
Investment in Subsidiary		440,000

EXHIBIT 15–10

PARENT CORPORATION AND SUBSIDIARY
Consolidation Work Sheet—Purchase Method
January 1, 19x1

	Parent	Subsidiary	Eliminations		Con-solidated
			Debits	Credits	
Assets					
Investment in Subsidiary	440,000	—		(1) 440,000	—
Other assets	4,960,000	500,000			5,460,000
Goodwill	—	—	(1) 120,000		120,000
Total	5,400,000	500,000			5,580,000
Liabilities and Owners Equity					
Liabilities	1,000,000	100,000			1,100,000
Shareholders' equity:					
Common stock	1,200,000	50,000	(1) 40,000 (2) 10,000		1,200,000
Additional paid-in capital	800,000	100,000	(1) 80,000 (2) 20,000		800,000
Retained earnings	2,400,000	250,000	(1) 200,000 (2) 50,000		2,400,000
Minority interest	—	—		(2) 80,000	80,000
Total	5,400,000	500,000			5,580,000

To repeat, this entry is made in neither company's ledger—the only place it appears is on the consolidation work sheet, and the only statement the goodwill appears in is the consolidated balance sheet. It would probably be listed under some caption such as "investment in subsidiary in excess of equity in tangible assets."

The second eliminating entry is one we saw before, to put the entire minority interest in Subsidiary's owners' equity under a single heading:

(2)

Common Stock (Subsidiary)..............	10,000	
Additional Paid-in Capital (Subsidiary) ...	20,000	
Retained Earnings (Subsidiary)	50,000	
Minority Interest.....................		80,000

The consolidated balance sheet would then reflect the figures shown in the right-hand column of Exhibit 15–10.

Notice what we've done in this consolidation. We've taken out the $440,000 investment asset and substituted the following, which net out at $440,000:

Assets:

Tangible assets	$500,000
Goodwill	120,000
Total Assets	$620,000

Liabilities and Minority Interest:

Liabilities	$100,000	
Minority interest	80,000	
Total Liabilities and Minority Interest		$180,000

Amortization of goodwill. The price Parent paid for its share of Subsidiary's stock exceeded the book value of the underlying equity by $120,000. Although it can be argued that with proper care Parent can maintain the economic value of Subsidiary's goodwill indefinitely, the required practice in the United States is to amortize purchased goodwill systematically over a period not to exceed 40 years.[5] The reasoning is that the factors that created the goodwill will disappear gradually, perhaps to be replaced by others, perhaps not. Since the original goodwill will dissipate gradually, its cost should be amortized gradually.

Parent decided on a 20-year amortization period, leading to an amortization of $6,000 a year. Thus, in consolidation, $6,000 had to be deducted from revenues for the year and from the balance sheet figure for goodwill. This reduced the consolidated net income figure to $934,000.

Appraisal values. The method of accounting for the acquisition would have to be modified slightly if appraisals revealed that the fair value of the acquired company's net tangible assets was greater or less than the amounts at which they were carried on the acquired company's books. In such cases, the appraised values should be substituted for the reported amounts.

For example, suppose an appraisal indicated that Subsidiary's assets had a fair value of $550,000 at the time Parent bought its shares. The fair value of the liabilities was $100,000. These appraisals would change three figures:

1. Individual tangible assets would be restated at their appraised values in the consolidated balance sheet.
2. The minority interest would be 20 percent of $550,000 − $100,000, or $90,000 (instead of $80,000, as before).
3. Goodwill would be the excess of the $440,000 cost over 80 percent of $550,000 − $100,000, or $80,000, instead of $120,000 as before.

Negative goodwill. A corporation's equity in a controlled subsidiary may have been purchased at a price per share *less than* the

---

[5] APB, "Opinion No. 17," para. 29 in AICPA, *Professional Standards—Accounting*, sec. 5141.29.

fair value of the subsidiary's net assets. Sometimes this means that the stock was obtained at a bargain price, far less than its true worth, but, in general, the implication is that the subsidiary was worth less than the fair value of its net assets. The amount of this difference is known as *negative goodwill.*

Current practice is to deduct the negative goodwill from the calculated cost of the noncurrent assets. If the cost assigned to the noncurrent assets is less than the amount of the negative goodwill, the difference is shown as a "deferred credit" to be amortized over a period not to exceed 40 years.[6] "Deferred credits" are typically shown on the balance sheet either as liabilities or in a separate category between the liabilities and the owners' equity. In this case, however, it would seem more logical to show the unamortized negative goodwill, if any, as a deduction from the consolidated asset total.

Purchase Method: Acquisition by Exchange of Stock

The purchase method is also used in some circumstances when stock is acquired in exchange for shares of stock of the acquiring corporation. This presents only one additional problem: how to measure the cost of the investment?

The accepted rule is to measure the cost of the investment either by the fair value of the stock given up or by the fair value of the stock acquired, whichever is more clearly evident.[7] When the acquiring company's stock is traded actively, the market price of this stock is usually the best evidence of market value available. For example, instead of paying cash for its 80 percent interest in Subsidiary Corporation, Parent issued 10,000 new shares of its own $10 par common stock, which then had a market value of $44 a share. The acquisition was recorded on Parent's books as follows:

Investment in Subsidiary	440,000	
Common Stock		100,000
Additional Paid-In Capital............		340,000

The consolidation then proceeds in the usual manner.

Pooling of Interests

The amortization of goodwill under the purchase method reduces reported income. The impact is even greater because amortization of goodwill is not recognized as an expense for tax purposes. This means that the *full* amount of the amortization is a deduction from

---

[6] Ibid., "Opinion No. 16," para. 91, sec. 1091.91.
[7] Ibid., para. 67, sec. 1091.67.

net income. If earnings are not exceptionally high otherwise, the amortization may convert an apparently favorable financial record into a picture embarrassing to management.

This provides a substantial incentive for the merging corporations to structure the exchange of stock so that the transaction can be regarded as a *pooling of interests*. In a pooling of interests, it is assumed that the operations of the combining corporations are continued in the joint enterprise. The recorded costs of the assets of the constituent companies prior to the pooling remain the basis for measurement in the consolidated statements. No additional goodwill is recognized.

The pooling-of-interests method is to be used only when the acquisition satisfies a number of conditions, of which the following are the most important:[8]

1. Each of the combining corporations is independent of the other.
2. The combination is effected by a single stock transaction, and the stock issued and accepted must be identical with already-outstanding voting common stock of the acquiring corporation.
3. Substantially all of the pooled company's stock (at least 90 percent) is obtained in exchange for stock of the acquiring corporation.
4. The acquiring corporation expects to continue the operation and activities of the pooled corporation.

To illustrate this method, let us assume that all of the shares of Subsidiary's stock were exchanged for 10,000 shares of Parent's stock. The accounting assumption underlying the pooling method is that both companies pool their assets, their liabilities, their paid-in capital, and their retained earnings. This means that the paid-in capital of both companies constitutes the paid-in capital of the pooled group; consolidated retained earnings is the sum of the retained earnings of the combined companies. Because Subsidiary's paid-in capital amounted to $150,000, this was the amount to be added to Parent's paid-in capital in consolidation. With Parent's stock at a par value of $10 a share, Subsidiary's paid-in capital was added to Parent's as follows:

Common stock	$100,000
Additional paid-in capital	50,000

The full $250,000 balance in Subsidiary's retained earnings account was included in the consolidated retained earnings at the time of acquisition.

---

[8] Ibid., paras. 45–49, sec. 1091.45–49.

In other words, the assets, liabilities, and owners' equity of the two companies were added together as follows:

	Parent	Subsidiary	Consolidated
Assets	$5,400,000	$500,000	$5,900,000
Liabilities	$1,000,000	$100,000	$1,100,000
Shareholders' equity:			
Common stock	1,200,000	100,000	1,300,000
Additional paid-in capital	800,000	50,000	850,000
Retained earnings	2,400,000	250,000	2,650,000
Total	$5,400,000	$500,000	$5,900,000

The total paid-in capital was $2.15 million, just equal to the combined paid-in capital of the two companies prior to the pooling ($2,000,000 + $150,000). Similarly, the combined retained earnings was the sum of the retained earnings of the constituent companies.

The distribution of Subsidiary's paid-in capital between Parent's common stock and additional paid-in capital is governed by the number and par value of Parent's shares issued in the pooling. In the illustration, the par value of Subsidiary's stock was $50,000, but it was exchanged for Parent Corporation stock with a par value of $100,000. This required a transfer of $50,000 from consolidated additional paid-in capital to the common stock. The total paid-in capital remained unchanged, however.

FINANCIAL REPORTING FOR BUSINESS SEGMENTS

The merits of consolidated financial statements have become so widely recognized in the United States that advocates of reporting on a parent-company-only basis are hard to find. Many business corporations have extended their operations into many different products and markets, however, and these companies are now required to provide separate financial information for each of their major lines of business, *in addition to* consolidated statements.

Arguments for Separate Disclosure

The basic argument for the disclosure of separate financial information for each segment of a multisegment corporation is that investors need such information to evaluate the past properly and forecast the future. For instance, a given net income figure combines the results of profitable and unprofitable business segments. If these are developing at different rates, the outsider will be hard pressed to identify the component trends on which forecasts of the future need to be based.

A second argument is that diversification has specific benefits as well as costs, and that to evaluate the company's management the investor is entitled to know something about the company's efforts to diversify. As one writer suggests, "It is . . . fair to assume that investors would want to measure both flexibility achieved and its cost in terms of profits forgone in order to avoid undervaluation of their investment."[9]

Required Disclosure

The accounting profession has decided, in the light of the above arguments, to require disclosure of certain information about the segments of multisegment businesses.[10] The criteria used to decide which segments require separate reporting leave management a good deal of room for judgment. The Financial Accounting Standards Board recognized the difficulties to be overcome in determining in a precise fashion what, in fact, constitute independent business segments and the portion of the company's costs that should be assigned to each; these questions were left to the corporations themselves, subject to certain guidelines.

Briefly stated, a *reportable segment* (a segment requiring separate reporting) is a significant component of an enterprise providing related products or services primarily to unaffiliated customers. Reportable segments are identified by (*a*) grouping products or services on a worldwide basis into industry segments and (*b*) determining which of these industry segments is of significant size. (A significant segment is one that represents at least 10 percent of combined revenue, profits or losses, or assets). Industry segments can be identified in any of three ways:

1. Segments producing related products or services that have similar purposes or end uses and, consequently, similar degrees of risk, profitability, and opportunity for growth.
2. Segments sharing common or interchangeable production or sales facilities, equipment, labor force, or raw materials.
3. Segments that are similar in geographic marketing areas, types of customers, or marketing methods.

The information to be disclosed for each reportable segment includes revenues, operating profit or loss, identifiable assets, and

---

[9] Leopold Schachner, "Corporate Diversification in Financial Reporting," *Journal of Accountancy*, April 1967, pp. 43–50.

[10] FASB, Statement No. 14, in AICPA, *Professional Standards—Accounting*, sec. 2081.

other related disclosures such as depreciation and capital expenditures. In determining the operating profit or loss, the company's operating costs are to be divided among the segments on the same bases used for internal reporting and decision-making purposes in the company.

In addition to the information on industry segments, companies are required to disclose information on their foreign operations by geographic areas, including data on revenues, profit or loss, and identifiable assets. Moreover, each enterprise is to report its export sales separately if they constitute at least 10 percent of consolidated revenue. If 10 percent or more of total revenue is derived from sales to a single customer, domestic government agencies, or foreign governments, these facts and amounts should also be disclosed.

SUMMARY

Nonfinancial corporations often hold government and commercial securities as a means of earning a return on temporarily idle funds. Securities held for this purpose ordinarily earn relatively low yields but are highly liquid. They are called *marketable securities.* Most of these temporary investments are in notes, bonds, or other credit instruments with relatively early maturities, and these are stated at their costs.

A company's primary motive for holding securities for longer-term investment is to produce income, and short-term marketability is seldom a consideration. When these investments are too small to give their owners any significant influence over the companies they represent, they are stated at the lower of cost or market. When the investments are large enough to give their owners some influence but not control, they are reported on an equity basis. That is, the investor reports as investment revenue the proportionate share of the investee's earnings, not just the dividends received, and measures the investment at cost plus the investor's equity in the investee's retained earnings since the acquisition was made.

When an investment constitutes a majority of the voting power in the other corporation, the holder is referred to as a parent company. Its financial statements will ordinarily represent the consolidated results and position of parent and subsidiary combined. This means, for example, that instead of an "investments" figure on the balance sheet, the assets and liabilities of the subsidiary will be merged with those of the parent.

Companies are now required to supplement their consolidated financial statements by publishing information on the results of individual segments of the business, foreign operations, export sales, and sales to major customers.

KEY TERMS

Business combinations
Business segment
Consolidated financial
  statements
Eliminations
Equity method
Goodwill

Intercompany transactions
Marketable securities
Minority interest
Pooling-of-interests method
Purchase method
Reportable segment

INDEPENDENT STUDY PROBLEMS (Solutions in Appendix B)

1. Minority investment. The Cantara Company on January 1, 19x1, bought 2,500 shares of the common stock of the Denby Corporation. These shares constituted 25 percent of Denby's outstanding common shares. Cantara paid $30 a share for this stock.

Denby reported a net income of $30,000 in 19x1 and declared dividends of $1.60 a share on its common stock.

a. How much investment income should Cantara report in 19x1 from its investment in Denby?

b. At what amount should Cantara report its investment in Denby on its December 31, 19x1, balance sheet?

2. Intercompany transactions. Alcon Corporation owns 100 percent of the shares of Nonon Company. In 19x1 the two companies had the following income:

	Alcon	Nonon
Sales revenues	$5,000,000	$1,000,000
Investment income (from Nonon)	50,000	—
Cost of goods sold	(3,000,000)	(700,000)
Other expenses	(1,500,000)	(200,000)
Net Income	$ 550,000	$ 100,000

You have the following additional information:

1. The price Alcon paid for Nonon's shares was equal to the appraised value of Nonon's net assets at the time the shares were bought.
2. Nonon sold merchandise to Alcon for $250,000 during 19x1. This merchandise had cost Nonon $180,000.
3. Alcon's inventory on December 31, 19x1, included $100,000 of merchandise bought from Nonon. Nonon's cost of this merchandise was $70,000.
4. On December 31, 19x1, Alcon owed Nonon $35,000 for merchandise purchases. This amount was included in Alcon's accounts payable and in Nonon's accounts receivable.
5. Income tax effects of intercompany transactions can be ignored.

a. Prepare a consolidated income statement for Alcon Corporation and its subsidiary for the year 19x1.
b. Prepare appropriate elimination entries to reflect the information supplied above.

3. 100 percent ownership; goodwill.   On January 1, 19x4, the Wolfe Corporation bought all the outstanding common stock of the Lamb Company (1,000 shares), at a price of $95 a share, paid in cash. The appraised value of Lamb's tangible assets at that time equalled their book value.

Lamb had a net income of $15,000 in 19x4, but declared no dividends during the year. On December 31, 19x4, the Wolfe Corporation's retained earnings amounted to $190,000. Its own accounts showed its investment in Lamb at $95,000. The shareowners' equity section of the Lamb Company's balance sheet on December 31, 19x4, was as follows:

Common stock	$90,000
Retained earnings (deficit)	(5,000)
Total	$85,000

No additional purchases or sales of common stock took place during 19x4, and no adjustments to retained earnings other than net income and dividends were made during the year.

In preparing consolidated statements, Wolfe decided to amortize goodwill at a straight-line rate of 10 percent a year.

a. Calculate the shareowners' equity in the Lamb Company on January 1, 19x4.
b. Calculate the amount of purchased goodwill on January 1, 19x4.
c. Identify the eliminations Wolfe would have to make in preparing a consolidated balance sheet as of December 31, 19x4.
d. Calculate consolidated retained earnings on December 31, 19x4.

4. Calculating consolidated income, retained earnings, and minority interest.   Company X purchased an 80 percent interest in Company Y on January 1, 19x2. The price was $80,000, paid in cash, and the purchase was recorded in the Investments account of Company X. The appraised value of Y's tangible assets was equal to their book value at the time the stock was bought.

The directors of Company Y declared cash dividends in the amount of $10,000 during 19x2.

When Company X received its share of Company Y's dividends, it debited Cash and credited Dividend Income. Company X's unconsolidated reported earnings for 19x2 amounted to $55,000, including dividend income. No other transactions between Company X and Company Y took place during the year.

Company X declared cash dividends of $30,000 during 19x2.

The stockholders' equity sections of the beginning and ending balance sheets of the two corporations showed the following:

	Company X		Company Y	
	1/1/x2	12/31/x2	1/1/x2	12/31/x2
Common stock	$100,000	$100,000	$ 30,000	$ 30,000
Premium on common stock	20,000	20,000	10,000	10,000
Retained earnings	375,000	400,000	60,000	65,000
Total	$495,000	$520,000	$100,000	$105,000

Goodwill, if any, was to be amortized in 20 equal annual installments.

a. Calculate consolidated net income for 19x2.
b. At what amount would the minority interest be reported on the December 31, 19x2, consolidated balance sheet?
c. Show the stockholders' equity section of the consolidated balance sheet as of December 31, 19x2.

5. Purchase or pooling? Two companies had the following balance sheets on December 31, 19x1:

	Company X	Company Y
Current assets	$ 5,500	$1,000
Plant and equipment, net	7,000	1,700
Total	$12,500	$2,700
Current liabilities	$ 2,500	$ 500
Common stock ($5 par)	2,000	250
Additional paid-in capital	3,000	750
Retained earnings	5,000	1,200
Total	$12,500	$2,700

These balance sheets included $200 that Company Y owed Company X for goods Company Y purchased during 19x1 and sold to its customers.

These two companies merged on January 1, 19x2, Company X issuing 100 shares of its common stock in exchange for all of the common shares of Company Y. The fair value of a share of Company X's stock at that time was $30.

In 19x2, Company X reported unconsolidated net income of $1,000, including $100 in cash dividends from Company Y. Company X paid $400 in cash dividends to its shareholders. Company Y reported unconsolidated net income of $180. No intercompany sales were made during the year, and the $200 beginning-of-year debt was paid by Company Y during the year.

The appraised value of Company Y's tangible assets was equal to their book value on the date of the merger. As a matter of policy, X's directors insist that any purchased goodwill be amortized in 20 equal annual installments.

a. Should the merger have been accounted for as a purchase or as a pooling of interests? Explain why.
b. Prepare a consolidated balance sheet immediately after the merger.
c. Calculate consolidated net income for the year 19x2.

d. Prepare the owners' equity section of the consolidated balance sheet at December 31, 19x2.

e. How would your answers to (b) and (c) have differed if you had answered (a) differently?

EXERCISES AND PROBLEMS

6. Pooling versus purchase: discussion question. Company P has just acquired all of the assets of Company Q by an exchange of stock. Company Q has achieved a notable rate of growth in recent years, both in sales and in earnings, and its stock has been selling at market prices considerably in excess of its book value. The financial statements of Company P are footnoted to indicate that this acquisition was treated as a pooling of interests.

In what ways would next year's reported net income and the end-of-year balance sheet have differed if the acquisition had been treated as a purchase rather than as a pooling of interests?

7. Measurement basis: minority investment. The market price of the common stock of Epstein Drugs had ranged from $23 to $35 a share during 19x1 and 19x2. Its price in January 19x3 was $32. At that point, Harlow Enterprises offered to buy any or all of the common shares of Epstein Drugs at a price of $40 a share. Epstein's management advised its shareholders to reject this offer, saying the company was worth more than $40 a share, but 350,000 shares were sold to Harlow at that price. Epstein had 1 million shares outstanding at that time.

At the time Harlow made these purchases, Epstein's shareowners' equity was as follows:

Common stock, $5 par	$ 5,000,000
Additional paid-in capital	8,000,000
Retained earnings	4,000,000
Total	$17,000,000

During 19x3, Epstein had a net income of $5 a share and distributed cash dividends of $3 a share.

a. Calculate Harlow's investment income in 19x3 from its ownership of Epstein shares. Harlow amortizes goodwill in 40 equal annual installments.

b. At what amount should Harlow report its investment in Epstein on its December 31, 19x3, balance sheet?

c. An investment analyst commented that consolidated financial statements for Harlow would have been more meaningful than the statements it actually issued. How would consolidated statements differ from nonconsolidated statements? State your reasons for agreeing or disagreeing with the analyst.

8. Consolidated sales and cost of goods sold. On March 1, 19x1, Company P sold merchandise to its wholly owned subsidiary for $120. Company P had bought this merchandise on February 1, 19x1, for $80. The subsidiary paid Company P on April, 19x1, and sold the merchandise on account to an outside customer for $150 on December 15, 19x9.

a. How were these transactions reflected in the unconsolidated income statements for Company P and its subsidiary for the year ended December 31, 19x1?

b. How should these transactions be reflected in the company's consolidated income statement for the year? Prepare a worksheet elimination entry to produce this result.

c. How would your answers to (a) and (b) have differed if the merchandise had remained in the subsidiary's inventory on December 31, 19x1?

9. Goodwill; minority interest. On December 31, 19x1, the Pilot Company paid $92,000 in cash for an 80 percent interest in the Essex Company. The Essex balance sheet on that date showed the following balances in the shareholders' equity:

Common stock	$ 40,000
Additional paid-in capital	20,000
Retained earnings	50,000
Total	$110,000

The appraised value of Essex's tangible assets was equal to their book value on the date of acquisition.

a. What was the amount of the goodwill on the date of the purchase?
b. What was the amount of the minority interest on this date?

10. Business combination: alternative methods. On December 31, 19x5, the Ajax Company purchased 8,000 shares of the common stock of the Achilles Company from John and Alfred Achilles, the majority shareholders. The purchase price was $11 a share, paid in cash. These shares constituted 80 percent of the Achilles Company's outstanding common stock. The Achilles Company balance sheet on that date showed the following balances in its stockholders' equity accounts:

Common stock	$ 60,000
Additional paid-in capital	10,000
Retained earnings	50,000
Total	$120,000

The Achilles Company had only one asset, the patent rights to a hair-coloring compound, listed on the December 31, 19x5, balance sheet at $120,000. The company had no liabilities on that date.

a. Show how the assets and owners equity of the Achilles Company would appear on the Ajax Company's consolidated balance sheet on January 1, 19x6, immediately after the purchase.

b. What alternative accounting treatment(s) did you consider? Give your reasons in favor of the treatment you selected.

11. Consolidated net income, minority interest, retained earnings. The Homer Company bought 8,000 shares of the common stock of the Cicero

Corporation on December 31, 19x3. The purchase price was $12 a share, paid in cash. These shares constituted 80 percent of the Cicero Corporation's outstanding common stock. Cicero's balance sheet on that date showed the following shareholders' equity:

Common stock	$ 60,000
Additional paid-in capital	25,000
Retained earnings	35,000
Total	$120,000

The appraised value of Cicero's assets was equal to their book value on the date of the acquisition.

In 19x4, the Cicero Corporation had net income of $30,000 and paid $20,000 in dividends to its stockholders. The Homer Company's net income for the year amounted to $50,000, including dividends from Cicero. Neither company included any intercompany profit in the inventory it reported at the end of the year.

a.   What was the amount of the consolidated net income for 19x4, after providing for minority interests?

b.   At what amount would minority interest be shown on the December 31, 19x4, consolidated balance sheet?

c.   How much of Cicero's retained earnings would be shown in consolidated retained earnings as of December 31, 19x4?

12.   Business combination: alternative methods.   Company A and Company B were two completely independent companies. Neither had invested in the other; neither had ever bought goods or services from the other. These two companies merged with each other at the beginning of this year. Immediately before the merger, their balance sheets showed the following:

	Company A	Company B
Cash	$290	$ 30
Other current assets	90	60
Property and equipment (net)	120	60
Total	$500	$150
Liabilities	$100	$ 50
Common stock	50	15
Additional paid-in capital	150	45
Retained earnings	200	40
Total	$500	$150

The amounts shown for common stock were the total par values of the shares.

a.   Assume Company A purchased the net assets of Company B for $160 cash and operated B as one of its divisions. The book value of Company B's net assets was $150 − $50 = $100. Company A paid a higher price because B's property and equipment was appraised at $120. What would A's balance sheet show immediately after this purchase?

b. Assume Company A purchased all of the outstanding common stock of Company B for $160 cash and operated B as a subsidiary (thereby preserving B as a separate legal entity). The appraised value of the property and equipment was equal to its book value. What would A's consolidated balance sheet show immediately after the acquisition?

c. Assume Company A acquired all of the outstanding stock of Company B, issuing in exchange its own stock with a market value of $160 (par $40). The merger of the two companies was treated as a pooling of interests. After the merger, what would appear on A's consolidated balance sheet?

d. For the year preceding the merger, net income was $50 for Company A and $11 for Company B (after depreciation of $6). Assuming the same operating revenues and expenses for the year after merger except as they may be affected by the accounting method, what net income would be reported under each of the three circumstances described above? (Where appropriate, assume that company policy calls for goodwill to be written off on a straight-line basis over a five-year period.)

e. Compare the results under the three sets of circumstances. Which is most attractive to a management that is interested in putting its best foot forward?

13. Business combination. On November 30, 19x3, the Fair Deal Corporation exchanged 10,000 shares of its $5 par common stock for a 100 percent ownership in Strate & Shute, Inc. At that time, Fair Deal stock was selling at a market price of $40 per share; Strate & Shute was a family-owned corporation, and there was no market in its shares. The acquisition was treated as a pooling of interests.

Balance sheets drawn up for the two corporations as of November 30, 19x3, just before the acquisition transaction was consummated, showed the following (in summary form):

	Fair Deal	Strate & Shute
Assets		
Assets	$1,000,000	$250,000
Owners' Equity		
Common stock	$ 200,000	$100,000
Additional paid-in capital	300,000	70,000
Retained Earnings	500,000	80,000
Total Owners' Equity	$1,000,000	$250,000

Earnings for the two companies for 19x3 were:

	Fair Deal	Strate & Shute
January 1–November 30	$120,000	$40,000
December 1–December 31	20,000	5,000
Total	$140,000	$45,000

There were no intercompany sales during the year. No dividends were declared by either company during the year. A set of consolidated financial statements was prepared at the end of 19x3.

a.   At what amounts would goodwill and retained earnings appear on the consolidated balance sheet at December 31, 19x3?

b.   Calculate consolidated net income for the year. (Goodwill, if any, is to be amortized in equal amounts for 20 years.)

c.   How would your answers to (a) and (b) have differed if the Strate and Shute stock had been acquired in exchange for $394,000 in cash?

14.   Business combination.   Below are the balance sheets of the Single and Multiple Product Corporations as of December 31, 19x3:

	Single	Multiple
Assets	$156,000	$3,400,000
Liabilities	$ 50,000	$ 650,000
Capital stock, 32,000 shares	32,000	
Capital stock, 800,000 shares		800,000
Capital contributed in excess of par value	17,000	600,000
Retained earnings	57,000	1,350,000
Total	$156,000	$3,400,000

The appraised value of Single's tangible assets was equal to their book value at that time.

At the start of 19x4, Multiple paid $190,000 in cash for the 32,000 shares of Single. The two companies' income statements for 19x4 prior to consolidation showed the following:

	Single	Multiple
Sales	$800,000	$10,000,000
Expenses	700,000	8,700,000
Operating income	$100,000	$ 1,300,000
Dividend received		40,000
Income before Taxes	$100,000	$ 1,340,000

No intercompany sales took place during 19x4, and consolidated income before taxes was taxed at a rate of 50 percent.

a.   Would the merger have been accounted for as a purchase or as a pooling of interests? Why?

b.   Prepare a consolidated balance sheet at the beginning of 19x4.

c.   Present a consolidated income statement. Goodwill, if any, was to be amortized equally over seven years.

d.   How, if at all, would your answers to the questions above have differed if the shares of Single had been obtained in exchange for 20,000 shares of Multiple's stock, valued at $9.50 a share?

15.   Advantages of consolidated statements.   Indico, Inc., has its headquarters in a country in which corporations are not required to follow generally accepted accounting principles in preparing their financial statements. Indico has one subsidiary, Dilex, Inc. Indico established Dilex in 19x1 by buying 100,000 shares of its $1 par common stock for $500,000. No other shares were issued, either then or later.

The income statements of the two companies for the year 19x7 were as follows:

	Indico	Dilex
Sales revenues	$150,000	$600,000
Dividend income (from Dilex)	40,000	—
Total Revenue	$190,000	$600,000
Cost of goods sold	85,000	420,000
Selling and administrative expenses	45,000	53,000
Interest expense	—	22,000
Income tax expense	10,000	30,000
Net Income	$ 50,000	$ 75,000

Dilex's sales revenues included $50,000 in sales to Indico; the cost of goods sold attributable to these sales was $35,000.

The two companies' statements of financial position as of December 31, 19x7, contained the following information:

	Indico	Dilex
Current Assets:		
Cash	$ 10,000	$ 25,000
Accounts receivable	20,000	170,000
Inventories	30,000	205,000
Total Current Assets	$ 60,000	$400,000
Investment in subsidiary	500,000	—
Plant and equipment (net)	140,000	670,000
Total Assets	$700,000	$1,070,000
Current Liabilities:		
Accounts payable	$ 5,000	$ 35,000
Taxes payable	5,000	10,000
Total Current Liabilities	$ 10,000	$ 45,000
Bonds payable	—	275,000
Total Liabilities	$ 10,000	$ 320,000
Common stock	$200,000	$ 100,000
Additional paid-in capital	100,000	400,000
Retained earnings	390,000	250,000
Total Shareowners' Equity	$690,000	$ 750,000

On December 31, Indico owed Dilex $2,000 for purchases of merchandise, and this amount was included in the figures given above. Indico's inventory included merchandise purchased from Dilex at a price of $3,000. Dilex's cost of this merchandise was $1,800.

a. Prepare a set of consolidated financial statements for Indico and its subsidiary.
b. Indico has never published either consolidated financial statements or the separate financial statements of Dilex. A group of Indico's

shareholders has asked management to publish consolidated state-ments for 19x7. The company's treasurer has opposed this, but has sug-gested meeting the shareowners' needs by shifting to the equity method in the parent company's statements. Evaluate this suggestion, indicat-ing the benefits, if any, consolidated statements would give the share-holders and indicating whether the equity method would be an adequate substitute for consolidation. Use figures from the problem to support your arguments.

16. _Preparing consolidated statements._ The Sutton Company is a wholly owned subsidiary of the Porter Company. The assets, liabilities, and stock-holders' equities reported by these two companies as of December 31, 19x9, were as follows:

	Porter Company	Sutton Company
Cash	$ 250,000	$ 130,000
Marketable securities	400,000	150,000
Accounts receivable—customers	1,250,000	540,000
Allowance for doubtful accounts	(25,000)	(10,000)
Accounts receivable—subsidiary	100,000	
Inventories	1,100,000	550,000
Stock of Sutton Company (at cost)	150,000	
Advances to subsidiary	420,000	
Plant, property, and equipment (net)	1,525,000	760,000
Total	$5,170,000	$2,120,000
Accounts payable—trade	$ 575,000	$ 185,000
Accounts payable—parent		90,000
Accrued liabilities	350,000	100,000
Taxes payable	525,000	275,000
Advances from parent		420,000
Common stock	300,000	100,000
Additional paid-in capital	700,000	40,000
Retained earnings, 1/1/x9	2,420,000	835,000
Net income, 19x9	650,000	250,000
Dividends declared, 19x9	(300,000)	(175,000)
Treasury stock	(50,000)	
Total	$5,170,000	$2,120,000

The two companies showed the following figures on the income statements for 19x9 prepared for the use of the managers of the two individual companies:

	Porter Company	Sutton Company
Net sales	$10,000,000	$4,600,000
Other income	250,000	20,000
Cost of goods sold	(6,700,000)	(3,210,000)
Selling, general, and administrative expenses	(2,400,000)	(900,000)
Income taxes	(500,000)	(260,000)
Net Income	$ 650,000	$ 250,000

Further information:

1. Porter purchased the Sutton stock on January 1, 19x1, for $150,000 in cash. As shown on Sutton's books, the book value of Porter's equity at that time was $120,000. The appraised value of Sutton's tangible assets was equal to their book value at that time.
2. Merchandise in transit from the Porter Company to the Sutton Company on December 31, 19x9, was recorded by Porter as a sale transaction, billed at $10,000. This transaction had not yet been recorded by Sutton.
3. Sales by Porter to Sutton in 19x9 totaled $1.7 million, including the transaction described in item (2) above. Sutton made no sales to Porter during the year.
4. Porter's billings for merchandise shipped by Porter to Sutton during the year but not sold by Sutton prior to December 31, 19x9, included an intercompany profit of $20,000.
5. The company's policy was to amortize any goodwill in the consolidated statements in 15 equal annual installments, starting in 19x1.
6. Porter Company sometimes prepares financial statements on a nonconsolidated basis. In preparing these statements it is required to use the equity method of accounting for its investment in Sutton. For this purpose it eliminates the effects of intercompany transactions and amortizes the excess of purchase cost over the underlying book value of its equity in Sutton Company in 15 equal annual installments, starting in 19x1.

a. Calculate Sutton's retained earnings on the date Porter bought its stock.
b. Calculate Porter's equity in Sutton's net income for the year ended December 31, 19x9. No adjustments of income tax expense or taxes payable are necessary.
c. Calculate Porter's equity in the earnings retained by Sutton from the date of the acquisition to December 31, 19x9.
d. Calculate the amount at which Porter should report its investment in Sutton on a nonconsolidated, parent-company statement of financial position as of December 31, 19x9.
e. Determine and describe the adjustments Porter would have to make to reflect the information in items (2), (3) and (4).
f. Make other necessary adjustments and prepare a consolidated income statement for the year ended December 31, 19x9.
g. Make other necessary adjustments and prepare a consolidated statement of financial position as of December 31, 19x9.

17. Segment reporting: discussion question. Combustion Equipment Associates, Inc., markets, designs, builds, and operates systems to abate pollution, recycle wastes, and produce energy. The company also manufactures a variety of products used for dust control, filtration, separation, classification, and drying of grain; cereal foods, minerals, fibers, solid wastes, and fossil fuels; and energy conversion and conservation equipment.

The following segment data were provided in a footnote to the financial statements in the company's 1978 annual report (in thousands of dollars):

	Environmental Systems	Energy Products and Services	Environmental Products	Agricultural Products and Other	Adjustments and Eliminations	Consolidated
Net sales from unaffiliated customers	$49,100	$24,995	$44,200	$36,650		$154,945
Intersegment sales ..	—	1,200	4,200	4,200	($9,600)	—
Other revenues	4,060	3,845	—	—	—	7,905
Total revenue .	$53,160	$30,040	$48,400	$40,850	($9,600)	$162,850
Operating profit	$13,436	$ 6,786	$ 5,291	$ 4,791		$ 30,304
General corporate expenses						(4,569)
Unrealized foreign currency exchange loss						(491)
Interest expense, net						(3,541)
Income before income taxes ...						$ 21,703
Identifiable assets at March 31, 1978 ...	$73,657	$22,486	$26,840	$16,099		$139,082
Corporate assets						11,275
Total Assets at March 31, 1978						$150,357
Depreciation and amortization	$ 794	$ 362	$ 781	$ 361		$ 2,298
Capital expenditures	$ 4,264	$ 1,120	$ 841	$ 534		$ 6,759

Environmental Systems—designs, constructs and operates large scale facilities that abate pollution on energy producing projects, such as power plant scrubbers, and that recycle wastes and produce energy, as with resource recovery projects.

Energy Products and Services—manufactures products that convert fuels to heat energy, such as coal-fired hot water and steam generators and fuel oil and solid waste gasifiers, and also markets various forms of fuel and energy sources to customers, such as low grade coal and waste oils.

Environmental Products—manufactures air pollution control and material handling equipment including fabric filters for grain terminals, wood and mineral processing facilities, coal-fired industrial steam plants and also a variety of materials separation, classification conveying and handling devices.

Agricultural Products and Other—includes: manufacture of devices that attach to farm combines and harvest, separate, and dry grain and legumes; manufacture of small oil and gas combustors; and, a specialized contracting operation.

Intersegment sales are made at prices comparable to transactions with unaffiliated parties. An environmental systems contract with a governmental agency accounted for approximately 11% of consolidated revenues in 1978.

Identifiable assets are those assets used by each of the respective industry segments. Investments in and advances to partnerships and other entities principally relate to the East Bridgewater Associates limited partnership, which operates a resource recovery project in the United States. Such investments are included in the identifiable assets of the Environmental Systems segment. Corporate assets consist primarily of cash and short-term investments.

Consolidated foreign operations in Canada, United Kingdom, and Germany for 1978 were as follows: net sales, $19,546,000; operating loss, $174,000 (excluding unrealized foreign currency exchange losses of $491,000); net loss, $1,070,000. At March 31, 1978, balances relating to these operations were as follows: net current assets, $4,235,000; net assets, $4,838,000; total identifiable assets, $12,369,000.

a. How might these segment data help investors decide whether to buy or sell shares of this corporation's common stock? Illustrate your argument with figures drawn from the data provided by the company.

b. Is this information adequate, in your opinion, or should the company have included additional information on these segments in its 1978 annual report? Comment on the likely costs and benefits of any additional information you would like to see.

16

Statements of Changes in Financial Position

THE INCOME STATEMENT provides information about the results of the company's operations during a particular time period. The statement of financial position (balance sheet) provides information about the company's assets, liabilities, and owners' equity on a particular date. A third statement, the statement of changes in financial position, or funds statement, shows where the company has obtained resources ("funds") during a specified period of time and what it has done with these additional resources during that period. The purpose of this chapter is to explain how the funds statement is constructed, how it relates to the income statement and the statement of cash flows, and how it can be used.

CASH FLOWS AND FUNDS FLOWS

The term *funds* has many meanings. For example, we speak of pension funds, meaning the assets that have been or will be accumulated to pay pensions to specified individuals or groups or classes of individuals. Or, we may say we have funds in the bank, meaning that we have an asset we think of as cash.

The term has a very special meaning in the statement of changes in financial position. This section will try to make this meaning clear by contrasting a simple statement of cash flows with an equally simple statement of changes in financial position.

Statement of Personal Cash Flows

John Prout is a junior executive in a large corporation. His salary last year was $24,000, and he received $2,000 in dividends and interest on his investments. He paid $18,000 for day-to-day living expenses, $7,000 for income taxes, and ended the year owing $500 for a suit of clothes, gifts, and restaurant meals he had bought using various credit cards during November and December. He had owed nothing for credit-card purchases at the beginning of the year.

Mr. Prout bought a house for $60,000 at the end of December, paying $20,000 in cash and borrowing the remaining $40,000 from a mortgage institution. He received an inheritance of $15,000 from the estate of a great-aunt, who had died during the previous year, and bought a new sports car with part of the proceeds, paying $7,000 in cash at the time of delivery. Finally, he discovered he had paid the government $1,300 too much in income taxes during the year, thereby entitling him to a $1,300 refund sometime within the next few months. He had $12,000 in his bank account at the beginning of the year and $1,000 at the end.

The cash flows in these transactions are summarized in Exhibit 16–1. Cash receipts totaled $41,000, but cash disbursements

EXHIBIT 16–1

JOHN PROUT
Summary of Cash Receipts and Disbursements
For Last Year

Cash Receipts:		
Cash received from earnings:		
Salary	$24,000	
Interest and dividends	2,000	$26,000
Cash received from inheritance		15,000
Total Cash Receipts		$41,000
Cash Disbursements:		
For living expenses	$18,000	
For income taxes	7,000	
For new house	20,000	
For new car	7,000	
Total Cash Disbursements		52,000
Net Decrease in Bank Balance		$11,000

amounted to $52,000, thereby bringing the cash balance down by $11,000.

Statement of Changes in Personal Financial Position

Exhibit 16–1 omits three of Mr. Prout's financial transactions most observers would regard as significant. For one thing, he borrowed $40,000 to help him buy his new house. Even though he never handled this amount of cash, it was just as useful to him as cash in obtaining the house. Furthermore, by borrowing, he assumed an obligation to make a series of payments in the future, an obligation that could have a severe effect on his behavior in the years to come.

The cash-flow statement also overlooks the $500 in unpaid bills outstanding at the end of the year and the tax refund Mr. Prout was entitled to. These also arose from transactions that affected his financial position. They are reflected in the statement of changes in financial position in Exhibit 16–2.

EXHIBIT 16–2

JOHN PROUT
Statement of Changes in Financial Position

Inflows of Financial Resources:		
Funds from current operations:		
Salary	$24,000	
Interest and dividends	2,000	$26,000
Inheritance		15,000
Mortgage loan		40,000
Total Inflows of Financial Resources ...		$81,000
Uses of Financial Resources:		
For living expenses	$18,500	
For income taxes	5,700	
To buy a new house	60,000	
To buy a new car	7,000	
Total Uses of Financial Resources		91,200
Net Decrease in Working Capital ..		$10,200

This statement shows all of the flows of financial resources arising out of Mr. Prout's transactions last year, not just the flows of cash. First, the full purchase price of the house is shown as a use of financial resources, and the mortgage loan is shown as a source. Second, the $500 in unpaid bills has been added to the $18,000 Mr. Prout paid for living expenses during the year, yielding a revised total of $18,500 expended for this purpose. Third, the $1,300 due as an income tax refund has been deducted from the amount of taxes paid and only the net amount is shown on the statement.

Perhaps the best way to explain these differences is to point out that the statement of changes in financial position is often described as a summary of inflows and outflows of the firm's *working capital*. Funds, in other words, is defined as working capital, and the funds statement shows how much working capital has flowed in and how much has flowed out during the period. For example, the two income tax transactions had the following effects:

Payment made	$7,000	decrease in cash
Refund due	1,300	increase in receivables
Net Effect on Working Capital	$5,700	decrease in working capital

The $5,700 is the figure to be shown on the funds statement, because this is how this set of transactions affected the working capital.

The $40,000 mortgage loan is the only figure in this statement that had no direct effect on Mr. Prout's working capital. We include it because the mortgage transaction can be viewed as a two-stage process: (1) an inflow of working capital through borrowing and (2) an outflow of working capital to acquire the house. This isn't a bad assumption. Mr. Prout's borrowing power is a valuable resource and is far from unlimited. By borrowing to buy a house, he used some of this resource, thereby reducing his ability to borrow later for other purposes. A statement of changes in financial position that overlooked this fact would be far from complete and much less useful.

In summary, to finance all of his purchases during the year, Mr. Prout had to reduce his working capital by $10,200.

USING FUND-FLOW ANALYSIS

Funds statements are useful mainly because they throw light on management's investing and financing practices. The uses a company makes of its funds have a considerable influence on its future profitability and on the risks investors in the company are exposed to. Knowledge of how management gets the funds to finance these activities is important for the same reason.

In a sense, the balance sheet is a summary of the net effects of all the company's investing and financing activities since the company was formed. Analysis of the structure of assets, liabilities, and owners' equities at any given time, therefore, can reveal a good deal about the company's management of its sources and uses of funds. Analysis of *changes* in structure may be even more revealing, however; and this is the domain of *funds-flow analysis*. By examining the changes in balance-sheet items between balance-sheet dates, one may determine the sources of the funds obtained and the ways in which these funds were used during this *limited time period*.

Sources of Funds

The sources of business funds can be grouped into four main categories:

1. Current operations.
2. Borrowing.
3. Issuance of additional shares of the company's capital stock.
4. Sale of assets not originally acquired for resale.

The most important (though not necessarily the largest) of these is the company's current operations. It is the most important for four reasons: (1) it is a continuing source, the result of a myriad of individual actions and decisions, not the result of intermittent activity; (2) it is the source most completely within management's control; (3) it provides a base that is essential if management wishes to raise additional funds by borrowing or by issuing additional shares of stock; and (4) its use exposes the company to no additional risk of the kind generally associated with borrowing.

Risk is an important factor in any financing decision. When a company borrows, it increases the risks its owners (and managers) are exposed to. Interest or principal may fall due for payment just when the company finds itself temporarily short of cash. The company may have to curtail its other activities to make these payments or, in extreme cases, may fail to make the payments, causing it to fall into bankruptcy or receivership.

Finally, funds obtained from shareholders through the sale of stock or retention of earnings carry no risk of insolvency. The company has no contractual obligations to make payments on specified dates, even to the preferred shareholders. In return for removing this risk from the corporation, the stockholders expect a higher yield on their investment than that earned by the company's creditors. This desired yield can and should be considered a cost of obtaining capital from the shareholders. In other words, by increasing its reliance on current operations and other owner-supplied funds, the company can reduce the risks it is exposed to; in exchange, it must forgo the cost advantages of using borrowed money.

Outside investors study funds statements to see what combinations of risk and cost management is accepting. If the risk pattern is changing, this will be a factor in the investors' decisions. Outsiders are also interested in the ability of the company's normal operations to generate a reliable stream of funds. Other things being equal, a larger stream of funds flows from current operations reduces the risk of investing in the company and provides the basis for additional investment in potentially profitable ventures.

Uses of Funds

The other side of the funds statement may be equally revealing. The major uses of funds are:

1. Cash dividends and other distributions to shareholders.
2. Retirement of long-term debt.
3. Purchases of plant and equipment.
4. Additional investments in other companies.

A review of the percentage of funds going into each of these uses can be very informative to the investor. A high ratio of dividends to current operating-funds flows, for example, is evidence that management has adopted a strategy of little or no growth, or even gradual liquidation. Large purchases of plant and equipment indicate a strategy of internal growth, while large outside investments signal a strategy of growth through acquisition.

The two sides of the funds statement also have to be considered in relation to each other. For example, a high-risk financing strategy (heavy borrowing) means one thing if most of the funds are used to purchase plant and equipment or investments in other companies. It may take on an entirely different meaning, however, if the cash dividends and stock repurchases bulk large in the uses of funds.

The accounting profession has concluded that the reasons for preparing statements of changes in financial position are so compelling that one of these statements must accompany the income statement and statement of financial position whenever audited financial statements are prepared for external use.[1]

PREPARING THE STATEMENT: AN INFORMAL APPROACH

Formal worksheet procedures can be used to develop statements of changes in financial position. We'll describe a procedure of this kind in the next section. Before doing that, however, we'll go through a simple illustration in a less-formal way, to stress the logic of the analysis rather than the mechanics. This informal approach has three main phases:

1. Developing a schedule of balance-sheet changes.
2. Using additional information.
3. Choosing a format in which to present the results of the analysis.

First Approximation: Balance-Sheet Changes

The first step in funds statement preparation is to tabulate the changes in individual balance-sheet items that have occurred between two successive balance-sheet dates. For example, the balance sheets of Peabody, Inc., on January 1 and December 31, 19x1, are shown in Exhibit 16–3.

---

[1] APB, "Opinion No. 19," para. 7, in AICPA, *Professional Standards—Accounting, Current Text* (New York: Commerce Clearing House, Inc., 1978), sec. 2021.07.

EXHIBIT 16–3

PEABODY, INC.
Comparative Statements of Financial Position
January 1 and December 31, 19x1

	January 1	December 31	Increase (Decrease)
Current Assets:			
Cash	$ 30,000	$ 14,000	
Accounts receivable	70,000	85,000	
Inventories	90,000	95,000	
Total Current Assets	$190,000	$194,000	
Current Liabilities:			
Accounts payable	$ 79,000	$ 69,000	
Salaries payable	1,000	1,000	
Income taxes payable	10,000	12,000	
Total Current Liabilities	$ 90,000	$ 82,000	
Working capital	$100,000	$112,000	$ 12,000
Plant and equipment, net	200,000	235,000	35,000
Total	$300,000	$347,000	$ 47,000
Long-Term Liabilities:			
Bonds payable	$ 90,000	$ 80,000	$(10,000)
Deferred taxes	15,000	20,000	5,000
Shareowners' Equity:			
Common stock	100,000	150,000	50,000
Retained earnings	95,000	97,000	2,000
Total	$300,000	$347,000	$ 47,000

To facilitate the analysis, current assets and current liabilities are grouped at the top of the statement. Details of changes in individual current assets and current liabilities do not enter into the calculation of the figures on the funds statement. For this reason they have been omitted from the third column of figures.

EXHIBIT 16–4

PEABODY, INC.
Statement of Balance Sheet Changes
For the Year Ended December 31, 19x1

Sources of Funds:		
Increase in common stock		$50,000
Increase in retained earnings		2,000
Increase in deferred taxes		5,000
Total		$57,000
Uses of Funds:		
Increase in plant and equipment	$35,000	
Decrease in bonds payable	10,000	
Total		45,000
Increase in Working Capital		$12,000

The changes shown in the right-hand column are the basic raw materials from which funds statements are prepared. These figures have been assembled in the rudimentary funds statement shown in Exhibit 16–4. This statement implies that the company obtained $50,000 in funds by issuing additional shares of stock to its share-holders, $2,000 by retaining net assets generated by the operations of the period, and $5,000 by using its rights to defer portions of its income taxes to a later period. It used $35,000 to buy plant and equipment and another $10,000 to retire long-term debt, leaving $12,000 to strengthen the working-capital position.

The rules by which the balance-sheet changes were assembled in this statement are simplicity itself:

1. An increase in a noncurrent asset is the result of a *use* of funds.
2. A decrease in a noncurrent liability or in the owners' equity is the result of a *use* of funds.
3. An increase in a noncurrent liability or in the owners' equity arises because a *source* of funds has been tapped.
4. A decrease in a noncurrent asset is interpreted as a *source* of funds.

Put in its simplest terms, this says that we use funds to acquire assets or to pay off creditors and owners; we get funds by selling assets, by borrowing, or by inducing the owners to invest more funds in the company.

Additional Information: The Income Statement

Unfortunately, a statement like the one in Exhibit 16–4 doesn't reveal very much about the sources and uses of the company's resources. Most of the increases and decreases were net changes, the result of offsetting the increases originating in some transactions against the decreases coming from others. We can almost always improve the statement by bringing in information from sources other than the balance sheets.

For example, although retained earnings increased by only $2,000, we find from the income statement for the year that net income was $39,000. This means that the resources flowing into the firm during the year as a result of the year's operations brought $39,000 more net assets into the firm than they took out. We might say, therefore, that net income was a $39,000 source of funds in 19x1. This already tells us more than the $2,000 net increase in retained earnings showed us.

Net income, however, is likely to be a poor measure of the amount of funds generated by current revenue-producing operations. The relationship between net income and the amount of funds provided by operations is illustrated in a simple way in Exhibit 16–5. This

EXHIBIT 16-5

PEABODY, INC.
Income Statement
For the Year Ended December 31, 19x1

Sales revenue		$400,000
Less: Cost of goods sold	$240,000	
Selling and administrative salaries	56,000	
Sundry selling and administrative expenses	20,500	
Interest	7,000	
Income taxes—current portion	21,000	344,500
Funds provided by operations		$ 55,500
Less: Depreciation	$ 11,000	
Income taxes—deferred portion	5,000	
Loss on sale of equipment	1,000	(17,000)
Add: Gain on debt retirement		500
Net Income		$ 39,000

exhibit shows how Peabody's income statement for the year might have been drawn up if expenses, gains, and losses not representing expenditures or receipts of current funds had been separated from other income-statement items. The amount of funds provided by operations is calculated by subtracting the amount of "funds-consuming" expenses—that is, those requiring increases in current liabilities or decreases in current assets—from current revenues, as in the upper portion of Exhibit 16-5.

Notice that four items on the income statement didn't enter into the calculation of the amount of funds provided by operations: depreciation, the deferred portion of income tax expense for the year, the loss on the sale of equipment, and the gain on debt retirement. Take depreciation, for example. It is a legitimate expense and, therefore, must be on the income statement, but it doesn't stand for a current use of funds. Therefore, it shouldn't be deducted from revenues in the calculation of the amount of funds provided by operations.

In other words, the analysts start with net income as their *first approximation* to the amount of funds provided by operations. They then have to *add back* such items as depreciation, the deferred portion of current income taxes, losses, and other amortizations of long-life assets, and *subtract* such items as nonoperating gains. Peabody's statement for 19x1 would show the following:

Net income		$39,000
Add: Depreciation		11,000
Deferred portion of current income tax expense		5,000
Loss on sale of equipment		1,000
Subtract: Gain on debt retirement		(500)
Funds Provided by Operations		$55,500

Depreciation, income tax deferrals, and losses have to be added back because they do not measure current outflows of funds. They are not appropriate deductions from revenues in the calculation of the amount of funds provided by operations. Gains, on the other hand, may measure inflows of current funds, but it is better to report them as part of the funds flows arising from the transactions which led to the recognition of the gain. We'll consider this point at greater length later in this section.

Other Changes in Retained Earnings

In our preliminary statement of balance-sheet changes (Exhibit 16–4), we listed "Increase in retained earnings, $2,000" as a source of funds. In the last section, we replaced this with the net income figure, $39,000. Now it's time to explain the $37,000 difference between these two numbers. Our information this time comes from the statement of changes in retained earnings:

Retained earnings, January 1		$ 95,000
Add: Net income		39,000
		$134,000
Less: Cash dividends	$17,000	
Stock dividends	20,000	37,000
Retained Earnings, December 31		$ 97,000

The $17,000 in cash dividends certainly was a use of funds. The stock dividend, however, merely represented a transfer from one owners'-equity category to another. No resources flowed into or out of the firm, and the stock dividend, therefore, doesn't appear on the funds statement.

Sale of Stock

The stock dividend accounted for $20,000 of the increase in the company's common stock. This means that we should amend our original statement of increases and decreases. Instead of showing $50,000 as a source of funds from increases in common stock, we should subtract the $20,000 stock dividend and list only $30,000. Since this amount didn't arise as a result of a stock dividend, we have to assume it came from the sale of additional shares of stock, very clearly a source of funds.

Notice what we have done. We have replaced two figures in our original statement, the $2,000 increase in retained earnings and the $50,000 increase in common stock, with three different figures:

Sources of Funds		Uses of Funds	
Net income	$39,000		
Sale of stock	30,000	Cash dividends	$17,000

Net Change in
Owners' Equity
+$52,000

The algebraic total remains the same as it was before, +$52,000, but we have a much better picture of what actually happened than we did when we had information only on net increases and decreases.

Purchases and Sales of Fixed Assets

The next item in our illustration to call for analysis is the company's investments in its plant and equipment. Again, the procedure is to start with the increase or decrease in the balance-sheet amount and adjust this to reflect any additional information we can find.

In Exhibit 16–3 we saw that net plant and equipment had increased from $200,000 to $235,000 during the year. In our analysis of the flow of funds from the company's ordinary operations, we noted that depreciation for the year amounted to $11,000. If this had been the only factor affecting the plant and equipment, the net balance would have *decreased* by $11,000. In other words, to achieve the net increase of $35,000, gross increases in plant and equipment must have amounted to $46,000:

Plant and Equipment

Bal. 1/1	200,000	Depreciation for the year	11,000
???	46,000		
Bal. 12/31 235,000			

Without further information, the likeliest explanation of this $46,000 change is that it represented purchases of plant and equipment during the year. The figures in Exhibit 16–6 permit us to go farther, however. The figure for additions to gross plant and equipment shows that equipment purchased during the year cost $50,000. This $50,000 enters the funds statement as a use of funds.

The other change in plant and equipment during the year was the retirement of equipment with an original cost of $30,000 and a net

EXHIBIT 16-6

PEABODY, INC.
Statement of Plant and Equipment Changes
For the Year Ended December 31, 19x1

	Original Cost	Accumulated Depreciation	Net Plant and Equipment
Balance, January 1	$290,000	$90,000	$200,000
Additions	50,000	11,000	39,000
Retirements	(30,000)	(26,000)	(4,000)
Balance, December 31	$310,000	$75,000	$235,000

book value of $4,000. If no further information on these retirements is provided in the financial statements, the $4,000 can be assumed to approximate the proceeds from the sale of these assets. In this case, however, we know that Peabody's income statement listed a $1,000 loss on the sale of equipment. This means that the equipment must have been sold for $1,000 less than its book value—that is, for $3,000—and two items have to be reflected in the funds statement: the $3,000 proceeds from the sale of equipment and the $1,000 loss on that sale. The $3,000 is clearly a nonoperating source of funds; the $1,000 loss, as we saw earlier, has to be included in the calculation of the amount of funds provided by operations. In other words, it isn't an outflow of funds.

The original $35,000 increase in plant and equipment can now be replaced on the funds statement by the following four items:

Sources of Funds		Uses of Funds	
Obtained from sale of plant and equipment	$ 3,000	Used to acquire plant and equipment	$50,000
Added to net income in calculating the amount of funds provided by operations:			
Depreciation	11,000		
Loss on sale of equipment	1,000		

Net Change in
Plant and Equipment
+$35,000

Depreciation Is Not a Source of Funds!

The mechanics of adding depreciation back to net income on the funds statement may lead to the hasty conclusion that depreciation is a source of funds. It must be emphasized most strongly that this is not the case. Funds, if any, come from operations. If no sales are made, then no funds are derived from operations no matter how big the annual depreciation charge.

Similarly, although losses must be added back to net income to get a correct measure of the funds provided by operations, these losses are not sources of funds. Depreciation and losses allowed in the computation of taxable income do affect the amount of taxes currently payable, but even here the funds flow is reflected in the tax figure and not in the write-off or amortization of the cost.

Retirement of Long-Term Debt

We have now replaced all but one of the balance sheet changes in Exhibit 16–4 with more detailed information. The one remaining item is the change in the amount of bonds payable, which decreased by $10,000. Without further information, we would enter this in the funds statement as a use of funds. From the income statement, however, we know that the company realized a $500 gain on debt retirement. Thus the bonds must have been repurchased at a cost of $9,500, and instead of one entry in the funds statement, we have two:

Funds used to retire debt	$ 9,500
Amount to be subtracted from net income in computing funds provided by operations	500
Total	$10,000

Format of the Statement

The statement of changes in financial position for Peabody, Inc., is shown in Exhibit 16–7. Notice how much more information this statement contains than the rudimentary summary of balance sheet changes we presented in Exhibit 16–4.[2] It shows us that the main internal source of funds, current operations, was inadequate to cover both the cash dividend and the company's purchases of plant and equipment. The company was growing faster, in other words, than its internal sources could support.

---

[2] Some of the nonoperating sources and uses of funds affect the amount of income taxes reflected in the net-income figure. The calculations necessary to adjust the pretax figures for their tax effects are beyond the scope of this introductory discussion.

EXHIBIT 16–7

PEABODY, INC.
Statement of Changes in Financial Position
For the Year Ended December 31, 19x1

Sources of funds:
From operations:

Net income		$39,000
Add: Depreciation		11,000
Deferred portion of income tax expense		5,000
Loss on sale of equipment		1,000
Total		$56,000
Less: Gain on debt retirement		500
Funds Provided by Operations		$55,500
From sale of common stock		30,000
From sale of plant and equipment		3,000
Total Sources of Funds		$88,500

Use of Funds:

To purchase plant and equipment	$50,000	
To pay cash dividends	17,000	
To retire debt	9,500	
Total Uses of Funds		76,500
Net Increase in Working Capital		$12,000

The statement also shows us that the company retired debt, meeting its needs for additional funds by issuing common stock. In other words, despite its growth, the company was moving its capital structure toward a less-risky mixture of more owners' equity and less debt.

The statement in Exhibit 16–7 uses a residual format, in which the change in working capital is listed at the bottom of the statement, as the difference between the total sources and the total uses of funds. We actually prefer what is known as a *balanced format*, in which the change in working capital is treated either as a source or as a use of funds, depending on the direction of the change. Exhibit 16–8 shows a statement in this format, eliminating only the detailed breakdown of the operating funds section we provided in Exhibit 16–7.

The issue is of no great moment, but we prefer the balanced format because the residual format focuses attention unduly on the change in working capital, which may be the least important figure in the statement. *The purpose of the funds statement is not to explain the change in working capital, but to show how management obtained resources during the period and how it used them.* In this case, it used $12,000 of the available funds to strengthen its working-capital position. This surely is just as clearly a use of funds as the $9,500 the company used to retire outstanding bonds payable.

EXHIBIT 16–8

PEABODY, INC.
Statement of Changes in Financial Position
For the Year Ended December 31, 19x1—Balanced Format

Sources of Funds:

From operations	$55,500
From sale of common stock	30,000
From sale of plant and equipment	3,000
Total Sources of Funds	$88,500

Uses of Funds:

To purchase plant and equipment	$50,000
To pay dividends	17,000
To retire debt	9,500
To increase working capital	12,000
Total Uses of Funds	$88,500

Funds Flow versus Cash-Flow Statements

Companies pay their bills with cash, not with "funds." It may come as some surprise, therefore, to find that corporations publish funds statements, not cash-flow statements, in their annual reports. We can suggest several reasons for this practice. First, cash-flow statements don't include several significant kinds of resource flows—issuing common stock to acquire a minority interest in another company, for example, or using long-term leases to finance the acquisition of equipment.

Another reason is that the amount of funds generated by operations isn't affected by customers' decisions to pay their bills early or late or by management's decisions to affect the timing of purchases and payments to the company's suppliers. If management pays $10,000 to a short-term trade creditor, for example, working capital doesn't change, but the amount of cash flow from operations decreases. Cash-flow figures, in other words, are likely to fluctuate more erratically than the flow of working capital from operations. Long-term investors may prefer to use funds-flow figures because they smooth out the erratic fluctuations in the timing of cash receipts and payments. While conversions of net current noncash assets into cash and vice versa do indicate changes in liquidity, investors' interest is usually focused on fundamental relationships rather than on short-term variations in liquidity.

We can always study changes in liquidity by examining the schedule of changes in the components of working capital that accompanies the funds statement. For example, Peabody's schedule for 19x1, reproduced in Exhibit 16–9, shows that the $12,000 increase in working capital was accompanied by a substantial reduc-

EXHIBIT 16-9

PEABODY, INC.
Schedule of Changes in Current Assets and Current Liabilities
For the Year Ended December 31, 19x1

	January 1	December 31	Increase (Decrease)
Current Assets:			
Cash	$ 30,000	$ 14,000	$(16,000)
Accounts receivable	70,000	85,000	15,000
Inventories	90,000	95,000	5,000
Total	$190,000	$194,000	$ 4,000
Current Liabilities:			
Accounts payable	$ 79,000	$ 69,000	$(10,000)
Salaries payable	1,000	1,000	—
Income taxes payable	10,000	12,000	2,000
Total	$ 90,000	$ 82,000	$ (8,000)
Working Capital	$100,000	$112,000	$ 12,000

tion in the company's liquidity. Accounts receivable and inventories increased by $15,000 and $5,000, offsetting the $16,000 reduction in the cash balance. This may have been a temporary, short-term phenomenon, or it may have been an early warning of a future liquidity problem.

Irregularities in the structure of working capital may be important enough to justify redefining funds to exclude one or more components of the working capital. Many companies, for example, rely heavily on short-term bank borrowing, year after year. In such cases this is really part of the firm's long-term capital structure, and changes in the outstanding bank debt may be very significant portions of the funds-flow picture.

For analytical purposes, therefore, short-term notes payable might be classified as a form of long-term debt, with increases being treated as sources of funds and decreases coming through as uses of funds. "Funds," in such cases, would consist of all the current assets, less all the current liabilities except short-term notes payable.[3]

Cash Flow from Operations

"Funds from current operations" is sometimes referred to in the financial press and even in some finance textbooks as the firm's cash flow, but it is worth reemphasizing at this point that this is a mis-

---

[3] Short-term obligations the company intends to refinance on a long-term basis are classified as noncurrent liabilities if the company can demonstrate its ability to carry out the refinancing. FASB, Statement No. 6, in AICPA *Professional Standards— Accounting*, sec. 2033.09–14.

nomer. Current revenues are inflows of *funds*, even if they are not currently realized in *cash;* current expenses are treated as operating outflows of funds if they represent expenditures of current assets or creation of current liabilities.

Funds flow differs from cash flow mainly to the extent that inventories, current receivables, and current payables change during the period. Peabody's revenues, for example, totaled $400,000 but its receivables were $15,000 greater at year end than on January 1—collections from customers thus amounting to only $385,000. Similarly, the current portion of income tax expense was $21,000, but only $19,000 of this was actually paid out in cash during the year—the balance in accrued income taxes having gone up by $2,000.

Salary and interest payments during the year were equal to salary and interest expense because no changes in the liabilities for these items were reported. Payments for merchandise and other goods and services used in operations differed from the amounts shown as expense, however. First, we know from Exhibit 16–3 that inventories increased by $5,000. Thus purchases must have exceeded the cost of goods sold by this amount, bringing the total up to $245,000. Next we find that current accounts payable went down by $10,000, indicating that cash payments exceeded the cost of purchased goods and services by that amount. Total cash payments, therefore, amounted to $245,000 + $20,500 + $10,000 = $275,500, or $15,000 more than the total of the cost of goods sold and the sundry selling and administrative expenses. The cash flow from operations can now be calculated as follows:

Funds provided by operations	$55,500
Add: Increase in current income taxes payable	2,000
Less: Increase in current receivables	(15,000)
Increase in inventories	(5,000)
Decrease in current accounts payable	(10,000)
Cash Flow from Operations	$27,500

PREPARING THE FUNDS STATEMENT: A WORK-SHEET APPROACH

The analysis in the previous section was conducted informally, more or less on the back of an envelope. In simple situations this procedure is adequate, but in the more common practical case, some kind of organized approach is generally necessary to keep the analysis under control: (1) to prevent errors and (2) to discover information that might otherwise go unnoticed.

The Work-Sheet Method

All formal methods of statement preparation start with a list of balance-sheet changes between two dates or, what amounts to the

EXHIBIT 16–10

PEABODY, INC.
T-Account Work Sheet for Funds Statement Preparation
For the Year Ended December 31, 19x1

Working Capital		Bonds Payable	
Net change 12,000		Net change 10,000	

Plant and Equipment		Deferred Income Taxes	
Net change 20,000			Net change 5,000

Accumulated Depreciation		Common Stock	
Net change 15,000			Net change 50,000

Funds Provided by Operations		Retained Earnings	
			Net change 2,000

Other Sources of Funds		Uses of Funds	

same thing, the beginning and ending balances in each balance-sheet item.

Peabody's balance-sheet changes for 19x1 are shown in T-account form in Exhibit 16–10, based on the balances listed in Exhibit 16–3. Our objective will be to reproduce the journal entries that together produced these balance-sheet changes. (The three blank T-accounts at the bottom of the exhibit are analytical accounts, inserted explicitly for use in statement preparation.)

Reconstructing Transactions

The first item to be examined is Common Stock. This showed an increase of $50,000 during the year. Of this amount, $30,000 represented the proceeds from the sale of new shares of stock to outside investors. The entry that would have been made to record this is:

Cash.....................................	30,000	
Common Stock		30,000

Since cash is a component of working capital and the sale of stock produced an inflow of cash, the sale of stock was a source of funds. Therefore we can restate this entry as follows on the work sheet:

(1)

| Other Sources of Funds | 30,000 | |
| Common Stock | | 30,000 |

This can be translated into a general rule: *each work-sheet entry should be identical to the entry that was made to record the transaction on the company's books, with one slight change: whenever a transaction embodies a funds flow or a correction of a funds-flow item in another transaction, one of the three analytical accounts—Funds Provided by Operations, Other Sources of Funds, or Uses of Funds—is debited or credited instead of the working-capital account that was actually affected.*

The remaining $20,000 increase in the Common Stock account resulted from a stock dividend issued during the year. The entry to record this is:

(2)

| Retained Earnings | 20,000 | |
| Common Stock | | 20,000 |

This transaction had no effect on funds flows and, therefore, requires no entry in any of the funds-change accounts on the work sheet. It was simply a paper transaction, transferring figures from one owners' equity account to another.

The Common Stock T-account on the work sheet now shows the following:

Common Stock

	Net change	50,000
	(1)	30,000
	(2)	20,000

Since the total of the amounts "below the line" just equals the net change in this account balance, and since no further information is available, it is safe to assume that the change in this account has been completely explained. We can move on to another account.

The next account we shall examine is Retained Earnings. One entry in this account has already been made (entry 2); another can be made to reflect the $39,000 net income for the year:

(3)

| Funds Provided by Operations | 39,000 | |
| Retained Earnings | | 39,000 |

This reflects a fact that should be totally familiar by now: although the determinants of net income are recorded in owners'-equity accounts, net income arises because more net assets were earned during the year than were consumed in the process. The debit to Funds Provided by Operations in entry (3) identifies this increase in net assets.

Another change in the Retained Earnings account reflected the declaration of cash dividends for the year. This was clearly a use of funds and can be entered in the work sheet by means of the following entry:

(4)

Retained Earnings	17,000	
Uses of Funds		17,000

The Retained Earnings account on the work sheet now shows the following:

Retained Earnings

		Net change	2,000
(2) Stock dividend	20,000	(3) Net income	39,000
(4) Cash dividend	17,000		

The three changes recorded in this account fully explain the net change in the account balance, and thus we can once again pass on to the analysis of another account.

It will be recalled that the $10,000 reduction in bonds payable was accomplished by repurchasing bonds at a price of $9,500. The entry to record this was:

Bonds Payable	10,000	
Cash		9,500
Gain on Debt Retirement		500

The $9,500 outlay of cash was definitely a use of funds, and the work-sheet entry is to debit Bonds Payable and credit Uses of Funds. The appropriate treatment of the $500 gain, on the other hand, is to subtract it from the net-income figure in computing the amount of funds provided by operations. Because the net-income figure was debited in entry (2) to the Funds Provided by Operations work sheet account, the $500 gain should be credited to that account. The composite work sheet entry is:

(5)

Bonds Payable	10,000	
Uses of Funds		9,500
Funds Provided by Operations		500

This leaves only the fixed-asset accounts to be analyzed. The next work-sheet entry records the purchase of plant and equipment during the year:

(6)

Plant and Equipment	50,000	
Uses of Funds		50,000

The next entry records depreciation:

(7)

Funds Provided by Operations	11,000	
Accumulated Depreciation		11,000

(Remember again that the depreciation amount is placed in the Funds Provided by Operations account as an adjustment to net income—it is not a source of funds in its own right.)

Finally, the entry that was made to record the retirement and sale of equipment during the year was:

Cash.....................................	3,000	
Loss on Sale of Equipment	1,000	
Accumulated Depreciation	26,000	
Plant and Equipment		30,000

On the funds-statement work sheet this would appear as:

(8)

Other Sources of Funds	3,000	
Funds Provided by Operations	1,000	
Accumulated Depreciation	26,000	
Plant and Equipment		30,000

With these three entries, we have accounted for all of the changes in the plant and equipment accounts.

This leaves only two balance sheet changes to be accounted for. The first of these, the $5,000 increase in the balance in the Deferred Income Taxes account, was produced by nonfunds charges against revenues and must be added back to net income. The work sheet entry is:

(9)

Funds Provided by Operations	5,000	
Deferred Income Taxes		5,000

The final item to be entered on the work sheet is the change in working capital. Because this figure is not to be subjected to further analysis, it can be accounted for by a single entry:

(10)

Working Capital.........................	12,000	
Uses of Funds		12,000

In other words, resources amounting to $12,000 were used to increase working capital during the year.

The Completed Work Sheet

   This completes the analysis. The work sheet now appears as in Exhibit 16–11. Notice that for each of the original accounts the sum of the entries below the line is equal to the net change in the account balance shown in the upper part of the account. The other three accounts contain all the items that will go into the funds statement itself. The funds statement in Exhibit 16–7 is simply a formal presentation of the amounts shown in these three analytical accounts.

EXHIBIT 16–11

PEABODY, INC.
Completed Funds Statement Work Sheet
For the Year Ended December 31, 19x1

Working Capital

Net change	12,000		
(10)	12,000		

Bonds Payable

Net change	10,000		
(5)		10,000	

Plant and Equipment

Net change	20,000		
(6)	50,000	(8)	30,000

Deferred Income Taxes

		Net change	5,000
		(9)	5,000

Accumulated Depreciation

Net change	15,000		
(8)	26,000	(7)	11,000

Common Stock

		Net change	50,000
		(1)	30,000
		(2)	20,000

Retained Earnings

		Net change	2,000
(2)	20,000	(3)	39,000
(4)	17,000		

Funds Provided by Operations

(3) Income	39,000	(5) Gain on	
(7) Depreciation	11,000	debt retirement	500
(8) Loss on sale of equipment	1,000		
(9) Deferred income taxes	5,000		

Uses of Funds

		(4) Dividends	17,000
		(5) Debt retirement	9,500
		(6) Equipment purchases	50,000
		(10) Increase working capital	12,000

Other Sources of Funds

(1) Sale of stock	30,000		
(8) Sale of equipment	3,000		

SUMMARY

The objective of the income statement is to summarize the economic productivity of the firm's resources during the period. Cash-flow statements summarize the receipts and disbursements of cash, and are intended to measure the firm's ability to meet its short-term needs for cash. Statements of changes in financial position, in contrast, are designed to show how the firm obtained and used financial resources during the period. The relationships between the structure of the resources provided and the amounts devoted to such uses as dividends, property additions, and debt retirement are important pieces of information for the evaluation of the firm's financial management, and for future planning by management.

This chapter has tried to explain what funds flows are and has presented a simple method that can be used to develop funds statements from income-statement and balance-sheet information. The method itself is less important, however, than the relationships between the funds statement and the other financial statements with which it is coupled.

KEY TERMS

Fund-flow analysis   Sources of funds
Funds from current operations   Uses of funds

INDEPENDENT STUDY PROBLEMS (Solutions in Appendix B)

1. **Analysis of plant and equipment changes.** Below are certain balances from the Placque Corporation's financial statements:

Balance Sheet

	19x3	19x2
Plant and equipment	$8,900	$8,500
Allowance for depreciation	3,600	3,300

Income Statement

Depreciation expense	$ 900
Loss on retirements	400

A note to the statement reports that property with an original cost of $1,300 and accumulated depreciation of $600 was sold during 19x3 for $300.

a. List the transactions that affected the plant and equipment and allowance for depreciation during the year.
b. Indicate how, if at all, each of these would be shown on a statement of changes in financial position.

2. Preparing a funds statement. The following figures (in thousands of dollars) have been taken from the Anderson Company's balance sheets for the beginning and end of the year 19x1:

	Beginning	Ending
Current assets	$56,746	$ 77,091
Long-term marketable securities, at cost	—	1,005
Property, plant and equipment, at cost	31,414	49,096
Accumulated depreciation	(13,237)	(18,421)
Total	$74,923	$108,771
Current liabilities	$42,536	$ 48,898
Bonds payable	—	7,000
Deferred income taxes	4,362	4,899
Total Liabilities	$46,898	$ 60,797
Preferred stock, at par ($100 per share)	1,347	1,123
Common stock, at par ($1 per share)	4,317	4,492
Additional paid-in capital	7,179	19,014
Retained earnings	15,182	23,345
Total	$74,923	$108,771

Additional information on transactions during 19x1:

1. Net income for the year, $8,243,000.
2. Preferred dividends declared and paid, $80,000.
3. Preferred stock repurchased and retired, 2,240 shares; the purchase price exceeded the par value by $37,000, and this excess was charged to additional paid-in capital.
4. Common stock issued, 175,000 shares.
5. Depreciation (on income statement), $5,501,000.
6. Cost of property, plant and equipment acquired, $18,082,000.

a. Use a work sheet to analyze the flows of funds this year.
b. Prepare a statement of changes in financial position for the year, using a balanced format.

3. Preparing a funds statement; identifying cash flows. The following information was taken from an annual report (all figures are in thousands of dollars):

Balance Sheet

		August 31 This Year		August 31 Last Year
Current Assets:				
Cash		$ 883		$ 954
U.S. government securities		1,222		1,704
Accounts receivable	$1,504		$1,553	
Allowance for uncollectible accounts	119	1,385	115	1,438
Inventories		1,946		2,651
Prepaid expenses		170		88
Total Current Assets		$5,606		$ 6,835

Balance Sheet

		August 31 This Year		August 31 Last Year
Long-Life Assets (at Cost):				
Land		295		295
Building, machinery, and equipment	$6,610		$5,998	
Allowances for depreciation	2,685	3,925	2,410	3,588
Total Assets		$9,826		$10,718
Current Liabilities:				
Accounts payable		$ 505		$ 609
Accrued taxes		556		$ 896
Total Current Liabilities		$1,061		$ 1,505
Mortgage bonds payable		710		1,260
Deferred income taxes		290		240
Total Liabilities		$2,061		$ 3,005
Stockholders' Equity:				
Capital stock		7,000		7,000
Retained earnings		765		713
Total Liabilities and Stockholders' Equity		$9,826		$10,718

Schedule of Changes in Plant Asset Accounts

	August 31 Last Year	Increase	Decrease	August 31 This Year
Cost	$5,998	$894 (additions)	$282*	$6,610
Allowance for depreciation	2,410	350 (depreciation)	75*	2,685
Balance	$3,588			$3,925

* Sale of equipment.

Statement of Income and Retained Earnings
For the Year Ended August 31, This Year

Net sales		$13,380
Less: Cost of goods sold	$10,880	
Selling and administrative expenses	1,623	
Loss on sale of equipment	100	
Income taxes	367	
Total deductions*		12,970
Net income		$ 410
Retained earnings, beginning of year		713
		$ 1,123
Less: Dividends declared	$ 300	
Settlement of prior years' taxes	58	358
Retained Earnings, End of Year		$ 765

* Includes depreciation, $350,000.

a. Prepare a statement of changes in financial position.
b. Calculate the amount of cash provided by operations. What additional information does this figure provide?

EXERCISES AND PROBLEMS

4. Changes in plant and equipment. The Granada Corporation's income statement for 19x1 showed depreciation of $150,000 and a $42,000 loss on the sale of equipment. The amount of accumulated depreciation increased by $37,000 between the beginning and the end of the year, and the original cost of the company's plant and equipment went from $1 million at the beginning of the year to $2 million on December 31, 19x1. The original cost of the equipment retired during the year amounted to $175,000.

Which changes in plant and equipment would appear on the funds statement for the year? Where would they appear and in what amounts?

5. Changes in plant and equipment. A note to the financial statements of Solo Corporation revealed the following:

	Plant and Equipment	Accumulated Depreciation
Beginning balance	$650,000	$200,000
Additions	210,000	45,000
Retirements	(140,000)	(110,000)
Ending balance	$720,000	$135,000

One item on the company's income statement for the year was a gain on the sale of equipment, $15,000.

Which of these items would appear on the statement of changes in financial position for the year, and how would they be shown?

6. Changes in contributed capital. A footnote to the financial statements of Eaton Enterprises identified the following changes in contributed capital during 19x1:

	Preferred Stock (Par Value)	Common Stock (Par Value)	Additional Paid-in Capital	Treasury Stock
Beginning balance	$120	$450	$375	$(12)
Retirement of preferred	(60)	—	(10)	—
Issue of common stock		100	250	—
Executive stock options	—	10	15	—
Stock dividend	—	28	70	—
Sale of treasury stock	—	—	5	12
Ending balance	$ 60	$588	$705	—

Which of these items would appear on the statement of changes in financial position for the year, and how would they be shown?

7. Interpretation: funds flow versus income flow. The Arkville Transit Company operates a network of bus lines in a small city. Last year it reported a small operating loss, and earnings are unlikely to improve in the near future. The following income statement for last year is likely to be typical of those to be prepared for the next few years:

Fares and other revenues		$1,000,000
Expenses:		
Salaries and wages	$650,000	
Fuel and lubricants	170,000	
Depreciation	100,000	
Tires and batteries	20,000	
Repair parts	30,000	
Other expenses	40,000	
Total Expenses		1,010,000
Net Income (Loss)		$ (10,000)

The company's balance sheet showed the following amounts at the beginning and end of last year:

	Beginning of Year	End of Year
Assets		
Current Assets:		
Cash	$ 100,000	$ 90,000
Receivables	150,000	140,000
Inventories	50,000	60,000
Total Current Assets	$ 300,000	$ 290,000
Plant and equipment (net)	940,000	920,000
Total Assets	$1,240,000	$1,210,000
Liabilities and Stockholders' Equity		
Current liabilities	$ 70,000	$ 150,000
Bonds payable	100,000	—
Common stock	260,000	260,000
Retained earnings	810,000	800,000
Total Liabilities and Stockholders' Equity	$1,240,000	$1,210,000

Mr. John Bergson recently bought an 80 percent interest in this company for $200,000. When shown the income statement above, he replied, "Good! That's just what I'd hoped for."

Mr. Bergson is a professional investor, not given to letting sentiment or emotion affect his investment decisions. Furthermore, he has little time to devote to active participation in the management of the companies he invests in.

a. How did he probably justify his decision to invest in the Arkville Transit Company?

b. What plans does he probably have for his investment in Arkville Transit? How do these plans differ from the actions of the previous owners? Do you think that he is likely to achieve his objectives? Support your answers with figures from the problem.

8. Preparing a funds statement. The General Ferry Corporation reported the following balance sheets in a recent year:

	Beginning of Year		End of Year	
Cash		$ 15		$ 10
Accounts receivable		10		15
Inventory		40		60
Current Assets.........................		$ 65		$ 85
Plant and equipment........................	$100		$113	
Less: Accumulated depreciation	40	60	45	68
Total Assets		$125		$153
Accounts payable............................		$ 10		$ 12
Bank loan payable		20		40
Current Liabilities......................		$ 30		$ 52
Deferred income taxes		5		7
Shareholders' equity:				
Common stock ($1 par)	$ 25		$ 29	
Capital paid-in in excess of par	15		20	
Retained earnings	50	90	45	94
Total Liabilities and Shareholders' Equity...............................		$125		$153

Additional information:

1. Net income for the year (including $3 gain on sale of plant and equipment), $5.
2. Cash dividends declared and paid during the year, $10.
3. Depreciation on plant and equipment during the year, $8.
4. Plant and equipment acquired during the year:
   For cash, $10.
   For four new shares of common stock, $9.

Prepare a statement of changes in financial position.

9. Preparing funds statement; contrast with cash flow statement. Hartwell Stores operates a chain of retail hardware stores. Its income statement for 19x5 showed the following:

Gross sales		$120
Less: Estimated customer defaults	$ 2	
Cost of goods sold	80	
Wages and salaries	15	
Depreciation	5	
Income tax expense	4	
Miscellaneous operating expense	8	114
Net Income		$ 6

The following figures were taken from the company's statements of financial position at the beginning and end of 19x5:

	January 1	December 31
Assets:		
Cash	$10	$ 8
Accounts receivable (net)	20	23
Inventory (at cost)	15	19
Plant and equipment (net)	30	35
Total Assets	$75	$85
Liabilities and Owners' Equity:		
Accounts payable	$11	$17
Bonds payable (long-term)	22	21
Deferred income taxes	3	4
Common stock	25	31
Retained earnings	14	12
Total Liabilities and Owners' Equity	$75	$85

You have the following additional information:

1. The company declared and paid $5 in cash dividends to its shareholders in 19x5.
2. A stock dividend of $3 was declared and distributed.
3. Equipment with an original cost of $7 and accumulated depreciation of $6 was sold. There was neither a gain nor a loss on this transaction.
4. All accounts payable arose from the purchase of merchandise.

a. Prepare a statement of changes in financial position for 19x5. The statement should list each source of funds, including funds provided by operations, and each use of funds.
b. How does this differ from a cash-flow statement? You should quantify your answer, but you need not prepare a full cash flow statement.

10. Preparing a funds statement; cash flow from operations.   You have the following information about the financial affairs of the XYZ Company:

1. Balance sheets:

	Beginning of Year		End of Year	
Current Assets:				
Cash		$ 2		$ 1
Accounts receivable		3		4
Inventories		5		6
Total Current Assets		$10		$11
Land, plant, and equipment, cost	$20		$29	
Less: Accum. depreciation	8	12	9	20
Total Assets		$22		$31
Current Liabilities:				
Accounts payable		$ 4		$ 3
Taxes payable		1		2
Notes payable		—		2
Total Current Liabilities		$ 5		$ 7

	Beginning of Year		End of Year
Bonds payable		—	5
Deferred taxes		3	4
Total Liabilities		$ 8	$16
Common stock	$ 4		$ 5
Additional paid-in capital	2		4
Retained earnings	8		6
Total Owners' Equity		14	15
Total Liabilities and Owners' Equity		$22	$31

2. Income statement:

Sales Revenues		$48
Operating expenses:		
Cost of goods sold	$25	
Depreciation	4	
Other	15	44
Operating Income		$ 4
Gain on sale of equipment		5
Income Before Taxes		$ 9
Income tax expense		4
Net Income		$ 5

3. Footnotes:
(1) Land purchased during the year in exchange for bonds, $5.
(2) Cash dividends declared and paid, $4.
(3) Stock dividends, capitalized at $3.
(4) Original cost of plant and equipment retired and sold during the year, $7.

a. Prepare a statement of changes in financial position.
b. Was the amount of cash flow from operations greater or less than the amount of funds provided by operations? Explain briefly.

11. Preparing and interpreting a funds statement. The Traydown Corporation's financial position went from bad to worse during 19x8, although net income showed a satisfactory increase over that of prior years. Despite the company's negotiation of a $100,000 bank loan early in 19x8, the cash balance decreased to a dangerous point by the end of the year. The balance sheets showed the following:

TRAYDOWN CORPORATION
Comparative Balance Sheets
(thousands of dollars)

	December 31, 19x7	December 31, 19x8
Assets		
Current Assets:		
Cash	$ 50	$ 30
Receivables	200	220
Inventories	150	200
Total Current Assets	$400	$450

	December 31, 19x7	December 31, 19x8
Buildings and fixtures......................	$300	$280
Less: Allowance for depreciation	(90)	(70)
Net Buildings and Fixtures	$210	$210
Total Assets	$610	$660

Liabilities and Stockholders' Equity		
Current Liabilities:		
Accounts and wages payable	$200	$180
Bank loan payable	50	150
Total Current Liabilities	$250	$330
Mortgage payable	70	55
Deferred income taxes	20	23
Long-term note payable	10	12
Total Liabilities	$350	$420
Stockholders' Equity:		
Common stock (par)	$140	$130
Retained earnings	120	110
Total Stockholders' Equity	$260	$240
Total Liabilities and Stockholders' Equity...............................	$610	$660

Notes (All figures are in thousands of dollars):

1. Net income for 19x8 was $29.
2. Total sales were approximately the same in 19x8 as in 19x7.
3. A building with an original cost of $52 and accumulated depreciation of $30 was sold for $56, cash.
4. Depreciation for the year was $10.
5. Cash dividends paid were $23.
6. One stockholder sold his common stock back to the company for $26, cash. The par value of this stock was $10, and the remaining $16 of the repurchase price was charged to retained earnings.

a. Prepare a statement of changes in financial position, with a supplementary schedule of working-capital changes.

b. Prepare a brief report, addressed to the loan officers of the company's bank, commenting on any items in your statement you think would help them reach a decision on renewing or increasing the size of the bank's loan to the company. They have a statement of forecasted cash flows for 19x9, but feel that the 19x8 funds statement can provide additional information the forecast does not provide.

12. *Preparing a funds statement; impact of inflation.* A company's annual report showed the following balance sheets for the beginning and end of its most recent fiscal year:

Current Assets:	Beginning		End		Change	
Cash		$ 10		$ 20		+$10
Accounts receivable		30		51		+ 21
Inventory		50		45		− 5
Total Current Assets		$ 90		$116		+$26
Investments in other corporations		80		50		− 30
Fixed assets	$220		$228		+$8	
Less: Accumulated depreciation	120		124		+ 4	
Fixed Assets, Net		100		104		+ 4
Total Assets		$270		$270		−
Current Liabilities:						
Accounts payable		$ 40		$ 35		−$ 5
Dividends payable		−		2		+ 2
Total Current Liabilities		$ 40		$ 37		−$ 3
Bonds payable		40		−		− 40
Deferred income taxes		20		23		+ 3
Total Liabilities		$100		$ 60		−$40
Shareowners' Equity:						
Common stock (par).................	$ 25		$ 30		+$ 5	
Additional paid-in capital	65		90		+ 25	
Retained earnings	80		90		+ 10	
Total Shareowners' Equity		170		210		+ 40
Total Liabilities and Share-owner's Equity		$270		$270		−

You have the following additional information:

1. Net income for the year, $30.
2. Cash dividends declared during the year, $8.
3. Stock dividends declared during the year (par value $2), $12.
4. Depreciation on fixed assets for the year, $18.
5. Purchases of fixed assets during the year:
   For cash, $21.
   In exchange for stock (par value $3), $18.
6. Cash proceeds from sale of fixed assets during the year, $2.
7. Cash proceeds from sale of investments during the year, $42; no investments were purchased during the year, and all investments are shown on the balance sheet at cost.
8. All accounts payable were to vendors of merchandise bought for resale.

a. Prepare a statement of changes in financial position.
b. The year in question was a year of severe inflation. Judging from the funds statement and from information in the problem, do you think the actions taken by the management of this company were appropriate in an inflationary situation?

13. Preparing a funds statement. The net changes in the balance sheet of X Company for the year 19x0 are shown at the top of the next page.

	Debit	Credit
Investments		$25,000
Land	$ 3,200	
Buildings	35,000	
Machinery	6,000	
Office equipment		1,500
Allowance for depreciation:		
Buildings		2,000
Machinery		900
Office equipment	600	
Discount on bonds	2,000	
Bonds payable		40,000
Capital stock—preferred	10,000	
Capital stock—common......................		12,400
Premium on common stock		5,600
Retained earnings		6,800
Working capital	37,400	
Total	$94,200	$94,200

Additional information:

1.   Cash dividends of $18,000 were declared December 15, 19x0, payable January 15, 19x1. A 2 percent stock dividend on the common stock was issued March 31, 19x0, when the market value was $12.50 per share.
2.   The investments were sold for $27,500.
3.   A building which cost $45,000 and had a depreciated basis of $40,500 was sold for $50,000.
4.   The following entry was made to record an exchange of an old machine for a new one:

Machinery..	13,000	
Allowance for Depreciation—Machinery	5,000	
Machinery		7,000
Cash		11,000

5.   A fully depreciated office machine which cost $1,500 was written off.
6.   Preferred stock of $10,000 par value was redeemed for $10,200.
7.   The company sold 1,000 shares of its common stock (par value $10) on June 15, 19x0, for $15 a share. There were 13,240 shares outstanding on December 31, 19x0.

Prepare a statement of changes in financial position for the year 19x0.
(AICPA adapted)

14.   Preparing and interpreting a funds statement.   The Apex Company's financial statements for 19x2 showed the following (all figures are in thousands of dollars):

Balance Sheets

Assets	December 31, 19x2	December 31, 19x1
Current Assets:		
Cash	$ 2,133	$ 2,250
Accounts receivable, net	1,382	1,064
Inventories	1,179	936
Total Current Assets	$ 4,694	$ 4,250

Balance Sheets

	December 31, 19x2	December 31, 19x1
Long-Term Assets:		
Land	273	198
Buildings, machinery, and equipment	6,700	6,750
Less: Allowance for depreciation	(2,270)	(2,000)
Investments in subsidiaries	3,018	3,002
Goodwill	90	100
Total Assets	$12,505	$12,300
Liabilities and Shareowners' Equity		
Current Liabilities:		
Accounts payable	$ 1,080	$ 2,350
Taxes payable	550	650
Dividends payable	350	—
Total Current Liabilities	$ 1,980	$ 3,000
Long-Term Liabilities:		
Bonds payable	1,000	—
Bond premium	72	—
Provision for pensions	150	150
Provision for deferred income taxes	110	90
Total Liabilities	$ 3,312	$ 3,240
Shareowners' Equity:		
Common stock, at par	1,510	1,500
Premium on common stock	2,000	1,910
Appropriation for contingencies	400	300
Retained earnings	5,283	5,350
Total Liabilities and Shareowners' Equity	$12,505	$12,300

Income Statement
For the Year Ended December 31, 19x2

Sales		$ 9,880
Income from unconsolidated subsidiaries		206
Gain on sale of land		15
Total		$10,101
Less: Cost of goods sold	$7,414	
Selling and administrative expenses	1,843	
Amortization of goodwill	10	
Interest expense	97	
Income taxes	354	
Total expenses		9,718
Net Income		$ 383

Notes to financial statements:

1. All the company's subsidiaries were located in the United States. Income on investments in unconsolidated subsidiaries was recognized on an equity basis.
2. Expenses for the year included depreciation in the amount of $496,000.
3. The only dividend declared during the year on Apex common stock was the cash dividend declared during December and payable on January 20, 19x3.

4. Buildings, equipment, and machinery purchased in 19x2 cost $246,000.
5. The Apex Company issued stock during the year in exchange for land. No other common stock transactions occurred during the year.
6. Bonds were issued on January 2, 19x2, with a 10 percent coupon rate.

   a. Prepare a statement of changes in financial position for the year,
   b. What does this funds statement tell you about management's financial policies and practices?

15. *Using funds statements to explain changes in financial status.* The Mastik Company was incorporated in 1972 by two young electronics engineers, Frank Orsini and Rosemary Newman, to manufacture and market a new electronic relay they had developed. The initial share capital consisted of 10,000 shares, divided equally between the two founders. Each of the founders paid the company $10,000 in cash for those shares. An additional block of 2,000 shares was issued in 1974 to a friend of the founders in exchange for $5 a share, paid in cash.

The company's first product was highly successful, and in 1974 operations were transferred to a larger building which the company leased for five years. Purchase of additional equipment at that time was financed by a five-year loan from an equipment finance company. This same company also granted loans for equipment purchased in subsequent years.

Mastik's sales continued to grow at a rapid rate as new products and services were introduced. Net income grew even faster, as shown in the following table:

	1975	1976	1977
Sales	$194,000	$318,000	$390,000
Expenses:			
Wages and salaries	$ 87,000	$178,000	$191,000
Materials and supplies	58,000	75,000	94,000
Rent	12,000	12,000	12,000
Depreciation	5,000	7,000	8,000
Other operating expenses (including interest)	20,000	22,000	31,000
Income taxes	4,000	8,000	18,000
Total Expenses	$186,000	$302,000	$354,000
Net Income	$ 8,000	$ 16,000	$ 36,000

In March 1978, Mastik's commercial bank notified management that the company's bank balance had fallen to less than the minimum required by the bank. The bank was unwilling to extend additional credit unless the company was able to broaden its ownership base and attract more stockholder capital. The company's balance sheets for the previous four years were as follows:

Assets	1974	1975	1976	1977
Current Assets:				
Cash	$18,000	$ 21,000	$ 15,000	$ 8,000
Accounts receivable	20,000	29,000	48,000	74,000
Inventories	11,000	15,000	30,000	55,000
Prepayments	2,000	3,000	4,000	5,000
Total Current Assets	$51,000	$ 68,000	$ 97,000	$142,000
Long-Term Assets:				
Machinery and equipment	$50,000	$ 60,000	$ 65,000	$ 82,000
Less: Accumulated depreciation	(6,000)	(11,000)	(18,000)	(26,000)
Net Long-Term Assets	$44,000	$ 49,000	$ 47,000	$ 56,000
Total Assets	$95,000	$117,000	$144,000	$198,000
Liabilities and Stockholders' Equity				
Current Liabilities:				
Accounts payable	$ 3,000	$ 6,000	$ 10,000	$ 14,000
Wages and taxes payable	4,000	5,000	9,000	20,000
Notes payable to bank	2,000	7,000	12,000	20,000
Total Current Liabilities	$ 9,000	$ 18,000	$ 31,000	$ 54,000
Equipment loan payable	30,000	35,000	30,000	25,000
Notes payable to stockholders	4,000	4,000	7,000	12,000
Total Liabilities	$43,000	$ 57,000	$ 68,000	$ 91,000
Stockholders' Equity:				
Common stock	$30,000	$ 30,000	$ 30,000	$ 30,000
Retained earnings	22,000	30,000	46,000	77,000
Total Stockholders' Equity	$52,000	$ 60,000	$ 76,000	$107,000
Total Liabilities and Stockholders' Equity	$95,000	$117,000	$144,000	$198,000

Mr. Orsini and Ms. Newman were stunned by this news. They didn't understand how they had gotten into such a difficult position, since they had never reported a loss, even in their first year of operations, their customers were all good credit risks, and finished goods were always shipped soon after completion.

Prepare a report for Mr. Orsini and Ms. Newman explaining to them what had happened.

17

Financial-Statement Analysis

CORPORATE FINANCIAL STATEMENTS summarize part of the company's history. Their main purpose, however, is to help managers and investors make decisions that will affect the company's future. The study of financial statements for this purpose is known as *financial-statement analysis*. The purpose of this chapter is to explain what financial-statement analysis is and what it is expected to accomplish. We'll also introduce some of the devices financial analysts use. The chapter has four parts:

1. The basic tools of analysis: financial ratios.
2. Measures of profitability.
3. Measures of debt-paying ability and risk.
4. Measures of efficiency.

THE BASIS: THE ROLE OF RATIOS

The basic building block in financial-statement analysis is the *ratio*, a percentage or decimal relationship of one number to another. Ratios are used in three different ways: (1) to examine the relationships between two financial-statement items or groups of items in the same time period, such as the amount of cash on hand and the total of the current liabilities (structural analysis); (2) to compare individual financial-statement items of the same company in different time periods (time-series analysis); and (3) to compare the company's financial-statement items with those of other firms in the same industry or with some market-wide measure or measures (cross-sectional analysis).

The advantage of ratios is that they bring the numbers being expressed as ratios down to a common scale. A company may be twice as large as it was ten years ago, for example, so comparing total expenses in the two periods won't be as useful as comparing the expense/revenue ratios in the two periods.

Stating relationships on a common scale doesn't necessarily make them perfectly comparable, however. A high ratio may be appropriate for a company in one industry but not for a company in another industry or for a company at a different stage in its development or for a much larger or smaller company.

Both time-series analysis and cross-sectional analysis may be distorted by inflation or unusual business conditions. Time-series comparisons tend to be distorted by inflation to a larger extent than cross-sectional comparisons because all observations in a cross-sectional analysis are made in the same time period, with the same resource price structure. The analyst's problem is to decide how serious these distortions are and how to adjust for them.

For these reasons, we can't prescribe an ideal value for any ratio. The ideal varies with the circumstances the individual company finds itself in. Our objective will be to provide some insight into whether high ratios are likely to signal strengths or weaknesses in different circumstances.

To do this, we'll use the financial statements of a hypothetical company, the Alpha Company. Exhibit 17–1 presents Alpha's balance sheets as of the end of 19x1 and 19x2. Exhibit 17–2 shows the company's income statement for 19x2, and Exhibit 17–3 is the statement of changes in retained earnings for 19x2. We'll introduce the company's funds statement later in the chapter.

MEASURES OF PROFITABILITY

Investors become and remain stockholders in a company because they believe that dividends and capital gains (increases in the market price of the stock) will compare favorably with the amounts they can earn on alternative investments of comparable risk. The most important determinant of future dividends and capital gains is the corporation's future earnings, and the first source of data for use in forecasting future earnings is the corporation's past-earnings record.

Three ratios used widely as measures of the company's past-earnings record are:

1. Earnings per share of common stock.
2. Return on common equity.
3. Return on assets.

EXHIBIT 17–1

ALPHA COMPANY
Statements of Financial Position
December 31, 19x1, and 19x2

Assets

	19x2	*19x1*
Current Assets:		
Cash	$ 2,600	$ 4,300
Receivables	19,800	17,100
Inventories	35,900	28,700
Total Current Assets	$58,300	$50,100
Long-Term Assets:		
Buildings and equipment	$49,100	$42,900
Less: Accumulated depreciation	19,400	18,100
Net buildings and equipment	$29,700	$24,800
Land	1,400	1,900
Total Assets	$89,400	$76,800

Liabilities and Shareholders' Equity

	19x2	*19x1*
Current Liabilities:		
Accounts payable	$ 6,600	$ 4,800
Notes payable	15,500	6,200
Federal income taxes	2,100	2,200
Total Current Liabilities	$24,200	$13,200
Long-term debt	11,700	17,400
Total Liabilities	$35,900	$30,600
Shareholders' Equity:		
5% preferred stock, par value $10 (700 shares)	$ 7,000	$ 7,000
Common stock, par value $5 (2,000 shares in 19x2, 1,800 shares in 19x1)	10,000	9,000
Capital in excess of par value	12,600	9,900
Retained earnings	23,900	20,300
Total Shareholders' Equity	$53,500	$46,200
Total Liabilities and Shareholders' Equity	$89,400	$76,800

We'll discuss each of these in turn and then describe a way of breaking the return-on-assets ratio down into two component ratios, the asset-turnover ratio and the profit-margin ratio. We'll also discuss the concept of the quality of earnings and the dividend-payout ratio.

Earnings per Common Share

The most widely used measure of financial performance is net after-tax earnings per common share, usually referred to as *earnings per share*. As we saw in Chapter 14, dividends the holders of preferred stock are entitled to must be subtracted from net income to

EXHIBIT 17–2

ALPHA COMPANY
Income Statement
For the Year Ended December 31, 19x2

Sales revenue		$105,200
Expenses:		
Cost of goods sold (except depreciation)	$57,700	
Depreciation	2,500	
Research and development	4,700	
Selling and administration	27,400	92,300
Income before interest and taxes		$ 12,900
Interest expense		1,400
Income before taxes		$ 11,500
Income taxes		5,750
Net income		$ 5,750

get earnings applicable to the common stock. The 19x2 calculation for the Alpha Company is:

$$\frac{\text{Net income} - \text{Preferred dividends}}{\text{No. of common shares}} = \frac{\$5,750 - \$350}{2,000}$$
$$= \$2.70 \text{ per share.}$$

Earnings per share figures are used to compare one year's earnings with those of prior years. They are also combined with other figures, such as market price per share, to reveal relationships the analyst wishes to examine. The relationship between a company's earnings per share and a market index of earnings (total earnings of a large sample of corporations) can be particularly useful in predicting the company's future earnings.

Both the numerator and the denominator of this ratio need to be studied carefully. The dilution adjustments we discussed in Chapter 14 are now made routinely and we needn't dwell on them here. What we need to concentrate on is the earnings numerator. For one

EXHIBIT 17–3

ALPHA COMPANY
Statement of Changes in Retained Earnings
For the Year Ended December 31, 19x2

Retained earnings, January 1, 19x2		$20,300
Add: Net income, 19x2		5,750
		$26,050
Less: Dividends on preferred stock	$ 350	
Dividends on common stock	1,800	
Total dividends		2,150
Retained earnings, December 31, 19x2		$23,900

thing, analysts distinguish between earnings from ordinary, continuing operations and earnings from operations about to be discontinued or from extraordinary events. In fact, even ordinary operating earnings have to be examined carefully because many items that used to be reported as extraordinary items, at the bottom of the income statement, must now be included in ordinary income. The total amount of income or loss from these sources is likely to fluctuate more widely than income from other sources. The analyst should be alert to identify the underlying movements in earnings behind these fluctuations.

Quality of Earnings

Analysts now study the company's financial statements to appraise what they refer to as the *quality of earnings*. Quality has many dimensions. Some of these refer to the company's accounting policies. Companies using Fifo for inventories, straight-line depreciation, the flow-through method of accounting for the investment credit, and pooling-of-interests accounting for business combinations are likely to report greater earnings than companies using Lifo, accelerated depreciation, investment-credit deferral, and the purchase method of accounting for business combinations.

Quality also depends on the nature of the company's products and markets. It is important to know whether the bulk of current earnings comes from growing business segments or from declining segments, from domestic markets or foreign markets, from a few large customers or many small ones, and so on. The publication of segment-income data, including a geographic breakdown, provides analysts with the raw material for analyzing these aspects of quality.

A third aspect of earnings quality is the extent to which current earnings are affected by current expenditures on research and development or missionary marketing activities. Sales revenues from these activities won't be recognized until some time in the future, but their costs show up among the current year's expenses. Similarly, if equipment-replacement prices have been rising rapidly, current depreciation charges are likely to be much lower than they will be in the future when the present equipment is replaced. In fact, a good deal of our discussion in Chapters 8–15 was designed to provide the foundation for an analysis of the quality of earnings.

Return on Common Equity

The absolute amount of income is an inadequate measure of profitability because it does not indicate how much had to be invested to achieve it. One way to put earnings and investment figures together is to compute the rate of return on common equity, that is, the ratio of net income available to the common shareholders to the *book value* of the common shareholders' equity in the company. In Alpha, the book value of the common equity was the total of capital stock at par value, capital in excess of par value, and retained earnings, adding up to $46,500 at the end of 19x2.[1] The rate of return on common equity, therefore, was as follows:

$$\frac{\text{Net Income} - \text{Preferred Dividends}}{\text{Common Equity}} = \frac{\$5,750 - \$350}{\$46,500} = 11.6 \text{ percent.}$$

In reaching a judgment as to whether this represents good or bad performance, a number of questions must be answered. For example, how does this figure compare with the return of other firms in the industry and in industry in general? Is this company's rate of return holding steady, going up, or declining? How wide are the year-to-year fluctuations in rate of return?

The rate of return on common equity can also be calculated in another way, with the market value of the common shares as the denominator of the ratio. After all, book value represents investment decisions investors made in the past. The current question is how large a return the company is making on the amounts investors are now willing to invest in this company.

This ratio is calculated routinely, but in an inverted form. That is, one of the most widely quoted ratios in the financial press is the *price/earnings ratio*, usually referred to simply as the *P/E ratio*. For example, if Alpha's common stock was being traded on the market at a price of $27 a share at the end of 19x2, the P/E ratio was $27/$2.70 = 10. This is simply the reciprocal of the earnings/market value ratio: $2.70/$27 = 10 percent.

Return on Assets and the Leverage Effect

A corporation's return on its common equity is a consequence of two factors: (1) its return on assets and (2) the extent to which *leverage* is employed by the company. Return on assets is defined as the ratio of earnings before interest to total assets. Leverage is the percentage of total assets that is supplied by creditors and preferred shareholders.[2]

---

[1] Earnings may be related to the investment at the beginning of the year, the investment at the end of the year, or an average of the two. We have used year-end investment because it is generally the most convenient.

[2] Leverage can also be defined as the ratio of *long-term* debt and preferred stock to the book value of the common stock, or as the ratio of *interest-bearing* debt and preferred stock to common equity. Our definition, which uses total liabilities in the numerator and total assets in the denominator, is appropriate when the comparison is to be made between return on total assets and return on the common shareholders' equity in those assets, as it is here.

Pretax analysis. The leverage effect can be seen most easily in an analysis of pretax figures. For example, The Alpha Company had $89,400 in assets and $12,900 in income before interest and taxes in 19x2 (from Exhibits 17–1 and 17–2). Its pretax rate of return on assets was:

$$\frac{\text{Income before Interest and Taxes}}{\text{Total Assets}} = \frac{\$12,900}{\$89,400} = 14.4\%.$$

The reason for using earnings before interest and dividends as the numerator in this ratio is that the denominator represents all assets, not just those supplied by the shareholders. To be comparable, the earnings figure should measure earnings before distributions either to creditors (interest) or shareholders (dividends).

By using leverage, the company was able to earn a much higher return on its common equity than it earned on its total assets. If the income tax rate had been zero, the earnings available to the common stockholder would have been the $12,900, less the $1,400 in interest expense and the $350 in dividends on the preferred stock, or $11,150:

Income before Interest and Income Taxes	− Interest Expense	− Preferred Dividends =	Pretax Leveraged Income
$12,900	$1,400	$350	$11,150

The book value of the common stockholders' equity was $46,500 (from Exhibit 17–1). The pretax rate of return on common equity therefore was:

$$\frac{\text{Pretax Income on Common Equity}}{\text{Common Stockholders' Equity}} = \frac{\$11,150}{\$46,500} = 24.0\%.$$

The leverage effect in this case is illustrated in Exhibit 17–4. This was successful leverage because the 3.9 percent average interest cost of debt and 5 percent cost of preferred stock were less than the overall earnings rate on total assets (14.4 percent). The common shareholders, in other words, gained the full 14.4 percent on their own investment plus more than half of the return on the assets financed by creditors and preferred stockholders. To get this additional return, the common stockholders had to assume the greater *risk* (uncertainty of the rate of return on their investment) arising from the increased fixed burden of debt service. ("Debt service" is the total of the payments for interest and principal in any period.)

Three technical aspects of this analysis are worth noting. First,

EXHIBIT 17–4.   Pretax Effect of Financial Leverage

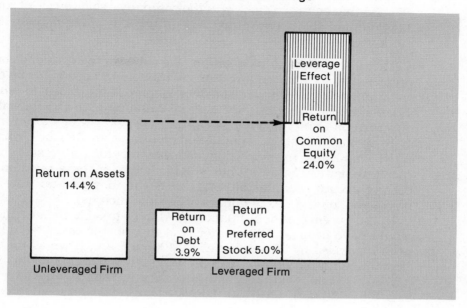

some liabilities, such as accounts payable and accrued taxes payable, lead to no recognized interest expense. The presence of these liabilities in the mix reduces the average interest cost of the company's debts to less than the interest rate on those liabilities which give rise to recognized interest expense.

Second, year-end liability balances may be a very poor approximation to the *average* amount of liabilities outstanding during the year, which may have been much larger or much smaller than the year-end amounts. These variations within the year make leverage analysis much less precise than it appears to be.

Finally, both interest and preferred-dividend rates are the historical rates in effect when the debt was incurred or preferred stock was issued. They don't necessarily represent the current costs of those kinds of capital. Alpha's pretax costs of *new* borrowing in 19x2 may have been much higher than the historical rates reflected in this analysis. For current leveraging decisions, management has to compare current borrowing rates with the anticipated returns on additional investments in assets.

After-tax analysis.   The after-tax analysis is likely to be even more dramatic than the pretax analysis because tax deductibility reduces the nominal after-tax cost of debt. The analysis is in three steps:

1.   Calculate the after-tax rate of return on common equity for the actual capital structure.

2. Recalculate the after-tax rate of return on equity on the assumption that common stock was the company's sole source of funds.
3. Compare these two rates; the difference between them is the leverage effect.

The first of these steps is simple. We subtract the dividends on any preferred stock outstanding from net income and divide the difference by the common shareholders' equity. We performed this calculation in the preceding section and came up with an after-tax rate of return on equity of 11.6 percent.

To make the second calculation, we have to find out what tax rate is applicable to the portion of earnings before interest and taxes that interest deductibility has shielded from income taxation. The correct tax rate for this adjustment is the marginal-tax rate—that is, the rate on the next i dollars of taxable income.

In the absence of debt financing, Alpha's taxable income in 19x2 would have been $1,400 greater, and the income taxes would have been increased by 50 percent of $1,400, or $700, if we assume a 50 percent marginal-tax rate. Income taxes, therefore, would have been $5,750 + $700 = $6,450, and after-tax income would have been $12,900 − $6,450 = $6,450. The after-tax return on assets therefore was:

$$\frac{\text{Adjusted after-tax income}}{\text{Total assets}} = \frac{\$6,450}{\$89,400} = 7.2\%$$

This is the return Alpha would have earned on the common equity if no debt or preferred financing had been employed.

The after-tax leverage effect is illustrated in Exhibit 17–5. As this shows, the use of debt and preferred stock raised Alpha's return on its common equity from 7.2 percent to 11.6 percent. The after-tax cost of debt was only 1.95 percent, because the interest was deductible from taxable income.

The same calculations could be performed with market values substituted for book values in the denominator.

Successful versus unsuccessful leverage. Leverage works both ways, of course. If the overall return on assets is smaller than the rates of return on debt and preferred stock, the rate of return on the common equity will be smaller than the return on assets and may even be negative.

The relationship between return on assets and return on equity is diagrammed in Exhibit 17–6. In this case, with total debt of $35,900, a 1.95 percent average after-tax cost of debt and a 5 percent preferred stock, the average return on assets has to be only 2.5 percent for the return on common equity to be equal to return on assets. If

EXHIBIT 17–5. After-Tax Effect of Financial Leverage

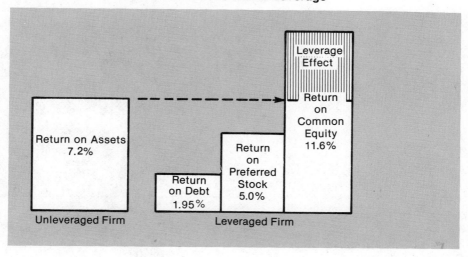

return on assets is higher than that, leverage will be successful; if return on assets is lower, leverage will be unsuccessful.

The line of relationship in Exhibit 17–6 is shown as a straight line. This won't always be true, partly because different tax rates are likely to apply to different portions of the taxable income and partly because the tax status of losses depends on the company's tax history. The basic relationship holds, however; the success or failure of leverage depends on the relationship between the return on assets and the after-tax book rate of return on senior securities.

The possibility of unsuccessful leverage adds to the risks of investment in this company, and the market will adjust the prices it is willing to pay for the company's stocks and bonds to reflect this risk. In simple terms, the common stock will have a lower price/earnings ratio than a comparable company with no leverage.

Percentage of Sales Ratios

The rate of return on assets is the product of two factors: (1) the rate of asset turnover and (2) the profit margin. This relationship can be stated in the form of an equation:

$$\text{Return on Assets} = \text{Asset Turnover} \times \text{Profit Margin}$$
$$= \frac{\text{Sales}}{\text{Assets}} \times \frac{\text{Income}}{\text{Sales}}$$

EXHIBIT 17–6.   Effect of Variations in Return on Assets on Leveraging Success

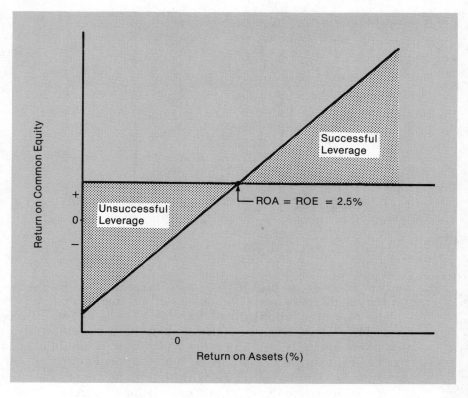

We'll discuss profit-margin ratios here, leaving asset-turnover ratios for the final section of this chapter.

The profit-margin ratio and other percentage of sales ratios are widely used in profitability analysis, mainly to identify trends or intercompany differences. In calculating the overall profit-margin ratio, we need to use the same income figure we are using in the return-on-investment comparisons. If return on investment is calculated as a return on assets, as in our present example, then the income figure should be before interest but after taxes, the tax figure being adjusted to eliminate the leverage effect, as described in the preceding paragraph.

Alpha's adjusted income after taxes, as we saw a moment ago, was $12,900 − $6,450 = $6,450. Its profit margin for 19x2 was:

$$\frac{\text{Adjusted Net Income}}{\text{Sales Revenue}} = \frac{\$6,450}{\$105,200} = 6.1 \text{ Percent.}$$

If return on investment is measured by the rate of return on equity, the numerator should be the amount of income available to the common stockholders (net income minus preferred dividends).

The overall profit-margin ratio is usually supplemented by various subordinated ratios, such as the *operating ratio* (the ratio of operating expenses to operating revenues), the *gross-margin ratio* (the ratio of the total gross margin to gross revenues), and the *research-and-development ratio* (the ratio of research and development expenses to gross revenues). These ratios are useful both in intercompany comparisons and in analyzing trends in the company's own performance. A rising operating ratio, for example, may be a signal of operating difficulties; an operating ratio higher than competitors' ratios may be a signal of competitive weakness. Alternatively, a high and rising operating ratio may signal a shift by the company to an aggressive marketing strategy, in which low profit margins are accompanied by large increases in sales volume, now or in the future.

This dual interpretation reinforces a point we made earlier. The ratio is only an analytical tool. A high ratio may be a good sign or a bad sign, and the analyst can only decide which it is by placing it in the context of other ratios and other available information.

The Payout Ratio and the Rate of Growth

Potential purchasers of a company's stock are buying not only dividends at the current rate but prospects of future growth (or decline). This growth is provided, in large part, by the reinvestment of funds provided by operations. An index of the company's commitment to growth is the *payout ratio*:

$$\text{Payout Ratio} = \frac{\text{Dividends per Share}}{\text{Earnings per Share}}$$

At Alpha in 19x2, the payout ratio was $0.90/$2.70 = 33\frac{1}{3}$ percent.

The companion of the payout ratio is the *retention ratio*, the percentage of the current year's earnings the company retains. Technically, it's the difference between the payout ratio and 100 percent—in Alpha's case, $66\frac{2}{3}$ percent.

The real question is how effectively the company can use the funds it retains and reinvests in the business. Financial analysts sometimes calculate a figure they call the *sustainable-growth ratio,* as follows:

$$\text{Sustainable-Growth Ratio} = \text{Return on Equity} \times \text{Retention Ratio.}$$

For Alpha in 19x2, the sustainable-growth ratio was 11.6 × 0.67 = 7.7 percent. This says that the book value of the stock was growing at a rate of 7.7 percent a year; if all other relationships were steady, earnings presumably were growing at the same rate. The higher the return on equity and the higher the retention rate, the higher the rate of growth in earnings the company can sustain.

The rate of return on equity is likely to be reflected in the *market-value ratio*:

$$\text{Market-Value Ratio} = \frac{\text{Market Price per Share}}{\text{Book Value per Share}}$$

Problems of asset measurement aside, companies with higher rates of return on equity will have higher stock prices relative to the current book value of the stock than comparable companies (with similar risk characteristics) having lower return-on-equity ratios, as long as the market believes the company can continue to generate these returns on the funds reinvested in the business. Earnings retention means the stockholders are exchanging current cash dividends in the expectation of receiving greater cash dividends or increased market prices in the future. If the company can't use the cash effectively, the return on equity will fall, the growth rate will drop, and the market-value ratio will decline.

The size of the market-value ratio depends on investors' appraisals of the ability of book values to measure the present value of the company's future cash flows. The book value of Alpha's common stock in 19x2 was $46,500/2,000 = $23.25 a share. The market price was $27, and the market-value ratio was $27/$23.25 = 1.16. This could reflect a relatively low asset-measurement profile—Lifo inventory measurement, for example. Alternatively, it could mean that the company's assets promised to yield a higher rate of return than investors considered normal.

MEASURES OF DEBT-PAYING ABILITY AND RISK

Both lenders and investors in stocks are interested not only in profitability but also in the risks associated with investments in individual companies. Lenders think of risk as the uncertainty as to whether they will receive the amounts due them and on time; equity investors see it as the degree of uncertainty surrounding their estimates of the rate of return on their investments. Financial-statement analysis includes three kinds of techniques for evaluating risk:

1. Analysis of the funds structure.
2. Analysis of the sources and uses of funds.
3. Coverage analysis.

Analysis of the Asset-Liability Structure

One kind of analysis of the sources and uses of funds is a study of the *structure* of the firm's assets and of its liabilities and owners' equities.

Debt structure. The order in which the sources of funds are listed in the balance sheet corresponds to two important characteristics: the interest cost of obtaining the funds and the risk they bring with them. Current liabilities are an attractive source of funds because the interest cost of this capital is low. However, since they fall due in a relatively short period, the risk cost is high. They may fall due for payment just when the company finds itself temporarily short of cash. Long-term debt, in contrast, typically carries a higher interest rate but poses a smaller immediate threat of insolvency. Furthermore, the company ordinarily can pick a convenient time to refinance long-term debt before it falls due, thereby minimizing the likelihood that it will fall due when the company lacks ready cash.

Finally, funds obtained from shareholders through the sale of stock or retention of earnings carry no risk of insolvency. The company has no contractual obligations to make payments on specified dates, even to the preferred shareholders. In return for removing this risk from the corporation, the stockholders expect a higher yield on their investment than that earned by the company's creditors. This desired yield can and should be considered a cost of stockholder capital.

The relative importance of debt in the capital structure is measured by a number of different ratios, of which we'll consider only three. The first of these, the *long-term-debt ratio*, is obtained by dividing the book value of the long-term debt by the book value of the owners' equity. For Alpha at the end of 19x2 this ratio was:

$$\frac{\text{Long-Term Debt}}{\text{Pfd. Stock + Common Equity}} = \frac{\$11,700}{\$7,000 + \$46,500} = 21.9 \text{ Percent.}$$

The long-term-debt ratio is used as a measure of risk. Because only the near-term debt retirement and interest requirements constitute an immediate threat to the company's solvency, however, this ratio applies more to long-term than to short-term risks.

A variant of the debt/equity ratio is the *debt/assets ratio,* the ratio of total liabilities to total assets. This is a more inclusive measure of risk than the long-term-debt ratio and more quickly responsive to changes in risk. Pressure for additional funds ordinarily can be relieved faster by increasing short-term debt than by any other means.

In 19x2, for example, the Alpha Company increased its short-term debt and decreased its long-term debt. As a result, the debt/assets ratio remained almost constant, but the *short-term-debt ratio* (current liabilities divided by total liabilities plus owners' equity) increased from 17.2 percent at the end of 19x1 to 27.1 percent a year later. Other things being equal, this represented an increase in risk.

The main difficulty in interpreting these ratios is that they are highly affected by the company's asset-measurement policies. The choice of inventory method, consolidation policy, and similar matters affect the equity-structure ratios just as they affect the profitability ratios.

One way to get around this difficulty is to calculate the debt structure on a market-value basis. The advantage of market values is that they provide a more up-to-date measure of the debt burden. Market values of debt represent the present value of future debt service payments under current market conditions. For example, if the market rate of interest is 9 percent, a company with $1 million of 5 percent debt incurred when the market yield was 5 percent has a smaller debt burden than a company with a $1 million issue of 9 percent bonds of the same maturity but issued when the market yield was 9 percent. Each will appear on the balance sheet as a $1 million liability, but the market value of the 5 percent issue will be much smaller, reflecting its smaller burden to the company.

Asset structure.   The way the firm's funds have been used is also significant. Current assets are more liquid than plant and equipment, for example—that is, they can be made available more quickly to meet unexpected cash needs. Investments in current assets may also be highly profitable if they enable the company to increase total revenues or reduce total operating costs. Beyond some point, however, additional investments in current assets add less than enough to income to provide an adequate rate of return on the additional investment—idle cash balances, for example, earn a very low rate of return.

With these relationships in mind, analysts can use asset structure ratios to see how management is using the company's funds. For instance, two of Alpha's asset structure ratios for 19x2 reflected a clear decline in the company's liquidity:

	19x1	19x2
Cash/assets	5.6%	2.9%
Cash and receivables/assets	27.9	25.1

This was a favorable change if it resulted from a reduction in the amount of idle assets, an unfavorable change if it resulted from the company's inability to generate enough cash to meet its needs.

Working-capital ratios.   Whether a company is liquid enough depends on its ability to meet short-term demands for cash. Analysts frequently use two balance-sheet ratios to throw light on this question: the current ratio and the quick ratio or acid-test ratio.

The *current ratio* is the ratio of total current assets to total current liabilities. Looking back at Exhibit 17–1, we see that Alpha Company's current ratio at the end of 19x2 was:

$$\frac{\text{Current Assets}}{\text{Current Liabilities}} = \frac{\$58,300}{\$24,200} = 2.41.$$

Since the comparable ratio at the beginning of the year was $50,100/$13,200 = 3.80, the company's activities during the year obviously caused a substantial weakening in its current position.

A high current ratio isn't an unmixed blessing. It shows that the company is financing a large proportion of its current assets from long-term sources—long-term debt and owners' equity. This provides a cushion or margin of safety against possible short-term downswings in the company's business, thereby reducing financial risk, but it is also costly. As we pointed out earlier, short-term credit is likely to be cheaper than long-term credit, and a high current ratio means the company is either unable or unwilling to use this cheaper credit as extensively as a company with a low ratio.

One defect of the current ratio is that its level depends on the method used to measure inventories. Other things being equal, a company using Fifo or average costing will have a higher current ratio after purchase prices have been rising than a company measuring inventories on a Lifo basis. Fortunately, inventory-replacement-cost data are now available for many companies, and these data give the analyst the raw materials to make adjustments to eliminate this source of noncomparability.

Another defect of the current ratio is that it conveys no information on the *composition* of the current assets. Clearly, a dollar of cash or even of accounts receivable is more readily made available to meet obligations than a dollar of most kinds of inventory. A measure designed to overcome this defect is the *quick ratio*. This is the ratio of cash, short-term marketable securities, and short-term receivables to current liabilities. This ratio for Alpha was as follows at the end of 19x2:

$$\frac{\text{Quick Assets}}{\text{Current Liabilities}} = \frac{\$2,600 + \$19,800}{\$24,200} = 0.93.$$

This represented a sharp decline from the previous year's value of ($4,300 + $17,100) ÷ $13,200 = 1.62, reflecting the large increase in inventory and notes payable. This shift might be regarded as a cause for some concern.

Funds-Flow Analysis

The main defect of all the balance-sheet ratios is that they represent static relationships. Very few companies have enough cash or liquid assets at the beginning of the year to cover all the payments they will have to make during the year. Nor should they, because this would tie up the company's funds unnecessarily. Instead, they rely on the cash coming in during the year to cover most of their needs to pay cash.

For this reason, the best guarantee that the company will be able to pay its bills when they come due is an ample excess of cash receipts from operations over cash disbursements required by operations. Whether Alpha's current ratio of 2.41 or its quick ratio of 0.93 represented an adequate margin of safety depended on the variability of the cash-flow stream, its ability to renew or replace its existing short-term obligations with other short-term obligations, and its ability to reduce the amount of its current assets without impairing its operating performance.

Management uses a *cash budget* to determine whether the anticipated cash receipts from operations are likely to be adequate to meet the company's needs for cash during the coming period. We'll discuss cash budgets in the next chapter. Outside investors have no access to the cash budget, however, and must try to approximate it by other means. The handiest tool for this purpose is the statement of changes in financial position (funds statement).

Alpha's funds statement for 19x2, prepared by the methods we described in Chapter 16, is presented in Exhibit 17–7. Since this company had no deferred taxes and no reported nonoperating gains and losses, funds from operations was the total of net income and depreciation. If this continued at the same level in 19x3, it wouldn't be big enough to cover dividends and plant and equipment expendi-

EXHIBIT 17–7

ALPHA COMPANY
Statement of Changes in Financial Position
For the Year Ended December 31, 19x2

Sources of Funds:

From operations:

Net income	$ 5,750
Depreciation	2,500
Total	$ 8,250
From sale of common stock	3,700
From sale of land	500
From working capital	2,800
Total Sources of Funds	$15,250

Uses of funds:

To retire long-term debt	$ 5,700
To pay dividends	2,150
To purchase plant and equipment	7,400
Total Uses of Funds	$15,250

tures at the 19x2 level. The analyst would have to estimate (*a*) how large the company's capital expenditures would be in 19x3 and (*b*) whether other sources of funds would be available in 19x3 to meet those needs.

The funds statement, of course, isn't a cash-flow statement, but it can usually serve the same purpose. Some changes in short-term receivables and payables are temporary, and, in the absence of growth, increases in one period will be offset by decreases in the next period. If the company's growth rate is rapid, however, the analyst will have to make explicit forecasts of the effect of this growth on the company's cash flows.

Coverage Ratios

Although the funds-flow statements and cash-flow statements are probably the most valuable single basis for judging debt-paying ability, certain *coverage ratios* are also widely used for this purpose. Like the funds statement, the coverage ratio deals with *dynamics*, measuring a relationship between two sets of *flows*. The basic coverage ratio is the *times-charges-earned ratio*, the ratio of income before taxes and interest to interest and preferred dividend requirements. On this basis, the Alpha ratio for 19x2 was:

$$\frac{\text{Income before Interest and Taxes}}{\text{Interest} + \text{Preferred Dividends}} = \frac{\$12,900}{\$1,750} = 7.4.$$

In other words, the company's earnings could shrink to one seventh of their 19x2 size and still be adequate to cover the interest and preferred dividend requirements.[3]

The times-charges-earned ratio is obviously incomplete. Interest and preferred-dividend payments aren't the only payments the company is committed to make on a continuing basis. A company's fixed obligations also include such items as property taxes, rentals, scheduled retirements of maturing debt, and even management salaries and other operating costs that wouldn't shrink quickly in the face of a reduction in the company's operating volume. A better ratio therefore is a ratio of the cash flow available to cover fixed-cash payments of all kinds. This is the *fixed-charges ratio*. To calculate the amount of cash flow available, we must identify the fixed costs we subtracted in calculating the cash flow from operations and add them back. In other words, the fixed-charges ratio is calculated as follows:

$$\frac{\text{Cash Flow from Operations} + \text{Fixed Operating Cash Payments}}{\text{Fixed Operating Cash Payments} + \text{Other Fixed Cash Payments}}$$

Outsiders don't have full access to the figures entering into the calculation of this ratio, but they have enough information to approximate it. We'll return to this idea in Chapter 21, in which we discuss a technique known as *break-even analysis*.

No matter what coverage ratio is used, however, it has to be examined in conjunction with some measure of *volatility*—that is, the amplitude of fluctuations in annual earnings or operating cash flows before taxes and interest. Presumably, the higher the earnings volatility, the higher the coverage ratio should be.

MEASURES OF EFFICIENCY

As we pointed out earlier, a company's profitability depends on the profit margin on sales and on the amount of assets required to support a given sales volume. The main danger in focusing profitability analysis on revenue-based income or expense ratios is that they don't measure economic efficiency in any absolute sense. Businesses such as grocery chains and meat-packing companies operate with exceptionally narrow margins on sales and rely on a large sales volume to

---

[3] Preferred dividends are not deductible from revenues in computing taxable income. Therefore, the amount entered in the coverage ratio formula ought to be the *pretax* amounts necessary to provide for preferred dividends. This added refinement can be left for more advanced texts on the grounds that it will be important only if the coverage ratio is very low.

cover operating expenses and yield a satisfactory return on investment. Others, such as high-fashion clothing shops and yacht manufacturers, take the opposite tack and operate with low volume and high markups.

The solution to this problem is to supplement the profit-margin ratios with *asset-turnover ratios*. We'll take a brief look at three of these:

1. Total-asset turnover.
2. Receivables turnover, or collection period.
3. Inventory turnover.

Total-Asset Turnover

The principal turnover ratio is the ratio of total sales to total assets. Using year-end total assets as the base, this ratio for Alpha in 19x2 was:

$$\frac{\text{Sales Revenue}}{\text{Total Assets}} = \frac{\$105,200}{\$89,400} = 1.18.$$

In other words, $1 of assets was required to support every $1.18 of sales.

Once again, the main use of this kind of ratio is to identify ways in which the company is departing from its own previous operating pattern or from that of its competitors. Turnover and percentage-of-sales ratios must be examined together, in parallel—the significance of a change in one can be appraised only if movements in the other are known.

The main shortcoming of these ratios is that they are sensitive to variations in asset-measurement and revenue-recognition practices. We've said enough about these in general to make repetition here unnecessary, but if all the accounting-policy differences between two companies run in the same direction—that is, one company's policies all lead to higher asset figures than the other's—the asset-turnover ratios may be very difficult to compare.

Receivables Turnover and the Collection Period

The efficiency of individual kinds of assets may be easier to appraise than overall efficiency. Again, we use turnover ratios to measure efficiency. For example, the *receivables-turnover ratio* is the ratio of annual credit sales to accounts receivable. Based on 19x2 year-end-receivables balances, this ratio for Alpha was:

$$\frac{\text{Sales Revenues}}{\text{Receivables}} = \frac{\$105,200}{\$19,800} = 5.3.$$

What this says is that the receivables "turned over" 5.3 times during the year.

A related and perhaps more easily understood statistic is the *collection period*—the number of days' sales in accounts receivable. On the basis of a 360-day year, $105,200 ÷ 360 = $291.60 is the average daily sales. Dividing the accounts-receivable balance by this figure produces $19,800 ÷ $291.60 = 68, the number of days' sales in accounts receivable. This can also be calculated by dividing the number of days by the receivables-turnover ratio: 360/5.3 = 68 days.

These ratios are regarded as indicators of (1) the liquidity of the receivables, (2) the quality of the receivables, and (3) management's credit-granting policies. A low turnover ratio—that is, a long collection period—means that in the normal course of business receivables are turned into cash only slowly. A collection period that is long relative to the normal credit period in the industry indicates either that the firm is using a liberal credit policy to stimulate sales or that the receivables are of low quality, with many customers failing to pay their bills on time. If Alpha's terms of sale call for payment within 30 days, for example, its collection period would be regarded as quite long.

Neither ratio is very precise. The year-end receivables may be lower than their average for the year; sales revenues may include revenues from cash sales. An aging of the receivables would give a much better indication of the quality of those receivables; a weighted average of the collection times during the year would be more indicative of the collection period. What this means is that once again the emphasis must be less on the absolute size of the ratio than on trends and intercompany comparisons.

A high turnover of receivables may not always be the most efficient policy for a firm. It may be the consequence of a tight credit policy and a vigorous collection program that unduly restricts the volume of sales. A loosening of credit standards will often increase receivables by a larger percentage than the increase in sales, but the increase in profit may be considerably higher than the company's desired rate of return on the added investment.

Inventory Turnover

Another ratio similar in purpose to the receivables-turnover ratio is the inventory-turnover ratio. Inventory and revenue figures are not precisely comparable: the former are on a cost basis, while the latter represent selling prices. Strictly speaking, therefore, the number-of-days' inventory on hand can be calculated only if the cost of goods sold is known, in which case the ratio is cost of goods sold per day, divided by inventory. The same purpose can be served by a sales/inventory ratio, however, and inventory turnover is often calculated on this basis.

Fortunately, we have Alpha's cost of goods sold figure for 19x2. Based on the year-end inventory, the 19x2 inventory-turnover ratio for Alpha was:

$$\frac{\text{Cost of Goods Sold}}{\text{Inventories}} = \frac{\$57,700}{\$35,900} = 1.6.$$

A low ratio is indicative of slow-moving inventory, and a ratio that is falling or lower than competitors' or both is a sign of potential danger. On the other hand, a company may deliberately carry large inventories to reduce the loss of sales caused by inadequate stocks and to avail itself of economies of large purchase or production lots. Nevertheless, a falling ratio is presumptive evidence of a decline in liquidity, high carrying costs, and potential future losses from obsolescence.

Inventory-turnover ratios are subject to the same defects as receivables-turnover ratios. They say little about the quality of the year-end inventory mix, nor do they reflect seasonal variations in sales and inventories. Probably even more important, however, are the effects of the company's inventory-measurement methods. During and after a period of generally rising prices, for example, Lifo inventories will have higher turnover ratios than Fifo inventories. When replacement cost data are available, they can be substituted for the historical cost figures to make the ratios more comparable over time and among companies.

SUMMARY

Outside financial analysts use the data in corporate financial statements to help them predict corporations' future earnings (profitability analysis) and its debt-paying ability (solvency analysis). Various ratios are calculated for these purposes. Other ratios indicating the efficiency of asset utilization are related both to profitability analysis and to solvency analysis. A representative set of ratios in each of these three categories is listed in Exhibit 17–8.

EXHIBIT 17–8.   Selected Financial Ratios

Profitability

Profit-Margin Ratio
$$\frac{\text{Net Income}}{\text{Total Revenue}}$$

Operating Ratio
$$\frac{\text{Cost of Goods Sold + Other Operating Expenses}}{\text{Operating Revenues}}$$

Earnings per Common Share
$$\frac{\text{Net Income–Preferred Dividends}}{\text{No. of Common Shares Outstanding}}$$

Return on Common Equity
$$\frac{\text{Net Income–Preferred Dividends}}{\text{Common Equity}}$$

Return on Assets
$$\frac{\text{Adjusted Net Income}}{\text{Total Assets}} \quad \text{or} \quad \left(\frac{\text{Sales}}{\text{Assets}} \times \frac{\text{Income}}{\text{Sales}}\right)$$

Payout Ratio
$$\frac{\text{Common Dividends}}{\text{Income Applicable to Common Shareholders}}$$

Price/Earnings Ratio
$$\frac{\text{Market Price per Common Share}}{\text{Earnings per Common Share}}$$

Debt-Paying Ability and Risk

Current Ratio
$$\frac{\text{Current Assets}}{\text{Current Liabilities}}$$

Quick Ratio
$$\frac{\text{Cash + Marketable Securities + Receivables}}{\text{Current Liabilities}}$$

Debt/Asset Ratio
$$\frac{\text{Total Liabilities}}{\text{Total Assets}}$$

Long-Term-Debt Ratio
$$\frac{\text{Long-Term Debt}}{\text{Preferred Stock + Common Equity}}$$

Times Interest Earned
$$\frac{\text{Net Income Before Interest + Taxes}}{\text{Interest + Preferred Dividends}}$$

Fixed-Charges Ratio
$$\frac{\text{Cash Flow Before Fixed Charges}}{\text{Total Fixed Charges}}$$

Efficiency

Accounts-Receivable Turnover
$$\frac{\text{Sales Revenue}}{\text{Receivables}}$$

Inventory Turnover
$$\frac{\text{Cost of Goods Sold}}{\text{Inventories}}$$

Total-Asset Turnover
$$\frac{\text{Sales Revenues}}{\text{Total Assets}}$$

The validity of these kinds of analysis is conditioned not only by the comparability of past and future but also by the quality of the underlying data. The measurement methods used in preparing company financial statements have great effects on the ratios discussed in this chapter, and these effects must be considered when the ratios are being interpreted.

KEY TERMS

Collection period	Payout ratio
Coverage ratios	Price/earnings ratio
Current ratio	Profit-margin ratio
Debt/assets ratio	Quality of earnings
Earnings per share	Quick ratio
Fixed-charges ratio	Receivables turnover
Inventory turnover	Return on assets
Leverage	Return on common equity
Long-term-debt ratio	Retention ratio
Market-value ratio	Sustainable growth
Operating ratio	Times-charges-earned ratio

INDEPENDENT STUDY PROBLEMS (Solutions in Appendix B)

1. Calculating return on equity. The Barnes Company had net income after taxes of $106 million for 19x4, $11.3 million for 19x5, and $109.1 million for 19x6. Preferred dividends were $10 million in each year. The shareholders' equity section of the company's balance sheets during this period showed the following:

	12/31/x3	12/31/x4	12/31/5	12/31/x6
Preferred stock	$ 170,000,000	$ 170,000,000	$ 170,000,000	$ 170,000,000
Common stock, $1 par	50,000,000	50,000,000	52,000,000	52,000,000
Additional paid-in capital	200,000,000	200,000,000	238,000,000	238,000,000
Retained earnings	580,000,000	626,000,000	677,300,000	724,400,000
Total	$1,000,000,000	$1,046,000,000	$1,137,300,000	$1,184,400,000

a. Compute the earnings per common share in 19x4, 19x5, and 19x6, basing your calculations on the number of shares outstanding at the end of the year.

b. Compute the book value per common share at each balance-sheet date.

c. Compute the return on common equity for 19x4, 19x5, and 19x6. In each case, base your calculations on average common equity for the year.

2. Effect of transactions on ratios. A company has just sold one of its buildings at a price equal to its book value and has used the proceeds from the sale to retire long-term bonds payable. The price paid to retire the bonds was equal to the amount at which they were shown on the balance sheet. Upon selling the building, the company entered into a lease with the new owner.

a. If the new lease is treated as an operating lease, not requiring lease capitalization, how will this series of transactions affect:
1. The debt/equity ratio?
2. The current ratio?
3. The asset-turnover ratio?
b. If the new lease is treated as a repurchase of the property (requiring lease capitalization), how will this series of transactions affect these three ratios?

3. Effect of leverage. The following data have been taken from the financial statements of a manufacturing company:

Total assets	$100,000
Interest expense	$ 2,000
Tax rate	45%
Return on common equity	7.2%
Debt/equity ratio	0.25

The company had no preferred stock outstanding.

a. Calculate the overall rate of profitability (return on assets).
b. Did the company use leverage successfully?

4. Interfirm comparisons of profitability. Companies A, B, and C are three of the largest merchandising companies in the United States. We have the following data on these companies for a recent year (dollars in thousands):

	Company A	Company B	Company C
Rank (by sales) among merchandising firms	26	11	2
Sales revenues	$627,349	$1,293,765	$5,458,824
Assets	120,363	274,603	884,001
Shareholders' equity	43,554	163,317	627,366
Net income	11,477	8,327	55,897
Interest expense	3,994	5,342	13,088

a. Calculate income as a percentage of sales, asset turnover, return on assets, return on equity, and debt/asset ratio for each company. You should assume a 50 percent income tax rate.
b. For return on common equity, Company A ranked first, Company B ranked 46th, and Company C ranked 39th among the merchandising companies on the list. Basing your analysis on the financial statement data alone, prepare an explanation of the difference between the relative sales ranking and the relative return on common equity ranking.

EXERCISES AND PROBLEMS

5. Effects of transactions on selected ratios. The Casey Company has a current ratio of 3.0, a quick ratio of 1.5, a receivables turnover of 6.1, and an inventory turnover of 4.5. How will each of the transactions listed below affect these ratios?

a. Purchase of merchandise for cash.
b. Purchase of merchandise on credit.

   c. Sale of a marketable security at cost (that is, at zero gain or loss).
   d. Sale of merchandise at a profit for cash.

   6. Using ratios to determine balance sheet amounts. The December 31, 19x5, balance sheet of Ratio, Inc., is presented below, with some omissions. The items listed are the only items in the balance sheet. Amounts indicated by question marks can be calculated from the additional information given.

Assets:

Cash	$ 25,000
Accounts receivable (net)...	?
Inventory	?
Plant and equipment (net)	294,000
	$432,000

Liabilities and Stockholders' Equity:

Accounts payable (trade)	$?
Income taxes payable (current)	25,000
Long-term debt	?
Common stock	300,000
Retained earnings	?
	$?

Additional Information:

Current ratio (at year-end)	1.5 to 1
Total liabilities divided by total stockholders' equity (at year-end)...........	0.8
Inventory turnover:	
Based on sales and ending inventory....................................	15 times
Based on cost of goods sold and ending inventory	10.5 times
Gross margin for 19x5...	$315,000

   a. Calculate Ratio's trade accounts payable on December 31, 19x5.
   b. Calculate retained earnings on December 31, 19x5.
   c. Determine the cost of Ratio's inventory on December 31, 19x5.

                                                (AICPA adapted)

   7. Leverage exercise. Company X and Company Y are identical in all respects except for their capital structure. Company X obtained $1 million in assets from the issuance of 100,000 shares of common stock. It has no debt. Company Y obtained $500,000 in assets by issuing 20-year, 8 percent bonds at their face value; it obtained another $500,000 by issuing 50,000 shares of common stock. Each company had $1 million in sales revenue and earnings before interest and income taxes (EBIT) of $150,000. The income tax rate was 50 percent.

   a. Calculate earnings per share for each company. Did Company Y use leverage successfully?
   b. How would your answer change if each company had sales of $350,000 and EBIT of $60,000?

   8. Effects of transactions on ratios. A company's current ratio was in excess of 1.0, the times-charges-earned ratio was 3.0, and the ratio of earnings before interest and income taxes to net sales was 0.15. Net income was positive. Each of the following transactions occurred independently of the others:

1. Issued common stock in exchange for cash.
2. Sold building for cash at a price in excess of book value.
3. Declared and paid cash dividend on common stock.
4. Paid cash to retire long-term debt.
5. Paid accounts payable 30 days after receipt of merchandise.
6. Issued a long-term note payable in exchange for land.
7. Sold goods costing $10,000 on current account for $15,000.
8. Issued common stock in exchange for outstanding convertible preferred stock.
9. Issued common stock in exchange for outstanding convertible bonds.

For each of these transactions, *taken by itself* (all other things unchanged), state whether each of the following ratios will increase, decrease, or remain the same:

a. Current ratio.
b. Times-charges-earned ratio.
c. Debt/assets ratio.
d. Net income/sales ratio.

9. *Leverage exercise.* The Doud Company has a return on common equity of 12 percent, based on net income of $12,000 (after income taxes). Its debt/owners'-equity ratio is 50 percent and the income tax rate is 40 percent. Interest expense is $4,600 a year.

a. Calculate total assets.
b. Calculate earnings before interest and income taxes (EBIT).
c. Calculate the before-tax rate of return on total assets.
d. Calculate the after-tax rate of return on total assets.
e. Is this company using leverage successfully? Explain.

10. *Trend analysis: interpretation of ratios.* Analysis of a company's financial statements reveals the following information for three consecutive years:

	19x1	19x2	19x3
Return on common equity	8.1%	9.7%	10.5%
Current ratio	2.5:1	2.7:1	2.6:1
Earnings per share	$1.62	$2.04	$2.31
Times charges earned	10.0	4.2	3.9
Debt/equity ratio	1:5	2:3	9:11

The tax rate was 50 percent in each of these years, and 50,000 shares of common stock were outstanding throughout the entire three-year period.

a. Did the company's basic profitability increase during this period? Support your position with figures developed from the information supplied above.
b. Did the shareowners' risk increase? Cite figures to support your position.

11. *Effect of financing method.* A company needs approximately $1 million in new capital to finance its expansion program. Management is undecided whether to obtain the needed funds from the sale of bonds or from the sale of additional shares of common stock. You have the following information:

1. Number of shares of stock now outstanding: 300,000.
2. Current annual earnings after taxes: $1.2 million ($4 a share).
3. Anticipated increase in earnings (before interest and income taxes) from investment of additional capital: $400,000.
4. The proposed bond issue would consist of 20-year, 8 percent bonds with a face value of $1 million, to be sold to an insurance company at their face value.
5. The proposed stock issue would consist of 40,000 shares of common stock, to be sold at a price of $25 a share.
6. The effective income tax rate is 40 percent.
7. The company now has no long-term debt.

a. Calculate the anticipated earnings per share under each method of financing.

b. How great an effect is this decision likely to have on the riskiness of investments in the company's common stock?

12. Quality of earnings: effect of inventory method. The Alpha Company and the Omega Company are both engaged in the smelting and refining of copper. The year 19x8 was a poor year for the copper industry in general, with rates of return on assets clustering mainly between 1 and 2 percent. The following data were taken from the balance sheets of these two companies as of the beginning and end of that year:

	December 31, 19x7	December 31, 19x8
Alpha Company inventories (Lifo)	$ 32,825,000	$ 26,450,000
Omega Company inventories (Fifo, lower of cost or market)..............	77,140,000	63,750,000
Alpha Company total assets..................	128,448,000	119,856,000
Omega Company total assets	312,660,000	285,918,000

Neither company had any interest-bearing debt at any time during 19x8.

Alpha adopted Lifo 15 years before 19x8, when copper prices were about half the level they had reached at the beginning of 19x8. Its inventories had grown about 10 percent in that period.

The market prices of copper and copper ores were at the same level on December 31, 19x8, as they had been on January 1, 19x8.

The income statements for the two companies for the year ended December 31, 19x8 were as follows:

	Alpha	Omega
Sales	$95,000,000	$215,000,000
Cost of goods sold	$74,300,000	$180,000,000
Depreciation	3,700,000	9,000,000
Other expenses	9,000,000	20,000,000
Total Expenses	$87,000,000	$209,000,000
Income before taxes	$ 8,000,000	$ 6,000,000
Income taxes	4,000,000	3,000,000
Net Income	$ 4,000,000	$ 3,000,000

a. Using the average of the beginning-of-year and end-of-year figures as the base, calculate each company's return on assets in 19x8.

b. Which of these companies appears to have been more profitable than the other in 19x8? Support your answer with figures insofar as you can and indicate how the differences in the companies' inventory methods influenced your conclusion.

c. How would your answer to (b) have differed if the prices of copper and copper ores had been 10 percent lower throughout 19x8 than at the end of 19x8?

13. Evaluating receivables and credit policy. Delta Company and Gamma Company sell similar lines of products. The manager of Delta Company has collected the following statistics:

	Delta	Gamma
Sales, 19x3	$7,000,000	$5,000,000
Estimated customer defaults, 19x3	35,000	50,000
Income before interest and taxes, 19x3	600,000	500,000
Total assets, December 31, 19x3	4,800,000	4,000,000
Accounts receivable, December 31, 19x3	800,000	750,000

The manager wants the answers to the questions stated below. You are expected to answer the questions if possible. If the information provided is not adequate for a satisfactory answer, you are to state the additional information you need and explain how you would use this information to answer the questions.

a. Which company has the more liberal credit policy?
b. Which company has the more liquid receivables?
c. By how much will Delta's accounts receivable increase during 19x4?
d. Which company is managing its accounts receivable more profitably?

14. Manipulation of financial ratios. On December 15, 19x1, the controller of Redwood, Inc., gave the president a copy of an estimated year-end balance sheet for the company, containing the following figures:

Assets:

Cash	$ 300,000
Accounts receivable	120,000
Inventories	180,000
Plant and equipment (net)	900,000
Total	$1,500,000

Liabilities and Shareowners' Equity:

Accounts payable	$ 300,000
Long-term debt	100,000
Common stock	800,000
Retained earnings	300,000
Total	$1,500,000

The president was concerned that the quick ratio was so low and asked the controller to suggest some way of improving this ratio in the two weeks remaining before the end of the year.

a. Calculate the quick ratio.
b. What suggestion probably would be the easiest to implement? Would carrying out this suggestion impose any costs on the company?
c. What action might analysts take that would either neutralize this kind of year-end "window dressing" or make it unnecessary?

15. Inadequacy of position ratios. At the beginning of 19x1, the Davis Company's current ratio was 3.25, the quick ratio was 1.25, and the ratio of long-term debt to the common shareholders' equity was 0.3. The return on equity in 19x0 was 15 percent. All of these ratios were well within the range regarded by financial analysts as satisfactory for this industry.

The Davis Company had begun a plant-expansion program in 19x0. To finance the completion of that program in 19x1 and 19x2, the company negotiated an additional long-term loan of $7 million early in 19x1. Market conditions deteriorated during 19x1, however. Sales volume fell from $25 million in 19x0 to $20 million in 19x1, while net income fell from $3 million to $400,000. Davis's cash position deteriorated even more severely, and in December, 19x1, it was unable to make its scheduled payments to its creditors.

Davis's income statement for 19x1 and condensed balance sheets for the beginning and end of the year were as follows:

DAVIS COMPANY
Statement of Income for the Year Ended December 31, 19x1
(in millions of dollars)

Sales revenues	$20.0
Expenses:	
Cost of goods sold*	$13.7
Selling and administrative expense	4.1
Interest expense	1.5
Income tax expense	0.3
Net Income	$ 0.4

* Schedule of the cost of goods sold:

Materials inventory, January 1	$ 2.7
Purchases of materials	10.8
	$13.5
Materials inventory, December 31	4.9
Cost of Materials Used	$ 8.6
Factory labor	5.9
Factory depreciation	0.5
Other factory costs	2.3
Total Costs of Production	$17.3
Less: Cost of added finished goods inventory	3.6
Cost of Goods Sold	$13.7

DAVIS COMPANY
Condensed Statements of Financial Position, December 31, 19x1 and 19x2
(in millions of dollars)

	19x1	19x2		19x1	19x2
Cash	$ 1.0	$ .2	Accounts payable	$ 1.0	$ 4.7
Accounts receivable	4.0	6.3	Notes payable	3.0	3.0
Inventory	8.0	13.8	Taxes payable	—	0.3
Plant and equipment	17.0	20.5	Interest payable	—	0.4
			Long-term debt	6.0	13.0
			Common stock	5.5	5.5
			Add'l paid-in capital	2.5	2.5
			Retained earnings	12.0	11.4
			Total Liabilities and Shareholders'		
Total Assets	$30.0	$40.8	Equity	$30.0	$40.8

a. Calculate the current ratio, quick ratio, and long-term debt-to-equity ratio at the end of 19x1.

b. Prepare an analysis to explain what led to Davis's inability to pay its creditors on schedule in 19x1.

c. Comment on the usefulness of position ratios such as the quick ratio as indicators of short-term bill-paying ability.

16. Comparison of two companies. Below are the income statements and balance sheets of the Franklin Company and the Morgan Company, taken from their annual reports for the year ended December 31, 19x1:

Income Statement
For the Year 19x1

	Franklin Company	Morgan Company
Sales	$8,000,000	$7,000,000
Cost of goods sold	$6,000,000	$4,700,000
Selling, general, and administrative expenses	1,200,000	1,900,000
Interest on debt	—	70,000
Income before taxes	$ 800,000	$ 330,000
Income taxes	390,000	160,000
Net Income	$ 410,000	$ 170,000
Dividends Declared	$ 100,000	$ 70,000

Condensed Statements of Financial Position
As of December 31, 19x1

Assets	Franklin Company	Morgan Company
Cash	$ 300,000	$ 300,000
Accounts receivable	800,000	650,000
Inventory	1,300,000	850,000
Net plant and equipment	2,100,000	1,500,000
Total	$4,500,000	$3,300,000

	Franklin Company	Morgan Company
Liabilities and Owners' Equity		
Accounts payable	$ 710,000	$ 400,000
Taxes payable	390,000	160,000
Long-term debt	—	1,400,000
Common stock	2,200,000	800,000
Retained earnings	1,200,000	540,000
Total	$4,500,000	$3,300,000

On the basis of the available information, which do you consider to be (1) more liquid? (2) more solvent? (3) more profitable? Explain your conclusions.

17. Effect of accounting methods. Dalton Company two years ago established two subsidiary corporations to develop two new markets. The two companies started with identical sets of assets and no liabilities. Dalton distributed the stock of these two companies to its shareholders, and, thereafter, they operated independently of each other and of Dalton.

One of these companies, Littler, Inc., elected to use the Lifo inventory method, the deferral method of accounting for the investment credit, and accelerated depreciation. The other company, Bigler Enterprises, used Fifo, the flow-through method, and straight-line depreciation.

The balance sheets of the two companies at the end of last year, their second year of operation, contained the following information:

	Littler	Bigler
Current Assets:		
Cash	$ 4,000	$ 3,100
Accounts receivable	7,000	7,000
Inventory	10,000	12,000
Total Current Assets	$21,000	$22,100
Plant and equipment	20,000	20,000
Less: Accumulated depreciation	(7,200)	(4,000)
Total Assets	$32,800	$38,100
Current Liabilities:		
Accounts payable	$ 2,500	$ 2,500
Taxes payable	1,000	1,100
Total Current Liabilities	$ 3,500	$ 3,600
Long-term debt	10,000	10,000
Deferred income taxes	—	1,600
Total Liabilities	$13,500	$15,200
Deferred investment tax credits	1,600	—
Common stock	5,000	5,000
Additional paid-in capital	10,000	10,000
Retained earnings	3,700	7,900
Total Liabilities and Shareowners' Equity	$32,800	$38,100

The two companies' income statements for last year showed the following:

	Littler	Bigler
Sales revenues	$75,000	$75,000
Cost of goods sold	51,000	50,000
Gross Margin	$24,000	$25,000
Selling and administrative expenses	10,000	8,800
Interest expense	1,000	1,000
Income tax expense	6,300	7,600
Net Income	$ 6,700	$ 7,600

The two companies have had identical sales volumes and have paid identical amounts as dividends each year. Inventory replacement costs have been rising at a rate of about 10 percent a year. Neither company made any capital expenditures last year.

Prepare an analysis comparing the profitability of these two companies, taking into consideration the differences in their accounting policies insofar as you are able.

(Suggested by Charles W. Bastable)

18. Interfirm comparisons: profitability analysis. Anderson, Ltd., and Zoysia, Inc., are incorporated and operate in a country in which generally accepted accounting principles are followed but the income tax rate is only 25 percent. The two companies offer the same general line of products to the same potential customers.

The following data were taken from the 19x1 financial statements of these two companies:

	Anderson	Zoysia
Cash	$ 8,000	$ 24,000
Accounts receivable	17,000	19,200
Inventories	27,200	29,568
Prepaid expenses	2,000	4,000
Property and equipment	100,000	220,000
Accumulated depreciation	(62,400)	(57,152)
Total	$ 91,800	$239,616
Current liabilities	$ 20,000	$ 40,000
Long-term debt—6%	40,000	—
Long-term debt—9%	—	20,000
Stockholders' equity	31,800	179,616
Total	$ 91,800	$239,616
Sales	$204,000	$460,800
Cost of goods sold	(163,200)	(354,816)
Other expenses	(22,440)	(46,080)
Interest	(2,400)	(1,800)
Income taxes	(3,990)	(14,526)
Net Income	$ 11,970	$ 43,578

a. All sales are on account and there are only minor seasonal variations in sales. Compare the current debt-paying ability of the two firms. To what extent can the inventories be looked upon as a means of paying debts due in 30 days? In 60 days?

b. Compare the profitability of the two firms. What factors account for the difference?

c. Compare the long-term debt-paying ability of the two firms.

part III

ACCOUNTING DATA FOR MANAGEMENT PLANNING AND CONTROL

18

Budgetary Planning

ACCOUNTING INFORMATION serves two major ongoing purposes: (1) to help investors decide where to invest their money and (2) to help the managers of individual organizations plan and control those organizations' activities. The second of these is the domain of managerial accounting, our main concern from here on.

As we pointed out in Chapter 1, managerial planning and control are really separate stages of one overall control process. Each has its own features, however, and each places its own demands on the accounting system. Accounting's contribution to managerial planning is the main concern of Chapters 18 through 22; the remaining chapters will then examine the role of accounting in helping management control the execution of these plans. This introductory chapter has four main parts:

1. A brief description of planning processes generally.
2. An examination of one of these processes, the development of the annual operating and financial plan, or budget.
3. A step-by-step illustration of the budgetary planning process.
4. A survey of accounting's role in budgetary planning.

PLANNING PROCESSES

Control always begins at the planning stage. Planning is the process of deciding on a course of action, of finding and choosing among the alternatives available. It takes five forms:

547

1. *Strategic planning*—establishing the basic directions top management wants the organization to take.
2. *Long-range periodic planning*—translating the strategic plan into a set of preliminary action proposals and making rough estimates of the resources required to carry them out.
3. *Short-range periodic planning (budgeting)*—developing a coordinated program to govern the use of all the organization's resources in a single short period, usually the first year of the long-range plan.
4. *Project and situation planning*—making final decisions to use specific portions of the organization's resources in specific ways.
5. *Scheduling*—determining in detail what needs to be done to carry out the planned program, establishing timetables for the performance of these tasks, and seeing to it that people, materials, facilities, and funds are available in the necessary quantities at the necessary times and places to carry out the plan.

The diagram in Exhibit 18–1 traces the relationships among these processes. The progression moves from the top of the chart toward

EXHIBIT 18–1.   Managerial Planning Processes

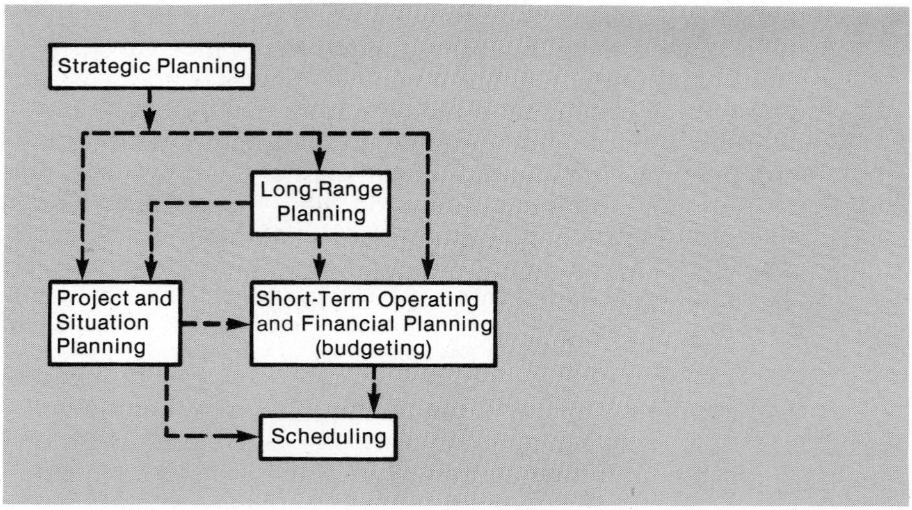

the bottom, from the general to the specific, from the tentative to the firm commitment. What the diagram doesn't show is that project and situation planning often take place within the context of the annual budgeting process, as well as at other times.

BUDGETARY PLANNING: FORM AND PURPOSE

The short-term operating and financial plan, or *budget*, shows what resources the organization has decided to use during a specific time period, where it plans to get them, where and how it plans to use them, and what it expects to accomplish during this period. It assembles the project and situation decisions that have already been made, incorporates a preliminary forecast of those to be made and implemented during the period, and presents the results as an integrated, coordinated plan for the period.

The best way to understand budgeting is to follow the steps an organization takes in developing a budget. Before we get into an example, however, we need to look briefly at four questions:

1. What are the various parts of the budget?
2. How does the budget relate to the structure of the organization?
3. What are the goals budgeting is expected to attain?
4. What criteria should be applied in budgeting?

Components of the Budget

We usually classify the parts of the budget into two groups, operating budgets and financial budgets. *Operating budgets* list the amounts of goods and services the organization plans to consume during the operating period and the benefits it expects these activities to produce. In most organizations, the resources consumed are generally represented by cost figures as well as by physical quantities; in a profit-oriented company, benefits are represented by revenues. The *financial budgets*, on the other hand, show how much money the organization plans to spend during the period and where it plans to get it.

Exhibit 18–2 describes the budget of a manufacturing firm. Each block in the diagram represents one or more parts of the overall budget. For convenience, we shall refer to each part as a budget, although we find it useful to remember that these are all part of a single budgetary plan.

The Organizational Dimension

The budget also has an organizational dimension. All but the smallest organizations are subdivided, with different individuals responsible for the operation of the various subdivisions. In small organizations, one layer of subdivisions is enough—one *department* for purchasing, another for production, another for selling, and so forth. In larger organizations, the departments will be subdivisions of larger

EXHIBIT 18–2.   Budget Components

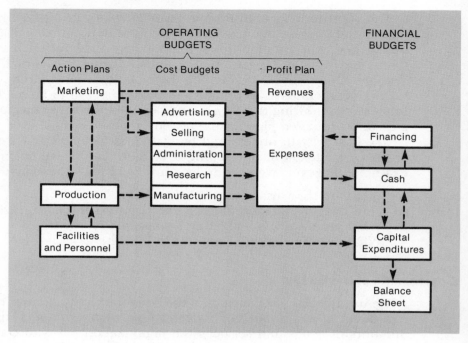

units, each one a subdivision of the whole. A sales *division*, for example, may include a dozen or more branch offices. And if the branches are numerous, they are likely to be grouped into regions, each with a regional manager reporting to the division manager.

The organizational dimension of the budget doesn't appear in Exhibit 18–2. Each division, each department has its own portion of the overall plan. Departmental budgets are narrow in scope, dealing with only one or two elements. Divisional budgets are more comprehensive—divisions with both sales and production operations even have their own profit plans and may have divisional balance sheets and partial financing plans. Overall financing remains a head-office responsibility, however, and most organizations control cash mainly in the head office.

The Purposes of Budgeting

The annual budgetary planning process has at least six major objectives:

1.   To force managers to *analyze* the company's activities critically and creatively.

2. To direct some of management's attention from the present to the *future*.
3. To enable management to *anticipate* problems or opportunities in time to deal with them effectively.
4. To reinforce the managers' *motivation* to work to achieve the company's goals and objectives.
5. To give managers a continuing *reminder* of the actions they have decided on.
6. To provide a *reference point* for control reporting.

The first four of these are advantages of the budgeting *process*. The final two items in the list are advantages of the budget documents themselves. For example, the budget is intended to serve the managers as a constant reminder of the plan they have adopted. As such, it provides a blueprint they can consult from time to time as they work to implement the plan. In this sense, it serves as a set of general instructions to the departmental and divisional managers, reflecting the actions they have agreed to take and the results they have agreed to strive for.

Decision Criteria in Budgeting

Budgeting, like other forms of planning, is a process focusing on a set of decisions. For this purpose, each manager typically submits proposals to higher management. Higher management then decides whether to approve these proposals as they stand, modify them in some way, or return them to the originators for revision and resubmission.

Higher management needs to examine individual proposals from four points of view: (1) Do the anticipated *benefits* of proposed expenditures justify the costs? (2) Are the estimates *realistic*? (3) Is the proposal *consistent* with the company's strategic plans and with the proposals of other parts of the organization? and (4) Is it *feasible* in the light of the company's financial, marketing, and production capacities?

This process is more iterative than the above description is likely to imply. That is, tentative budgets are proposed, discussed, and revised again and again as they move upward toward final approval. The process is one of progressive dialogue; an executive seldom receives a budget proposal from a subordinate without having discussed vital aspects of it ahead of time. Through vertical and horizontal communication within the management group, these plans are adjusted and readjusted until they become a set of integrated and realizable objectives consistent with overall company policies.

In none of this has any mention been made of the use of budgets as *limits*. Some of the figures embodied in the budget may indeed be used in this way—for example, budgeted advertising expenditures may be the maximum amount the advertising manager can spend—but budgeting is in its essence a planning process, not a limiting process. The budgeting procedure should allow for changes in the amount or pattern of the budgeted expenditures as conditions change or as management gains more knowledge of its resources and opportunities.

PREPARING THE ANNUAL BUDGET

The development of a formal budgetary plan requires a careful examination of the interrelationships among its various components. Although the complexity of this process cannot be conveyed effectively in a few pages, a very simple example may at least identify the problems. Since a manufacturing illustration would be too complex for our purposes at this point, let us see how the management of a small publishing house, Darwin Books, Inc., developed its annual budget for 19x1.

The Organization

Activities at Darwin Books fall broadly into three major categories: manuscript procurement, production, and sales. "Production," in this case, consists mainly of editing manuscripts, preparing them for typesetting, proofreading, and designing book covers and dust jackets. All printing and binding of books is done on contract by outside printers.

The company has two main product lines—textbooks for college and university use and textbooks for secondary schools, and this provides the basis for the company's organization chart, portions of which are shown in Exhibit 18–3. The vice president in charge of each of the textbook divisions is responsible for both manuscript procurement and sales. Each has a force of field representatives, organized into four regional groups, each headed by a regional manager with the title of field editor. The financial vice president is in charge of all financial activities, including the coordination of the annual budget.

The Marketing Plan

Darwin's fiscal year begins on July 1 each year. Early in March, 19x1, John Truro, the company's president, asked each textbook division manager to submit a tentative marketing plan, showing the size and composition of the field organization, the promotional pattern to be followed, and the anticipated revenues and expenses.

EXHIBIT 18–3

DARWIN BOOKS, INC.
Partial Organization Chart

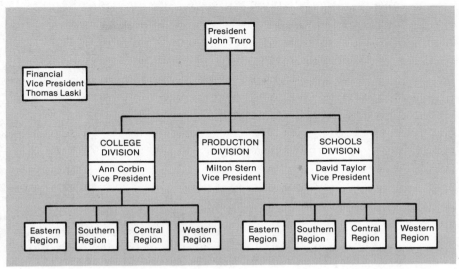

Ann Corbin, the manager of the college division, started by preparing an up-to-date list of the book titles that were then available or were scheduled for production in time for use during the next fiscal year. She gave copies of this list to each of her field editors and asked each of them to spell out in detail a promotional program for the coming year, estimate its cost, and predict the resulting sales volume. Dave Taylor, the schools-division manager, followed a similar procedure.

Both division managers reviewed the projected sales and the underlying marketing plans with their field editors. Ms. Corbin, for example, compared the proposed expense/sales ratio for each region with the 19x0 ratio and with the ratios in other regions. She compared the proposed increase in selling expense in each region with the projected increase in sales volume. She prompted her western-region field editor to hire an additional field representative to work actively in locating new manuscripts for textbooks in the natural sciences, and her comments and suggestions led to various changes in all of the regional plans.

At one point, she turned down a proposal of the southern-region field editor to expand the field staff to increase the number of contacts with junior colleges in the area. Darwin Books had few titles that were appropriate for use in the junior-college market. She felt that any promotional effort in this market should be concentrated on a few departments in a few of the larger junior colleges. This would not require an increase in the size of the field sales force.

After working with the field editors, the two division managers presented the following tentative sales and expense budgets to Tom Laski, the financial vice president:

	College Division	Schools Division
Sales revenues	$4,200,000	$2,700,000
Less: returns	150,000	50,000
Net sales	$4,050,000	$2,650,000
Marketing expenses:		
Division office salaries	$ 100,000	$ 85,000
Field salaries	400,000	300,000
Travel and entertainment	200,000	120,000
Advertising	50,000	50,000
Other	70,000	60,000
Total Marketing Expenses	$ 820,000	$ 615,000

Mr. Laski questioned Dave Taylor, the schools-division manager, on the slow growth in sales in his division and the high ratio of marketing expenses to sales. Mr. Taylor blamed both of these on the lack of any large-volume titles in the list. Darwin Books was a relative newcomer in the schools market, with a line of innovative texts, but none of these had broken through with sales to the large school districts which accounted for the bulk of textbook purchases. Mr. Laski remarked that Mr. Truro would want to discuss the schools division's future with Mr. Taylor at the final budget review session in June.

The Production Plan

At this point, Mr. Laski asked the textbook division managers to meet in his office with Milt Stern, the production manager. The textbook division managers gave Mr. Stern their proposed schedule for new books and new editions and their estimates of sales for each title in the active list. They reviewed inventory figures and identified titles that should be allowed to go out of print as soon as present stocks were exhausted.

Mr. Stern complained that the manuscript-preparation schedules were too heavily concentrated in the autumn months. Many of his copy editors were part-time employees, but some things had to be done by full-time personnel, and they simply could not handle the projected peak load. Darwin Books had solved this problem occasionally in the past by delaying the publication dates for several books, but this time it seemed more profitable to authorize an increase in the size of Mr. Stern's full-time staff.

The Profit Plan and the Cash Budget

After his meeting with the division vice presidents, Mr. Laski assembled the available data into a tentative profit plan for the coming year. This tentative plan is summarized in Exhibit 18–4. He also

EXHIBIT 18–4

DARWIN BOOKS, INC.
Tentative Profit Plan
For the Year Ending June 30, 19x2

	College Division	Schools Division	Total
Net sales	$4,050,000	$2,650,000	$6,700,000
Divisional expenses:			
Printing and binding	$2,400,000	$1,700,000	$4,200,000
Copy editing	100,000	80,000	180,000
Advertising and selling	650,000	470,000	1,120,000
Authors' royalties	500,000	250,000	750,000
Administration	70,000	65,000	135,000
Total Divisional Expenses	$3,720,000	$2,565,000	$6,285,000
Divisional profit	$ 330,000	$ 85,000	$ 415,000
General administrative expenses			300,000
Income before income taxes			$ 115,000
Income taxes			50,000
Net Income			$ 65,000

assembled proposals for such items as dividends and purchases of furniture and equipment and prepared the following tentative cash budget for the coming year:

Cash Receipts:		
Customers		$6,500,000
Other sources		100,000
Total Cash Receipts		$6,600,000
Cash Disbursements:		
Salaries	$1,350,000	
Printing	4,500,000	
Other suppliers	210,000	
Authors' royalties	700,000	
Taxes	50,000	
Dividends	40,000	
Furniture and equipment purchases	60,000	
Total Cash Disbursements		6,910,000
Cash Deficit		$ 310,000

As this shows, anticipated cash receipts were $310,000 less than anticipated disbursements. This left management with several options to investigate, mainly the following:

1. Reduce existing cash balances.
2. Defer payments to suppliers.
3. Press customers for prompter payment.
4. Curtail discretionary spending plans.
5. Borrow.
6. Revise marketing plans.
7. Reduce dividends.

Although the choices here are top management's responsibility, the financial executives are usually expected to analyze the alternatives and make recommendations. In practice, they are likely to work closely with the division managers and other senior operating managers, so that the final budget already reflects the consensus of top management's views before it is presented to the board for approval.

The main problem at this point is to find adequate criteria to guide management's choices among these alternatives. In this case, management felt that any reduction in the dividend would have had an unacceptable effect on the market price of the company's stock. This alternative, therefore, was regarded as a last resort.

Unless the company's collection efforts have been lax, faster collections from customers ordinarily can be achieved only at the cost of lost sales, usually a very costly effect. Slower payments to suppliers may weaken the company's credit rating and increase purchasing costs. In this case, however, Mr. Laski felt that payments to the company's printers could be cut back by $100,000 without adverse effects.

Ordinarily the cheapest way of covering a cash deficit is to reduce the company's bank balances or liquidate any holdings of short-term marketable securities. In this case, Mr. Laski's analysis indicated that reduction of the cash balance would jeopardize the company's ability to meet its payrolls and other obligations on time, and Darwin Books had no marketable securities to liquidate. Fortunately, its credit rating was very good, however, and Mr. Laski was able to get a commitment for a $200,000 line of credit from a local bank, at 8 percent interest. By deferring $15,000 in equipment purchases, the anticipated deficit would be covered. These changes can be summarized as follows:

Borrowing	$200,000
Less: after-tax interest on borrowing	4,000
Net Cash from Borrowing	$196,000
Reduction in payments to printers	100,000
Deferral of equipment purchases	15,000
Net Cash Effect	$311,000

Both the tentative profit plan and the tentative cash budget were modified to reflect these changes. The board of directors reviewed and approved the revised plans, but indicated their dissatisfaction with the profit level being achieved. Mr. Truro was asked to work with his division managers on ways to improve profit performance, with particular attention to the schools division. A full-fledged review of the schools division was scheduled for an autumn board meeting.

Budgeting as a Decision-Making Process

This brief discussion should make it quite clear that budgeting is a creative, decision-oriented process. It may also be the most important single phase in the management-control process, in that much of what the organization will do is settled at this time.

Budget approval is top management's signal that the methods selected and the ends to be achieved are acceptable. When management receives a proposed profit plan, it can either (1) accept it, (2) send it back for revision, or (3) take steps to terminate the operation. In practice, some question is almost always raised about the adequacy of the plan, thus ruling out immediate acceptance. Termination, on the other hand, is unlikely to be ordered unless such a decision has been considered before and deferred to give the division manager an opportunity to come up with a viable alternative.

The result is a response pattern like that schematized in Exhibit 18–5. Management's rejection of an initial proposal, represented by the "No" arrow under the top diamond, ordinarily starts the process again, as lower management seeks ways to improve the anticipated results. This is shown by the arrows looping back into the block at the upper left-hand corner of the exhibit.

Notice that three of the blocks at the right of the diagram represent decisions to accept and implement the budget. These decisions reflect top management's conclusion that existing management can't be expected to surpass the performance levels embodied in the proposals being accepted. This is important because one purpose of the budget, as we mentioned earlier, is to serve as a standard against which the performance of divisional and departmental managers can be evaluated. Top management's approval of a budget, therefore, carries with it a commitment to recognize the budgeted performance levels as satisfactory if actual conditions are as anticipated. If top management is unwilling to make this commitment, the proposal should be routed back into the loop for another revision and review.

THE ROLE OF ACCOUNTING

Although we have ignored the accounting staff until now, accounting and other financial personnel have important roles to play in the planning process:

1. They provide data for use in preparing estimates.
2. They analyze and interpret these data.
3. They design and operate the budgeting procedures.
4. They consolidate and review the budgetary proposals originating in various parts of the organization.

A few words about each of these activities are in order before we move on.

1. *Data collection.* The estimates managers use in making budgeting decisions reflect their forecasts of the future consequences of those decisions. To make those estimates, however, managers usually draw very heavily on records of what happened in the past. The future may be very different from the past, but it is likely to be closer to the past than to some set of estimates drawn at random.

EXHIBIT 18–5.   System Responses to Proposed Profit Plan

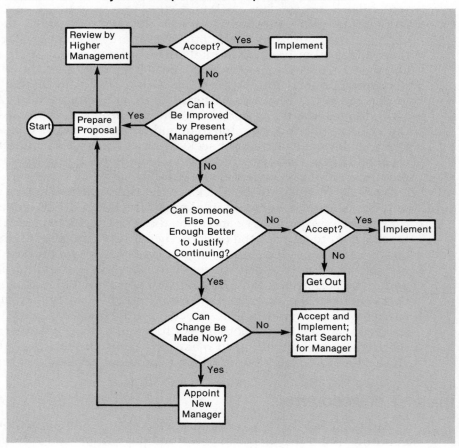

In other words, managers are more comfortable adjusting past figures than starting fresh, with no underlying data at all.

One function of the accounting system, therefore, is to provide a record of the costs and benefits of the company's various activities in considerable detail. Ideally, these data should enable management to identify the responses of costs, expenses, revenues, and cash flows to various kinds of managerial actions. For example, the management of our illustrative company, Darwin Books, would like to know how sales and expenses in the college division responded in the past to increases in advertising and field-selling effort. It probably would also like to know what would happen to net income if revenues were to fall, say, 10 percent short of their forecasted levels.

2. Data analysis. Accounting's contribution doesn't stop with data collection. The accounting numbers need to be interpreted, adjusted to allow for changes in conditions, and recombined in various ways. Since the accountants know more about their own figures than anyone else, it is inevitable that they do a good deal of this analytical work.

3. Budget administration. The headquarters financial staffs, often including others as well as accountants, play two other roles in the budgeting process. The first of these is that they are responsible for designing and securing support for the procedural aspects of periodic planning, mainly the questions of what is to be budgeted, when, and by whom. This is ordinarily done by the budget staff, working closely with operating executives. The final installation is likely to be summarized in a budget manual, spelling out deadlines for various budget components, assigning responsibilities for budget preparation, prescribing forms, and describing the overall budget pattern.

4. Consolidation and review. The final role of accountants and others on the central financial staff is in the review and coordination phase of budgeting. Although the operating managers have the main responsibility for developing operating and financial plans, the central financial staff are responsible for putting the pieces together.

Even if budget proposals have been reviewed carefully and critically all the way up the line within a given segment of the organization, the corporate financial staff members often have the authority to subject these proposals to their own tests of feasibility and profitability. They are always free to seek clarification or question whether other alternatives have been investigated, and, in some cases, they even have the power to ask individual managers to revise their proposals.

We must emphasize, however, that in taking any action of this sort, the controller, budget director, or other financial executive is acting as the agent of the chief executive. Planning is a managerial function first, a technical operation second.

SUMMARY

Periodic planning, or budgeting, is not simply a matter of forecasting what the future has to offer. It is a creative process in which executives at all levels are expected to evaluate and compare different possible courses of action, selecting those which seem most likely to meet company goals. Budgeting, in other words, is a form of decision making.

In this chapter we have tried to convey a feeling for the complexity and dynamism of the budgeting process without getting bogged down in complex numerical examples. In our illustration, budget preparation was initiated by top management, but the major effort took place at the divisional level as the division managers developed their marketing plans and translated them into production requirements and profit estimates. These plans were reviewed, revised, and consolidated before being presented to top management for final approval. They came together eventually in a profit plan and cash budget that were both feasible and acceptable to top management.

Accounting and other financial personnel have vital roles to play in all this. They provide, interpret, and analyze data, design and administer the budgeting procedures, review the proposals submitted by managers in various parts of the organization, and consolidate the final set of proposals into a feasible, workable plan. Our tasks in the next few chapters will be to outline some of the kinds of information the accountants can supply and to indicate how this information can and should be used.

KEY TERMS

Budget	Production plan
Budgeting	Profit plan
Cash budget	Project and situation planning
Long-range planning	Scheduling
Marketing plan	Strategic planning

INDEPENDENT STUDY PROBLEM (Solution in Appendix B)

1.   Developing a profit plan and cash budget; feasibility test.   The Darnell Company is organized in three divisions, each with a division manager, a small office staff, and its own sales force. The various divisions sell different kinds of products and deal with different groups of customers.

The company's budget director has received the following proposals and estimates for next year from the division managers:

	Division A	Division B	Division C
Divisional marketing costs amounting to	$ 150	$ 500	$ 300
Will produce revenues of	1,000	3,000	2,100
And cost of goods sold of....................	650	1,650	1,260
Administrative expenses to support these activities will total	150	300	200
Accounts receivable will increase by	10	200	50
Inventories will exceed this year's ending balances by	50	100	50
Accounts payable will increase by	15	50	80

The expenses of the company's central management are tentatively budgeted at $400 for the year, to be paid in cash. Cash purchases of equipment amounting to $130 and cash dividends of $350 are also proposed. Of the equipment purchases, $60 is to replace existing equipment and $70 is for expansion. The expansion proposals, which management has approved in principle, will have no effect on next year's income statement.

Depreciation is included in the administrative expense figures above as follows: central management, $10; Division A, $5; Division B, $15; Division C, $20.

a. Prepare a tentative profit plan and cash budget for next year, on the assumption that all of these proposals are approved.

b. The company will start next year with a cash balance of $290 and an unused line of bank credit of $100. The minimum cash balance is 5 percent of sales. Is the tentative plan feasible?

EXERCISES AND PROBLEMS

2. **Product-line budgeting.** Hammersmith, Ltd., has three regional factories, each of which manufactures all of the company's products. The sales force is also organized geographically, in ten regional divisions, and each sales representative has a geographic territory in which he or she is the company's sole representative.

In the past, the annual budgeting process started with the development of tentative sales and marketing plans by the regional sales managers. These were then used to estimate the requirements for production and for administrative support. After review and revision, the final budget was structured along organizational lines.

Hammersmith's management became convinced in the late 1970s that this approach was preventing the development of coherent, aggressive marketing plans for individual products. Four product managers were appointed, each one responsible for setting objectives and developing marketing programs for one of the company's four main product groups. The regional manufacturing and sales organizations remained in being; the product managers were planners and coordinators without direct-line authority over factory or sales personnel.

In line with this change, top management decided that all future budgets would be drawn up on a product-line basis. Each product manager would draw up a proposed marketing and production plan for his or her line, working closely with the head-office sales and production staffs.

What problems do you foresee in the new system? How would you try to anticipate them and minimize their importance?

3. Tentative cash budget. The Management of the Cranmore Manufacturing Company at the beginning of 19x1 anticipated (1) a decrease in sales as compared with 19x0 because of production time lost in converting to new products, and (2) a considerably smaller profit margin due to higher material and labor costs. The controller was asked to prepare a cash budget based on estimated 19x1 sales of $2.4 million (a decrease of $300,000) and, in particular, to forecast the cash position at the close of 19x1.

The treasurer's forecast of certain balance sheet and other items was as follows:

Accounts receivable (net)	$ 35,000 decrease
Accounts payable	20,000 decrease
Inventories	17,000 increase
Additions to plant (gross)	125,000
Additions to retained earnings appropriated for contingencies	25,000
Income for 19x1 (after depreciation but before income taxes)	95,000
Depreciation expense, 19x1	48,000
Income taxes for 19x1 (payable in 19x2)	45,000
Dividend payments (at 19x0 rates)	30,000

The cash balance on January 1, 19x1, was $54,000, and the accrued tax liability on that date, arising from 19x0 taxable income, amounted to $93,000. The company had no bank loans outstanding.

a. Assuming that any balance-sheet items not listed above would be unchanged, prepare a schedule of forecasted cash receipts and cash disbursements for 19x1 and determine the expected cash balance as of December 31, 19x1.

b. What action would you expect management to take when it sees the cash flow estimates for the year?

4. Budgeting decisions: identifying criteria and data required. A consulting firm has a professional staff of ten, giving it a capacity to provide 1,500 hours of consulting service in an average month. Commitments to and from the company's present clients will require the firm to provide them with approximately 1,000 hours of service in each of the next six months, yielding revenues of approximately $40,000 a month and project-related expenses of $10,000 a month. Salaries of the professional staff amount to $25,000 a month; rent and other office expenses average $8,000 a month.

The firm would like to submit bids for four additional consulting projects to be completed during the next six months. The staff have been working closely on each of these with the prospective clients and are quite convinced that the firm will be given the assignments if it can promise completion within the six-month period. The estimates for these four projects are as follows:

	Project A	Project B	Project C	Project D
Hours per month	125	250	375	450
Consulting fees to be charged to the client each month	$5,000	$6,000	$16,500	$22,500
Unreimbursed project expenses per month (other than salaries of professional staff, rent, and other office expenses)	$ 100	$ 500	$ 7,500	$ 9,000

a. What should the firm do? Show your calculations.
b. What criterion or criteria did you use in reaching your conclusions?
c. What other kinds of information about these projects would you, as the budget officer, find useful and perhaps essential in the development of a budget for the next six months?

5. Budgeting decisions: ranking competing proposals. You have just been appointed budget director of a manufacturing company, responsible for reviewing and coordinating the budget proposals submitted by the company's operating executives. On your first day on the job you are given the following summaries of budget proposals for each of the company's three products:

	Product A	Product B	Product C
Sales revenues	$240,000	$120,000	$40,000
Expenses:			
Manufacturing cost of the goods sold	$120,000	$ 72,000	$28,000
Sales salaries	32,000	12,000	4,000
Travel and entertainment	48,000	16,000	4,800
Advertising	20,000	4,000	2,400
Total Product Expenses	$220,000	$104,000	$39,200
Product profit margin	$ 20,000	$ 16,000	$ 800

All three products are sold by the same sales force. The advertising costs in each of the budget proposals are specific to the particular product line, however—that is, each advertising figure in the table above is the amount the company proposes spending to advertise that particular product.

The three products are manufactured in the same factory, but each product has its own production line within the factory. The finishing operation on each product must be performed on highly sophisticated equipment, however, and this equipment is so expensive that separate installations for each product line would be uneconomical. For this reason the factory has only one finishing department, which performs the finishing operations on all of the company's products.

The manufacturing cost of goods sold figures in the budget proposals summarized above were made up as follows:

	Product A	Product B	Product C
Direct materials............................	$ 16,000	$10,000	$ 4,500
Direct labor:			
Finishing department	8,000	12,800	2,000
Other departments	28,000	10,000	6,000
Overhead:			
Finishing department	12,000	19,200	3,000
Other departments	56,000	20,000	12,500
Total Cost of Goods Sold	$120,000	$72,000	$28,000

The finishing department has a total practical capacity of 2,500 hours a month. The budget proposals summarized above call for the following amount of time in the finishing department:

Product A .... 1,000 hours
Product B .... 1,600 hours
Product C .... 250 hours

Finishing work can also be performed by independent local firms at a cost of $25 an hour.

a. Outline the steps you would take in reviewing the proposed budgets for the three product lines. Illustrate each step, using figures supplied here, and indicate how you would decide how much finishing work should be performed by outside contractors.

b. What additional classifications of these costs would help you in making the budgeting decisions your review procedures would require? Explain how these classifications would help.

6. Budgeting decisions: profitability and feasibility.   The president of Ethelred, Inc., has a commitment from the company's bank for a loan of $100,000, if the company needs it during the coming year. No other outside source of cash will be available during the year.

Ethelred provides bookkeeping services to local business firms and other organizations and has been growing rapidly in recent years. Its experience has been that accounts receivable increase as its sales volume increases. A $10 increase in annual sales volume will require a $1 increase in accounts receivable.

If the company continues its present operations, maintaining its sales force at current levels, total sales volume will increase next year by $100,000 and reported income will be:

Sales $1,100,000
Expenses (including $10,000 depreciation) 980,000
Net Income .... $ 120,000

The company's present facilities will be adequate to handle this sales volume, requiring expenditures of only $12,000 for routine replacement of furniture and equipment.

The company's president would like to add another sales representative to contact a new group of potential customers. Additional data-processing equipment would have to be rented to handle any business the new sales representative brought in. These changes would increase Ethelred's annual operating expenses by the following amounts:

Sales representative's salary and expenses	$22,000
Equipment rental	30,000
Other expenses	60,000 + 10% of added sales

The president believes that the additional sales volume from this market would amount to $50,000 in the first year, but it might amount to nothing at all. If the operation proved successful, revenues in later years would be substantially higher.

Ethelred's shareholders have received cash dividends of $50,000 in each of the last three years, and the board of directors has tentatively decided to increase the dividend next year to $60,000 if the cash flow is adequate. It also wishes to contribute $20,000 to the local art museum as a community service.

a. Are these proposals feasible? Prepare a tentative profit plan and a tentative cash budget to support your answer. You may assume that all expenses other than depreciation and all equipment expenditures must be accompanied by immediate cash payments.

b. What action should the president take?

7. Revising a proposed budget. Noting substantial increases in the proposed levels of marketing and administrative costs over those of the current year, the Darnell Company's budget director asked the company's three division managers for additional information to be used in reviewing the divisional budget proposals summarized in Independent Study Problem 1. It wasn't clear how much of the increases were due to changes in prices and how much resulted from changes in the amount or structure of marketing effort.

To supplement the forecasted results for the proposed marketing plans, the budget director asked each division manager for estimates of the following:

1. This year's results.
2. The results to be expected next year if this year's marketing program were to be continued unchanged.
3. The results to be expected next year if marketing and administrative expenses were to be kept at this year's levels (an "austerity budget"):

With the help of personnel from the central market research and controller's departments, the division managers supplied the following additional data:

	Division A	Division B	Division C
Expected results this year from this year's program:			
Sales	$800	$2,000	$2,000
Cost of goods sold	496	1,200	1,200
Marketing expenses	120	380	280
Administrative expenses	110	200	190
Accounts receivable, year end	40	350	330
Inventories, year end	195	320	360
Accounts payable, year end	60	120	550
Expected results next year if this year's program were to be repeated:			
Sales	840	2,400	2,000
Cost of goods sold	546	1,392	1,260
Marketing expenses	125	400	300
Administrative expenses	120	220	200
Accounts receivable, year end	42	400	330
Inventories, year end	215	368	360
Accounts payable, year end	64	141	550
Expected results under austerity budget:			
Sales	820	2,100	1,900
Cost of goods sold	533	1,218	1,197
Marketing expenses	120	380	280
Administrative expenses	110	200	190
Accounts receivable, year end	41	360	314
Inventories, year end	205	324	332
Accounts payable, year end	62	124	517

Central administrative expenses for the current year are expected to total $380, cash purchases of equipment will amount to $120, and cash dividends of $300 will be paid. Depreciation expenses included in the administrative expenses are: central management, $10; division A, $5; division B, $15; division C, $20.

a. Calculate expected net income for the current year.

b. Prepare a profit plan on the assumption that current marketing programs will be continued next year. (Central administrative expenses would be at their proposed level, $400.)

c. Prepare an austerity budget profit plan on the assumption that marketing and administrative expenses next year are held to this year's level. (Under an austerity budget, central administrative expenses would amount to $395.)

d. Assuming that these estimates are sound, and basing your recommendations solely on the figures given in these two problems, what action should Darnell's management take on the budget proposals?

8. Budgeting: benefits and implementation problems. "This budget is a big nuisance," said Hiram Baumgartner, president of Colleyford, Inc., the U.S. subsidiary of a large European manufacturer of electrical and electronic products. "I have to spend most of my time on it for the better part of a month, and I don't know how many hours my controller puts in on it. As far as I'm concerned, it's just another report I have to make."

Colleyford operated one small electronics factory in upstate New York, but otherwise imported all of its needs from parent-company factories in Europe and Japan. It operated primarily in the northeastern United States and on the West Coast and had fairly large product-distribution warehouses in New York and San Francisco.

For budgeting purposes, Colleyford used the parent company's product classification scheme. It marketed products in six of the parent's product categories:

1. Lighting products.
2. Electronic tubes and transistors.
3. Components for computers and industrial communications equipment.
4. Radios, television receivers, and phonographs.
5. Industrial equipment and parts.
6. Service and repair.

Some products were marketed through wholesalers, while others were sold directly to industrial consumers by the company's own sales force. Colleyford had a sales force of approximately 40 men and women. Although some of them tended to concentrate on one or two product groups, they all handled all of the company's lines.

Mr. Baumgartner was allowed to manufacture any product his plant was equipped to produce. The types and amounts of this production were included in the budget that he submitted to headquarters each November. The parent-company headquarters then informed him which factories would supply his remaining requirements. The prices charged for these intergroup transfers were established by the head office in advance of budget preparation.

Two or three staff executives from the parent company's headquarters ordinarily spent a week or so at the Colleyford offices while the budget was being prepared and were also in frequent communication by telephone. They offered their advice and suggestions and raised questions about parts of the budget proposal as it was in process. Mr. Baumgartner usually presented his budget to the parent company in person at the end of November; and the final budget received from headquarters in December was ordinarily almost identical to the one Mr. Baumgartner submitted.

a. What benefits might Mr. Baumgartner reap from the company's system of budgetary planning? Comment on possible reasons for his attitude toward the budget and offer suggestions as to what might be done to give him a more favorable view of the budgetary process.

b. Discuss the problems of data classification in Colleyford, Inc. What kinds of data should the profit plan include, and how should these data be subdivided and classified?

19

Analyzing Short-Term Planning Problems

IN DESIGNING SYSTEMS to accumulate data for planning purposes, accountants need to understand how these data will be used. The purpose of this chapter is to explain what kinds of data are relevant to a major class of decisions, decisions determining how a business organization should use its capacity to produce goods and services in the short term. The chapter has three parts:

1. Basic concepts for resource-allocation decisions
2. Short-term, cost-volume relationships.
3. Applying the incremental principle.

BASIC CONCEPTS FOR RESOURCE-ALLOCATION DECISIONS

Decision making starts when someone sees a problem to be solved or an opportunity to do something new. In either case, the next step is to identify two or more possible solutions to the problem—that is, two or more alternative courses of action management might take. In this section we'll study seven basic concepts management needs to understand in choosing among these alternatives:

1. Cash flow.
2. The incremental principle.
3. Incremental cost.

4. Different costs for different purposes.
5. Sunk cost.
6. Opportunity cost.
7. Uncertainty and expected value.

Cash Flow

From the decision maker's point of view, each alternative is described by the costs it will entail, the benefits management expects it to yield, and the degree of certainty management attaches to these estimates. In a business organization, costs and benefits are measured by the cash flows associated with the specific alternative being examined. The *net benefit* (benefit minus cost) of any course of action is the difference between the amount of cash it will bring in and the amount of cash management must spend to get it.

The reason for this emphasis on cash flows is simple. In most circumstances, cash is the only resource management can use to get productive goods and services or to reward the shareholders. If the firm has no cash and can't get any, it won't be able to meet its payroll, no matter how many receivables or how much equipment it has. On the other hand, if cash is coming in, it can be used to buy materials and pay the employees. Noncash resource outflows, such as depreciation on existing equipment, reduce the income figure for financial reporting, but they don't reduce management's current purchasing power.

The Incremental Principle

Decisions are always choices: if management has no choice, no decision is necessary. What matters is whether the cash flow from one alternative is better than the cash flow from any other. The decision affects only the *differences* between the cash flows of that alternative and those of the alternative against which it is being compared.

This fact is the basis for the *incremental principle*, which states that the choice of one alternative instead of another should be based on an analysis of the differences between them. This idea is illustrated in Exhibit 19–1. In financial terms, each alternative can be described by the total cash flow associated with it. The differences between them is then described by the difference between these two cash-flow totals. We refer to this as the *differential cash flow*, *incremental cash flow*, or *incremental profit*. Again, the timing of these differences should be identified if differences in timing are important to the decision.

EXHIBIT 19-1. Cash Flow Attributable to a Proposed Action

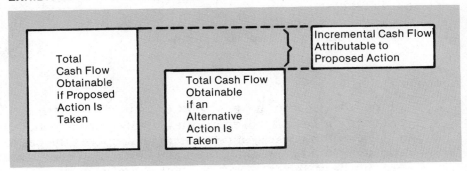

Incremental Cost

One component of incremental profit, sometimes the only one, is *incremental cost*—the difference between the total cash outlay necessary to operate the company if a proposed action is taken and the total outlay required by the alternative the company will accept if the proposal is rejected. This definition is sometimes expanded to include the opportunity costs we'll discuss later in this section.

Incremental cost is likely to be very different from the cost figures emerging from accounting systems designed for public financial reporting. For example, the business of the Apollo Trucking Company is to carry freight between Chicago and Cleveland. Exhibit 19-2

EXHIBIT 19-2

APOLLO TRUCKING COMPANY
Costs of Carrying Freight

	Actual Cost, Last Year		Incremental Cost	
Cost Element	Total	Per Trip	Loaded	Empty
Labor	$168,000	$112	$112	$112
Fuel	90,000	60	65	40
Maintenance and repairs	22,500	15	11	8
Depreciation	12,000	8	—	—
Taxes and insurance	6,000	4	—	—
Administration	16,500	11	—	—
Total	$315,000	$210	$188	$160

summarized the costs incurred by the company last year. The first column shows the total cost of operating the company during the year. The company's trucks made 1,500 one-way trips between these two cities last year, and the figures in the second column were obtained by dividing total cost by 1,500.

The average cost of $210 may be a useful approximation to incremental cost under certain circumstances. For example, it may be a fairly good basis for estimating the incremental cost of doubling the size of the company and doubling the number of trips each year. For other comparisons, however, it is likely to be wide of the mark. The incremental cost figures in the two right-hand columns are based on a comparison of operating the trucks the company now has and leaving them idle.

To begin with, the estimated incremental cost of the first cost element, labor cost, is equal to last year's average cost, $112, and is the same whether the truck is loaded or empty. Fuel costs, however, are expected to amount to $65 whenever a truck is fully loaded but only $40 when it makes the run empty. The $60 average in the second column indicates that the company's trucks made many trips either empty or with partial loads.

Continuing down the list, we find that the average cost of truck maintenance and repairs last year was $15 a trip. Some of these costs will be necessary even if a truck stands unused all year-round. Use of the truck adds to these standby costs: as the table shows, the company's maintenance and repair costs increase by $11 on the average for each fully loaded trip and by $8 for each empty trip. These are incremental costs of truck usage.

Depreciation, taxes and insurance, and administrative expenses for the year are independent of the number of trips made, given the number of trucks in the fleet. The consequence is that the incremental cost per trip for these cost categories is zero, up to the present capacity of the fleet.

Summing up the various incremental costs, we find that the cost of a trip from one city to another is not the $210 full cost but $188 if the truck is loaded and $160 if the truck is empty.

Different Costs for Different Purposes

The concepts of differential cost and differential profit apply to all resource–allocation decisions. Should we take on more business? Should we expand the plant? Should we withdraw a product from the market? Each of these requires a different definition of what is differential, however. No part of the plant manager's salary is a differential cost in a decision to accept an order for 400 door panels, but it certainly is a differential cost if management is considering closing the plant.

Differences, in other words, relate to specific decisions and specific sets of alternatives. The motto, "Different costs for different purposes," should be emblazoned on every accountant's office wall.

Sunk Cost

A term frequently used in decision analysis is *sunk cost*. Although some people use the term differently, we prefer to define sunk cost as any cost that will be unaffected by the decision to be made. For any given decision, all costs can be divided into two classes—sunk costs and differential costs.

The amounts paid in the past to buy a plot of land are sunk costs. Nothing management can do now can change that amount. The same is true of costs that have already been incurred to develop a new product that management is now considering placing on the market. Even the plant manager's salary is a sunk cost in an analysis of whether to take on another order. In other words, the term is used to identify costs that are irrelevant to a particular decision. "These costs are sunk, and we don't need to consider them."

Opportunity Cost

Proposals sometimes call for the use of resources the company already controls. No cash outlay has to be made to obtain them. They have a differential cost, however, measured by the net cash inflow that will be lost if they are diverted from their best alternative use. This differential cost is known as the *opportunity cost* of these resources. It is the value of an opportunity forgone. It belongs in the analysis because *an action that eliminates a cash inflow is exactly equivalent to an action that requires a cash outflow.* The effect on the company's cash position is identical.

For example, a variety chain paid $500,000 ten years ago for a plot of land as a site for a shopping center. Uncertainty as to state highway relocation plans forced management to postpone the project, and the land has lain idle ever since. The route of the new highway has now been established, and the company is again considering the possibility of using the land as a shopping-center site.

The original purchase price of the land is a sunk cost, irrelevant to the decision. The shopping-center proposal must be charged for the land, however, because building the shopping center would prevent the company from using it to generate cash in other ways. If we find that the land can be sold for a net price of $800,000, after deducting all commissions, fees, and taxes, and if the chain has no other use for the land, then $800,000 is its opportunity cost for the purpose of this decision. This amount should be included among the cash outflows required by the shopping center proposal.

Uncertainty and Expected Value

A truck can't make a one-way trip from one city to the other; it must make a round trip. If freight is carried both ways, the incremental cost of a round trip is $188 + $188 = $376. If the backhaul is empty, the cost of a round trip is $188 + $160 = $348. Finally, the incremental cost of carrying freight on a trip that would otherwise be an empty backhaul is $188 − $160 = $28.

These are the cost figures that management should use whenever it knows with certainty which of these three situations it faces. For example, if the decision is whether to accept a shipment in Cleveland and management knows that it has a return load waiting in Chicago, the incremental cost is $188. If it knows that it has no return load waiting in Chicago and that the truck will have to return empty to Cleveland, the incremental cost is $348. Finally, if a truck is now in Cleveland, ready to head back to Chicago empty, the incremental cost of taking a Chicago-bound shipment is $28.

In many decision situations, however, Apollo's management is uncertain whether a load of freight will be available for the backhaul. In these situations, management uses a decision technique known as *expected value analysis*. This requires the assignment of probabilities to the various possible situations that may exist and the use of these probabilities to weight the costs that will prevail in these situations.

To illustrate, suppose that Apollo has been offered a one-year contract to haul freight from Chicago to Cleveland. The contract will require it to carry at least two and at most four loads of freight per week. The management has decided that when a Chicago truck is dispatched to carry a load, the incremental cost is the cost of a fully loaded trip to Cleveland plus the cost of an empty backhaul. When a Cleveland truck is available in Chicago to carry a backhaul, the cost of the trip is the incremental cost of a loaded trip over the cost of an empty backhaul, or $28. Management has also estimated that when a load has to be shipped from Chicago to Cleveland, a Cleveland truck will be available for a backhaul 30 percent of the time and a Chicago truck will have to be dispatched for that purpose 70 percent of the time.

This rather complicated set of assumptions is summarized in Exhibit 19–3, together with the calculation of the "expected value" of the incremental cost. This shows that 70 percent of the trips will have an incremental cost of $348, while 30 percent will have an incremental cost of only $28. On the average, therefore, the incremental cost will be somewhere between these two figures, in this case $252.

(Notice that if the reverse probabilities hold in Cleveland, the expected value of the cost of carrying a load from there to Chicago is 0.3 × $348 + 0.7 × $28 = $124. The sum of the expected values of the costs each way ($252 + $124 = $376) is just equal to the cost of a round trip for a loaded truck.)

EXHIBIT 19–3. Calculation of Expected Value

	(1) Cost per Trip	(2) Percentage of Total Trips	(3) Weighted Cost per Trip (1) × (2)
Chicago-based truck: cost of full load plus empty backhaul	$348	70%	$243.60
Cleveland-based truck: added cost of loaded backhaul ($188–$160)	28	30	8.40
Expected Value of Haulage Cost per Trip			$252.00

SHORT-TERM, COST-VOLUME RELATIONSHIPS

Many resource-allocation decisions focus on management's efforts to use existing capacity profitably. Increasing or decreasing the amount of capacity takes time, and, in the meantime, management must try to do its best with what it has.

The question in a decision of this kind is whether to increase or decrease the rate of output of a particular product or service within existing capacity limits. For this purpose, management needs to estimate how costs will change when the rate of output increases or decreases.

Variable Costs

All organizations engage in *responsive activities*—that is, activities imposed on a part of the organization by activities outside it. Manufacturing is a responsive activity, meeting demands arising out of marketing activities. Preparing payrolls is a responsive activity, meeting demands arising out of all the firm's activities.

Some costs of responsive activities go up or down almost automatically in response to small changes in operating volume. Operating volume, or level of activity, is the rate at which resources are used (pounds of materials per hour) or at which goods or services are produced (meals served per week). Any cost that must be increased in total if the firm is to achieve a small increase in the level of activity is a *variable cost*.

The diagram in Exhibit 19–4 represents the behavior of a cost element that is proportionally variable with volume. Each dot stands for the cost and volume recorded in one particular month in the past.

EXHIBIT 19–4. Proportionally Variable Cost

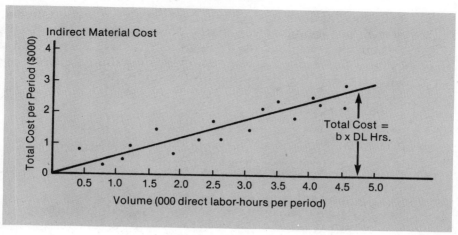

The line drawn through the dots indicates the cost of the indirect materials this firm might be expected to use at each level of activity if future conditions are like those of the past.

TERMINOLOGY REMINDER

Direct materials are materials that are fully and readily traceable to the individual production orders they are used on. *Indirect materials* are all other materials used in the factory in support of production but not traceable to individual production orders.

Direct labor is the amount of labor that is fully and readily traceable to individual production orders. *Indirect labor* consists of all other factory labor.

The line fitted to the observations plotted in Exhibit 19–4 is described by the equation:

$$C = bV$$

in which

C = total cost per month
V = the volume of activity, measured by direct labor hours
b = the rate of variable cost per direct labor hour.

In this case, average variable cost is constant (and equal to b) per unit of output throughout the entire volume range.

Fixed Costs

   Costs that don't change as a necessary result of small changes in
volume are known as *fixed costs*. Some of these are the fixed costs of
responsive activities, also known as *capacity costs*. They are the
costs of the resources used to provide or maintain current operating
capacity. The horizontal line in the upper half of Exhibit 19–5, for

EXHIBIT 19–5.   Fixed Cost

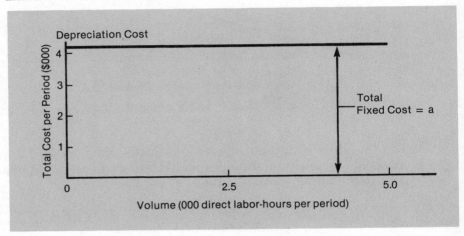

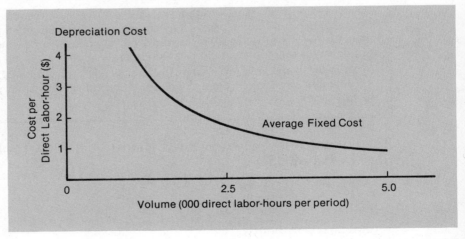

example, represents the relationship between total depreciation cost
and the volume of activity. The line of relationship is given by the
formula:

$$C = a$$

in which a represents total depreciation cost per month. Since the total depreciation cost doesn't vary as a result of output changes, the cost per unit of output falls as the rate of output per period increases. At any output (V), the average cost is a/V. This is shown in the lower half of Exhibit 19–5.

Every organization has a second group of fixed costs, fundamentally different from the first. These are the costs of *programmed activities*, undertaken at management's initiative to meet objectives other than meeting demands for service imposed on the organization from the outside. Research and development are programmed activities; so is sales promotion; so are methods-improvement studies.

Programmed activities determine the organization's scope and direction. Some of them are *innovative*, designed to enable the organization to change the way it operates—by developing new products, acquiring other firms, improving operating methods, and so forth. Others are *promotional*, intended to stimulate demands for the organization's goods and services—most selling activities fall in this category.

Programmed activities are very different from responsive activities. Responsive activities are more or less imposed on the organization by the success of its programmed activities. The costs of responsive activities must adapt to changes in volume if the organization is to meet its commitments; the costs of programmed activities need not go up if responsive activities expand.

The costs of programmed activities are known by many names, including programmed costs, discretionary costs, and managed costs. They tend to be budgeted at constant levels for individual time periods. Once the budget is set, programmed costs per unit will be low if volume is high and high if volume is low.

Semivariable and Stepped Costs

Not all cost elements can be described as totally fixed or proportionally variable. Many other relationships are possible, and two of these are worth mentioning here.

Some costs are partly fixed and partly variable. The diagram in Exhibit 19–6 pictures the cost-volume relationship of one of these elements. In this case, indirect labor cost falls as volume falls toward zero, but it does not fall proportionately with the change in volume. This kind of cost can be described by an equation which combines the elements included in the other two equations cited earlier:

$$C = a + bV,$$

in which both a and b are positive. Dividing both sides by V, we get:

$$\text{Average cost} = C/V = a/V + b.$$

EXHIBIT 19–6.   Semivariable Cost

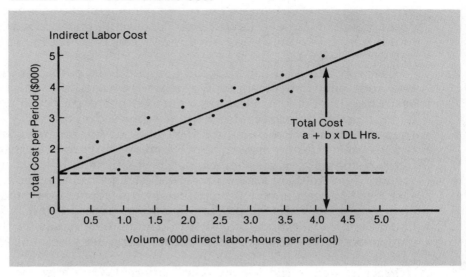

As output (V) increases, a/V decreases and so does average overhead cost per unit (C/V).

Other cost elements may behave in the manner represented in Exhibit 19–7. As this shows, costs rise in a step-like fashion. The basic supervisory staff can handle all levels of volume up to 1,500 direct labor-hours a month. For sustained operations above this level, additional supervisory personnel must be employed, and total cost jumps up. Average cost falls as volume expands as long as the in-

EXHIBIT 19–7.   Stepped Cost

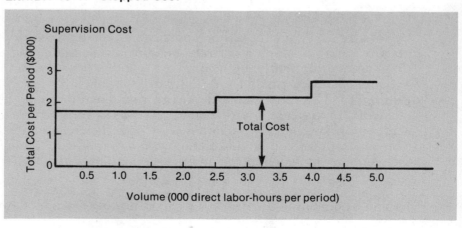

crease is not big enough to move supervisory costs to the next level. The average rises at this point and then begins to fall again as volume continues to expand while total cost remains constant.

Stepped costs such as these are generally classified as fixed costs on the grounds that volume generally moves within fairly narrow ranges in the short run. Substantial volume changes require careful planning and conscious decisions to move to higher or lower plateaus.

Estimating Cost Variability

Estimating the rate at which costs vary with volume isn't easy. For one thing, it isn't always clear how volume should be measured. If a department produces only one kind of product or service, volume can be measured by the number of units produced. In the more typical multiproduct situation, however, the units produced are so dissimilar that physical output totals are meaningless—one automobile plus one bicycle doesn't add up to two of anything. The usual solution in this situation is to use some measure of input, such as the number of direct labor-hours (as in the diagrams in this chapter) or the weight of the materials processed.

Having chosen a measure of volume, we still have to develop a method of estimating the rate at which costs will change in response to changes in volume. Most analysts prefer a statistical approach known as *least-squares regression analysis*. This approach uses a mathematical formula to position a line of relationship on a diagram like the one in Exhibit 19–6. This line, known as a *regression line*, is drawn in such a way that the dots in the diagram are closer to this line than to any other that might be drawn in its place.[1]

A simpler approach is to rely on the judgment of experienced personnel. This approach, known as the *inspection-of-accounts* method, requires someone to classify each kind of cost as wholly fixed, wholly variable, or a mixture of the two. The analyst then estimates the monthly amount for each fixed cost element and the average unit cost for each proportionally variable element.

The inspection-of-accounts method is less scientific than regression analysis, but it can be used when historical data are inadequate for some reason. It should also be used to check the results of regression analysis—statistics sometimes lie, and a little personal judgment may be necessary to find the truth.

---

[1] This method is described in any standard statistics text. For example, see William A. Spurr and Charles P. Bonini, *Statistical Analysis for Business Decisions*, rev. ed. (Homewood, Ill.: Richard D. Irwin, Inc., 1973), chaps. 16–17.

Cost Variability and Incremental Costs

Our interest in cost variability arises mainly because the only incremental costs for many decisions are the wholly variable costs and the variable components of semivariable cost elements. This is not always true, however. For many decisions, some or all of the fixed costs are incremental.

The reason for this apparent contradiction in terms is not hard to find. Fixed costs remain constant only so long as capacity is unchanged. Whenever a decision is large in scope or has a long time horizon, at least two of the alternatives will differ in total capacity. This means that some of the fixed costs are likely to differ between alternatives—that is, fixed costs will be incremental costs.

For example, suppose Apollo has seven trucks, all licensed, insured, and in good operating condition. The costs of licensing and insuring the trucks are fixed costs, in that they will be the same in total whether the trucks operate 50,000 miles this year or 100,000 miles.

In deciding whether to accept a particular shipment, requiring the movement of a truck from Cleveland to Chicago and back, Apollo's management should ignore the costs of licensing and insuring the truck. These costs are sunk costs with respect to this decision.

Suppose, however, that traffic on the Chicago-Cleveland route has declined to such an extent that management is considering the possibility of placing one of the company's trucks in storage for the rest of the year. If this is done, the insurance company will refund the insurance premiums already paid on this truck for the remainder of the year, but the state government will not refund any portion of the license fee. For this decision, therefore, the license fee is a sunk cost, but the insurance premium is an incremental cost.

APPLYING THE INCREMENTAL PRINCIPLE

A study of two illustrative problems will throw additional light on the uses of financial data in resource allocation decisions: (1) pricing additional business and (2) discontinuing a product. Examination of these problems will also show that all of the relevant considerations cannot always be quantified, so that the data themselves do not determine what the decision should be.

Pricing Additional Business

Most business firms do most of their business with a group of fairly regular customers who buy the products and services that are the firm's regular stock in trade. Opportunities sometimes arise, however, to fill special orders for products that are not part of the regular line.

An opportunity of this sort came to the management of the Van Horn Company, a manufacturer of lawn mowers. The purchasing agent of the Wilde Company, which operated a chain of automotive and hardware stores, asked Van Horn's sales manager whether Van Horn would be interested in manufacturing 2,000 power mowers to be sold by Wilde under its own brand name, Wilcut. Van Horn could have this order at a price of $48 a unit. Production capacity was easily adequate to handle this order.

The Wilcut mower would be very similar to one of Van Horn's regular mowers, and the company's controller prepared the following estimate of unit cost, based on the company's usual full-cost accounting methods:

Manufacturing cost:	
Direct materials	$25.80
Direct labor	7.00
Overhead	9.35
Total	$42.15
Selling expense	1.45
Administrative expense	2.90
Total Cost	$46.50

This was only $1.50 less than the estimated price, a margin that the controller regarded as inadequate.

TERMINOLOGY REMINDER

Factory overhead consists of all factory costs other than direct materials and direct labor. A *factory overhead rate* is an average determined by dividing total factory-overhead cost by some index of volume, such as the number of direct labor hours. A factory overhead rate reflecting all factory overhead costs, both fixed and variable, is a *full-cost* overhead rate.

The manufacturing vice president prepared an alternative profit estimate, based on the estimates of cost variability shown in the first column of the following table:

	Per Unit	Total
Incremental variable cost:		
Direct materials	$25.80	$51,600
Direct labor	7.00	14,000
Factory overhead	5.00	10,000
Administration	.20	400
Incremental Variable Cost	$38.00	$76,000
Incremental fixed factory overhead		2,000
Total Incremental Cost		$78,000
Incremental sales revenues	$48.00	96,000
Incremental Profit		$18,000

In this analysis, the manufacturing vice president accepted the original estimates of direct labor and direct materials costs as fully incremental costs because they represented employee salaries and materials-purchase costs that would not be incurred if the proposal were rejected.

The variable portions of factory overhead also seemed likely to be fully incremental, and these were estimated at $5 a unit. Fixed factory overhead was mostly sunk, however, and the manufacturing vice president excluded that portion of the overhead rate from the analysis. The idea was to include only those fixed overhead costs likely to be added to the total by acceptance of the order. The only likely increment here seemed to be a slight increase in supervisory costs, adding up to about $2,000 for the contract as a whole. Fixed costs, in other words, can be incremental, but not necessarily in the proportions implied by the regular full-cost overhead rate.

The selling and administrative expense figures in the original estimates, like the $9.35 in factory overhead, were based on average cost/revenue ratios for the company as a whole. The only selling and administrative costs to be affected by the acceptance of this order were clerical costs in the accounting department, which seemed likely to go up by about 20 cents for each additional unit manufactured and sold. This increment was also included in the estimates of variable costs summarized above.

Collection of figures such as these doesn't necessarily settle the managerial problem. The sales manager pointed out that Van Horn had been losing market share in recent years by not participating in the rapidly growing portion of total mower sales handled by mail-order houses and other large retail distributors. This initial order would give the company valuable experience in dealing in this market and might lay the groundwork for a substantial penetration of the market in the future.

The president, on the other hand, was afraid that the company's regular customers, mostly small independent dealers, would regard this as unfair to them and might shift to competitors' lines. The controller suggested that the low price might lead competitors to retaliate by price cutting on models that competed directly with Van Horn's own branded models. Another worry was that if the sales force were encouraged to cut the price this time it would want to do so again and again. This would undermine the company's entire pricing structure.

How this argument was resolved is unimportant here, but it does illustrate two things. First, a purely quantitative analysis is unlikely to resolve the issues in decision-making situations involving major policy questions. Second, the arguments summarized above represent the typical range of managerial reactions to the use of incremental cost data. How the issues are resolved in any case will depend on management's considered judgment on the validity of the arguments raised in this illustration.

Dropping an Unprofitable Product

Van Horn's management also faced another problem at the same time. One of its regular products, the Estate power mower, was selling at a price that was $4.10 less than the average cost assigned to that product. Van Horn's president asked the controller to prepare an estimate of the financial impact of withdrawing the Estate mower from the line.

The controller's first step was to ask the sales manager whether withdrawal of the Estate mower would affect the company's sales of any of its other mowers. The sales manager reported that if this item were dropped, many buyers would switch to the company's Suburban mower, a slightly cheaper model with many of the same features as the Estate mower. Sales of the Suburban mower seemed likely to increase by about 3,000 units a year if the Estate mower were dropped. None of the company's other models would be affected.

The controller's next step was to prepare estimates of the variable cost of manufacturing and selling these two mowers. These estimates were as follows:

	Estate	Suburban
Variable factory costs:		
Direct materials	$32.00	$27.50
Direct labor	12.00	7.50
Overhead	6.00	5.00
Total	$50.00	$40.00
Variable selling cost	3.50	3.00
Variable administrative cost	.20	.20
Total Variable Cost	$53.70	$43.20

Variable selling costs in this table represented the commissions which the company's sales force received on all sales of the regular lines of mowers.

Finally, the controller tried to estimate how dropping the Estate mowers would affect the fixed factory overhead. This effect was not measured by the overhead rate, but had to be estimated from an item-by-item analysis of overhead costs. After careful study, the manufacturing vice president reported that $27,000 of the factory's overhead costs, which were fixed as long as *any* Estate mowers were manufactured, could be eliminated if *none* were produced. Production of an additional 3,000 Suburban mowers a year wouldn't lead to any increases in fixed overhead.

The analysis of this proposal is summarized in Exhibit 19–8.

EXHIBIT 19–8

VAN HORN COMPANY
Incremental Cash Flows from Estate Mowers

	(1)		(3)	(4)	(5)
					Net Loss from
			Suburban Mower		*Dropping*
	Losses Due to		*Gains if the*		*the*
	Dropping the		*Estate Mower*		*Estate*
	Estate Mower		*Is Dropped*		*Mower*
	Per Unit	*Total*	*Per Unit*	*Total*	*(2) – (4)*
Incremental costs:					
Variable cost.................	$53.70	$268,500	$43.20	$129,600	$138,900
Fixed factory overhead cost.......................		27,000		—	27,000
Total		$295,500		$129,600	$165,900
Incremental revenue	70.00	350,000	60.00	180,000	170,000
Incremental Profit..........		$ 54,500		$ 50,400	$ 4,100

The figures in column (1), taken alone, indicate that the company would lose $54,000 by dropping the Estate Mower. (Fixed costs aren't shown in column (1) because they vary only in one large lump sum, not gradually as the number of units increases or decreases.) This loss would be partially offset, however, by gains from increased sales of the Suburban mower. Column (4) shows that the increase in profit in the Suburban line would be about $50,400. The estimated incremental loss from dropping the Estate mower therefore was only $4,100, or about 1 percent of sales revenues from this line.

This analysis shows that the Estate mower was not a dead loss, as the original full-cost estimate had implied, but neither was it a great contributor to profit, as the figures in column (2) seemed to indicate. It was of borderline importance, and management probably should have looked at it very carefully to see whether its profitability could be improved or whether management's efforts should be expended in other directions.

SUMMARY

The basic approach to quantitative analysis for management decisions is to estimate the incremental cash flows, the *differences* between the anticipated results of a proposed course of action and the anticipated results of the action the company would take if the proposal were rejected.

This *incremental analysis* is a simple and powerful concept, but one which is by no means easily applied in all cases. In simple situations, for example, a product's variable cost may be a good estimate of the cost of increasing product output, but revenue effects may be extremely difficult to forecast. In other cases, many fixed costs will also be affected, particularly if large amounts of business are affected by the decision.

Although the future is uncertain, it is sometimes possible to estimate the probability of each possible future outcome of a decision and get the expected value of the payoff. In other situations, these uncertainties are more intractable and have to be dealt with in a qualitative way, after the incremental calculations have been made.

This chapter has indicated how costs can be classified into fixed and variable costs to make them more readily usable in decision making. We have examined a number of cost concepts, such as sunk costs and opportunity costs, to obtain a richer understanding of how costs are used in decision making.

KEY TERMS

Capacity costs
Expected value
Fixed cost
Incremental cost
Incremental profit
Opportunity cost

Programmed activities
Regression analysis
Responsive activities
Sunk cost
Variable cost

INDEPENDENT STUDY PROBLEMS (Solutions in Appendix B)

1. **Cost-volume relationships.** The Johnson Works has prepared the following estimates of average total factory cost at different volumes:

Weekly Volume (Units)	Average Cost per Unit
1	$11.00
2	6.00
3	4.33
4	3.50
5	3.00
6	2.67
7	2.43
8	2.25
9	2.22
10	2.30

a. Calculate average variable cost at each volume. (For this purpose, assume that total fixed cost is the same at all volumes.)

b. Calculate average fixed cost at each volume.

c. Assuming the company is now operating at a weekly volume of nine units, calculate the cost relevant to a decision on increasing the rate of operations to ten units a week.

2.   Opportunity cost.   Nancy Smith bought 100 shares in Hydrophonics, Ltd., on January 15, 19x1, paying $15 a share. She bought an additional 100 shares on March 18, 19x4, paying $20 a share. The market price of this stock fell rapidly in 19x5, reaching a low point of $6 a share. Early in 19x6 the market price had recovered to $8 a share. At that point General Enterprises, Inc., offered to buy all shares tendered to it at a price of $10 a share.

What cost figure should Ms. Smith use in evaluating this offer?

3.   Uncertainty: choosing a source of supply.   A company uses 100,000 pounds of material X every month. A supplier has offered to supply the company's requirements of this material for the next year at a fixed price of 80 cents a pound. The current market price is 75 cents, but if the facilities of one of this material's principal foreign suppliers are expropriated by the foreign government, total output will fall and the world price is likely to go to 90 cents a pound.

In management's judgment, there is about a 40 percent chance the supplier will be nationalized during the next year. Would you advise management to accept the proposed contract?

4.   Identifying incremental costs.   Marmon, Inc., owns two delivery trucks. The costs of owning and operating these trucks are as follows:

	Truck A	Truck B
Yearly fixed costs:		
Garage space	$ 400	$ 400
Depreciation	600	400
Registration and insurance	1,400	1,300
Maintenance	300	300
Variable costs:		
Drivers' wages and benefits	$10 an hour	$10 an hour
Gasoline and oil	.10 a mile	.11 a mile
Maintenance	.05 a mile	.06 a mile

Marmon normally operates truck A 1,800 hours a year; truck B is used only 650 hours. On the average, trucks in service cover 15 miles in an hour. The company rents garage space for its trucks in a nearby garage. The garaging contract for either truck can be cancelled on one month's notice. Maintenance is provided by a local truck-repair shop.

Marmon has just purchased merchandise in a liquidation sale and must pick this merchandise up next week. Unfortunately truck A is now fully scheduled for regular deliveries all next week, and truck B can't be used because it is too wide for the loading platform where the merchandise is located. Truck B can be used for truck A's regular deliveries, however, and this will let the company use truck A to pick up the merchandise, if the costs are acceptable.

Management estimates this job will take one full week and require 40 hours of a driver's time. The truck will travel 400 miles. Truck B, in the regular delivery service, will operate 40 hours and cover 600 miles. The additional truck driver would be hired for the week on a contract basis at the regular cost of $10 an hour.

As an alternative, an independent trucking company has offered to pick up and deliver the purchased merchandse to Marmon's warehouse for $500.

a. Should Marmon use truck A to pick up this merchandise, or should it use the independent trucker? Show your calculations and indicate how you treated each cost element. (You may assume a year of 50 weeks.)

b. Because truck B is used so little, management is considering scrapping it and using an independent trucker to make the deliveries it is now used for. Assuming truck B now has no significant scrap value, what is the highest annual amount Marmon could afford to pay an independent trucker each year instead of using truck B? Show your calculations. (Ignore income taxes.)

EXERCISES AND PROBLEMS

5. Effect of special order. Relay Corporation manufactures batons. Relay can manufacture 300,000 batons a year at a total variable cost of $750,000 and a total fixed cost of $450,000. Relay's prediction is that 240,000 batons will be sold at the regular price of $5 each. In addition, a special order has been placed by a customer for 60,000 batons at a 40 percent discount off the regular price.

By what amount will income before income taxes be increased or decreased as a result of this special order?

(AICPA)

6. Make or buy decision. Buck Company manufactures Part No. 1700 for use in its production cycle. The costs per unit for 5,000 units of Part 1700 are as follows:

Direct materials	$ 2
Direct labor	12
Variable overhead	5
Fixed overhead	7
Total	$26

Hollow Company has offered to sell Buck 5,000 units of Part No. 1700 for $27 a unit. If Buck accepts this offer, some of the facilities presently used to manufacture Part No. 1700 can be used in the manufacture of Part No. 1211, thereby reducing the company's cost of manufacturing Part No. 1211 by $40,000. In addition, if the company stops making Part No. 1700, it can reduce its total fixed factory overhead by $15,000.

What is the incremental profit or loss to be obtained by accepting Hollow's offer?

(AICPA adapted)

7.   *Identifying sunk costs.* The Meredith Machine Company entered into a contract to manufacture certain specially designed processing equipment for a foreign buyer. When the equipment was completed and in the testing stage, currency controls which nullified all import contracts were instituted by the government to which the purchaser was subject. The manufacturing costs incurred by the Meredith Company up to that time amounted to $700,000. The scrap value of the equipment was estimated to be approximately $80,000.

No purchaser could be found for the equipment in its existing form, but one company was interested if certain major modifications were made. This company offered $500,000; the estimated cost of modification to fit the revised specifications was $200,000.

What action should the Meredith Company have taken? To what extent was the decision affected by the amount of manufacturing cost the company had already incurred?

8.   *Drawing a regression line.* The following table summarizes the departmental direct labor-hours and indirect labor cost for a factory department for the past 12 months:

Direct Labor-Hours	Indirect Labor Cost
14,400	$5,520
10,650	4,140
14,100	5,640
15,000	6,600
13,650	4,680
13,050	5,100
13,350	4,860
13,500	4,740
13,500	5,460
14,250	4,800
13,200	4,140
13,350	4,800

a.   Plot these data on a sheet of graph paper and draw a straight-line regression line which seems to fit the observations most closely.

b.   Derive the mathematical equation that describes this line.

c.   What difficulties do you foresee in trying to determine cost-volume relationships by this method? Would you use the method, despite these difficulties?

9.   *Taking on additional business.* A printing company is considering an opportunity to print a new monthly magazine for an organization of professional social workers. The organization is not wealthy, and it cannot pay more than 50 cents a copy to have its new magazine printed, or $5,000 a month. The printing firm would like to help out, but only if it can recover its costs, plus a margin of 5 percent of cost to allow for contingencies. If the contingencies did not materialize, the firm would make a small profit.

The costs of direct labor, paper stock, and ink would be completely variable. Printing the magazine would bring the monthly volume in the print shop from 8,000 direct labor-hours to 8,500 direct labor-hours a month, and average overhead costs would drop from $2 an hour at 8,000 hours to $1.95 an hour at 8,500 hours. Management has drawn up the following profit estimate for the new magazine:

Revenue per hour......................		$10.00
Costs per hour:		
Direct labor	$6.00	
Paper stock and ink	2.50	
Printing overhead	1.95	10.45
Profit/(Loss) per Hour		$ (0.45)

The print shop manager says the print shop overhead is a sunk cost and should be ignored. Since the anticipated margin over direct costs amounts to $1.50, the job should be taken on.

Prepare an analysis and make a recommendation. If your analysis indicates the proposal should be rejected, prepare a response to be made to the social workers' representative.

10. Identifying incremental costs. A company has four large presses of approximately the same capacity. Each was run at close to its full capacity during 19x8. Each machine is depreciated separately; a declining-charge method is used. Data for each press are:

	No. 1	No. 2	No. 3	No. 4
Date acquired	1/1/x0	1/1/x4	1/1/x6	1/1/x7
Cost	$100,000	$120,000	$145,000	$175,000
Operating costs—19x8				
Labor	$ 11,000	$ 10,500	$ 10,000	$ 9,500
Maintenance	3,800	2,400	2,000	1,000
Repairs	600	1,200	800	500
Depreciation	3,500	5,400	7,800	10,800
Total	$ 18,900	$ 19,500	$ 20,600	$ 21,800

It is expected that activity in 19x9 will be substantially less than in 19x8. As a result, one machine is to be put on a standby basis. It has been proposed that No. 4 should be that machine on the grounds that it has the highest operating cost. A standby machine would require neither maintenance nor repairs.

Do you agree with this proposal? Explain, citing figures from the problem.

11. Desirability of reducing prices. The manager of the university print shop is trying to decide whether to meet the prices and delivery-time performance of local commercial printing shops on small printing jobs. The commercial shops quote prices that are 10 percent lower than the university shop's schedule and also offer faster delivery at no extra charge. Until now, university departments have been required to use the university shop for this sort of work, but a mounting volume of complaints has led the university controller to authorize the use of off-campus shops. The university shop will continue to do large-volume jobs and confidential work, such as examinations and research reports. The university shop would require the same amount of equipment it now has, even if it were to let small jobs go outside.

At its present operating volume of 2,000 labor-hours a month, the operating costs of the university print shop are:

Paper stock .... Varies with nature of work
Labor .... $8 a labor-hour
Other processing costs .... $6 a labor-hour

All labor is regarded as wholly variable with volume; other processing costs include $8,000 of fixed costs, the remainder being wholly and proportionally variable with volume, volume being measured in terms of labor-hours.

Approximately 600 labor-hours a month are now being spent on the work affected by the decision. Materials cost on this work is approximately $6,000 a month, and the amount now being charged by the university shop to other university departments for this work is $15,000 a month.

The shop manager is convinced the shop will lose the work unless it meets both the competitive price and the competitive delivery time. To permit faster deliveries, an additional 80 hours of labor a month would be required in excess of the 600 labor-hours now devoted to this work. Fixed costs would not be affected by this choice between these two alternatives.

Which alternative should the manager choose? Show your calculations.

12.   Discontinuing a product.   Company X manufactures and sells more than 200 products to industrial customers. Management is now reviewing one of these, product T. Although this product seemed highly promising when it was introduced two years ago, competitive developments have cut into its market, and the marketing manager says no one at all will be buying it three years from now. You have been given the following estimates:

	This Year	Next Year	Year After Next
Sales	$1,000,000	$ 600,000	$ 200,000
Costs:			
Variable factory	$ 500,000	$ 300,000	$ 100,000
Fixed factory	250,000	150,000	50,000
Development	200,000	200,000	200,000
Direct selling	150,000	120,000	60,000
Total costs	$1,100,000	$ 770,000	$ 410,000
Product Margin	$ (100,000)	$(170,000)	$(210,000)

Further investigation reveals that:

1.   The charges for fixed factory costs in the table shown above are based on average overhead rates. When production of this product is discontinued, $70,000 in fixed factory overheads will be eliminated each year.
2.   The company spent $1 million to develop this product. This amount is being amortized over a five-year period at $200,000 a year, and $600,000 remains unamortized today.

3. Direct selling costs are all traceable to this product and consist of items such as sales-force salaries and travel expenses.
4. Investment in working capital to support this product is negligible.

Prepare an analysis to help management decide whether to discontinue manufacturing and selling product T right now or keep it in the line for one, two, or three years.

13. Make or buy; maximum purchase price; long term versus short term.
The Grandview Corporation has been manufacturing a chemical compound known as corolite. Its entire output of this compound, about 100,000 gallons a year, has been used in the production of several of the company's finished products.

Grandview uses 10,000 gallons of corolite a year in the manufacture of blivets in a separate factory. A gallon of corolite is used for each dozen blivets manufactured. You have the following cost estimates:

	Corolite	Blivets
Annual volume	100,000 gal.	10,000 doz.
Direct materials	$4/gal.	$2/doz.*
Direct labor	8/gal.	5/doz.
Variable overhead	6/gal.	3/doz.
Fixed overhead	5/gal.	4/doz.
Total	$23/gal.	$14/doz.*

* Plus one gallon of corolite per dozen.

The Boxboro Corporation has just developed a substitute for corolite, known as formulane, and has offered to sell 10,000 gallons of this product to Grandview for use in the manufacture of blivets during the coming year. The price would be $20.50 a gallon. Formulane has one advantage over corolite: it can be used directly in the manufacture of blivets without further processing in the blivet plant. Management estimates this would reduce the direct labor cost of manufacturing blivets by $1 a dozen, or 20 percent of the total direct labor cost in the blivets factory.

Manager of the blivets factory has asked management to approve the purchase of 10,000 gallons of formulane from Boxboro, on the basis of the following cost comparison:

Purchase price of formulane	$20.50
Less: Reduction in processing time ($1 + 20 percent of overhead)	2.40
Net Cost of Formulane	$18.10
Cost of corolite	23.00
Net Saving	$ 4.90

The manager of the corolite plant has objected, saying the corolite plant's fixed costs would go on anyway; therefore, the net cost of formulane to Grandview would be $18.10 + $5.00 = $23.10.

Total fixed costs in the blivets plant wouldn't change if formulane were to be substituted for corolite. Variable overhead costs in each factory vary in proportion to changes in direct labor costs.

    a. Should Grandview buy formulane from the Boxboro Company? Summarize the figures on which your answer is based and show how you calculated them.

    b. Calculate the maximum price Grandview could afford to pay Boxboro for an order of 10,000 gallons of formulane.

    c. Suppose Grandview was considering discontinuing the manufacture of corolite entirely, using formulane obtained from Boxboro in all products now based on corolite. Formulane has the same advantages over corolite in all these products as in the manufacture of blivets. Would the maximum purchase price of formulane probably be greater, less, or equal to the maximum purchase price you calculated in your answer to (*b*)? Explain.

14.   Closing a factory.   Arcadia Corporation has its home office in Ohio and leases factory buildings in Texas, Montana, and Maine, all of which produce the same product. The operations of the Maine factory have been marginal for a number of years. The lease on the Maine building will expire at the end of this year, and Arcadia's management has decided to cease operations there rather than renew the lease. This factory's machinery and equipment will be sold. Arcadia expects the proceeds from the sale of these assets will exceed their book value by an amount just adequate to cover all termination costs.

Prior to the decision to close the Maine plant, Arcadia's management had prepared the following projection of operating results for the next year:

	Total	Texas	Montana	Maine
Sales revenue	$4,400,000	$2,200,000	$1,400,000	$800,000
Fixed costs:				
Factory	$1,100,000	$ 560,000	$ 280,000	$260,000
Selling and administrative	350,000	210,000	110,000	30,000
Variable costs	1,450,000	665,000	425,000	360,000
Home office costs	500,000	225,000	175,000	100,000
Total Operating Expense	$3,400,000	$1,660,000	$ 990,000	$750,000
Operating income before taxes	$1,000,000	$ 540,000	$ 410,000	$ 50,000

The selling price is $25 a unit.

Home office costs are divided among the factories in proportion to their labor costs. They will remain at $500,000 even after the Maine factory is closed.

Arcadia would like to continue serving the customers now being served by the Maine factory, if it can do this economically. Accordingly, management is considering the following alternatives:

1. Close the Maine factory and expand the operations of the Montana factory by using space presently idle there. This move would result in the following changes in Montana's operations:

    a. Sales revenue would increase by 50 percent.

    b. Factory fixed costs would increase by 20 percent.

    c. Selling and administrative fixed costs would increase by 10 percent.

    d. Average variable costs would be $8 per unit sold by the Montana factory.

2. Close the Maine factory and enter into a long-term contract with an independent manufacturer to serve the area's customers. This manufacturer would pay Arcadia a royalty of $4 a unit based on an estimate of 30,000 units being sold.

3. Close the Maine factory and discontinue serving its present customers.

Prepare an analysis to help management decide which of these three alternatives is the most desirable for Arcadia.

(AICPA adapted)

15. Special order. Anchor Company manufactures several different styles of jewelry cases. Management estimates that during the third quarter of 19x6 the company will be operating at 80 percent of maximum capacity. Because the company desires a higher utilization of plant capacity, the company will consider accepting a special order.

Anchor has received special-order inquiries from two companies. The first order is from JCP, Inc., which would like to market a jewelry case similar to one of Anchor's cases. The JCP jewelry case would be marketed under JCP's own label. JCP, Inc., has offered Anchor $5.75 per jewelry case for 20,000 cases to be shipped by the end of the quarter. The cost data for the Anchor jewelry case which is similar to the specifications of the JCP special order are as follows:

Regular selling price per unit	$9.00
Costs per unit:	
Raw materials	$2.50
Direct labor: 0.5 hours × $6	3.00
Overhead: 0.25 machine-hours × $4	1.00
Total	$6.50

According to the specifications provided by JCP, Inc., the special order case requires raw materials that are less expensive than those in Anchor's regular case. Consequently, the raw materials would cost only $2.25 a case. Management has estimated that the remaining costs, labor time, and machine time would be the same as on the Anchor jewelry case.

The second special order was submitted by the Krage Company for 7,500 jewelry cases at $7.50 a case. These cases would be marketed under the Krage label and would have to be shipped by the end of the quarter. The Krage jewelry case is different from any jewelry case in the Anchor line, however. The estimated unit costs of this case are as follows:

Raw materials	$3.25
Direct labor: 0.5 hours × $6	3.00
Overhead: 0.5 machine-hours × $4	2.00
Total	$8.25

In addition, Anchor would incur $1,500 in additional set-up costs and would have to purchase a $2,500 special device to manufacture these cases; this device would be discarded once the special order was completed.

The Anchor manufacturing capabilities are limited to the total machine-hours available. The plant's maximum capacity under normal operations is 90,000 machine-hours a year or 7,500 machine-hours a month. The budgeted fixed overhead for the current year amounts to $216,000. All manufacturing overhead costs are applied to production on the basis of machine-hours at $4 an hour.

Anchor will have the entire third quarter to work on the special order, if it decides to accept one of them. Production of its regular products will increase in the fourth quarter, leaving no capacity available for filling a special order. Management doesn't expect any repeat sales to be generated by either special order, and company policy precludes Anchor from subcontracting any portion of an order which isn't expected to generate repeat sales.

Should Anchor Company accept either special order? Justify your answer and show your calculations.

(IMA adapted)

20

Cost Measurement: Full Costing

Two MAJOR COMPONENTS of the budgetary plan are the operating plan and the capital plan. The operating plan summarizes the actions management intends to take in connection with the production and sale of goods and services during the period covered by the budget, the anticipated costs of these actions, and their anticipated results. The capital plan summarizes management's intentions to acquire and retire equipment, inventories, and other assets during the period.

The expenditures the company actually makes can be classified into the same two classes: (1) operating costs, the costs of carrying out the operating plan during the period and (2) capital expenditures, the costs of the assets the company buys or builds during the period. Our purpose in this chapter is to examine the most important features of a system used by accountants to classify and record an organization's operating costs. The chapter has four parts:

1. Classifying operating costs when they take place, based on their traceability to specific activities and specific units of the organization.
2. Using predetermined overhead rates to assign factory overhead costs to individual job orders.
3. Using separate overhead rates for individual production centers.
4. Assigning costs to individual products when a production operation yields two or more different products.

INITIAL COST CLASSIFICATION

When a company incurs a cost in its operations, it may try to classify that cost in three ways:

1. By organization segment.
2. By object of expenditure.
3. By activity.

Organizational Classification

From an accounting viewpoint, an organization can be regarded as a group of interrelated *cost centers*. A cost center is any department or other unit of the organization or any portion of such a unit for which management chooses to accumulate operating costs. When incurred, costs are assigned to the cost centers they are immediately traceable to.

When an organization unit engages in two or more activities that have different effects on the costs of that organization unit, it should be subdivided into smaller cost centers. A factory department, for example, may have both mechanized and manual operations. The costs of the mechanized operations are likely to be so different from those of the manual operations that management will expect the accountant to be able to separate them.

Object-of-Expenditure Classification

Many of management's decisions affect its operating costs. This suggests that accounting data should be collected in ways that make it easier to identify the relationships between costs and their determinants. One way of doing this is to divide the organization into cost centers. Another is to classify a cost-center's costs into their "natural elements," such as salaries, supplies, electric power, and so on. This is often referred to as classification by *object of expenditure*. (*Supplies* are the *object* obtained by the *expenditure* of funds.)

The first two dimensions of the cost-accumulation system are illustrated in Exhibit 20–1. Each column contains the costs of a

EXHIBIT 20–1.   Two-Dimensional Account Structure

Object of Expenditure \\ Cost Center	Factory Management	Machine Shop	Assembly Department	
Salaries				
Supplies				
Depreciation				

specific cost center; each row contains the costs of a given object of expenditure. The costs in any given cell are the amounts of a specific object used in a specific cost center. Every operating cost can be assigned to one of the cells in the full diagram. (To save space, only a portion of the account structure appears here.) The organizational classification shows *where* the cost was incurred; the object-of-expenditure classification shows *what* resources were used.

Increasing the number of object-of-expenditure categories increases both the cost of the accounting system and the probability that costs will be misclassified. The accountants should only increase the number of categories if the determinants of cost are very likely to be different. For example, if the costs of lubricating oil vary with the number of machine-hours and the costs of cleaning supplies vary with the number of labor-hours, putting them in the same account would be likely to obscure the underlying cost-volume relationships.

Activity Classification

The third dimension of the account structure is the activity classification. Activities fall into three main classes:

1. *Order-getting activities*, designed to induce customers to buy merchandise or place orders.
2. *End-product activities*, undertaken to provide services to outside customers, manufacture finished products and parts, or carry out research projects.
3. *Service and support activities*, undertaken to support activities in the other two classes.

Our concern in this chapter is with end-product activities. Most of these consist of the production of goods or services for outside clients or customers—automobiles, restaurant meals, and hospital patient care are useful examples. Other end-product activities include research projects for the organization's own future benefit, and the construction of productive facilities for the organization's own use. Our illustrations will be located in manufacturing organizations, but most of the discussion applies to other kinds of organizations as well. Bank managers, hospital administrators, and even museum managers need cost information just as much as factory managers do.

The end-product activities in factories result in the production of identifiable quantities of individual products. The process of measuring the costs of these activities is known as *product costing*; the total amount of cost assigned to a particular product or job order is known as *product cost*.

The methods of product costing fall into two broad categories: process costing and job-order costing. *Process costing* is applicable when the production process turns out a single kind of product for long periods of time at a stretch (cement, flour, and so forth). In this case, product cost is equal to the cost assigned to the cost centers in which the product is manufactured. Product cost per unit can be computed easily from the formula:

$$\text{Average Unit Cost} = \frac{\text{Total Production Costs for the Period}}{\text{Total Units of Product Manufactured}}$$

Job-order costing, in contrast, is used when the production facilities produce many different kinds of products simultaneously or in rapid succession (job printing, furniture manufacture, and so forth). Since each cost center engaged in production works on many different products, assigning costs to individual production cost centers isn't enough. Some other mechanism has to be found if costs are to be assigned to individual projects or batches or job lots of products. The rest of this chapter will be devoted to an examination of some of the methods accountants use for this purpose.

JOB-ORDER COSTING WITH PREDETERMINED OVERHEAD RATES

Most product costing systems are *full costing* or *absorption costing* systems, in which product cost includes a share of all factory costs, not just a portion of them. The job-order costing system we outlined in Chapter 6 was a simple example of this kind of system. In this section we'll see how the accountant collects the data a job-order costing system is based on and what happens when a predetermined overhead rate is used to assign factory overhead costs to individual job orders.

REMINDER: ELEMENTS OF JOB-ORDER COST

Job-Order Cost Sheet Job No. 111	
Direct materials	$ 853
Direct labor	156
Factory overhead	185
Total	$1,194

Direct materials: the costs of materials that can be traced readily to individual job orders.

Direct labor: the costs of the time employees spend working directly on individual job orders.

Factory overhead: all factory costs not readily traceable to individual job orders; assigned to jobs by means of averages known as overhead rates.

Classifying Labor and Materials Costs

To identify direct labor and direct materials costs, the accountants need some way of metering the amounts of labor and materials used on the job. For direct labor, the usual device is the *time ticket*. Each employee fills in a time ticket for each different job or each kind of indirect labor he or she engages in during the day. It identifies the amount of time worked, the job or class of indirect labor, and the hourly labor rate. Direct labor cost is determined by multiplying the rate by the amount of time shown on the time ticket. The dollar amount is then entered on the job cost sheet.

The flow of materials is most likely to be identified by *materials requisitions,* showing the kinds of materials used, the quantities, the cost per unit, and the job number or class of indirect materials. The direct materials cost of a job is the total of the costs of all the materials traced to that job. It, too, is entered on the job cost sheet.

Most costs classified as overhead can't be traced to individual job orders. Two groups of costs are included in overhead for other reasons, however. For the first of these, the reason is that tracing the cost to the job would cost more than the added accuracy would be worth. For example, a dressmaker would find it possible but not economical to measure the amount of thread or buttons consumed on each production order. The costs of these items are classified as overhead costs.

Second, some costs are treated as overhead because it would be *unsound* to treat them as direct costs. For instance, factory employees are paid more than their regular wage rate for hours they work in excess of some specified amount. The difference between the regular wage rate and the special rate is the *overtime premium.* For example, if the regular wage rate is $6 an hour, the employee ordinarily will be paid $9 (time and a half) for overtime work. The overtime premium is $3 an hour.

Overtime premium almost always should be classified as overhead—that is, the cost of an overtime hour spent on a specific job order should be distributed as follows:

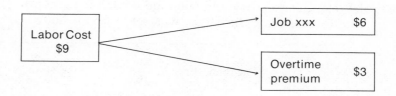

The reason for treating the premium as overhead is that overtime results from the *total* demand on the production facilities. *All* production shares equally in the responsibility for the overtime.

Whenever workers can be transferred from job to job, overtime premiums are just as much the result of sticking to the original production schedule on the first jobs scheduled as they are to the decision to accept the last order received.

Predetermined Overhead Rates

As we saw in Chapter 6, factory overhead is assigned to job orders by means of overhead rates. The overhead rate is usually a ratio of cost to some characteristic of individual job orders, such as the number of direct labor-hours:

$$\text{Overhead Rate} = \frac{\text{Overhead Cost}}{\text{Direct Labor-Hours}}.$$

Although overhead rates representing actual average costs are often used in costing government contracts, *predetermined* rates are more common elsewhere. A predetermined overhead rate is based on *estimates* of overhead cost and production volume—that is, the rate is not the average overhead cost of each individual period, but the average cost in a "normal" or typical period:

$$\text{Overhead Rate} = \frac{\text{Estimated Overhead Costs in a Normal Month}}{\text{Estimated Total Volume in a Normal Month}}$$

These estimates are made before the beginning of the period, usually the company's fiscal year, and the resulting rates are generally used without change throughout the period, no matter what the actual cost experience is.

The Lion Corporation's factory was designed to operate most efficiently at a volume of 16,000 direct labor-hours a month. In 19x1, management estimated that if this volume were achieved, factory overhead would average $96,000 a month. The overhead rate for the year, therefore, was set at $6 an hour:

$$\text{Overhead Rate} = \frac{\$96,000}{16,000} = \$6 \text{ an Hour.}$$

Using this rate, the accountant would assign $60 in factory overhead cost to a job requiring ten direct labor-hours.

Overhead Over- or Underabsorbed

The process of assigning factory overhead costs to individual job orders is commonly called the *application* or *absorption* of overhead. Every time work is performed on a job order, some overhead is assigned to it or "absorbed" by it. The total amount absorbed in any period is the sum of the amounts assigned to individual job orders during the period. This amount can also be determined by applying the following formula:

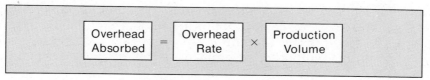

For example, suppose the Lion Corporation used a predetermined overhead rate of $6 a direct labor-hour in 19x1. Direct labor during the year amounted to 15,000 hours. The total amount absorbed by production in 19x1—that is, the amount assigned to job orders during the year—therefore amounted to 15,000 × $6 = $90,000. The company's system, in other words, identified $90,000 as the overhead cost of creating new inventory assets during the year.

The amounts absorbed are recorded on the individual job cost sheets for the job orders on which the work was done. This isn't enough, however. Remember that the individual job cost sheets are represented in the ledger by one or more work in process accounts. This relationship is illustrated in Exhibit 20–2. The balance in a work in process account should always equal the total of the costs shown on the job cost sheets it summarizes.

EXHIBIT 20–2. Relationship between Work in Process Account and Job-Order Cost Sheets

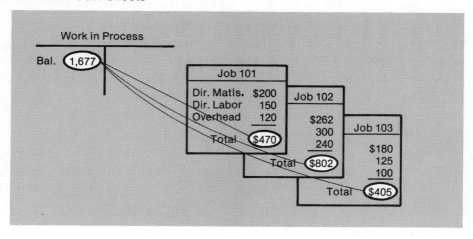

The assignment of overhead costs to job orders, therefore, requires the assignment of identical amounts to a work in process account. In our example, this could be accomplished by the following entry:

Work in Process......................   90,000
    Factory Overhead   90,000

Remember from our discussion in Chapter 6 that the Factory Overhead account is used to accumulate the actual factory overhead costs each period. We described this account as a temporary asset account. The credit to this account merely represents the transfer of $90,000 from this temporary account to a permanent asset account, Work in Process.

Suppose the actual overhead cost in the Lion Corporation's factory amounted to $95,000. The Factory Overhead account would show the following:

Factory Overhead

Actual overhead costs →	95,000	90,000	Overhead costs absorbed →
Bal. 5,000			

The costs enter at the left and leave in a slightly different guise at the right. The account itself is simply a mechanism to make this movement easier.

Notice what has happened, though. Remember that we *predetermined* the overhead rate before we knew that overhead costs for the year would amount to $95,000. Using this predetermined rate, we *absorbed* only $90,000, or $5,000 less than the $95,000 we actually spent. This $5,000 difference is known as the factory overhead cost *variance* or the over- or underabsorbed overhead. In this case the company didn't have enough production volume to absorb all of the overhead costs it actually incurred, and the $5,000 was referred to as *underabsorbed*. If the amount absorbed had exceeded the total overhead cost for the period, the excess would have been labeled *overabsorbed*.

Over- or underabsorption of overhead arises in two ways:

1. *Actual costs differ* from the amounts that would normally be expected at the production volume actually achieved during the period.

2. *Production volume differs* from the volume used to set the overhead rate.

The first of these effects is probably self-evident. If volume holds steady but the company spends more than it expected to when it set the overhead rate, it won't absorb the extra costs. And if it spends less than it expected, it will overabsorb its overhead.

The volume effect works the same way. The Lion Corporation's $6 overhead rate, for example, was based on the assumption that volume would amount to 16,000 direct labor-hours, on the average. At that volume, the full $96,000 in estimated overhead costs will be absorbed. If volume is smaller than that, however, the amount absorbed will be smaller. In the extreme case, if volume falls to zero, no overhead costs will be absorbed at all. Low volume, in other words, is likely to lead to underabsorption; volume greater than normal will lead to overabsorption.

External Reporting of Under- or Overabsorbed Overhead

When overhead is either over- or underabsorbed, the company has to decide how to treat the over- or underabsorbed portion in the financial statements it prepares for its shareholders and others outside the organization. Three alternatives might be considered:

1. Divide the under- or overabsorption in any period between the income statement and balance sheet in direct proportion to the distribution of the overhead absorbed during the period.
2. Report the under- or overabsorption in full as a loss or gain on the income statement for the period in which it arises.
3. Carry any such amounts to the balance sheet for the end of the period, to be added to or offset against similar amounts arising in preceding or succeeding periods.

1. Dividing the underabsorbed balance. Choice of the first alternative implies that the amount of overhead cost assigned to any product should be based on the actual overhead costs during the period in which it was produced, not on the predetermined overhead rate. In our illustration, $90,000 in overhead costs was actually assigned to production during the period. If one fourth of the $90,000 was included in the cost of goods sold for the period and three quarters remained in the inventory at the end of the period, then one fourth of the variance ($1,250) would be added to the cost of goods sold, and three fourths ($3,750) would be included in the reported inventory figure on the end-of-period balance sheet:

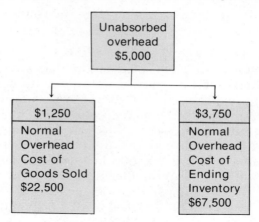

The amount of overhead assigned to the ending inventory would be $71,250 instead of the $67,500 normal amount.

2.   *Variance taken to the income statement.*   The second possibility is to take the entire amount over- or underabsorbed to the income statement for the period in which it arises. If this is done, the overhead cost assigned to a unit of product in inventory will reflect (1) a competitively efficient level of output and (2) a reasonably attainable level of production efficiency—that is, its *normal cost.*

The argument supporting this solution is that inefficiencies due to overspending or underproduction are costs of the period rather than costs of the products manufactured during the period. If volume is low, for example, some of the fixed costs incurred to provide the capacity to produce will go unabsorbed. In other words, these are the costs of the goods are *weren't* produced, not costs of the goods that *were* produced.

The cost of providing the idle portion of capacity fits the definition of a *loss*—a cost unaccompanied by any benefit. Since losses are taken to the income statement when they are identified, unabsorbed overhead costs should be treated as expenses or losses of the current period. A predetermined overhead rate, in other words, is the *preferred* basis for product costing, not a poor substitute adopted for reasons of convenience.

3.   *Deferring the variance.*   The third alternative is to carry over- or underabsorbed balances forward from period to period on the assumption that underabsorption in one period will be offset by overabsorption in another. This approach is often taken in interim reporting when seasonal variations are strong, but the unlikelihood that over- and underabsorption will actually cancel each other out over any reasonable number of years rules out this approach for external reporting.

In practice, all overhead variances are likely to be taken in full to the income statement if they are small enough to be classified as immaterial. If they are large, they will probably be divided between the inventory and the cost of goods sold.

REMINDER: COST DISTRIBUTION

The factory costs to be accounted for in any period are the costs of the beginning inventories, the costs of materials purchased, and the factory operating costs of that period. These costs are accounted for by assigning them either to the ending inventories, to the cost of goods sold, or to the over(under)absorbed overhead. This requirement is illustrated in the following diagram, using a simple set of hypothetical costs:

Beginning Inventory: Raw Materials Work in Process Finished Goods	$40		Cost of Goods Sold	$75
Materials purchased	$30		Underabsorbed Overhead	$10
Labor and Other Resources Used in the Factory	$50		Ending Inventory: Raw Materials Work in Process Finished Goods	$35
Costs to be Accounted for			Costs Accounted for	$120
	$120			

The over(under)absorbed overhead is either assigned in its entirety to the cost of goods sold or is divided between the cost of goods sold and the ending inventory.

DEPARTMENTAL OVERHEAD RATES

Companies seldom use a single overhead rate for an entire factory. Instead, they use departmental overhead rates, one for each production center or department. (For ease of expression, we'll refer to these as departmental rates, even though in many cases individual departments will be subdivided into two or more cost centers, each with its own overhead rate.) We'll discuss four questions arising from this practice:

1.　The reasons why companies use departmental rates.
2.　The need for interdepartmental cost allocations for this purpose.
3.　How allocations are made.
4.　How relevant allocations are to managerial decisions.

The Reasons for Departmental Rates

Companies use departmental overhead rates to produce more accurate product costs. Different products take different routes through the factory. Some may require only assembly work where overhead costs are relatively low, while others require extensive work in the machine room, where overhead costs are high. The use of a single, factory-wide overhead rate in these circumstances would assign some of the machine-room overhead to the products of the assembly department. To avoid this, departmental overhead rates are used.

For example, the Lion Corporation's factory has three production departments: A, B, and C. The budgeted overhead cost for the entire factory was $6 a direct labor-hour in 19x1. A great deal of diversity lay behind this average, however. Exhibit 20–3 lists the budgeted

EXHIBIT 20–3

LION CORPORATION
Budgeted Monthly Factory Overhead Costs at Normal Volume
For the Year 19x1

| Type of Cost | Department | | | |
	A	B	C	Total
Indirect labor	$ 7,000	$15,000	$ 6,000	$28,000
Indirect materials	3,000	8,000	2,000	13,000
Depreciation	5,000	6,000	5,000	16,000
Power	3,000	2,000	4,000	9,000
Other costs	14,000	9,000	7,000	30,000
Total	$32,000	$40,000	$24,000	$96,000
Direct labor-hours	4,000	10,000	2,000	16,000
Overhead rate per hour	$8	$4	$12	$6

overhead costs at normal volume for each of these three departments. It shows average overhead costs of $8 an hour in department A, $4 in department B, and $12 in department C.

To illustrate the significance of these variations, let us suppose that two of the products manufactured in this factory require five hours of direct labor for each unit. Product X is produced entirely in department B; product Y is manufactured in department C.

A factory-wide overhead rate would assign an overhead cost of $6 × 5 = $30 to each of these products. Using departmental rates, however, product X would be assigned a cost of $4 × 5 = $20, while the overhead cost of a unit of product Y would be $12 × 5 = $60. This is a substantial difference.

Accuracy is important not for its own sake but for its impact on the user of accounting data. Automobile manufacturers, for example, make exhaustive analyses of the costs of manufacturing component parts. Each automobile model is aimed at a particular segment of the market, and its price must fall in a narrow range appropriate to that market. If the estimated manufacturing cost is too high to leave an adequate profit margin in that price range, management must either find ways to reduce costs, move to an outside source of supply, or redesign the automobile. Cost estimates for this purpose should reflect the costs of the specific resources to be used, not some broad factory average.

The Need for Interdepartmental Cost Allocations

Some of the costs of operating a factory aren't specifically traceable to the production departments in which the products are actually manufactured. Depreciation on the factory building and the plant manager's salary are two examples; the cost of production scheduling is another.

Each of these costs can be traced unequivocally to some cost center. The plant manager's salary, for example, can be traced to the factory's administrative office; production-scheduling costs can be traced to the production-scheduling department. This isn't enough for product costing, however. These cost centers are *service* centers, not production centers. As Exhibit 20–4 shows, products pass through the production centers, picking up direct materials, direct

EXHIBIT 20–4.   Product Flows versus Service Flows

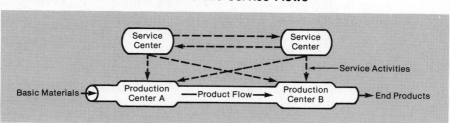

labor, and production-center overhead costs as they go. They don't go through the service centers. Production couldn't take place if the costs of these services weren't incurred, however, and this means that they are definitely part of the full cost of production. Our problem is to find some means of getting these costs from the service centers where they originate to the job orders they make possible.

Accountants have two ways of assigning service-department costs to individual job orders:

1. Direct apportionment.
2. Interdepartmental allocation and absorption.

Direct apportionment.   Under the direct apportionment method, the accountant calculates a separate overhead rate for each group or pool of service-center costs. For example, suppose that service overheads amount to $7,000 a month, production center A operates at 5,000 direct labor-hours a month, and production center B has 2,000 direct labor-hours a month. A plantwide direct apportionment rate based on direct labor would be $1 a direct labor-hour. A product needing ten direct labor-hours would be charged $10 for service overhead.

Allocation-absorption.   Many accountants argue that direct apportionment is not accurate enough. They point out what we saw in Exhibit 20–4, that the service centers serve other cost centers, not products, and that some cost centers need much more service than others. A direct labor-hour in a machining department ordinarily will be supported by much more maintenance cost than a direct labor-hour in assembly, where the ratio of equipment to people is much smaller.

To reflect these differences, most cost accountants would suggest taking the allocation-absorption route. This is a three-stage method:

1. Allocate budgeted service-center costs to production centers.
2. Include the amounts allocated to each production center in that production center's overhead rate.
3. Use these overhead rates to assign overhead costs to products, including allocated overheads as well as the overhead costs directly traceable to the production centers.

The Allocation Process

Returning to our illustration, we find that the Lion Corporation's factory had three service departments—factory management, building services, and equipment maintenance—as well as the three production departments. The budgeted monthly costs of these three departments were as follows:

	Factory Manage-ment	Building Service	Equipment Mainte-nance
Wages and salaries	$4,800	$1,300	$8,400
Supplies.............................	200	200	500
Depreciation	50	1,200	200
Power	—	400	200
Property taxes	—	700	—
Other costs	950	200	300
Total	$6,000	$4,000	$9,600

The accountant's task was to find a way of allocating these costs among the three production departments so that the allocations would most closely approximate the amount of service-department cost attributable to each production department.

Allocations in this case were based on the statistics given in Exhibit 20–5. To begin with, the accountants distributed the expected

EXHIBIT 20–5

LION CORPORATION
Estimates Used in Distributing Estimated Service-
Department Costs for Overhead Rate Determination

Department	Number of Employees	Floor Space Occupied (Square Feet)	Number of Equipment Maintenance Labor-Hours to Be Used Each Month
Department A	36	24,000	450
Department B	81	36,000	350
Department C	18	20,000	400
Subtotal	135	80,000	1,200
Factory management	4	2,000	—
Building service	2	1,000	50
Equipment maintenance	10	3,000	—
Total	151	86,000	1,250

factory-management costs among the three production departments in proportion to the total number of employees (direct and indirect) in those departments. This produced the following:

Department	(1) Number of Employees	(2) Fraction of Production Employees	(3) Allocation of Factory Management Cost (2) × $6,000
Department A	36	4/15	$1,600
Department B	81	9/15	3,600
Department C	18	2/15	800
Total	135		$6,000

The justification for using the number of employees as the allocation basis was that this was judged to be the major determinant of the size of the factory-management department.

Next, building services costs were allocated among the production departments on the basis of relative floor space occupied:

Department	(1) Floor Space Occupied (Square Feet)	(2) Percent of Floor Space Occupied	(3) Allocation of Building Service Cost (2) × $4,000
Department A	24,000	30%	$1,200
Department B	36,000	45	1,800
Department C	20,000	25	1,000
Total	80,000	100%	$4,000

Once again, the assumption was that the cost of providing building service was closely related to the amount of floor space occupied.

Finally, budgeted equipment-maintenance costs were allocated in proportion to each department's estimated consumption of maintenance-department services. The maintenance department's budgeted cost amounted to $9,600 a month. Spreading this over the 1,200 hours of maintenance services to be provided to the three production departments during an average month gave a budgeted cost rate of $8 per maintenance-hour. Using this rate, the budgeted allocation was:

Department	Estimated Number of Maintenance Hours Used	Allocation of Maintenance Service Costs at $8 per Maintenance-Hour
Department A	450	$3,600
Department B	350	2,800
Department C	400	3,200
Total	1,200	$9,600

After all these allocations were made, the estimated costs of the three production departments were as shown in the last three columns of Exhibit 20–6. The overhead rates shown at the bottom of these columns are larger than the overhead rates in Exhibit 20–3

EXHIBIT 20–6

LION CORPORATION
Factory Overhead Cost Allocation for 19x1

	Factory Management	Building Service	Equipment Maintenance	Production Department A	B	C
Indirect labor	$4,800	$1,300	$8,400	$ 7,000	$15,000	$ 6,000
Indirect materials	200	200	500	3,000	8,000	2,000
Depreciation	50	1,200	200	5,000	6,000	5,000
Power.	—	400	200	3,000	2,000	4,000
Property taxes	—	700	—	—	—	—
Other costs	950	200	300	14,000	9,000	7,000
Total Traceable	$6,000	$4,000	$9,600	$32,000	$40,000	$24,000
Allocated charges:						
Factory management	(6,000)	—	—	1,600	3,600	800
Building service	—	(4,000)	—	1,200	1,800	1,000
Equipment maintenance . .	—	—	(9,600)	3,600	2,800	3,200
Total Budgeted Cost	—	—	—	$38,400	$48,200	$29,000
Direct labor-hours				4,000	10,000	2,000
Overhead rate (per direct labor-hour.)				$9.60	$4.82	$14.50

because they include provision for all factory costs, not just those that were directly traceable to the production departments. The service departments had no overhead rates because no production work was done there.

Relevance of Allocations to Managerial Decisions

The idea behind interdepartmental cost allocations is to produce overhead rates that more accurately represent the factory overhead costs attributable to the operations of individual direct-production departments. That is, the amount of service-department cost allocated to a production department should measure the amount of cost that would not have been incurred if the factory had never included that production department.

This has both a short-term and a long-term meaning. From a short-term point of view, the allocation to any production center should measure the amount of service-department cost that could be avoided if the production center were to keep its existing capacity idle. A long-term allocation should indicate the amount of service-department cost that could be avoided if the production center were to be eliminated entirely and the service department's capacity reduced accordingly.

The first of these quantities consists mostly of the short-term variable costs of operating the service center; the longer-term figure includes an allocation of the fixed costs of providing service-department capacity. In other words, variable costs should be allocated to the departments requiring current service *activity*, while service-department fixed costs should be allocated to the departments which create the need for *capacity*.

Valid allocation bases reflecting these concepts are hard to find. The result is that allocations are often at least partly arbitrary, thereby reducing their relevance to managerial decisions. Allocations of plant management salaries among production departments on the basis of the relative amounts of time spent in them, for example, do not measure the amounts by which plant management salaries could be reduced if the various departments were to be eliminated. For decision purposes it would be better not to allocate at all then to use an arbitrary allocation base such as this.

THE COSTS OF JOINT PRODUCTS

Overhead costing is difficult in the first instance because overhead costs are *common costs*—that is, they can't be traced clearly to any one product but are common to all of the products manufactured in a particular set of facilities. Common costs are also encountered in another situation, in which the processing of a single raw material or set of materials yields two or more different products simultaneously. The outputs of such processes are known as *joint products*, and their costs are known as *joint costs*.

A full explanation of joint-product costing would require more space than we are able to give it here, but the basic problem can be sketched rather quickly. Joint costs can be traced to the joint process but not to the individual products that emerge from it. The labor cost of slaughtering a hog is a cost both of the hams and of the pigskin gloves that eventually emerge from production.

Accountants usually divide joint costs among the joint products in proportion to their relative values. For example, suppose the cost of a joint process amounts to $600. It yields 100 pounds of product A, worth $5 a pound, and 250 pounds of product B, worth $1 a pound. The total value of the output is $500 + $250 = $750. Product A would be assigned two thirds of the total cost; product B would get the rest, as Exhibit 20–7 shows.

Costing formulas of this sort provide measures of inventory cost that are adequate for external financial reporting. They are useless

EXHIBIT 20-7. Value-Based Allocation of Joint Cost

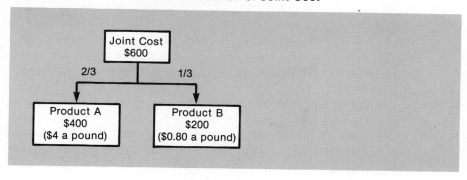

for decision making, however. Suppose management has an opportunity to spend an additional $100 to convert 100 pounds of product B into a more valuable product C, worth $1.95. A "cost" comparison would show:

Cost of product B: 100 pounds × $0.80	$ 80
Conversion costs	100
Total Cost	$180
Sale value of product C: 100 pounds × $1.95	195
Conversion Gain	$ 15

The real cost of product B, however, is $1, not 80 cents. This is its opportunity cost, the amount the company would sacrifice by not selling it in its present form. When the opportunity cost is considered, the proposal is a $5 loser: $195 in revenue, obtained at a sacrifice of $100 from product B, and conversion cost of $100.

SUMMARY

Most accounting systems provide for a three-way classification of operating costs: by organization unit, by object of expenditure, and by activity—the where, what, and why dimensions of operations.

Assigning costs to individual activities is the most difficult aspect of these systems—and the most important for managerial decision making. The main problem centers on the overhead costs, those not directly traceable to individual end-product activities. These are assigned to products by means of averages known as overhead rates or burden rates.

Most overhead rates are predetermined; once the amount of materials, labor, or machine time used on a job is known, the overhead cost of the job can be calculated, even if actual overhead costs are still unknown at that time. Overhead rates are also likely to be departmentalized—that is, each department or cost center is given its own rate, used for assigning overhead costs to the work done within its borders. This requires the allocation of the costs of service departments to the various direct-production departments. Development of meaningful allocation bases is difficult, however, and these cost allocations are often not very useful in the estimation of incremental costs.

An even more difficult problem arises when the direct materials and direct labor in a given process are the joint costs of two or more products. In such cases, incremental costs for individual products are difficult and sometimes impossible to estimate, and the analyst must work directly with estimates of opportunity cost.

KEY TERMS

Cost allocation	Object of expenditure
Cost center	Overtime premium
Departmental overhead rate	Predetermined overhead rate
Direct apportionment	Product cost
End-product activity	Production center
Joint cost	Service center
Joint products	Time ticket
Materials requisition	Traceability
Normal cost	Under/overabsorbed overhead

INDEPENDENT STUDY PROBLEMS (Solutions in Appendix B)

1. Job cost and overhead variance.   Chailly, Inc., uses a job-order costing system in its factory with a predetermined overhead rate based on direct labor-hours. You are given the following information:

1. Job No. 423 was started on March 3, finished on March 28.
2. Other data:

	Job No. 423	All Jobs (in March)	Annual Budget at Normal Volume
Direct labor-hours	60	10,000	100,000
Direct labor cost	$400	$ 60,000	$ 350,000
Direct materials cost	$800	$150,000	$1,300,000

3. Factory overhead budgeted for the entire year was $900,000; actual overhead for the month of March was $106,000.

a.   Compute the cost of Job No. 423.
b.   Calculate the overhead variance for the month of March.

2. Job-order costing: predetermined overhead rate.   The Webber Corporation has a job-order costing system and a plant-wide predetermined overhead rate of $4 a direct labor-hour. You have the following data:

1. Inventory balances on December 1:

Materials $10,000
Work in process 15,000
Finished goods 20,000

2. Data recorded during December:

Materials purchased $16,000
Direct materials issued 18,000
Direct labor, 5,000 hours 48,000
Manufacturing overhead (actual) 17,000
Cost of goods finished 80,000

3. Finished goods inventory on December 31: $23,000.

a. Calculate the cost of the materials inventory and the cost of the work in process inventory on December 31.
b. What was the cost of goods sold during December?
c. What was the over- or underabsorbed overhead in December?
d. Prepare entires, in two-column journal form, to record the transactions for the month.

3. Departmental overhead rates. The Robertson Company has been using a single overhead rate for its entire factory. An alternative has been proposed: departmental overhead rates. You are given the following information:

1. Three products (A, B, C) are produced in three departments (1, 2, 3).
2. Labor-hours required for a unit of each product are:

	Department			
	1	2	3	Total
Product A	2	1	1	4
Product B	0	2	2	4
Product C	2	3	3	8

3. Products produced in a normal year: A—40,000 units; B—40,000 units; and C—10,000 units.
4. Overhead incurred in a normal year: department 1—$400,000; department 2—$300,000; and department 3—$100,000.

Should the company use a plantwide overhead rate or departmental overhead rates? Why? (In either case, the overhead rate or rates would be based on direct labor-hours.)

4. Interdepartmental allocations. The Hubbard Woods Company applies manufacturing overhead costs to all job orders by means of departmental overhead rates. Separate rates are prepared for each of four production centers: (1) melting and pouring, (2) molding, (3) core making, and (4) cleaning and grinding. Monthly factory overhead costs at normal volume are expected to be as follows:

Indirect labor:
Melting and pouring	$3,000
Molding	900
Core making	300
Cleaning and grinding	900

Supplies used:
Melting and pouring	150
Molding	150
Core making	600
Cleaning and grinding	300
Taxes (machinery and equipment, $36; building, $72)	108
Compensation insurance	195
Power	150
Heat and light	240
Depreciation—building	192
Depreciation—machinery and equipment	180
Total	$7,365

You have the following information about the production centers:

Department	Floor Space (Sq. Ft.)	Cost of Machinery and Equipment	Direct Labor per Month	Compensation Insurance*	Power Consumption
Melting and pouring	500	$ 6,000	$ —	$2.00	10
Molding	2,000	1,500	3,600	1.00	—
Core making	500	4,500	1,500	1.00	10
Cleaning and grinding	1,000	6,000	3,900	1.50	30
Total	4,000	$18,000	$9,000	—	50

* Rate per $100 of direct and indirect labor payroll.

a. Prepare a schedule in which you allocate the overhead costs among the four production centers for the purpose of deriving a set of full-cost overhead rates.

b. Prepare predetermined overhead rates based on the following estimates of normal volume: (1) melting and pouring, 10,000 pounds; (2) molding, 420 direct labor-hours; (3) core making, 150 direct labor-hours; and (4) cleaning and grinding, 520 direct labor-hours.

EXERCISES AND PROBLEMS

5. Fill in the blanks. The Dowbar Company manufactures candlesticks on a job-order basis, using a plantwide overhead rate based on normal volume. You have the following data for three recent years:

	19x1	19x2	19x3
Overhead rate per direct labor-hour	$?	$?	$ 3.20
Actual direct labor-hours	?	9,000	8,000
Normal direct labor-hours	8,000	8,500	?
Overhead absorbed	$30,000	$27,900	$?
Actual overhead	29,000	?	27,000
Overhead over(under)absorbed	?	(600)	?
Overhead cost at normal direct labor-hours	24,000	?	28,800

Make the necessary calculations and supply the figures missing from this table.

6. Effect of predetermined overhead rate. The Bates Company has been using a relatively small percentage of its capacity for the past year, and this situation is likely to persist. You have the following data:

1. Estimated factory overhead cost at normal volume (10,000 direct labor-hours a month), $40,000.
2. Estimated factory overhead cost at estimated actual volume (8,000 direct labor-hours a month), $36,000.
3. Actual factory overhead cost at actual volume for April (7,500 direct labor-hours), $37,000.

a. Calculate a predetermined overhead rate on the basis of normal volume.
b. Calculate the amount of overhead under- or overabsorbed during April.
c. Would the amount of overhead under- or overabsorbed have been increased or reduced if the overhead rate had been based on estimated actual volume? Would you have preferred this alternative? Explain.

7. Classifying labor costs. A factory department has four direct production workers. They work an eight-hour day plus occasional overtime. The pay for overtime hours is 150 percent of the regular time rate.

Three jobs (Nos. 125, 127, and 129) were in process when the employees reported for work on the morning of July 6. Operations were begun during the day on four new jobs (Nos. 126, 128, 130, and 131). Work was completed on Jobs 125, 126, 127, and 130. The following time tickets were filed for the day's work:

Employee	Hourly Wage Rate	Job No.	Hours
Abt, J.	$4.00	127	1
		126	5
		Lubrication	1
		128	1
Davis, P.	6.00	125	1
		127	2
		130	2
		Training	3
		Clean-up	1
Rogers, L.	5.00	128	4
		Sweeping	1
		130	3
		128	2
Thomas, G.	7.00	129	1
		Maintenance	2
		129	1
		131	4
		130	2

These time tickets are listed in the sequence in which the work was performed.

Prior labor costs on jobs in process at the beginning of the day were as follows: Job 125, $28; Job 127, $73; Job 129, $48. Completed jobs were transferred to the finished-goods storeroom.

a.   Calculate the total direct labor cost for the day. How much should be entered on each of the job-order cost sheets? How much would you classify as overhead cost?

b.   Indicate any alternative(s) you considered and rejected in answering part (a) and give your reasons for your choice(s).

c.   Calculate the direct labor cost of the goods finished.

d.   Calculate the direct labor cost of the work in process at the end of the day.

8.   Classifying operating data.   Twelve citizens of Des Moines organized a corporation, International Friendship, Inc., (IFI) to provide scholarships and other assistance to students participating in an international exchange program. The following transactions are representative of the transactions that took place during IFI's first year:

1.   Cash contribution received from Mr. and Mrs. Earl Brown, $100.

2.   Cash payment to Midwest Travel Agency for airline ticket for Hector Johnson, exchange student, $510.

3.   Crumpled receipts presented for reimbursement by Carl Thoreau, president of IFI, as evidence of his payments for cookies and soft drinks purchased for reception for local high school students to acquaint them with the exchange program, $14.

4.   Check received from David Wallace for two tickets to fund-raising dance, $20.

5.   Cash payment to Andrew McDonald for printing: IFI stationery, $23; tickets for fund-raising dance, $18; programs and tickets for benefit variety show, $47.

6.   Cash payment for postage stamps: to mail 1,000 letters requesting donations to support IFI programs, $150; for use of president and treasurer in routine correspondence, mailing checks and so forth, $15.

7.   Payment to Hosts International, Inc., as scholarship for Nancy Brendon, exchange student, $1,300.

What structure should the operating revenue and operating cost section of IFI's chart of accounts have? Identify as many account titles as you deem necessary to illustrate the structure you have in mind and indicate in each case why a separate data category should be recognized.

9.   Calculating over(under)absorbed overhead.   Grace Manufacturing Company uses a job-order costing system with a predetermined factorywide overhead rate based on normal volume. The factory's normal operating volume is 100,000 pounds of direct material a month, and its estimated overhead cost at that volume is $93,000 a month.

Calculate the amount of over(under)absorbed overhead in a month in which the following data were recorded:

a.   Volume, 90,000 pounds; overhead cost, $90,000.

b.   Volume, 110,000 pounds; overhead cost, $99,000.

c.   Volume, 80,000 pounds; overhead cost, $86,000.

d.   Volume, 100,000 pounds; overhead cost, $95,000.

10. Distributing manufacturing costs. The Eagleby Company uses a job-order costing system with a predetermined factorywide overhead rate based on normal volume. The overhead rate in 19x1 was $2.50 a direct labor hour. Over(under)absorbed overhead is included in full each month as a component of the cost of goods sold.

On May 1 and May 31, 19x1, the company had the following inventories:

	May 1	May 31
Raw materials	$20,000	$17,000
Work in process	13,000	15,000
Finished goods	32,000	32,500

You have the following information about the factory's transactions during the month of May, 19x1:

1. Raw materials purchased: $8,000.
2. Direct labor used: 5,000 hours, $45,000.
3. Factory overhead cost: $14,000.
4. Indirect materials used: None.

a. Calculate the cost of direct materials used during May.
b. Prepare a schedule showing (1) the costs to be accounted for during May and (2) the amounts of these costs to be assigned to each inventory category and to the cost of goods sold.
c. How much of the cost of goods sold represented over(under)absorbed overhead?

11. Discussion question: interdepartmental cost allocations. A company's power department provides electric power to four factory departments. Power consumption is measured indirectly by the number of horsepower-hours used in each department. Consumption data are shown in the following schedule:

SCHEDULE OF HORSEPOWER HOURS

	Producing Departments		Service Departments	
	A	B	X	Y
Needed at capacity production	10,000	20,000	12,000	8,000
Used during an average month	8,000	13,000	7,000	6,000

The cost of operating the power department was expected to total $4,000 + $0.40 per horsepower-hour.

The company wishes to establish overhead rates for the two producing departments. What dollar amounts of power-department costs should be included in the budget of each producing and service department? Give reasons for your answer. Indicate why you either did or did not allocate power-department costs to the two service departments.

12. Single versus multiple overhead rates. The Franklin Company's factory has a drill-press department with six style A, three style B, and two style C machines. These machines have the following characteristics:

	Machine Style A	Machine Style B	Machine Style C
Cost—each machine	$2,000	$3,000	$4,500
Space occupied—each machine (sq. ft.)	20	50	60
Horsepower-hours per month—each machine	850	1,600	3,000
Hourly wage rate, machine operators	$5.50	$6.60	$7.80
Operating hours per month at normal volume—each machine	184	160	150

A machine operator operates only one machine at a time; the number of direct labor-hours is, therefore, equal to the number of machine-hours.

The normal overhead costs of the drill press department for one month are as follows:

Depreciation, taxes and insurance—buildings	$ 910
Depreciation, taxes and insurance—machinery	600
Heat and light	260
Power	795
Miscellaneous	330
Total	$2,895

a.   Calculate a full-cost overhead rate applicable to all of the machines in this department, expressed as a percentage of direct labor cost.

b.   Allocate the departmental overhead costs among the three machine styles and calculate a separate full-cost overhead rate for each machine style, expressed as a rate per machine-hour. (Miscellaneous costs are to be divided equally among the 11 machines in the department.)

c.   Job No. 2051 was run on one of the style C machines and required 15 hours of machine time. Compare the amount of overhead costs that would be assigned to this job under the two different costing systems implicit in (a) and (b) above. How would you choose between the two?

13.   Calculating interdepartmental allocations.   Minkin Enterprises, Inc., operates a factory with two production departments; a service department and a factory office. All factory overhead costs except the costs of building ownership and operation are assigned initially to the departments they are traceable to. The costs of building ownership and operation are accumulated in a separate set of accounts.

In developing predetermined departmental overhead rates, Minkin Enterprises first distributes the estimated building ownership and operation costs among the four factory departments in proportion to the amount of floor space each occupies. The estimated costs of the factory office, including its share of building ownership and operation costs, are then reassigned to the other three factory departments in proportion to the number of employees in each department. Finally, the estimated costs of the factory service department are divided between the two production departments in proportion to the amount of service it is expected to provide.

Estimated overhead costs and statistics for next year are as follows:

	Produc- tion No. 1	Produc- tion No. 2	Factory Service	Factory Office	Building Ownership & Operation
Traceable overhead costs per month	$10,925	$6,550	$5,975	$3,150	$7,000
Floor space (sq. ft.)	9,000	7,000	3,000	1,000	—
Number of employees	35	60	5	3	2
Service-hours used per month	400	200	—	—	—
Machine-hours per month	5,000	—	—	—	—
Direct labor-hours per month	—	9,000	—	—	—

a. Using the company's method, allocate the estimated costs.

b. Calculate predetermined overhead rates for the two production departments: No. 1, based on machine-hours; No. 2, based on direct labor-hours.

14. Calculating inventory costs; proposed allocation of overhead variance.
On November 30, a fire destroyed the plant and factory offices of the Swadburg Company. The following data survived the fire:

1. From the balance sheet at November 1, you find the beginning inventories: materials, $5,000; work in process, $15,000; finished goods, $27,500.

2. The factory overhead rate in use during November was 80 cents per dollar of direct material cost.

3. Total sales for the month amounted to $60,000. The gross profit margin constituted 25 percent of selling price.

4. Purchases of materials during November amounted to $30,000.

5. The payroll records show wages accrued during November as $25,000, of which $3,000 was for indirect labor.

6. The charges to factory overhead accounts totaled $18,000. Of this, $2,000 was for indirect materials and $3,000 was for indirect labor.

7. The cost of goods completed during November was $52,000.

8. Underabsorbed overhead amounted to $400. This amount was not deducted in the computation of the gross profit margin (item 3 above).

a. Calculate the amount of cost that had been assigned to the inventories of raw materials, work in process, and finished goods that were on hand at the time of the fire on November 30.

b. The Swadburg Company's management has claimed that a portion of the underabsorbed overhead should be assigned to the inventory, thereby increasing the amount due from the insurance company. The insurance company has denied this claim, and you have been called upon to arbitrate the dispute. What answer would you give? What arguments would you advance to support it?

15. Joint cost allocation. During the past year the Atom Chemical Company converted certain raw materials into 500,000 pounds of material A and

1 million gallons of liquid B. The total joint cost of production was $388,000. After separation, material A was processed further and converted into material C at an additional cost of 3 cents a pound. The selling price of material C was 40 cents a pound and that of liquid B 30 cents a gallon.

For inventory measurement, the joint costs were allocated between the joint products in proportion to their values before separate processing. For this purpose, the value of material A was measured by the value of material C less the costs of separate processing.

The inventory on December 31 contained 20,000 pounds of material A, 50,000 gallons of liquid B, and 35,000 pounds of material C.

a.   Calculate the unit cost and total cost of the December 31 inventories of these three products.

b.   After computing your answer to (a), you discover that the company's inventories of C have been increasing by about 15,000 pounds a year for the past two years because customers have been abandoning the process for which it is an essential raw material. This trend is likely to continue, and price reductions would not be an effective means of increasing the sales volume of material C. Sales volume of B is relatively constant from year to year. The purchasing agent of Molecule, Inc., has just offered to sign a contract to buy 25,000 pounds of A during each of the next three years. The price for the first year would be 26 cents a pound; prices for later years would be negotiated later. Prepare a short statement indicating whether the offer should be accepted. Be sure to indicate how you used the unit cost figure you obtained in (a) above.

16.   Analyzing effects of transactions; clerical errors.   The Sandrex Company uses a job-order cost accounting system. Direct labor costs are charged daily to Work in Process and credited to Accrued Wages Payable on the basis of time tickets. Direct materials costs are charged to Work in Process and credited to Materials Inventory. Factory overhead costs are charged initially to a Factory Overhead account. Overhead costs are charged to the Work in Process account by means of a predetermined overhead rate of $2 a direct labor-hour. The costs of goods finished are transferred from Work in Process to a Finished Goods account at the time each job is completed. A perpetual inventory system is used for both materials and finished goods.

Following are some of the events that took place in 19x1:

1.   Goods manufactured in 19x0 at a cost of $8,000 were sold on credit for $14,000. The job cost sheets for these goods showed a total of $2,000 for materials, $3,000 for direct labor, and $3,000 for overhead.
2.   Factory overhead was charged to a job on which 480 direct labor-hours were recorded during 19x1. The job was still unfinished at the end of the year.
3.   It was discovered prior to the end of 19x1 that an error in analyzing a batch of time cards resulted in treating 500 hours of direct labor at $5 an hour as indirect labor (that is, the charge was made to Factory Overhead). The job on which this labor was used was finished but not sold in 19x1.
4.   Materials costing $5,000 and supplies costing $500 were issued from the

factory storeroom. Of the materials, $1,000 was for use in constructing new display cases in the company's salesrooms. The display cases were completed and placed in use during 19x1. The remaining materials were issued to the factory for specific job orders which were still in process at the end of 19x1. Of the supplies, $100 was for the immediate use of the sales office, and the remainder was for general factory use.

5. Prior to the end of 19x1, it was discovered that $1,000 of direct materials had been charged to the wrong job. At the time this error was discovered, both jobs had been completed but not yet sold.

6. Prior to the end of the year, it was discovered that an error had been made in adding up the direct labor-hours on a certain job order which had been completed and the products sold during 19x1. The dollar amount of direct labor was added correctly, but the hours were overstated by 100.

7. At the end of 19x1, factory wages earned but still unpaid amounted to $3,000 for direct labor and $1,000 for indirect labor. Time tickets for these amounts of labor had not yet been processed. Employer's payroll taxes on these wages were 9 percent. This company treats all payroll taxes as overhead.

a. Indicate how discovery of these facts would affect the cost assigned to the work in process inventory at the end of the year, the cost of the finished goods inventory, or the cost of goods sold. Each event should be regarded as independent of the others.

b. Prepare journal entries to record these events. If no entry is required, explain why.

17. Costing individual jobs. The Broxbo Manufacturing Company uses a job-order costing system. On July 1, the cost of the work in process was $2,700, made up as follows:

Job No.	Materials	Labor	Overhead
101	$ 620	$640	$340
102	730	250	120
Total	$1,350	$890	$460

Finished goods on this same date amounted to $4,000, representing the cost of Job No. 100.

During July, material cost, labor cost, and labor-hours were:

Job No.	Material Cost	Labor Cost	Labor-Hours
101	$ 100	$ 860	200
102	200	1,900	300
103	1,500	780	150
104	2,000	820	200
105	3,000	245	50
Total	$6,800	$4,605	900

In a normal month, the factory is expected to operate at a volume of 1,000 labor-hours, and factory overhead is expected to amount to $3,000. Actual factory overhead cost for July was $2,950.

Job Nos. 101, 102, and 103 were completed during July and were placed in the finished-goods storeroom.

Job Nos. 100, 101, and 102 were delivered to customers during July at a billed price of $15,000.

a. Calculate the total cost assigned to each job order.
b. What was the total gross margin on Job Nos. 100, 101, and 102?
c. What was the amount of the over- or underabsorbed overhead for the month?
d. For what purposes might management wish to use the information summarized in your answers to (a), (b), and (c) above? Is this information well suited to these purposes?

18. Interpreting job cost data. Dan Roman is a contractor specializing in small house remodeling jobs. Most of his employees are specialists who work for other contractors as well, so that the size of his payroll rises and falls with fluctuations in the amount of work to be done. Higher wage rates are paid to the more highly skilled workers, but the average wage rate in the construction industry in Mr. Roman's area is about $7 an hour.

Mr. Roman recently installed a job-order costing system and now has the following labor cost data:

Job Number	Estimated Labor-Hours	Estimated Labor Cost	Actual Labor-Hours	Actual Labor Cost
47	600	$4,200	650	$4,900
48	400	2,800	380	3,050
50	900	6,300	1,000	8,200
51	200	1,400	210	1,450
52	500	3,500	460	3,450
54	700	4,900	750	5,200
55	800	5,600	820	7,000

During the period covered by these figures, Mr. Roman submitted bids on 18 jobs. Other contractors underbid him on 11 of these; he was the low bidder on the seven jobs shown above. Mr. Roman's profit margin was considerably lower than that of most of his competitors during this period.

a. What advice can you give Mr. Roman on the basis of these figures? Do they help explain his low profit margin? Is there anything he can do about it?
b. What further data would you probably find in Mr. Roman's job cost sheets that would throw further light on these questions?
c. Would charging overhead costs to individual job orders provide Mr. Roman with useful information?

19. Departmental overhead rates; allocations. The Sender Company has four production departments (machine No. 1, machine No. 2, assembly, and painting) and three service departments (storage, maintenance, and office), but uses a plantwide overhead rate based on direct labor-hours. At normal volume, 100,600 direct labor-hours would be used and factory overhead costs would be as follows:

Indirect labor and supervision:	
Machine No.1	$33,000
Machine No. 2	22,000
Assembly	11,000
Painting	7,000
Storage	44,000
Maintenance	32,700
Indirect materials and supplies:	
Machine No. 1	2,200
Machine No. 2	1,100
Assembly	3,300
Painting	3,400
Maintenance	2,800
Other:	
Rent of factory	96,000
Depreciation of machinery and equipment	44,000
Insurance and taxes on machinery and equipment	2,400
Compensation insurance at $2 per $100 of labor payroll	19,494
Power	66,000
Factory office salaries	52,800
General superintendence	55,000
Miscellaneous office costs	21,620
Heat and light	72,000
Miscellaneous storage charges (insurance and so forth)	3,686

You have the following additional information about the various departments:

Department	Area (Sq. Ft.)	Cost of Machinery and Equipment	Raw Materials Used	Horsepower Rating	Direct Labor-Hours	Direct Labor Payroll	Number of Employees
Machine No. 1	65,000	$220,000	$520,000	2,000	48,000	$440,000	100
Machine No. 2	55,000	110,000	180,000	1,000	17,600	220,000	60
Assembly	44,000	55,000		100	24,000	110,000	30
Painting	32,000	22,000	90,000	200	11,000	55,000	15
Storage	22,000	11,000					14
Maintenance	11,000	16,500					10
Office	11,000	5,500					11
Total	240,000	$440,000	$790,000	3,300	100,600	$825,000	240

a. Calculate a plantwide overhead rate on a full-cost basis.
b. Calculate departmental overhead rates based on full costing. For this purpose you will need to distribute some of the general overhead costs among the seven departments and then allocate the costs of the service departments among the four production departments. You should allocate office and general superintendence costs on the basis of direct

labor-hours, maintenance on the basis of machinery and equipment cost, and storage costs on the basis of materials (direct and indirect) used.

c. How would the use of these departmental overhead rates instead of the plantwide rate affect the amount of cost assigned to a job order requiring 100 direct labor-hours in machine No. 1, 200 direct labor-hours in machine No. 2, 20 hours in assembly, and 10 hours in painting?

20. *Review problem; use of T-accounts.* The Lasill Company manufactures several types of pumps, partly to order and partly for stock. In both cases, work is done on the basis of production orders, and costs are recorded by job. The company's balance sheet as of August 31, 19x4, and its transactions for the month of September 19x4, are shown below.

THE LASILL COMPANY
Statement of Financial Position
August 31, 19x4

Assets

Current Assets:

Cash	$ 23,280	
Accounts receivable	31,070	
Materials and supplies	15,120	
Work in process	8,300	
Finished goods	6,730	$ 84,500

Long-Life Assets:

Machinery and equipment	$248,600	
Less: Allowance for depreciation	83,200	165,400
Total		$249,900

Liabilities and Shareholders' Equity

Current Liabilities:

Accounts payable	$ 27,650	
Accrued wages and salaries	1,830	$ 29,480

Shareholders' Equity:

Common stock	$150,000	
Retained earnings	70,420	220,420
Total		$249,900

Transactions during September:

1. Purchased: Materials and supplies $28,310
                      Machine .... 21,000 $ 49,310

2. Issued materials and supplies:

Direct materials—Job No. 17	$ 2,530	
No. 18	7,120	
No. 19	6,690	
Indirect materials	4,060	20,400

3. Accrued wages and salaries:

Direct labor—Job No. 16, 1,200 hrs.	$ 6,440	
No. 17, 3,600 hrs.	17,370	
No. 18, 5,600 hrs.	30,580	
No. 19, 800 hrs.	4,000	
Indirect labor and supervision	9,420	
Office salaries (administration and sales)	14,590	82,400

4.	Depreciation on equipment: Plant	....	$ 2,040	
	Office	....	120	$ 2,160
5.	Other manufacturing costs:			
	Power, light, and heat	....	$ 3,830	
	Repairs	....	1,160	
	Sundry	....	790	5,780
6.	Other administrative and sales expenses	....		2,770
7.	Jobs finished during month: Nos. 16–18			
8.	Sales during month: Job No. 15 (balance)	....	$ 8,350	
	No. 16 (all)	....	21,300	
	No. 17 (all)	....	30,300	
	No. 18 (20 out of 50 pumps)	.....	28,400	88,350
9.	Received payments from customers on account	....		87,800
10.	Paid: Accounts payable	....	$43,690	
	Wages	....	80,850	124,540
11.	Received loan from bank on September 30			
	(90–day note)	....		30,000

Additional information:

1. Payroll deductions and taxes are omitted for purposes of simplification.
2. All costs incurred other than payrolls and depreciation are in the first instance credited to Accounts Payable.
3. Manufacturing overhead is charged to jobs at the rate of $2 per direct labor-hour.
4. The opening balance of Finished Goods represents part of Job Order No. 15; that of Work in Process, Job No. 16 (materials, $4,500; direct labor, $2,600; overhead, $1,200).

a. Enter the above transactions in T-accounts and job-order cost sheets. (Use a single T-account for all factory overhead costs.)
b. Prepare financial statements for the month. Over- or underabsorbed overhead is to be entered as a special item on the income statement.

21

Cost Measurement: Variable Costing

UNIT COSTS produced by the methods described in Chapter 20 will seldom approximate incremental costs. They are particularly inappropriate when management's decisions have such a short time horizon and such narrow scope that the only incremental costs are the short-run variable costs of utilizing existing production capacity.

To provide unit costs that are more directly useful in such situations and to introduce more flexibility into the cost files generally, many companies calculate product cost on a *direct-costing* or *variable-costing* basis. This chapter has a three-part mission:

1. To explain variable costing and illustrate how it might be useful to management.
2. To apply variable-costing data to the construction of break-even charts and other profit-volume diagrams.
3. To examine the relevance of variable-costing and full-costing data to product pricing decisions.

VARIABLE COSTING

Variable costing is a device to permit the segregation of the variable component of manufacturing costs in product cost records and subsequently in internal profit performance reports. *Under variable costing, unit cost is defined as the average variable cost* of manufacturing the product. Fixed manufacturing costs are excluded from product cost completely.

Application to Job-Order Costing

Variable costing differs from full costing in job-order costing only in the treatment of factory overhead. Direct labor and direct materials are typically assumed to be fully variable with volume and, therefore, are assigned to product units in the manner described in Chapters 6 and 20. Factory overhead is then included in product cost by means of overhead rates that cover only the variable components of the overhead cost elements.

For example, suppose that an analysis of the overhead costs in the Lion Corporation's department C has provided the estimates tabulated in Exhibit 21–1. In this case, the overhead rate would be $5.60

EXHIBIT 21–1. LION CORPORATION, DEPARTMENT C: Estimates of Fixed and Variable Costs

	Fixed Cost per Month	Variable Cost per Direct Labor-Hour
Indirect labor	$ 4,000	$1.00
Indirect materials	500	.75
Depreciation	5,000	—
Power	—	2.00
Other direct departmental costs	3,500	1.75
Allocated costs:		
Factory management	800	—
Building services	1,000	—
Equipment maintenance	3,000	.10
Total	$17,800	$5.60

a labor-hour. A job order requiring ten labor-hours in this department would be charged $56 (10 hours × $5.60) for variable overhead, and no charge would be made for any portion of the $17,800 in fixed costs.

Both indirect labor and equipment-maintenance costs in this case are semivariable. Indirect labor, for example, has a minimum monthly expenditure of $4,000 plus increments of $1 a labor-hour in response to the use of the department's facilities. The variable and fixed components can't be recorded separately because the accountant has no way of labeling a particular indirect labor expenditure as fixed or variable at the time it is made. Fortunately, this is no barrier to variable costing. Since the overhead rate is predetermined, the only requirement is that a *rate of variability* can be determined for each cost element.

Variable Costing for Easier Cost Estimation

The main argument for variable costing is that it provides a clearer, more versatile set of data on which to build estimates of incremental costs. For example, Department C has a good deal of idle capacity. Its normal volume is 2,000 direct labor-hours a month; it is now using only 1,500 hours. Of this, 300 hours are devoted to the manufacture of product Y, with an output of 30 units a month.

The company's management is considering a proposal to sell product Y in a new market area, with an estimated sales volume of 20 units a month in the first year. This would require about 200 additional direct labor-hours a month in department C, an increment clearly within existing capacity limits.

The full-cost overhead rate for this department is $14.50 a direct labor-hour, derived from the following formula:

$$\text{Overhead Rate} = \frac{\text{Estimated Cost at Normal Volume}}{\text{Normal Volume}}$$

$$= \frac{\$17,800 + \$5.60 \times 2,000 \text{ DLH}}{2,000 \text{ DLH}} = \$14.50/\text{DLH}$$

Using this rate, the accountants would assign $2,900 of department C's overhead costs to the proposal:

Overhead cost = 200 DLH × $14.50/DLH = $2,900.

Using the variable-costing rate, they would come up with a $1,120 estimate:

Overhead cost = 200 DLH × $5.60/DLH = $1,120.

It should be obvious that variable costing gives a more relevant cost estimate if fixed costs are not expected to be affected by the decision on this proposal. But what if the addition of 200 direct labor-hours would require increases in fixed costs as well as increases in variable costs? Neither average full cost nor average variable cost measures the increment in this case. Variable costing does have an advantage, however—it places the fixed costs in a separate category, where they can be studied explicitly, line by line.

For example, an increase in volume from 1,500 to 1,700 direct labor-hours a month isn't huge, but it may be big enough to cause increases in some of the fixed costs. Remember that some fixed costs are only fixed within certain volume limits. If volume moves outside those limits, fixed costs will either increase or decrease.

Variable costing also makes it easier to give management a clear view of the effect of changes in volume on the company's profits. It does this by facilitating the calculation of *contribution-margin* figures. Suppose, for example, that product Y has direct material costs of $80, direct labor costs of $50, and no variable-selling and administrative costs at all. It would be sold to a distributor for $300

TERMINOLOGY

Contribution margin is the difference between the net revenue from a product or service and the short-term variable costs of producing and selling that product or service.

---

a unit, and the distributor would pay all freight, taxes, and marketing costs. The contribution margin from the production and sale of additional units of product Y would be $114 a unit:

Selling price		$300
Less variable costs:		
Direct materials	$80	
Direct labor	50	
Overhead (10 hours × $5.60)	56	186
Contribution Margin		$114

In evaluating this proposal, management is interested in estimating the sensitivity of profit to variations in sales volume. Using the contribution margin figures, it is a simple matter to prepare incremental profit estimates for three different volume levels:

	10 units	20 units	30 units
Sales ($300)	$3,000	$6,000	$9,000
Less: Variable costs ($186)	1,860	3,720	5,580
Contribution margin ($114)	$1,140	$2,280	$3,420
Less: incremental fixed cost	1,000	1,000	1,000
Incremental Profit	$ 140	$1,280	$2,420

Average Cost versus Incremental Cost

These arguments for variable costing should not be misinterpreted. The unit costs produced by job-order costing are average costs, no matter whether variable costing or full costing is used. These averages are general-purpose figures, and should not be used as direct measures of incremental cost without careful analysis.

For example, suppose the $50 estimate for direct labor costs applies only to a total production volume of 30 units a month. Expansion of volume by an additional 20 units would reduce average direct labor cost to $45. An unwary analyst might possibly be trapped into using the new average to calculate incremental cost: $20 \times \$45 = \$900$. In fact, the calculation should be:

Total direct labor cost at 50 units a month: 50 × $45	$2,250
Total direct labor cost at 30 units a month: 30 × $50	1,500
Incremental Direct Labor Cost of 20 Additional Units	$ 750

Incremental direct labor cost, in other words, is expected to average $37.50 for each additional unit.

Costs for Inventory Measurement

Some accountants have suggested that variable costing should be an acceptable or even the preferred basis for measuring the costs of manufactured goods in inventory for public financial reporting. This view isn't widely shared, however, and variable costing isn't a "generally accepted accounting principle"—that is, it can't be used in preparing financial statements for external use.

As a result, companies using variable costing for internal cost measurement must find ways to add a provision for average fixed cost to the variable costs assigned to the units in inventory on any balance-sheet date. Separate overhead rates covering fixed factory costs can be prepared for this purpose and used when necessary.

BREAK-EVEN CHARTS

The relationships among costs, volume, and profit are often described graphically in *break-even charts* or *profit graphs*. These are drawn to help management visualize the sensitivity of profit to errors in the forecasts of volume or to demonstrate the potential gains from volume-generating activities. We'll study five aspects of this kind of analysis:

1. Locating the break-even point.
2. Constructing a basic profit-volume chart.
3. Incorporating estimated investment requirements in the chart.
4. Constructing charts to represent multiproduct operations.
5. Allowing for dynamic effects.

The Break-Even Point

Profit graphs are based on estimates of total fixed costs and of revenues and variable costs per unit of volume. For example, Seaton Chemicals, Inc., has just developed a new plastic and is about to market it commercially. The product, still identified by its laboratory code number, X-250, is very similar to Thor, a product of another chemical company, currently selling at $1.30 a pound. Thor's annual sales are about five million pounds.

On the basis of data obtained in part from the engineering department, a cost analyst on the controller's staff has estimated the costs of producing and selling X-250, as follows:

Item	Total Fixed Cost	Variable Cost per Pound
Direct material	$ —	$0.34
Direct labor	—	0.27
Manufacturing overhead	800,000	0.21
Selling and administrative costs	400,000	0.08
Total	$1,200,000	$0.90

The fixed costs in this table are the additions to the company's total annual fixed costs that would result from the decision to introduce and market X-250.

This information may be stated mathematically as follows. If X-250 is sold at $1.30 a pound, then total revenue, R, at a level of output, V, is

$$R = \$1.30V.$$

The total cost, C, at an output of V is

$$C = \$1,200,000 + \$0.90V.$$

The firm will *break even* at the output at which $R = C$. This is found by equating the above two expressions and solving for V:

$$1.30V = 1,200,000 + 0.90V$$
$$V = 3,000,000 \text{ pounds.}$$

We can get the same result using contribution margin figures. At a price of $1.30, X-250 would have a contribution margin of $1.30 − $0.90 = $0.40 a pound. The break-even point can be located by finding out how many pounds must be sold to produce a *total* contribution margin equal to the anticipated fixed costs. This is obtained by dividing the fixed costs by the contribution margin per unit:

Break-even volume = $1,200,000/$0.40 = 3,000,000 pounds.

A companion figure to the break-even volume is the *margin of safety*, the difference between the break-even volume and the actual or anticipated volume of activity. In making its decision to introduce X-250 commercially, for example, Seaton's management saw marketing possibilities its competitor had overlooked. It forecasted a sales volume of 3,500,000 pounds in the first year alone, with rapid expansion in the years to follow. The margin of safety therefore was:

Margin of safety = 3,500,000 − 3,000,000 = 500,000 pounds.

In other words, the company would cover its total costs even if volume turned out to be 500,000 pounds smaller than management had anticipated.

The Basic Chart

This same information can be presented in graphic form, in a *profit-volume chart* or *break-even chart.* Exhibit 21–2 shows one

EXHIBIT 21–2.   SEATON CHEMICALS, INC.:   Profit-Volume Chart, Product X-250

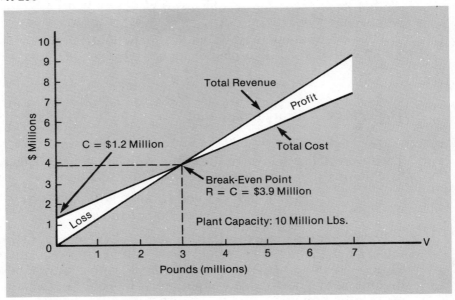

form this kind of chart can take. A glance at this chart reveals three key estimates:

1. At zero volume, the operation will lose $1 million because the fixed costs will be uncovered.
2. The operation will just cover its costs at an annual volume of 3 million pounds.
3. The vertical distance between the two lines at any volume measures the estimated profit margin at that volume.

The Linearity Assumption

Both the revenue line and the cost line in Exhibit 21–3 were *linear*—that is, we drew them as straight lines. We could just as well have drawn them as curves or as step-functions, as follows:

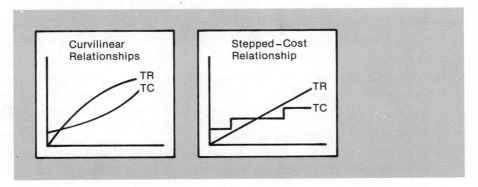

We ought to draw the relationships in these forms if we know or can estimate in advance that a change in physical volume will cause either revenue or cost to change in a predictable, nonlinear way. For example, if contracts with our customers provide for a reduction in our selling price if our total volume exceeds some specified quantity, we should draw the revenue line with a bend in it.

Most charts are drawn with straight lines, not because management believes the relationships are linear from zero volume to capacity but because the charts are used to describe cost and revenue behavior within a limited portion of this total range, as in the following diagram:

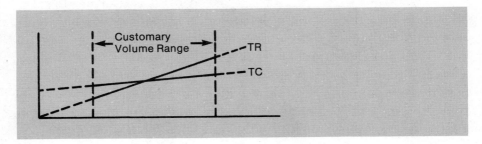

Within this range, the responses of costs and revenues to changes in physical volume are likely to be linear or very close to it. The portions of the lines extending outside the customary range aren't used. Extending them in this way allows us to describe the relationships within the customary range in simple, linear equations like those we're using in this section.

After-Tax Analysis

Many modifications of the basic profit chart are available. For one thing, management is likely to want the chart to reflect the impact of volume on income taxes. If the figures in our previous illustration were pretax figures, and if income taxes are levied at a flat rate of 40 percent, the profit equation will take the following form:

$$\text{Net income} = (1 - 0.4)(\$1.30V - \$0.90V - \$1,200,000)$$
$$= 0.6 \times \$0.40V - 0.6 \times \$1,200,000$$

(In our example, we used a selling price of $1.30 a unit, average variable costs of $0.90 a unit, and total fixed costs of $1,200,000.)

In other words, on an after-tax basis the contribution margin per unit is $0.6 \times \$0.40 = \$0.24$ and the fixed costs are $0.6 \times \$1,200,000 = \$720,000$. This relationship is diagrammed in Exhibit 21–3. As this shows, the breakeven volume is still the same, but the profit spread is much narrower.

EXHIBIT 21–3.   SEATON CHEMICALS, INC.:   After-Tax Break-Even Chart

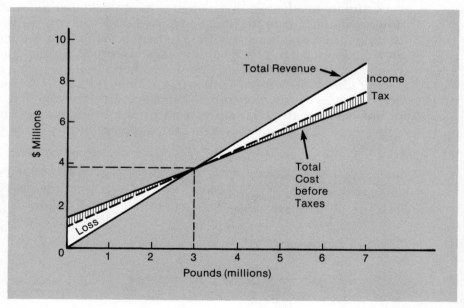

Drawing in the tax relationships can get fairly complicated if the tax rate isn't constant at all volumes. We have assumed, for example, that if volume is so low the company reports a net loss, the company will get a tax refund. Ordinarily this will be true only if the company has accrued or paid taxes in the past. If tax refunds are unavailable, then the spread between the cost and revenue lines will be at a wider angle below the break-even point than above it.

Charting Dividend and Investment Requirements

The chart may also be modified by adding a specified amount of dividends to the after-tax fixed costs. The two lines then will intersect at a volume we might refer to as a "target volume."

Alternatively, management may wish to identify a specified rate of return on investment as its target, and may want the chart to show the volume at which this target will be met. For example, suppose Seaton Chemicals has introduced X-250 and has invested $6 million in plant, equipment, and working capital to support it. Management wants to know whether the contribution at the anticipated sales volume will cover the fixed operating costs and a 10 percent rate of return on the investment as well.

The target figure can be represented by the expression: Target income $= rI$, in which r is the target rate of return and I is the amount of the investment. If r is 10 percent and I is $6,000,000, then the target income is $600,000. The after-tax income formula now takes the following form:

$$\text{Income above (below) target} = \$0.24V - \$720,000 - \$600,000$$
$$= \$0.24V - \$1,320,000$$

The target volume is:

$$\text{Target volume} = \$1,320,000/\$0.24 = 5,500,000 \text{ pounds.}$$

This analysis is diagrammed in Exhibit 21–4.

The only way the company can reach this target volume is to expand the total market far beyond the 5 million pounds its principal competitor supplied before Seaton came on the scene. Management's decision to make the investment was based on its confidence it could do just that.

Multiproduct Profit Charts

By the addition of other revenue and cost lines, the profit chart can be used to diagram the anticipated results of alternative pricing policies or marketing methods. It can also be used for rough profit forecasting in multiproduct situations.

To illustrate the multiproduct break-even chart, let's assume (1) that the same plant could be used to produce both X-250 and another new chemical, Y-78; (2) that total fixed costs would be, as before,

EXHIBIT 21–4. SEATON CHEMICALS, INC.: Profit Chart Incorporating a 10 Percent Target Rate of Return on Investment in Product X-250

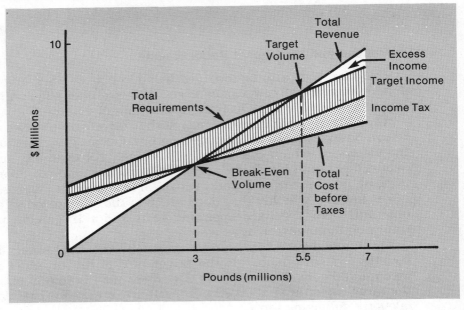

$1.2 million a year; and (3) that the estimated volume, revenue, and variable cost data for the two products are as follows:

		Per Unit		Total	
Item	Sales Volume	Price	Variable Cost	Revenue	Variable
X-250	2,000,000 lbs.	$1.30	$0.90	$2,600,000	$1,800,000
Y-78	3,000,000 lbs.	1.80	1.50	5,400,000	4,500,000
Total				$8,000,000	$6,300,000

The $6 million total variable cost is 78.75 percent of the $8 million total revenue for the stated sales volumes. Therefore, as sales volume varies in total *with the product mix unchanged,* cost will increase or decrease by $0.7875 per dollar of sales revenue. These assumptions are reflected graphically in Exhibit 21–5. (Tax effects are omitted to keep the diagram simple.) Volume (V) is measured on the horizontal axis by sales revenue because physical volume mea-

EXHIBIT 21–5. SEATON CHEMICALS, INC.: Break-Even Chart for Two Products

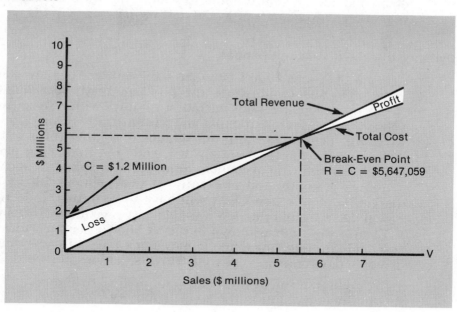

sures for the two products aren't added together easily. The total-cost line is described by the equation:

$$C = \$1,200,000 + \$0.7875V.$$

The total-revenue line is $R = V$. The break-even point is found where total revenue (R) equals total cost (C):

$$V = \$1,200,000 + \$0.7875V$$
$$V = \$5,647,059.$$

The same calculation can be made using contribution-margin averages. Here the average contribution margin is ($8,000,000 − $6,300,000)/$8,000,000, or 21.25 percent of sales revenue. The break-even point is again calculated by dividing this ratio into total fixed cost:

Break-even volume = $1,200,000/0.2125 = $5,647,059.

Break-even charts may be used to describe a wide variety of situations, but care must always be taken to bear in mind the assumptions on which such charts are based. In the present case, the conditions under which the plant will earn the indicated profit at any given level of volume are (1) that the costs and prices for each product are as estimated and (2) that the mix in which the two products sell is in the ratio of two pounds of X-250 to three pounds of Y-78.

Dynamic Effects of Volume Changes

Profit charts shouldn't be taken too literally. They are static devices, designed to illustrate the profit normally associated with steady operation at various operating volumes within the customary volume range given marketing and administrative plan. They show what will happen to the profit margin if volume turns out to be different from the level anticipated when the marketing plan was established and if management adjusts the scope of its responsive activities promptly and efficiently. If management adopts a new marketing plan, a new chart will have to be drawn, reflecting the new fixed costs and the new variable cost-revenue relationship.

Even if the chart is drawn to reflect known nonlinearities in the cost and revenue functions, it may not fit actual experience in a dynamic environment very well. Three situations are worth noting:

1. A rapid movement from one volume level to another.
2. A temporary shift in the level of activity.
3. A persistent shift in product demand.

Transitional effects. When volume moves rapidly from one level to another, the costs of responsive activities may respond either faster or more slowly than the chart indicates. A volume expansion may be sustained for a while without moving up to a new step in certain semivariable costs such as supervision. At the same time, variable costs may rise even more sharply than the chart indicates as the firm has to buy materials on rush orders or has to hire untrained personnel.

Temporary volume shifts. Management may choose to support an excessive cost structure for a short period if volume has declined and the decline seems likely to be temporary. Layoffs of personnel are expensive, and the company may be better off to pay standby salaries for a while than to pay severance wages and train new workers when volume picks up again. By the same token, if volume increases temporarily, the company may find it more economical to resort to abnormal overtime, subcontracting, or other costly practices than to add to its permanent staff. Again, actual costs will depart from the levels indicated on the chart.

Persistent shifts in demand. The usual profit charts reflect a specific economic climate, a specific management attitude. If the climate changes, management's attitudes will change, too. Cost behavior is likely to be affected.

For example, as volume moves down toward or even below the break-even point, management's attitudes toward activities it has thought of as essential are likely to change. Discretionary activities such as window washing and even some responsive activities may feel the hot breath of the cost cutter. For this reason, the actual zero-profit volume is likely to be a good deal lower than the break-even volume on the chart.

By the same token, if demand has shifted upward, fixed costs are likely to inch up, a movement sometimes referred to as "creep." Cost control seems less urgent, and fringe activities seem more attractive because "after all, the company can afford it."

THE RELEVANCE OF FIXED COST: CATALOG-PRICING DECISIONS

Variable costing has been developed to meet management's needs for data relevant to decisions with a short-term impact. Many decisions have a longer time horizon or a larger scope, however, entailing at least some increments in the fixed costs. The question is whether average full cost should be used to approximate average incremental cost in these situations. The purpose of this section is to examine this question in the context of a pricing decision.

Catalog-Pricing Decisions: A Simple Model

Many pricing decisions apply not to a single order but to a substantial number of customer orders or inquiries during a period of many months. We'll refer to these as catalog-pricing decisions.

An economist would say that the best approach to catalog pricing is to estimate the effect of price on volume and the effect of volume on cost, selecting the price that seems likely to produce the greatest spread between total revenue and total cost. For example, suppose a company estimates the following price-volume relationship:

Price	Units Sold	Revenue
$1.25	10,000	$12,500
1.50	8,000	12,000
1.75	6,000	10,500

Estimated costs, including production, selling, and administrative costs, are as follows:

Units Sold	Total Cost
10,000	$10,000
8,000	9,000
6,000	8,000

Putting these two sets of estimates together yields the following profit estimates:

Price	Units Sold	Revenue	Cost	Profit
$1.25	10,000	$12,500	$10,000	$2,500
1.50	**8,000**	**12,000**	**9,000**	**3,000**
1.75	6,000	10,500	8,000	2,500

The optimal price in this case is $1.50.

Price-volume relationships, unfortunately, are very difficult to identify or predict. Without this information, management is likely to use cost figures alone, at least to calculate what it considers to be a *normal price*. The normal price is determined by adding to cost a standard percentage mark-up. The actual price charged may differ from the normal price for different items in the product line because of demand and other considerations, but the starting point is cost.

This approach is called *cost-based formula pricing*. The issue we'll consider in the next few pages is whether the cost figures underlying formula prices should be defined as full factory cost, variable cost, or some other figure.

The Full-Cost Fallacy

No business can report a net income if the prices of its products don't cover the costs of developing, manufacturing, and selling them, together with the costs of administering and financing the company. If the price of every product covers the costs assigned to it, with at least a little left over, the company will report a profit. A pricing formula that adds a markup to full cost, therefore, would seem to guarantee profitable operations.

Unfortunately, this isn't the case. The company will make a profit only if enough products sell at or near the volume levels the cost estimates were based on. For example, suppose a company has only one product, with fixed costs of $5,000 a month and variable costs of $1 a unit. The profit necessary to produce a normal rate of return on investment is $2,000 a month. The plant was designed to operate efficiently at volumes between 8,000 and 12,000 units a month, 10,000 units being regarded as normal.

At a 10,000-unit level, total costs will be $5,000 + $1 \times 10,000 = $15,000. Average cost will be $15,000/10,000 = $1.50. The desired profit margin is $2,000/10,000 = $0.20 a unit. A formula-based price therefore might be $1.70:

Average variable cost	$1.00
Average fixed cost	.50
Profit mark-up	.20
Normal Price	$1.70

Suppose the company prices the product at this level, but its competitors offer their comparable products at prices near $1.50. As a result, our company sells only 7,000 units. The income statement will show the following:

Revenues (at $1.70)		$11,900
Expenses:		
Variable costs (at $1)	$7,000	
Fixed costs	5,000	12,000
Net Loss		$ (100)

The reason is that at the lower volume the fixed costs must be spread over a smaller number of units, thereby increasing average fixed cost. This effect is illustrated in Exhibit 21–6.

EXHIBIT 21–6. Effect of Low Volume on Average Cost

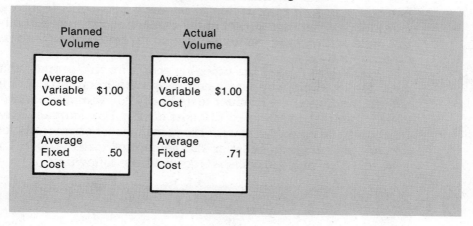

Our company might try to prevent this by recalculating average cost and the desired profit margin at a 7,000-unit volume:

Average variable cost	$1.00
Average fixed cost: $5,000/7,000	.71
Normal profit margin: $2,000/7,000	.29
Adjusted Price	$2.00

Unfortunately, this would probably drive even more customers into the competitors' arms, volume would fall to less than 7,000 units, and the company would still lose money. Cost-plus pricing, in other words, is far from a sure road to profitability.

The Case for Full-Cost Pricing

Full-cost pricing formulas can't be justified on the grounds that they guarantee profits. Recognizing this leaves us free to seek other reasons why these formulas are so widely used in practice. Many plausible explanations can be found, but we have room to mention only two:

- 1. Full-cost formulas appear to reduce uncertainty.
- 2. Prices based on full-cost formulas won't attract new entrants to the industry.

Reducing market uncertainty.   The first argument is that full-cost formula pricing may appear to reduce the uncertainty surrounding the pricing decision. One company's sales depend as much on the prices its competitors charge as on its own prices. Competitors' cost structures for a given product are likely to be quite similar, however, and the full-cost formula may help the company forecast its competitors' prices. It may decide to set the price at this level and concentrate on other ingredients of the marketing mix, such as advertising, field selling, and customer service, to get customers to buy the company's wares.

Variable-cost figures are probably poorer for this purpose than full cost. For example, suppose a company with many products is considering adding a new product to its line. The estimated variable cost is $15 a unit; the estimated full cost is $20. The company's average markup on other products with the same market characteristics is 30 percent of average full cost or 120 percent of variable cost. The two cost-based pricing formulas would yield the following:

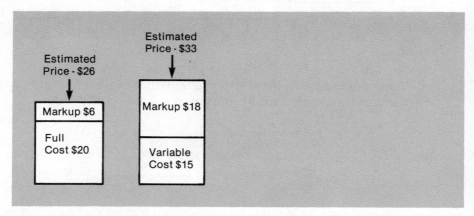

The full-cost price is lower than the variable-cost price in this case because this new product uses less-expensive capacity than the average product. We can see this by calculating the average ratio of full cost to variable cost. If P = price, F = full cost, and V = variable cost, we have the following two normal relationships:

Variable Cost	Full Cost
$P = 2.2V$	$P = 1.3F$

The relationship between variable cost and full cost for the average product can be derived by putting these two formulas together:

$$2.2V = 1.3F.$$

Full cost for an average product, in other words, is 2.2/1.3, or about 170 percent of its variable cost. The full cost of the new product, in contrast, is only $20/$15 = 133 percent of variable cost.

Why is this significant? If this company can produce this product in facilities with a low full-cost/variable-cost ratio, so can its competitors. A price based on the average for all products, therefore, very likely would be higher than the prices competitors will charge for comparable products. A variable-cost pricing formula, therefore, will be a poorer prediction of market price than a full-cost pricing formula.

Deterring new entrants. A third argument for full-cost pricing is that full-cost data may help management identify a price that won't be unduly attractive to potential competitors. In other words, cost data may help management forecast what sacrifices competitors are making or would have to make to manufacture a similar product and thereby provide management with a means of estimating a competitive price level.

Flexible Solutions

Not even the most hardened advocate of full cost as a basis for pricing would claim that average full cost is the appropriate basis for all managerial decisions or even for all pricing decisions. Full cost may approximate incremental cost in some cases but may be far wide of the mark in others.

To provide management with a more useful data base for decisions, the accountant can design the system to produce "full-cost" figures that represent the average cost required for each particular product, including both variable cost and an allowance for the fixed costs attributable to that product. These figures can be subcoded into fixed and variable components, so that variable-cost figures can be used when they seem more relevant.

SUMMARY

To provide more useful data for incremental cost estimation, accountants have developed a system of factory-overhead costing known as variable costing or direct costing, in which only variable costs are assigned to products. Although incremental cost with respect to a particular decision may not be equal to either variable cost or full cost, it is easier to move from variable cost to incremental cost than to take full-cost figures and convert them into estimates of incremental cost. Furthermore, estimates of short-run variability often can be taken directly from a variable-costing data bank, whereas special studies are necessary to obtain these data if full costing is used.

Variable-costing systems help management construct profit-volume diagrams of various sorts. These show the estimated relationship between profit and volume under a prescribed operating plan. They also show the location of the break-even point, the volume at which the total contribution margin will just cover the total fixed cost. They are used mainly to demonstrate the sensitivity of profits to variations in volume and errors in estimation or to show how different marketing plans differ in profit sensitivity.

Variable cost isn't the only measure of cost management will ever need in decision making. Product pricing, for example, often requires estimates of costs that include fixed costs as well as variable costs. The objective is to identify the price the market can support on a long-term basis. This suggests the development of a data base that includes product-cost figures both on a variable-costing basis and on a basis that includes some provision for fixed costs.

KEY TERMS

Break-even point
Catalog-pricing decisions
Contribution margin
Cost-based formula pricing
Margin of safety

Normal price
Product mix
Profit-volume chart
Target volume
Variable costing

INDEPENDENT STUDY PROBLEMS (Solutions in Appendix B)

1. Profit-volume diagrams. The Cranby Company manufactures and sells a single product. You have the following data:

Fixed costs	$32,000 a month
Variable costs	$3 a unit
Selling price	$5 a unit
Anticipated sales	20,000 units

   a.   Construct a profit-volume chart.

   b.   Calculate the break-even point, the margin of safety, and the anticipated profit at the anticipated sales volume.

   c.   The company is considering increasing the selling price to $5.50. At this price it expects to sell 18,000 units.

       1.   Recalculate the break-even point, the margin of safety, and the anticipated profit.

       2.   Redraw the profit-volume chart, showing both the old and the new profit spreads.

       3.   How many units would have to be sold at the new price to produce a 10 percent increase in total profit before taxes?

   d.   The sales manager has offered a counterproposal. The price would be reduced to $4.60, and an additional $4,000 a month would be spent on advertising.

       1.   Recalculate the break-even point.

       2.   How many units would have to be sold at the new price to produce a 10 percent increase in total profit before taxes?

2.   Variable costing.   A company manufactures many products. Each product passes through two production departments, which have the following cost structures:

	Department A	Department B
Normal monthly volume	5,000 direct labor-hours	10,000 pounds of material
Monthly fixed costs at normal volume	$10,000	$40,000
Monthly variable costs at normal volume	15,000	20,000

Two of the job orders that went through the factory last month had the following results:

	Job 1 (Product X)		Job 2 (Product Y)	
	Quantity	Cost	Quantity	Cost
Direct inputs:				
Direct materials	480 lbs.	$2,400	1,500 lbs.	$4,800
Direct labor:				
Department A	180 hrs.	1,620	100 hrs.	900
Department B	60 hrs.	420	40 hrs.	280
Output	600 units		1,000 units	

   a.   Calculate the unit cost of each of these jobs on a full-costing basis.

   b.   Recalculate unit costs on a variable-costing basis.

   c.   Why are the relative variable costs of these two products so different from their relative full costs?

3.   Using average costs in decisions.   The manager of a department in a social welfare agency has proposed the inauguration of a new social service, requiring the addition of 15 social workers to the department's payroll. The costs of other departments in the agency would not be affected by the addition of this new service, except as noted below.

   The director of the agency agrees that the social service would fill an important need and that providing it would be consistent with the agency's charter. The director can make $200,000 available to finance this service by discontinuing one of the services now being provided by one of the agency's other departments, but will do so only if the new service can be provided for $200,000 or less.

The department head has developed the following figures:

	If the Service Is	
	Provided	Not Provided
Total number of social workers in the department	25	10
Average cost of the department's operations	$14,000	$15,500

Calculate differential cost. Should the proposal be approved?

4. Use of contribution-margin ratios. The Carillo Company sells two products, A and B, with contribution-margin ratios of 40 and 30 percent and selling prices of $5 and $2.50 a unit. Fixed costs amount to $72,000 a month. Monthly sales average 30,000 units of product A and 40,000 units of product B.

a.   If the company spends an additional $9,700 on sales promotion, sales of product A can be increased to 40,000 units a month. Sales of product B will fall to 32,000 units a month if this is done, however, as some customers shift from one product to the other. Should this proposal be accepted?

b.   As an alternative to the proposal in (a), management is considering redesigning product A and reducing the price of product B to give both products more market appeal. The variable cost of product A would be increased by ten cents a unit; the price of product B would be reduced by ten cents a unit. Unit sales of each product would increase by 5,000 units a month. What action would you recommend?

EXERCISES AND PROBLEMS

5. Profit/volume exercises. Each of the following exercises is independent of the others.

Exercise A:

The Oliver Company plans to market a new product. Based on its market studies, Oliver estimates it can sell 5,500 units in 19x1. The selling price will be $2 a unit. Variable costs are estimated to be 40 percent of the selling price. Fixed costs are estimated to be $6,000.

a.   Calculate the break-even point (in units).
b.   Calculate the margin of safety.

Exercise B:

The Breiden Company sells rodaks for $6 a unit. Variable costs are $2 a unit. Fixed costs are $37,500.

a. How many rodaks must be sold if the company is to realize income before income taxes of 15 percent of sales revenue?
b. How many rodaks must be sold if the company is to realize income before taxes of $10,000?

Exercise C:

At a break-even point of 400 units sold, the variable costs were $400 and the fixed costs were $200. How much will the 401st unit sold contribute to income before income taxes?

(AICPA adapted)

6. *Profit/volume exercises.* Each of the following exercises is independent of the others.

Exercise A:

Label Corporation's product A has sales of $300,000, variable costs of $240,000 and fixed costs of $40,000.

a. Assuming the cost relationship is linear, calculate the break-even volume.
b. How much income before taxes would product A generate if its sales volume increased by 20 percent?

Exercise B:

Dallas Corporation wishes to market a new product for $1.50 a unit. Fixed costs to manufacture and market this product are $100,000 if volume is smaller than 500,000 units and $140,000 if volume is 500,000 units or more. The contribution margin is 20 percent. How many units must be sold to realize income before taxes from this product of $100,000?

Exercise C:

Freedom, Inc., has projected the following annual costs based on 40,000 units of production and sales:

	Total Annual Costs	Variable Portion's Percent of Total Annual Costs
Direct material	$400,000	100%
Direct labor	360,000	75
Manufacturing overhead	300,000	40
Selling and administrative	200,000	25

a. Compute Freedom's unit selling price that will yield income before taxes of 10 percent if sales are 40,000 units.
b. Assume management selects a selling price of $30 a unit. Compute Freedom's dollar sales that will yield a projected 10 percent margin on sales, assuming the above variable fixed-cost relationships are valid.

(AICPA adapted)

7. *Calculating variable product cost.* A company has three production departments, each with its own full-cost overhead rate:

Department A	$2 per pound of materials
Department B	$3 per machine-hour
Department C	$4 per direct labor-hour

You are told that at normal volume variable costs account for 40 percent of the overhead cost in department A, 30 percent of the overhead cost in department B, and 60 percent of the overhead cost in department C.

A job lot of 1,000 units of product X was manufactured in April. This job used 2,000 pounds of materials (in department A), 400 machine-hours in department B, and 200 direct labor-hours in department C.

a. Calculate the overhead cost of this job lot on a full-costing basis.
b. Calculate the overhead cost of this job lot on a variable-costing basis.
c. What do you do with the costs that are included in (a) but excluded in (b)?

8. Use of average cost in decisions. Brown manufactured a single product known as a "hyperflange" and sold it to industrial and commercial users. Brown's total volume was 100,000 hyperflanges a month.

Smith was one of Brown's best customers. Every month Brown sold 10,000 hyperflanges to Smith, at a price of $5 each. Last week, however, Smith gave Brown a chance to increase the size of the monthly shipment to 15,000 units, *provided* that Brown would quote a price of $4 on each of the additional 5,000 units. The price of the first 10,000 units would not change. Smith argued that this would be extra business for Brown, meaning that Brown need charge no overhead against these additional units. In this case, a $4 price should be adequate.

Brown disagreed because the $4 price wouldn't cover the company's costs, which averaged $4.46 a unit. Brown's figures were as follows:

	At 100,000 Units a Month	At 105,000 Units a Month
Direct labor and materials	$3.00	$3.00
Other factory costs	1.00	.97
Selling and administrative costs	.50	.49
Average Total Cost	$4.50	$4.46

What unit cost figure should Brown use in deciding whether to take on the added business? Show your calculations.

9. Break-even exercise: multiproduct company. The Danvers Corporation has two products, for which you have the following data:

	Product A	Product B
Sales volume (units)	200,000	300,000
Selling price per unit	$2	$3
Contribution-margin ratio	30%	40%
Traceable fixed costs	$120,000	$200,000
Common fixed costs.....................	30,000	60,000

a. Calculate a break-even dollar sales volume for each product. State any assumptions you had to make.
b. Calculate a break-even dollar sales volume for the company as a whole. State any assumptions you had to make.

c. Compare the break-even point you calculated in (*b*) with the sum of the break-even points you calculated in (*a*). Explain why these two figures are or aren't identical.

10. Effect of changes on break-even point. During 19x1, the Arapahoe Company sold 300,000 units of product and had a net income (after taxes) of $60,000. The contribution margin was $1 a unit before taxes, and the selling price was $2.50. Fixed costs were $200,000, and the income tax rate was 40 percent.

For 19x2, variable costs went up 10 cents a unit, fixed costs went up $22,000, and income taxes increased to a rate of 50 percent.

a. What was the break-even sales volume for 19x1, in dollars?
b. What will be the break-even sales dollars for 19x2 if the selling price is not changed?
c. How many units will have to be sold to make a net income of $60,000 in 19x2 if the selling price is not changed?
d. By how much will the selling price have to be increased if the break-even point, in units, is to be the same in 19x2 as in 19x1?
e. At what selling price would the company continue to make $60,000 net income after taxes on sales of 300,000 units?

11. Simple pricing model. Middleton Enterprises, Inc., owns a baseball stadium with a seating capacity of 5,000. The fixed costs of operating this stadium are $15,000 a year, and variable costs are ten cents per spectator per game. These variable costs actually increase in steps, an increase of 500 spectators requiring a $50 increase in costs, but management sees no harm in converting this $50 increment into an average.

One hundred games are played each year, and the average attendance is 1,000 spectators a game. Fixed costs, therefore, average 15 cents per spectator per game. The stadium is adequate for all games except a special series of five exhibition games with major-league teams. For each of these five games, the estimated demand is as follows:

If the Price Is—	Then Estimated Attendance Is—
$3.00	2,000
2.50	6,000
2.00	9,000
1.75	11,000
1.50	16,000
1.00	20,000

The company can rent a nearby stadium (25,000 capacity) for a fee of $2,000 for each game plus 10 percent of gross receipts. In addition, the company would still have the variable costs of ten cents per spectator per game.

Assuming that the price charged will be one of the six alternatives above, present a table that will indicate the admission price that will be most profitable for the company and also whether the larger stadium should be rented. Show all calculations.

12. Contribution-margin analysis.   The Davis Company produces two products and anticipates, with no changes in prices or programs from the previous year, the following relationships for costs, prices, and volume:

	Product A	Product B
Revenues	$3.00 a unit	$5.00 a unit
Variable costs	$1.50 a unit	$2.00 a unit
Traceable fixed costs	$45,000	$60,000
Common fixed costs	$57,000	
Volume	60,000 units	40,000 units

Although no relationship between common fixed cost and any other variable has been established, the Davis Company allocates common fixed costs between the two products in proportion to their dollar sales volumes.

Management is considering each of the following independent proposals:

1. An outlay of $20,000 for advertising which would result in anticipated volume of 50,000 units of A and 50,000 units of B. The individual who proposes this move states that "B is the high-margin product—this is what we want."
2. A change in production methods which would increase the annual outlay for common fixed costs by $10,000 but would reduce the variable costs of product A by ten cents a unit and the variable costs of product B by 15 cents a unit. This change would also expand the capacity of production of A from 70,000 units to 80,000 units, but the sales would not be expected to increase.
3. A reduction of the price of B to $4.75 which would increase the volume of B to 45,000 units. This would require a $5,000 increase in B's fixed costs. Sales volume of A would be unaffected.
4. An increase in wage rates for the direct labor. This increase would raise the variable costs of A by ten cents a unit and of B by 15 cents a unit. If the increase were granted, management would increase the selling price of each product by 15 cents. Sales of A would decrease by 5,000 units; sales of B would decrease by 2,000 units.

a. Calculate the effect of each of these proposals on the company's income before taxes.
b. Indicate in each case whether the change would be likely to increase the margin of safety, decrease it, or leave it unchanged.

13. Covering minimum return on investment requirements.   The Degas Company sells products with an average pretax contribution margin of 40 percent of sales. Fixed costs amount to $500,000 a year, and the income tax rate is 40 percent.

To support its production and marketing activities, the company must maintain net assets of $700,000 plus an amount equal to 10 percent of sales. The company's management wishes to maintain a rate of return on net assets of at least 12 percent after taxes.

a. Calculate the minimum dollar sales volume at which the company can generate its desired rate of return on investment.
b. What is the company's net income at this volume? What is the margin of safety?

14. Overhead rates under variable costing. The management of the Leininger Company has decided to use variable costing for cost-estimating purposes. Full-cost figures will be entered on the job-order cost sheets and in the financial accounts. The estimated overhead costs of factory department 77 at a normal volume of 4,000 direct labor-hours a month are as follows:

Supervision	$ 4,000
Indirect labor	6,000
Fringe benefits	8,400
Supplies	1,200
Power	1,000
Depreciation	800
Miscellaneous	600
Total	$22,000

You have the following additional information:

1. Supervision costs remain at $4,000 a month for any volume between 3,000 and 5,000 direct labor-hours. If volume drops below 3,000 hours, supervision can be cut to $2,800; if volume exceeds 5,000 hours, supervision costs will go up to $5,000 a month.
2. One third of indirect labor costs at normal volume are fixed; two thirds are proportional to the number of direct labor-hours.
3. Fringe benefits amount to 20 percent of labor cost, including direct labor, supervision, and indirect labor. Direct labor wage rates average $8 an hour.
4. Supplies and power costs should be proportional to the number of direct labor-hours.
5. Depreciation and miscellaneous overhead costs are entirely fixed.
6. The volume of activity ordinarily fluctuates between 3,200 and 4,600 direct labor-hours.

Calculate overhead rates for this department, both for variable costing and for full costing.

15. Product cost under variable costing. The Gaddis Corporation owns and operates two factories. One of these manufactures component parts, either for sale to outside customers or for use in the company's other factory.

Each factory uses a job-order costing system with a factory-wide predetermined overhead rate based on estimated overhead costs at normal volume, determined as follows:

	Factory A	Factory B
Overhead cost at normal volume:		
Variable	$10,000	$ 8,000
Fixed	50,000	12,000
Total	$60,000	$20,000
Normal monthly volume	20,000 machine-hours	10,000 direct labor-hours
Overhead rate	$3 per machine-hour	$2 per direct labor-hour

Management is considering the possibility of using Factory B to manufacture a new product, product X. Annual volume would amount to 5,000 units, which would require 1,000 direct labor-hours in factory B at a direct labor wage rate of $8 an hour, add $25,000 to factory B's direct materials costs, and increase factory B's fixed overhead by $500 a month. Factory B's variable overhead costs would vary in proportion to the number of direct labor-hours used.

All the direct materials for product X would be component parts manufactured in factory A. Their costs would be:

Direct materials	$11,000
Direct labor	8,000
Factory overhead	6,000
Total	$25,000

Fixed overhead costs in factory A would be unaffected by the manufacture of the parts necessary to make product X.

Gaddis Corporation's marketing vice president asked the controller for cost estimates to be used in an analysis of the sensitivity of the company's income to errors in the forecasts of sales volume for product X. The controller provided these estimates from the data supplied above. When asked why the company didn't use variable costing to determine product costs on a regular basis, the controller replied that prices had to cover fixed costs, too. Besides, full-cost data could be adjusted to a variable-costing basis any time management needed estimates of variable cost.

a. Calculate the unit cost of product X on a variable-costing basis.
b. Comment on the controller's argument, including an analysis of the differences between your answer to (a) and the cost of product B on a full-costing basis.

16. Inventory measurement under variable costing. The Anthrax Company uses variable costing to measure product costs for managerial purposes, but measures its inventories at full cost for financial reporting to outsiders, using a predetermined overhead rate for this purpose.

The company's profit plan for 19x1 showed the following estimates:

Sales		$10,000
Manufacturing cost of goods sold:		
Direct materials	$1,500	
Direct labor	2,000	
Variable factory overhead	1,000	
Fixed factory overhead	1,300	5,800
Gross margin		$ 4,200
Selling and administrative expense:		
Variable	$ 400	
Fixed	1,600	2,000
Income Before Taxes		$ 2,200

Variable overhead costs were assigned to products by means of a predetermined overhead rate, stated as a percentage of direct labor cost.

You have the following information for 19x1:

1. The costs assigned to the company's inventories as of January 1, 19x1, were as follows: variable costs, $2,400; fixed costs, $360; total costs, $2,760. The company uses the Fifo method of inventory costing.
2. Sales revenues in 19x1 amounted to $11,000.
3. Operating costs for the year were:

Direct materials	$1,800
Direct labor	2,400
Variable factory overhead	1,200
Fixed factory overhead	1,000
Variable selling and administrative	480
Fixed selling and administrative	1,600

4. The inventory on December 31, 19x1, was as follows:

Raw materials	$ 600
Work in process and finished goods:	
Direct materials	360
Direct labor	1,200
Overhead	?

a. Calculate the variable cost of goods sold for 19x1 and the variable overhead cost of the December 31, 19x1, inventory.
b. Calculate the Fifo cost of the December 31, 19x1, inventory for outside financial reporting purposes.
c. What was the effect on income before taxes in 19x1 of using full costing instead of variable costing to measure inventories?

17. Contribution-margin analysis: interdependent products. The Mazzini Company manufactures a number of products, three of which can be described as follows:

	Rinsol	Sudsit	Sansgrit
Price per case	$7.60	$12.00	$15.00
Cost per case:			
Direct materials	$3.00	$ 3.50	$ 6.00
Direct labor	1.00	1.00	1.50
Factory overhead	2.00	2.00	3.00
Administration	.38	.60	.75
Total cost	$6.38	$ 7.10	$11.25
Marketing profit per case	$1.22	$ 4.90	$ 3.75
Total marketing costs	$400,000	$4,000,000	$800,000
Number of cases sold	400,000	1,000,000	200,000

You have the following additional information:

1. Factory overhead is assigned to products by means of an overhead rate of 200 percent of direct labor cost.
2. The variable portion of factory overhead cost amounts to 60 percent of direct labor cost.
3. Fixed factory overhead costs will remain constant for all feasible production volumes of these three products. If production of any one of them

were to be discontinued entirely, however, the company could reduce its fixed factory overhead by $200,000.

4. Administrative costs are assigned to products at amounts equal to 5 percent of sales. Investigation shows that the variable portion of this amounts to 30 cents a case.

5. The marketing costs are all fixed. Discontinuation of any product would reduce the amounts shown by 75 percent.

a. Using the company's methods of cost assignment, calculate income before taxes for each of these three products.

b. Judging solely from the information provided above, would you recommend that any of these three products be discontinued? Show your calculations.

c. You are told further that sale of a case of Rinsol causes the company to lose the sale of three tenths of a case of Sudsit. Sale of a case of Sansgrit, however, increases sales of Sudsit by one tenth of a case. No other interproduct relationships can be identified. What recommendation would you make now? Show your calculations.

18. *Costs for pricing.* The Hardy School is a nonprofit organization providing educational programs for gifted children. The school as two divisions: a lower school, for children six to nine years old, and an upper school, for ten-to thirteen-year-old children. Both divisions and the school's administrative offices are located in a single building. This building is occupied under a lease which still has two years to run. The annual rental is $12,000, which is less than the school would have to pay to lease comparable facilities today.

The school year has just ended, all bills have been paid, and the school has $4,700 in its bank account. The board of trustees is meeting next week to set the tuition rates for next year. Tuition this past year was a flat $3,800 per pupil, and 60 pupils were enrolled in each division. Space is available to take as many as 70 pupils in each division, and no more.

The school's treasurer has just finished drawing up a tentative cost budget for next year. This shows the following:

Upper school	$234,000
Lower school	222,000
Administration (including rent, heat, light, and so forth)	60,000
Total	$516,000

Based on past experience, the treasurer expects to raise $18,000 next year in charitable contributions from alumni and educational foundations. The school has no endowment funds of its own.

The chairman of the finance committee plans to recommend an increase in the tuition rate to $4,150 because that will balance the budget. The treasurer wants to set the tuition at $4,300 because this represents full cost. The headmaster is reluctant to see any increase in the tuition rate because some of the gifted children in the school might not be able to continue. More importantly, parents of six-year-old children might be less willing to enroll these children because the total commitment for the next eight years would be even greater than it is now. Those with children in the upper school might be less likely to withdraw these children from the school because their future commitment would be smaller. No one has any firm estimate of the effect of a tuition increase on enrollment, however.

   a. Prepare an estimate or estimates of average costs the board might use in reaching a decision on the tuition question.

   b. Prepare your own recommendation, including a concise statement of your reasons for favoring the action you are recommending.

   19. *Using contribution-margin data; interdependent products.* The Albegata Company produces four products, Alpha, Beta, Gamma, and Delta. Its income statement for the past year showed the following (in thousands of dollars):

	Alpha	Beta	Gamma	Delta	Total
Units sold	400	300	200	2,000	—
Sales revenues	$4,000	$3,000	$2,000	$1,000	$10,000
Cost of goods sold:					
Direct material	$1,500	$1,000	$ 500	$ 500	$ 3,500
Direct labor	1,000	1,000	300	200	2,500
Factory overhead absorbed	400	400	120	80	1,000
Total	$2,900	$2,400	$ 920	$ 780	$ 7,000
Gross margin	$1,100	$ 600	$1,080	$ 220	$ 3,000
Selling expenses:					
Sales commissions	$ 120	$ 90	$ 60	$ 30	$ 300
Traceable fixed costs	200	60	60	60	380
Common fixed costs	480	360	240	120	1,200
Administrative expenses:					
Order processing	30	50	20	20	120
General administration	320	240	160	80	800
Total Operating Expense	$1,150	$ 800	$ 540	$ 310	$ 2,800
Net Income (Loss) Before Tax	$ (50)	$ (200)	$ 540	$ (90)	$ 200

   It is believed that no external force in the foreseeable future will alter the picture. At the board of directors' meeting, it is decided that something must be done in view of the low overall profit rate (2 percent on sales) and the net loss on all except one product line.

   Upon your request, the following additional information is furnished by the company:

1. Sales commissions are paid to the company's sales force at the rate of 3 percent of sales.
2. Order-processing costs are assigned to products on the basis of the amount of time spent by office employees in recording orders, preparing invoices, and recording the amounts collected from customers. Order-processing costs increase in steps, but the steps are narrow enough to justify classifying these costs as variable.
3. Analysis of factory overhead and fixed operating expenses:

	Alpha	Beta	Gamma	Delta
Factory overhead:				
Variable (with direct labor cost)	$150	$200	$100	$ 60
Fixed, but escapable if the line is				
shut down	150	100	10	10
Fixed and inescapable if the line is				
shut down	100	100	10	10
Traceable selling expense:				
Fixed, escapable only by shutdown	180	60	50	60
Fixed, inescapable by shutdown	20	—	10	—
Common fixed selling expense:				
Escapable by shutdown	200	210	200	110
Inescapable by shutdown	280	150	40	10
General administrative expense:				
Fixed, escapable only by shutdown	20	40	10	50
Fixed, inescapable by shutdown	300	200	150	30

4. Products Beta and Alpha share the same equipment, and this is now fully utilized. A unit of Alpha requires the same number of machine-hours as a unit of Beta. For competitive reasons, the selling price of neither product can be increased. The marketing manager has no doubt the company could get enough additional orders of either of these products to utilize the equipment fully if production of the other were to be discontinued, with no change in any marketing costs except sales commissions.

5. Product Delta is looked on as a loss leader, since it is feared that sales of Gamma would fall by as much as 20 percent if Delta were dropped from the company's line. Alpha and Beta, on the other hand, are sold to other types of buyers, and their sales would not be affected.

a. Give recommendations when only the additional information in (1), (2), and (3) is known. (All recommendations must be supported by computations showing estimated improvement in profits.)

b. Give recommendations when only the additional information in (1), (2), (3), and (4) is known.

c. Give recommendations when all of the above information is known.

22

The Capital-Expenditure Decision

THE DECISIONS DESCRIBED in Chapter 19 could be based on estimates of their effects on the organization's cash flows in a single time period no longer than a year. This approach is inadequate when management is faced with an *investment problem.* An investment problem is a situation requiring management to decide whether to expend cash in one or more time periods to obtain cash inflows in another time period or periods.

One of the most important types of investment problems is the *capital-expenditure decision,* in which an initial cash outlay (the capital expenditure) is made in the expectation that it will produce cash receipts in a later year or years. Typical examples are proposals to build, acquire, replace, or expand long-lived productive assets. The purpose of this chapter is to see how management can analyze and solve problems of this sort.

THE PRESENT-VALUE APPROACH

The most widely recommended method of evaluating proposals to make capital expenditures is to calculate for each proposal the present value of the anticipated cash flows, using a discount rate representing the company's minimum acceptable rate of return on investment. This is referred to as *discounted-cash-flow (DCF)* analysis.

659

> ### TERMINOLOGY REMINDER
>
> The *present value* of a future sum is the amount which, if invested now at compound interest at the specified rate, will grow to an amount equal to the future sum at the specified future date.

The method we'll describe in this section is simpler and less complete than the approach now favored by investment theorists, which requires adjustments of individual cash-flow estimates to allow for risk.[1] The method described here can serve as an introduction to that more complex approach; furthermore, it is the method most likely to be encountered in practice.

The Procedure

In its basic form, this kind of analysis consists of four steps:

1. Identify the proposal and at least one alternative to accepting it.
2. Estimate the cash flows, year by year, that would result if the proposal were accepted; make a similar set of estimates for each alternative being considered.
3. Discount the cash flows for each alternative to determine their present values and add these together to derive the *net present value* of this alternative.
4. Choose the alternative with the greatest present value.

Step 1:   Identify the alternatives.   A company is considering a proposal to invest $34,000 (proposal A). To evaluate this proposal, management has to identify at least one alternative to accepting it. If it has no alternative, it has no decision to make. In this case management has decided to introduce only one alternative: *reject proposal A.*

Step 2:   Estimate the cash flows.   One way to proceed would be to estimate the cash flows for the entire company under each alternative. This might be necessary for truly major capital-expenditure proposals that would affect the basic nature and structure of the company's operations. A simpler approach, adequate for most capital-expenditure decisions, is to select one alternative as a benchmark and measure the cash flows of each other alternative as differences from that benchmark. In this case management has se-

---

[1] See Jan Mossin, *Theory of Financial Markets* (Englewood Cliffs, N.J.: Prentice-Hall, Inc., 1973), chap. 7.

lected "reject proposal A" as the benchmark alternative. The cash flows relative to this benchmark are as follows:

Years from Now	Cash Flow
0	−$34,000
1	+ 10,000
2	+ 10,000
3	+ 10,000
4	+ 10,000
5	+ 10,000
Total	+$16,000

In this table, cash receipts are identified by (+) signs; the cash outlay is identified by a (−) sign.

Step 3: Discount the cash flows. This company regards 10 percent as the minimum acceptable rate of return on investment. Present-value multipliers can be taken from the 10 percent column of Table 3 in Appendix A. These multipliers and the present values of the cash flows from Proposal A are shown in Exhibit 22–1.

EXHIBIT 22–1.   Calculating the Net Present Value of Proposal A

Years from Now	(1) Cash Flow	(2) Present Value at 10 Percent Multiplier (Table 3)	(3) Present Value at 10 Percent Amount (1) × (2)
0	−$34,000	1.0000	−$34,000
1	+ 10,000	0.9091	+ 9,091
2	+ 10,000	0.8264	+ 8,264
3	+ 10,000	0.7513	+ 7,513
4	+ 10,000	0.6830	+ 6,830
5	+ 10,000	0.6209	+ 6,209
Net Present Value			+$ 3,907

Step 4: Choose the best alternative. Exhibit 22–1 shows that proposal A has a positive net present value. This means that the cash flows it is expected to generate will be more than enough to return the $34,000 initial outlay and to provide a 10 percent rate of return on the company's investment. Since the company finds 10 percent an acceptable rate of return, it should be happy to accept proposal A.

Step 5: Verify the results. Although the decision itself requires the managers to go beyond the raw figures and apply their judgment, the basic calculations need go no farther than Step 4. It may be useful this time, however, to check the truth of the statement that proposal A will yield a rate of return greater than 10 percent.

To do this, we need to examine the process from the other end. The initial investment is $34,000. The first year's interest at 10 percent, therefore, would amount to $3,400. Since $10,000 in cash is received, the remaining $6,600 can be treated as a partial recovery of the original investment. This leaves an unrecovered balance of $27,400 at the end of the first year. Interest on that in the second year is $2,740, leaving $7,260 of the second year's cash receipts to be treated as a recovery of another portion of the initial outlay. Continuing these calculations for three more years produces the following table:

Year	(1) Unrecovered Investment, Beginning of Year	(2) Interest at 10 Percent	(3) Amortization of Investment [$10,000 − (2)]	(4) Unrecovered Investment, End of Year (1) − (3)
1	$34,000	$3,400	$6,600	$27,400
2	27,400	2,740	7,260	20,140
3	20,140	2,014	7,986	12,154
4	12,154	1,215	8,785	3,369
5	3,369	337	9,663	(6,294)

By the end of the fifth year, the entire investment has been recovered, despite annual interest payments at a 10 percent rate, and the firm still has $6,294 left over (see Exhibit 22–2). In other words, the

EXHIBIT 22–2. The Investment-Recovery Pattern

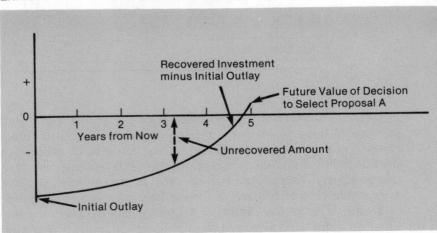

company could have paid more than 10 percent interest from the cash flows from this investment.[2]

The Internal Rate of Return

Net present value is sometimes an awkward figure to use in discussing the merits of individual capital-expenditure proposals. For this reason some companies prefer to use the *internal rate of return,* defined as that rate of discount at which the net present value is zero. Calculating the internal rate of return is a three-step, trial-and-error process:

Step 1. **Discount all cash flows at a trial rate.** We have already performed this step. The net present value of the cash flows at 10 percent is $3,907. This indicates that the rate of return is greater than 10 percent, but it doesn't show how much greater.

Step 2. **Discount all cash flows at a second trial rate.** Since we know that the internal rate of return is higher than 10 percent, a reasonable second trial rate is 15 percent. To simplify the calculations, we can use the present-value multiplier from Table 4 in Appendix A; this is simply the sum of the multipliers in Table 3 for the first five years. The multipliers and present values at this rate are:

Years from Now	Cash Flow	Present Value at 15 Percent Multiplier	Amount
0	−$34,000	1.000	−$34,000
1–5	+ 10,000 per year	3.352	+ 33,520
Net Present Value			−$ 480

The present value of the cash receipts at a 15 percent discount rate is only $33,520, producing a negative net present value. This means that the cash flows are not big enough to produce a rate of return as high as 15 percent.

Step 3. **Interpolate.** The true rate of return is somewhere between 10 percent and 15 percent. It is the rate of return at which net present value equals zero. We can approximate this by interpolating between two points on a graph, as shown in Exhibit 22–3. We can do

---

[2] The $6,294 residual is the future value of $3,907 five years later, compounded annually at 10 percent.

EXHIBIT 22-3. Interpolating to Approximate the Internal Rate of Return

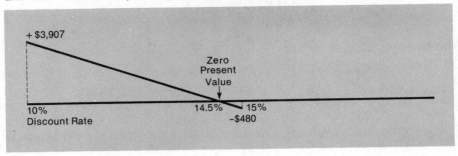

the same thing algebraically, again rounding the answer to the nearest tenth of a percent.

$$\text{Approximate Rate} = 10\% + \frac{\$3,907}{\$3,907 + \$480} \times (15\% - 10\%)$$

$$= 14.5\%$$

($\$3,907 + \$480 = \$4,387$ is the total distance between $+\$3,907$ and $-\$480$.)

The Reason for the Present-Value Approach

Present value is a useful measure of the desirability of a capital expenditure proposal because it is sensitive to the timing of the anticipated cash flows. For example, a company can invest in any or all of the following proposals:

Years from Now	Net Cash Receipts (+) or Cash Outlays (−)		
	Proposal X	Proposal Y	Proposal Z
0	−$13,000	−$13,000	−$13,000
1	+ 1,000	+ 5,000	+ 9,000
2	+ 5,000	+ 5,000	+ 5,000
3	+ 9,000	+ 5,000	+ 1,000
Total Cash Flow	+$ 2,000	+$ 2,000	+$ 2,000

These three proposals have identical lifetime total cash flows, but they are far from equally desirable. Proposal Z is the best proposal because cash is received earlier under this proposal than under either of the others. Proposal X is the worst of the three.

These differences appear clearly in present-value calculations. Assuming an 8 percent discount rate, the present values of these proposals are:

Years from Now	Present-Value Multipliers	Proposal X	Proposal Y	Proposal Z
0	1.0000	−$13,000	−$13,000	−$13,000
1	0.9259	+ 926	+ 4,630	+ 8,332
2	0.8573	+ 4,286	+ 4,286	+ 4,286
3	0.7938	+ 7,144	+ 3,969	+ 794
Net Present Value		−$ 644	−$ 115	+$ 413

The present-value multipliers in this table came from the 8 percent column of Table 3 in Appendix A.

In this case, proposals X and Y promise a return on investment of less than 8 percent; only proposal Z promises a return in excess of 8 percent. Only proposal Z should be accepted. The present-value measure, in other words, permits management to compare proposals that differ in the timing of their cash flows.

Multiple Alternatives

So far, we have assumed that the decision maker has only two alternatives: accept the proposal or reject it. For major capital-expenditure proposals, management should insist that a real effort be made to identify one or more substitute proposals that might fill the same needs in different ways. Once this has been done, management should select the proposal with the greatest positive net present value; if none of the proposals has a positive net present value, all should be rejected.

For example, we saw earlier that Proposal A has an estimated present value of $3,907. Instead of accepting this proposal, however, management could accept either proposal B or proposal C. The cash flows and multipliers for proposals B and C are as follows:

	(1)	(2)	(3)	(4)	(5)
		Proposal B		Proposal C	
Years from Now	Present-Value Multiplier at 10 Percent	Cash Flow	Present Value (1) × (2)	Cash Flow	Present Value (4) × (1)
0	1.0000	−$56,000	−$56,000	−$45,000	−$45,000
1	0.9091	+ 16,000	+ 14,546	+ 15,000	+ 13,636
2	0.8264	+ 16,000	+ 13,222	+ 15,000	+ 12,396
3	0.7513	+ 16,000	+ 12,021	+ 15,000	+ 11,270
4	0.6830	+ 16,000	+ 10,928	+ 10,000	+ 6,830
5	0.6209	+ 16,000	+ 9,934	+ 5,000	+ 3,105
Net Present Value			+$ 4,651		+$ 2,237

Proposal B offers a higher net present value than Proposal A; the net present value of proposal C is lower than that of either of the other two. Proposal B therefore should be chosen.

Disinvestment Decisions

All the investment problems we have looked at so far have focused on proposals to tie up company funds in plant, equipment, and working capital. A similar kind of problem arises when someone proposes to sell a factory, withdraw from a market area, or discontinue selling a product, converting the amounts invested in those activities into ready cash. These are *disinvestment problems*.

For example, a company has an opportunity to realize $500,000 in cash by closing and selling one of its factories. It can refuse this offer and continue to operate the plant, but cash flows from the sale of the products made in the plant will decline rapidly, and the resale value of the land, building, and equipment will fall even faster.

Again the best way to start is to set up a timetable of cash flows, this time with one column for each of the two alternatives and another for the differential cash flows:

(1) Years from Now	(2) Cash Flows from Abandoning the Plant	(3) Cash Flows from Keeping the Plant	(4) Differential Cash Flows (2) − (3)
0	+$500,000	0	+$500,000
0–1	0	+$250,000	− 250,000
1–2	0	+ 200,000	− 200,000
2–3	0	+ 150,000	− 150,000
3–4	0	+ 100,000	− 100,000
4–5	0	+ 50,000	− 50,000
Total	+$500,000	+$750,000	+$250,000

This problem is no different from any of the other problems we have been looking at. To see why this is true, let's turn the problem around. Instead of thinking of this as a proposal to sell the plant, we can think of it as a proposal to keep it in operation. To do that, the company must forgo an immediate cash inflow of $500,000. Doing that is just like investing $500,000 to keep the plant going. If we look at it this way, we get the following timetable:

Years from Now	Differential Cash Flows
0	−$500,000
0–1	+ 250,000
1–2	+ 200,000
2–3	+ 150,000
3–4	+ 100,000
4–5	+ 50,000

If the minimum acceptable rate of return is 10 percent, and if we assume that cash flows are concentrated at the end of each year, the present value is as follows:

Time	Cash Flow	Multiplier	Present Value
0	−$500,000	1.0000	−$500,000
1	+ 250,000	0.9091	+ 227,275
2	+ 200,000	0.8264	+ 165,280
3	+ 150,000	0.7513	+ 112,695
4	+ 100,000	0.6830	+ 68,300
5	+ 50,000	0.6209	+ 31,045
Net Present Value			+$104,595

The same calculation can be made each year until it finally gives the signal to disinvest.

THE MINIMUM ACCEPTABLE RATE OF RETURN

Business firms must be careful to make investments that will produce an adequate rate of return. The money they have to invest comes from their stockholders and from lenders. These investors expect to be rewarded for letting the firm use their money.

The cost of attracting funds into the company has two components: (1) the cost of debt capital and (2) the cost of equity capital.

Cost of Debt Capital

The cost of debt capital is the rate of interest that equates the present value of the future stream of interest payments (after allowing for income tax effects) and maturity date repayment of face value to the current net proceeds from sale of the debt instruments. For example, assume that bonds with a coupon rate of 9 percent and a 20-year maturity can be sold at their face value. After providing for the tax deductibility of interest at a tax rate of 50 percent, the after-tax cost of this debt offering is 4.5 percent.

Cost of Equity Capital

The cost of equity capital can be defined as the rate of discount stockholders apply to the expected future receipts from stock ownership to determine the price they are willing to pay. To determine this rate, we need data on the market price of the stock and the stockholders' future expectations. The latter information being unavailable, the analyst typically falls back on a study of past relationships between market prices, dividends, and capital appreciation.

As a simple illustration of the concept, if a stock is selling for $50 per share and the company's earnings are stable at $5 a share, this is some evidence that the marginal stockholders in the company are willing to pay $10 for each dollar of earnings. To attract additional funds into the firm, therefore, the company must be able to communicate an expectation that these funds will also earn a return of at least 10 percent on investment, and perhaps more.

The cost of equity capital for any company includes a risk premium in addition to the cost of risk-free capital. The size of this premium depends on the perceived risks of investing in that company relative to the risks of investing in the market generally. The so-called capital-asset pricing model links the size of the risk premium to the contribution the stock makes to the variability of a diversified portfolio. Companies whose stock prices are very sensitive to movements in the stock market will have high-risk premiums, and vice versa.[3]

Weighted Average Cost of Capital

Most companies use both debt and equity capital. Utility companies have a high proportion of debt, mining companies relatively little. A company's average cost of capital will depend not only on the costs of the two kinds of capital but also on the proportions in which they are to be used.

What this means is that the minimum acceptable rate of return should be based on a weighted average of the costs of debt and equity capital. The weights should represent the relative place each has in the company's financing plans:

	After-Tax Capital Cost	Weight	Weighted Cost
Debt	4.5%	40%	1.8%
Equity	12.0	60	7.2
Total			9.0%

---

[3] James H. Lorie and Mary T. Hamilton, *The Stock Market: Theories and Evidence* (Homewood, Ill.: Richard D. Irwin, 1973).

If the company's investments do not yield a rate of return at least as great as the cost of capital, they will dilute the company's earnings and impair its ability to secure funds on a balanced basis in the future.

ESTIMATING THE CASH FLOWS

The most difficult part of present-value analysis is the estimation of cash flows. We'll study four components of the cash flow stream:

1. The initial outlay.
2. Secondary investment outlays.
3. Operating cash flows.
4. End-of-life salvage values.

We'll finish this section by putting all the cash flows in a timetable so they can be discounted to their present values.

The Initial Outlay

The initial outlay includes all cash flows necessary to carry out the proposal. It consists of some or all of the following:

1. Cash outlays for plant and equipment.
2. Opportunity costs of existing facilities to be incorporated in the proposal.
3. Outlays for working capital.
4. Disposal values of facilities to be displaced by the proposal.
5. Immediate income tax effects.

Plant and equipment. For most proposals, the major outlays are for the acquisition and installation of physical facilities. For example, a proposal to modernize a factory is expected to require the following outlays before the investment begins to bring in cash receipts:

Equipment	$80,000
Installation	10,000
Training and test runs	7,000
Total	$97,000

If these outlays are spread over a period longer than six months, they should be divided and dated at the nearest year-end. In most cases, it is accurate enough to assume that all these cash flows take place at one time. In this case we'll assume they all take place within a very short period. This period will be referred to as the *zero date* for present-value calculations.

Existing facilities used. One of the company's present machines, now idle, will be put back in service only if the modernization proposal is approved. No cash needs to be paid for this machine—the company already owns it. Even so, it belongs in the timetable. By accepting the proposal, management will make this machine unavailable for any other use. This proposal, therefore, should be charged for the machine's value in its best other use—that is, its opportunity cost.

In this case, management agrees that the machine will be sold if it is not needed for the modernization proposal. The estimated sale price is $12,000. This is part of the investment outlay because, in accepting the proposal, the company is depriving itself of $12,000 in cash:

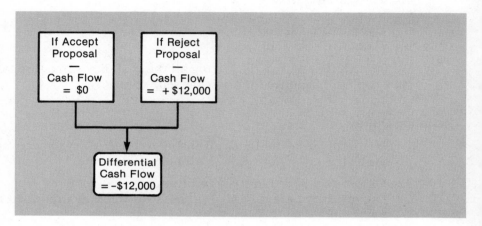

A *cash receipt forgone is always equivalent to a cash outlay.* The book value of the equipment doesn't measure either current or future cash flows, of course, and therefore should be ignored.

Working capital.   Once the new equipment is in operation, management expects it will support a larger volume of sales. These will require additional working capital which should be reflected in the timetable:

Inventories: the amount spent to increase the size of the average inventory $10,000
Receivables: the difference between net revenues and collections in the first year (inserted as part of the initial outlay because estimates of operating cash flows usually reflect revenues rather than collections)   4,000
Cash: any additional balances immobilized because they are necessary to support the additional volume of activity resulting from the proposal   2,000
Trade payables and other short-term, noninterest-bearing liabilities: any increments in these items arising from the additional volume of activity . . .   11,000

These amounts should be entered in the timetable as they occur. Because the net increase in this case is small ($10,000 + $4,000 + $2,000 − $11,000 = $5,000), management has decided to simplify the calculation by putting the entire amount in the timetable as a cash outlay at zero date.

Displaced facilities. The cash flows we have mentioned overstate the amount of investment that will be necessary. If the proposal is accepted, a machine now serving a standby purpose can be disposed of. This machine has a tax basis (book value) of only $1,000, but once again opportunity cost, not book value, is the right measure of the cash flow. Opportunity cost is measured by the machine's scrap value, $6,000. The displaced machine, in other words, can finance $6,000 of the gross pretax outlays the proposal will require.

This may become clearer if we point out once again that we are really comparing two alternatives in our cash flow estimates:

A Accept the Proposal and Dispose of Existing Standby Equipment +$6,000	B Reject the Proposal and keep the Standby Equipment +$0

The only way to get the $6,000 cash inflow is to accept this proposal. It therefore becomes a cash inflow attributable to the proposal and must be included in the timetable.

Tax effects. The net incremental pretax initial outlay amounts to $108,000, the sum of the six items we just discussed:

New equipment	$ 80,000
Installation	10,000
Training and test runs	7,000
Existing equipment	12,000
Working capital	5,000
Less: Disposal of displaced machine	(6,000)
Net Pretax Outlay	$108,000

Some of these amounts will affect the company's income taxes immediately. In fact, we have designed the illustration to include four separate tax effects: a tax credit, a tax deduction, a tax-deductible loss, and a taxable gain. (A tax credit is a direct reduction in the amount of tax due; a tax deduction is a reduction in the amount of taxable income.)

Tax credit. Many governments offer tax credits to induce business firms to invest in facilities or to increase their inventories, thereby providing jobs and stimulating the economy. In our illustration, the $80,000 outlay for new equipment is eligible for a 10 percent tax credit. This will reduce the tax by $8,000, and this amount should be deducted in calculating the initial outlay.

Tax deduction. Both the purchase price and the installation cost of the new equipment will be capitalized and depreciated for tax purposes over a period of years. The $7,000 in training and test-run costs, however, will be fully deductible from taxable revenues right away. At a 40 percent tax rate, this will reduce current taxes by $2,800. The after-tax outlay for these items therefore is $7,000 − $2,800 = $4,200.

Tax-deductible loss.   The idle machine to be used in the proposal also has a tax impact. We have already seen that accepting the proposal will deprive the company of the $12,000 cash flow from selling this machine. It will also deprive the company of the right to enter the loss from the sale of the machine on the current income tax return. The loss for tax purposes is the difference between the proceeds from the sale and book value for tax purposes (the "tax basis"), which in this case happens to be $20,000:

Sale value	$12,000
Tax basis	20,000
Tax-Deductible Loss	$ 8,000

Since this would reduce taxable income, it would also reduce taxes. Using the machine will deprive the company of this tax reduction. It thus becomes another cash outflow arising from the proposed investment. At a tax rate of 40 percent, the tax effect is $3,200. The after-tax cash flow is:

Sale value	$12,000
Tax reduction due to loss	3,200
After-Tax Cash Flow	$15,200

Taxable gain.   The final element in the initial outlay calculation, the sale of the displaced machine, also has a tax effect. The market value of this machine is $6,000, and the tax basis is $1,000, so the taxable gain is $5,000. The cash flows are:

Market value	$6,000
Tax on the gain: 40% × $5,000	2,000
After-Tax Cash Flow	$4,000

EXHIBIT 22–4. Calculation of After-Tax Initial Outlay

Item	Outlay before Tax	Tax Effect	Outlay after Tax
Equipment, installed	$ 90,000	$(8,000)	$ 82,000
Working capital	5,000	0	5,000
Training and test runs	7,000	(2,800)	4,200
Surplus equipment used	12,000	3,200	15,200
Equipment displaced	(6,000)	2,000	(4,000)
Total	$108,000	(5,600)	$102,400

The after-tax investment outlay.   All these figures are summarized in Exhibit 22–4. In this case the net difference between the pretax and after-tax amounts is relatively small, less than 6 percent; in other cases it will be much higher.

Secondary Investment Outlays

Management can often predict special outlays that will have to be made in later time periods to keep the investment alive. These, too, may be for equipment or for additional working capital. Each has to be examined for its tax implications.

Secondary investment outlays of this sort are no different in concept from the initial outlay, and need no further discussion here. The only secondary investment outlay management anticipates for the plant modernization proposal is $20,000 to replace equipment at the end of the fifth year. This will have no immediate impact on taxes, and $20,000 is the after-tax cash flow.

Operating Cash Flows

The benefits from most investments come from increased revenues or from lower operating costs. Two of the many possible cash flow patterns are illustrated in Exhibit 22–5. In the upper diagram, initial operating outflows are followed by several years of positive cash flows, rising to a flat peak in the fifth and sixth years, then declining slowly. Negative cash flows (net outflows) during the first year or so are typical of investments in new products or new markets. The lower diagram depicts a mining investment with a high immediate payoff but declining cash flows as the resources become more and more difficult to exploit.

The benefit pattern in our modernization proposal is much simpler. The main benefits are expected to take the form of reduced operating costs. Although the cash costs of operating the plant will undoubtedly rise as the facilities grow older, the difference between the before-tax cash flows associated with the company's current facilities and those incurred in operating and renovated facilities will be relatively constant at $25,000 a year.

The next step in the analysis is to calculate the effect of the project on income taxes. To do this, we have to identify two sets of figures:

1.   Incremental cash flows not appearing on the current tax return.
2.   Incremental accounting charges and credits appearing on the current tax return but unaccompanied by current pretax cash flows.

EXHIBIT 22–5.   Operating Cash Flow Patterns

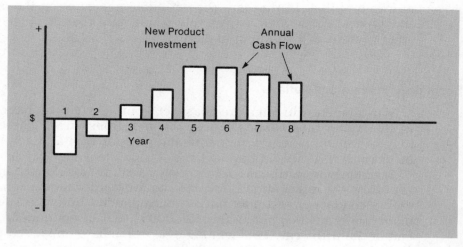

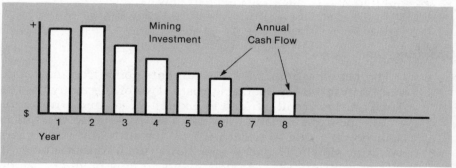

In this case incremental taxable income is equal to the pretax cash flow less the incremental tax depreciation. Incremental depreciation is the difference between two amounts:

Depreciation on Property Required by the Project		Tax Basis	Depreciation
	New Equipment	$90,000	20% of Declining Balance
	Existing Machine ...	20,000	
	Secondary Investment	20,000	

Depreciation on Property Displaced by the Project		Tax Basis	Depreciation
	Displaced Machine .	$1,000	$500 a Year for Two Years

The calculation of depreciation on the equipment required by the project is summarized in Exhibit 22–6. The initial tax basis of this equipment is $110,000, as shown at the top of column (1). The first year's depreciation is 20 percent of this, or $22,000. This reduces

EXHIBIT 22–6. Tax Depreciation on New and Retained Facilities

Year	(1) Tax Basis, Start of Year	(2) Additions	(3) Tax Depreciation 20% × [(1) + (2)]	(4) Tax Basis, End of Year (1) + (2) − (3)
1	$110,000	—	$22,000	$88,000
2	88,000	—	17,600	70,400
3	70,400	—	14,080	56,320
4	56,320	—	11,264	45,056
5	45,056	—	9,012	36,044
6	36,044	$20,000	11,209	44,835
7	44,835	—	8,967	35,868
8	35,868	—	7,174	28,694
9	28,694	—	5,739	22,955
10	22,955	—	4,591	18,364

the tax basis to $88,000 (the second figure in column [1]), and the tax depreciation for the second year is 20 percent of $88,000, or $17,600.

For simplicity, we have used a single declining-balance calculation for all three types of costs in all years. In practice, tax depreciation would be converted to a straight-line write-off for each of the costs at different times. We have also assumed that retirements of equipment will be zero prior to the end of the ten years.

The tax depreciation figures in Exhibit 22–6 do not measure incremental tax depreciation. If the proposal is rejected, the equipment it would displace will be kept. Tax depreciation of $500 a year will be recorded for the first two years, until the equipment is fully depreciated. This means that *incremental* tax depreciation for each of the first two years is $500 less than the figures shown in Exhibit 22–6:

Year	Depreciation if Proposal Is Accepted	Depreciation if Proposal Is Rejected	Incremental Depreciation
1	$22,000	$500	$21,500
2	17,600	500	17,100
3	14,080	—	14,080

This last calculation may be easier to understand if it is recognized as a simple time shift. If the proposal is accepted, the equipment will be replaced, and $1,000 will be deducted immediately from taxable income. If the proposal is rejected, on the other hand, the equipment will be retained, and the $1,000 will be deducted from taxable income during the next two years.

Given the before-tax cash flows and the tax-depreciation figures, it is a simple matter to calculate taxable income, income tax effects, and after-tax cash flows. Exhibit 22–7 summarizes these calcula-

EXHIBIT 22–7. Calculation of After-Tax Operating Cash Flows

Year	(1) Cash Flow before Taxes	(2) Tax De- preciation*	(3) Taxable Income (1) − (2)	(4) Income Tax 40% × (3)	(5) Cash Flow after Taxes (1) − (4)
1	$ 25,000	$ 21,500	$ 3,500	$ 1,400	$ 23,600
2	25,000	17,100	7,900	3,160	21,840
3	25,000	14,080	10,920	4,368	20,632
4	25,000	11,264	13,736	5,494	19,506
5	25,000	9,012	15,988	6,395	18,605
6	25,000	11,209	13,791	5,516	19,484
7	25,000	8,967	16,033	6,413	18,587
8	25,000	7,174	17,826	7,130	17,870
9	25,000	5,739	19,261	7,704	17,296
10	25,000	4,591	20,409	8,164	16,836
Total	$250,000	$110,636	$139,364	$55,744	$194,256

* The figure for each of the first two years differs from that shown in Exhibit 22-6 by $500, placing it on an incremental basis, as explained in the text.

tions for the plant modernization proposal. With the before-tax figures in the left-hand column, the three middle columns are used to compute the income tax effect. The after-tax cash flow is then found by deducting the tax from the before-tax cash flow.

Notice how the declining-charge depreciation has changed the constant annual before-tax cash flow into a stream of gradually declining amounts. This makes this proposal more valuable than if only the straight-line method were available.

End-of-Life Salvage Value

The final cash flow associated with a capital expenditure proposal is the cash value of the facilities and working capital remaining when the project's life comes to an end. This value is usually referred to as the residual value or, less elegantly, salvage value. Salvage values are quite important for short-lived investments, less so for projects with long lives. To find out whether salvage values are important, we should always prepare rough estimates except for extremely long-lived projects.

The plant modernization expenditures are expected to be product-ive for ten years. The expected incremental salvage value is as fol-lows:

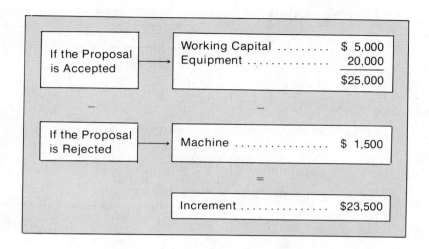

The $1,500 deduction needs some explanation. If the proposal is rejected, the company will keep its standby machine instead of sell-ing it now. The estimated sale value of the equipment ten years from now is $1,500. The current salvage value of this machine, $6,000, was entered into the timetable through Exhibit 22–4 as a cash re-ceipt (deduction from the initial cash outlay); its value ten years from now should be classified as an outlay (deduction from the end-of-life salvage value), as in the following table:

Years from Now	If Proposal Is Accepted	If Proposal Is Rejected	Incremental Cash Flows
0	+$6,000		+$6,000
10	—	+$1,500	− 1,500

The estimated liquidation value of the incremental working capi-tal, $5,000, is equal to its book value. The equipment required by the proposal, however, will have a tax basis of $18,364 at the end of ten years, as we can see in the bottom line of Exhibit 22–6. This is $1,636 less than the market value, and this amount is taxable. At a tax rate of 40 percent, the tax will be $654.

The standby machine the company will still have if the proposal is rejected will be fully depreciated ten years from now. The $1,500 liquidation value, therefore, will be fully taxable. The tax will be $600. The incremental after-tax salvage value is $23,446:

	Pretax Cash Flow	Income Tax	After-Tax Cash Flow
Working capital	$ 5,000		$ 5,000
Equipment	20,000	$ 654	19,346
Standby equipment	(1,500)	(600)	(900)
Net Salvage Value	$23,500	$ 54	$23,446

The net tax impact in this case is negligible.

Calculating Present Value

Once the cash flows have been estimated, calculating present value is a simple matter. The first step is to enter the cash flows in a timetable, as in the first three columns of Exhibit 22–8. The first

EXHIBIT 22–8.   Calculation of Present Value

	(1)	(2)	(3)	(4)	(5)
			Total	Present Value at 10%	
Years from Now	Investment Cash Flow after Taxes	Operating Cash Flow after Taxes	Cash Flow after Taxes (1) + (2)	Multiplier*	Amount (3) × (4)
0	−$102,400	—	−$102,400	1.0000	−$102,400
1	—	+$23,600	+ 23,600	0.9091	+ 21,455
2	—	+ 21,840	+ 21,840	0.8264	+ 18,049
3	—	+ 20,632	+ 20,632	0.7513	+ 15,501
4	—	+ 19,506	+ 19,506	0.6830	+ 13,323
5	− 20,000	+ 18,605	− 1,395	0.6209	− 866
6	—	+ 19,484	+ 19,484	0.5645	+ 10,999
7	—	+ 18,587	+ 18,587	0.5132	+ 9,539
8	—	+ 17,870	+ 17,870	0.4665	+ 8,336
9	—	+ 17,296	+ 17,296	0.4241	+ 7,335
10	+ 23,446	+ 16,836	+ 40,282	0.3855	+ 15,529
Net Present Value					+$ 16,800

* From Table 3, Appendix A.

column shows the initial outlay, the renovation outlay five years later, and the end-of-life salvage value. These are added to the operating cash flows to get the total cash flow figures in column (3).

The second step is to calculate the minimum acceptable rate of return. For our illustrative company, this is 10 percent after taxes.

The third step is to take present-value multipliers from present-value tables and apply these to the cash flows. The result of this step is shown in the right-hand column of the exhibit.

These calculations show that the present value of the moderniza-tion proposal is $16,800, the total of the figures in the right-hand column. This means that, if the estimates are correct, the future operating cash receipts will be big enough to pay back the amounts invested ($102,400 and $20,000) and pay interest on these amounts at an annual rate of 10 percent after taxes, with enough left over to increase the company's value now by $16,800. Other things being equal, the proposal should be accepted.

ECONOMIC LIFE

Cash flows in the preceding example were estimated for a ten-year period. This period was selected because management estimated that the investment had an economic life of ten years. The economic life of an investment is the length of time before the combination of assets, people, and purposes it embodies will have to be reconsti-tuted or disbanded.

In practice, the economic life of an investment is often defined to coincide with the economic life of one or more of the major tangible assets acquired at the time the investment is made. These assets may be replaced at the end of this period, either because the costs of owning and operating them are high relative to the costs of owning and operating replacement assets then available, or because the re-placement assets can produce a greater quantity or variety of output. Alternatively, economic life may come to an end because the reve-nues from the products or services provided can no longer cover the costs of providing them, including a return on the investment. In such cases, the assets may be sold or diverted to other uses.

SOME RECURRING QUESTIONS

The measures of costs or of revenues and expenses prepared for financial reporting sometimes affect investment decisions even though they don't measure current cash flows. Similarly, some cash flows, though not project related, are sometimes incorrectly included in cash-flow timetables.

Our analysis of the plant modernization proposal has dealt with four of these situations:

1. The unamortized costs of existing facilities or programs have been ignored.
2. No deductions have been made for depreciation on new equip-ment.
3. Internal cost allocations and absorptions have been ignored un-less they approximate the differential cash flows.

4.   No provision has been made for cash flows arising from borrowing or debt repayment transactions.

A brief review of each of these should help avoid misunderstandings
later on.

Unamortized Costs

Management often finds it difficult to ignore amounts spent in the
past to provide equipment or to develop new products. Suppose, for
example, an automobile company has spent $400 million to design,
test, tool, and market a new automobile model. Sales have been
disappointing, and management is considering discontinuing the
model. Only $220 million of the development and marketing costs
have been amortized, however, leaving $180 million in tooling costs
to be written off now if the company decides to drop the model from
the line.

The $180 million in unamortized costs is irrelevant to the decision
to discontinue the model—it is not a cash flow. Even so, it may influence the decision:

1.   Money is always spent to create value. Belief that a value has
been created is slow to die, and managers are often reluctant to
terminate an old project. ("It's a shame to write off all that
money. If we just put in another $100 million, the model is sure
to take hold.")
2.   Managers often think of costs as amounts to be recovered. If not
recovered as originally intended, they have to be charged against
something else. ("We can't accept that proposal. It won't cover
amortization of the costs of tooling we already have.") Result:
proposals that don't bring in enough cash to cover depreciation of
past outlays as well as future cash outlays may be turned down.

These are two examples of the *sunk-cost fallacy*, the notion that
costs not yet amortized are somehow relevant to decision making.
One of these makes it harder to get rid of old projects; the other
makes it harder to adopt new ones. The relevant concept in both
cases is opportunity cost: What is the present salvage value of the
investment, and by how much will that salvage value decline if the
investment is not liquidated now? The amounts invested in the past
are sunk costs; neither they nor amortization of them are relevant to
today's decisions.

Depreciation on New Facilities

Annual depreciation charges on the equipment required by the
plant modernization proposal were not reflected in the $25,000 an-

nual cash flow. Depreciation charges don't measure cash flows. This doesn't mean that present-value calculations overlook depreciation, however. Depreciation is real and can't be ignored. It is the difference between the initial outlay and the end-of-life salvage value:

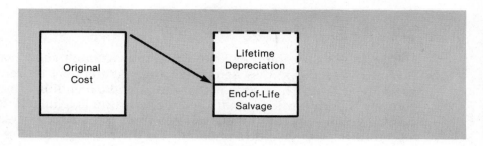

Accountants recognize depreciation for financial reporting by spreading it in some fashion over the assets' estimated lives. They reflect it in present-value analysis by entering two amounts in the cash-flow timetable—the initial outlay and the end-of-life salvage value—at the times these cash flows take place.

For example, on an investment proposal calling for an outlay of $60,000 now and a residual value of $3,000 in three years, the lifetime depreciation amounts to $57,000. This enters the timetable in the following way:

Time	Cash Flow
0	−$60,000
3	+ 3,000
Total	−$57,000

Entering depreciation again in the form of annual deductions from cash receipts would be double counting.

Allocations and Cost Absorption

A third source of difficulty is the practice of reassigning overhead costs by means of overhead rates and interdepartmental cost allocations. One company, for instance, applies factory overhead to products by means of a predetermined overhead rate of $2 a direct labor-dollar. It is very unlikely, however, that the company will save $2 in overhead for every dollar of direct labor it saves. In fact, most labor-saving investments actually increase total company overhead rather than the other way around.

Interdepartmental cost allocations can be misleading in a very similar way. In our example, plant modernization will decrease the amount of floor space required by the operations affected by the pro-

posal. This will reduce the amount of building occupancy costs allocated to these operations. The opportunity cost of the space saved is
zero, however, because the company has no way of using it or renting
it out. The cash-flow estimates must ignore this apparent difference
in costs.

The Treatment of Interest

Timetables for capital expenditure proposals don't show borrow-
ings as cash inflows; they don't show interest and debt retirements
as cash outflows. The reason is that the capital-expenditure decision
controls the investment of *all* the long-term funds available to the
company, not just the funds available from the shareowners. The
discounting process allows implicitly for the rewards the long-term
lenders and shareowners require—they don't have to be deducted a
second time.

For example, take a proposal with an initial cash outlay of $34,000
and cash receipts of $10,000 a year for five years. The left-hand block
in Exhibit 22–9 shows that the net cash flow for the five-year period

EXHIBIT 22–9.   Calculation of Implicit Interest

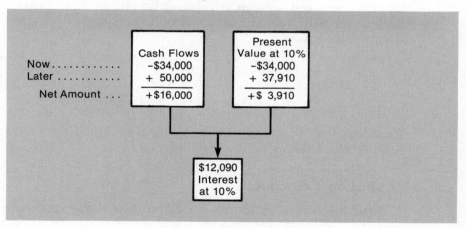

is +$16,000; the right-hand block shows that the present value is
only +$3,910. The $12,090 difference between these two figures represents interest at 10 percent on the investment for the full life of the
project.

The explanation is that the figures in the left-hand block represent
the present values of the cash flows at a *zero* rate of interest. The
figures in the right-hand column are smaller because interest at 10

percent has been subtracted. This being the case, charging interest explicitly against the cash flows generated by a proposal would be double counting.

SUMMARY

Many of management's resource-allocation problems can be classified as investment problems. Decision models for investment problems must provide a mechanism for comparing incremental cash outflows in one or more time periods with the incremental cash inflows in another time period or periods.

The model that does this most satisfactorily is the present-value model, in which all anticipated incremental cash flows are discounted to their present equivalents at a discount rate based on the cost of capital. Other things being equal, the alternative with the greatest positive net present value should be selected; proposals with negative net present values should be rejected. A related technique is the calculation of each project's internal rate of return, which can then be compared directly with the cost of capital.

In calculating net present value or the internal rate of return, the analyst has to estimate the economic life of the investment, the amount and timing of the investment outlays, the amount and timing of the operating cash flows, and the end-of-life salvage value attributable to the proposal. All of these estimates should reflect differential or incremental cash flows, not accounting allocations made for other purposes. Sunk costs should be ignored. The differentials should be measured from a bench mark that will be acceptable to the company, and opportunity costs must not be neglected.

KEY TERMS

Capital expenditure	Internal rate of return
Cost of capital	Investment problem
Discounted cash flow (DCF)	Minimum rate of return
Economic life	Net present value
End-of-life salvage value	Zero date

APPENDIX: SIMPLER MEASURES OF INVESTMENT VALUE

Two simpler measures than present value and the internal rate of return are sometimes used in the evaluation of capital expenditure proposals: (1) payback period and (2) average return on investment.

Payback Period

The payback period is the time that will elapse before net cash receipts will cumulate to an amount equal to the initial outlay. The shorter the payback period, the better the project, or so it is assumed.

If cash flows are uneven, the payback period should be calculated by adding cash flows until the total equals the initial outlay. Otherwise it can be calculated by applying the following formula:

$$\text{Payback period (years)} = \frac{\text{Investment outlay}}{\text{Average annual cash receipts}}$$

For example, if the installed cost of a piece of equipment is $50,000 and it will produce cash operating savings of $10,000 a year, it has a payback period of five years:

$$\frac{\text{Investment}}{\text{Annual cash receipts}} = \frac{\$50,000}{\$10,000} = 5 \text{ years}$$

The main defect of payback period is that it ignores the estimated useful life of the proposed facilities. If the facilities will have to be replaced five years from now, the project will have achieved no net earnings for the company. The company will have invested $50,000 at a zero rate of return. Or, if a large portion of the investment outlay is for working capital with a high end-of-life recovery value, the project may be more desirable than another with a lower payback period but no end-of-life salvage value.

Average Return on Investment

A second method is to compute for each proposal the expected average return on investment. This may be defined in many ways, perhaps most commonly by the following formula:

$$\frac{\text{Average}}{\text{return}} = \frac{\text{Average cash receipts} - \text{average annual depreciation}}{\text{Average lifetime investment}}$$

The average lifetime investment figure depends on the method used to calculate depreciation. The use of straight-line depreciation for accounting purposes presumes that investment declines in a linear fashion as facilities age. The average investment under this assumption is halfway between the amount of the initial outlay and the residual investment at the end of the project's life, measured by the recoverable value of the facilities and working capital at that time.

For example, the project for which payback period was computed earlier required an initial outlay of $50,000 and had no end-of-life salvage value. Average investment is thus $25,000. Assuming that the life of this project is expected to be ten years, average annual depreciation is $5,000, and the average before-tax return on investment is 20 percent:

$$\frac{\text{Average net earnings}}{\text{Average investment}} = \frac{\$10,000 - \$5,000}{\$25,000} = 20\%$$

This method does consider the expected life of the facilities, and it does consider the amount of end-of-life salvage. It fails, however, to allow for differences in timing of outlays and receipts. By this method, a project in which no receipts appear until the tenth year will appear to be just as profitable as a project in which most of the cash is received in the first few years of the project's life, as long as the average is the same.

INDEPENDENT STUDY PROBLEMS (Solutions in Appendix B)

1. **Estimating cash flows: make or buy decision.** The Arnold Machine Company has been having a neighboring company perform certain operations on a part used in its product at a cost of 50 cents per piece. The annual production of this part is expected to average 6,000 pieces.

The Arnold Machine Company can perform this operation itself by bringing into operation two machines: a spare lathe which has a net tax basis of $2,000 and a new machine which can be purchased at a price of $7,000. The new machine is expected to last seven years. The old machine has a remaining physical life of at least ten years and could be sold now for approximately $1,500. The final salvage value of both machines is considered negligible. In performing the operation itself, the Arnold Company will incur out-of-pocket costs for direct labor, power, supplies, and so forth, of 20 centers per piece.

The old machine is being depreciated for tax purposes at a straight-line amount of $500 a year. The new machine would be depreciated for tax purposes in seven years by the sum-of-the-years'-digits method. The income tax rate is 40 percent.

a. Arrange the pretax cash flows in a timetable.
b. Calculate the after-tax cash flows and arrange them in a timetable.

2. **Estimating after-tax cash flows.** Under a new proposal just submitted by the production manager of the Romano Company, the proposed facilities will cost $100,000, half of which will be capitalized for tax purposes. The rest will be expensed immediately. A government investment incentive device known as an investment credit allows the company an immediate tax rebate of 10 percent of the capitalized portion of the outlay. Depreciation charges for subsequent years will be based on the full amount capitalized, however.

The proposal will also require a $10,000 increase in working capital.

Cash operating savings are expected to amount to $20,000 a year. Expected life for tax purposes is eight years, and the double-rate, declining-balance method is used in computing depreciation. The tax rate is 50 percent.

a. Compute the after-tax initial cash outlay for this proposal.
b. Compute the after-tax cash saving for each of the first two years of the life of the facilities.

3. *Calculating present value and internal rate of return.* The expected life of a facility proposal is ten years, the installed cost will be $65,000, and the expected end-of-life salvage value is zero. The equipment will replace facilities now in use that have a book value of $30,000 and a market value of $10,000. The remaining tax life of the old facilities is eight years.

Double-rate, declining-balance depreciation will be used for tax purposes on the new facilities. No "investment credit" is available, but $15,000 of the new facility's installed cost can be expensed immediately for tax purposes. The present facilities are being depreciated for tax purposes by the straight-line method down to an end-of-life salvage value of zero.

Estimated before-tax, before-depreciation cash savings amount to $20,000 a year. The tax rate is 50 percent, and all savings are assumed to take place at the end of each year.

a. Compute the incremental after-tax present value of this proposal at 10 percent, compounded annually.
b. Compute the incremental after-tax internal rate of return on this proposal.

4. *Calculating present value: equipment replacement.* The Walpole Cotton Company is currently considering the installation of weaving equipment with a total cost including freight and installation of $44,000. If this proposal is accepted, this equipment will replace equipment which three years before cost $55,000 and is still in good running order. Because of the greater efficiency of the new equipment, the present equipment now has a resale value of only $5,000. The cost of removing the old equipment and revamping the machine service facilities will be $15,000, of which $5,000 is considered a part of the installation cost and is included in the $44,000 to be capitalized, while the remaining $10,000 is to be charged to expense.

The manufacturing cost tabulation shows a substantial reduction in annual operating cost, as follows:

	At Present	After New Installation
Annual costs:		
Labor	$ 12,500	$ 3,000
Depreciation (10% of cost, straight-line)	5,500	4,400
Supplies, repairs, and power	4,000	3,400
Taxes, insurance, and miscellaneous	900	1,000
Total	$ 22,900	$ 11,800
Annual Production—Units	500,000	500,000

The original life estimate on the present equipment was based on a forecast that a major technical improvement would be introduced in equipment that would become available at the end of ten years from the date of installation. This major technical improvement has been incorporated in the new equipment now available, seven years ahead of time. If the equipment is not replaced now, management believes that another ten years will pass before replacement is justifiable.

The present equipment is being depreciated for tax purposes by the sum-of-the-years'-digits method over a ten-year period. Tax depreciation on the new equipment would be calculated in a similar fashion.

If a 10 percent return on investment after taxes is required, would you recommend the expenditure? Assume a tax rate of 50 percent.

EXERCISES AND PROBLEMS

5. Present-value exercises.   Heslin, Inc., invested in a machine with a useful life of five years and no salvage value. The machine was depreciated for tax purposes by the straight-line method. The annual cash inflow from operations, net of income taxes, was $1,000. Heslin used a minimum acceptable rate of return of 12 percent.

a. Assuming this investment just satisfied the company's minimum rate of return on investment, what was the amount of the original investment?
b. Assuming the amount of the original investment was $3,500, what was the net present value, rounded to the nearest dollar?

(AICPA adapted)

6. Present-value exercise.   Ludington, Inc., has just purchased a new machine for $350,000. The machine is expected to have a useful life of eight years and no salvage value. The present value of the after-tax cash flows generated by this machine is $371,120, if the minimum annual rate of return on investment is 14 percent.

What annual cash inflow, net of income taxes, has been used in the calculation of the present value?

(AICPA adapted)

7. Value of tax benefits.   Freedom Corporation acquired a fixed asset at a cost of $100,000. The estimated life was four years, and the estimated salvage value was zero. The relevant interest rate was 8 percent after taxes and the income tax rate was 40 percent.

What was the present value of the tax benefits resulting from using sum-of-the-years'-digits depreciation instead of straight-line depreciation for tax purposes?

(AICPA adapted)

8. Discussion question: effect of past purchase price.   David and Zelda are co-owners of 1,000 shares of the common stock of Arlington Farms, Inc., an industrial conglomerate. They bought these shares five years ago at a price of $46 a share. The market price of a share of Arlington Farms common stock is now $12.50.

Zelda thinks the stock should be sold now because the company's future seems dim. David agrees with Zelda's forecast but thinks the stock should be kept because selling it now would prevent them from recovering their investment. Their tax advisor thinks they should keep the stock because they have no capital gains to offset the tax loss against on their tax return. Without capital gains, David and Zelda would get no immediate tax benefit from the sale.

Which side, if any, do you take in this argument? What flaws do you find in the positions you have rejected?

9. Disinvestment proposal: estimating cash flows.   J. T. Long, owner of the Long Office Building, was recently approached by a buyer for that property. The offer consisted of $200,000 down plus $50,000 at the end of each of the next five years—a total of $450,000.

Mr. Long had bought the land and built the building 15 years earlier. The land had cost $40,000; the building had cost $600,000. Annual depreciation for tax purposes had been charged at a straight-line rate of $20,000 a year.

The appraised value of the land at the time of the offer was $100,000. The remaining useful life of the building at that time seemed to be about ten years. At the end of that time, the land and building probably could be sold to a developer for $150,000. The amount of working capital required to support the operation of this building was negligible and seemed likely to remain so.

Mr. Long expected future income to be about $30,000 a year for the remaining life, calculated as below:

Yearly revenues from office rental		$79,000
Yearly expenses:		
Taxes	$ 4,000	
Repairs	12,000	
Depreciation	20,000	
Heat and miscellaneous	13,000	49,000
Total Income		$30,000

The cash flows from ownership of the property each year would become available to Mr. Long at the end of the year.

a. Prepare a time table of the pretax cash flows associated with this proposal.

b. Disinvestment decisions of this sort should take into consideration the tax consequences of the different alternatives. Which of the cash flows you identified in (*a*) would have to be adjusted, and what information would you need to have to make these adjustments?

10. Calculating cash flows.   Company X is considering a proposal to increase the degree of automation in one of its manufacturing departments. The following estimates have been made:

1. Initial outlay, $100,000, of which $20,000 would be expensed immediately for tax purposes. No investment credit would be applicable.
2. The capitalized portion of the initial outlay would be depreciated for tax purposes at a straight-line rate of 10 percent a year, starting the first year.
3. The net annual before-tax cash savings would be $22,000, starting immediately after installation.
4. The facilities would be obsolete at the end of six years of operation, at

which time they would be dismantled at a cash cost of $5,000 and sold for scrap. Scrap recovery at that time would be $1,000.

5. The company's effective income tax rate is expected to be 50 percent.
6. All cash flows after the initial outlay are expected to take place at year-end.

a. Calculate the after-tax initial outlay.
b. Calculate the expected after-tax cash inflow for the second year.
c. Calculate the anticipated effect of this proposal on the company's net income for the third year.
d. Calculate the after-tax cash flow from dismantling and scrap recovery at the end of six years.

11. *Sensitivity of rate of return.* The initial investment outlay is $40,000, of which $30,000 will be capitalized for tax purposes. The remaining $10,000 of the initial outlay will be expensed immediately for tax purposes. Before-tax operating cash receipts will be $12,000 a year for five years; these amounts will be received at the end of each year. Estimated end-of-life salvage value is zero.

Straight-line depreciation and a five-year life are to be used for tax purposes. The tax rate is 40 percent. Taxes are paid or tax credits are received immediately, as soon as the taxable or tax-deductible transaction takes place.

a. What is the present value of this proposal at an annual interest rate of 8 percent?
b. What is the after-tax internal rate of return?
c. What would be the internal rate of return if end-of-life salvage were to be $5,000 but annual depreciation for tax purposes continued to be based on zero salvage?
d. What would be the rate of return on investment if economic life and tax life were both six years, with zero salvage value?
e. What would be the rate of return if economic life and tax life were five years, salvage were zero, and double-rate, declining-balance depreciation were used for tax purposes?
f. Prepare a short commentary on the relationships indicated by your answers to the previous parts of this question.

12. *Estimating cash flows.* R. Oliver and J. Rand have formed a corporation to franchise a quick-food system for shopping malls. They have just completed experiments with the prototype of the machine which will be the basis of the operation. The machine has never been tested under commercial operating conditions, however, and a test of this sort must be conducted before any franchises can be offered for sale.

To conduct this test, Oliver and Rand plan to have a commercially usable machine built to their specifications and installed in a vacant store in a nearby shopping mall. They will be willing to make this investment and run the test even if the test operation itself isn't likely to meet their minimum rate-of-return requirement because they expect to make their money on the sale and servicing of franchises later on. They need estimates of the cash flows associated with the test operations, however, because if the expected results are extremely poor, franchising probably won't be feasible, and they won't make the investment now. If the test is undertaken and if it proves successful, they will market the franchises aggressively.

Oliver and Rand's best estimates of income from the test operation for the next four years are as follows:

	19x1	19x2	19x3	19x4
Sales revenues	$120,000	$150,000	$200,000	$230,000
Operating expenses:				
Cost of goods sold	$ 60,000	$ 75,000	$100,000	$110,000
Wages	24,000	30,000	40,000	44,000
Supplies	2,000	2,300	2,400	3,200
Personal property				
taxes	1,000	1,200	1,600	1,800
Annual rental (1)	12,000	12,000	12,000	12,000
Depreciation (2)	11,000	11,000	11,000	11,000
Development costs (3)	20,000	20,000	20,000	20,000
Total	$130,000	$151,500	$187,000	$202,000
Income (loss) before				
income taxes	$ (10,000)	$ (1,500)	$ 13,000	$ 28,000
Income taxes @ 40%	— (4)	— (4)	600(4)	11,200
Net Income	$ (10,000)	$ (1,500)	$ 12,400	$ 16,800

Notes:
(1)   The shopping mall requires each tenant to sign a ten-year lease. Three years' rental is payable at the beginning of the lease period with an annual payment at the end of each of the next seven years.
(2)   Construction of the commercially usable machine is expected to be completed on January 1, 19x1. The $130,000 purchase price will be paid at that time. The salvage value of this machine at the end of its ten-year life is estimated to be $20,000. Straight-line depreciation is to be used for statement purposes and sum-of-the-years'-digits depreciation will be used for tax purposes.
(3)   The prototype machine cost $200,000 to develop and build two years ago. These costs weren't classified as research and development costs as the machine was being built; instead, they were capitalized as equipment costs. The machine isn't suitable for commercial use, but Oliver and Rand expect to use it for demonstration purposes during the next ten years. Its cost will be amortized at $20,000 a year, both for statement purposes and for income taxation.
(4)   The losses of the first two years will be offset against the $13,000 pretax income in 19x3.

At the end of the four-year period Oliver and Rand intend to sell the pilot operation and concentrate on the sale and supervision of franchises. Based on the projected income stream from this pilot operation, they believe they can sell it for $190,000; the income tax liability arising from the sale will be $40,000.

Investments in working capital are expected to be negligible.

a. Calculate the cash flow for the mall operation for each year of the four-year period beginning January 1, 19x1, ignoring income tax implications. End-of-life salvage values should be listed separately from the operating cash flows.

b. Adjust the cash flows for the tax consequences, as appropriate.

(IMA adapted)

13. Make or buy decision. Griffa Machine Company has been purchasing from a neighboring company a part used in one of its products. The purchase price of this part is 95 cents each, and the expected average annual production is 6,000 parts.

The methods department of the Griffa Machine Company has submitted a proposal to manufacture this part in the company's own plant. To do this, the company would have to purchase a new machine at a price of $10,800. It would also use a lathe now owned by the company but not in current use. This lathe has an estimated market value now of $1,000, but its book value is $2,000. Depreciation for tax purposes on the old lathe is at a straight-line rate of $400 a year. The new machine would be depreciated for tax purposes by the sum-of-the-years'-digits method over an eight-year period. Griffa's management believes that both machines would be usable for ten years if the proposal were accepted, and the final salvage value of both machines is assumed to be negligible.

The incremental costs of operating the two machines, other than depreciation costs, would be as follows:

	Unit Cost
Direct labor, 0.1 hour at $4 an hour	$0.40
Direct materials	$0.10
Power, supplies, and so forth	$0.05

All other factory costs would be unaffected by the decision to manufacture this part. The company uses an overhead rate of $3 per direct labor-hour to absorb factory overhead costs.

Assuming an income tax rate of 50 percent and a minimum acceptable rate of return on investment of 10 percent after taxes, should this proposal be accepted?

14. Expansion proposal. The management of the Taunton Cotton Company is considering the acquisition of new spinning machinery, partially to replace certain less-efficient equipment and partially to increase total productive capacity. Market surveys indicate that the anticipated increase in productive capacity can be disposed of only by additional sales effort coupled with a price reduction. Pertinent data are as indicated below:

Cost of new equipment, including freight and installation	$55,000
Cost of removal of equipment replaced, rearrangement and re-vamping, and so forth, to be charged to expense for tax purposes	25,000
Net book value of equipment replaced (original cost: $40,000)	8,000
Amount to be realized from sale of equipment replaced	5,000

	Present		Proposed	
Annual Processing Costs	Dollars	Per Lb.	Dollars	Per Lb.
Labor	$120,000	$0.0600	$135,000	$0.0540
Supplies, repairs, and power	80,000	0.0400	93,000	0.0372
Taxes, insurance, and miscellaneous	20,000	0.0100	22,000	0.0088
Depreciation (10% of cost, straight-line)	4,000	0.0020	6,000	0.0024
Total	$224,000	$0.1120	$256,000	$0.1024

Annual production:
Present .... 2,000,000 lbs.
Proposed .... 2,500,000 lbs.
Estimated manufacturing margin (estimated selling price minus
  estimated material cost):
Present .... $ 0.150
Proposed (allowing for reduction of ½¢ in selling price) 0.145
Estimated additional selling and administrative expenses:
Commissions .... $ 5,000
Branch office sales expense (including advertising)....................... 11,000
Billing and miscellaneous administrative.................................. 1,500
  Total $17,500

Depreciation for tax purposes on present equipment has been by the straight-line method at 10 percent of cost. Tax depreciation on the new equipment would be by the sum-of-the-years'-digits method over a ten-year period. Expected salvage value is zero, and the income tax rate is 50 percent.

a. Prepare a timetable of the estimated pretax cash flows, and make the necessary adjustments for the effects of income taxation.
b. Would you recommend the expenditure if a 10 percent return after taxes is required?

15. Maximum purchase price. Company Z has contracted to supply a governmental agency with 50,000 units of a product each year for the next five years. A certain component of this product can be either manufactured by Company Z or purchased from the X Corporation, which has indicated a willingness to enter into a subcontract for 50,000 units of the component each year for five years if the price offered is satisfactory. These alternative methods of procurement are regarded as equally dependable.

If Company Z decides to manufacture the component, it expects the following to occur:

1. A special-purpose machine costing $110,000 will have to be purchased. No other equipment will be required.
2. For tax purposes, this machine will be assumed to have a ten-year life, but management does not expect the machine to be useful beyond the contract period. Estimated salvage value at the end of five years is $10,000.
3. Depreciation for tax purposes will be by the double-rate, declining-balance method. There will be no "investment credit."

4. The manufacturing operation will require 1,000 feet of productive floor space. This space is available in a building owned by Company Z and will not be needed for any other purpose in the foreseeable future. The costs of maintaining this building (including repairs, utilities, taxes, and depreciation) amount to $2 per square foot of productive floor space per year.

5. Variable manufacturing costs—materials, direct labor, and so forth—are estimated to be 50 cents a unit.

6. Fixed factory costs other than those mentioned in (1) through (4)—such as supervision and so forth—are estimated at $20,000 a year.

7. Income taxes are computed at the rate of 50 percent of taxable income or taxable savings.

8. The policy of Company Z is to subcontract if and only if the costs saved by manufacturing instead of subcontracting provide less than a 10 percent annual return on investment. For this purpose, return on investment is defined as the relationship between cost saving, after provision for income taxes, and the capital investment that will have to be made to permit Company Z to manufacture the component in its own plant.

What is the maximum price per unit which Company Z should be willing to offer to the X Corporation? Make explicit any assumptions which you believe to be necessary in solving the problem.

16. Equipment-replacement proposal. Diane Adams burst into the office of her supervisor, the works manager, to announce that a new machine which had just come out should be bought to replace the one used in the manufacture of product W. To support her argument, she presented the following comparative income statements for product W:

	Using the Present Machine	Using the New Machine
Expenses:		
Factory direct materials	$ 50,000	$ 50,000
Factory direct labor	40,000	30,000
Machinery depreciation	5,000	10,000
Other factory overhead (200% of direct labor)	80,000	60,000
Selling and administrative expenses (15% of sales)	30,000	30,000
Total	$205,000	$180,000
Sales revenues	200,000	200,000
Income (Loss) before taxes	$ (5,000)	$ 20,000
Less: Income taxes	(2,500)	10,000
Net Income (Loss)	$ (2,500)	$ 10,000

"The cost of the present machine is a sunk cost," Ms. Adams said. "The new machine will cost us $105,000, and since it will increase our net income by $12,500 a year, it will bring us a good deal more than the 8 percent annual after-tax return on investment we want."

Upon investigation, you discover the following additional information:

1. Machine data:

	Present Machine	New Machine
Expected life	Not applicable	10 years
Original cost	$55,000	$110,000
Tax depreciation to date	27,000	0
Present trade-in value	10,000	Not applicable
Expected trade-in value after 7 years	5,000	35,000
Expected trade-in value after 10 years	0	10,000
Capacity in units per year	60,000	80,000
Expected output (units per year)	50,000	50,000

2. Several products are manufactured in the same factory. Product W is now being assigned 25 percent of the total factory overhead cost other than equipment depreciation. Factory overhead other than equipment depreciation can be predicted from the following formula:

$$\$240,000 + 0.5 \times \text{Direct labor cost.}$$

Installation of the new machine would add $500 a year in electric power costs over and above the amounts indicated by this formula.

3. Tax depreciation on the old machine has been calculated on the sum-of-the-years'-digits method, based on a ten-year life and zero salvage. Tax depreciation on the new equipment would follow the same pattern. Gains and losses on the sale of equipment would be taxed at the regular tax rate, and no "investment credit" is available. Depreciation for internal financial reporting is calculated on a straight-line basis.

4. If production of product W were discontinued, the present machine could be disposed of. None of the fixed factory overhead costs other than equipment depreciation would be affected by discontinuation of product W, nor would any saving in selling and administrative expenses be made. Working capital of $10,000 would be released for use elsewhere, however.

Present and support a recommendation as to the desirability of continuing the manufacture of product W and purchasing the new machine. Establish the alternatives clearly and indicate the consequences of each.

17. Meeting expansion requirements. The Caldwell Manufacturing Company is using a special-purpose A-16 machine in the manufacture of a certain product. Because of expected increases in sales volume, additional capacity will have to be acquired. Two possibilities are under review:

A. Purchase an additional A-16 machine identical to the present one and operate the two machines.
B. Purchase a new high-speed B-32 machine with double the capacity of the present machine and keep the present A-16 machine as standby equipment.

The following information is available:

1. Production requirements are expected to average 70,000 units a year.
2. All machines are assumed to have a ten-year life from date of installa-

tion, with zero salvage value at the end of that time. Sum-of-the-years'-digits depreciation is used for tax purposes.

3. The present A-16 machine had a cost of $8,800 four years ago. Its present market value is $4,800.

4. The price of the new A-16 machine is $9,900. Unless the B-32 machine is bought now, the present A-16 will have to be replaced six years from now at a cost of $11,000. The market value of this replacement machine will be about $5,000 when it is four years old.

5. The price of a new B-32 machine is $39,600.

6. Repair and maintenance costs for an A-16 machine used regularly during the year are $2,800 a year.

7. Repair and maintenance costs for the B-32 machine and an A-16 machine used for standby purposes would total $4,000 a year.

8. Comparative variable costs per unit of output are:

	A–16	B–32
Materials	$0.136	$0.208
Supplies	0.052	0.024
Labor	0.212	0.088
Total	$0.400	$0.320

9. The minimum acceptable rate of return is 8 percent after taxes. Income tax rate is 50 percent.

a. Which alternative would you choose? Show your calculations.

b. Indicate for *each* of the following whether the purchase of the B-32 machine would become more or less desirable. Explain your answer.

1. New labor contract raises wage rates.
2. After-tax minimum acceptable rate of return increases.
3. Demand for product increases, so machine usage is increased to 80,000 units a year.
4. Materials prices increase.

18. Introducing a new product. Early in 1975, the Nonon Company was considering whether to begin the manufacture and sale of a new product. Information on the new product is summarized below:

1. Development costs through the end of 1974 were $80,000. Further development costs of $100,000 in 1975 and $200,000 in 1976 would be required.

2. A manufacturing facility would be built in 1976. The plant would cost $1.2 million and have a life of 25 years. The equipment would cost $2 million and have an average life of 15 years.

3. The estimated price and cost data developed on the new product were:

Sales price per pound	$ 0.90
Variable manufacturing cost per pound	0.40
Variable selling and administrative cost per pound	0.10
Fixed factory cost per year exclusive of depreciation	225,000
Fixed selling and administrative cost per year	150,000

4. The sales forecast for the product was:

1977	500,000 lbs.
1978	1,500,000
1979	2,000,000
1980	2,700,000
1981	3,000,000

5. The plant had a capacity of 3.5 million pounds, but it could readily be increased if the demand should go above that level. It was expected that sales would continue to grow after 1981 at a modest rate. However, a forecast of sales for the first five years was difficult, and forecasting beyond that year was largely guess work. It was therefore decided to make the analyses on the assumption that sales of 3 million units would be maintained through the year 2001.

6. The company is subject to a 50 percent tax rate and has been quite profitable. It uses double-rate, declining-balance depreciation for book and tax purposes.

7. From 1977 to 1981 the expenditures on plant and equipment not included in the above costs were expected to be negligible. From 1982 to 2001, they were expected to be about equal to the depreciation expense which would be maintained at about the 1982 level by these expenditures.

8. Introduction of the new product would require additional working capital totaling $700,000, but not all of this would be necessary immediately. The working capital would be built up according to the following schedule (increments would be required as of the *beginning* of each year):

1977	$200,000
1978	300,000
1979	150,000
1980	50,000

9. In 2001, the plant was expected to be worth $300,000, the equipment $1.4 million, and the working capital the amount invested.

10. The corporation requires a 10 percent return on investment after taxes.

Should the Nonon Company have continued the development of this new product in 1975? (Except for the increments in working capital, all cash flows should be assumed to take place at the *end* of the year.)

23

The Control Process: Standard Costing

ONCE MANAGEMENT HAS ESTABLISHED its plans, it needs to keep informed on the organization's successes and failures in implementing these plans. Providing this kind of *feedback information* is a key accounting responsibility, and the subdivision of managerial accounting that deals with these matters is known as *responsibility accounting*. The purpose of this chapter is to explain how management can use feedback information and how the accountant can generate it.

To avoid unnecessary confusion, we'll concentrate here, very narrowly, on the problems of developing and using feedback data in the control of factory direct labor and direct materials costs. Before doing so, however, let's look briefly at the management process in which feedback information is used.

BASIC ASPECTS OF CONTROL REPORTING

Control reporting is tied closely to the concept of *responsibility*—that is, results should be reported to those executives who are responsible for achieving them. This introduces three questions:

1. What is the responsibility structure?
2. What performance standards should be used?
3. How should deviations from performance standards be used?

697

The Responsibility Structure

The authority/responsibility patterns in an organization are usually drawn in the shape of a pyramid, as in Exhibit 23–1. Each block in this chart represents an executive, and each of these executives is responsible for the use of the resources in that segment. Putting this

EXHIBIT 23–1.   Organization Chart

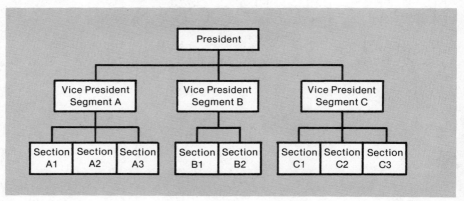

another way, each block represents a *responsibility center*—an organization unit headed by a single person, answerable to higher authority and obligated to perform certain tasks.

The executive in each block is also responsible for the use of resources by the executives in the blocks farther down in the pyramid. The president is responsible for the whole organization. The vice president of segment A is responsible for that segment, including the activities of the people in sections A1, A2, and A3. The manager of section A1 is responsible only for what goes on in that small area. Responsibility centers of the lowest level are known by different names in different companies, *department* being perhaps the most common.

Performance Standards

The purpose of control information is to direct management's attention to situations that aren't what they ought to be or what management expected them to be. This calls for a *performance standard,* defined as a statement of the level of results management regards as appropriate under a specified set of circumstances. It may be stated as a rate per period of time, as a ratio of input to output (or output to input), or as a ratio of one input to another. (An *input* is any material or service used in a process. An *output* is any useful result of a process. Output is also referred to as the amount of *work done*.)

The performance standard for the president's responsibility center is the profit plan, adjusted to allow for changes in economic conditions since the plan was adopted. The profit plan is a poor performance standard for managers at the departmental level, however. Managers at this level aren't responsible for many of the factors that lead actual performance away from planned levels. They do the work assigned to them, and this may be very different from the work loads management anticipated when it drew up the profit plan in the first place. The standards, in other words, have to be adjusted to reflect the tasks assigned to the managers at this level.

Management by Exception

Managers need performance reports for either or both of two reasons. First, they may need reports to keep them informed about what is going on; this is called *attention-directing* information. Second, they may need information to confirm or quantify the effects of events and actions they have observed or taken; information of these kinds is called *scorecard* information.

In either case, management's interest focuses on the *deviations* of actual performance from the standard performance level. A simple exception-based report is illustrated in Exhibit 23–2. Each district

EXHIBIT 23–2. Exception Report: Actual Sales versus Planned Sales

District	Actual Sales This Month	Deviation from Plan (Percent)
Boston	$ 140,000	− 3%
New York	263,000	+ 2
Atlanta	202,000	−11◄—
Pittsburgh	105,000	− 4
Cleveland	306,000	+ 5
Chicago	183,000	+ 3
Minneapolis	58,000 ◄—	+ 1
St. Louis	125,000	−18◄—
New Orleans	95,000 ◄—	− 4
Dallas	274,000	+ 1
Denver	198,000	+ 6
Seattle	102,000	− 7
San Francisco	161,000	+ 1
Los Angeles	423,000	+15◄—
Total	$2,635,000	+ 1%

total less than $100,000 and each deviation greater than 7 percent is highlighted. An explanation of each figure designated by an arrow must be made within three days.

This emphasis on deviations is part of what is known as *management by exception*, which states that management should devote its scarce time only to operations in which results depart significantly from the performance standards. Operations in which results are close to the performance standard are presumed to be under control.

At any given level, the manager needs to divide the deviations from the performance standards into two groups:

1. Those arising from environmental conditions different from those implicit in the standard.
2. Those arising from internal causes.

If the deviations result from environmental conditions, management needs to reexamine its plans. This replanning is an *adaptive response*. For example, if the price of copper falls sharply or fails to rise as rapidly as management had anticipated, a manufacturer of electrical wire may reshape its production and marketing plans to emphasize copper wire instead of aluminum wire.

If the deviations result from internal causes, however, management may decide to find ways of identifying and removing these

EXHIBIT 23–3. Adaptive and Corrective Responses

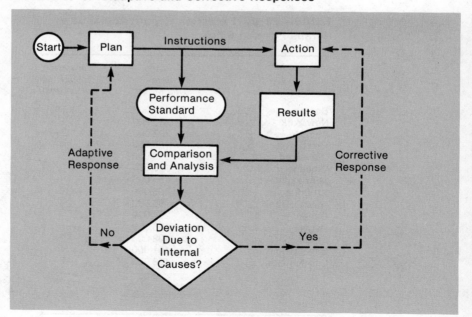

causes. This kind of action is a *corrective* response. For example, low productivity on an assembly line may be due to a high rate of absenteeism, stemming from dissatisfaction with working conditions and a lack of effective managerial leadership. This situation calls for management to decide whether to accept the low productivity—that is, either decide the problem is external and revise the plan accordingly or decide that further investigation and control actions aren't worthwhile—or take action to identify and correct the causes of high absenteeism.

What we're saying is that although a departure from a plan may arise from controllable causes, the cost of finding out what these causes are and how to counteract them may be greater than the reduction in costs or increase in gross margin the corrections would achieve. If so, corrective action is inadvisable.

In Exhibit 23–3, for example, the adaptive response is shown as an instruction to change the plan; the corrective response appears as an instruction to the manager in charge to change the department's action pattern.

STANDARD COSTS

Factory managers have several kinds of performance standards. They have quality standards, safety standards, delivery standards, cost standards, and many others. Their cost standards come from the company's *standard-cost* file. A standard cost is management's estimate, prepared in advance, of the costs of the inputs that should be necessary to obtain a specific material, product, or service. The standard-cost file has three main sections:

1. *Standard prices and labor rates.* These are the prices management estimates should be necessary to obtain a unit of each item of material the company buys and the estimated hourly cost of each class of labor employed in the factory.
2. *Standard operations costs.* These are the quantities of the various inputs management estimates should be necessary to perform each production operation within the factory's capability, multiplied by their standard prices.
3. *Standard product costs.* The quantities of the various inputs that management estimates should be necessary to manufacture units of specific products in specified production lots, multiplied by the standard prices of these inputs.

The most important part of this file for cost reporting purposes is the file of standard product costs. These are embodied in *standard cost sheets*, one for each product or component part. Exhibit 23–4, for example, shows the standard cost sheet for "Door Front No.

Exhibit 23–4. A Standard Cost Sheet

Department	Machining				Quantity	1,000
Description	Door Front No. 6948					
Standard Cost	$457.00			Standard Cost per Unit	$0.457	

Operation or Item	Materials			Labor		
	Quantity	Price	Total	Hours	Rate	Total
Steel Sheet	3,600	$0.08	$288.00			
Cut				4.8	$3.50	$ 16.80
Drill				16.0	3.75	60.00
Stamp				7.3	4.00	29.20
Finish				18.0	3.50	63.00
Total			$288.00			$169.00

6948," a product manufactured by the Landau Company, a small manufacturer of industrial equipment. The first column lists all the items of direct material and all the direct labor operations required in the manufacture of the product. The next three columns contain information on standard materials costs; the final three columns show the amount and composition of standard direct labor cost.

Standard cost sheets also contain information on the standard overhead costs of individual products. Because these play a different role in the cost reporting process, we've omitted them from this exhibit. We'll discuss standard factory overhead costs separately in the next chapter.

VARIANCES FROM STANDARD COST

As we have already pointed out, accounting-control reports emphasize the differences between actual results and the results embodied in performance standards. These differences, or any subdivisions of them, are known as *variances*. For example, the direct labor cost variance is the difference between the actual cost of direct labor and the standard direct labor cost of the work done.

Many events lead to direct materials and direct labor cost variances. Some of these lead the company to use either more or fewer *units* of materials or labor than the standards call for:

The portion of the total variance attributable to these causes is the *quantity variance,* defined as the difference between actual and standard input quantities for the output actually achieved.

Others affect the *prices* the company pays for materials or the *wage rates* of its employees:

> A variance arising in this way is known as a *price variance* or a *rate variance*, defined as the difference between actual and standard input prices for a specified quantity of resource inputs.

In this section we shall see how to (1) calculate quantity variances, (2) measure price variances, and (3) decide which variances to report to management.

Calculating Quantity Variances

Quantity variances are indexes of physical efficiency. They show the relationships between the quantities of resources used and the quantities of the outputs derived from them. Given enough data, we can always measure the quantity variances in physical units.

For example, suppose that combining 1.2 pounds of material *A* with 0.3 hours of labor is expected to yield one unit of product *Y*. This relationship can be expressed in a formula:

$$1.2 \text{ pounds } A + 0.3 \text{ labor-hours} \rightarrow 1 \text{ unit } Y$$

Suppose, further, that on April 18, a batch of ten units of *Y* was produced from 14 pounds of material *A* and required four labor hours. In schematic terms:

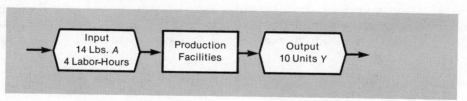

But ten units of product *Y* can also be expressed in terms of their *standard input* content of 12 pounds of *A* (ten times 1.2) and three hours of labor (ten times 0.3). Substituting these equivalents and separating the materials from the labor, we have:

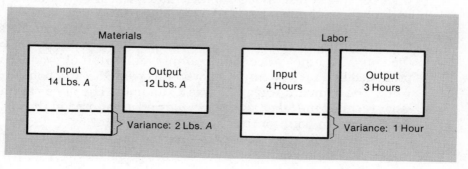

The quantity variances are the differences between actual input quantities (14 pounds and 4 hours) and the standard input quantities for the work that has been done (12 pounds and 3 hours). In this example, the company used more materials (2 pounds) and more labor (1 hour) than the standards called for. These are called *unfavorable* variances. If the actual input quantities had been less than the standard quantities, we would refer to the differences as *favorable* variances.

Although quantity variances represent physical quantities, they are usually measured in dollars. To get these dollar figures, the accountant multiplies the physical quantities by standard prices. If the standard price of material A is $7 a pound, the materials quantity variance can be calculated in dollars as follows:

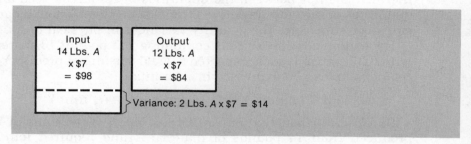

Quantity variances are measured at standard prices rather than at actual prices, first, because standard prices are clerically simpler to use, as we shall demonstrate shortly, and, second, because they make it easier to compare the quantity variances from month to month.

Measuring Price Variances

Direct materials and direct labor cost variances also arise because actual purchase prices or actual wage rates differ from standard prices or wage rates. Since the wage rate is the price of labor services, both of these can be classified as *price variances*.

We generally calculate price variances by multiplying the actual input quantity by the difference between the actual input price and the standard input price. For example, our batch of product Y was produced by a factory employee who was paid $5.25 an hour to do the work. The standard wage rate was $5 an hour. The price variance for labor is called the *labor rate variance* and amounted in this instance to 25 cents an hour for four hours, or $1 in total.

Schematically, the labor variances on this operation can be summarized as follows:

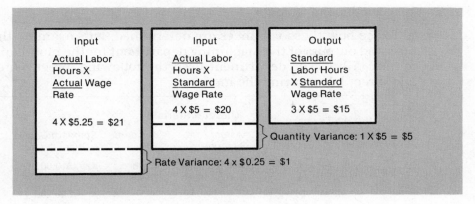

Again the variance was unfavorable in that the company paid more than the standard allowed for.

Variances for Scorecard Reports

In deciding which variances to report to a particular manager, we generally apply the *controllability criterion*—that managers should be assigned only those variances they are expected to control. The managers of production centers are expected to control quantity variances; price variances are usually outside their jurisdiction and, therefore, are not reported to them.

We also have to find out how the manager plans to use the variance information. For example, Landau's factory manager, Mr. A. C. Surrey, needs information on direct labor and direct materials costs in the factory's two production departments (machining and assembly) for one purpose only—to provide a measure of how effectively the department heads have controlled these costs. If one department does well on this score, Mr. Surrey offers praise and encouragement. If costs seem to have gone out of control, he asks for an explanation and a plan to bring them back into line.

For their part, the department heads in this factory don't need accounting reports to tell them when control efforts are needed—they are close enough to their own operations to identify problems as they arise and respond to them. They need reports only as scorecards, to reinforce their motivation to control costs and to indicate how successful their efforts have been.

This means that the company doesn't need to accumulate and report quantity variances in great detail. Instead, variances are calculated monthly, in total for each department. Actual quantities of labor and materials used are classified by department only; no job-order cost sheets are used.

Determining Inputs and Outputs

To see how these variances are determined, let's examine the inputs and outputs of the machining department for the month of September, 19x1. The department used the following direct materials and direct labor during the month:

Direct Materials			
Class of Materials	Actual Quantity	Standard Price	Standard Cost of Quantity Used
A	5,000 lbs.	$2/lb.	$10,000
B	800 units	$54/unit	43,200
Total			$53,200
Direct Labor			
Labor Grade	Actual Quantity	Standard Rate	Standard Cost of Quantity Used
9	1,420 hours	$10/hour	$14,200
7	900 hours	$ 8/hour	7,200
Total			$21,400

Since the quantity variances are to be measured at standard input prices, we don't need to know the actual prices or the actual labor rates of the materials and labor used during the month.

Measuring the department's output is slightly more complicated. The jobs completed by this department during September had a total standard direct materials cost of $57,250 and a standard direct labor cost of $19,400. These figures don't measure the output, however—that is, the standard cost of the work actually done during the month—unless the amount of work in process was the same at the end of September as at the beginning.

Suppose, for example, that the standard materials cost of the work in process at the end of September was $760 greater than the standard cost of materials in process at the beginning of the period. This means that the department accomplished two things:

1. It completed jobs with a standard materials cost of $57,250
2. It added to the standard materials cost of the work in process 760

   Standard Materials Cost of the Work Done during September $58,010

This output calculation is diagrammed in Exhibit 23–5. The blocks at the left of the equal sign represent the total amount of

EXHIBIT 23–5. Output, Product Completions, and Work in Process

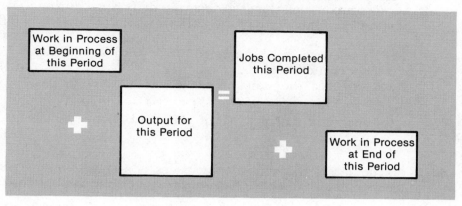

output in the department at some time during the period, including some of the output contributed by last month's operations (opening work in process); the blocks at the right show how much of this output went out of the department and how much remained in process at the end. In this diagram the ending work in process is larger than the beginning work in process—therefore, the *total* amount of work done (the output) is greater than the number of units *completed* during the period.

In standard costing calculations, all of the quantities in this diagram are measured by their standard costs—that is, the standard input quantities multiplied by their standard prices. The equation can be restated as follows:

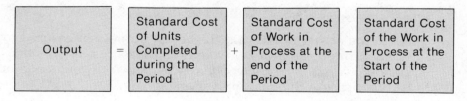

The same calculation can be performed on labor costs. The standard labor cost of the work already done on the work in process at the start of operations on September 1 was $8,500. This figure was obtained by counting the items in process at that time and multiplying the number of units by the standard labor costs of the operations already performed on them in this department. Using the same procedure at the end of the month, the accountants found that the standard labor cost of the work in process at that time was only $7,700, a decrease of $800.

This means that the department's direct labor employees turned out *less* production than the department *finished* during the month. The standard labor cost of the work done was calculated as follows:

1. The department completed work with a standard labor cost of $19,400
2. It reduced the standard labor cost of work in process by .... (800)

Standard Labor Cost of the Work Done during September $18,600

Calculating the quantity variances is a simple matter once the inputs and outputs have been measured in comparable units:

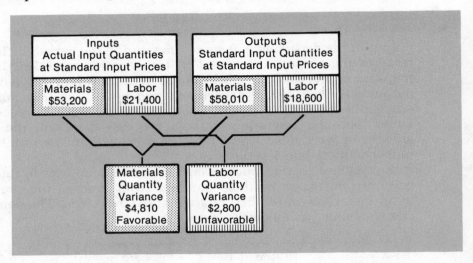

Since the actual inputs and the actual outputs (measured by their standard input quantities) were both measured at the *same* set of standard input *prices,* the differences between inputs and outputs had to measure the quantity variances only.

A STANDARD COSTING SYSTEM

Although standard cost variances can be generated outside the ledger accounts, through calculations like those we have just illustrated, we usually find it more convenient or more economical to tie them into the regular factory cost accounts. This is done by installing and using a *standard costing system,* a set of accounts, procedures, files, and reports incorporating measurements of inputs and outputs at their standard costs.

Standard costing systems differ from each other in many ways. Each has its own distinguishing characteristics; each uses its own account structure to accumulate data. We'll see how one of these, a simple system we call a *basic plan* system, uses accounts to trace the following:

1. Purchases of materials.
2. Issues of direct materials.
3. Direct labor costs.
4. Transfers of completed work.
5. Direct materials and direct labor quantity variances.

Recording Purchases of Materials

Most standard costing systems start with the departmentalization of cost and output data. The Landau Company, for example, has separate work in process accounts and separate output records for each cost element in each of its two production departments. It also has a raw materials inventory account and an account for the finished goods inventory. This makes six factory inventory accounts in all, and these are shown with their September 1, 19x1, balances in Exhibit 23–6.

EXHIBIT 23–6

LANDAU COMPANY
Factory Inventory Account Balances
September 1, 19x1

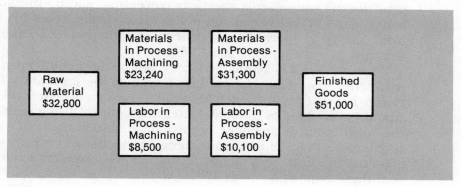

Each inventory in this list is measured at standard cost. Separate work in process accounts are used for labor and materials costs to facilitate the isolation of the quantity variances. (Overhead costs are ignored in this illustration and will be considered in Chapter 24.)

The Landau Company, like other companies with basic-plan standard costing systems, identifies materials price variances when the materials are bought. To accomplish this, it has to reprice each item on each vendor's invoice at its standard cost, obtained from the standard cost file. The difference between this and the actual cost, the amount payable to the supplier, is charged or credited to a materials price variance account.

The actual cost of the materials the Landau Company bought during September was $63,800; the total standard cost of these materials was $60,250. A summary entry covering these purchases is:

(1)

Raw Material	60,250	
Materials Price Variance	3,550	
Accounts Payable		63,800

A debit to the variance account means that the company has had to pay more than the standard cost; by definition, this is classified as an unfavorable variance. A credit to the account is made whenever the goods were acquired at less than standard cost; in other words, it represents a favorable variance.

Recording Issues of Materials

When we studied job-order costing in Chapter 19, we saw that the costs of direct materials were charged both to a work in process account and to individual job-order cost sheets. The Landau Company doesn't use job-cost sheets, however, and doesn't measure the actual costs of individual job orders. It classifies costs by department, not by job, because cost-control activities center on individual departments, not on individual jobs.

When material is requisitioned by one of the manufacturing departments, therefore, the *standard cost* of the quantity issued is charged to that department's Material in Process account; this same amount is credited to the Raw Material account. During September, the machining department requisitioned direct materials with a standard cost of $53,200; no materials were issued to the assembly department during the month. The entry the company made to record these requisitions was as follows:

(2)

Material in Process—Machining	53,200	
Raw Material		53,200

This entry established the machining department's responsibility for these materials.

Recording Direct Labor Costs

Direct labor costs, like direct materials costs, are charged to departments, not to individual job orders. Each department is charged with the direct labor-hours it uses, multiplied by the standard wage rate for each labor grade. Direct labor in the Landau Company's factory was as follows during September:

Pay Grade	Standard Labor Rate	Machining Department		Assembly Department	
		Hours	At Standard Labor Rate	Hours	At Standard Labor Rate
9	$10	1,420	$14,200	—	—
7	8	900	7,200	1,000	$ 8,000
5	5	—	—	2,400	12,000
Total			$21,400		$20,000

These figures were reflected in the following entry:

(3)

Labor in Process—Machining	21,400	
Labor in Process—Assembly	20,000	
Accrued Labor		41,400

The Accrued Labor account is a temporary clearing account. The credit balance in this account after entry (3) was made was a first approximation to the liability arising from the use of direct labor during the month. The company's actual liability, however, was for the actual wages earned by the employees, not the standard rate of pay. This was determined when the payrolls for the period were prepared, reflecting the actual hours worked and the actual wage rate for each employee. The direct labor payroll for the month showed the following:

Pay Grade	Hours	Actual Wages
9	1,420	$14,320
7	1,900	14,100
5	2,400	10,800
Total		$39,220

The Landau Company didn't departmentalize these figures because the department heads didn't need to know the actual wage rates of the workers in their departments. The entry recording the payroll was as follows:

(4)

Accrued Labor	39,220	
Wages Payable		39,220

The credit to Wages Payable recorded the correct amount of the company's wage liability. The debit to Accrued Labor would have returned the balance in this account to zero if actual and standard wage rates had been identical. Because actual rates differed from standard, however, the account had a nonzero balance at the end of the month. This measured the *labor rate variance*.

This can be seen by looking at a schematic representation of this account:

Accrued Labor

Actual hours × actual wage rates 39,220	Actual hours × standard wage rates 41,400

Since the same number of hours appears on both sides of this account, any account balance must be due to differences between the standard and actual wage rates. This account therefore was closed out by entry (5):

(5)

Accrued Labor   2,180

    Labor Rate Variance   2,180

In this case the labor rate variance was favorable (credit balance), indicating that the actual wage rates, on the average, were less than the standard wage rates for the labor used during the month.

Transferring Completed Work

The completion of a production order by a department is evidenced in the Landau Company by a *transfer slip* which identifies the item, the quantity transferred, the department that produced the item, and the department or inventory location to which the item was transferred. These transfers are all recorded at standard cost. The accounting department refers to the standard product cost file to establish the standard labor and material cost per unit. The quantity transferred is then multiplied by these unit figures to establish the relevant totals.

The machining department in the Landau Company's factory transfers part of its completed production to the assembly department; the remainder, consisting of machined parts, is placed in the finished-goods storeroom in the factory. The standard costs of the products completed by the machining department during September were as follows:

	Standard Direct Materials Cost	Standard Direct Labor Cost	Total Standard Cost
To assembly department	$52,050	$16,300	$68,350
To finished-goods storeroom	5,200	3,100	8,300
Total	$57,250	$19,400	$76,650

The transfers from the machining department to the finished-goods storeroom were recorded by the following entry:

(6a)

Finished Goods	8,300	
Materials in Process—Machining		5,200
Labor in Process—Machining		3,100

This reduced the balances in the machining department's accounts and established the accountability of the finished-goods clerk for the parts transferred to that location.

The entry to record the transfers to the assembly department was very similar to entry (6a):

(6b)

Materials in Process—Assembly	68,350	
Materials in Process—Machining		52,050
Labor in Process—Machining		16,300

Notice that the *entire* standard cost of the items transferred to the assembly department was charged to the assembly department as *materials* costs. The reason is that the assembly department regards these items as materials. The assembly manager neither knows nor cares whether labor cost in the machining department amounted to 10 percent or 90 percent of the total standard cost of these materials. If a worker destroys materials by careless handling, the cost of the items lost is part of the materials quantity variance, not partly labor and partly materials.

The assembly department, in turn, completed work on a number of jobs during the month and transferred the finished products to the finished-goods stockroom. We only need to study one department to understand how the basic plan works, however; the remainder of the illustration, therefore, will leave the assembly department alone.

Deriving Quantity Variances

Our last task in basic-plan standard costing is to calculate the quantity variances and remove them from the work in process accounts. Deriving the quantity variances is a three-step process:

1. Calculate the balances in the work in process accounts.
2. List the jobs in process at the end of the period and calculate the standard cost of the work that has already been done on these jobs.
3. Compare each account balance with the standard cost of the work in process; the difference between these two figures is the quantity variance.

For example, after all of the machining department's transactions for the month had been recorded, its Materials in Process account showed the following:

Material in Process—Machining

Bal. 9/1	23,240	(6)	57,250
(2)	53,200		
	76,440		
Bal. 9/30	19,190		

As this shows, the department was responsible for materials with a total standard cost of $76,440. By completing a number of jobs and transferring products to the assembly department or to the finished-goods stockroom, it received credit for $57,250 in standard costs, leaving $19,190 unaccounted for.

The next step was to list the jobs in process at the end of the month and calculate the standard cost of the work done on these jobs before that time. A count of this kind showed that the machining department had the following work in process at the end of September:

Standard materials cost of work in process $24,000
Standard labor cost of work in process   7,700

The differences between these amounts and the account balances measured the quantity variances. For example, the $24,000 standard materials cost of the work in process was $4,810 *greater* than the $19,190 account balance. This shows that the department used *less* direct material than the standards called for; in other words, the materials quantity variance was *favorable*.

We can demonstrate this by treating both the beginning balance and the materials issued to the department during the month as *resources available* and the ending balance and work completed as the *results* of using them:

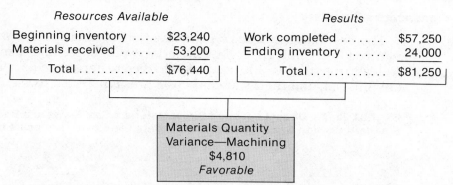

Resources Available

Beginning inventory $23,240
Materials received 53,200

| Total .... | $76,440 |

Results

Work completed $57,250
Ending inventory 24,000

| Total .... | $81,250 |

Materials Quantity
Variance—Machining
$4,810
Favorable

The $4,810 variance is also the amount by which the balance in the work in process account was understated at the end of the month. The following entry served to transfer the variance to its own account and to restore the work in process account to its correct end-of-month balance:

(7a)

Materials in Process—Machining   4,810
    Materials Quantity Variance—Machining   4,810

The credit to the variance account indicated that the variance this month was favorable.

We can analyze the department's labor in process account the same way. The account showed the following figures after the month's transactions were recorded:

Labor in Process—Machining

Bal. 9/1	8,500	(6a)	3,100
(3)	21,400	(6b)	16,300
	29,900		19,400
Bal. 10,500			

To get from the $10,500 balance shown here to the correct balance of $7,700 (revealed by the inventory count we mentioned earlier), the accountants had to make a $2,800 credit to the account:

(7b)

Labor Quantity Variance—Machining   2,800
    Labor in Process—Machining   2,800

This transferred the unfavorable quantity variance from the work in process account to the variance account where it belonged.

Transactions Summary

The cost flows in a basic-plan standard costing system are summarized in Exhibit 23–7. Raw material is purchased and then issued to departments. Labor is used and charged to departments. Products are finished, and their standard costs are transferred to the finished

EXHIBIT 23–7.   Direct Labor and Direct Materials Cost Flows in a Basic-Plan Standard Costing System (departmental detail and overhead costs omitted)

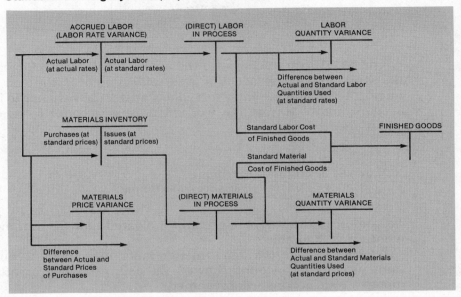

goods inventory account. Finally, variances are computed and transferred to variance accounts.

Summary: Characteristics of the Basic Plan

This brief example illustrates all of the main features of basic-plan standard costing systems:

1. Materials price variances are identified and segregated when the materials are acquired; actual prices don't enter the inventory accounts.
2. Each department is charged with the quantities of the direct labor and direct materials it uses, multiplied by standard wage rates and standard materials prices.

3. Each department is credited with the standard cost of the products it completes during each month.
4. Labor and materials quantity variances aren't identified until the end of the measurement period. At that time the work in process in each department is counted and measured at its standard materials and labor costs; to determine the quantity variances the accountants compare these figures with the balances in the work in process accounts.
5. Little detailed information on the labor and materials quantity variances is available. They are identified as departmental totals for the month as a whole; they aren't calculated for individual job orders or individual workers.
6. All work in process inventory account balances are restated at standard cost at the end of each month.

A standard costing system of this sort won't be good enough if management relies on the system to provide prompt, detailed information on the quantity variances in specific departments. As the fourth and fifth characteristics in the list indicate, the basic plan provides variance information only after the end of a period and then only as departmental totals for the period as a whole. If management wants to rely on its standard costing system to identify problems as soon as they arise and locate them very precisely, it should insist on a more elaborate system.[1]

One unusual feature should be noted. The total materials variance for any given period arises in connection with two different sets of materials quantities. Materials price variances arise from the quantities of materials *purchased* during the period, while materials quantity variances arise from variations in the quantities of materials *used* during the period. In our example:

Materials purchased (at standard prices)	$60,250		Materials used (at standard prices)	$53,200
Materials price variance	(3,550)		Materials quantity variance	4,810

Total Materials
Variance .... $ 1,260

The total labor variance for the period is much more straightforward, because the quantities purchased and the quantities used are identical.

---

[1] A system designed to provide this more detailed information on a timely basis is described in Gordon Shillinglaw, *Managerial Cost Accounting*, 4th ed. (Homewood, Ill.: Richard D. Irwin, Inc., 1977), chap. 20.

PROBLEMS WITH STANDARD COSTING

Standard costing systems may be very useful, but they are not without problems. The three main problems are system cost, the difficulty of developing standards for all operations, and the danger of unfavorable employee reactions to the standards.

System Cost

Standard costing systems can provide useful information, but getting this information may cost more than it is worth. We have already suggested that the cost of preparing detailed engineered cost standards for all products and all operations may exceed the value of the benefits they will generate. Developing standards of this kind also takes time, and management may not be willing to wait a year or more to get the standard costing system going.

One way to get the system going quickly and at a low cost is to develop preliminary standards from historical data already on file. These standards can then be refined as further information becomes available. Variance data in the early periods will be used more to identify standards that may be out of line than to evaluate operating performance.

Operating the standard costing system offers some cost-saving opportunities over historical costing systems, mainly by eliminating the need to use actual materials prices and wage rates to record the use of resources inputs. Individual inventory records can be kept in physical units only—total standard cost can always be calculated by multiplying the physical quantities on hand by their standard prices.

Whether operating costs will be greater or less than in historical costing systems depends in large measure on the kind of standard costing system used. Many systems are designed to provide information frequently and in great detail. These systems tend to be relatively expensive because getting the extra detail calls for a more elaborate data-collecting system.

Since the basic plan is not designed to provide large quantities of steering-control information, it can be justified only if it can be installed and operated at a relatively low cost. Basic-plan systems deliberately sacrifice information in the interest of reducing clerical costs. The main clerical costs peculiar to the basic plan are the costs of recording interdepartmental transfers and the costs of measuring the work in process at the end of each period.

Nonstandard Products

Some portion of each month's output in job-order production is typically of new products or product modifications for which no standards have been set. Most of these are merely new combinations of operations and materials already listed in the standard cost file, and standards can be derived fairly easily. When this is not the case, two solutions are possible. First, new standards might be developed for the new operations. If accuracy is attempted, the establishment of new standards is costly and could even delay production. Using rough approximations avoids these problems but may cloud the meaning of overall departmental variances.

The widely used alternative is to grant actual time allowances for unrated work. Actual costs can be accumulated on time tickets and totaled either for each job order or for each department in total. Job-order totals can be compared with estimates, if desired, but the latter are not used as the basis for departmental reports. Departmental variances, therefore, pertain only to that portion of total production represented by input-rated operations.

Behavioral Problems

Most problems in employee relations under standard costing arise from poor execution or a basic misunderstanding of the system. The purpose of standard costing is to help management control costs, but management may try to use it as a means of inducing employees to reduce costs. Cost reduction is a laudable objective, and it may be achieved as a result of the development of standards, but it is not an automatic result. Cost reduction generally requires methods changes, and it cannot be assumed that employees will change their methods simply because someone tells them that they are not performing up to standard.

SUMMARY

Control reports compare actual results with performance standards. For factory direct materials and direct labor costs, standard costs can be the performance standards. Differences between standard costs and actual costs are known as cost variances, and the accountant uses standard costing systems to generate variance information for management. Variances due to differences between actual and standard input quantities are referred to as quantity variances; price and rate variances reflect differences between actual and standard materials prices or wage rates.

Standard costing systems differ from each other in many ways, but the most significant differences are in when and how variances are isolated. The simplest standard costing systems are basic-plan systems, and the quantity variances produced under these systems are in the form of departmental totals—the differences between the actual quantities of the inputs consumed in the department and the standard input equivalents of the department's actual output in each time period. When these physical quantities are multiplied by standard input prices, the result is the dollar quantity variance that appears on the periodic performance report.

The basic plan is relatively inexpensive. It identifies the departments in which quantity variances occur and provides management with a summary measure of cost-control effectiveness in each department. It is appropriate when the department head relies on the standard costing system for scorecard control information only. Its main weakness is that it fails to provide detailed information from which management can identify the products, operators, machines, or operations in which the bulk of the variances occur. If management needs this information, a more expensive system may be justified.

KEY TERMS

Adaptive response	Quantity variance
Basic-plan standard costing	Rate variance
Controllability criterion	Responsibility
Corrective response	Responsibility accounting
Feedback information	Responsibility center
Management by exception	Scorecard reports
Performance standard	Standard cost
Price variance	Standard costing system

INDEPENDENT STUDY PROBLEMS (Solutions in Appendix B)

1. **Calculating and analyzing labor cost variances.** You have the following information about the operations of department Y during the month of March:

	Product A	Product B
Units finished	5,000	10,000
Units in process:		
March 1	1,000	1,000
March 31	600	1,200
Standard direct labor cost per unit	$2	$1

Products in process on any date are presumed to be half-processed by department Y's labor force.

Direct labor cost in department Y amounted to $23,500 in March. The standard cost of this amount of labor totaled $22,000.

a. Compute the total direct labor cost variance for the month.
b. Analyze this variance in as much detail as you can and clearly label each component that you have identified.

    c. Compute the standard direct labor cost of the inventory in process at the end of the month.

    2. *Calculating and analyzing materials cost variances.* The Hillman Company manufactures a single product known as Quik-Tite. Material A is the only raw material used in the manufacture of Quik-Tite. Transactions in material A for the month of June are as follows:

	Standard	*Actual*
Units of Quik-Tite produced		61,000
Pounds of material A required to produce one		
unit of Quik-Tite	1.6 lbs.	1.5 lbs.
Cost of material A purchases during June	$2.00/lb.	$2.05/lb.
Inventory of material A on June 1		4,000 lbs.
Material purchased during June		95,000 lbs.

Calculate and analyze the materials variances for the month.

    3. *Standard costing system; use of T-accounts.* The Continental Company uses a basic plan system of standard costing. Its factory consists of a single department. Account balances relating to factory materials and labor were as follows on May 1:

	Dr.	*Cr.*
Raw materials	$29,460	
Materials in process	18,400	
Labor in process.......................	9,650	
Finished goods	35,000	
Accrued wages payable		$1,620

The balance in the Finished Goods account represented the labor and materials cost of the goods on hand; overhead costs were accounted for separately and are not covered by this problem. All inventories were measured at their standard cost.

    The transactions for the month were:

1. Material costing $36,500 and with a standard cost of $37,900 was purchased.
2. Material with a standard cost of $41,300 and an actual cost of $40,500 was put into process.
3. Labor used during the month amounted to $28,400 at standard rates.
4. The output transferred out of the department had the following standard costs: material, $42,600; labor, $28,300.
5. Finished goods with a standard labor and materials cost of $79,200 were sold.
6. The standard cost of the work in process at the end of the month was found by physical inventory to be: material, $15,200; labor, $11,000.
7. The wages paid during the month totaled $32,180, and there were no unpaid wages as of the end of the month.

    Open T-accounts for the balances at the start of the month, account for the month's transactions, and make any entries necessary to adjust the inventory accounts to their correct level at the end of the month. Variances should be transferred to a Variance Summary account at the end of the month. Indicate the nature of each variance and state whether it was favorable or unfavorable.

EXERCISES AND PROBLEMS

4. *Supplying missing information.* You have the following data on Goodman Company's direct labor costs:

Standard direct labor-hours	30,000
Actual direct labor-hours	29,000
Direct labor quantity variance—favorable	$ 4,000
Direct labor rate variance—favorable	5,800
Total direct labor payroll	110,200

a. What was Goodman's actual direct labor rate?
b. What was Goodman's standard direct labor rate?

(AICPA adapted)

5. *Calculating departmental output.* Department X completed work during June on 4,300 units of product A and 2,700 units of product B. The standard material and labor costs of these two products were as follows:

	Product A	Product B
Standard materials cost per unit ...	$5	$ 2
Standard labor cost per unit	6	10

The standard costs of the amounts of these two products in process in department X at the beginning and end of June were as follows:

	Product A	Product B
June 1:		
Standard materials cost	$5,000	$1,000
Standard labor cost	3,000	2,500
June 30:		
Standard materials cost	4,000	1,200
Standard labor cost	3,200	3,500

Calculate department X's output for the month, as measured by its standard materials cost and by its standard labor cost.

6. *Recording transactions; basic plan.* The framing department in Scotco's factory receives direct materials from the materials storeroom, processes it, and transfers the processed material to the edging department for further processing.

Each department has two work in process accounts, one for materials costs and one for labor costs. (Overhead costs are ignored in this problem.) The factory has a single control account for its materials inventories; materials purchased are entered in the Materials Inventory account at their standard cost.

The following information includes all the transactions relating to the framing department's labor and materials during the month of August and all purchases and issues of materials during that time:

1. Inventories, at standard cost:

	August 1	August 31
Materials	$500	$525
Materials in process—framing	200	55
Labor in process—framing	100	80

2. Materials purchased for cash: actual cost $300; standard cost $285.
3. Materials issued to framing: actual cost $250; standard cost $260.
4. Labor used in framing and paid for in cash: actual cost $320; standard cost $330.
5. Standard cost of goods finished by framing and transferred to edging: materials, $400; labor, $380.

a. Set up appropriate T-accounts, enter the opening balances, and record the month's transactions.

b. Prepare the necessary entries to transfer the variances to a Variance Summary account; accompany each entry by the name or description of the variance being transferred and indicate whether it is favorable or unfavorable.

7. Sequential standard-costing exercises. Follow the instructions given for each of the four exercises presented below. You should do these exercises in the sequence given.

Exercise A:

Tapscott Enterprises, Inc., reports materials and labor quantity variances to factory department heads each month. One of its departments worked on only two products during January. Its standard inputs and actual outputs were as follows:

	Standard Material Quantity per Unit (Pounds)	Standard Labor-Hours per Unit	Units of Product Manufactured During January
Product A	6	4	2,000
Product B	10	2	3,000

The following quantities of materials and labor were used during January: materials, 44,000 pounds; labor, 13,500 hours.

a. Calculate materials and labor quantity variances for the month in terms of pounds of materials and hours of labor. Indicate whether each variance is favorable or unfavorable.

b. The standard materials price is $3 a pound. The standard wage rate is $5 an hour.
   1. Calculate standard unit cost for each product in dollars.
   2. Restate your quantity variances (from a) in monetary terms.

Exercise B:

Preston Pans, Ltd., manufactures cookware. All of its factory operations are performed in a single department. The department's facilities were used during February to manufacture the following three products:

	Standard Materials Quantity (Pounds per Unit)		Standard Labor-Hours per Unit	Units of Product Manufactured
	Material X	Material Y		
Product A	1	3	1	1,000
Product B	2	1	1	3,000
Product C	3	4	6	2,000

You have the following additional information:

1. Standard materials prices: material X, $2 a pound; material Y, $5 a pound.
2. Standard wage rate: $5 an hour.
3. Direct materials purchased during February:
    Material X: 10,000 pounds, $21,000.
    Material Y: 15,000 pounds, $77,000.
4. Direct material used during February:
    Material X: 12,600 pounds.
    Material Y: 15,000 pounds.
5. Direct labor used during February: 16,800 hours, $80,000.

a. Calculate labor and materials variances, in dollars, in whatever detail you think is appropriate.
b. Indicate to whom each of your variances should be reported.

Exercise C:

Block Houses, Inc., manufactures prefabricated housing modules. The following information was collected for one department for the month of March:

1. Inventory of work in process, March 1 (at standard cost):
    Materials: $28,000.
    Labor: $16,000.
2. Direct materials with a standard cost of $22,000 were received in the department from the storeroom during the month.
3. Direct labor cost for the month was $8,000 at actual wage rates and $7,500 at standard wage rates.
4. The standard cost of products finished and transferred out of the department during the month was as follows:
    Standard direct materials cost: $21,200.
    Standard direct labor cost: $7,800.
5. Inventory of work in process, March 31 (at standard cost):
    Materials cost: $24,000.
    Labor cost: $15,000.

a. Calculate the standard labor and materials costs of the work done during the month.

 b. Calculate the labor and materials variances for the month.
 c. Comment on the department head's cost-control performance during the month.

Exercise D:

Anderson Products Company manufactures two products in a factory with three production centers—the preparing, bonding, and finishing departments. The head of each department is responsible for controlling the quantity of labor and materials used in that department.

Materials are issued from the storeroom to the preparing department. After processing there, they are transferred to the bonding department. After bonding, they go to finishing and from finishing to the finished-goods warehouse. You have the following additional information:

1. Output of the preparing department ("intermediate products") during April:

	Product A	Product B
Standard cost per pound:		
Materials	$2.00	$5.00
Labor	.50	2.00
Pounds transferred to bonding	10,000	15,000

2. Actual unit cost of intermediate product in preparing department during April:

	Product A	Product B
Materials	$2.05	$5.20
Labor	.50	2.10

3. Standard costs per unit in bonding department:

	Product A	Product B
Intermediate product (from preparing department)	1.1 lbs.	1.5 lbs.
Direct labor (standard wage rate, $6 an hour)	0.5 hrs.	0.8 hrs.

4. Direct labor cost in bonding department during April: 13,000 hours, $80,000.
5. Units completed and transferred to finishing department during April:
   Product A: 8,000 units.
   Product B: 10,500 units.
6. Work in process inventories, bonding department, April 1 and April 30: negligible.

Calculate labor and materials quantity variances for the bonding department for the month of April.

8. Calculating and analyzing labor variances. You have the following information for a factory department for the month of September:

1.

	Product X	Product Y
Units finished	2,000	1,500
Units in process:		
September 1	1,000	500
September 30	2,000	800
Standard direct labor cost per unit		
(at $5 an hour)	$20	$30

2. One half of the required departmental direct labor had been performed on each unit in process on the indicated dates.

3. Actual direct labor cost, month of September: 19,000 hours, $100,000.

a. Calculate the standard direct labor cost of the work done in this department during September.

b. Calculate the total direct labor cost variance for the month.

c. Analyze this total variance. Which portion of the variance is likely to be subject to the department head's control?

9. Supplying missing figures. You have the following information on direct labor and materials costs in two factory departments in the month of March:

	Department A	Department B
Actual wage rate	$8.30 an hour	$9.00 an hour
Standard wage rate	?	$9.20 an hour
Actual labor quantity used	9,200 hours	?
Standard labor quantity required by work done	9,600 hours	4,600 hours
Labor rate variance	$2,760 Unfav.	?
Labor quantity variance	?	$1,840 Unfav.
Actual materials quantity used	10,000 pounds	?
Standard materials quantity required by		
work done	?	31,000 gallons
Standard materials cost of work finished and		
transferred out of department	$17,500	?
Standard price of materials	$2 a pound	$5 a gallon
Historical cost of materials	$1.90 a pound	$4.90 a gallon
Materials quantity variance	?	$5,000 Fav.
Materials in process, March 1, at		
standard cost	$12,500	$25,000
Materials in process, March 31, at		
standard cost	$14,000	$23,200

Supply the information missing from these two columns.

10. Preparing a control report. The Neptune Company operates a small factory which makes only one product. Four production operations are necessary, one in each of the factory's four departments. The company's engineers have determined that these operations should require the following labor-hour allowances under normal conditions:

	Labor-Hours per Unit of Product			
	Operation No. 1	Operation No. 2	Operation No. 3	Operation No. 4
Operators...............	1.0	3.0	1.5	0.5
Helpers	0.5	2.5	2.0	0.1
Handlers...............	0.2	0.5	1.0	0.3

Operators are paid $6 an hour, helpers $4 an hour, and handlers $3 an hour. During August, the factory's operations were:

	Operation No. 1	Operation No. 2	Operation No. 3	Operation No. 4
Units produced	2,000	1,800	2,100	2,000
Labor-hours:				
Operators.............	1,100	5,200	3,400	980
Helpers	550	4,600	4,600	190
Handlers.............	210	1,000	2,200	610

a.   Prepare a report for management, summarizing labor operations for the month in terms of both hours and dollars, and write a brief paragraph commenting on the effectiveness of labor control during the month.

b.   What advantages, if any, do you see in including dollar figures on this report? Explain.

11.   **Report format; interpreting the variances.**   The following materials and labor cost-variance report was prepared for a factory during July:

	Material		Labor	
Raw material inventory, July 1	$10,000		$ —	
Work in process inventory, July 1	4,000		4,500	
Materials purchased during July	24,000		—	
Labor used during July	—		45,000	
Total Cost to Be Accounted For		$38,000		$49,500
Raw material inventory, July 31	$ 8,000		$ —	
Work in process inventory, July 31	3,000		3,750	
Goods completed during July	29,000		44,700	
Total Cost Accounted For		40,000		48,450
Variance		$ 2,000		$ (1,050)

Additional data were as follows:

Materials purchased during July:
   At actual cost......................... $24,000
   At standard cost 26,400
Materials used during July:
   At standard cost 28,400
Labor used during July:
   At actual cost......................... 45,000
   At standard cost 44,250

a.   Compute the price and quantity variances for materials and labor.

b.   Suggest ways to improve the format of the variance report that is presented to the factory manager each month. What purpose would this report serve?

c.   What action would you recommend as a result of the information revealed by your analysis of variance? The action might be to acquire certain additional information; in that case assume the necessary facts and then state what action should be taken on the basis of these facts.

12.   T-accounts; evaluating the system.   The Jiffy Dinner Company manufactures 15 types of frozen dinners. A standard menu priced at predetermined food prices, labor rates, and standard processing times for each operation is the basis for a standard cost system in which the entire plant is treated as one department.

Work in process is small and subject to little fluctuation from one month to the next. Therefore, to avoid the job of counting and costing it, the in-process inventory is assumed to be the same and equal to the following amounts at the end of each month:

Food, trays, and so forth in process	$18,000
Labor in process	3,000

Actual overhead is charged to expense each month and is not included in product cost. The cost of goods and services purchased for factory use is credited to Accounts Payable; the cost of labor services used is credited to Accrued Wages Payable as the work is performed.

The relevant factory account balances on April 1 were as follows:

Cash	$34,000
Raw food and supplies	33,000
Food, trays, and so forth, in process	18,000
Labor in process	3,000
Frozen dinners	67,000
Accrued wages payable	1,800
Accounts payable	28,000

The transactions for the month were as follows:

1.   Food and supplies purchased: actual cost $73,000; standard cost, $70,300.
2.   Direct labor cost: at standard wage rates, $26,400.
3.   Payrolls paid, $25,000; accrued wages as of the end of the month, $1,300.
4.   Actual overhead costs incurred, $42,000, including $4,000 of supplies at standard prices.
5.   Food, trays, and other direct material transferred out of the storeroom: standard cost, $63,000.
6.   Standard cost of frozen dinners produced:

Food, trays, and so forth	$60,200
Direct labor	27,500
Total	$87,700

7. Standard cost of dinners sold: $115,000.

a. Open T-accounts for the opening balances, account for the above transactions, and transfer all variances to the Cost of Goods Sold account. Identify and label each variance.

b. How would the cost of goods sold have been different if the company had measured its inventory on a Fifo actual-cost basis?

c. Is a system of this kind likely to provide management with information that is detailed enough to be useful? What conditions must be present to justify an affirmative answer to this question?

13. Using T-accounts. A factory has two production departments and a basic-plan standard costing system. The inventories on May 1 had the following standard costs:

Raw materials	$40,000
Department A:	
Materials in process ...., ...	10,000
Labor in process	6,000
Department B:	
Materials in process	8,000
Labor in process	9,000

The following transactions took place during May:

1. Raw materials purchased: standard cost, $25,000; actual cost, $25,800.
2. Materials issued (at standard cost):
   To department A, $12,000.
   To department B, $15,000.
3. Direct labor cost (at standard wage rates):
   Department A, $11,000.
   Department B, $17,000.
4. Actual direct labor payroll for the month, $30,100.
5. Products completed by department A (at standard cost):

	Materials	Labor
Transferred to department B for further processing	$ 8,600	$5,800
Transferred to finished-goods storeroom	4,700	3,400
Total	$13,300	$9,200

6. Products completed by department B and transferred to finished-goods storeroom (at standard cost): materials, $28,200; labor, $15,800.
7. Work in process inventories on May 31, at standard cost:

	Materials in Process	Labor in Process
Department A	$9,000	$7,000
Department B	9,000	8,000

a. Enter the opening balances in appropriately titled T-accounts, record the transactions, and make the necessary adjustments to restore the account balances to their correct May 31 levels.

b. Prepare a summary of the variances for the month.

14. *Determining and reporting variances.* Tufwun Products Company manufactures a limited line of machined products in its Albany factory. A basic plan of standard costing is in use at the factory, with materials inventories being carried at their standard prices. The following information pertains to the operations of the Milling Department for the month of September:

1. Direct labor in the department is divided into three pay grades, as follows:

Grade	Standard Wage Rate per Hour
101	$ 7
102	8
105	10

2. Wages actually earned by employees differ from these standard rates due to seniority provisions. Actual hours worked and actual gross pay during the month were as follows:

Grade	Hours	Gross Wages
101	1,250	$ 9,050
102	1,500	12,150
105	1,520	15,100
Total	4,270	$36,300

3. Production and product cost standards for the month:

	Standard Materials Cost per Unit	Standard Milling Department Labor per Unit 101 Hours	102 Hours	105 Hours	Standard Labor Cost	Units Produced, September
Product						
A	$ 6	0.5	1.0	—	$11.50	400
B	12	1.0	0.5	1.5	26.00	800
C	15	0.5	1.0	0.5	16.50	600

4. Direct materials costs charged to the department, at standard prices, $22,800.
5. The department had no unfinished work in process either at the beginning or at the end of the month.

a. Analyze the department's cost variances in September and prepare a summary for the factory manager's use in evaluating the department head's effectiveness in controlling costs.

b. If you identified any variance that wouldn't enter into the evaluation of the department head's performance, indicate who might be interested in it and for what purpose?

c. Under what circumstances would the department head need more information than this system provides? What kinds of additional information would be required, and what would have to be done to provide it?

24

Control of Overhead Costs

WITH THE GROWTH of automation in the factory and the growing importance of the service sector of the economy, factory direct labor and materials costs account for an ever smaller percentage of total business costs. The problem of controlling overhead costs, both inside and outside the factory, therefore assumes greater and greater significance. The purpose of this chapter is to see what techniques might be useful in the control of overhead costs and how these tie into the accounting system. Our discussion is divided into five parts:

1. The distinction between supportive and discretionary overhead costs.
2. Controlling discretionary overhead costs.
3. The flexible budget as a performance standard.
4. Analyzing factory overhead cost variances.
5. Behavioral issues in cost control systems.

SUPPORTIVE VERSUS DISCRETIONARY OVERHEAD COSTS

Overhead costs can be divided into two broad classes: supportive overheads and discretionary overheads. Supportive overhead costs are the overhead costs of the responsive activities we identified in Chapter 19. They are incurred to enable the organization to fill demands that are placed on the system from outside. Like direct

731

labor and direct materials, they are volume-determined—that is, they are necessary to service the volume of orders that have entered the system. Factory rent, factory supervision, and the costs of preparing customers' invoices are examples of supportive overheads.

Discretionary overheads are the costs of programmed activities. They are incurred to secure some future benefit or to meet some independent objective set by management. In this category we have such costs as advertising, research, contributions to charitable organizations, and management consultants' fees.

CONTROLLING DISCRETIONARY OVERHEAD COSTS

Most of our discussion in this chapter will focus on supportive overheads, partly because accounting techniques are more fully developed for these and partly because the profit-reporting systems we'll discuss in Chapter 25 focus on certain kinds of discretionary activities. To put this material in perspective, however, we need to see in general terms how management can use accounting information at two stages of the process of controlling discretionary overheads:

1. In planning discretionary activities.
2. In responding to subsequent events.

Planning Criteria

Discretionary costs are fixed costs—by definition, since only costs that vary in response to volume changes are variable costs. This being the case, most of the decisions that determine the level of discretionary costs are made when the budget is established. People are hired, commitments are made, and orders are placed on the strength of budget authorizations.

This means that the most crucial control process for discretionary overheads is budget review and approval. The basic criterion underlying these decisions is the cost-benefit criterion: do the anticipated benefits justify the cost? For major self-standing activities, such as new product development projects, approval often comes in two stages, as diagrammed in Exhibit 24–1. The project is reviewed initially as part of the regular budgetary planning process. If it passes muster at that time, it is incorporated in the budget. Much can happen between the date the budget is approved and the date the first commitment of resources is made, however. Management is likely to take advantage of any additional information generated during this

EXHIBIT 24–1.   Two-Stage Approval Process for Product-Development Projects

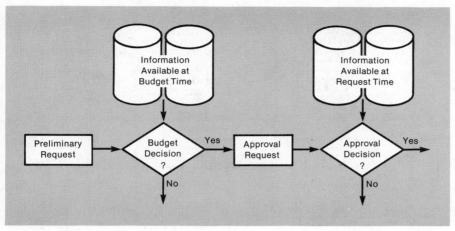

period before making the final decision to go ahead with the project or put it on the shelf.

Feedback Reporting

Feedback reporting is no less important than budgetary planning in the control of discretionary overhead costs. First, although these are fixed costs, they do change in response to the decisions management makes about the activities they support. Reporting the costs and benefits from these activities calls management's attention to situations that may call for replanning. Second, even without any change in management's plans, actual expenditures may deviate from the fixed budgets. Feedback reports call such deviations to management's attention.

Discretionary or programmed activities are of many types, each calling for its own reporting structure. Most of these, except marketing which we'll review in Chapter 25, are similar in structure to product-development activities. The key to feedback reporting in product development and in similar types of discretionary activities is to break the overall objective down into a number of identifiable subobjectives—cost can then be compared with the amount of cost management planned to incur to achieve each of these subobjectives.

The breakdown of a simple project might take the form illustrated in Exhibit 24–2. This shows a project that was started on March 1 and scheduled for completion on October 31 of the same year. Each of the circles in this diagram represents a significant *milestone*

EXHIBIT 24–2.   Project Milestones and Budget Allowances

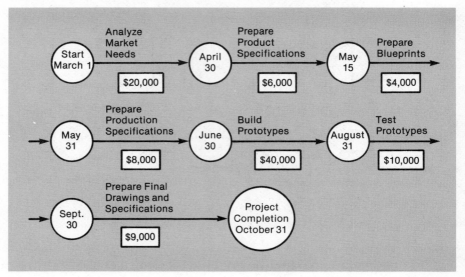

along the road to the completion of the project. The arrows between milestones represent *activities,* each with its own budgeted cost. Most of the activities, in turn, can be further subdivided into sub-activities and intermediate milestones if management wants this additional detail.

In this case, the analysis stage proceeded as planned and was completed on April 30 at a cost of $19,500. Snags were encountered in the development of product specifications, however, and this activity wasn't completed until May 31, at a cost of $12,000. Our first inclination might be to prepare a cost report comparing the amount spent ($31,500) with the amount originally budgeted for March, April, and May ($20,000 + $6,000 + $4,000):

	Actual Expenditures	Budgeted Expenditures	Expenditure Variance
March–April	$19,500	$20,000	$ 500
May	12,000	10,000	(2,000)
Year to Date...............	$31,500	$30,000	$(1,500)

Unfortunately, management wouldn't find this report very useful. The reason: the budget figures in this table were based on the expectation that the third milestone would be reached by the end of May. The company actually reached only the second milestone in this period. The budget, in other words, ought to be cut back to $26,000, the amount planned for the first two activities. If this is done, we'll have the following report:

	Actual Cost	Budgeted Cost	Cost Variance
Analysis	$19,500	$20,000	$ 500
Product specifications	12,000	6,000	(6,000)
Total to Date	$31,500	$26,000	$(5,500)

This is an activity-centered report, showing clearly that the company has spent $5,500 more to do the work than it had planned to, a signal of a serious cost overrun on this project.

This cost overrun is much more significant than the $1,500 over-spending shown in the first report. It's easy enough to keep spending close to the amount budgeted—even if salary rates go up, for example, management can hold to the budget by using fewer people. The really important question is whether management got as much for its money as it had bargained for.

To implement this approach, management has to divide the over-all project into activities, each with its own budget estimate. Reports then can be issued either when key milestones are reached or periodically, at the end of each month or quarter. These reports require the following:

1. Accumulate costs by project, using some form of job-order costing.
2. Record each milestone as it is passed and estimate any progress that has been made toward the next milestone as of the date of the report.
3. Estimate the amount of cost budgeted for the amount of progress made during the period.
4. Compare actual costs with budgeted costs for the progress that has been achieved, explaining major variances whenever possible.

Reports of this kind focus exclusively on the past. Because discretionary activities can always be discontinued if the anticipated costs exceed the perceived benefits, a strong case can be made for incorporating revised forecasts of future costs and completion dates in the reports. Management can then decide whether to continue the project and, if so, whether to increase or decrease the rate of spending to advance or defer the estimated completion date.

CONTROLLING SUPPORTIVE OVERHEAD COSTS

Supportive overheads are similar to factory direct labor and direct materials in that they are incurred to enable management to service the sales or production orders that are presented to it. They differ in other respects, however, and these differences call for a separate structure of feedback information. We'll examine five questions:

1. What performance standards are appropriate.
2. How the performance standards should be developed.
3. What form the overhead cost reports should take.
4. How the controllability criterion can be applied.
5. What role interdepartmental cost allocations should play.

To keep the chapter from getting too long, we'll restrict ourselves to a discussion of factory overhead costs, leaving nonmanufacturing supportive overheads to more advanced texts.

Performance Standards: The Flexible Budget

Except in special circumstances, the performance standard for direct labor and direct materials costs is determined by multiplying the number of units produced in the period by the standard cost per unit. This implies that direct materials and direct labor costs will be strictly proportional to volume as long as they are kept under control.

The standard cost of a unit of product usually includes a provision for standard overhead cost, too. For example, suppose the overhead rate is $5 a direct labor-hour and the standard direct labor time for product X is two hours a unit. The standard overhead cost for a unit of this product, therefore, is $10. This figure is totally unaffected by the number of hours actually used to manufacture the product.

We can't use this standard cost as a performance standard, however, mainly because overhead costs are partly fixed. For example, multiplying standard overhead cost by the number of units produced gives us the dashed line in Exhibit 24–3, labeled "Standard Overhead Cost." A performance standard drawn from this line at a low volume of 2,000 units a month (point P) would be too tight because more overhead is required to support this volume, as the solid line shows. By the same token, the standard overhead cost figure will be too lenient a performance standard at any volume in excess of 2,500 units a month, such as point M. Volumes in this upper portion of the range require less overhead than the standard product cost implies.

Our conclusion from all this is that we need to prepare not one performance standard but a series of them, one for each possible level of operating volume. This series of standards is known collectively as the *flexible budget*. The applicable performance standard in any given period is the specific budget for the level of output achieved in that period.

An example of a flexible budget is shown in Exhibit 24–4. This shows the overhead budget for the molding department in the Lester

EXHIBIT 24–3. Standard Overhead Cost as a Cost Control Standard

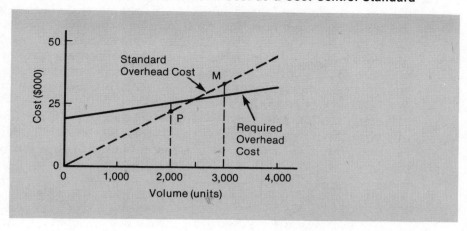

Plastics Company's factory. This department consists of 60 injection molding machines and certain auxiliary equipment. It has a department manager, two general supervisors, one for each of the two shifts it operates, and two section chiefs, each responsible for supervising the operation of the department's manual machines on one shift. Supervision of the automatic machines is performed directly by the general supervisor. In addition, the department has a maintenance supervisor to keep the machines in operation and a material control supervisor to keep the machines supplied with material and to inspect and move the finished product out of the molding room.

EXHIBIT 24–4

LESTER PLASTICS COMPANY, MOLDING DEPARTMENT
Overhead Budget

Item	Monthly Fixed Cost	Variable Cost per Standard Machine-Hour
Indirect labor:		
Supervision	$ 8,400	x
Floor service	x	$0.37
Maintenance service	1,600	0.07
Material control and testing	1,000	0.02
Idle time	x	0.04
Overtime premiums	x	0.05
Other direct charges:		
Employee benefits	2,200	1.11
Indirect materials	800	0.28
Machine setup	1,500	0.05
Power	x	0.09
Depreciation	700	x
Allocated service department costs	3,200	x
Total	$19,400	$2.08

The first column of Exhibit 24–4 lists the categories into which the department's overhead is classified; the second column shows the monthly fixed cost for each of these overhead items; and the third gives the variable cost per hour of machine operation. Standard machine-hours were selected as being the most accurate measure of production, because the number of standard machine-hours is the most important determinant of how much factory overhead cost is necessary.

Notice that a linear cost-volume relationship is assumed in this case, as it was in Exhibit 24–3—that is, the cost budget can be represented on a chart by a straight line, fitting a formula of the form:

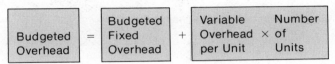

As Exhibit 24–4 shows, the department's estimated fixed costs amount to $19,400 a month, while its variable costs total $2.08 per standard machine-hour. The total budgeted overhead cost at any level of output for any month is found by substituting the number of standard machine hours required by the department's output for the month in the equation,

$$\text{Budgeted Overhead} = \$19,400 + \$2.08 \times \text{Standard Machine-Hours}$$

and solving for budgeted cost.

Although it is almost always used for simplicity in textbook illustrations, the straight-line budget is not necessarily applicable in all cases. Budgeted overtime premium, for example, could be zero for all volumes up to 10,000 standard machine-hours a month, 50 cents an hour for the next 5,000 hours, and then $1.50 a hour for all hours in excess of 15,000. The flexible budget allowances should conform to the anticipated facts and need not be squeezed out of shape to conform to some universally applicable formula.

Choosing a Measure of Volume

Throughout this discussion, we have used standard machine-hours as the basis for calculating the flexible budget allowances. This is appropriate if overhead costs correlate more closely with standard machine-hours than with any other measure of volume. The number of standard machine-hours is a measure of *output*, in that it is unaffected by variations in the number of machine-hours actually used per unit of output. It is quite possible, however, that overhead will depend more on the number of input units actually used than on the output of the period. If so, the actual input quantity should be used to calculate the flexible budget allowances.

For example, suppose the overhead costs in the molding department vary with the number of machine-hours actually used. The budget formula for indirect materials costs is:

Indirect Materials Cost = $800 + $0.28 × Machine-Hours

If the department uses 13,800 machine-hours, its flexible budget for indirect materials costs should be $800 + $0.28 × 13,800 = $4,664, no matter how many standard machine-hours its output in that month calls for.

Sources of Budget Estimates

A variety of information sources are used to develop the flexible budgets for individual departments. The primary source is managerial experience, the block at the left in Exhibit 24–5. The operating

EXHIBIT 24–5. Sources of Flexible Budget Data

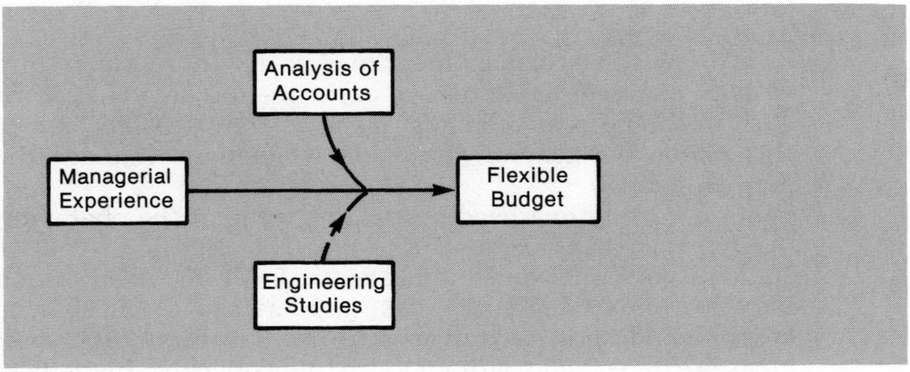

managers are likely to know their operations better than anyone else, and their estimates of their needs for indirect labor, services, and supplies are likely to be a good place to start.

Even the experienced manager is likely to need data of some sort to help quantify the qualitative impressions left by past experience. The most valuable data are likely to come from the company's historical records. The manager can often classify many costs as essentially variable or essentially fixed; past data can provide the basis for estimates of average variable cost or for the monthly amount of fixed costs.

This kind of inspection of historical data can be supplemented in some cases by statistical analyses of the same data. Mathematical equations can be solved, for example, to find a line to describe the relationship between cost and volume in the observations represented by the dots in Exhibit 24–6.

EXHIBIT 24–6.   Line of Relationship Fitted to Historical Observations

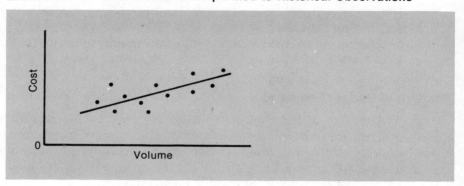

In a few cases, management may be able to rely on a third source of data, engineering studies of experimental data. Experimentation with overhead cost relationships is seldom feasible, however, and this approach is generally used only when major changes in methods are being made.

Many factory overhead costs have some of the characteristics of discretionary overheads. This is particularly true of staff activities such as personnel and industrial engineering. Neither analysis of historical cost records nor time studies can establish what these costs should be at any given volume. Substantial increases or decreases can be made without any really noticeable immediate effects on the factory's ability to meet delivery schedules efficiently.

The source of information for these costs is management. As we pointed out earlier, management must decide what it wants to achieve. It must try to appraise the benefits of such things as personnel management programs and decide how large an effort it wishes to make in each area. Once this has been done, historical analysis or discussions with authoritative personnel can be used to try to determine reasonable cost allowances to achieve management's objectives.

Departmental Feedback Reports

Although preparation of the flexible budget has merit for its own sake, the primary payoff comes in periodic cost-performance reporting. Some overhead cost reports are issued daily; some weekly, and some at longer intervals. A month is the typical reporting period for the main departmental cost summaries.

The monthly overhead cost summaries consist of *comparisons* of the actual costs for the month with the budget allowances appropriate to the volume actually achieved during the month. For example, the report shown in Exhibit 24–7 was issued to the head of the mold-

EXHIBIT 24–7

LESTER PLASTICS COMPANY, MOLDING DEPARTMENT
Overhead Cost Report

MONTHLY COST SUMMARY

Department Molding

Month October

Volume this month 14,300 standard machine-hours

Item	Budget	Actual	(Over) Under
Indirect labor:			
Supervision	$ 8,400	$ 8,524	$ (124)
Floor service	5,291	6,156	(865)
Maintenance service	2,601	3,081	(480)
Material control and testing	1,286	1,145	141
Idle time	572	899	(327)
Overtime premiums	715	1,293	(578)
Other controllable direct charges:			
Indirect materials	4,804	4,500	304
Machine setup	2,215	2,179	36
Power	1,287	1,240	47
Total Controllable Costs	$27,171	$29,017	$(1,846)
Noncontrollable costs:			
Employee benefits	18,073	19,806	(1,733)
Depreciation	700	705	(5)
Allocated service-department costs	3,200	3,200	
Total Department Overhead	$49,144	$52,728	$(3,584)

ing department, covering this department's operations for the month of October. During this month, the department operated at a volume of 14,300 standard machine-hours. This figure, applied to the budget formulas of Exhibit 24–4, provides the budget allowances shown in the "budget" column of Exhibit 24–7. Except for the allocated service-department costs, the costs in the "actual" column are those which were recorded in the departmental accounts on the basis of requisitions, time tickets, and the like.

The differences between actual costs and the flexible budget allowances are most commonly referred to as *spending variances,* although other terms such as *budget variances* and *performance variances* are also used.

The Controllability Criterion

The structure of the report in Exhibit 24–7 is another application of the controllability criterion we described in Chapter 23. Variances the manager can't control are listed, but they are shown "below the line," in a section clearly labeled "noncontrollable." An alternative that many prefer is to eliminate these noncontrollable items from the departmental reports altogether.

The only major spending variance classified here as noncontrollable is in employee benefits, accounting for almost half of the overhead spending variance in October. Employee benefits costs arise from the use of direct as well as indirect labor. The variance is controllable, but only as a by-product of actions to control the use of labor time, not by separate actions focused on benefits alone. Reporting these costs as a separate item, as Lester Plastics does, is a common practice, but it is selected for convenience rather than for managerial relevance. A much better approach is to include provisions for benefits in the rates at which labor time is charged to the department.

Exhibit 24–7 also illustrates another application of the controllability criterion. Several of the items classified as controllable are wholly or partially fixed. The department uses substantial quantities of indirect materials, for example, even when production volume is very low. The manager is expected to be just as economical and careful in the use of these materials as in the use of materials to facilitate increases in production volume.

Interdepartmental Cost Allocations

The final item in Exhibit 24–7 was for allocated service-department costs. Management may choose to allocate these costs for any of four reasons:

1. To measure the costs of individual products by the average costs actually incurred during the period instead of by predetermined overhead rates or standard costs.
2. To provide a record of the amount of service consumed by individual departments for use in later decisions on proposals that, if accepted, would affect service consumption.
3. To reflect each manager's effectiveness in controlling the amount of service used.

4.   To make managers aware of costs incurred elsewhere to support the operations of their departments.

Only the third of these reasons calls for showing a service variance in the controllable section of the report.

Management need make no monthly allocations at all if none of the four purposes listed above is important. The product-costing objective can be met by including provisions for service costs in predetermined overhead rates, using the methods we described in Chapter 20. If management chooses to make monthly allocations, however, it has four main choices:

1.   Charge a flat amount each month, fixed in advance.
2.   Charge a flat rate per unit of service.
3.   Charge a flat rate per unit of activity in the departments receiving the service.
4.   Charge a varying rate per unit of service or per unit of activity in the departments receiving the service, each month's rate calculated so as to distribute the service department's full cost that month.

If the allocation is for control, a flat-rate per unit of service should be used. Variations in the amount charged then will reflect variations in the quantity of service consumed, not variations in the average cost of providing it. The managers of the departments using the service may be able to control the amount of service used, but they have little influence over its average cost.

The Lester Plastics Company used a set of flat monthly charges. As a result, the allocation was not only shown below the line, as a noncontrollable item, but the charge was exactly equal to the amount budgeted at the start of the year. When allocations are made on this basis, the amounts charged to other departments will differ from the costs of the service center itself. Suppose, for example, that a scheduling department charges other departments a total of $9,000 each month. During September, the department incurred $9,420 in costs. A summary T-account for the department would show the following:

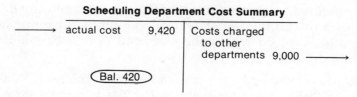

Scheduling Department Cost Summary

→ actual cost	9,420	Costs charged to other departments	9,000 →
Bal. 420			

In other words, predetermining the amount other departments were charged for scheduling services left $420 of this department's costs unallocated. This is the service department's counterpart of the underabsorbed production department overhead we encountered in Chapter 20. It can be analyzed by the methods we'll describe in the next section.

Following Up the Reports

Cost reports of this type are only the first step in effective responsive control. Although the advantage of the flexible budget is that it adjusts the cost standard to current volume conditions, it can't allow for changes in other factors such as wage rates, purchase prices, or manufacturing methods. Furthermore, management may deliberately incur excessive costs when volume is changing rapidly, to avoid even greater cost penalties in future periods.

The issuance of the report should be followed, therefore, by an attempt to identify the causes of major deviations. Whenever the deviations are unfavorable and the causes are controllable, corrective action should be initiated; other portions of the deviation are likely to call for replanning the future.

VOLUME VARIANCES IN FACTORY
OVERHEAD COSTS

Most factory costing systems are integrated into the company's regular historical accounting records. In these, as we saw in Chapter 20, the factory is charged for its actual overhead costs and is given credit for the amounts charged to individual products, referred to as *absorbed overhead*. The difference between total overhead cost and the amount of overhead absorbed is known as the *total overhead variance*.

Spending variances account for only part of the total. The purpose of this final section is to bridge the gap between the spending variance and the total overhead variance in a factory which uses standard overhead costs on a full-costing basis.

Calculating the Overhead Variance

In a standard costing system the total overhead cost charged to individual products (absorbed) is the predetermined overhead rate times the number of standard labor-hours, machine-hours, or other input factor on which the overhead rate is based. In the molding department:

1. The overhead rate was ($19,400 + $2.08 × 20,000)/20,000 = $3.05 a machine-hour at the department's normal volume of 20,000 standard machine-hours.

2. The department's output in October was equivalent to 14,300 standard machine-hours.
3. The amount of overhead absorbed was $3.05 × 14,300 = $43,615.

The department's actual overhead cost in October was $52,728, as we saw in Exhibit 24–7. The total overhead variance, therefore, was $43,615 − $52,728 = $9,113 and was unfavorable (see Exhibit 24–8).

EXHIBIT 24–8. Derivation of Total Overhead Variance

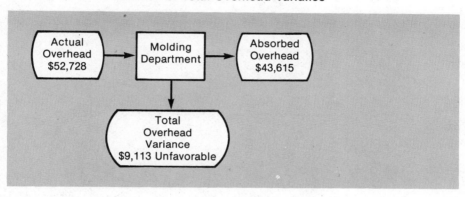

Reasons for the Overhead Variance

The total overhead variance, also referred to as the amount of overhead over- or underabsorbed, arises mainly as a result of two forces:

1. *Spending* variations: actual costs differ from the amounts that would normally be expected at the production volume actually achieved during the period.
2. *Volume* variations: production volume during the period differs from the volume used in setting the overhead rate.

We know from the monthly overhead cost report (Exhibit 24–7) that $3,584 of the total overhead variance in October was accounted for by spending variances; the remaining $5,529 was the overhead *volume variance,* attributable to the difference between the 20,000-hour normal volume and the 14,300-hour actual volume for the month.

The explanation is quite simple. The amount of fixed overhead absorbed in a full absorption costing system is proportional to volume. The overhead rate in this case included 97 cents to absorb fixed costs. This figure can be calculated from the data in Exhibit 24–4:

$$\frac{\text{Total Fixed Cost}}{\text{Normal Volume}} = \frac{\$19,400}{20,000 \text{ Standard Hours}} = \$0.97 \text{ a Standard Hour}$$

If volume had reached 20,000 standard hours, then all the budgeted fixed costs would have been absorbed, as Exhibit 24–9 shows. In

EXHIBIT 24–9. The Overhead Volume Variance

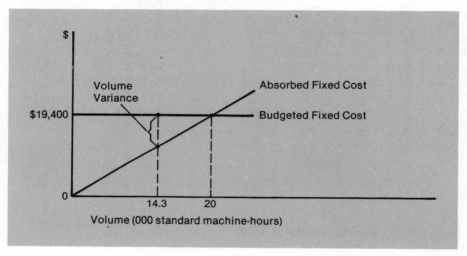

stead, actual volume was 5,700 standard machine-hours less than normal. This means that the fixed costs that would have been absorbed by these 5,700 hours had no place to go, no product to absorb them. Low volume, therefore, accounted for $5,700 \times \$0.97 = \$5,529$ of the unabsorbed fixed overhead. We call this a volume variance.

Interpreting the Volume Variance

The volume variance must be interpreted carefully. It does not mean that costs were $5,529 greater than expected because volume was lower than normal. It merely says that no production was available to absorb $5,529 of the costs that were expected to occur. Expressed differently, $5,529 was spent to provide production capacity the company did not use.

The department heads don't establish their own production schedules. The volume of activity is determined outside the factory, on the basis of the number of customer orders in hand or anticipated. This being so, volume variances are not controllable by the department head or even by the plant manager. They should be reported to plant managers only to help them explain the total overhead variance to higher management, and they shouldn't be reported to the department managers at all.

Reconciling the Variances

The overall variance computation can be summarized in the following manner:

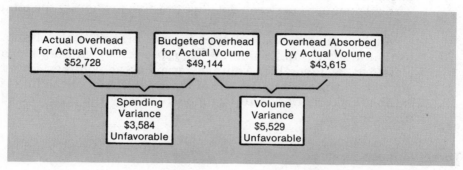

Exhibit 24–10 presents this same information in graphic form. This is like Exhibit 24–9 except that it includes the variable over-

EXHIBIT 24–10. Overhead Cost Variances

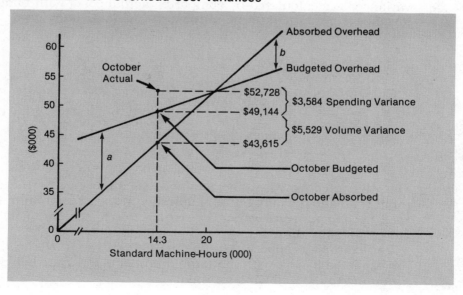

head costs as well as the fixed overheads. The amounts of overhead absorbed are shown by the height of the straight line rising from the lower left-hand corner of the chart. The amounts budgeted are shown by the height of the other line. Because some of the department's costs are fixed, this line has a gentler slope than the Absorbed Overhead line. Variable costs in this case are proportional to volume—$2.08 in budgeted variable costs for each standard machine hour—and thus the flexible budget is shown as a straight line.

The amounts budgeted and absorbed at this month's volume of 14,300 standard hours are shown as large dots on these two lines. The actual amount spent is shown by another dot. By measuring the vertical distances between dots, we are able to identify the total variance and its two components parts.

Volume variances at volumes in excess of normal volume, such as that marked *b* in Exhibit 24–10, represent overabsorption and are classified as favorable. Volume variances at volumes lower than normal, in the zone to the left of the intersection of the lines in the exhibit, represent underutilization of capacity and are referred to as unfavorable.

Three-Variance Analysis

The division of the total overhead variance into spending and volume components is appropriate only if overhead costs are expected to vary with *standard* inputs, in this case standard machine-hours. If overhead costs vary with *actual* inputs, however, the spending variances are calculated by comparing actual costs with budget allowances appropriate to the number of inputs actually used:

Spending Variances if Overhead Costs Vary with Actual Inputs	*Spending Variances if Overhead Costs Vary with Standard Inputs*
Actual Costs—Budgeted Costs Appropriate for Actual Input Quantities	Actual Costs—Budgeted Costs Appropriate for Standard Input Quantities

The difference between the total budget allowance at the actual input level and the total budget allowance at the standard input level then becomes a third variance, attributable to the company's efficiency in using these inputs.

For example, suppose the molding department's overhead costs are expected to vary with the actual number of machine-hours used, according to the following formula:

> Total Overhead Cost = $19,400 + $2.08 × Actual Machine-Hours

This means that every time the department saves a machine-hour, it ought to be able to save $2.08 in overhead costs. In October, the department saved 500 hours, because it used only 13,800 machine-hours instead of the 14,300 hours allowed by the standard costs of the work done during the month. Efficiency in machine usage, in other words, reduced the allowed amount of overhead cost by 500 × $2.08 = $1,040. We call this a *machine efficiency variance*. (When volume is measured by the amount of direct labor, we refer to this variance as a *labor efficiency variance*.)

This new variance fits into the total overhead variance as shown in the following diagram:

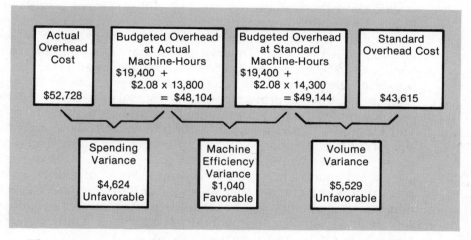

The volume variance is the same as in the two variance system, but the spending variance is different. The difference lodges in the new third variance, the machine efficiency variance. The sum of the spending and machine efficiency variances is equal to the spending variance in a two-variance system.

BEHAVIORAL ISSUES IN COST CONTROL SYSTEMS

The technical problems encountered in the design and use of standard costs and flexible budgets for the control of overhead are small in comparison with the behavioral or human relations problems in employing such systems to aid management control in large organizations. Solutions to these problems are often elusive, and in any case space does not permit discussion of more than a few of them. We shall give brief attention to five questions:

1. How can the accountant deal with shared responsibility for cost control?
2. Do budgets serve automatically as operational objectives?
3. What is the role of participation in the budgeting process?
4. How far down in the organization should budget responsibility be pushed?
5. What problems can be created by poor system administration?

Identifying Cost Responsibility

Assigning costs to organizational units whose managers are responsible for controlling them is not as easy as we may have implied. A cardinal rule in management is that department heads can't be held responsible for personnel not under their supervision or for material or services they haven't requisitioned. For example, if workers and material under the supervision of Jones are used to provide a service used by Smith, Smith can't be held responsible for the cost of providing the service. Smith may be held responsible for the usage of the service, but the primary point for control of the cost is Jones.

One problem is that actual authority and responsibility relationships typically depart in significant respects from those embodied in the formal organization structure. This can't be blamed on management incompetence in establishing the organization structure. Organization charts are a gross oversimplification of reality. Even the plant manager has more than one boss, and to represent the connection between a staff worker or a department manager and other personnel in a company, one would have to draw a number of lines upward, laterally, and at various angles.

Given this, it is especially important for all levels of management to recognize that (1) department managers aren't *solely* responsible for the costs assigned to them and (2) they aren't *without* responsibility for these costs. Once these points are recognized, it should be a simple matter to recognize that budgetary control systems should be used more to identify problem areas and effective actions than to assign absolute credit or absolute blame.

Budgets as Operational Objectives

Responsibility accounting is built on the assumption that management at all levels will strive to reach or surpass budgeted performance levels. In this view, the budget identifies the goals of the organization and establishes a standard of performance which everyone will attempt to achieve.

Not everyone in a company is automatically motivated to achieve budgeted goals. The goals may or may not be shared by particular individuals, since individuals' goals are based on their own needs, and achieving budgeted performance may make little or no contribution to the satisfaction of these needs. Individuals for whom this is true don't accept or *internalize* the budget. Their aspiration levels are below the levels required by the budget and it doesn't motivate them. By contrast, when managers internalize the budgets for their departments, they accept the organization's goals; we may say that *goal congruence* has been achieved.

Goal congruence is the most critical behavioral problem that management faces in the budgetary process. The prospect of promotion, incentive pay schemes, participation in setting the budget, and other means are employed to bring about goal congruence. Aspiration levels differ among individuals, however. Some value the "good life" and the approval of their subordinates more than organizational success. Policies that achieve goal congruence for one individual may not succeed for another. Changes in operating conditions or in a person's thinking as time goes by may influence his or her aspiration level. This makes it difficult to use aspiration levels as the basis for performance standards.

Participation

One way to get subordinate managers to internalize performance standards is to have them participate in setting the standards. Participation means that decisions are, to some extent, joint decisions of the managers and their superiors. It doesn't mean that both must be in full agreement on every decision, but the subordinates must be convinced that they are given a fair shake.

Participation doesn't automatically insure the internalization of performance standards. The gap between the individual's goals and those of the organization may be too great to be bridged. Furthermore, conditions may be such that a more authoritarian managerial style will be more effective in raising the aspiration levels of subordinates. Even so, participation may be very useful. First, it can be used to strengthen the bonds among the members of the group by providing more effective communication. Second, it can increase the visibility of the progress that each member of the group is making toward internalization of organizational goals. The first of these increases the desire of individuals to share the goals of others in the group; the second increases their ability to do this.[1]

Level of Budgetary Control

Another behavioral issue is how far down in the organization structure cost control responsibility should be pushed. For example, Lester Plastics Company's molding department could be treated as a single responsibility center or as four separate responsibility centers, one for each machine group in each of the two shifts the factory is operating. The choice between these two alternatives depends on answers to two questions:

1. Does the department head's day-to-day contact with the supervisors provide adequate control over their areas, or is control and cost consciousness better served by putting each of the four supervisors in direct contact with the budget?
2. Can the supervisors operate from a budget, or is their ability limited to dealing with people and material—that is, do budgets confuse and frighten them?

Since the variation in costs with output may differ between the two machine groups, or even between the two shifts of one machine group, budgets on the supervisory level may make better bench marks for control. Certain manufacturing costs, however, such as the costs of the department's maintenance staff, are common to the whole department. To push control responsibility down to the supervisory level, the maintenance force would either have to be split into four groups, which might not be economical, or would have to remain the responsibility of the department head in a separate cost center of its own. If costs of this kind are substantial, the overhead costs directly chargeable to each supervisor and not common to the whole department may not be important enough to warrant the additional bookkeeping and other costs necessary to bring the budget down to that level.

System Administration

Behavioral problems are sometimes created or enhanced by the ways in which control systems are administered. One factor may be that budget administrators regard their jobs as purely technical and are insensitive to the needs of the line executives. As a consequence they may create defensiveness, hostility, and conflict.

Another factor may be that higher management may misuse the

[1] For a further examination of these and related issues, see Edward E. Lawler III and John Grant Rhode, *Information and Control in Organizations* (Pacific Palisades, Calif.: Goodyear Publishing Co., 1976).

budget, regarding it as a device to exert pressure on subordinates. The result is likely to be increased tension, interdepartmental warfare, resentment, and a good deal of other counterproductive behavior. The problem is a confusion of cost control with cost reduction. Cost control is the process of achieving planned performance under existing conditions; *cost reduction* is a process by which the underlying conditions of production are changed. Unless management recognizes the differences between these two processes, it will have difficulties with its budgetary control system.

SUMMARY

Control of overhead costs, both in and out of the factory, can be even more important than control of factory direct labor and direct materials. For control purposes, overheads can be divided into two broad categories—discretionary costs and supportive costs. Supportive costs are made necessary by production orders or sales; discretionary costs are incurred to obtain sales orders or to achieve other benefits or objectives that are technologically independent of current volume levels.

Controlling discretionary costs is largely a matter of cost-benefit analysis, an essential ingredient of the budgetary planning process. This should be followed up by a system of feedback reporting that relates costs incurred to the amount of progress achieved toward the goals of the programs.

Control of supportive overheads requires the estimation of standard input/output relationships. Because many overhead costs are fixed in the short period, different input/output ratios are appropriate at different volumes. The set of alternative overhead budgets for different volume levels is known as the flexible budget. Differences between actual overheads and the flexible budget allowances for the volume actually achieved are known as spending variances. Most of the remainder of the total overhead variance arises from the existence of fixed costs and the use of predetermined overhead rates at nonstandard volumes; it is called a volume variance. In some cases a third variance arises, representing the effect on overhead cost of a variance in the input factor on which the flexible budget allowances are based; depending on the nature of the input factor, this variance is called a machine efficiency variance, a labor efficiency variance, or a materials efficiency variance.

Use of standard costs and budgetary controls may increase or even create behavioral problems in the organization. Care must be taken to avoid misuse of the systems and to try to induce managers at all levels to internalize standards that represent good organizational performance.

KEY TERMS

Cost overrun	Milestones
Cost reduction	Participation
Discretionary overhead	Programmed costs
Flexible budget	Spending variance
Goal congruence	Standard overhead cost
Labor efficiency variance	Supportive overhead
Machine efficiency variance	Volume variance

INDEPENDENT STUDY PROBLEMS (Solutions in Appendix B)

1. Calculating and analyzing factory overhead variances. The Cotton Company uses a standard costing system and develops volume and spending variances in its overhead costs. You are given the following information for one of the company's factory departments:

1. The opening balance in Overhead in Process was $6,680.
2. The actual overhead for the month was $17,400.
3. The overhead budget was $4,680 a month plus $1.15 per standard direct labor-hour.
4. The normal level of production was 9,000 standard direct labor-hours.
5. The department worked 10,800 direct labor-hours during the month.
6. The standard labor content of the products completed and transferred out of the department during the month was 10,500 hours.
7. The standard labor content of the work in process was 4,000 hours at the start of the month and 3,600 hours at the end.
8. Overhead costs are expected to vary with output rather than with actual direct labor-hours.

a. Calculate the standard overhead cost of the work done in this department during the month.

b. What was the standard overhead cost of the work in process at the end of the month?

c. Develop the department's overhead spending and volume variances for the month.

2. Variances in allocated costs. A service department's budget includes the following summary figures:

$$\text{Budgeted costs} = \$3,000/\text{month} + \$7 \times \text{service-hours}.$$

Normal volume is 3,000 service-hours a month.

The flexible budget for production department X allows for the use of 100 service-hours a month and the manager is expected to control the department's usage of this service.

During August the service department provided 2,400 service-hours to other departments at a cost of $22,000. Department X used 95 service-hours this month.

a. How much service-department cost should be charged to department X for the month of August?
b. What variance in service-department costs should be reported to the manager of department X?
c. What can you say about the cost performance of the service-department manager during the month?

3. Cost performance reporting: supportive overheads. The Riptide Company uses full-cost overhead rates and departmental flexible budgets for cost reporting. The fiscal year is divided into 13 "months" of four weeks each. Department T has a normal production volume of 4,000 direct labor-hours a month and the following flexible budget, valid for volumes between 3,000 and 4,500 direct labor-hours a month:

	Fixed per Month	Variable per Direct Labor- Hour
Nonproductive time, machine operators	—	$0.25
Other indirect labor	$2,000	0.50
Operating supplies	—	0.15
Depreciation	2,000	—
Rent	700	—
Total	$4,700	$0.90

Actual costs and volumes in two successive months were as follows:

	Month 4	Month 5
Direct labor-hours	4,000	3,000
Nonproductive time	$ 800	$1,200
Other indirect labor	3,700	3,600
Operating supplies	650	430
Depreciation	2,100	2,150
Rent	770	730

a. Calculate budget allowances and prepare a cost performance report for each of these months. This report should include each of the five overhead cost elements, arranged in any way you find appropriate.
b. Comment on the various items in these reports, indicating which items are likely to be of greatest significance in evaluating the cost-control performance of the department supervisor.
c. Looking only at those items for which cost performance was poorer in month 5 than in month 4, what would be your reaction to the statement that the manager of this department had been lax in enforcing cost control during month 5? What remedial action would you suggest, if any?
d. Calculate the volume variances for these two months. What is the significance of the volume variance? Would it have arisen if the company had been using variable costing?

EXERCISES AND PROBLEMS

4. Discussion question: communicating with managers. "What do you mean, I'm over my budget?" said Bob Dietz, shop supervisor. "It says right here in the annual budget that my regular monthly indirect labor allowance is $3,300. I didn't make up the budget; you did. I only spent $3,200, so where do you get off telling me I'm $200 over? Maybe it's those birds up in the · accounting department, fouling me up again."

a. As Dietz's boss, how would you explain the situation to him? Was he right? Should he have had an allowance of $3,300?
b. If Dietz is typical of the shop supervisors, what do you think should be done to strengthen the factory's overhead cost-control system?

5. Calculating departmental volume. A standard costing system is used. The department's overhead cost budget is based on standard labor-hours. Normal volume for the department is 20,000 standard labor-hours a month, and the overhead rate is $3 a standard labor-hour. Overhead cost fluctuations correlate more closely with product output than with direct labor input.

During the month, 21,300 actual labor-hours were used. The department finished and transferred to other departments products with a standard overhead cost of $69,000. The standard departmental overhead cost of work in process was $16,200 on the first of the month and $18,000 at the end of the month.

Calculate the number of hours on which the flexible budget allowances for the month should be based.

6. Variance calculation exercise. Overhead costs in one of the Bastian Corporation's factory departments are expected to total $8,000 a month plus $1.40 per standard direct labor-hour. The normal level of output is 11,000 standard direct labor-hours a month.

During the month of June, the actual overhead costs were $22,100, and the actual level of activity was 9,300 standard direct labor-hours.

a. Establish a standard overhead rate for the department.
b. Calculate the volume and spending variances for the month.
c. Using T-accounts, show how these facts would be reflected in the factory accounts.

7. Variance calculation exercise; reporting to management. A standard costing system is in use, and standard factory overhead cost is $2 per standard direct labor-hour. Overhead costs vary with the number of standard direct labor-hours, according to the following formula:

Budgeted Costs = $11,000 per Month + $0.90 per Standard Direct Labor-Hour.

Actual overhead costs for October totaled $22,140, and 11,200 direct labor-hours were recorded. Product standard costs and actual production volumes for October were:

Product	Standard Overhead Cost per Unit	Units Produced, October
A	$ 5	100
B	6	500
C	10	1,000
D	3	1,200
E	2	2,000

a. Compute the total overhead variance, an overhead spending variance, and an overhead volume variance for the month. Indicate in each case whether the variance is favorable or unfavorable.

b. How, if at all, should the volume variance be reported to management? To what management level would you report it?

8. Performance reporting: discretionary overheads. A research plan called for the expenditure of $48,000, to be spread evenly over a six-month period. At the end of two months, $16,200 had been spent, the project was one quarter complete, and management estimated that the project would be completed successfully seven months after it was begun, at a total cost of $60,000.

a. Present a brief financial report to the project manager's immediate superior, highlighting the financial performance of the project team.

b. What responses might management take in this situation? What criteria might it use in choosing among these? What data might it reasonably ask for to aid in this choice?

9. Service department variances. Cardwell Company has its own management consulting department which provides advisory services to other departments within the company. It charges the other departments for its time at a predetermined hourly rate equal to its estimated average cost at normal volume. You have the following information:

1. In a normal month, the department provides 500 hours of service. Its costs are entirely fixed and are budgeted at $8,000 a month.
2. The quality control department's budget for June included a provision for 30 hours of management consulting services.
3. The management consulting department's costs amounted to $8,400 in June. The department provided 525 hours of service during the month, including 25 hours to the quality control department.

a. Calculate the amount of cost charged by the management consulting department to the quality control department and to all other departments combined in June.

b. Calculate the total variance for the management consulting department in June and break it down into its component parts.

c. Calculate the quality control department's variance in management consulting service charges for the month of June. What does this variance mean?

10.   Supplying missing information: two-variance analysis.   Manchester Tool Works has a standard costing system. Variable factory overhead costs in each department vary with departmental output, measured by the number of standard direct labor-hours. You have the following data for two departments for the month of June:

	Department S	Department T
Standard overhead rate per standard direct labor-hour	?	$4.50
Actual direct labor-hours	1,900	4,500
Standard direct labor-hours (June)	1,800	?
Standard direct labor-hours at normal volume	?	4,000
Budgeted fixed cost	$5,000	?
Budgeted variable overhead cost for each standard direct labor-hour	$1	$2.50
Actual overhead cost	$6,700	$20,300
Standard overhead cost	?	$21,600
Overhead spending variance	?	?
Overhead volume variance	?	?
Total overhead variance	$400 unfavorable	?

Make the necessary calculations and supply the information missing from this table.

11.   Supplying missing information: three-variance analysis.   Dorset, Inc., has a factory with 15 production departments. A standard costing system is in use. The following data apply to two factory departments during the month of May:

	Department A	Department B
Standard overhead rate per standard direct labor-hour	$?	$8
Actual direct labor-hours (May)	2,200	?
Standard direct labor-hours (May)	2,000	5,500
Normal volume (standard direct labor-hours)	2,500	?
Budgeted fixed overhead cost	$10,000	$25,000
Budgeted variable overhead cost for each actual direct labor-hour	$2	$3
Total overhead variance	$3,000 unfavorable	?
Overhead spending variance	?	?
Overhead labor efficiency variance	?	$900 favorable
Overhead volume variance	?	?
Actual overhead cost	?	$42,000
Standard overhead cost of actual work done	?	?

Make the necessary calculations and supply the information missing from this table.

12.   Interpreting changes in average overhead cost.   The Dearborn Company manufactures product X in standard batches of 100 units. A standard cost system is in use. The standard costs for a batch are as follows:

Direct materials—60 pounds at 45 cents a pound	$ 27.00
Direct labor—36 hours at $2.15 an hour	77.40
Overhead—36 direct labor-hrs. at $2.75 an hour	99.00
Total Standard Cost per Batch	$203.40

Dearborn's normal monthly output is 240 batches (24,000 units). Factory fixed costs are budgeted at $4,752 a month.

The Dearborn Company's management is worried by the size of the factory overhead costs, which make up almost half of the standard costs of product X. Accordingly, when the actual average overhead cost for April fell to $2.60 per actual direct labor-hour, management felt somewhat encouraged.

Actual production in April amounted to 210 batches. Actual overhead cost totaled $20,592. Variable overhead costs vary with the number of standard direct labor-hours.

a.   Should Dearborn's management be encouraged by the reduction in average overhead cost? Prepare an analysis of the overhead costs in April that will help management understand the causes of the reduction.

b.   Would average overhead cost per direct labor-hour be a useful index of production efficiency for the factory manager? For the president? Comment.

13.   Labor and overhead variance exercise.   The data below relate to the month of April, 19x1, for Marilyn, Inc., which uses a standard costing system:

Actual total direct labor cost	$43,400
Actual direct labor-hours used	14,000
Standard direct labor-hours allowed for good output	15,000
Direct labor rate variance—unfavorable	$ 1,400
Actual total overhead cost	$32,000
Budgeted fixed overhead costs	$ 9,000
Normal volume in standard direct labor-hours	12,000
Total predetermined overhead rate per standard direct labor-hour	$2.25

Variable overhead costs are expected to vary with departmental output, measured by the number of standard direct labor-hours.

a.   Calculate the direct labor quantity variance for the month and indicate whether it was favorable or unfavorable.

b.   Calculate the spending variance for the month and indicate whether it was favorable or unfavorable.

c.   Calculate the volume variance and indicate whether it was favorable or unfavorable.

(AICPA adapted)

14.   Service department cost allocations; effect of using actual average costs.   Department X is a factory service department. It provides labor services on request to all other factory departments.

Department X's flexible budget for overhead costs is $5,000 a month plus $4 per hour of service provided to other departments. Its normal volume is 5,000 hours a month.

Department A is a factory production department. Its normal monthly volume is 20,000 machine-hours. Its flexible budget includes a provision for department X services: 100 service-hours a month plus one hour for every 50 department A machine-hours.

Each month, the factory accountants find department X's actual cost per service-hour. Department A is then charged for its use of department X by multiplying this actual unit cost by the number of department X hours used in department A during the month.

During the month of June, department X recorded 4,500 hours, of which 500 were charged to department A. Operating costs in department X for the month totaled $24,300. Department A recorded 20,500 machine-hours during the month.

a.   What purpose, if any, is served by allocating service-department costs to other departments? Is this likely to be a valid purpose in this case?

b.   Develop a department A budget formula from which flexible budget allowances, in dollars, can be derived for department A's consumption of department X services.

c.   Compute the amount of department X cost charged to department A for the month of June and compare this with the flexible budget allowance for department A derived from (b) above.

d.   Analyze the costs of department X and explain the reasons for the deviation between the allocated and budgeted cost.

e.   Suggest a way or ways by which the company's interdepartmental service-cost allocation method could be improved.

15.   Analyzing, reporting, and interpreting overhead variances.   The Tumbler Company uses a system of departmental flexible budgets to provide overhead cost-control information for its factory department managers. The machining department of this company's factory assigns overhead to products by means of an overhead rate of 78 cents a machine-hour. The monthly flexible budget for the machining department is as follows:

	Volume (Machine-Hours)				
	10,000	12,000	14,000	16,000	18,000
Supervision	$ 1,900	$ 1,900	$ 1,900	$ 2,200	$ 2,200
Indirect labor	2,000	2,200	2,400	2,600	2,800
Supplies	500	600	700	800	900
Payroll taxes	1,210	1,430	1,660	1,930	2,210
Overtime premiums	50	70	220	400	1,000
Depreciation	800	800	800	800	800
Floor space charges	3,000	3,000	3,000	3,000	3,000
Engineering services	600	650	700	750	800
Total	$10,060	$10,650	$11,380	$12,480	$13,710

During May, this department operated at a rate of 16,000 machine-hours and was charged the following amounts:

Supervision	$ 2,500
Indirect labor	2,710
Supplies	720
Payroll taxes	2,000
Overtime premiums	900
Depreciation	850
Floor space charges	2,700
Engineering services	820
Total	$13,200

The following additional information is available:

1. The departmental supervision account is ordinarily charged for the straight-time wages earned by assistant supervisors. Although these assistant supervisors are paid on an hourly basis, they usually work a full workweek. When the department head deems it necessary, a senior machinist is given additional supervisory duties, and a proportional part of that person's wages is charged to the supervision account.

2. The plant manager assigned a quality-control supervisor to this department for one week during May to assist the department manager in the production of a long run of parts with very tight specifications. The departmental supervision account was charged $330 for the supervisor's services during this period.

3. The indirect labor account is charged for the wages of departmental materials handlers and helpers and also for the nonproductive time of machine operators. During May, machine operators were idle for approximately 100 hours because of machine breakdowns and delays in receiving work from other departments. The account was charged $420 for this idle time. The indirect labor budget figure includes an allowance for such costs in the amount of 1 cent per machine-hour.

4. Departments are charged for payroll taxes on all departmental wages, both direct and indirect. Payroll taxes are charged to the departments at a predetermined rate per labor-dollar. This rate is not changed during the year.

5. Overtime work in each department is scheduled monthly by the production scheduling department, on the basis of scheduled production for the month. The department manager's primary responsibility is to meet the production schedule and may use whatever amount of overtime premium is necessary to accomplish this objective.

6. The depreciation charge is computed monthly on the basis of the original cost of the equipment located in the department as of the first day of the month.

7. Floor-space charges are computed monthly by multiplying the number of square feet of floor space occupied by each department by the average cost of building depreciation, insurance, utilities, and janitorial and maintenance services for that month.

8. Engineering services are provided to production departments by the factory engineering department. These services consist primarily of methods studies prepared at the request of the plant manager or on the initia-

tive of the chief engineer. The charge for these services is based on a predetermined rate per engineering-hour.

a. What is the normal operating volume for this department?

b. Compute the total overhead variance for this department for the month of May.

c. Prepare an analysis of the May overhead variance in as much detail as possible. Indicate what you would report to the department manager and why. Prepare a report for the department manager to show the format that you would use.

d. Would the figures for May seem to warrant any action by the department manager? By anyone else? Explain.

25

Reporting Profits to Management

THE PERFORMANCE REPORTS in most organizations can be arranged in pyramids. By far the largest number of reports are likely to be directed at the activities of managers at relatively low levels—factory department heads, sales branch managers, research project directors, and so forth. Because these managers' responsibilities are generally limited to the performance of single functions—manufacturing, sales, research, and so forth—the reports at this level are narrow in scope.

Managerial responsibilities broaden at higher levels of the organization, and the periodic performance reports, therefore, are larger in scope than those below them in the pyramid. In business organizations, the principal performance reports at higher managerial levels are profit performance reports because profit is the primary measure of business success. The purpose of this chapter is to see how internal profit reports can be used and how they may be constructed and interpreted.

PURPOSES OF INTERNAL PROFIT REPORTING

The basic unit for profit performance reporting is the *business segment*, defined as any group of current revenue-generating activities management chooses to identify. Companies are likely to recognize two or more kinds of segments. For example, a company may group its products into several product lines, each with its own reported profit; at the same time, it may also recognize as segments

763

the individual geographical regions the company operates in or the different industries it serves or both.

Although ultimate profit responsibility rests with top management, at least some of this responsibility is usually shared with managers at lower levels. Profit reports to these subordinate managers have two main purposes:

1. To reinforce their motivation by keeping them informed on the effectiveness of their efforts to generate profits.
2. To direct their attention to aspects of their operations in which special problems or opportunities have arisen.

For example, the monthly profit report may tell a branch manager that the branch has been generally successful in generating profits but that two sales territories have fallen far below the performance level they should have reached. The report of overall success should help maintain the manager's motivation or commitment to profit-oriented activity; the detailed segment information should lead the manager to devote time to finding out what went wrong in the low-yield territories and taking whatever action seems called for.

Higher management's interest in internal profit reports is similar but somewhat broader. At the very top, management is likely to use these reports in three ways:

1. To evaluate the profit-generating performance of subordinate managers (*managerial evaluation*).
2. To evaluate the profit-generating performance of the resources invested in individual segments (*investment evaluation*).
3. To evaluate the methods used to generate profit in individual business segments (*operations evaluation*).

The reports are also intended to give top management the same kind of motivational reinforcement they are designed to provide at lower levels.

PROFIT REPORTING FOR OPERATIONS EVALUATION

The most fundamental use of internal profit reports is to provide profit-responsible executives with information they can use in improving their effectiveness in generating profits for the company. Four aspects of profit reporting for this purpose deserve discussion at this time:

1. Measuring profit contribution.
2. Reporting segment investment.
3. Analyzing profit variances.
4. Choosing the segment structure.

Measuring Profit Contribution

The profit report for any given business segment should identify the amount the segment has contributed to total company profit. The question is how this contribution is to be measured.

Most reporting systems use one of the following two definitions: (1) profit contribution and (2) net profit. The relationship between these two measures is illustrated in Exhibit 25–1. We start with the

EXHIBIT 25–1. Contribution Margin, Profit Contribution, and Net Profit

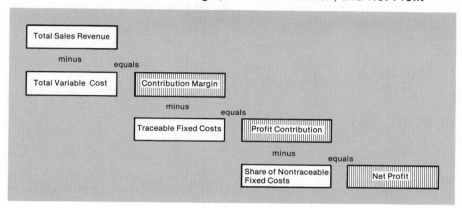

contribution-margin figure we introduced in Chapter 19, the revenues of the segment less the variable costs occasioned by these revenues. To get profit contribution, we subtract the fixed costs traceable to the segment. Finally, if we want to calculate a net profit figure for the segment, we deduct a pro rata share of the fixed costs we can't trace specifically to any individual segment.

Exhibit 25–2 shows how the profit-contribution concept may be used in reporting segment profit to the top management of a simple, two-segment firm. Separate columns are provided for each of the firm's two business segments: regular products and custom products. The top half of the statement summarizes the revenues and variable costs for each segment. Custom products, for example, had variable costs of $476,000, or 75.6 percent of the revenues for this segment. This left only $154,000 in contribution margin and a contribution-margin ratio of 24.4 percent, about half the margin obtained from the company's regular products.

The next two lines show the amount of fixed costs specifically traceable to the individual segments, leading to the profit-contribution figures on the line below. Other fixed costs, much larger in total, were not distributed between the two segments—that is, net

EXHIBIT 25–2

SADDLER PRODUCTS CORPORATION
Product Profit-Contribution Statement
For the Month of March, 19x1
(000 omitted)

	All Products	Regular Products Amount	Regular Products % of Net Sales	Custom Products Amount	Custom Products % of Net Sales
Net sales	$3,495	$2,865	100.0	$630	100.0
Standard variable costs:					
Factory	$1,910	$1,456		$454	
Order filling	115	93		22	
	$2,025	$1,549	54.0	$476	75.6
Contribution margin	$1,470	$1,316	46.0	$154	24.4
Product-traceable fixed costs	195	148	5.2	47	7.4
Profit contribution	$1,275	$1,168	40.8	$107	17.0
Common fixed costs:					
Factory	318				
Selling and administrative	624				
Income before Tax	$ 333				

income was calculated and reported only for the company as a whole. *Under the profit-contribution approach, company net income is the sum of the segment profit contributions, less the total of the fixed costs not traceable to individual product-line segments.* This set of relationships is diagrammed in Exhibit 25–3.

To move from profit contribution to net income for individual segments, we have to find some way of allocating the common fixed costs shown at the bottom of Exhibit 25–2. An ideal solution would be to allocate to each segment the amount of fixed costs the company could eliminate if it were to withdraw from that segment. To try to approximate this, we might subdivide the common fixed costs into groups, each of which has its own set of determinants, and then allocate the costs in each group to the segments in proportion to the segments' shares of these determinants. The cost of office space in a company's headquarters, for example, might be divided among the company's divisions in proportion to the amount of space each of them occupies.

This approach can't succeed completely, however, because many common fixed costs can't be identified clearly with determinants that can also be identified with individual segments. Take the costs of headquarters office space, for example. Allocating them to divisions may be feasible because the amount of floor space occupied by

EXHIBIT 25–3. Relationship between Segment Profit Contribution and Company Net Income

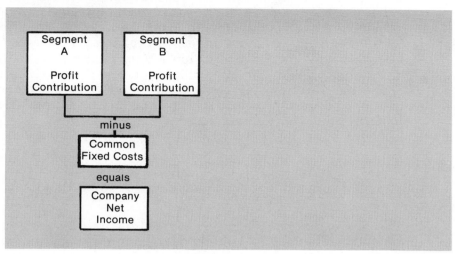

each division is easily identified, but allocating them to individual product lines or individual regions of the country is much more questionable because product lines and regions don't occupy floor space.

As a result, some or all of the common fixed costs are typically allocated in proportion to some broad measure of segmental activity, such as sales volume or the number of employees.

The argument for the profit-contribution approach is that most allocations of the nontraceable fixed costs are, to a large extent, arbitrary. How much of the president's salary should be charged to regular products and how much to custom products is a question of metaphysics, not of management. General percentage allocations are the worst of all because they make no pretense of measuring the amount of fixed cost the company could avoid by abandoning the segment. In general, the profit contribution of a segment is likely to be a better measure of the amount of profit generated in that segment, the amount available to contribute toward the coverage of common fixed costs, and, once these have been covered, the company's net income.

Reporting Segment Investment

One way of increasing the profit contribution from a business segment is to invest more money in it—in inventories, in receivables, in plant and equipment. Any evaluation of the profitability of a segment's operations, therefore, should include an examination of the amount invested to support their operations.

For example, suppose the investment in special equipment, inventories, and receivables for the custom products business was only $2 million, whereas a total investment of $50 million was directly traceable to the regular product lines. Suppose, further, that the cost of invested capital was 12 percent a year, or 1 percent a month. Under these circumstances, it would be both reasonable and informative to deduct 1 percent of the traceable investment from the monthly profit-contribution figure:

	Regular Products	Custom Products
Profit contribution	$1,168,000	$107,000
Interest on direct investment	500,000	20,000
Residual Profit Contribution	$ 668,000	$ 87,000

This shows that both segments covered the implicit costs of the investment resources specifically devoted to them, but much of the profit contribution from regular products was consumed by the heavy capital requirements of that segment. At a minimum, management should examine the investment structure to see whether the markets could be served effectively with a smaller capital commitment.

Analyzing Profit Variances

To evaluate the operations of individual segments, management needs to have some idea of how large a profit contribution the segment ought to be making. Various standards are available for this purpose: the segment's profit contribution in a previous period, the profit contributed by other segments of the company, or the profit generated by comparable segments in competing firms, if that information is available.

Since many of these factors are taken into consideration when the current operating plan was developed, *planned profit contribution* is likely to be a useful bench mark in evaluating the results of current operations. Exhibit 25–4, for example, shows that the regular products line failed by a wide margin to meet its objectives during March. The cumulative performance for the year to date was also poor.

This statement throws very little light on the reasons for the product line's poor profit performance this year. To fill this void, most internal profit statements include some form of analysis or commentary on the deviations between actual and budgeted performance. The commentary may call attention to unusual events that had sig-

EXHIBIT 25–4

SADDLER PRODUCTS CORPORATION, REGULAR PRODUCTS
Comparative Profit-Corporation Report
For the Month of March, 19x1
(000 omitted)

	This Month			Year to Date	
	Actual Results	Budgeted Results	Variance Over/ (Under)	Actual Results	Variance Over/ (Under)
Net sales	$2,865	$3,025	$(160)	$7,124	$(520)
Standard variable cost:					
Factory	$1,456	$1,519	$ (63)	$3,520	$(327)
Order filling	93	95	(2)	246	21
Total	$1,549	$1,614	$ (65)	$3,766	$(306)
Contribution margin	$1,316	$1,411	$ (95)	$3,358	$(214)
Product-traceable fixed costs ...	148	144	(4)	450	18
Profit contribution	$1,168	$1,267	$ (99)	$2,908	$(196)
Interest on traceable investment .	51	53	2	158	(5)
Residual Profit Contribution	$1,117	$1,214	$ (97)	$2,750	$(201)

nificant favorable or unfavorable effects on reported income during the period, and it may indicate whether these effects are expected to continue and what actions management is taking to cope with or capitalize on the situation.

These qualitative commentaries are often supported and supplemented by quantitative breakdowns of the aggregate profit variance in each segment of the business. The variance can be subdivided to identify whatever influences management thinks are likely to be significant.[1]

Choosing the Segment Structure

So far we have been dealing with what seems to be a very simple operating structure—only two business segments, with all profit responsibility assigned to top management. Even here, management would ordinarily want more detail. Subdivision of the regular products line into related product groups, classification of results by geographical areas, and a more complete descriptive classification of costs are all possible forms this additional detail might take.

In practice, additional detail is imperative because profit responsibility is shared with managers at a number of different levels. In

---

[1] For one analytical scheme, see Gordon Shillinglaw, *Managerial Cost Accounting,* 4th ed. (Homewood, Ill.: Richard D. Irwin, Inc., 1977), chap. 25.

this situation, the greatest amount of detail is usually provided only to managers at the lowest level of profit responsibility. Reports received routinely by top management show very little detail because responsibility for managing the details has been delegated to subordinates. Top management is likely to see detailed figures only when specific problems or opportunities call for top management attention.

Exhibit 25–5, for instance, shows a report that might be issued to the district sales manager as an overall summary of that district's

EXHIBIT 25–5

SADDLER PRODUCTS CORPORATION, BOSTON DISTRICT
Profit Performance Report
For the Month of March, 19x1

	Actual	Budget	Variance Over/(Under)
Net sales	$514,000	$500,000	$14,000
Standard variable cost of goods sold	286,000	280,000	(6,000)
Contribution margin	$228,000	$220,000	$ 8,000
District expenses:			
Branch salaries	$ 2,800	$ 2,800	—
Sales salaries	24,900	24,200	$ (700)
Travel	5,200	6,300	1,100
Entertainment	1,300	800	(500)
Local advertising	1,000	1,100	100
Storage and delivery	6,800	6,500	(300)
Branch office expenses	1,100	1,000	(100)
Interest on investment	2,600	2,200	(400)
Other	300	100	(200)
Total District Expenses	$ 46,000	$ 45,000	$ (1,000)
Profit Contribution	$182,000	$175,000	$ 7,000

profit contribution. The business segment in this case is the company's sales in its Boston district rather than company-wide sales of a specific product line as in Exhibit 25–4.

A glance at this report will tell the district manager that the actual sales volume was $514,000, that this produced a contribution margin $8,000 larger than the profit plan called for, and that the district profit contribution for the month was $7,000 greater than the profit objective. It also shows that although travel expenses were down substantially, most of the other district expenses ran ahead of the budget. The entertainment expenses and interest on investment were particularly high. The manager probably would want to investigate.

Districtwide totals fail to give the district manager any explanation of the sources of the main deviations from the profit plan. For this reason, the accountant might prepare another report like the one in Exhibit 25–6. This shows the five items traceable to individual salespeople—sales, cost of goods sold, sales salaries, travel, and entertainment—and calculates the deviation from planned profit performance for each sales representative.

EXHIBIT 25–6

SADDLER PRODUCTS CORPORATION, BOSTON DISTRICT
Sales Force Performance Summary
For the Month of March, 19x1

Sales Representatives	Net Sales	Standard Variable Cost of Goods Sold	Salary and Direct Expenses	Profit Contribution		
				Amount	Variance Over/ (Under)	% of Sales
Brown	$ 40,000	$ 21,900	$ 2,500	$ 15,600	$ (800)	39.0
Cannon	31,000	18,300	3,200	9,500	(1,900)	30.6
Evars	63,000	32,000	4,300	26,700	3,700	42.4
Johnson	30,000	18,100	2,900	9,000	(2,400)	30.0
Kelly	54,000	30,600	4,200	19,200	400	35.6
Lusso	47,000	25,800	3,100	18,100	2,800	38.5
McGregor	76,000	42,200	3,800	30,000	4,000	39.5
Nelson	55,000	31,400	3,400	20,200	1,500	36.7
Stern	68,000	38,700	3,600	25,700	2,200	37.8
Williams	50,000	27,000	3,000	20,000	(1,600)	40.0
Total	$514,000	$286,000	$34,000	$194,000	$ 7,900	37.7
General branch expenses				12,000	(900)	2.3
District profit contribution				$182,000	$ 7,000	35.4

Charging the sales representatives with the direct expenses of their own operations, as in this report, is a very useful feature. Kelly, for example, sold $4,000 more than Williams, but when all the costs traceable to these sales were deducted, Kelly's profit contribution was $800 less than Williams's. Kelly more than met the planned profit contribution, though, while Williams and three others fell short of theirs.

The district managers in the marketing division all report to the division's general sales manager. Managers at this level are farther removed from the day-to-day operations of individual sales branches, and, therefore, are less likely to be aware of problems and opportunities as they emerge. As a result, they must rely heavily on accounting reports to direct their attention in the right directions.

The general sales manager's needs might be met by preparing a set of district profit-contribution reports, together with a short report on the costs of operating the central office. This would have two disadvantages. First, important figures might be lost in a welter of detail. Second, the general sales manager might be tempted to run individual branches by remote control, undermining the authority and motivation of the district managers.

The usual solution is to give the middle manager a more condensed set of reports. One such report is illustrated in Exhibit 25–7.

EXHIBIT 25–7

SADDLER PRODUCTS CORPORATION
Marketing Division Profit Performance Summary
For the Month of March, 19x1

	Net Sales	Standard Variable Cost of Goods Sold	District Expenses*	Profit Contribution	
				Amount	Variance
Boston	$ 514,000	$ 286,000	$ 46,000	$ 182,000	$ 7,000
New York	946,000	453,000	84,000	409,000	25,000
Baltimore	472,000	287,000	51,000	134,000	(33,000)
Atlanta	348,000	197,000	42,000	109,000	15,000
Pittsburgh	588,000	328,000	63,000	197,000	3,000
Cleveland	627,000	359,000	58,000	210,000	(2,000)
Total	$3,495,000	$1,910,000	$344,000	$1,241,000	$15,000
Central marketing expenses:					
Administration				$ 40,000	$ 1,000
Market research ...				26,000	(1,000)
Advertising				103,000	10,000
Other				23,000	(3,000)
Total				$ 192,000	$ 7,000
Profit Contribution...				$1,049,000	$22,000

* Includes interest on investments in district facilities and working capital.

Again the profit-contribution format is used. Each district's results are summarized on a single line. Net sales, profit contribution, and the variance in profit contribution for each branch are taken directly from the District Sales and Expense Summary, illustrated for the Boston district in Exhibit 25–5.

General selling expenses for the marketing department as a whole and the costs of administering the general sales manager's office are grouped together in the lower half of the departmental report but are not charged to individual districts. The bottom line in Exhibit 25–7 shows the amounts left to cover corporate overheads and to provide a profit for the company.

INTERNAL PROFIT REPORTING FOR MANAGERIAL EVALUATION

Top management's second major use for periodic internal profit reports is in evaluating the ability of subordinate managers to generate profits, given the resources at their disposal and the environment in which they have to work. We shall look briefly at the evaluation of managerial profit performance in one specific kind of organization unit, the profit center.

The Profit-Center Concept

Organizations in which the managers reporting to the chief executive officer are responsible for generating profits in specific business segments are generally referred to as *decentralized* companies. Their major operating divisions are known as *profit centers*. A profit center has four main characteristics:

1. It has a profit objective.
2. Its management has authority to make decisions affecting the major determinants of profit, including the power to choose its markets and sources of supply.
3. Its management is expected to use profit-based decision rules.
4. Its management is accountable to higher management for the amount of profit generated.

Decentralization is at its best whenever a division's operations come closest in scope and depth to those of separate independent companies. Under these circumstances, the profit reported by each division is largely independent of operating performance in other divisions of the company, thus facilitating the interpretation of reported profits. Organization units that come closest to meeting these specifications are those that are responsible for the manufacture and sale of individual product lines or groups of related product lines, although in some industries divisionalization on a regional basis is feasible.

Service Centers

Many organization units in decentralized companies are classified as service centers. A service center is a unit providing services or support to other units in the organization within the limits set by its capacity and being judged on the quality and cost of the service provided. The relationship between service centers and profit centers in diagrammed in Exhibit 25–8.

EXHIBIT 25–8.   Relationships between Service Centers and Profit Centers

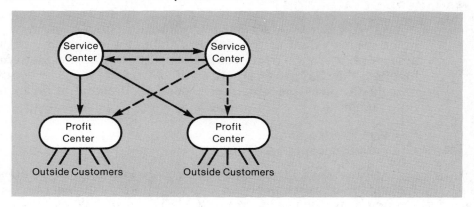

Organization units are classified as service centers for either of two reasons:

1. The unit has little or no access to outside customers (for example, the controller's department).
2. Top management is unwilling to give the profit-center managers the authority to decide how much of the unit's output they are to use or whether they are to use it at all (for example, a legal department).

As the diagram indicates, true service centers do no significant amount of business with outside customers. A service department which provides services to outsiders is an organizational hybrid. Special arrangements have to be made to define their managers' responsibilities for revenues as well as for costs and to establish appropriate performance standards.

Reasons for Profit Decentralization

The creation of profit centers and the delegation of profit responsibility has three major objectives:

1. To provide a basis for delegating portions of top management's decision-making responsibility to executives who have closer operating familiarity with individual products or markets.
2. To bring subordinate executives into more direct contact with the ultimate profit objectives of the firm.

3. To provide an integrated training ground for the top managers of the future.

In other words, decentralization aims to recreate in the large organization the conditions that give life and flexibility to the small company without sacrificing the advantages of size.

Standards for Managerial Evaluation

Standards to be used in evaluating division managers' profit performance need to meet two major requirements:

1. Current attainability by competent division managers.
2. Consistency with the degree of profit controllability.

Both of these are necessary if the managers are to internalize the standards as their own and accept responsibility for achieving them.

Attainability. Each division is to some extent unique. Profit differences can be created by variations in the age or condition of production facilities; by differences in local wage structures, transportation costs, and raw material prices; by differences in the types of products handled or customers served; or by differences in the degree of competition faced in the marketplace. Each manager's performance should be evaluated in the light of the situation facing the division. This means that the standard must be different from division to division and must be changed from period to period as conditions change.

Controllability. Profit performance should be defined to exclude any variances that are not to some significant extent within the control of the division manager. At the same time, we must recognize that no measure of profit can be a precise reflection of a manager's effectiveness in profit control. Too many other factors enter in. The danger lies in trying to avoid this problem by adopting a profit definition that eliminates so many of the possible sources of variances that the manager is relieved of most profit-control responsibilities. No variable is ever completely controllable; controllability always means the ability to influence a cost or revenue within limits.

Variations in divisional sales, for example, are an important aspect of managerial performance even though they may result in large part from changes in general business conditions. Changes in the business environment can and should be considered in evaluating profit performance but not in calculating the profit figures on which the evaluation is to be based.

The profit standard that meets these criteria is the current *profit plan*. As we indicated earlier, most profit plans are established jointly by profit-responsible executives, their subordinates, and their immediate superiors. Once established, they become commitments—by the profit-center manager to strive to carry them out, and by higher management to accept the achievement of planned results as satisfactory managerial performance. If superiors are unwilling to make this commitment, they should reject the plan and either demand a new one or find a new manager for the profit center.

This being the case, the inescapable conclusion must be that budgeted profit is the appropriate bench mark or standard against which managerial profit performance is to be judged. This means that a large reported profit in one profit center may earn the manager few laurels, while a small profit in another may be regarded as a great managerial feat. Two safeguards are essential, however:

1. Active top management participation in budget setting.
2. Inclusion of improvement targets in the budgeting process.

Top management has to carry out a rigorous, critical review of all budget proposals, usually with strong central-staff participation. It also has to work for performance improvement. Low profit levels may be acceptable for a while, but they can't be tolerated in the long run. Recognizing this, top management should judge division managers' performance at least as much by the quality of their budget proposals as by their success in carrying them out.

Measuring Profit Performance

In general, the profit measures that serve for operations evaluation will serve for managerial evaluation as well. The only difference is the addition of the controllability criterion. The profit-performance measure for managerial evaluation must reflect all the profit determinants the profit-center manager can control. By the same token, it should exclude variances in elements that are not controllable at the profit center level.

Good examples of noncontrollable variances are variances in the amount of head office expenses that are allocated to individual profit centers. Unless these allocations represent charges for services requested by the profit-center managers, no variances in these allocations should be reflected in the evaluation of the profit-center managers.

INTERNAL PROFIT REPORTS FOR INVESTMENT EVALUATION

The third use of segment profit reports is in investment evaluation. This is related to operations evaluation but deals with a more fundamental question: Are the segment's activities generating enough income to support the resources invested in it?

The Profit Standard

Since investment capital is usually the scarcest of the resources management must deal with, the performance standard for this kind of evaluation must relate the amount of the segment's earnings to the amount of invested capital—that is, it should be a *return on investment* standard. Since a decision to continue an activity has the same effect as a decision to invest in it, the appropriate performance standard is the minimum rate of return management is willing to accept for new capital expenditures. This standard should be based on the company's cost of capital and should be the same for all segments in a given risk category. Management has no reason to regard 8 percent as a satisfactory return on money invested in one segment but an unsatisfactory return in another unless the two segments differ widely in risk.

Focus of the Analysis

Investment analysis of a segment's performance can be either prospective or retrospective:

> *Prospective.* Are this segments' activities profitable enough to warrant maintaining or increasing the current investment commitment?

> *Retrospective.* Are this segments' activities profitable enough to support the investments management has already made in the segment?

Prospective analysis requires a comparison of the present value of the cash flows from continued operation with the cash flows to be generated by withdrawing from the segment now. For example, an analysis based on operating a segment for another three years might be diagrammed as in Exhibit 25–9.

EXHIBIT 25–9.   Investment Analysis on a Prospective Basis

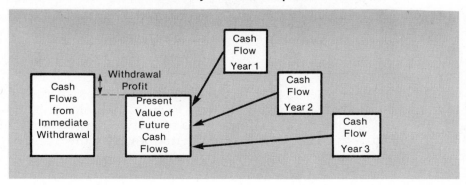

The cash flows from immediate withdrawal come from the after-tax liquidation value of the facilities and working capital attributable to the segment, less any liquidation costs (employee severance pay and so on), also adjusted for the tax effects. The cash flows from continued operation are the net receipts the company would lose if it were to drop out of the market now.

Routine segment profit reports do not and cannot provide these cash flow estimates. Performance reports are by their very nature retrospective, based on observations of actual results. As such, they can play only two roles:

1. To direct top management's attention to segments that persistently earn less than the target return on investment.
2. To show how viable the segment is likely to be on a continuing basis—that is, are the revenues covering all the costs attributable to them; if not, the future is bleak, no matter how favorable the current cash flow relationships.

Measuring Investment Performance

To measure segment profit performance for investment evaluation, we need to relate the amount of profit attributable to the segment to the amount of investment used to support it. Most companies meet this requirement by summarizing a segment's profit performance in a single figure, the ratio of the segment's net income to the amount invested in it. This ratio is the segment's rate of return on investment, or *ROI*.

An alternative is to calculate *residual income,* defined as the segment's income less an investment carrying charge, determined by multiplying the investment in the segment by an interest rate based on the cost of capital. For example, if the cost of capital is 9 percent and the investment in the segment is $10 million, the monthly carrying charge is as follows:

> Annual Rate/12 × Investment = Monthly Charge
>   9%/12   × $10,000,000 = $75,000 a Month

If the segment's profit is too small to cover the investment charge, the segment isn't paying its way. Eventually, unless conditions improve or management finds ways of cultivating the segment more effectively, management should withdraw from the segment and invest its funds elsewhere.

Either ROI or residual income is subject to a number of measurement problems. We have space to mention only two of these. First, measurements of the income and investment attributable to individual segments require allocations of centrally administered assets and expenses. Allocations of these items are often highly arbitrary, as we saw earlier. The more important they are to an individual segment, the less reliance can be placed on the ROI or residual income.

Second, the relevant measure of investment in calculating the rate of return on investment is the segment's market value, measured by the proceeds the company could obtain by selling the plant and equipment and liquidating the working capital supporting the segment's activities. The book value of the company's investment in the segment is likely to be very different from this market value, thereby biasing the ROI ratio. Moreover, this bias will be stronger in some segments than in others, depending on the age and composition of the assets in the segments and on the structure of the markets in which these assets would be sold.

Even so, as long as the reported return on investment is at levels management considers satisfactory, a more rigorous analysis of investment profitability is probably unnecessary. Estimates of current liquidation values are costly and difficult to make, and they should be made only if management has some reason to believe that liquidation might be preferable to continued operation.

We shall leave further discussion of these questions to more advanced texts. In passing, however, we should note one hidden danger in return-on-investment reporting. Faced with persistently low return on investment ratios in some of its operations, management may find it extremely difficult to remember that the failure of these segments to meet minimum profitability standards is a suitable topic for investment evaluation, not managerial appraisal. The appropriate standard for managerial evaluation is planned profit, not the average or minimum acceptable percentage rate of return on investment. No manager should be rewarded for being placed in charge of a profitable operation or stigmatized for being assigned to activities that are inherently unprofitable.

SUMMARY

Feedback information on the profit performance of individual company segments is of vital importance to management. It is used in evaluating the methods used to generate profit in the segment (operations evaluation), the performance of its management (managerial evaluation), and the profitability of the resources invested in it (investment evaluation).

Profit-contribution figures—revenues minus variable expenses and traceable fixed costs—provide a useful basis for operations evaluation. The deduction of implicit interest on segment investment to produce residual profit contribution is a useful refinement. Allocations of nontraceable fixed costs and investments are unnecessary and may be misleading.

The same figures, classified between controllable and noncontrollable items, can be used for managerial evaluation. The appropriate standard for managerial evaluation is the profit plan, accepted both by those directly responsible for the segment and by top management. This is particularly true in the profit centers of decentralized companies in which the segment manager is given substantial authority over the determinants of profit. Deviations from profit plans must be scrutinized to separate those attributable to managerial actions from those arising from other sources.

Return on investment or residual income is the appropriate profit performance measure for investment evaluation. For managerial decisions, this should reflect estimates of present liquidation values and future cash flows. Estimates of liquidation values are too expensive to make routinely, however, and management generally makes them only when the historical return on investment figures are persistently low or negative. The historical figures are used in the interim to provide a rough index of the profitability of past investment decisions in the aggregate.

KEY TERMS

Business segment	Profit center
Decentralization	Profit contribution
Investment carrying charge	Profit variance
Investment evaluation	Residual income
Managerial evaluation	Return on investment (ROI)
Operations evaluation	Service center

INDEPENDENT STUDY PROBLEMS (Solutions in Appendix B)

1. Profit contribution statement. The Dorsey Corporation has prepared the following performance summary for its industrial division for the month of December:

Net sales		$2,000,000
Cost of goods sold:		
Labor	$ 400,000	
Materials	100,000	
Overhead (actual)	1,000,000	
Costs incurred	$1,500,000	
Overhead overabsorbed	100,000	
Product costs	$1,600,000	
Decrease in inventory	160,000	
Cost of goods sold		1,760,000
Gross margin		$ 240,000
Less: Selling expenses........................	$ 300,000	
Administrative expenses	50,000	350,000
Profit (loss) on sales		$ (110,000)
Add: Factory overhead overabsorbed		100,000
Net Income (Loss) before Taxes..................		$ (10,000)

1. Manufacturing overhead costs are all traceable to the division.
2. At normal operating volumes, variable manufacturing overhead costs are approximately 30 percent of total manufacturing overhead costs in the industrial division. Variable overhead cost per labor-dollar is not affected by fluctuations in production volume.
3. The volume variance in manufacturing overhead costs in the industrial division was favorable, amounting to $20,000.
4. Variable selling expenses amount to 4 percent of industrial sales. All administrative expenses are fixed.
5. $50,000 of fixed selling expense and $5,000 of administrative expense are traceable to the industrial division; all other fixed selling and administrative expenses come from allocations.
6. An absorption costing system is in use in the factory. The ratio of the variable cost content of work in process and finished goods inventories to the total costs of these inventories is the same as the ratio of variable manufacturing cost to total "product costs" for the division for the period. Price-level changes may be assumed to be negligible.

a. Compute the following:
  1. Factory overhead spending variance.
  2. Budgeted fixed manufacturing cost.
  3. Contribution margin ratio.
b. Prepare a profit-contribution statement in good form, summarizing the results of the month's operations.

2. Managerial evaluation; residual income. The investment in division A consists of $200,000 in traceable working capital, $400,000 in traceable plant and equipment, and $100,000 in centrally administered assets, allocated to the division at a rate of one sixth of traceable investment. The budgeted amounts for these three totals were $150,000, $420,000, and $95,000.

Division A's net income for the year is $63,000, after deducting $30,000 in traceable depreciation, $40,000 in head office charges (allocated to the division at the rate of 5 percent of sales) and income taxes at 50 percent. The budgeted amounts were $70,000, $32,000, $45,000, and 50 percent.

The company estimates that its cost of capital is 12 percent, after taxes.

a. Calculate budgeted and actual return on investment.
b. Calculate budgeted and actual residual income.
c. Discuss the division manager's performance.
d. What action should management take in response to your evaluation of this division's activities, based on the figures supplied here?

EXERCISES AND PROBLEMS

3. Interpreting a profit-contribution report. A marketing vice president received the following summary report on the operations of the company's sales districts during the month of October (in thousands of dollars):

	Sales		Profit Contribution	
District	Amount	Over/(Under) Budget	Amount	Over/(Under) Budget
Boston	$ 220	$ (10)	$ 59	$ 4
New York	380	(20)	110	1
Pittsburgh	170	(30)	24	(16)
Atlanta	340	20	91	6
Chicago	210	(40)	46	(9)
New Orleans	140	(10)	18	(6)
Denver	90	(30)	10	—
Dallas	120	—	21	11
Los Angeles	290	(10)	66	6
Seattle	130	(30)	25	(15)
Total	$2,090	$(160)	$470	$(18)

Expenses other than those reflected in the district profit-contribution figures averaged 12 percent of sales.

a. How would you expect the marketing vice president to use this report? What significant facts does it reveal?
b. What further information would you expect the marketing vice president to ask for? What managerial action would you expect to observe?

4. Preparing a profit-contribution statement. Morgan Wicker Company has three products for which you have the following information:

	Product A	Product B	Product C
Contribution-margin ratio	40%	30%	45%
Sales revenues	$10,000	$8,000	$6,000
Traceable fixed expenses	1,000	1,500	2,500
Allocated fixed expenses	1,000	800	600

a. Prepare a profit-contribution statement, with a separate column for each product and one column for the company as a whole.

b. Comment briefly on the profitability of each product.

5. Calculating and interpreting residual income and return on investment. Thompson Enterprises regards 10 percent after taxes as the minimum acceptable rate of return on capital expenditures. You have the following figures for the Digby division for the last three years:

	19x1		19x2		19x3	
	Actual	*Budget*	*Actual*	*Budget*	*Actual*	*Budget*
Net income	$ 500	$ 480	$ 700	$ 650	$1,000	$ 950
Net investment	2,500	2,500	4,000	3,800	6,400	6,300

a. Calculate budgeted and actual residual income and return on investment for each year.

b. Assuming that allocations of common costs haven't influenced the division's results materially, what do these figures tell you about managerial performance and investment performance in this division?

6. Allocating common fixed costs. Localio Products Company has three divisions operating as profit centers and three central administrative departments operating as service centers. You have the following information on the three profit centers:

	Western Division	Central Division	Eastern Division	Total
Sales revenues	$2,000,000	$5,000,000	$3,000,000	$10,000,000
Profit contribution	300,000	1,200,000	1,100,000	2,500,000
Investment	1,500,000	4,000,000	3,500,000	9,000,000
Number of employees	1,250	2,500	1,250	5,000

The operating costs of the three administrative departments were:

Accounting	$300,000
Marketing	250,000
Executive offices	360,000

The income tax rate is 40 percent.

a. Calculate the return on investment in each division, allocating the costs of the three administrative departments on the following bases: accounting, number of employees; marketing, sales revenues; executive offices, investment.

b. Do these allocations give you a better basis for managerial evaluation or investment evaluation than you would have in their absence? As part of your answer, identify the criterion you believe should underlie allocations for each of these purposes.

7. Discussion question: identifying profit centers. Carnegie Improvements, Inc., buys parcels of land and builds condominium housing developments on them. Once a parcel of land has been bought, a manager is appointed to supervise construction and marketing operations at that development and to manage the commercial and recreational facilities in the development until the development is completed and all facilities are sold.

Building plans for each development are drawn up by a headquarters design department. Most building materials are selected and bought by a central purchasing department, and the terms of sale of condominium units are established by Carnegie's central management. Central management also establishes the selling-price schedule, although the local manager is authorized to reduce individual offering prices by as much as 10 percent if this seems necessary to get condominium units sold.

a.   What problems would have to be solved before income or return on investment could be calculated for a condominium development?

b.   Should the individual developments be classified as profit centers? Indicate the elements in this situation affecting your answer to this question.

8.   Preparing profit-contribution statement; sensitivity analysis.   Lee Merritt is manager of a division which has its own production facilities and its own sales force. He received the following monthly income statement on one of his product lines:

Sales revenues		$700
Expenses:		
Cost of goods sold	$490	
Marketing and distribution	70	
Research and development	15	
Administration	35	610
Income before Taxes		$ 90

Surprised by the size of the income figure, Mr. Merritt has asked you to prepare a statement in a format that will help him see the impact of volume and other factors more readily. You are given the following additional information:

1.   All of the products in this product line are manufactured in a single factory, which is devoted exclusively to this product line.

2.   The $490 cost of goods sold included the following:

Standard direct materials	$ 95
Standard direct labor	200
Standard overhead	160
Factory overhead volume variance	30
Factory overhead spending variance	(5)
Price and wage rate variances	(12)
Other factory cost variances	22
Total	$490

3.   Budgeted factory overhead = $90 + $0.50 × standard direct labor cost.

4.   Production volume was equal to sales volume during the month.

5.   The marketing and distribution expenses were as follows:

Sales commissions	$14
Variable distribution costs	21
Product-traceable fixed marketing costs	18
Common marketing costs, allocated to product lines as a percentage of sales	17
Total	$70

6. Research and development costs consisted of $3 in general research costs, allocated among the product lines as a percentage of sales, and $12 in the costs of projects for the development of new products for this line specifically.
7. Of the administrative expense, $5 was a fixed cost traceable to the product line, and the remainder consisted of allocated divisional and corporate headquarters expenses, entirely fixed.

a. Prepare a profit-contribution statement in good form. The bottom line on this statement should be the same as on the report originally submitted to Mr. Merritt. Factory cost variances other than the overhead volume variance should be classified as variable costs.
b. How would the product line's income before taxes be affected by a 10 percent decrease in sales and production volume? Prepare a revised profit-contribution statement based on this assumption. Did the profit-contribution format help you in any way?

9. Interpreting profit contribution. Georgia Ellis was the marketing manager for her company's cosmetic products. She reported to David Thompson, the company's marketing vice president. Ms. Ellis supervised a field sales force engaged exclusively in marketing the cosmetics line. Factory operations, however, were within the jurisdiction of the manufacturing vice president. Many steps in the production process for the cosmetics products were performed on a job-order basis by the personnel of factory departments also engaged in the manufacture of other company products.

Ms. Ellis received the following income statement for the cosmetics line for the month of August (in thousands of dollars):

	July Actual	*August Actual*	*August Budget*	*August Variance*
Sales	$1,000	$1,300	$1,200	$100
Standard cost of goods sold	600	800	720	(80)
Gross margin	$ 400	$ 500	$ 480	$ 20
Direct marketing expenses	150	155	150	(5)
Marketing margin	$ 250	$ 345	$ 330	$ 15
Favorable/(Unfavorable) factory variances:				
Overhead volume variance	10	(50)	—	(50)
Overhead spending variance	5	(6)	—	(6)
Direct cost variances	(12)	(54)	—	(54)
Profit Contribution	$ 253	$ 235	$ 330	$ (95)

Inventories of cosmetics products remained constant and at budgeted levels throughout July and August.

Mr. Thompson called Ms. Ellis into his office shortly after this report was issued and told her that in view of her poor performance in August, a scheduled promotion to the title of assistant vice president would be post-poned. "We'll see how you do in September and October," she was told.

a. You are a consultant on retainer for this company and you happened to overhear this conversation. Draft a statement, outlining your evaluation of Ms. Ellis's performance. If you would like to have additional information, say what you would like to have, but you must give a tentative answer to this question before this additional information becomes available.

b. List changes, if any, that you would like to make in the company's reporting system and explain why you would make them.

10. Evaluating managerial performance. Harry Keeler was the president of Anorak, Inc., a manufacturer of consumer goods. The income statements for the company's two divisions indicated that division A was highly profitable; division B was a break-even operation at best.

Mr. Keeler was due to retire soon, and the board of directors were examining the credentials of the two division managers. Both had been with the company for many years and had created enviable performance records in other positions before being named to head their respective divisions.

Both division managers seemed to have organizational ability, and employee morale in both divisions was extremely good. Both were well liked by the board members and seemed capable of representing the company effectively in dealings with outsiders.

The main difference between the two seemed to be that the manager of division A was able to generate profits, while the manager of division B could not. The following divisional income statements were prepared for the month of September:

	Division A		Division B	
	Budget	Actual	Budget	Actual
Sales	$1,050	$1,000	$490	$500
Cost of goods sold	630	600	395	400
Gross margin	$ 420	$ 400	$ 95	$100
Operating expenses:				
Marketing and selling	$ 95	$ 100	$ 50	$ 50
Divisional administration	48	50	45	40
Head office expense	41	42	19	21
Income taxes	94	85	(8)	(5)
Total Operating Expenses	$ 278	$ 277	$106	$106
Net Income (Loss)	$ 142	$ 123	$(11)	$ (6)

The following assets and liabilities were traced or assigned to these divisions at the end of September:

	Division A		Division B	
	Budget	Actual	Budget	Actual
Directly traceable:				
Accounts receivable	$1,200	$1,200	$ 520	$ 500
Inventories	1,100	1,100	860	800
Plant and equipment (net)	700	700	300	300
Accounts payable	(900)	(900)	(580)	(600)
Net Traceable Assets	$2,100	$2,100	$1,100	$1,000
Allocated (% of sales):				
Cash	380	400	190	200
Headquarters buildings, furniture				
and equipment	300	300	150	150
Net Assets	$2,780	$2,800	$1,440	$1,350

Additional information:

1. Each division is operated as a profit center. Each division manufactures all of its products in its own factories and sells them through its own sales force.
2. The income-statement comparisons for the year to date revealed a similar set of relationships to those in the statements for September.
3. The company used a minimum after-tax rate of return on investment of 12 percent in evaluating new capital-expenditure proposals.
4. Head office expenses were allocated to product lines in proportion to actual sales.
5. Market conditions for the products sold by both divisions were very close to those forecast at the beginning of the year.
6. The market for division B's products appeared unlikely to show any major improvement for some time. Barring a radical change in the market or the introduction of a major new product, industry sales were likely to remain at or near their current levels for some time.
7. The market for division A's products had been growing dramatically for several years, but the industry's growth had abated during this year, as anticipated.

Do these statements indicate that the manager of division A had a clearly superior profit performance in September? Prepare a summary report, showing, insofar as you can, the relative profit performance of the two managers, with your interpretation of the figures.

**11.*   *Effect of return on investment measures on decisions.*   Mr. Percy Jones, managing director of Orkney Biscuit Company, Ltd., is trying to decide whether to expand the company by adding an entirely new and different product line. The proposal seems likely to be profitable, and adequate funds can be obtained from outside investors to finance the new venture.

---

* Copyright 1968 by l'Institut pour l'Etude des Méthodes de Direction de l'Entreprise (IMEDE), Lausanne, Switzerland. Published by permission.

Orkney Biscuit has long been regarded as a well-managed company. It has succeeded in keeping its present product lines up to date and has maintained a small but profitable position in a highly competitive industry.

The amount of capital employed by the company in support of its present operations is approximately $4 million, and it is expected to remain at this level whether the proposal for the new product line is accepted or rejected. Net income from these existing operations now amounts to about $400,000 a year, and Mr. Jones's best forecast of the future is that this will continue to be the income from present operations, regardless of whether the new product line is introduced or rejected.

Introduction of the new product line would require an immediate investment of $400,000 in equipment and $250,000 in additional working capital. A further $100,000 in working capital would be required a year later.

Sales of the new product line would be relatively low during the first year but would increase steadily until the sixth year. After that, changing tastes and increased competition would probably begin to reduce annual sales. After eight years, the product line would probably be withdrawn from the market. At that time, the company would sell the equipment for its scrap value and liquidate the working capital. The cash value of the equipment and working capital at that time would be about $350,000.

The low initial sales volume, combined with heavy promotional outlays, would lead to heavy losses in the first two years, and no net income would be reported until the fourth year. The profit forecasts for the new product line are summarized in Exhibit 1.

EXHIBIT 1. Income Forecast for New Product Line

Year	(1) Forecasted Incremental Cash Flow from Operations	(2) Depreciation on New Equipment	(3) Forecasted Incremental Income before Tax (1) − (2)	(4) Income Tax at 40%*	(5) Forecasted Incremental Net Income after Tax (3) − (4)
1	−$ 350,000	$50,000	−$400,000	−$160,000	−$190,000
2	− 100,000	50,000	− 150,000	− 60,000	− 90,000
3	0	50,000	− 50,000	− 20,000	− 30,000
4	+ 200,000	50,000	+ 150,000	60,000	90,000
5	+ 500,000	50,000	+ 450,000	180,000	270,000
6	+ 1,000,000	50,000	+ 950,000	380,000	570,000
7	+ 900,000	50,000	+ 850,000	340,000	510,000
8	+ 650,000	50,000	+ 600,000	240,000	360,000

* When income before taxes is negative, the company is entitled to a tax rebate at 40 percent, either from taxes paid in previous years or from taxes currently due on other company operations.

Using these figures, Mr. Jones has prepared the cash-flow analysis summarized in Exhibit 2. Investment cash flow, shown in the first column, is added to the operating cash flows in column 2 (from Exhibit 1, column 1). The total is then adjusted for income taxes and discounted to find its present value at a 10 percent rate. These present values are shown in the right-hand column of Exhibit 2.

EXHIBIT 2

ORKNEY BISCUIT COMPANY, LTD[*]
Present Value of New Product Proposal
($000 omitted)

Year	(1)[a] Investment Cash Flows	(2) Operating Cash Flows	(3) Total Cash Flow before Tax (1) + (2)	(4)[b] Tax Depreciation	(5)[c] Taxable Income (2) − (4)	(6) Income Tax 40% of (5)	(7) Cash Flow after Tax (3) − (6)	(8)[d] Present Value Factor at 10%	(9) Present Value at 10% (7) × (8)
1	− 650	− 350	−1,000	50	− 400	−160	− 840	.9516	−799
2	− 100	− 100	− 200	50	− 150	− 60	− 140	.8611	−121
3	0	0	0	50	− 50	− 20	+ 20	.7791	+ 16
4	0	+ 200	+ 200	50	+ 150	60	+ 140	.7050	+ 99
5	0	+ 500	+ 500	50	+ 450	180	+ 320	.6379	+ 204
6	0	+1,000	1,000	50	+ 950	380	+ 620	.5772	+ 358
7	0	+ 900	+ 900	50	+ 850	340	+ 560	.5223	+ 292
8	+ 350	+ 650	+1,000	50	+ 600	240	+ 760	.4726	+ 359
Total	− 400	+2,800	+2,400	400	+2,400	960	+1,440		+408

[*] *IMPORTANT NOTE:* This exhibit is provided for later reference. It need not be reviewed prior to an analysis of the questions raised at the end of the case.

[a] The first year's outlay consists of $400,000 for equipment and $250,000 for working capital. An additional working capital outlay of $100,000 is required in the second year. Working capital outlays are completely recovered in the eighth year.

[b] One eighth of the equipment costs are recorded each year as depreciation.

[c] When taxable income is negative, the company is entitled to a tax rebate at 40 percent, either from taxes paid in prior years or from taxes currently due on other company operations.

[d] These interest factors are based on the assumption that each year's cash flow is spread uniformly throughout the year. They differ slightly, therefore, from those in Appendix A.

As Exhibit 2 shows, the present value of the anticipated cash receipts from the new product line exceeds the present value of the anticipated cash outlays by $408,000.

Mr. Jones seldom has an opportunity to invest funds as profitably as this, and he would like to approve this investment proposal. He is concerned by its effect on Orkney Biscuit's reported rate of return on investment, however. His accountants have given him the following figures (in thousands):

Year	Total Investment Start of Year	Net Income After Tax	Reported Return on Investment
1	$4,000	$160	4.0%
2	4,600	310	6.7
3	4,650	370	8.0
4	4,600	490	10.7
5	4,550	670	14.7
6	4,500	970	21.6
7	4,450	910	20.4
8	4,400	760	17.3

The accountants explain that they have obtained the forecasted net income by adding the forecasted after-tax net income for the new product line (Exhibit 1, column 5) to $400,000, the forecasted net income on the company's other product lines. They have obtained the total investment figures by adding $4 million to the investment outlays on equipment and working capital (Exhibit 2, column 1, cumulated) and subtracting depreciation on the new equipment (Exhibit 2, column 4, cumulated).

a. To what extent, if any, would the low anticipated rate of return on investment in the first three years be likely to affect the decision to launch the new product line if Orkney Biscuit is a private company, owned entirely by Mr. Jones?

b. How would your answer differ if you found that the Orkney Biscuit Company is a publicly owned company, with shares owned by a large number of small investors, and Mr. Jones is purely a salaried administrator?

c. How would your answer differ if the Orkney Biscuit Company were a wholly owned profit center of a much larger company and Mr. Jones expects to be a candidate to succeed one of the parent company's top executives who will retire from the company about two years from now?

appendix A

Compound Interest and Bond Tables

THE TABLES in this appendix contain the multipliers or conversion factors necessary to convert cash flows of one or more periods into their equivalent values at some other point in time. The basic explanation of the reasons for conversion is given in Chapter 7; only the mechanical details of how the numbers in the tables should be used are explained here. If more extensive tables or specialized tables are needed, they can be found in readily available financial handbooks or can be derived from simple computer programs.

Table 1: Future Value of $1

Each figure in Table 1 is the future value to which one dollar will grow by the end of n periods at an interest rate r, compounded once per period. To obtain the future value of any sum:

1. Select a future date to serve as a reference date.
2. Determine the number of periods (n) between the receipt or payment of cash and the reference date.
3. Determine the interest rate (r) at which amounts are to be compounded.
4. Find the figure from Table 1 corresponding to these values of n and r.
5. Multiply the cash sum by this figure.

For example, suppose we have $10,000 now and expect to receive another $10,000 two years from now. We want to find the future values of these sums at a reference date five years from now, compounded annually at 10 percent.

The first of these sums will grow for five years, and the figure from the five-year row of the 10-percent column of Table 1 is 1.6105. This indicates that $1 now will grow to $1.6105 in five years. The future value of $10,000 therefore is 1.6105 × $10,000 = $16,105.

The second sum will have only three years to grow. The multiplier from the three-year row of the 10-percent column is 1.3310, and the future value at the reference date is 1.3310 × $10,000 = $13,310.

These calculations can be summarized in a timetable of cash flows and future values:

Years before Reference Date	Cash Flow	Future Value Multiplier at 10% (Table 1)	Amount
5	+$10,000	1.6105	$16,105
3	+ 10,000	1.3310	13,310
Total			$29,415

In using this table, care must be taken to insure that the *interest rate* is appropriate to the *period*. Thus, if an amount is compounded *semiannually* at r percent *per annum* for n years, the number of interest periods is $2n$, and the interest rate per period is $r/2$. To illustrate, if interest is compounded *annually* at 6 percent, $10,000 now will grow to $32,071 by the end of 20 years. If interest is compounded *semiannually* at 3 percent every six months, however, the future value is $32,620, reflecting interest at 3 percent per six-month period for 40 periods.[1]

Extending Table 1

Table 1 can be extended easily to provide multipliers for any number of periods. For example, suppose one wants to find the future value of $10,000 compounded annually at 6 percent for 21 periods. No 21-period row is in the table. However, it is known that at the end of 20 years, the future value will be $32,071. If reinvested for one more year at 6 percent, this sum will amount to 1.06 × $32,071 = $33,995. This is the future value of $10,000 21 periods hence at 6 percent per period.

---

[1] Interest of 3 percent each six months is equivalent to an annual interest rate of $(1.03)^2 - 1 = 6.09$ percent, because interest earned in the first six months will earn interest in the second six months of the year. The semiannual compounding rate equivalent to a 6 percent annual rate is $\sqrt{1.06} - 1 = 2.9563$ percent. Table 1 can be used only if the interest rate *per period* is equal to the rate in one of the column headings. Since no column is provided for future values at 6.09 percent, Table 1 can't be used to calculate these amounts.

Alternatively, $10,000 will grow to $17,908 in ten years, and this sum will grow to $17,908 × 1.8983 = $33,995 in 11 additional years. (The 1.8983 figure comes from the 6 percent column, 11-period row of Table 1.) These relationships are shown in Figure A–1.

FIGURE A–1.   Future Values of $10,000 at 6%

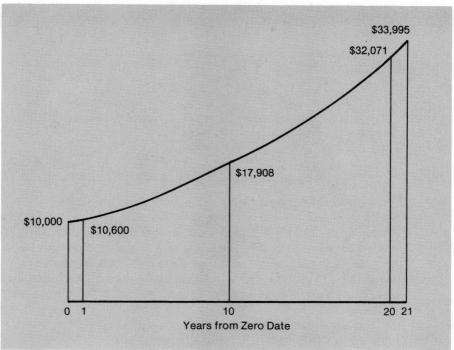

In other words, the future value of a dollar at any time in the future can be obtained by multiplying together any two or more multipliers for which the number of periods adds up to the desired number. Thus, the multiplier for 21 periods can be obtained by multiplying the factors for 1 and 20 periods, or 3 and 18 periods, or any other combination of periods totaling 21.

Table 2: Future Value of an Annuity of $1

The future value of a series of cash flows can always be determined with the aid of the multipliers in Table 1. This is time-consuming, however, and Table 2 has been developed for use as a computational shortcut whenever the cash flows in the series are identical in amount each period (an *annuity*).

The key to understanding this table is to realize that an annuity is really a combination of several cash flows, identical in amount and separated from each other by identical time intervals. Thus a two-year, $10,000 annuity is simply a series of two annual cash flows of $10,000 each. The future value of an annuity thus is simply the sum of the future values of the individual cash receipts or payments.

For example, the future value two years from now of $10,000 now and $10,000 a year from now, compounded annually at 6 percent, can be calculated with the aid of Table 1, as follows:

Years before Reference Date	Cash Flow	Future Value	
		Multiplier at 10% (Table 1)	Amount
2	+$10,000	1.1236	$11,236
1	+ 10,000	1.0600	10,600
Total			$21,836

The same answer can be found by multiplying the $10,000 annuity by the *sum* of the annual multipliers, 2.1836.

This is an example of an annuity *in advance*—that is, the cash flow took place at the *beginning* of each period. Suppose, instead, that the payments were made *in arrears*—that is, at the *end* of each period. The first payment would be made a year from now and would thus have only one year to grow before the two-year period ended. Thus, its future value would be only $10,600. The second payment, made at the end of the second year, would have no time at all to grow, and thus its future value would be $10,000.

The future value of a two-year, $10,000 annuity in arrears, compounded annually at 6 percent, therefore, is $10,600 + $10,000 = $20,600.

The multipliers in Table 2 are for annuities in arrears. The factor for a two-year, 6-percent annuity in arrears is 2.0600. Multiplying this by the $10,000 annual cash flow produces a future value of $20,600, the figure we derived in the preceding paragraph.

Converting Table 2 to Distant Future Equivalents

Table 2 consists of multipliers that can be used to calculate the future value of an annuity on the date the last payment is due to be made. Any multiplier in this table can also be translated into the multiplier that will determine future value as of some number of periods after the date of the final payment.

The procedure is to multiply the multiplier in Table 2 by the multiplier in Table 1 for the appropriate number of periods after the date of the last payment. For example, at 8 percent, the future value 15 years from now of a series of ten annual payments of $10,000 each, the first payment to be made one year from now, is calculated as follows:

$$\begin{array}{cccc} \$10,000 & \times \quad 14.4866 & \times \quad 1.4693 & = \quad \$212,852 \\ \text{(annuity)} & \text{(Table 2,} & \text{(Table 1,} & \text{(future value,} \\ & \text{10 years)} & \text{5 years)} & \text{15 years)} \end{array}$$

The first multiplier determines the sum that $10,000 a year will build up to by the end of ten years. Application of the second multiplier determines the amount that this sum will grow to in another five years.

Converting Table 2 for Annuities in Advance

The multipliers in Table 2 can also be used to calculate the future values of annuities in advance. To do this, we need to recognize that the interval between each payment and the future date is one year longer than in an annuity in arrears. The first payment in a three-year annuity in advance is made just three years before the future reference date. Since the first payment in a four-year annuity in arrears is also made exactly three years before the reference date, a three-year annuity in advance can be seen to be exactly the same as a four-year annuity in arrears without the final payment.

This relationship is diagrammed in Figure A-2. Future value is to be calculated as of the end of year 3. From a vantage point at the end of year 3, the only difference between a four-year annuity in arrears and a three-year annuity in advance is a single payment at the end of the third year. The calculation of the future value of a three-year,

FIGURE A–2

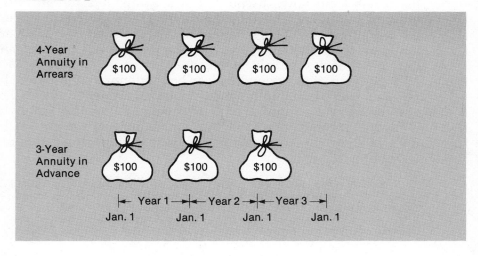

$10,000 annuity in advance, compounded at 8 percent to a reference date three years in the future, is as follows:

$$\begin{array}{cccc} \$10,000 & \times \quad 4.5061 & - \quad \$10,000 & = \quad \$35,061 \\ \text{(annuity,} & \text{(Table 2,} & \text{(omitted} & \text{(future value} \\ \text{4 years)} & \text{4 years)} & \text{final} & \text{3 years hence)} \\ & & \text{payment)} & \end{array}$$

An identical result would be obtained by subtracting 1.0000 from the multiplier in Table 2:

$$(4.5061 - 1.0000) \times \$10,000 = 3.5061 \times \$10,000 = \$35,061.$$

The general rule is: to obtain the multiplier for the future value of an n-period annuity in advance, *take the multiplier from Table 2 for an annuity of* (n + 1) *periods and subtract 1.0000.*

Table 3: Present Value of $1

Each figure in Table 3 is the present value on a given reference date of one dollar to be paid or received n periods later. To obtain the present value of any sum:

1. Select a date to serve as a reference date.
2. Determine the number of periods (n) between the reference date and the date on which the cash is to be paid or received.
3. Determine the interest rate (r) at which amounts are to be discounted.
4. Find the figure from Table 3 corresponding to these values of n and r.
5. Multiply the cash sum by this figure.

For example, to find the present value of $10,000 to be received five years from now, discounted at a compound annual rate of 8 percent, multiply $10,000 by the number 0.6806 from the 8 percent column of Table 3. This says that $6,806 invested now at 8 percent will grow to $10,000 in five years if the interest is left on deposit and reinvested each year at 8 percent interest.

Once again, if compounding is to be semiannual, the factor should be taken from the column for a semiannual interest rate equal to $r/2$ and the row for a number of periods equal to $2n$. If quarterly compounding is used, use $r/4$ and $4n$ (for example, 2 percent for 40 periods to show present value compounded quarterly at 2 percent a quarter for 10 years).[2]

---

[2] Quarterly compounding at 2 percent a quarter is equivalent to an annual rate of $(1.02)^4 - 1 = 8.24$ percent. The quarterly compounding rate equivalent to an 8 percent annual compounding rate is ($\sqrt[4]{1.08} - 1$), or approximately 1.94 percent each quarter. If this amount of precision is important, specially constructed quarterly tables, calculators, or computer programs should be used.

Extending Table 3

Table 3 can be extended easily to provide multipliers for any number of periods. The procedure is simple:

1. Select the column for the desired interest rate.
2. From this column select any two or more multipliers for which the number of periods adds up to the number of periods (n) for which a multiplier is needed.
3. Multiply these multipliers.

For example, the present value of $1 twenty years after the zero date at 5 percent compounded annually can be calculated in many ways. Three of these are:

Multiplier for (n = 10) × multiplier for (n = 10) = 0.6139 × 0.6139 = 0.3769
Multiplier for (n = 5) × multiplier for (n = 15) = 0.7835 × 0.4810 = 0.3769
Multiplier for (n = 1) × multiplier for (n = 19) = 0.9524 × 0.3957 = 0.3769

Why does this work? Suppose the company expects to receive $1 20 years from now. Multiplying it by the discount factor for $n = 10$ brings it to its present value *at a point ten years from now*, $0.614. That amount is not the present value today, however. It is the future value ten years from now. The present value today of any sum ten years in the future can be calculated by discounting it for ten years—in other words, by multiplying $0.6139 by 0.6139.

Table 4: Present Value of an Annuity of $1 per Period

The present value of a series of cash flows can always be determined by using the multipliers in Table 3. For example, a series of three payments of $10,000 each, the first one a year from now, the second a year later, and the third a year after that, has a present value at 8 percent, compounded annually, as follows:

Years After Reference Date	Cash Flow	Multiplier at 8% (Table 3)	Present Value at 8%
1	$10,000	0.9259	$ 9,259
2	10,000	0.8573	8,573
3	10,000	0.7938	7,938
Total			$25,770

Doing this for a large number of periods would be time consuming. Table 4 has been developed for use whenever the cash flows in a series are identical each period (an *annuity*). The multipliers in Table 4 for a three-year annuity at 8 percent is 2.5771. Multiplying this by the amount of the annuity, $10,000, produces a present value of $25,771, identical to the figure we derived above except for an insignificant rounding error. *Each multiplier in Table 4 is merely the sum of the multipliers in Table 3* for periods 1 through *n*.

Converting Table 4 to Earlier Equivalents

The multipliers in Table 4 are used to calculate the present value of a series of cash payments on a reference date exactly one period prior to the date of the first payment. To find the present value at a still earlier reference date, the present value of the annuity can be multiplied by the multiplier from Table 3 for the number of additional years desired.

For example, the present value at 8 percent of a ten-year, $10,000 annuity in arrears is:

$$\$10,000 \times 6.7101 = \$67,101.$$

Suppose, however, that the first payment in this annuity is five years from now and that we want to know its present value as of today. The $67,101 figure is the present value *one year before the first payment is made*, or four years from now:

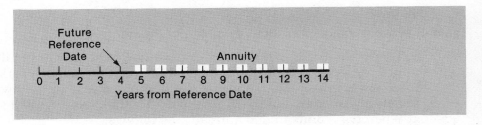

The present value today, therefore, can be obtained by multiplying $67,101 by the four-year multiplier from Table 3:

$$\$67,101 \times 0.7350 = \$49,319.$$

The same figure can be derived in a different way. A ten-year annuity starting five years from now is the same as a 14-year annuity in arrears minus the first four payments. The multiplier in Table 4 for 14 years at 8 percent is 8.2442, and the multiplier for four years is 3.3121. The appropriate multiplier, therefore, is:

$$8.2442 - 3.3121 = 4.9321.$$

Multiplying this by the $10,000 annuity produces a present value of $49,321, which differs only by an insignificant rounding error from the answer we derived earlier.

Converting Table 4 for Annuities in Advance

A somewhat similar procedure can be used to find the present value of an annuity in advance—that is, one in which the first payment is made on the date at which present value is to be calculated. A ten-year annuity in advance is simply a nine-year annuity in arrears plus one payment immediately. For $10,000 a year at 8 percent, the calculation is:

$$\underset{\substack{\text{(immediate} \\ \text{payment)}}}{\$10,000} + \underset{\substack{\text{(annuity,} \\ \text{9 years)}}}{\$10,000} \times \underset{\substack{\text{(Table 4,} \\ \text{9 years)}}}{6.2469} = \underset{\substack{\text{(present value,} \\ \text{10-year annuity)}}}{\$72,469.}$$

The general rule is: to convert a multiplier for the present value of an annuity in arrears to a multiplier for an annuity in advance, *take the multiplier for an interval one period shorter and add 1.0000.*

Finding Equivalent Annuities

It is sometimes useful to find the annuity that is equivalent to a given present sum. This is a simple arithmetic operation, once the present sum and the interest rate are known. The formula for the present value of an annuity can be expressed as:

Present value = Table 4 multiplier × annuity.

Turning this equation around, we find:

Annuity = Present value ÷ Table 4 multiplier.

The ten-year annuity in arrears that is equivalent at 8 percent interest to a present sum of $100,000 is:

Annuity = $100,000 ÷ 6.7101 = $14,903.

In other words, someone wanting to buy a ten-year annuity of $14,903 a year in an 8 percent market will have to pay $100,000.

Bond Value Tables

Tables 5 through 9 give the present values at various yield rates of bonds bearing various coupon rates from 5 percent to 9 percent and of various terms from six months to 30 years.

To find the present value of a bond when the yield to maturity is known, turn to the table with the appropriate coupon rate (for

TABLE 1. Future Value of $1

$$F_n = P(1 + r)^n$$

Pe-riods	2%	3%	4%	5%	6%	8%	10%	12%
1	1.0200	1.0300	1.0400	1.0500	1.0600	1.0800	1.1000	1.1200
2	1.0404	1.0609	1.0816	1.1025	1.1236	1.1664	1.2100	1.2544
3	1.0612	1.0927	1.1249	1.1576	1.1910	1.2597	1.3310	1.4049
4	1.0824	1.1255	1.1699	1.2155	1.2625	1.3605	1.4641	1.5735
5	1.1041	1.1593	1.2167	1.2763	1.3382	1.4693	1.6105	1.7623
6	1.1262	1.1941	1.2653	1.3401	1.4185	1.5869	1.7716	1.9738
7	1.1487	1.2299	1.3159	1.4071	1.5036	1.7138	1.9488	2.2107
8	1.1717	1.2668	1.3686	1.4775	1.5938	1.8509	2.1436	2.4760
9	1.1951	1.3048	1.4233	1.5513	1.6895	1.9990	2.3589	2.7731
10	1.2190	1.3439	1.4802	1.6289	1.7908	2.1589	2.5938	3.1059
11	1.2434	1.3842	1.5395	1.7103	1.8983	2.3316	2.8532	3.4785
12	1.2682	1.4258	1.6010	1.7959	2.0122	2.5182	3.1385	3.8960
13	1.2936	1.4685	1.6651	1.8856	2.1329	2.7196	3.4524	4.3635
14	1.3195	1.5126	1.7317	1.9799	2.2609	2.9372	3.7976	4.8871
15	1.3459	1.5580	1.8009	2.0709	2.3966	3.1722	4.1774	5.4736
16	1.3728	1.6047	1.8730	2.1829	2.5404	3.4259	4.5951	6.1304
17	1.4002	1.6528	1.9479	2.2920	2.6928	3.7000	5.0545	6.8660
18	1.4282	1.7024	2.0258	2.4066	2.8543	3.9960	5.5600	7.6900
19	1.4568	1.7535	2.1068	2.5270	3.0256	4.3157	6.1160	8.6128
20	1.4859	1.8061	2.1911	2.6533	3.2071	4.6610	6.7276	9.6463
22	1.5460	1.9161	2.3699	2.9253	3.6035	5.4365	8.1404	12.1003
24	1.6084	2.0328	2.5633	3.2251	4.0489	6.3412	9.8498	15.1786
26	1.6734	2.1566	2.7725	3.5557	4.5494	7.3964	11.9183	19.0401
28	1.7410	2.2879	2.9987	3.9201	5.1117	8.6271	14.4211	23.8839
30	1.8114	2.4273	3.2434	4.3219	5.7435	10.0627	17.4495	29.9599
32	1.8845	2.5751	3.5081	4.7649	6.4534	11.7371	21.1140	37.5817
34	1.9607	2.7319	3.7943	5.2533	7.2510	13.6901	25.5479	47.1425
36	2.0399	2.8983	4.1039	5.7918	8.1473	15.9682	30.9130	59.1356
38	2.1223	3.0748	4.4388	6.3855	9.1543	18.6253	37.4047	74.1797
40	2.2080	3.2620	4.8010	7.0400	10.2857	21.7245	45.2597	93.0510
50	2.6916	4.3839	7.1067	11.4674	18.4202	46.9016	117.3920	289.0022

example, Table 8 for an 8 percent coupon) and find the column corresponding to the number of years to maturity (for example, ten years). Finally, find the row identified by the known yield to maturity at the left (say, 9.4 percent), and read the present value from the appropriate column in that row (91.05). This indicates that a bond with a face value of $100 has a present value of $91.05 in a 9.4 percent market. To find the present value of any other face amount, multiply the face value by one one-hundredth of the factor shown in the table.

TABLE 2. Future Value of Annuity of $1 in Arrears

$$F = A \left[\frac{(1 + r)^n - 1}{r} \right]$$

Pe-riods	2%	3%	4%	5%	6%	8%	10%	12%
1....	1.0000	1.0000	1.0000	1.0000	1.0000	1.0000	1.0000	1.0000
2....	2.0200	2.0300	2.0400	2.0500	2.0600	2.0800	2.1000	2.1200
3....	3.0604	3.0909	3.1216	3.1525	3.1836	3.2464	3.3100	3.3744
4....	4.1216	4.1836	4.2465	4.3101	4.3746	4.5061	4.6410	4.7793
5....	5.2040	5.3091	5.4163	5.5256	5.6371	5.8666	6.1051	6.3528
6....	6.3081	6.4684	6.6330	6.8019	6.9753	7.3359	7.7156	8.1152
7....	7.4343	7.6625	7.8983	8.1420	8.3938	8.9228	9.4872	10.0890
8....	8.5830	8.8923	9.2142	9.5491	9.8975	10.6366	11.4360	12.2997
9....	9.7546	10.1591	10.5828	11.0266	11.4913	12.4876	13.5796	14.7757
10....	10.9497	11.4639	12.0061	12.5779	13.1808	14.4866	15.9376	17.5487
11....	12.1687	12.8078	13.4864	14.2068	14.9716	16.6455	18.5314	20.6546
12....	13.4121	14.1920	15.0258	15.9171	16.8699	18.9771	21.3846	24.1331
13....	14.6803	15.6178	16.6268	17.7130	18.8821	21.4953	24.5231	28.0291
14....	15.9739	17.0863	18.2919	19.5986	21.0151	24.2149	27.9755	32.3926
15....	17.2934	18.5989	20.0236	21.5786	23.2760	27.1521	31.7731	37.2797
16....	18.6393	20.1569	21.8245	23.6575	25.6725	30.3243	35.9503	42.7533
17....	20.0121	21.7616	23.6975	25.8404	28.2129	33.7502	40.5456	48.8837
18....	21.4123	23.4144	25.6454	28.1324	30.9057	37.4502	45.6001	55.7497
19....	22.8406	25.1169	27.6712	30.5390	33.7600	41.4463	51.1601	63.4397
20....	24.2974	26.8704	29.7781	33.0660	36.7856	45.7620	57.2761	72.0524
22....	27.2990	30.5368	34.2480	38.5052	43.3923	55.4568	71.4041	92.5026
24....	30.4219	34.4265	39.0826	44.5020	50.8156	66.7648	88.4989	118.1552
26....	33.6709	38.5530	44.3117	51.1135	59.1564	79.9544	109.1835	150.3339
28....	37.0512	42.9309	49.9676	58.4026	68.5281	95.3388	134.2119	190.6989
30....	40.5681	47.5754	56.0849	66.4388	79.0582	113.2832	164.4962	241.3327
32....	44.2270	52.5028	62.7015	75.2988	90.8898	134.2135	201.1402	304.8477
34....	48.0338	57.7302	69.8579	85.0670	104.1838	158.6267	245.4796	384.5210
36....	51.9944	63.2759	77.5983	95.8363	119.1209	187.1021	299.1302	484.4631
38....	56.1149	69.1594	85.9703	107.7095	135.9042	220.3159	364.0475	609.8305
40....	60.4020	75.4013	95.0255	120.7998	154.7620	259.0565	442.5974	767.0914
50....	84.5794	112.7969	152.6671	209.3480	290.3359	573.7702	1163.9209	2400.0180

Note: To convert this table to values of an annuity in advance, take one more period and subtract 1.0000.

These tables can also be used to find the yield to maturity when the market value and number of years to maturity are known. To find the yield to maturity of a fixed-payment bond, turn to the table for the bond's coupon rate, find the column for the number of years until the bond matures, and go down to the row on which the quoted market price is located. The yield is the figure at the left end of this row.

TABLE 3. Present Value of $1

$$P = F_n(1 + r)^{-n}$$

Periods	2%	3%	4%	4.5%	5%	6%	7%	8%	9%	10%	12%	14%	15%	20%	25%	30%
1	0.9804	0.9709	0.9615	0.9569	0.9524	0.9434	0.9346	0.9259	0.9174	0.9091	0.8929	0.877	0.870	0.833	0.800	0.769
2	0.9612	0.9426	0.9246	0.9157	0.9070	0.8900	0.8734	0.8573	0.8417	0.8264	0.7972	0.769	0.756	0.694	0.640	0.592
3	0.9423	0.9151	0.8890	0.8763	0.8638	0.8396	0.8163	0.7938	0.7722	0.7513	0.7118	0.675	0.658	0.579	0.512	0.455
4	0.9238	0.8885	0.8548	0.8386	0.8227	0.7921	0.7629	0.7350	0.7084	0.6830	0.6355	0.592	0.572	0.482	0.410	0.350
5	0.9057	0.8626	0.8219	0.8025	0.7835	0.7473	0.7130	0.6806	0.6499	0.6209	0.5674	0.519	0.497	0.402	0.328	0.269
6	0.8880	0.8375	0.7903	0.7679	0.7462	0.7050	0.6663	0.6302	0.5963	0.5645	0.5066	0.456	0.432	0.335	0.262	0.207
7	0.8706	0.8131	0.7599	0.7348	0.7107	0.6651	0.6227	0.5835	0.5470	0.5132	0.4524	0.400	0.376	0.279	0.210	0.159
8	0.8535	0.7894	0.7307	0.7032	0.6768	0.6274	0.5820	0.5403	0.5019	0.4665	0.4039	0.351	0.327	0.233	0.168	0.123
9	0.8368	0.7664	0.7026	0.6729	0.6446	0.5919	0.5439	0.5002	0.4604	0.4241	0.3606	0.308	0.284	0.194	0.134	0.094
10	0.8203	0.7441	0.6756	0.6439	0.6139	0.5584	0.5083	0.4632	0.4224	0.3855	0.3220	0.270	0.247	0.162	0.107	0.073
11	0.8043	0.7224	0.6496	0.6162	0.5847	0.5268	0.4751	0.4289	0.3875	0.3505	0.2875	0.237	0.215	0.135	0.086	0.056
12	0.7885	0.7014	0.6246	0.5897	0.5568	0.4970	0.4440	0.3971	0.3555	0.3186	0.2567	0.208	0.187	0.112	0.069	0.043
13	0.7730	0.6810	0.6006	0.5643	0.5303	0.4688	0.4150	0.3677	0.3262	0.2897	0.2292	0.182	0.163	0.093	0.055	0.033
14	0.7579	0.6611	0.5775	0.5400	0.5051	0.4423	0.3878	0.3405	0.2992	0.2633	0.2046	0.160	0.141	0.078	0.044	0.025
15	0.7430	0.6419	0.5553	0.5167	0.4810	0.4173	0.3624	0.3153	0.2745	0.2394	0.1827	0.140	0.123	0.065	0.035	0.020
16	0.7284	0.6232	0.5339	0.4945	0.4581	0.3936	0.3387	0.2919	0.2519	0.2176	0.1631	0.123	0.107	0.054	0.028	0.015
17	0.7142	0.6050	0.5134	0.4732	0.4363	0.3714	0.3166	0.2703	0.2311	0.1978	0.1456	0.108	0.093	0.045	0.023	0.012
18	0.7002	0.5874	0.4936	0.4528	0.4155	0.3503	0.2959	0.2502	0.2120	0.1799	0.1300	0.095	0.081	0.038	0.018	0.009
19	0.6864	0.5703	0.4746	0.4333	0.3957	0.3305	0.2765	0.2317	0.1945	0.1635	0.1161	0.083	0.070	0.031	0.014	0.007
20	0.6730	0.5537	0.4564	0.4146	0.3769	0.3118	0.2584	0.2145	0.1784	0.1486	0.1037	0.073	0.061	0.026	0.012	0.005
21	0.6598	0.5375	0.4388	0.3968	0.3589	0.2942	0.2415	0.1987	0.1637	0.1351	0.0926	0.064	0.053	0.022	0.009	0.004
22	0.6468	0.5219	0.4220	0.3797	0.3418	0.2775	0.2257	0.1839	0.1502	0.1228	0.0826	0.056	0.046	0.018	0.007	0.003
23	0.6342	0.5067	0.4057	0.3634	0.3256	0.2618	0.2109	0.1703	0.1378	0.1117	0.0738	0.049	0.040	0.015	0.006	0.002
24	0.6217	0.4919	0.3901	0.3477	0.3101	0.2470	0.1971	0.1577	0.1264	0.1015	0.0659	0.043	0.035	0.013	0.005	0.002
25	0.6095	0.4776	0.3751	0.3327	0.2953	0.2330	0.1842	0.1460	0.1160	0.0923	0.0588	0.038	0.030	0.010	0.004	0.001
26	0.5976	0.4637	0.3607	0.3184	0.2812	0.2198	0.1722	0.1352	0.1064	0.0839	0.0525	0.033	0.026	0.009	0.003	0.001
27	0.5859	0.4502	0.3468	0.3047	0.2678	0.2074	0.1609	0.1252	0.0976	0.0763	0.0469	0.029	0.023	0.007	0.002	0.001
28	0.5744	0.4371	0.3335	0.2916	0.2551	0.1956	0.1504	0.1159	0.0895	0.0693	0.0419	0.026	0.020	0.006	0.002	0.001
29	0.5631	0.4243	0.3207	0.2790	0.2429	0.1846	0.1406	0.1073	0.0822	0.0630	0.0374	0.022	0.017	0.005	0.002	0.001
30	0.5521	0.4120	0.3083	0.2670	0.2314	0.1741	0.1314	0.0994	0.0754	0.0573	0.0334	0.020	0.015	0.004	0.001	0.001
40	0.4529	0.3066	0.2083	0.1719	0.1420	0.0972	0.0668	0.0460	0.0318	0.0221	0.0108	0.005	0.004	0.001		
50	0.3715	0.2281	0.1407	0.1107	0.0872	0.0543	0.0339	0.0213	0.0134	0.0085	0.0035	0.001	0.001			

TABLE 4. Present Value of Annuity of $1 in Arrears

$$P_A = A\left[\frac{1 - (1 + r)^{-n}}{r}\right]$$

Periods (n)	2%	3%	4%	4.5%	5%	6%	7%	8%	9%	10%	12%	14%	15%	20%	25%	30%
1	0.9804	0.9709	0.9615	0.9569	0.9524	0.9434	0.9346	0.9259	0.9174	0.9091	0.8929	0.877	0.870	0.833	0.800	0.769
2	1.9416	1.9135	1.8861	1.8727	1.8594	1.8334	1.8080	1.7833	1.7591	1.7355	1.6901	1.647	1.626	1.528	1.440	1.361
3	2.8839	2.8286	2.7751	2.7490	2.7232	2.6730	2.6243	2.5771	2.5313	2.4869	2.4018	2.322	2.283	2.106	1.952	1.816
4	3.8077	3.7171	3.6299	3.5875	3.5460	3.4651	3.3872	3.3121	3.2397	3.1699	3.0373	2.914	2.855	2.589	2.362	2.166
5	4.7135	4.5797	4.4518	4.3900	4.3295	4.2124	4.1002	3.9927	3.8897	3.7908	3.6048	3.433	3.352	2.991	2.689	2.436
6	5.6014	5.4172	5.2421	5.1579	5.0757	4.9173	4.7665	4.6229	4.4859	4.3553	4.1114	3.889	3.784	3.326	2.951	2.643
7	6.4720	6.2303	6.0021	5.8927	5.7864	5.5824	5.3893	5.2064	5.0330	4.8684	4.5638	4.288	4.160	3.605	3.161	2.802
8	7.3255	7.0197	6.7327	6.5959	6.4632	6.2098	5.9713	5.7466	5.5348	5.3349	4.9676	4.639	4.487	3.837	3.329	2.925
9	8.1622	7.7861	7.4353	7.2688	7.1078	6.8017	6.5152	6.2469	5.9952	5.7590	5.3282	4.946	4.772	4.031	3.463	3.019
10	8.9826	8.5302	8.1109	7.9127	7.7217	7.3601	7.0236	6.7101	6.4177	6.1446	5.6502	5.216	5.019	4.192	3.571	3.092
11	9.7868	9.2526	8.7605	8.5289	8.3064	7.8869	7.4987	7.1390	6.8052	6.4951	5.9377	5.453	5.234	4.327	3.656	3.147
12	10.5753	9.9540	9.3851	9.1186	8.8633	8.3838	7.9427	7.5361	7.1607	6.8137	6.1944	5.660	5.421	4.439	3.725	3.190
13	11.3484	10.6350	9.9856	9.6829	9.3936	8.8527	8.3577	7.9038	7.4869	7.1034	6.4236	5.842	5.583	4.533	3.780	3.223
14	12.1062	11.2961	10.5631	10.2228	9.8986	9.2950	8.7455	8.2442	7.7861	7.3667	6.6282	6.002	5.724	4.611	3.824	3.249
15	12.8493	11.9379	11.1184	10.7395	10.3797	9.7122	9.1079	8.5595	8.0607	7.6061	6.8109	6.142	5.847	4.675	3.859	3.268
16	13.5777	12.5611	11.6523	11.2340	10.8378	10.1059	9.4466	8.8514	8.3126	7.8237	6.9740	6.265	5.954	4.730	3.887	3.283
17	14.2919	13.1661	12.1657	11.7072	11.2741	10.4773	9.7632	9.1216	8.5436	8.0216	7.1196	6.373	6.047	4.775	3.910	3.295
18	14.9920	13.7535	12.6593	12.1600	11.6896	10.8276	10.0591	9.3719	8.7556	8.2014	7.2497	6.467	6.128	4.812	3.928	3.304
19	15.6785	14.3238	13.1339	12.5933	12.0853	11.1581	10.3356	9.6036	8.9501	8.3649	7.3658	6.550	6.198	4.844	3.942	3.311
20	16.3514	14.8775	13.5903	13.0079	12.4622	11.4699	10.5940	9.8181	9.1285	8.5136	7.4694	6.623	6.259	4.870	3.954	3.316
21	17.0112	15.4150	14.0292	13.4047	12.8212	11.7640	10.8355	10.0168	9.2922	8.6487	7.5620	6.687	6.312	4.891	3.963	3.320
22	17.6580	15.9369	14.4511	13.7844	13.1630	12.0416	11.0612	10.2007	9.4424	8.7715	7.6446	6.743	6.359	4.909	3.970	3.323
23	18.2922	16.4436	14.8568	14.1478	13.4886	12.3034	11.2722	10.3711	9.5802	8.8832	7.7184	6.792	6.399	4.925	3.976	3.325
24	18.9139	16.9355	15.2470	14.4955	13.7986	12.5504	11.4693	10.5288	9.7066	8.9847	7.7843	6.835	6.434	4.937	3.981	3.327
25	19.5235	17.4131	15.6221	14.8282	14.0939	12.7834	11.6536	10.6748	9.8226	9.0770	7.8431	6.873	6.464	4.948	3.985	3.329
26	20.1210	17.8768	15.9828	15.1466	14.3752	13.0032	11.8258	10.8100	9.9290	9.1609	7.8957	6.906	6.491	4.956	3.988	3.330
27	20.7069	18.3270	16.3296	15.4513	14.6430	13.2105	11.9867	10.9352	10.0265	9.2372	7.9426	6.935	6.514	4.964	3.990	3.331
28	21.2813	18.7641	16.6631	15.7429	14.8981	13.4062	12.1371	11.0511	10.1161	9.3066	7.9844	6.961	6.534	4.970	3.992	3.331
29	21.8444	19.1885	16.9837	16.0219	15.1411	13.5907	12.2777	11.1584	10.1983	9.3696	8.0218	6.983	6.551	4.975	3.994	3.332
30	22.3965	19.6004	17.2920	16.2889	15.3725	13.7648	12.4090	11.2578	10.2737	9.4269	8.0552	7.003	6.566	4.979	3.995	3.332
40	27.3555	23.1148	19.7928	18.4016	17.1591	15.0463	13.3317	11.9246	10.7570	9.7791	8.2438	7.105	6.642	4.997	3.999	3.333
50	31.4236	25.7298	21.4822	19.7620	18.2559	15.7619	13.8007	12.2335	10.9617	9.9148	8.3045	7.133	6.661	4.999	4.000	3.333

Note: To convert this table to values of an annuity in advance, take one less period and add 1.0000.

TABLE 5.   Bond Values—Coupon Rate of 5 Percent (semiannual interest payments; semiannual compounding)

Annual Yield (%)	½	1	5	10	15	19½	20	30
				Years to Maturity				
4.0.........	100.49	100.97	104.49	108.18	111.20	113.45	113.68	117.38
4.1.........	100.44	100.87	104.03	107.32	110.01	112.00	112.20	115.45
4.2.........	100.39	100.78	103.57	106.48	108.84	110.58	110.75	113.57
4.3.........	100.34	100.68	103.12	105.64	107.68	109.18	109.33	111.74
4.4.........	100.29	100.58	102.67	104.81	106.54	107.80	107.93	109.94
4.5.........	100.24	100.48	102.22	103.99	105.41	106.45	106.55	108.19
4.6.........	100.20	100.39	101.77	103.18	104.30	105.11	105.19	106.47
4.7.........	100.15	100.29	101.32	102.37	103.20	103.80	103.86	104.80
4.8.........	100.10	100.19	100.88	101.57	102.12	102.51	102.55	103.16
4.9.........	100.05	100.10	100.44	100.78	101.05	101.25	101.27	101.56
5.0.........	100.00	100.00	100.00	100.00	100.00	100.00	100.00	100.00
5.1.........	99.95	99.90	99.56	99.22	98.96	98.77	98.76	98.47
5.2.........	99.90	99.81	99.13	98.46	97.93	97.57	97.53	96.98
5.3.........	99.85	99.71	98.70	97.69	96.92	96.38	96.33	95.52
5.4.........	99.81	99.62	98.27	96.94	95.92	95.21	95.14	94.09
5.5.........	99.76	99.52	97.84	96.19	94.94	94.06	93.98	92.69
5.6.........	99.71	99.42	97.41	95.45	93.96	92.94	92.84	91.33
5.7.........	99.66	99.33	96.99	94.72	93.00	91.82	91.71	89.99
5.8.........	99.61	99.23	96.57	93.99	92.06	90.73	90.60	88.69
5.9.........	99.56	99.14	96.15	93.27	91.12	89.65	89.51	87.41
6.0.........	99.51	99.04	95.73	92.56	90.20	88.60	88.44	86.16
6.1.........	99.47	98.95	95.32	91.86	89.29	87.55	87.39	84.94
6.2.........	99.42	98.85	94.91	91.16	88.39	86.53	86.35	83.74
6.3.........	99.37	98.76	94.50	90.46	87.50	85.52	85.33	82.57
6.4.........	99.32	98.66	94.09	89.78	86.63	84.53	84.33	81.43
6.5.........	99.27	98.57	93.68	89.10	85.76	83.55	83.34	80.31
6.6.........	99.23	98.48	93.28	88.42	84.91	82.59	82.37	79.21
6.7.........	99.18	98.38	92.88	87.75	84.07	81.65	81.42	78.14
6.8.........	99.13	98.29	92.48	87.09	83.24	80.72	80.48	77.09
6.9.........	99.08	98.19	92.08	86.44	82.42	79.80	79.55	76.06
7.0.........	99.03	98.10	91.68	85.79	81.61	78.90	78.64	75.06
7.1.........	98.99	98.01	91.29	85.14	80.81	78.01	77.75	74.07
7.2.........	98.94	97.91	90.90	84.51	80.02	77.14	76.87	73.10
7.3.........	98.89	97.82	90.51	83.88	79.24	76.28	76.00	72.16
7.4.........	98.84	97.73	90.12	83.25	78.47	75.43	75.15	71.23
7.5.........	98.80	97.63	89.73	82.63	77.71	74.60	74.31	70.33
7.6.........	98.75	97.54	89.35	82.02	76.96	73.78	73.49	69.44
7.7.........	98.70	97.45	88.97	81.41	76.22	72.97	72.67	68.57
7.8.........	98.65	97.36	88.59	80.80	75.49	72.18	71.87	67.72
7.9.........	98.61	97.26	88.21	80.21	74.77	71.39	71.09	66.88
8.0.........	98.56	97.17	87.83	79.61	74.06	70.62	70.31	66.06
8.1.........	98.51	97.08	87.46	79.03	73.36	69.86	69.55	65.26
8.2.........	98.46	96.99	87.09	78.45	72.67	69.12	68.80	64.48
8.3.........	98.42	96.89	86.72	77.87	71.98	68.38	68.06	63.71
8.4.........	98.37	96.80	86.35	77.30	71.30	67.66	67.33	62.95

TABLE 6. Bond Values—Coupon Rate of 6 Percent (semiannual interest payments; semiannual compounding)

Annual Yield (%)	\tfrac{1}{2}	1	5	10	15	19½	20	30
4.5	100.73	101.45	106.65	111.97	116.23	119.34	119.65	124.56
4.6	100.68	101.35	106.19	111.12	115.05	117.90	118.18	122.66
4.7	100.64	101.26	105.73	110.28	113.88	116.48	116.74	120.80
4.8	100.59	101.16	105.28	109.44	112.73	115.09	115.32	118.98
4.9	100.54	101.06	104.83	108.61	111.59	113.71	113.92	117.20
5.0	100.49	100.96	104.38	107.79	110.47	112.37	112.55	115.45
5.1	100.44	100.87	103.93	106.98	109.36	111.04	111.20	113.75
5.2	100.39	100.77	103.48	106.18	108.26	109.73	109.87	112.09
5.3	100.34	100.67	103.04	105.38	107.18	108.45	108.57	110.46
5.4	100.29	100.58	102.60	104.59	106.11	107.18	107.28	108.86
5.5	100.24	100.48	102.16	103.81	105.06	105.94	106.02	107.31
5.6	100.19	100.38	101.72	103.03	104.02	104.71	104.78	105.78
5.7	100.15	100.29	101.29	102.26	103.00	103.50	103.55	104.29
5.8	100.10	100.19	100.86	101.50	101.99	102.32	102.35	102.83
5.9	100.05	100.10	100.43	100.75	100.99	101.15	101.17	101.40
6.0	100.00	100.00	100.00	100.00	100.00	100.00	100.00	100.00
6.1	99.95	99.90	99.57	99.26	99.03	98.87	98.85	98.63
6.2	99.90	99.81	99.15	98.53	98.07	97.75	97.73	97.29
6.3	99.85	99.71	98.73	97.80	97.12	96.66	96.62	95.98
6.4	99.81	99.62	98.31	97.08	96.18	95.58	95.52	94.69
6.5	99.76	99.52	97.89	96.37	95.25	94.52	94.45	93.44
6.6	99.71	99.43	97.48	95.66	94.34	93.47	93.39	92.21
6.7	99.66	99.33	97.07	94.96	93.44	92.44	92.35	91.00
6.8	99.61	99.24	96.66	94.26	92.55	91.43	91.32	89.82
6.9	99.57	99.14	96.25	93.58	91.67	90.43	90.32	88.66
7.0	99.52	99.05	95.84	92.89	90.80	89.45	89.32	87.53
7.1	99.47	98.96	95.44	92.22	89.95	88.48	88.35	86.42
7.2	99.42	98.86	95.04	91.55	89.10	87.53	87.38	85.33
7.3	99.37	98.77	94.63	90.89	88.27	86.59	86.44	84.26
7.4	99.32	98.67	94.24	90.23	87.44	85.67	85.50	83.22
7.5	99.28	98.58	93.84	89.58	86.63	84.76	84.59	82.20
7.6	99.23	98.49	93.45	88.93	85.82	83.86	83.68	81.19
7.7	99.18	98.39	93.05	88.29	85.03	82.98	82.79	80.21
7.8	99.13	98.30	92.66	87.66	84.25	82.11	81.92	79.25
7.9	99.09	98.21	92.28	87.03	83.47	81.26	81.06	78.30
8.0	99.04	98.11	91.89	86.41	82.71	80.42	80.21	77.38
8.1	98.99	98.02	91.50	85.79	81.95	79.59	79.37	76.47
8.2	98.94	97.93	91.12	85.18	81.21	78.77	78.55	75.58
8.3	98.90	97.84	90.74	84.58	80.47	77.96	77.74	74.71
8.4	98.85	97.74	90.36	83.98	79.74	77.17	76.94	73.85

TABLE 7. Bond Values—Coupon Rate of 7 Percent (semiannual interest payments; semiannual compounding)

Annual Yield (%)	Years to Maturity							
	$^1/_2$	1	5	10	15	19$^1/_2$	20	30
5.0	100.98	101.93	108.75	115.59	120.93	124.73	125.10	130.91
5.1	100.93	101.83	108.29	114.74	119.75	123.30	123.65	129.03
5.2	100.88	101.73	107.84	113.90	118.59	121.89	122.22	127.19
5.3	100.83	101.63	107.38	113.06	117.44	120.51	120.81	125.40
5.4	100.78	101.54	106.93	112.24	116.31	119.15	119.42	123.64
5.5	100.73	101.44	106.48	111.42	115.19	117.81	118.06	121.92
5.6	100.68	101.34	106.03	110.61	114.08	116.48	116.72	120.23
5.7	100.63	101.25	105.59	109.81	112.99	115.18	115.40	118.58
5.8	100.58	101.15	105.14	109.01	111.91	113.90	114.10	116.97
5.9	100.53	101.05	104.70	108.22	110.85	112.64	112.82	115.39
6.0	100.49	100.96	104.27	107.44	109.80	111.40	111.56	113.84
6.1	100.44	100.86	103.83	106.66	108.76	110.18	110.32	112.32
6.2	100.39	100.76	103.39	105.90	107.74	108.98	109.10	110.84
6.3	100.34	100.67	102.96	105.14	106.73	107.80	107.90	109.38
6.4	100.29	100.57	102.53	104.38	105.73	106.63	106.72	107.96
6.5	100.24	100.48	102.11	103.63	104.75	105.48	105.55	106.56
6.6	100.19	100.38	101.68	102.89	103.77	104.35	104.41	105.20
6.7	100.15	100.29	101.26	102.16	102.81	103.24	103.28	103.86
6.8	100.10	100.19	100.84	101.43	101.86	102.14	102.17	102.55
6.9	100.05	100.10	100.42	100.71	100.93	101.06	101.08	101.26
7.0	100.00	100.00	100.00	100.00	100.00	100.00	100.00	100.00
7.1	99.95	99.91	99.59	99.29	99.09	98.95	98.94	98.77
7.2	99.90	99.81	99.17	98.59	98.18	97.92	97.90	97.55
7.3	99.86	99.72	98.76	97.90	97.29	96.91	96.87	96.37
7.4	99.81	99.62	98.35	97.21	96.41	95.91	95.86	95.21
7.5	99.76	99.53	97.95	96.53	95.54	94.92	94.86	94.07
7.6	99.71	99.43	97.54	95.85	94.68	93.95	93.88	92.95
7.7	99.66	99.34	97.14	95.18	93.84	92.99	92.92	91.85
7.8	99.62	99.24	96.74	94.52	93.00	92.05	91.96	90.78
7.9	99.57	99.15	96.34	93.86	92.17	91.12	91.03	89.72
8.0	99.52	99.06	95.94	93.20	91.35	90.21	90.10	88.69
8.1	99.47	98.96	95.55	92.56	90.55	89.31	89.19	87.67
8.2	99.42	98.87	95.16	91.92	89.75	88.42	88.30	86.68
8.3	99.38	98.78	94.77	91.28	88.96	87.54	87.42	85.70
8.4	99.33	98.68	94.38	90.65	88.18	86.68	86.55	84.75
8.5	99.28	98.59	93.99	90.03	87.42	85.83	85.69	83.81
8.6	99.23	98.50	93.61	89.41	86.66	85.00	84.85	82.88
8.7	99.19	98.40	93.22	88.80	85.91	84.17	84.02	81.98
8.8	99.14	98.31	92.84	88.19	85.17	83.36	83.20	81.09
8.9	99.09	98.22	92.46	87.59	84.43	82.56	82.39	80.22
9.0	99.04	98.13	92.09	86.99	83.71	81.77	81.60	79.36
9.1	99.00	98.04	91.71	86.40	83.00	80.99	80.82	78.52
9.2	98.95	97.94	91.34	85.81	82.29	80.23	80.04	77.70
9.3	98.90	97.85	90.97	85.23	81.59	79.47	79.28	76.89
9.4	98.85	97.76	90.60	84.66	80.91	78.73	78.53	76.09

TABLE 8. Bond Values—Coupon Rate of 8 Percent (semiannual interest payments; semiannual compounding)

Annual Yield (%)	Years to Maturity							
	$\frac{1}{2}$	1	5	10	15	$19\frac{1}{2}$	20	30
5.5......	101.22	102.40	110.80	119.03	125.31	129.68	130.10	136.53
5.6......	101.17	102.30	110.34	118.19	124.14	128.26	128.66	134.68
5.7......	101.12	102.21	109.89	117.35	122.98	126.86	127.24	132.88
5.8......	101.07	102.11	109.43	116.52	121.84	125.49	125.84	131.11
5.9......	101.02	102.01	108.98	115.69	120.71	124.14	124.47	129.37
6.0......	100.97	101.91	108.53	114.88	119.60	122.81	123.11	127.68
6.1......	100.92	101.82	108.08	114.07	118.50	121.50	121.78	126.01
6.2......	100.87	101.72	107.64	113.27	117.41	120.21	120.47	124.38
6.3......	100.82	101.62	107.20	112.47	116.34	118.93	119.18	122.79
6.4......	100.78	101.53	106.76	111.68	115.28	117.68	117.91	121.22
6.5......	100.73	101.43	106.32	110.90	114.24	116.45	116.66	119.69
6.6......	100.68	101.33	105.88	110.13	113.20	115.23	115.42	118.19
6.7......	100.63	101.24	105.45	109.36	112.18	114.04	114.21	116.72
6.8......	100.58	101.14	105.02	108.61	111.17	112.86	113.01	115.27
6.9......	100.53	101.05	104.59	107.85	110.18	111.70	111.84	113.86
7.0......	100.48	100.95	104.16	107.11	109.20	110.55	110.68	112.47
7.1......	100.43	100.85	103.73	106.37	108.22	109.42	109.54	111.11
7.2......	100.39	100.76	103.31	105.63	107.27	108.31	108.41	109.78
7.3......	100.34	100.66	102.89	104.91	106.32	107.22	107.30	108.47
7.4......	100.29	100.57	102.47	104.19	105.38	106.14	106.21	107.19
7.5......	100.24	100.47	102.05	103.47	104.46	105.08	105.14	105.93
7.6......	100.19	100.38	101.64	102.77	103.54	104.03	104.08	104.70
7.7......	100.14	100.28	101.23	102.07	102.64	103.00	103.04	103.49
7.8......	100.10	100.19	100.82	101.37	101.75	101.99	102.01	102.31
7.9......	100.05	100.09	100.41	100.68	100.87	100.99	101.00	101.14
8.0......	100.00	100.00	100.00	100.00	100.00	100.00	100.00	100.00
8.1......	99.95	99.91	99.60	99.32	99.14	99.03	99.02	98.88
8.2......	99.90	99.81	99.19	98.65	98.29	98.07	98.05	97.78
8.3......	99.86	99.72	98.79	97.99	97.45	97.13	97.10	96.70
8.4......	99.81	99.62	98.39	97.33	96.62	96.20	96.16	95.64
8.5......	99.76	99.53	98.00	96.68	95.81	95.28	95.23	94.60
8.6......	99.71	99.44	97.60	96.03	95.00	94.37	94.32	93.58
8.7......	99.66	99.34	97.21	95.39	94.20	93.48	93.42	92.58
8.8......	99.62	99.25	96.82	94.75	93.41	92.60	92.53	91.60
8.9......	99.57	99.16	96.43	94.12	92.63	91.74	91.66	90.63
9.0......	99.52	99.06	96.04	93.50	91.86	90.89	90.80	89.68
9.1......	99.47	98.97	95.66	92.88	91.09	90.04	89.95	88.75
9.2......	99.43	98.88	95.28	92.26	90.34	89.21	89.11	87.83
9.3......	99.38	98.79	94.89	91.65	89.60	88.40	88.29	86.94
9.4......	99.33	98.69	94.52	91.05	88.86	87.59	87.48	86.05
9.5......	99.28	98.60	94.14	90.45	88.13	86.79	86.68	85.19
9.6......	99.24	98.51	93.76	89.86	87.42	86.01	85.89	84.33
9.7......	99.19	98.42	93.39	89.27	86.71	85.24	85.11	83.50
9.8......	99.14	98.32	93.02	88.69	86.01	84.48	84.34	82.67
9.9......	99.09	98.23	92.65	88.11	85.31	83.72	83.59	81.87

TABLE 9.   Bond Values—Coupon Rate of 9 Percent (semiannual interest payments; semiannual compounding)

Annual Yield (%)	Years to Maturity								
	½	1	5	10	15	19½	20	30
6.5.....	101.21	102.38	110.53	118.17	123.73	127.41	127.76	132.82
6.6.....	101.16	102.29	110.08	117.37	122.63	126.11	126.44	131.18
6.7.....	101.11	102.19	109.64	116.57	121.55	124.83	125.14	129.57
6.8.....	101.06	102.09	109.19	115.78	120.49	123.57	123.86	128.00
6.9.....	101.01	102.00	108.75	114.99	119.43	122.33	122.60	126.46
7.0.....	100.97	101.90	108.32	114.21	118.39	121.10	121.36	124.94
7.1.....	100.92	101.80	107.88	113.44	117.36	119.90	120.13	123.46
7.2.....	100.87	101.71	107.45	112.68	116.35	118.71	118.92	122.01
7.3.....	100.82	101.61	107.02	111.92	115.34	117.53	117.74	120.58
7.4.....	100.77	101.52	106.59	111.17	114.35	116.38	116.57	119.18
7.5.....	100.72	101.42	106.16	110.42	113.37	115.24	115.41	117.80
7.6.....	100.67	101.32	105.73	109.68	112.40	114.12	114.28	116.46
7.7.....	100.63	101.23	105.31	108.95	111.45	113.01	113.16	115.13
7.8.....	100.58	101.13	104.89	108.23	110.50	111.92	112.05	113.84
7.9.....	100.53	101.04	104.47	107.51	109.57	110.85	110.97	112.56
8.0.....	100.48	100.94	104.06	106.80	108.65	109.79	109.90	111.31
8.1.....	100.43	100.85	103.64	106.09	107.73	108.75	108.84	110.08
8.2.....	100.38	100.75	103.23	105.39	106.83	107.72	107.80	108.88
8.3.....	100.34	100.66	102.82	104.69	105.94	106.71	106.78	107.70
8.4.....	100.29	100.56	102.41	104.01	105.06	105.71	105.77	106.54
8.5.....	100.24	100.47	102.00	103.32	104.19	104.72	104.77	105.40
8.6.....	100.19	100.38	101.60	102.65	103.34	103.75	103.79	104.28
8.7.....	100.14	100.28	101.20	101.98	102.49	102.79	102.82	103.18
8.8.....	100.10	100.19	100.80	101.31	101.65	101.85	101.87	102.10
8.9.....	100.05	100.09	100.40	100.65	100.82	100.92	100.93	101.04
9.0.....	100.00	100.00	100.00	100.00	100.00	100.00	100.00	100.00
9.1.....	99.95	99.91	99.61	99.35	99.19	99.09	99.09	98.98
9.2.....	99.90	99.81	99.21	98.71	98.39	98.20	98.19	97.97
9.3.....	99.86	99.72	98.82	98.07	97.60	97.32	97.30	96.99
9.4.....	99.81	99.63	98.43	97.44	96.82	96.45	96.42	96.02
9.5.....	99.76	99.53	98.05	96.82	96.04	95.60	95.56	95.06
9.6.....	99.71	99.44	97.66	96.20	95.28	94.75	94.71	94.13
9.7.....	99.67	99.35	97.28	95.58	94.53	93.92	93.87	93.20
9.8.....	99.62	99.26	96.90	94.97	93.78	93.10	93.04	92.30
9.9.....	99.57	99.16	96.52	94.37	93.04	92.29	92.23	91.41
10.0.....	99.52	99.07	96.14	93.77	92.31	91.49	91.42	90.54
10.1.....	99.48	98.98	95.76	93.17	91.59	90.70	90.63	89.68
10.2.....	99.43	98.89	95.39	92.59	90.88	89.93	89.84	88.83
10.3.....	99.38	98.79	95.02	92.00	90.18	89.16	89.07	88.00
10.4.....	99.33	98.70	94.65	91.42	89.48	88.40	88.31	87.18
10.5.....	99.29	98.61	94.28	90.85	88.79	87.66	87.56	86.38
10.6.....	99.24	98.52	93.91	90.28	88.11	86.92	86.82	85.59
10.7.....	99.19	98.43	93.55	89.71	87.44	86.19	86.09	84.81
10.8.....	99.15	98.34	93.18	89.15	86.77	85.48	85.37	84.04
10.9.....	99.10	98.24	92.82	88.60	86.12	84.77	84.66	83.29

appendix B

Solutions to Independent Study Problems

Chapter 1

1–1.
INCOME STATEMENT

Revenue from sales		$1,000
Cost of goods sold		700
Gross margin		$ 300
Operating expenses:		
Salaries and wages	$120	
Taxes	20	
Sundry	60	200
Net Income		$ 100

STATEMENT OF FINANCIAL POSITION

Assets			*Liabilities and Owners' Equity*		
Current Assets:			Current Liabilities:		
Cash	$ 100		Accounts payable	$ 250	
Accounts receivable	300		Wages payable	50	
Inventories	380		Taxes payable	5	
Prepaid rent	40		Note payable	350	
Total Current Assets		$ 820	Total Current Liabilities		$ 655
Furniture and fixtures		600	R. A. Copake, capital		765
Total		$1,420	Total		$1,420

809

1–2. *a.*

DINGY DIVE BAR
Statement of Financial Position
January 21, 19x4

Assets		Liabilities and Owners' Equity	
Current assets:		Current Liabilities:	
Cash	$ 1,500	Note payable	$11,500
Fixed Assets:		Owners' Equity:	
Bar equipment	1,000	Mr. Robinson	$ 1,500
Buildings	9,500	Mr. Griffiths	1,500
Improvements to		Mr. Thorndike	1,500
land	2,000	Total Owners'	
Land	2,000	Equity	$ 4,500
Total	$16,000	Total	$16,000

b.

DINGY DIVE BAR
Statement of Financial Position
February 21, 19x4

Assets		Liabilities and Owners' Equity	
Current Assets:		Current Liabilities:	
Cash	$ 1,000	Wages payable	$ 50
Accounts receivable	150	Accounts payable	200
Inventory	300	Note payable	11,500
Total Current		Total Current	
Assets	$ 1,450	Liabilities	$11,750
Fixed Assets:		Owners' Equity:	
Bar equipment	1,000	Mr. Robinson $1,400	
Buildings	9,500	Mr. Griffiths 1,400	
Improvements to		Mr. Thorndike 1,400	
land	2,000	Total Owners'	
Land	2,000	Equity	4,200
Total	$15,950	Total	$15,950

c. Since the partners have withdrawn a total of $600, it appears that the enterprise earned only $600 − $300 = $300 *before any charges for depreciation or any payments for services rendered by the proprietors.* The effect of the withdrawals has, therefore, been to reduce each partner's equity in the business.

Chapter 2

2–1. *a.* 1. Assuming that the equipment is equally useful in each of the 12 years, the annual depreciation should be $4,200/12 = $350. Since the furniture was purchased on July 1, only one half year's depreciation, or $175, should be taken in 19x3.

2. The timing of the payments is irrelevant. The sales representative worked three months in 19x3, and expense is 3 × $700 = $2,100.

3. The cost of goods sold is $220,000, and this is an expense, deductible from the revenues recognized in 19x3.

4. No expense. The payment merely canceled a liability that was assumed in 19x2.

  5. Rent expense = three months' rentals = $^3/_6$ × $22,500 = $11,250.

 b. 1. Asset, Furniture, increased by $4,200; Liability, Accounts Payable, increased by the same amount. Liability, Accounts Payable, decreased by $4,200; Asset, Cash, decreased by this amount. Asset, Furniture, decreased by $175; owners' equity decreased by this amount.

   2. Liability, Salaries Payable, increased by $2,100; owners' equity decreased by this amount. Asset, Cash, decreased by $1,400; Liability, Salaries Payable, decreased by this amount.

   3. Asset, Accounts Receivable, increased by $300,000; Asset, Inventory, decreased by $220,000; owners' equity increased by $80,000.

   4. Asset, Cash, decreased by $24,000; Liability, Accounts Payable, decreased by this amount.

   5. Asset, Cash, decreased by $22,500; Asset, Prepaid Rent, increased by $11,250; owners' equity decreased by $11,250.

2–2. *a.* Collections from customers = $100 + $500 − $80 = $520.
  b. Purchases on account = $250 + $40 − $50 = $240.
  c. Ending balance = $20 + $300 − $295 = $25.
  d. Beginning balance = $90 + $265 − $240 = $115.

2–3. *a.*

		Assets		
	Cash	Prepaid Rent	Equipment	Merchandise Inventory
(1)	$+300			
(2)	− 45	$+45		
(3)	−110		$+110	
(4)	−100			$+305
(5)	+650			−305
(6a)		−15		
(6b)			− 21	
(7)	−205			
Balance	$ 490	$ 30	$ 89	$ —

	Liabilities	Owners' Equity				
	Accounts Payable	Earl Holt, Proprietor	Sales Revenue (+)	Cost of Goods Sold (−)	Rent Expense (−)	Depreciation Expense (−)
(1)		$+300				
(4)	$+205					
(5)			$650	$305		
(6a)					$15	
(6b)						$21
(7)	−205					
Balance	$ —	$ 300	$650	$305	$15	$21

b.

BALANCE SHEET, AS OF MONDAY NIGHT

Assets			Liabilities and Owners' Equity	
Cash	$490		Liabilities	None
Prepaid Rent	30		Owners' equity	$609
Equipment	89			
			Total Liabilities and	
Total Assets	$609		Owners' Equity	$609

c.

INCOME STATEMENT FOR FIRST GAME

Sales revenue		$650
Less: Cost of goods sold	$305	
Rent	15	
Depreciation	21	341
Net Income		$309

2–4. *a.* 1. Asset, Merchandise, increased by $1,000,000; Liability, Accounts Payable, increased by $1 million.

2. Asset, Accounts Receivable, increased by $1.5 million; owners' equity increased by this amount. (Note: We know that the owners' equity didn't increase by this amount after all expenses were taken into consideration. This figure is a first approximation, to be corrected by additional information.)

3. Liability, Wages Payable, increased by $300,000; owners' equity decreased by this amount. [Note: This is one of the expenses offsetting the gross increase in owners' equity we identified in item (2).]

4. Liability, Accounts Payable, increased by $100,000; owners' equity decreased by this amount [just like (3)].

5. Asset, Cash, decreased by $1,050,000; Liability, Accounts Payable, decreased by the same amount.

6. Asset, Cash, decreased by $280,000; Liability, Wages Payable, decreased by this amount.

7. Asset, Cash, increased by $1.6 million; Asset, Accounts Receivable, decreased by this amount.

8. Asset, Equipment, increased by $40,000; Asset, Cash, decreased by $25,000; Liability, Accounts Payable, increased by $15,000.

9. Asset, Merchandise, decreased by $940,000; owners' equity decreased by this same amount, the cost of the goods that were sold. (We determine this by applying the transactions equation. Since the inventory increased by $60,000, the cost of goods sold must have been $60,000 less than the $1 million cost of the goods purchased [item (1)].

10. Asset, Equipment, decreased by $18,000; owners' equity decreased by the same amount.

11. Asset, cash, decreased by $10,000; owners' equity decreased by the same amount.

b.

A STORE
Income Statement
For the Year Ended December 31, 19x1

Sales revenue		$1,500,000
Expenses:		
Cost of goods sold	$940,000	
Wages	300,000	
Depreciation	18,000	
Other	100,000	1,358,000
Net Income		$ 142,000

c.

A STORE
Statement of Cash Flows
For the Year Ended December 31, 19x1

Cash provided by operations:		
Collections from customers		$1,600,000
Operating disbursements:		
Payments for merchandise and other current services	$1,050,000	
Payments to employees	280,000	1,330,000
Cash Provided by Operations		$ 270,000
Nonoperating uses of cash:		
Payments for equipment	$ 25,000	
Withdrawn by owners	10,000	
Total Nonoperating Uses of Cash		$ 35,000
Increases in cash balance		$ 235,000

Chapter 3

3–1. *a.* The way to solve this problem is to calculate the owners' equity at the beginning of the year, adjust it for the year's transactions other than income transactions, and then subtract this adjusted balance from the owners' equity at the end of the year, calculated by subtracting the year-end liabilities from the year-end assets:

	Assets	− Liabilities =	Capital Stock	Retained + Earnings
January 1	$120,000	$64,000	$20,000	$36,000
New stock			+ 6,000	
Dividends				− 24,000
Adj. balance				$12,000
December 31	140,000	68,000	26,000	46,000
Income				$34,000

b.

Capital stock: 2,100 shares	$26,000
Retained earnings	46,000
Total Shareowners' Equity	$72,000

3–2. *a.*

Trucks	4,000	
Cash		4,000

b.   Depreciation Expense   640
      Accumulated Depreciation   640

c.   Cash   1,100
      Accumulated Depreciation   1,920
      Gain or Loss on Truck Retirements .   980
      Trucks   4,000

3–3.   1.   Merchandise Inventory   5,000
        Notes Payable   5,000

   2.   Cash   4,000
        Accounts Receivable   4,000

   3.   Accounts Payable................   6,000
        Cash   6,000

   4.   Salaries Expense   1,000
        Salaries Payable   1,000

   5.   Salaries Payable   900
        Cash   900

   6.   Cash   50,000
        Note Payable   50,000

   7.   Accounts Receivable   8,000
        Revenue from Goods Sold   8,000
      Cost of Goods Sold...............   6,000
        Merchandise Inventory   6,000

   8.   Land   7,000
        Cash   7,000

   9.   Dividends Declared   3,000
        Dividends Payable   3,000

  10.   Office Supplies Expense   60
        Accounts Payable..............   60

  11.   Accounts Receivable   100
        Cash   100

3–4.   a.   To save space, the journal entries are not listed here. They can be identified easily from the numerals in parentheses in the T-accounts that follow.

b.

Cash				Capital Stock	
Bal.	12,510	(7b)	44,400		Bal.	50,000
(2)	296,000	(8)	248,850		(10)	60,000
(10)	60,000				Bal.	110,000
Bal.	75,260					

Accounts Receivable				Retained Earnings	
Bal.	23,060	(2)	296,000	(11)	25,000	Bal.	35,210
(1)	301,000					
Bal.	28,060					

Merchandise Inventory

Bal.	67,200	(1)	181,000
(3)	246,300		
Bal.	132,500		

Sales Revenues

	(1)	301,000

Equipment

Bal.	36,140	
(4)	3,800	
Bal.	39,940	

Cost of Goods Sold

(1)	181,000

Accumulated Depreciation

Bal.	17,120	
(9)	4,800	
Bal.	21,920	

Salaries Expense

(7)	43,000

Accounts Payable

(8)	248,850	Bal.	35,180
		(3)	246,300
		(4)	3,800
		(5)	15,000
		(6)	21,000
		Bal.	72,430

Rental Expense

(5)	15,000

Salaries Payable

(7b)	44,400	Bal.	1,400
		(7a)	43,000
		Bal.	0

Depreciation Expense

(9)	4,800

Dividends Payable

(11)	25,000

Miscellaneous Expenses

(6)	21,000

c.

HANDYMAN TOOL SHOP, INC.
Income Statement
For the Year Ended December 31, 19x2

Sales revenues		$301,000
Cost of goods sold		181,000
Gross Margin		$120,000
Operating expenses:		
Salaries	$43,000	
Rent	15,000	
Depreciation	4,800	
Other	21,000	83,800
Net Income		$ 36,200

HANDYMAN TOOL SHOP, INC.
Statement of Financial Position
December 31, 19x2

Assets			Liabilities and Shareowners' Equity			
Current Assets:			Current Liabilities:			
Cash		$ 75,260	Accounts payable			$ 72,430
Accounts receivable		28,060	Dividends payable			25,000
Merchandise inventory		132,500	Total Current Liabilities			$ 97,430
Total Current Assets		$235,820	Shareowner's Equity:			
Equipment	$39,940		Capital stock	$110,000		
Accumulated depreciation	21,920	18,020	Retained earnings	46,410		156,410
Total Assets		$253,840	Total Liabilities and Shareowners' Equity			$253,840

d. Sales Revenues 301,000

Cost of Goods Sold	181,000
Salaries Expense	43,000
Rental Expense	15,000
Miscellaneous Expenses	21,000
Depreciation Expense	4,800
Retained Earnings	36,200

Chapter 4

4–1. a. 2. Asset, accounts receivable, +$495,000; owners' equity, +$495,000.

3. Asset, cash, +$510,000; asset, accounts receivable, −$510,000.

4. No change in assets, liabilities, or owners' equity.

b. 2. Accounts Receivable 500,000
Sales Revenues 500,000

Estimated Customer Defaults ... 5,000
Allowance for Uncollectible Accounts 5,000

3. Cash 510,000
Accounts Receivable 510,000

4. Allowance for Uncollectible Accounts 8,000
Accounts Receivable 8,000

c.
Accounts receivable, gross	$932,000
Less: Allowance for uncollectibles	22,000
Accounts receivable, net	$910,000

d. Customer defaults should be reported at $5,000 unless the company has evidence that this estimate is incorrect. The $8,000 write-off this month was the result of sales in previous months and was deducted from revenues when those sales were made.

4–2. *a.* 1. Net cost of goods sold by Pacific: 5 × .98 × $50 = $245.
          2. Pacific's net revenue: 5 × .98 × $60 = $294.
          3. Pacific's income from discounts lost: 5 × .02 × $60 = $6.

b.   PACIFIC

Feb. 12	Inventory	1,000	
	Accounts Payable		1,000
Feb. 14	Accounts Receivable	600	
	Sales Revenue		600
	Cost of Goods Sold	500	
	Inventory		500
Feb. 16	Inventory	150	
	Loss from Damage	100	
	Cost of Gods Sold		250
	Sales Returns (or Sales		
	Revenue)	300	
	Accounts Receivable ..		300
Feb. 21	Accounts Payable	100	
	Loss from Damaged		
	Merchandise		100
	Accounts Payable	900	
	Purchases Discounts ..		18
	Cash		882

JONES ELECTRIC

Feb. 14	Inventory	600	
	Accounts Payable		600
Feb. 16	Accounts Payable	300	
	Inventory		300
Feb. xx	Accounts Receivable	500	
	Sales Revenue		500
	Cost of Goods Sold	300	
	Inventory		300

c. Pacific's inventory on February 28 was overstated by $13: $1 on each of the ten undamaged radios and 60 cents (2 percent of $30) on each of the five damaged radios. Assuming that Pacific classified the balance in the Purchases Discounts account as an income statement amount, income was also overstated by $13.

Pacific's sales revenue for February included $6 that arose not from sales but from Jones Electric's failure to take the cash discounts it was entitled to. This misclassification had no effect on net income because Jones Electric forfeited the discount in February, making the $6 an appropriate revenue item for Pacific.

Jones Electric's cost of goods sold included $6 that was really a form of interest expense arising from the loss of available cash discounts. This misclassification had no effect on net income because all 5 radios were sold in February.

4–3. *a.*

	Office	Sales	Warehouse	Total
Payments to employees.........	$ 7,590	$14,688	$ 9,836	$32,114
Income taxes withheld	1,500	3,500	1,200	6,200
F.I.C.A. tax withheld	650	1,300	780	2,730
Insurance withheld	260	512	184	956
Gross Pay	$10,000	$20,000	$12,000	$42,000
Employer's taxes:				
F.I.C.A.	650	1,300	780	2,730
Unemployment	300	600	360	1,260
Total Payroll Cost	$10,950	$21,900	$13,140	$45,990

b.

Salaries Expense—Office	10,000	
Salaries Expense—Sales	20,000	
Salaries Expense—Warehouse	12,000	
Salaries Payable		32,114
Taxes Payable		8,930
Accounts Payable		956

Tax Expense—Office	950	
Tax Expense—Sales	1,900	
Tax Expense—Warehouse	1,140	
Taxes Payable		3,990

Salaries Payable	32,114	
Cash		32,114

Taxes Payable	13,015	
Cash		13,015

Accounts Payable	585	
Cash		585

Chapter 5

5–1. *a.*

11/14	Interest paid, two months at 8 percent of $6,000 =	$ 80.00
12/14	Interest accrued, one month at 8 percent of $6,000 =	40.00
12/31	Interest accrued for 17 days:	
	17/360 × 8% × ($6,000 + $40 − $4,000) =	7.71
	Total interest expense	$127.71

b.

Interest Expense	7.71	
Interest Payable		7.71

c.

Interest Expense....................	5.89	
Interest Payable	7.71	
Note Payable	2,000.00	13.60
Cash		

Note: to simplify the clerical routine, the company might make a "reversing entry" on January 1, debiting Interest Payable and crediting Interest Expense for $7.71. The January 13 entry then would include only one debit, to Interest Expense, $2,013.60. The net effect would be the same.

5–2. *a.* Warranty expense = $3\% \times \$1,000,000 = \$30,000$.

   b. Warranty Expense 30,000

      Liability for Product

        Warranty   30,000

      Liability for Product Warranty 38,000

        Cash   38,000

5–3. *a.* To save space, a columnar worksheet is provided here instead of T-accounts.

Accounts	Trial Balance Dec. 31, 19x3		Adjustments		Adjusted Trial Balance	
Cash	28,800				28,800	
Notes receivable	17,700				17,700	
Accounts receivable	91,600			(1) 165	91,435	
Allowance for uncollectible accounts.........................		1,500	(1) 165	(2) 815		2,150
Inventory of merchandise	89,000		(3) 344,500 (4) 975	(3) 347,060	87,415	
Prepaid insurance	1,900			(5) 175	1,725	
Other prepayments	1,340				1,340	
Land	16,000				16,000	
Bldg. and equipment	45,800				45,800	
Allowance for depreciation		8,100		(5) 1,240		9,340
Accounts payable		18,800		(4) 975		19,775
Mortgage payable		45,000				45,000
Capital stock		150,000				150,000
Retained earnings		53,720				53,720
Sales revenues		412,000				412,000
Sales discounts, returns and allowances	12,000		(9) 890		12,890	
Customer defaults	2,100		(2) 815		2,915	
Interest income.....................		480				480
Purchases	344,500			(3) 344,500		
Advertising expense	1,200				1,200	
Salaries and wages expense	16,400		(8) 240		16,640	
Miscellaneous selling expense	5,800				5,800	
Property tax expense	3,300				3,300	
Insurance expense	525		(5) 175		700	
Miscellaneous general expense.......	8,435				8,435	
Interest expense	3,200		(7) 400		3,600	
Accrued interest payable				(7) 400		400
Accrued wages payable				(8) 240		240
Depreciation expense			(6) 1,240		1,240	
Cost of goods sold			(3) 347,060		347,060	
Allowance for sales discounts				(9) 890		890
Income tax expense			(10) 3,480		3,480	
Income tax payable				(10) 3,480		3,480
Total.......................	689,600	689,600	699,940	699,940	697,475	697,475

b.

THE GUYTON COMPANY
Income Statement
For the Year Ended December 31, 19x3

Sales revenues		$412,000
Less: Discounts, returns, and allowances	$ 12,890	
Estimated customer defaults	2,915	15,805
Net sales revenues		$396,195
Interest income		480
Total Revenue		$396,675
Expenses:		
Cost of goods sold	$347,060	
Salaries and wages	16,640	
Advertising	1,200	
Miscellaneous selling expense	5,800	
Insurance	700	
Depreciation	1,240	
Property taxes	3,300	
Miscellaneous general expenses	8,435	
Interest expense	3,600	
Income tax expense	3,480	391,455
Net Income		$ 5,220

THE GUYTON COMPANY
Statement of Financial Position
December 31, 19x3
Assets

Current Assets:		
Cash		$ 28,800
Notes receivable		17,700
Accounts receivable (net)		88,395
Inventory of merchandise		87,415
Prepaid insurance		1,725
Other prepaid expenses		1,340
Total Current Assets		$225,375
Fixed Assets:		
Land		16,000
Building and equipment	$ 45,800	
Less: Allowance for depreciation	9,340	36,460
Total Assets		$277,835

Liabilities and Stockholders' Equity

Current Liabilities:		
Accounts payable		$ 19,775
Accrued interest payable		400
Accrued wages payable		240
Income tax payable		3,480
Total Current Liabilities		$ 23,895
Mortgage on real estate		45,000
Total Liabilities		$ 68,895
Stockholders' Equity:		
Capital stock	$150,000	
Retained earnings	58,940	
Total Stockholders' Equity		208,940
Total Liabilities and Stock-		
holders' Equity		$277,835

c. Sales Revenues 412,000
  Interest Income 480
    Sales Discounts, Returns and
      Allowances 12,890
    Customer Defaults............. 2,915
    Advertising Expense 1,200
    Salaries and Wages Expense 16,640
    Miscellaneous Selling
      Expense 5,800
    Property Tax Expense.......... 3,300
    Insurance Expense 700
    Miscellaneous General
      Expense 8,435
    Interest Expense 3,600
    Depreciation Expense.......... 1,240
    Cost of Goods Sold 347,060
    Income Tax Expense........... 3,480
    Retained Earnings 5,220

Chapter 6

6–1. *a.* Direct materials:
  Issued $13,860
  Returned 528 $13,332
  Direct labor 13,360
  Factory overhead 8,000
    Total Cost $34,692

  Unit cost = $34,692/9,800 = $3.54

b. 1. Work in Process 13,860
       Materials Inventory 13,860

   2. Work in Process 13,360
       Wages Payable 13,360

   3. Work in Process 8,000
       Factory Overhead 8,000

   4. Materials Inventory 528
       Work in Process 528

   5. Finished Goods 34,692
       Work in Process 34,692

   6. Cost of Goods Sold 17,346
       Finished Goods 17,346

6–2. *a.*

Materials Inventory			
Bal.	11,650	(2)	7,250
(1)	4,500		
Bal.	8,900		

Work in Process			
Bal.	8,320	(7)	12,650
(2)	6,320		
(3)	3,300		
(6)	4,950		
Bal.	10,240		

Finished Goods			
Bal.	11,100	(8)	14,500
(7)	12,650		
Bal.	9,250		

Factory Overhead			
(2)	930	(6)	4,950
(3)	1,800		
(4)	400		
(5)	1,820		

Accumulated Depreciation			
		Bal.	xxx
		(4)	400
		(9)	100

Accounts Receivable			
Bal.	xxx		
(11)	19,350		

Accounts Payable			
		Bal.	xxx
		(1)	4,500
		(5)	1,820
		(10)	1,735

Salaries & Wages Payable			
		Bal.	xxx
		(3)	7,700

Sales Revenues			
		(11)	19,350

Cost of Goods Sold			
(8)	14,500		

Selling & Admin. Expenses			
(3)	2,600		
(9)	100		
(10)	1,735		

b.

KING APPLIANCE COMPANY
Income Statement
For the Month of October, 19xx

Sales revenues		$19,350
Less: Cost of goods sold	$14,500	
Selling and administrative expenses	4,435	18,935
Net Income		$ 415

6–3. *a.* Beginning receivables + sales − collections = ending receivables
$80,000 + $500,000 − Collections = $100,000
Collections = $480,000

b. Beginning inventory + purchases − (cost of goods sold − depreciation) = ending inventory
$60,000 + Purchases − $300,000 = $70,000
Purchases = $310,000

c. Beginning payables + purchases + other expenses − payments
= ending payables
$50,000 + $310,000 + $100,000 − payments = $30,000
Payments = $430,000

d.
Collections from customers	$480,000
Payments to suppliers, employees, and others	430,000
Cash Provided by Operations	$ 50,000

e. To answer this, several more calculations are necessary:
1. Ending retained earnings = beginning retained earnings
+ net income − dividends
$220,000 = $150,000 + $80,000 − Dividends
Dividends = $10,000
2. Capital stock increased by $30,000.
3. The original cost of plant and equipment on hand increased by $60,000; the change in accumulated depreciation was equal to depreciation for the year, indicating that no plant and equipment was retired during the year. Therefore, plant and equipment purchases amounted to $60,000.

f.

BEECHAM MANUFACTURING COMPANY
Statement of Cash Flows
For the Year Ended December 31, 19x1

Sources of cash:		
Operations		$50,000
Sale of stock		30,000
Total Sources of Cash		$80,000
Uses of cash:		
Purchase of plant and equipment	$60,000	
Dividends	10,000	
Total Uses of Cash		70,000
Increase in cash balance		$10,000

Chapter 7

7–1. a.
Present value of outlay	−$ 35,000
Present value of receipts: 0.3220 × $100,000 =	+ 32,200
Net Present Value	−$ 2,800

b.
Present value of 1/1/80 outlay	−$ 80,000
Present value of 1/1/85 outlay: 0.5674 × $20,000 =	− 11,348
Present value of receipt of $10,000 per period for six periods: 4.1114 × $10,000 =	+ 41,114
Present value of receipt of $20,000 per period for ten periods starting six periods hence: (6.9740 − 4.1114) × $20,000 =	+ 57,252
Net Present Value	+$ 7,018

c.
Present value of 1/1/80 outlay: 1.0000 × $20,000	−$ 20,000
Present value of next 10 outlays: 5.6502 × $20,000	− 113,004
Present value of receipt: 0.2567 × $250,000	+ 64,175
Net Present Value	−$ 68,829

7–2. *a.* Future value of outlay: 3.1059 × $35,000 .... −$108,706
Future value of receipt: 1.0000 × $100,000 .... + 100,000

Net Future Value .... −$ 8,706

Verification: Present value of $8,706 = .3220 × $8,706 = $2,803, which differs from the answer to (1*a*) by a rounding error only.

b. Future value of 1/1/80 outlay: 6.1304 × $80,000 .... −$490,432
Future value of 1/1/85 outlay: 3.4786 × $20,000 .... − 69,572
Future value of receipt of $10,000 per period for six periods:
(42.7533 − 17.5487) × $10,000 .... + 252,046
Future value of receipt of $20,000 per period for ten periods:
17.5487 × $20,000 .... + 350,974

Net Future Value .... +$ 43,016

Verification: 0.1631 × $43,016 = $7,061, which differs from the answer to (1*b*) by a rounding error only.

c. Future value of outlays: 20.6546 × $20,000 .... −$518,182
Future value of receipt: 1.0000 × $250,000 .... + 250,000

Net Future Value .... −$268,182

Verification: 0.2567 × $268,182 = $68,842, virtually identical to answer to (1*c*).

7–3. The annuity formula is: F = multiplier × A

A = F/multiplier
= $1,000,000/14.4866 = $69,029.31

7–4. The key here is to find a seven-year annuity in advance that will have the same present value as a five-year annuity in arrears which starts in year 4:
Present value of five-year annuity
= (5.7466 − 2.5771) × $4,000 = $12,678
Present value of seven-year annuity = (4.6229 + 1.0000) × Annuity
Annuity = $12,678/5.6229 = $2,255.

This can be checked by calculating the amount of interest accrued on the amount invested, and deducting the amounts repaid:

Year	Cash Flow Before Interest	Amount Invested After Cash Flow	Interest @ 8%	Amount Invested One Year Later
0........	−2,255	2,255	180	2,435
1........	−2,255	4,690	375	5,065
2........	−2,255	7,320	586	7,906
3........	−2,255	10,161	813	10,974
4........	{ −2,255 + 4,000 = +1,745 }	9,229	738	9,967
5........	+1,745	8,222	658	8,880
6........	+1,745	7,135	571	7,706
7........	+4,000	3,706	296	4,002
8........	+4,000	2*	0	0

* Rounding error.

The amounts invested, with interest, are just adequate to cover the five payments of $4,000 each.

7–5. Future value = 36.7856 × Annuity = $100,000
Annuity = $100,000/36.7856 = $2,718.18

7–6. *a.*

Year	Cash Flow	Multiplier (Table 3)	Present Value
1	$100,000	.9434	$ 94,340
2	180,000	.8900	160,200
Total			$254,540

b.

Year	Cash Flow	Multiplier (Table 3)	Present Value
0	$100,000	1.0000	$100,000
1	180,000	.9434	169,812
Total			$269,812

c. Income = $269,812 − $254,540 = $15,272.
(This can also be obtained by taking 6% of $254,540 = $15,272.)

d.

Present value, end of year 2	$180,000
Present value, beginning of year 2	169,812
Income, Year 2	$ 10,188

e. The richer opportunity elsewhere reduces the value of this asset slightly without changing the future cash flows. These cash flows then provide a greater annual income because they start from a smaller present value base.

Year	Cash Flow	Beginning of Year 1 Multiplier (Table 3)	Beginning of Year 1 Present Value	Beginning of Year 2 Multiplier (Table 3)	Beginning of Year 2 Present Value
1	$100,000	.9259	$ 92,590	1.0000	$100,000
2	180,000	.8573	154,314	.9259	166,662
Total			$246,904		$266,662

Income = $266,662 − $246,904 = $19,758 in year 1.
Income = $180,000 − $166,662 = $13,338 in year 2.

Chapter 8

8–1. *a.* We start with two basic calculations:

1. The profit on a unit is $25 − $12 − $6 = $7.
2. The inventory should be listed at sale price less future selling costs, $25 − $6 = $19.

Effect of producing one unit:
Cash descreased by $12.
Inventory increased by $19.
Owners' equity increased by $7.

Effect of shipping one unit:
Cash decreased by $6.
Inventory decreased by $19.
Receivables increased by $25.

Effect of collecting $25:
Cash increased by $25.
Receivables decreased by $25.

b.

	First Year	Second Year
Revenue	$1,500,000	$1,875,000
Cost of goods sold	$ 720,000	$ 900,000
Selling expense	360,000	450,000
Administrative expense	200,000	200,000
Net Income	$ 220,000	$ 325,000

8–2. *a.*

Gross revenues		$500,000
Customer defaults (2%)		10,000
Net revenue		$490,000
Manufacturing costs		350,000
Gross Margin		$140,000
Other expenses:		
Selling	$80,000	
Administrative	50,000	130,000
Income Before Taxes		$ 10,000

b. Inventory would be reported at $4.90 a unit, a total amount of $49,000.

c. Gross margin on a delivery basis would be 90,000 units × ($5.00 − $0.10 − $3.50) = $126,000. The company, therefore, would report a $4,000 *loss* before income taxes.

d. Inventory would be reported at $3.50 a unit (average manufacturing cost), or $35,000 in total. This is $14,000 less than the amount reported under the production basis.

Note: information on depreciation and production payments would be relevant if you had been asked to calculate the cash flow; it has no bearing on the measurement of income in an accrual-basis accounting system.

Chapter 9

9-1. *a.* Year	Lifo Cost of Goods Sold	Lifo Ending Inventory
19x1	55,000 × $3.10 = $170,500	10,000 × $3.00 = $ 30,000 5,000 × 3.10 = 15,500 $ 45,500
19x2	68,000 × $3.50 = $238,000	10,000 × $3.00 = $ 30,000 5,000 × 3.10 = 15,500 2,000 × 3.50 = 7,000 $ 52,500
19x3	80,000 × $3.75 = $300,000	10,000 × $3.00 = $ 30,000 5,000 × 3.10 = 15,500 2,000 × 3.50 = 7,000 10,000 × 3.75 = 37,500 $90,000
19x4	70,000 × $3.80 = $266,000 2,000 × $3.75 = 7,500 $273,500	10,000 × $3.00 = $ 30,000 5,000 × 3.10 = 15,500 2,000 × 3.50 = 7,000 8,000 × 3.75 = 30,000 $ 82,500
19x5	75,000 × $4.00 = $300,000	10,000 × $3.00 = $ 30,000 5,000 × 3.10 = 15,500 2,000 × 3.50 = 7,000 8,000 × 3.75 = 30,000 5,000 × 4.00 = 20,000 $102,500
19x6	70,000 × $4.25 = $297,500 5,000 × 4.00 = 20,000 5,000 × 3.75 = 18,750 $336,250	10,000 × $3.00 = $ 30,000 5,000 × 3.10 = 15,500 2,000 × 3.50 = 7,000 3,000 × 3.75 = 11,250 $ 63,750
19x7	85,000 × $4.40 = $374,000	10,000 × $3.00 = $ 30,000 5,000 × 3.10 = 15,500 2,000 × 3.50 = 7,000 3,000 × 3.75 = 11,250 15,000 × 4.40 = 66,000 $129,750
19x8	95,000 × $4.50 = $427,500	(same as 19x7) = $129,750

b.

Year	Fifo Cost of Goods Sold	Fifo Ending Inventory
19x1	10,000 × $3.00 = $ 30,000 45,000 × 3.10 = 139,500 $169,500	15,000 × $3.10 = $ 46,500
19x2	15,000 × $3.10 = $ 46,500 53,000 × 3.50 = 185,500 $232,000	17,000 × $3.50 = $ 59,500
19x3	17,000 × $3.50 = $ 59,500 63,000 × 3.75 = 236,250 $295,750	27,000 × $3.75 = $101,250
19x4	27,000 × $3.75 = $101,250 45,000 × 3.80 = 171,000 $272,250	25,000 × $3.80 = $ 95,000
19x5	25,000 × $3.80 = $ 95,000 50,000 × 4.00 = 200,000 $295,000	30,000 × $4.00 = $120,000
19x6	30,000 × $4.00 = $120,000 50,000 × 4.25 = 212,500 $332,500	20,000 × $4.25 = $ 85,000
19x7	20,000 × $4.25 × $ 85,000 65,000 × 4.40 = 286,000 $371,000	35,000 × $4.40 = $154,000
19x8	35,000 × $4.40 = $154,000 60,000 × 4.50 = 270,000 $424,000	35,000 × $4.50 = $157,500

c.

		Lifo		Fifo	
	Replacement Cost of Goods Sold	Cost of Goods Sold	Inventory Profit	Cost of Goods Sold	Inventory Profit
19x1 55,000 × $3.10 = $170,500		$170,500	—	$169,500	$ 1,000
19x2 68,000 × 3.50 = 238,000		238,000	—	232,000	6,000
19x3 80,000 × 3.75 = 300,000		300,000	—	295,750	4,250
19x4 72,000 × 3.80 = 273,600		273,500	$ 100	272,250	1,350
19x5 75,000 × 4.00 = 300,000		300,000	—	295,000	5,000
19x6 80,000 × 4.25 = 340,000		336,250	3,750	332,500	7,500
19x7 85,000 × 4.40 = 374,000		374,000	—	371,000	3,000
19x8 95,000 × 4.50 = 427,500		427,500	—	424,000	3,500
Total			$3,850		$31,600

The difference between these two totals ($31,600 − $3,850 = $27,750) is also the difference between the two ending inventory figures ($157,500 − $129,750 = $27,750).

9–2. *a.*

	Inventory			Cost of Goods Sold	
Date	Fifo	Lifo	Year	Fifo	Lifo
January 1, 1972	$1,875,000	$1,875,000			
			1972	$12,175,000	$12,350,000
December 31, 1972	2,700,000	2,525,000			
			1973	14,600,000	14,500,000
December 31, 1973	700,000	625,000			

b. The involuntary liquidation increased reported profit before taxes by $125,000. The liquidation amounted to 15,000 tons, but the first 5,000 of these were liquidated voluntarily. The involuntary part of the liquidation caused the transfer of 10,000 tons at $125 from the Lifo inventory. The effect on reported income was:

10,000 tons at current price of $140	$1,400,000
10,000 tons at inventory price of $125	1,250,000
Net Effect on Reported Income	$ 150,000

c. The effect is to increase the cost of the inventory by $200,000 over the level that would have prevailed if there had been no involuntary liquidation:

Base quantity, 5,000 tons	$ 625,000
1974 layer, 10,000 tons	1,450,000
Total..	$2,075,000
Lifo cost of 15,000 tons, 12/31/72	1,875,000
Net Effect on Inventory	$ 200,000

d.

	Pretax Income Difference	Tax Effect at 50%	
1972	$175,000	$87,500	Fifo pays more tax
1973	(100,000)	(50,000)	Lifo pays more tax
1974	25,000*	12,500	Fifo pays more tax

* Calculation:

	Fifo	Lifo
Beginning inventory	$ 700,000	$ 625,000
Purchases	14,500,000	14,500,000
Goods Available	$15,200,000	$15,125,000
Ending inventory	2,175,000	2,075,000
Cost of Goods Sold	$13,025,000	$13,050,000

Chapter 10

10–1. *a.* Straight-line depreciation:
Depreciable cost = $30,000 − $1,500 = $28,500
Rate = 1/5 = 20%
Depreciation = 20% × $28,500 = $5,700 a year.

b. & c.

Year	DDB Depreciation		SYD Depreciation	
	Beginning Balance	Depreciation at 40%	Fraction of Depreciable Cost	Depreciation
1..........	$30,000	$12,000	5/15	$9,500
2..........	18,000	7,200	4/15	7,600
3..........	10,800	4,320	3/15	5,700
4..........	6,480	2,592	2/15	3,800
5..........	3,888	1,555	1/15	1,900

d. Implicit-interest depreciation:

Year	Beginning Book Value	Cash Flow	Imputed Interest @ 10%	Depreciation
1..........	$30,000	$7,668	$3,000	$4,668
2..........	25,332	7,668	2,533	5,135
3..........	20,197	7,668	2,020	5,648
4..........	14,549	7,668	1,455	6,213
5..........	8,336	7,668	834	6,834

10–2. a. The sum-of-the-years' digits = 55
Depreciation per digit = $16,500/55 = $300
Depreciation schedule:

Year	Depreciation
1....................	10 × $300 = $3,000
2....................	9 × $300 = 2,700
3....................	8 × $300 = 2,400
Total	$8,100

b. Straight-line depreciation for three years = 3 × $1,650 = $4,950
Adjustment = $8,100 – $4,950 = $3,150
This would be deducted from the balance in Accumulated Depreciation and would be shown below any extraordinary items on the income statement for the year.

10–3. a. The conventional answer here is an accelerated depreciation formula, because cash flows are likely to decline rapidly as the textbook ages. If the time value of money is considered, an argument can be made for implicit-interest depreciation, but with sharply declining cash flows, this could be approximated by a diminishing-charge method or possibly by straight-line.

b. If we look at textbook A only, the accelerated methods will lead to lower reported income in the first two years and higher reported income in the last two years than straight-line depreciation would show. If we look at all the company's textbooks as a group, however, the effect of the choice depends on the rate of growth. If the company is growing, accelerated depreciation would reduce reported income in all years, unless the company stopped bringing out new textbooks in any quantity for a year or two. The assets' book value would be greater under straight-line depreciation than under any accelerated method.

Chapter 11

11–1. *a.* Current cost of goods sold:

January 1–May 15	55,000 × $2	$110,000
May 16–December 31	35,000 × $2.20	77,000
Total		$187,000
Current cost, ending inventory	60,000 × $2.20	$132,000

b. Holding gain:

Inventory on May 16: 50,000 − 15,000 = 35,000 units
Price increase: 20 cents a unit
Holding gain = 35,000 × $0.20 = $7,000

c. Current cost margin:

Revenues:

January 1–May 15	55,000 × $3	$165,000
May 16–December 31	35,000 × $3.10	108,500
Total		$273,500
Cost of goods sold [from (a)]		187,000
Current Margin		$ 86,500

11–2. *a.*

Current cost of goods sold [as in 11–1]	$187,000
Inventory holding gain	0
Current margin [as in 11–1]	86,500

b. The conclusion is that Company A benefitted by having an inventory position when prices went up. Company B had to rely entirely on its trading operations to generate income. The purpose of this question is to emphasize a very simple point which is often overlooked: companies without inventories have no inventory holding gains and losses, no matter what inventory costing method is used.

11–3. *a.*

	Units	Cost
Beginning inventory	50,000	$ 97,500
Purchases:		
January 1–May 15	40,000	80,000
May 16–December 31	60,000	132,000
Goods available	150,000	$309,500
Ending inventory	60,000	132,000
Cost of Goods Sold	90,000	$177,500

b.

	January 1	December 31
Current cost of inventory [from 11–1]	$100,000	$132,000
Fifo cost of inventory [from (a)]	97,500	132,000
Unrealized Holding Gain	$ 2,500	$ —

c. Inventory holding gain included in net income:

Current cost of goods sold [from 11-1]	$187,000
Fifo cost of goods sold [from (a)]	177,500
Inventory Profit	$ 9,500

Notice this is the total of the $7,000 holding gain for the year and the $2,500 change in the unrealized holding gain between the beginning and end of the year. It would be included in the gross margin and would not be identified separately.

11–4. *a.* Step 1: restate equipment at its January 1, 19x9 replacement cost:

Year of Purchase	Historical Book Value	Multiplier	Replacement Cost
19x0	$ 60,000	180/100	$108,000
19x2	24,000	180/110	39,273
19x5	44,000	180/150	52,800
Total	$128,000		$200,073

Step 2: subtract historical cost 128,000

Unrealized Holding Gain .... $ 72,073

b.

Year of Purchase	Historical Cost Depreciation	Multiplier	Replacement Cost Depreciation
19x0	$10,000	190/100	$19,000
19x2	3,000	190/110	5,182
19x5	4,000	190/150	5,067
Total	$17,000		$29,249

c. Realized holding gain = $29,249 − $17,000 = $12,249

d. Step 1: restate equipment at its December 31, 19x9, replacement cost:

Year of Purchase	Historical Book Value	Multiplier	Replacement Cost
19x0	$ 50,000	200/100	$100,000
19x2	21,000	200/110	38,182
19x5	40,000	200/150	53,333
Total	$111,000		$191,515

Step 2: subtract historical cost 111,000

Unrealized holding gain .... $ 80,515

e. The easiest way to calculate the holding gain for the year is to apply the formula:

Unrealized Holding Gain, End of Year	=	Unrealized Holding Gain Start of Year	+	Holding Gain for the Year	−	Holding Gain Realized during Year

Rearranging terms and substituting, we have the following:

Holding gain = $80,515 + $12,249 − $72,073 = $20,691

The same result can be achieved by calculating a half-year's increase in the replacement cost of the beginning equipment (from \$200,073 to \$211,188), subtracting \$29,249 of depreciation from the latter figure (bringing replacement cost down to \$181,939), and then calculating the increase in the replacement cost for the rest of the year on the remaining asset (from \$181.939 to \$191,515):

$$(\$211,188 - \$200,073) + (\$191,515 - \$181,939) = \$20,691$$

f. The percentage increase in the general price-level index (25/225) was the same as the percentage increase in the replacement-cost index (20/180). Therefore none of the holding gain represented a gain in purchasing power.

11–5. a.

	Dollars	Multiplier	Purchasing Power Units
Sales revenue	\$320	200/190	\$336.9
Expenses:			
Depreciation	\$ 20	*	\$ 29.5
Opening inventory	30	200/175	34.3
Other	235	200/190	247.4
Total expense	\$285		\$311.2
Net Income	\$ 35		\$ 25.7

* Each component of the depreciation charge must be restated separately:

Year of Purchase	Depreciation Historical Cost	Multiplier	Depreciation, Purchasing Power Units
19x0	\$ 8,000	200/110	\$14.5
19x3	4,000	200/130	6.2
19x8	3,000	200/170	3.5
19x9	5,000	200/190	5.3
Total	\$20,000		\$29.5

b. Net monetary position, December 31: \$55 − \$47 = \$8.
Net monetary position, January 1: \$30 − \$25 = \$5.
In purchasing power units:
   Beginning balance: \$5 × 200/180 = ... \$5.5
   Additions during year: \$3 × 200/190 = ... 3.2

   Total \$8.7
In ending purchasing power units 8.0

   Loss of Purchasing Power \$0.7

Purchasing power income, therefore, is \$25.7 − \$0.7 = \$25.

c.

	Dollars	Multiplier	Purch. Power
Current Assets:			
Cash	$ 15	200/200	$ 15.0
Accounts receivable	40	200/200	40.0
Inventory	35	200/195	35.9
Total Current Assets	$ 90		$ 90.9
Plant and equipment (net)	137	*	198.4
Total Assets	$227		$289.3
Current Liabilities:			
Accounts payable	$ 7	200/200	$ 7.0
Notes payable	30	200/200	30.0
Total Current Liabilities	$ 37		$ 37.0
Bonds payable	10	200/200	10.0
Total liabilities	$ 47		$ 47.0
Common stock	100	200/110	181.8
Retained earnings	80	Residual	60.5
Total Liabilities and Shareowners' Equity	$227		$289.3

* Calculated as follows:

Year of Purchase	Book Value, in Dollars	Multiplier	Purchasing Power Units
19x0	$ 49	200/110	$ 89.1
19x3	28	200/130	43.1
19x8	25	200/170	29.4
19x9	35	200/190	36.8
Total	$137		$198.4

Chapter 12

12–1. The cost of the shares was 21,600 × $15 = $324,000. This figure is obviously a very poor measure of the amount of resources sacrificed by Experimental Company to obtain the new building in 1977. Instead, the company should have used either the current market value of the stock or the current market value of the building, whichever could have been measured more accurately.

A market price of $105 a share gives an indicated market value of 21,600 × $105 = $2,268,000. A sale of this magnitude might very well have depressed the market price of the Respirator stock, however, so the market value of the 21,600 shares may have been lower. If the shares were traded actively, the amount of the price reduction would have been quite small; for small companies the reduction is often substantial.

Appraisal values, too, are often inaccurate, but urban building appraisals are usually quite reliable. Capitalization in the neighborhood of $2 million would seem reasonable here. A gain of $2 million − $324,000 = $1,676,000 should be recognized on this transaction.

12–2.

	Each Machine	All Machines
Asset Cost:		
Purchase price	$16,250	$ 97,500
Freight	700	4,200
Handling	200	1,200
Installation:		
Labor	800	4,800
Materials	100	600
Total	$18,050	$108,300

If the bookkeeping system is loosely designed, the installation
materials and perhaps even some of the installation labor might
be expensed. In concept, however, they should be capitalized.

12–3. *a.*

Original cost		$50,000
Accumulated depreciation	4 × $2,500 =	10,000
Book Value		$40,000

b.

Equipment	6,000	
Cash...........................		6,000

c.

Depreciation	2,875	
Accumulated Depreciation		2,875

The life of the machine wasn't extended, and the $40,000 +
$6,000 = $46,000 book value had to be depreciated during the
remaining 16 years of life.

d.

Accumulated Depreciation	12,000	
Cash...........................		12,000

This presumes the overhaul took the form of renewal or replacement of component parts; a debit to the Equipment
account would be double-counting.

e. Original cost: $50,000 + $6,000 $56,000

Accumulated depreciation:		
4 × $2,500	$10,000	
12 × $2,875	34,500	
Overhaul	(12,000)	32,500
Book Value		$23,500

Depreciation = $23,500/9 = $2,611 a year.

Chapter 13

13–1. *a.* The face value is $1 million, the payments each year will be
$80,000, and the amount paid equals the present value of the
future payments when the latter are discounted at 9 percent,
or 4.5 percent compounded semiannually.

b. $908,000, because the price must be less than the maturity
value to produce a yield in excess of the coupon rate.

c. The term is 20 years (the factor of 90.80 is found in the 20-year column, 9.0 percent row of Table 8).

d. Interest expense = 9%/2 × $908,000 = $40,860.
   Entry:

Interest Expense	40,860	
Cash		40,000
Unamortized Bond Discount		860

e. Principal = $908,000 + $860 = $908,860.
   Interest expense = 9%/2 × $908,860 = $40,899.
   Entry:

Interest Expense	40,899	
Cash		40,000
Unamortized Bond Discount		899

f.

Bonds payable, maturity value	$1,000,000
Less: Unamortized bond discount	90,241
Bonds payable, net	$ 909,759

13–2. Income calculation:

Income before depreciation and taxes		$6,000,000
Depreciation		850,000
Income after depreciation		$5,150,000
Income tax: Current	$2,375,000	
Deferred	200,000	2,575,000
Net Income		$2,575,000

Entries:

Depreciation	850,000	
Allowance for Depreciation		850,000
Income Tax Expense	2,575,000	
Income Taxes Payable		2,375,000
Provision for Deferred Income Taxes		200,000

Current taxable income = $4,750,000.

13–3. a. Annuity factor in advance at 12% = 3.037 + 1.000 = 4.037.
   Capitalized amount = 4.037 × $2,000 = $8,074.

Asset: Rights to leased property	$8,074
Liability: Liability for future lease payments = $8,074 − $2,000	6,074

b.

Depreciation = 1/5 × $8,074	$1,615
Interest = 12% × $6,074	729
Total	$2,344

    c. Book value of asset = $8,074 − $1,615 = $6,459.
Book value of liability = $6,074 − ($2,000 − $729) = $4,803.
Note: in practice, this method would not be used unless the lease payments entitled the lessee to virtually all of the lifetime service values of the leased equipment.

Chapter 14

14–1. *a.* Shares issued: par value $160,000; additional paid-in capital $480,000.
Added to retained earnings: $441,600 − $0.20 × 960,000 = $249,600.
The shareowners' equity at December 31, 19x1:

Common stock, 960,000 shares	$ 960,000
Additional paid-in capital	780,000
Retained earnings	749,600
Total	$2,489,600

    b. The book value of the common equity wasn't diluted because the new shares were issued at $4, whereas the book value of the earlier shares was only $2. The market value *may* have been diluted, if investors estimated that the company's return on the $4 was likely to be less than the return each previous share had been expected to earn before the new issue was offered for sale.

14–2. Retained earnings would decrease by $30,000, the total par value of the common stock would increase by $10,000, and additional paid-in capital would increase by $20,000.

14–3. Purchase of treasury stock: decreased cash by $3,000 and decreased the shareowners' equity by $3,000. Temporarily it is classified as a negative component of the shareowners' equity.

Dividend declaration: decreased retained earnings by $0.30 = 99,900 = $29,970; increased the liability, dividends payable, by this same amount.

Dividend payment: decreased the asset, cash, and the liability, dividends payable, by $29,970.

Sale of treasury stock: increased cash by $4,000 and increased the shareowners' equity by this amount, canceling the $3,000 negative component and adding $1,000 to additional paid-in capital.

14–4. *a.* Income available for common stock =
$$\$312,000 − \$50,000 = \$262,000.$$
Undiluted earnings per share = $262,000/100,000 = $2.62.

    b. Equivalent common shares =
$$100,000 + 2 \times 10,000 = 120,000.$$
Fully diluted earnings per share =
$$\$312,000/120,000 = \$2.60.$$

Chapter 15

15–1. *a.* Cantara's ownership interest in Cantara was large enough to require the use of the equity method. Cantara therefore should include 25 percent of $30,000 = $7,500 in its reported income for 19x1.

   b. Cantara's investment can be calculated as follows:

Purchase price	2,500 × $30 =	$75,000
Equity in 19x1 retained earnings*	2,500 × $1.60 =	3,500
Total		$78,500

* Equity in net income: ¼ × $30,000	$7,500
Less: Dividends received: 2,500 shares × $1.40	4,000
Equity in retained earnings	$3,500

15–2. *a.*

ALCON CORPORATION AND SUBSIDIARY
Consolidated Income Statement for the Year Ended
December 31, 19x1

Sales revenues	$5,750,000
Cost of goods sold	3,480,000
Gross margin	$2,270,000
Other expenses	1,700,000
Net income	$ 570,000

   b. The amount payable by Alcon has no effect on consolidated net income. The eliminating entry is:

Accounts Payable	35,000	
Accounts Receivable		35,000

The investment income represents dividends paid by Nonon during the year. Since this will be replaced on the consolidated income statement by Nonon's revenues and expenses, and since the dividends weren't paid to outsiders and therefore don't belong on a consolidated statement, the following elimination is appropriate:

Investment Income	50,000	
Dividends Declared		50,000

Sales revenue is overstated by $250,000, inventory is overstated by $40,000, and the cost of goods sold is overstated by $220,000. (The actual cost of goods sold was $180,000 − $70,000 = $110,000. Alcon showed a cost of goods sold of $250,000 − $100,000 = $150,000 and Nonon showed a cost of goods sold of $180,000, a total of $330,000. The difference between these two totals is $220,000.) The entry is:

Sales Revenues	250,000	
Inventory		30,000
Cost of Goods Sold		220,000

15–3.   *a.*   The owners' equity in the Lamb Company was $85,000 at the end of the year. Since its income for 19x4 was $15,000, the owners' equity must have been $70,000 at the beginning of the year, when Wolfe acquired the stock.

  b.   The price paid for the shares was $95,000. This was $25,000 greater than the appraised value of the net tangible assets at the date of acquisition ($70,000). Goodwill, therefore, was $25,000.

  c.   The $95,000 investment and Lamb's January 1, 19x1, owners' equity (common stock $90,000 less $20,000 accumulated deficit) must be eliminated. The $25,000 difference is goodwill, as we found in (*b*). Of this amount, $2,500 must be amortized in 19x4. A suitable entry is:

Amortization of Goodwill	2,500	
Goodwill	22,500	
Common Stock	90,000	
Investments		95,000
Retained Earnings		20,000

  d.   Calculation of consolidated retained earnings, December 31, 19x4:

Retained earnings, Wolfe Corporation	$190,000
Lamb Company, net income for 19x4	15,000
Less: Amortization of goodwill	(2,500)
Consolidated retained earnings	$202,500

15–4.   *a.*   Since the purchase price was equal to the appraised value of the underlying net tangible assets, no goodwill had to be recognized or amortized.

Company Y's net income for 19x2 was equal to the $10,000 it distributed plus the $5,000 increase in its retained earnings, a total of $15,000.

Company X's share in Company Y's income was 80 percent of $15,000, or $12,000. It recognized $8,000 as dividend income. Consolidated net income, therefore, was $4,000 greater than the income reported by Company X itself:

    Consolidated net income = $55,000 + $4,000 = $59,000.

  b.   Minority interest = 20% × $105,000 = $21,000.

  c.   Shareowners' equity:

Common stock	$100,000
Additional paid-in capital	20,000
Retained earnings	404,000
Total	$524,000

15–5.   *a.*   This would be treated as a pooling of interests because it was a straight exchange of stock and all of Y's stock was exchanged.

b. Consolidated balance sheet, January 1, 19x2:

Current assets	$ 6,300
Plant and equipment, net	8,700
Total Assets	$15,000

Current liabilities	$ 2,800
Common stock	2,500
Additional paid-in capital.......................................	3,500
Retained Earnings	6,200
Total Liabilities and Owners' Equity	$15,000

c. Consolidated net income = $1,000 − $100 + $180 = $1,080.

d.

Common stock	$ 2,500
Additional paid-in capital.......................................	3,500
Retained earnings	6,880
Total Owners' Equity	$12,880

e. If the merger had been treated as a purchase, the purchase price would have been recorded as 100 × $30 = $3,000. The appraised value of the net tangible assets was $2,700 − $500 = $2,200. Goodwill amounting to $800, therefore, would have been recognized. The shareowners' equity on January 1, 19x1, would have been as follows:

	Initial Amount	Added by Merger	Total
Common stock	$ 2,000	$ 500	$ 2,500
Additional paid-in capital	3,000	2,500	5,500
Retained earnings	5,000	—	5,000
Total	$10,000	$3,000	$13,000

Net income for 19x1 would have been $40 smaller due to the amortization of 5 percent of the goodwill.

Chapter 16

16–1. a. Transactions were:
Purchases of plant and equipment for $1,700.
Sale of plant and equipment for $300.
Depreciation of $900.

b. To be added back to net income to derive funds provided by operations:
Depreciation, $900.
Loss on retirements, $400.
To be listed with other sources of funds:
Sale of plant and equipment, $300.
To be listed as a use of funds:
Purchase of plant and equipment, $1,700.

16–2. a. To save space here, we've used a different type of work sheet, in which the opening balances are placed in the first pair of columns, the ending balances are placed in the third pair, and the transactions accounting for the differences between them are entered in the middle pair.

	Balances, January 1		Transactions		Balances, December 31	
	Debit	Credit	Debit	Credit	Debit	Credit
Working capital	14,210		(11) 13,983		28,193	
Long-term marketable securities	—		(8) 1,005		1,005	
Property, plant and equipment	31,414		(6) 18,082	(7) 400	49,096	
Accumulated depreciation		13,237	(7) 317	(5) 5,501		18,421
Bonds payable		—		(9) 7,000		7,000
Deferred income taxes		4,362		(10) 537		4,899
Preferred stock		1,347	(3) 224			1,123
Common stock		4,317		(4) 175		4,492
Additional paid-in capital		7,179	(3) 37	(4) 11,872		19,014
Retained earnings		15,182	(2) 80	(1) 8,243		23,345
Funds from operations: Net income Depreciation Deferred income tax			(1) 8,243 (5) 5,501 (10) 537			
Other sources: Common stock issue Sale of plant Long-term bonds			(4) · 12,047 (7) 83 (9) 7,000			
Uses of funds: Preferred dividends Retire preferred Buy plant Buy long-term marketable securities Increase working capital				(2) 80 (3) 261 (6) 18,082 (8) 1,005 (11) 13,983		
Totals	45,624	45,624	67,139	67,139	78,294	78,294

(4) The proceeds from the sale of common stock can be determined only after the retirement of the preferred has been accounted for; the remaining increase in additional paid-in capital must be attributed to the common stock.

(7) The proceeds from the sale of plant and equipment can be calculated only after the depreciation and equipment purchases have been accounted for. Once this has been done, we can see that $400 was subtracted from plant and equipment and $317 from accumulated depreciation during the year, indicating that the book value of the retired property was $83. The proceeds may have been either greater or less than this, but without data on the gain or loss we have chosen to assume that the selling price was equal to the book value of the property sold.

b.

ANDERSON COMPANY
Statement of Changes in Financial Position
For the Year Ended December 31, 19x1
(in thousands)

Sources:

From operations:

Net income	$ 8,243
Depreciation	5,501
Deferred income tax	537
Total from Operations	$14,281
From issue of common stock	12,047
From sale of long-term bonds	7,000
From sale of plant and equipment	83
Total Sources	$33,411

Uses:

To buy property, plant and equipment	$18,082
To buy long-term marketable securities	1,005
To retire preferred stock	261
To pay preferred dividends	80
To increase working capital	13,983
Total Uses	$33,411

16–3. a.

THE COMPANY
Statement of Changes in Financial Position
For the Year Ended August 31, 19xx

Sources:

From operations:

Net income	$ 410,000
Depreciation	350,000
Deferred income taxes	50,000
Loss on sale of equipment	100,000
Total from Operations	$ 910,000
From sale of equipment	107,000
From reduction in working capital	785,000
Total Sources of Funds	$1,802,000

Uses:

To purchase plant assets	$ 894,000
To reduce mortgage	550,000
To pay dividends	300,000
To settle prior years' taxes	58,000
Total Uses of Funds	$1,802,000

b. To convert funds from operations into an estimate of the cash flow from operations, we need to adjust it for the changes in accounts receivable and payable, inventories, accrued taxes, and prepaid expenses:

Funds from operations		$ 910,000
Add: Reduction of accounts receivable	$ 53,000	
Decrease of inventories..................	705,000	
Total Additions		758,000
		$1,668,000
Less: Increase in prepayments	$ 82,000	
Reduction of accounts payable	104,000	
Reduction of accrued taxes	340,000	
Total Subtractions		(526,000)
Cash Flow from Operations		$1,142,000

The $53,000 decrease in accounts receivable means that collections exceeded net sales revenues by this amount. The cash inflow, therefore, was $53,000 greater than the funds inflow. A useful exercise at this point is to phrase a similar explanation for each of the other adjustments.

In this case the cash-flow figure was slightly larger than the funds flow. Even so, the cash balance decreased, as did the company's investments in short-term marketable securities. These cash-flow figures provide useful supplementary information on short-term changes in the company's liquidity. When several years are taken as a whole, cash flow from operations and funds flow from operations will be very similar, any differences stemming mainly from the growth in the volume of business done.

Chapter 17

17–1.

		19x3	19x4	19x5	19x6
a.	Number of shares (000)	50,000	50,000	52,000	52,000
	Earnings available for common stock (000)		$96,000	$101,300	$99,100
	Earnings per share		$1.92	$1.95	$1.91
b.	Book value per share	$16.60	$17.52	$18.60	$19.50
c.	Average common equity (000) ...		$853,000	$921,650	$990,850
	Return on common equity		11.3%	11.0%	10.0%

17–2. *a.* 1. Debt decreases while equity remains unchanged; the debt/equity ratio therefore will fall.

2. Cash increases and then decreases by the same amount; current liabilities also remain unchanged. The current ratio will not be affected.

3. Since total assets have decreased, the ratio of sales to total assets (asset turnover) will increase.

b. 1. If the capitalized amount is equal to the book value of the building before the sale/leaseback, total debt will remain unchanged and the debt/equity ratio will be unaffected. If the capitalized amount is less than the former book value, the debt/equity ratio will fall.

2. If the first lease payment falls within the next 12 months or the next operating cycle, the present value of that payment will appear as a current liability. The current ratio therefore will fall.

3. Again, the effect depends on the amount capitalized. If this amount is equal to the book value of the building before the sale/leaseback, total assets will remain unchanged and the asset turnover ratio will be unaffected. If a smaller amount is capitalized, asset turnover will increase.

17–3. *a.* $$\text{Return on assets} = \frac{\text{Earnings Before Interest and Taxes (EBIT)}}{\text{Total Assets}}$$

Because this equation contains two unknowns, we must start by deriving one of them.

$$\text{Return on common equity} = \frac{(\text{EBIT} - \text{Interest}) \times (1 - \text{tax rate})}{\text{Common Equity}}$$

Again we have two unknowns, but we know that the common equity equals total assets minus total liabilities and that liabilities are 25 percent of the common equity. Putting these together, we find that:

Common equity = $100,000/1.25 = $80,000.

This permits the calculation of EBIT:

$$7.2\% = \frac{\text{EBIT} - \$2,000}{\$80,000} \times 0.55$$

EBIT = $10,473 + $2,000 = $12,473.

Return on assets (before taxes) = $12,473/$100,000 = 12.47%.
Return on assets (after taxes) = 12.47% × (1 − .45) = 6.86%.

b.   Since the after-tax return on assets is less than the return on common equity, the use of leverage succeeded in increasing the rate of return on the common equity.

17–4. *a.*   To separate the leverage effects completely, both the margin on sales and the return on assets ratios should be calculated on the basis of a debt-free capital structure. To do this, we need to make the following preliminary calculations:

	Company A	Company B	Company C
Net income/0.5	$22,954	$16,654	$111,794
Interest	3,994	5,342	13,088
EBIT	$26,948	$21,996	$124,882
Adjusted income (EBIT × 0.5)	13,474	10,998	62,441

The five required ratios are:

Return on equity	11,477/43,554	8,327/163,317	55,897/627,366
	= 26.4%	= 5.1%	= 8.9%
Return on assets......	13,474/120,363	10,998/274,603	62,441/884,001
	= 11.2%	= 4.0%	= 7.1%
Margin on sales	13,475/627,349	10,998/1,293,765	62,441/5,458,824
	= 2.1%	= 0.9%	= 1.1%
Asset turnover........	627,349/120,363	1,293,765/274,603	5,458,824/884,001
	= 5.2	= 4.7	= 6.2
Debt/asset ratio	76,809/120,363	111,286/274,603	256,635/884,001
	= 63.8%	= 40.5%	= 29.0%

b. We can give only a partial answer to this because we don't have more detailed information on the composition of the income statement, nor do we have a segment breakdown. One factor contributing to Company A's success is that its adjusted profit margin (income/sales) was twice as great as Company C's and more than twice as great as Company B's. Either its operating costs (salaries, rent, and so forth) were smaller or its gross margin was greater than those of either of the other companies.

A second factor is that Company A used leverage much more aggressively than either of the other companies. Whereas its return on assets was only about half again as great as Company C's, its return on equity was three times as great.

The only determinant in which Company C had an advantage over Company A was in asset turnover. Company C got $6.20 in sales for every dollar of assets, while Company A had to settle for $5.20 for each asset dollar. The difference in profit margin was far more than enough to offset this, however, and, in fact, Company A may have used big inventories, and big store investments (relative to sales) to achieve a higher mark-up.

Company B used debt more aggressively than Company C, but this was far from enough to offset its low profit margin and slow asset turnover. These kept its profitability ranking far below Company C's.

Another factor on which we have no information is the accounting measurement systems used by the three companies. Company C may have been on Lifo, for example, while Company B was on Lifo, and this could account for at least some of their differences in profit margin and return on assets. It is unlikely that accounting differences were great enough to account for the differences we can observe, however.

Chapter 18

18–1. *a.*

Profit Plan	Division A	Division B	Division C	Total
Sales revenues	$1,000	$3,000	$2,100	$6,100
Divisional expenses:				
Cost of goods sold	$ 650	$1,650	$1,260	$3,560
Marketing	150	500	300	950
Administrative	150	300	200	650
Total	$ 950	$2,450	$1,760	$5,160
Division margin	$ 50	$ 550	$ 340	$ 940
Headquarters expenses				400
Net Income				$ 540

Cash Budget				
Revenues	$1,000	$3,000	$2,100	$6,100
Less: Increase in receivables	10	200	50	260
Collections	$ 990	$2,800	$2,050	$5,840
Cost of goods sold	$ 650	$1,650	$1,260	$3,560
Add: Inventory increase	50	100	50	200
Purchases	$ 700	$1,750	$1,310	$3,760
Less: Increase in payables	15	50	80	145
Payments to suppliers	$ 685	$1,700	$1,230	$3,615
Division marketing costs	150	500	300	950
Division administration (expense less deprec.)	145	285	180	610
Total Divisional Disbursements	$ 980	$2,485	$1,710	$5,175
Division Cash Flow	$ 10	$ 315	$ 340	$ 665
Head office disbursements:				
Central administration				$ 390
Equipment purchases				130
Dividends				350
Total Head Office Disbursements				$ 870
Net Decrease in Cash				$ (205)

b.

Anticipated cash balance = $290 − $205 . . . . = $ 85
Minimum cash balance = 5% × $6,100 . . . . =   305
Cash shortage . . . . = $220

Since the company has only a $100 line of credit, the proposed plan is not financially feasible.

Chapter 19

19–1. *a. & b.*   The first step is to calculate total cost at each volume. The second step is to extrapolate this schedule backward, to estimate total cost at zero volume. This is the estimated total fixed cost. The third step is to subtract this amount from estimated total cost at each volume—the difference is total variable cost. The final step is to divide this total by the number of units to get average variable cost. Average fixed cost is calculated in the same manner, by dividing total fixed cost by the number of units:

Volume (Units)	Total Cost	Total Variable Cost	Average Variable Cost	Average Fixed Cost
0	$10(est.)	$ 0	—	—
1	11	1	$1.00	$10.00
2	12	2	1.00	5.00
3	13	3	1.00	3.33
4	14	4	1.00	2.50
5	15	5	1.00	2.00
6	16	6	1.00	1.67
7	17	7	1.00	1.43
8	18	8	1.00	1.25
9	20	10	1.11	1.11
10	23	13	1.30	1.00

    c. This calls for an estimate of incremental cost: total cost at ten units ($23) less total cost at nine units ($20), or $3.

19–2. The only relevant figure is opportunity cost, reflecting the cash flows Ms. Smith will receive in the future. None of the past prices is relevant to this decision because Ms. Smith can do nothing now to change them. The $6 figure was an opportunity cost in 19x5. Her decision not to sell then was the same as a decision to buy 200 shares at that price at that time. It no longer has any more relevance, however, than the $15 and $20 historical purchase prices. Even the $8 figure has no relevance because the $10 tender offer makes that the effective floor under the market price—it can't go lower as long as the tender offer is in effect, and it will go higher only if enough shareholders believe that the stock is worth more than $10.

19–3. Expected value of open market purchases:

$$0.6 \times \$0.75 + 0.4 \times \$0.90 = \$0.81.$$

This is virtually identical to the proposed contract price. The contract would provide a modest saving of $1,000 in cost each month and would also give management an opportunity to devote its attention to other matters, without worrying about the cost of its supplies for the next year. The contract should be accepted.

19–4. *a.* The first step is to identify the alternatives. One alternative is to operate trucks A and B; the other is to operate truck A and use the independent trucker.

The second step is to decide which costs will be totally unaffected by the choice (sunk costs). In this case all the fixed costs are irrelevant to the decision because they will be unaffected by it. (Both trucks will be in service during the whole period under either alternative.)

	Trucks A and B	Truck A and Independent
Truck A:		
Driver	$10 × 40 = $400	$10 × 40 = $400
Gas and oil	$.10 × 400 = 40	$.10 × 600 = 60
Maintenance	$.05 × 400 = 20	$.05 × 600 = 30
Truck B:		
Driver	$10 × 40 = 400	—
Gas and oil	$.11 × 600 = 66	—
Maintenance	$.06 × 600 = 36	—
Independent	—	500
Total	$962	$990

Since the use of both company trucks will reduce total cash outflows by $28, this alternative should be selected.

b. By disposing of truck B, the company could save the following annual cash outflows:

Fixed:	
Garage space	$ 400
Registration and insurance	1,300
Maintenance	300
Variable:	
Driver: $10 × 650	6,500
Gas and oil: $.11 × 650 × 15	1,072
Maintenance: $.06 × 650 × 15	585
Total	$10,157

If the independent trucker's charges would exceed $10,157, the company would find it profitable to keep truck B in service. At any lower price, the company should use the independent. (Depreciation was ignored in this calculation because it didn't represent a cash flow to be affected by the decision. If keeping the truck would affect its salvage or resale value, this effect would have to be considered, as we'll see in Chapter 22.)

Chapter 20

20–1. a. Cost of job No. 423:

Overhead rate = $900,000/100,000 = $9 a direct labor-hour

Materials	$ 800
Labor	400
Overhead ($9 × 60)	540
Total	$1,740

b.

Actual overhead	$106,000
Absorbed overhead (10,000 × $9)	90,000
Underabsorbed overhead	$ 16,000

20–2. *a.*

Materials:			Work in process:		
Beginning inventory	$10,000		Beginning inventory ...	$ 15,000	
Purchases	16,000		Additions:		
	$26,000		Direct materials	18,000	
Issues	18,000		Direct labor	48,000	
Ending inventory	$ 8,000		Overhead: 5,000 × $4	20,000	
				$101,000	
			Completions	80,000	
			Ending inventory	$ 21,000	

b.

Beginning finished goods inventory	$ 20,000
Completions	80,000
	$100,000
Ending finished goods inventory	23,000
Cost of Goods Sold	$ 77,000

c.

Actual overhead	$17,000
Absorbed overhead: 5,000 × $4	20,000
Overabsorbed Overhead	$ 3,000

d.
1. Materials 16,000
   Accounts Payable 16,000

2. Work in Process 18,000
   Materials 18,000

3. Work in Process 47,000
   Wages Payable 47,000

4. Manufacturing Overhead 17,000
   Accounts Payable, etc. 17,000

5. Work in Process 20,000
   Manufacturing Overhead 20,000

6. Finished Goods 80,000
   Work in Process 80,000

7. Cost of Goods Sold 77,000
   Finished Goods 77,000

20–3. First, calculate plantwide and departmental overhead rates:

		Hours			
Product	Output	Dept. 1	Dept. 2	Dept. 3	All Depts
A	40,000	80,000	40,000	40,000	
B	40,000		80,000	80,000	
C	10,000	20,000	30,000	30,000	
Total hours		100,000	150,000	150,000	400,000
Overhead		$400,000	$300,000	$100,000	$800,000
Overhead rate		$4.00	$2.00	$0.67	$2.00

Then calculate unit overhead cost for each product:

	Product A		Product B		Product C	
	Hours	Cost	Hours	Cost	Hours	Cost
Departmental rates:						
Department 1	2	$ 8.00	—		2	$ 8.00
Department 2	1	2.00	2	$4.00	3	6.00
Department 3	1	.67	2	1.34	3	2.01
Total Unit Cost ..		$10.67		$5.34		$16.01
Plantwide rate	4	$ 8.00	4	$8.00	8	$16.00

As this shows, the effect on the unit costs of products A and B is substantial, and the departmental overhead rates presumably indicate more accurately the amount of resources used to support production of the product. If production and sales are not equal, the difference will also affect reported income.

20–4. a.

	Allocation Basis	Melting and Pouring	Molding	Core Making	Cleaning and Grinding
Indirect labor	Traceable	$3,000	$ 900	$ 300	$ 900
Supplies used	Traceable	150	150	600	300
Taxes:					
Machinery and equipment ...	% of cost	12	3	9	12
Building	Floor space	9	36	9	18
Compensation insurance	% of payroll	60	45	18	72
Power	Usage	30	x	30	90
Heat and light	Floor space	30	120	30	60
Depreciation:					
Building	Floor space	24	96	24	48
Machinery	% of cost	60	15	45	60
Total		$3,375	$1,365	$1,065	$1,560

b.					
Overhead cost		$3,375	$1,365	$1,065	$1,560
÷					
Normal volume		10,000	420	150	520
=					
Overhead rate		$0.3375 a pound	$3.25 an hour	$7.10 an hour	$3.00 an hour

Chapter 21

21–1. *a.*

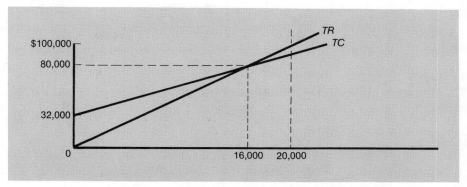

b. Break-even point: $32,000/($5 − $3) = 16,000 units
Margin of safety: 20,000 − 16,000 = 4,000 units

Anticipated profit:

Revenues at $5	$100,000
Variable costs at $3	$ 60,000
Fixed costs	32,000
Income before Taxes	$ 8,000

c. 1. Break-even point: $32,000/($5.50 − $3) = 12,800 units
Margin of safety: 18,000 − 12,800 = 5,200 units

Anticipated profit:

Revenues at $5.50	$99,000
Variable costs at $3	$54,000
Fixed costs	32,000
Income before Taxes	$13,000

2. The effect of the price increase is to increase the spread between total cost and total revenue at any given volume. When volume is measured in physical units, as it is in this case, this increased spread is reflected in the profit-volume chart as a steeper slope for the total revenue line. The revised chart is shown below:

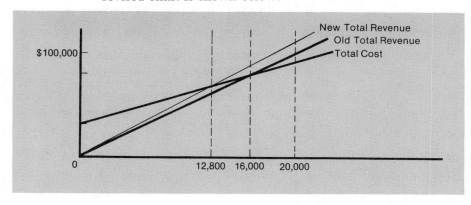

3. Profit target: 1.1 × $8,000 .... $ 8,800
   Total fixed costs 32,000

   Needed Contribution Margin $40,800

   Crossover volume = $40,800/$2.50 = 16,320 units

d. 1. Break-even point: $36,000/($4.60 − $3) = 22,500 units
   2. Profit target: 1.1 × $8,000 .... $ 8,800
      Total fixed cost 36,000

      Needed Contribution Margin $44,800

   Crossover point = $44,800/$1.60 = 28,000 units

21–2. a. Full costing overhead rates:
   Department A: $25,000/5,000 = $5 a direct labor-hour
   Department B: $60,000/10,000 = $6 a pound
   Job-order costs:

	Job 1	Job 2
Direct materials	$2,400	$ 4,800
Direct labor:		
Department A	1,620	900
Department B	420	280
Overhead:		
Department A at $5	900	500
Department B at $6	2,880	9,000
Total	$8,220	$15,480
Unit cost	$13.70	$15.48

b. Variable costing overhead rates:
   Department A: $15,000/5,000 = $3 a direct labor-hour
   Department B: $20,000/10,000 = $2 a pound
   Job-order costs:

	Job 1	Job 2
Direct materials	$2,400	$4,800
Direct labor:		
Department A	1,620	900
Department B	420	280
Overhead:		
Department A at $3	540	300
Department B at $2	960	3,000
Total	$5,940	$9,280
Unit cost	$9.90	$9.28

c. Variable unit cost of job 2 is less than that of job 1; full cost was greater for job 2 than for job 1. The main reason is that job 2 used much more of department B's capacity than job 1 and department B has a much higher proportion of fixed costs than department A. Total profit is thus much more sensitive to variations in sales of product Y (job 2) than to variations in sales of product X.

21–3. Differential cost is the effect of the decision on total cost:

Total cost if the service is provided: 25 × $14,000	$350,000
Total cost if the service is not provided: 10 × $15,500	155,000
Differential cost	$195,000

The proposal should be approved.

21–4. *a.*

		Present Program		Proposed Program	
	Contribution				
	Margin		*Profit*		*Profit*
Product	*per Unit*	*Volume*	*Contribution*	*Volume*	*Contribution*
A	$2.00	30,000	$60,000	40,000	$ 80,000
B	0.75	40,000	30,000	32,000	24,000
Total Contribution Margin			$90,000		$104,000
Fixed costs			72,000		81,700
Income before taxes			$18,000		$ 22,300

The proposal looks like a desirable one.

b.

	Contribution		
	Margin	*Units*	*Profit*
Product	*per Unit*	*Sold*	*Contribution*
A	$1.90	35,000	$66,500
B	0.65	45,000	29,250
Total Contribution Margin			$95,750
Fixed costs			72,000
Income before Taxes			$23,750

This alternative is even better than the one in (*a*). A good question to ask now, however, is what would happen if more selling effort [as in (*a*)] were devoted to the redesigned and repriced products; this might produce even better results.

Chapter 22

22–1. *a.* Pretax analysis: *Cash Flow*
Immediate cash flow (time = 0):

To make: cost of new machine	−$7,000
To buy: proceeds from sale of old machine	+ 1,500
Difference (incremental cash flow)	−$8,500

Annual cash flow (time = 1-7):

To make: out-of-pocket production, costs, at $0.20	−$1,200
To buy: purchase costs, at $0.50	− 3,000
Difference (incremental cash flow)	+$1,800 a year

b. After-tax analysis:

Investment outlay (time = 0):

To buy:	proceeds from sale of old machine	+$1,500
	Tax [40% of ($1,500 − $2,000)]	+ 200*
	Net proceeds from sale	+$1,700
To make:	cost of new machine	− 7,000
	Difference (incremental cash flow)	−$8,700

* A tax credit is equivalent to a cash inflow.

Annual cash flow (time = 1-7):

Year	Pretax Cash Flow	Tax Depreciation Old Machine	New Machine	Total	Taxable Income	Tax	After-tax Cash Flow
1	+$1,800	$500	$1,750	$2,250	$ (450)	$(180)	+$1,980
2	+ 1,800	500	1,500	2,000	(200)	(80)	+ 1,880
3	+ 1,800	500	1,250	1,750	50	20	+ 1,780
4	+ 1,800	500	1,000	1,500	300	120	+ 1,680
5	+ 1,800	—	750	750	1,050	420	+ 1,380
6	+ 1,800	—	500	500	1,300	520	+ 1,280
7	+ 1,800	—	250	250	1,550	620	+ 1,180

22–2. *a.*

Cost of machine		$100,000
Less:	Tax reduction on portion expensed ($50,000)	(25,000)
	10% tax credit on portion capitalized	(5,000)
Plus:	Working capital required	10,000
	Net Present Outlay	$ 80,000

b.

	Year 1	Year 2
1. Before-tax reduction in operating costs	$20,000	$20,000
2. Cost subject to depreciation for tax purposes, beginning of year	$50,000	$37,500
3. Tax-allowed depreciation [25% of (2)].............	12,500	9,375
4. Taxable saving [(1) − (3)]	7,500	10,625
5. Tax [50% of (4)]	$ 3,750	$ 5,312
6. After-tax cash flow [(1) − (5)]	$16,250	$14,688

22–3. *a.* Present outlay:

Cost of machine			$50,000
Less:	Sale value of old machine	$10,000	
	Tax reduction on retirement loss on old machine [50% of ($30,000 − $10,000)]	10,000	20,000
	Tax reduction on installation	7,500	27,500
	Net Present Outlay		$37,500
Present value of 10% of after-tax future cash savings (see table below)			68,453
	Net Present Value		+$30,953

Calculation of discounted cash flows from investment decision:

(1)	(2)	(3)	(4)	(5)	(6)	(7)	(8)	(9)
	Net Book		Deprecia-					
	Value of	Tax	tion	Increase in			After-	Present
Years	New	Deprecia-	on old	Deprecia-	Taxable	Income	Tax	Value
Hence	Machine	tion	Machine	tion	Income	Tax	Cash Flow	at 10%
1.......	$50,000	$10,000	$ 3,750	$ 6,250	$ 13,750	$ 6,875	$ 13,125	$11,932
2.......	40,000	8,000	3,750	4,250	15,750	7,875	12,125	10,020
3.......	32,000	6,400	3,750	2,650	17,350	8,675	11,325	8,508
4.......	25,600	5,120	3,750	1,370	18,630	9,315	10,685	7,298
5.......	20,480	4,096	3,750	346	19,654	9,827	10,173	6,316
6.......	16,384	3,277	3,750	− 473	20,473	10,237	9,763	5,511
7.......	13,107	2,621	3,750	− 1,129	21,129	10,564	9,436	4,843
8.......	10,486	2,097	3,750	− 1,653	21,653	10,826	9,174	4,280
9.......	8,389	1,678	—	1,678	18,322	9,161	10,839	4,597
10.......	6,711	1,342	—	1,342 ⎱	13,289	6,645	13,355	5,148
10.......	5,369	5,369	—	5,369 ⎰				
Total		$50,000	$30,000	$20,000	$180,000	$90,000	$110,000	$68,453

Derivation of amounts in columns (3) through (9):
  (3) 20% of col. 2.
  (4) 12.5% of $30,000 (remaining book value).
  (5) Col. 4 less col. 3.
  (6) $20,000 cash flow less increase in depreciation (col. 5).
  (7) 50% of col. 6.
  (8) $20,000 less col. 7.
  (9) Col. 8 × Table 3, Appendix A.

b. To find the internal rate of return, discount the cash flows in column 8 above, first at 40% and then at 50%:

		Present Value	
	Cash		
Year	Flow	at 25%	at 30%
0	−37,500	−37,500	−37,500
1	+13,125	+10,500	+10,093
2	+12,125	+ 7,760	+ 7,178
3	+11,325	+ 5,798	+ 5,153
4	+10,685	+ 4,381	+ 3,740
5	+10,173	+ 3,337	+ 2,737
6	+ 9,763	+ 2,558	+ 2,021
7	+ 9,436	+ 1,982	+ 1,500
8	+ 9,174	+ 1,541	+ 1,128
9	+10,839	+ 1,452	+ 1,019
10	+13,355	+ 1,429	+ 975
Total		+ 3,238	− 1,956

The internal rate of return is thus approximately 40.8%.

22–4. Initial cash flows:

Acquisition cost, new machine:

Invoice price	$39,000
Ancillary outlays, capitalized	5,000
Ancillary outlays, expensed	10,000
	$54,000
Less: tax effect, expensed portion	5,000
Net Cash Outlay, New Machine	$49,000

Proceeds, old machine:

Resale value	$ 5,000	
Tax basis: $55,000 − $10,000 −		
$9,000 − $8,000	28,000	
Tax Loss	$23,000	
Tax credit at 50%	(11,500)	
Net Proceeds, Old Machine		16,500
Incremental Cash Flow		$32,500

Annual cash flows:

Years from Now	(1) Present Machine	(2) New Machine	(3) Differ- ence	(4) Taxable Income $10,000 − (3)	(5) Incom Tax @ 50%	(6) After-Tax Cash Flow $10,000 − (5)	Multi- plier	Present Value
1..........	$7,000	$8,000	$1,000	$9,000	$4,500	$5,500	.9091	$ 5,000
2..........	6,000	7,200	1,200	8,800	4,400	5,600	.8264	4,628
3..........	5,000	6,400	1,400	8,600	4,300	5,700	.7513	4,282
4..........	4,000	5,600	1,600	8,400	4,200	5,800	.6830	3,961
5..........	3,000	4,800	1,800	8,200	4,100	5,900	.6209	3,663
6..........	2,000	4,000	2,000	8,000	4,000	6,000	.5645	3,384
7..........	1,000	3,200	2,200	7,800	3.900	6,100	.5132	3,131
8..........	—	2,400	2,400	7,600	3,800	6,200	.4665	2,892
9..........	—	1,600	1,600	8,400	4,200	5,800	.4241	2,460
10.........	—	800	800	9,200	4,600	5,400	.3855	2,082
Total								$35,483

The present value of the future cash flows exceeds the incremental outlay by $2,983. Other things being equal, the proposal should be accepted.

Chapter 23

23–1. *a.*

	Product A	Product B	Total
Equivalent units:			
Finished units	5,000	10,000	
Ending inventory	300	600	
	5,300	10,600	
Beginning inventory	500	500	
Total	4,800	10,100	
Standard labor cost per unit	× $2	× $1	
Total standard labor cost	$9,600	$10,100	$19,700
Actual labor cost			$23,500
Total Labor Cost Variance			$ 3,800

b. Standard labor cost $19,700
   Actual hours × standard rates 22,000
   Labor quantity variance.......................... $(2,300)
   Actual hours × actual rates 23,500
   Labor rate variance.............................. (1,500)

c. Ending inventory:
   Product A: 600 × ½ × $2 .... $ 600
   Product B: 1,200 × ½ × $1 600

   Total .... $ 1,200

23–2. Actual cost of materials purchased:
      95,000 × $2.05..................................... $194,750
      Standard cost of materials purchased:
      94,000 × $2.00 190,000

      Materials Price Variance .... $ (4,750)

      Actual quantity of materials used:
      61,000 × 1.5 × $2................................. $183,000
      Standard quantity of materials used:
      61,000 × 1.6 × $2................................. 195,200

      Materials Quantity Variance 12,200
      Total Materials Variance .... $ 7,450

The quantity variance could also be calculated at actual prices.
The arguments against doing it that way are: (1) it would increase
clerical costs and (2) it would make interperiod comparisons and
summaries more difficult—the change in the quantity variance
from one period to the next would include both quantity and price
components.

23–3.

Raw Materials and Supplies

Bal. 5/1	29,460	(2)	41,300
(1)	37,900	Bal. 6/1	26,060
Bal. 6/1	26,060		

Material in Process

Bal. 5/1	18,400	(4)	42,600
(2)	41,300	(6a)	1,900
		Bal. 6/1	15,200
Bal. 6/1	15,200		

Labor in Process

Bal. 5/1	9,650	(4)	28,300
(3)	28,400		
(6b)	1,250	Bal. 6/1	11,000
Bal. 6/1	11,000		

Accrued Wages

(7)	32,180	Bal. 5/1	1,620
		(3)	28,400
		(8)	2,160

Finished Goods

Bal. 5/1	35,000	(5)	79,200
(4)	70,900	Bal. 6/1	26,700
Bal. 6/1	26,700		

Material Price Variance

(9a)	1,400	(1)	1,400

Cost of Goods Sold

(5)	79,200		

Material Quantity Variance

(6a)	1,900	(9b)	1,900

Variance Summary				Labor Quantity Variance		
(9b) MQV	1,900	(9a) MPV	1,400	(9c)	1,250	(6b) 1,250
(9d) WRV	2,160	(9c) LQV	1,250			
(unfavorable)		(favorable)				

Accounts Payable, Cash, etc.		Wage Rate Variance		
	(1) 36,500	(8)	2,160	(9d) 2,160
	(7) 32,180			

Chapter 24

24–1.　*a.*　Overhead rate: ($4,680/9,000 = $.52) + $1.15 = $1.67 per
standard direct labor-hour
Standard overhead cost = (10,500 hrs. + 3,600 hrs. −
4,000 hrs.) × $1.67 = $16,867.

　　　b.　Month-end balance: 3,600 hrs. × $1.67 = $6,012.

　　　c.
Actual overhead	$17,400
Budgeted at standard hours (10,100)	16,295
Spending variance	$1,105 unfavorable
Standard overhead	16,867
Volume variance	572 favorable
Total Variance	$ 533 unfavorable

24–2.　*a.*　A predetermined charging rate should be used so that changes
in the monthly charge measure changes in consumption only.
The rate in this case would be:

$$($3,000 + $7 \times 3,000)/3,000 = $8 \text{ an hour.}$$

At this rate, the charge for August would be:

$$95 \times $8 = $760.$$

　　　b.　The budget is $100 \times $8 = 800. The manager is expected to
control usage, and the variance is $800 − $760 = 40. This
would be regarded as favorable unless it merely represents post-
ponement of necessary service.

　　　c.　Actual cost in the service department was $2,200 in excess
of the flexible budget allowance and $2,800 in excess of the
amount charged to other departments. Much of the $2,200 may
have resulted from an inability to reduce costs quickly to adapt
to a suddenly lower level of service demand. This may be economically and organizationally justifiable. What the variance
does is identify an out-of-line situation which management
must then decide to correct or live with.

24–3. *a.*

	Month 4			Month 5		
	Budget	*Actual*	*Variance*	*Budget*	*Actual*	*Variance*
Controllable:						
Nonproductive time	$1,000	$ 800	$ 200	$ 750	$1,200	$(450)
Other indirect labor	4,000	3,700	300	3,500	3,600	(100)
Operating supplies	600	650	(50)	450	430	20
Total controllable	$5,600	$5,150	$ 450	$4,700	$5,230	$(530)
Noncontrollable:						
Depreciation	2,000	2,100	(100)	2,000	2,150	(150)
Building service charges .	700	770	(70)	700	730	(30)
Total	$8,300	$8,020	$ 280	$7,400	$8,110	$(710)

b.   Only the first three overhead cost items listed are likely to be of any significance in evaluating the cost-control performance of the department supervisor, and, of these, nonproductive time and other indirect labor have the greatest impact. Depreciation and building service charges are noncontrollable and have no bearing on managerial evaluation in this department.

c.   Labor costs did not go down with decreasing volume. There are many possible reasons for this. This may merely be a time lag—management may have decided not to cut the labor force to meet the volume reduction in the hope that volume would recover quickly. This should be examined more critically if volume continues at these newer and lower levels. We cannot ignore any one month's reports, but we need to examine them in the context of a longer period of time. Even two months is likely to be too short a period for random forces to have averaged themselves out.

The other item in which the variance has increased is depreciation, and this should be labeled as noncontrollable.

d.   Overhead rate = $4,700/4,000 + $3,600/4,000
$$= \$1.175 + \$.90 = \$2.075/\text{DLHr.}$$

Volume variance:
Month 4: zero
Month 5: $1.175 × (4,000 − 3,000) = $1,175 Unfav.

Or:

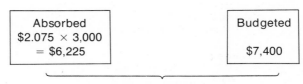

The main significance of the volume variance is that it is a charge against profits due to low volume, a charge not reflected in product cost.

Chapter 25

25–1. *a.* 1. Actual $1,000
Total variance .... 100 favorable

Absorbed $1,100
Volume variance .... 20 favorable

Budget $1,080
Spending variance .... 80 favorable

2. Budgeted fixed cost: $1,080 − 30% of $1,100 = $750

3. Variable cost:
Labor $400
Materials 100
Overhead (30%) 330

Total .... $830 = 830/1,600 of product cost

830/1,600 × $1,760 = ... $913
Selling expense (4%) 80

Total Variable $993

Contribution margin = $2,000 − $993 = $1,007 = 50.35%.

b.
DORSEY CORPORATION
Profit Contribution Statement
For the Month Ended December 31, 19xx
Sales $2,000
Variable costs:
Manufacturing $913
Selling 80   993

Contribution Margin $1,007
Traceable fixed costs:
Manufacturing $750
Selling and administrative 55   805

Spending variance (favorable) .... (80)

Profit Contribution .... $ 282

25–2. *a.*

	Budgeted	Actual
Income	$ 70,000	$ 63,000
Investment	665,000	700,000
Return on investment	10.5%	9.0%

b.

	Budgeted	Actual
Income	$ 70,000	$ 63,000
Investment charge at 12%	79,800	84,000
Residual Income (Loss)	$ (9,800)	$ (21,000)

c. Neither the ROI figures nor the residual income figures are
    relevant to managerial evaluation because of the changes in the
    allocated amounts and the changes in traceable investments
    and depreciation, none of which is controllable in any meaning-
    ful sense of the word. Using budgeted amounts to replace the
    actual amounts reported for these elements, we can calculate a
    revised residual income figure as follows:

Working capital (actual)		$200,000
Traceable plant and equipment (budgeted)		420,000
Allocated investments (budgeted)		95,000
Adjusted Investment		$715,000
Income as reported		$ 63,000
Less: Change in depreciation	$2,000	
Change in allocations	5,000	(7,000)
Add: Tax on the changes		3,500
Adjusted income		$ 59,500
Carrying charge (12% × $715,000)		(85,800)
Adjusted Residual Income (Loss)		$ (26,300)

This indicates that the division manager's performance was
actually a good deal worse than the initial comparisons indicated. One problem is that investment in working capital exceeded the plan by $50,000. Sales volume was $100,000 greater
than the budgeted amount (evidenced by the increase in the
allocation of head office costs), but this alone wouldn't account
for the increase in working capital. Furthermore, the increase
in sales volume was accompanied by a $10,500 after-tax de-
crease in divisional income (from $70,000 to $59,500). The
sources of this decrease should be investigated to see how much
of it was within the division manager's control.

d. The ratio of profit contribution to traceable investment is 13.8
    percent ($63,000 income plus 50 percent of $40,000 in head
    office charges, divided by $600,000 traceable investment). This
    indicates that the division may be paying its way. It is close
    enough to the minimum, however, to justify asking how many
    costs in the head office and how many investments administered
    by the head office are attributable to this division. If a study
    finds that attributable costs and investments in the head office
    are large enough to push the division's attributable return on
    investment substantially below 12 percent, then top manage-
    ment should analyze the division's incremental cash flows, both
    now and in the future when major capital investments are being
    considered. The purpose: to find out whether withdrawal would
    be desirable.

Index

This book has been set VIP in 10 and 9 point Primer, leaded 2 points. Part numbers and titles and chapter titles are Avant Garde Extra Light, and chapter numbers are Avant Garde Demi Bold. The size of the type page is 28 by 46½ picas.